FRO
SACRA

D0768884

RARY

N OF
RARY

The Pursuit of Power

THE PENGUIN HISTORY OF EUROPE
General Editor: David Cannadine

* not yet published

RICHARD J. EVANS

The Pursuit of Power

Europe 1815–1914

VIKING

VIKING
An imprint of Penguin Random House LLC
375 Hudson Street
New York, New York 10014
penguin.com

First published in Great Britain by Allen Lane, an imprint of Penguin Random House UK

Copyright © 2016 by Richard J. Evans
Penguin supports copyright. Copyright fuels creativity, encourages diverse voices, promotes free
speech, and creates a vibrant culture. Thank you for buying an authorized edition of this book and for
complying with copyright laws by not reproducing, scanning, or distributing any part of it in any form
without permission. You are supporting writers and allowing Penguin to continue to publish books
for every reader.

Maps drawn by Andras Bereznay

LIBRARY OF CONGRESS CATALOGING-IN-PUBLICATION DATA
Names: Evans, Richard J., author.
Title: *The Pursuit of Power: Europe 1815–1914* / Richard J. Evans.
Description: New York, New York: Viking, 2016. | Series: The Penguin history
of Europe; 7 | Includes bibliographical references and index.
Identifiers: LCCN 2016044050 (print) | LCCN 2016046539 (ebook) | ISBN
9780670024575 (hardcover: alk. paper) | ISBN 9780735221215 (ebook)
Subjects: LCSH: Europe—Politics and government—1815-1871. |
Europe—Politics and government—1871-1918. | Europe—History—1815-1871.
| Europe—History—1871-1918.
Classification: LCC D363 .E97 2016 (print) | LCC D363 (ebook) | DDC
940.2/8--dc23
LC record available at https://lccn.loc.gov/2016044050

Printed in the United States of America
3   5   7   9   10   8   6   4   2

Set in Sabon LT Std

Eric Hobsbawm
1917–2012
in memoriam

Contents

List of Illustrations

1. *Windmill near Norwich*, painting by John Crome, *c.* 1816. Tate Gallery, London. *Copyright © Tate, London, 2016*
2. *Le Gâteau des Rois*, satirical cartoon on the Congress of Vienna, French school, 1815. Private Collection. *The Stapleton Collection/ Bridgeman Images*
3. *The Massacre at Chios of 1822*, painting by Eugène Delacroix, 1824. Musée du Louvre, Paris. *Lanmas/Alamy*
4. *The Fighting Temeraire*, painting by Joseph Mallord William Turner, 1838. National Gallery, London. *Bridgeman Images*
5. *The Emancipation of Russian Serfs in 1861*, painting by Boris Mikhailovich Kustodiev, 1907. State Art Museum, Nizhny Novgorod, Russia. *Bridgeman Images*
6. *The Great Famine*, painting by George Frederick Watts, 1850. Watts Gallery, Compton, Surrey. *© Trustees of the Watts Gallery/Bridgeman Images*
7. Open-cast copper mine at Falun, Sweden, lithograph, *c.* 1850. *akg-images/ullstein bild*
8. *Arrival of the first train from St Petersburg to Tsarskoye Selo*, lithograph, 1837. *Heritage Image Partnership/Alamy*
9. *New Harmony, Indiana*, engraving by F. Bate, 1838. *Chronicle/Alamy*
10. Windischgraetz bombards Prague, lithograph, 1848. Wien Museum, Vienna. *akg-images*
11. The Battle of Sadowa or Königgrätz, engraving, 1866. *Interfoto/Alamy*
12. Napoleon III's army crosses the Mont Cénis pass, engraving, nineteenth century. Museo del Risorgimento, Milan. *Copyright © 2016. Photo Scala, Florence*
13. *The City of Vienna Ball*, painting by Wilhelm Gause, 1904. Wien Museum, Vienna. *akg-images*
14. *The Steam Hammer in Nasmyth's Foundry near Manchester*, print after a painting by James Nasmyth, 1871. *Hulton Archive/Getty Images*

List of Maps

Preface

This book is a history of Europe from 1815 to 1914, following on sequentially in the Penguin History of Europe from the previous volume in the series, *The Pursuit of Glory* (2007), which covers the period 1648 to 1815. As the author of that brilliant book, my Cambridge colleague Tim Blanning, remarks, every history of Europe has to start at some arbitrary date, but some dates are more arbitrary than others. We speak habitually of 'the nineteenth century' or 'the twentieth century', but historians know that the period 1801 to 1900 or 1901 to 2000 has no real meaning beyond the merely chronological. History is full of loose ends, and even the outbreak and conclusion of major wars that so often provide the terminal dates for histories covering discrete segments of the European past, including this one, leave many issues unresolved. Different aspects of history have different chronologies, and a date that has a meaning in political or military or diplomatic history may have very little significance in social or economic or cultural history. French historians of the *Annales* school have become accustomed to speaking of an *immobile history* which persisted well into modern times in many parts of Europe, so that despite the fall of the *ancien régime* in European political systems at the end of the eighteenth century, the *ancien régime économique et social* persisted well into the second half of the nineteenth century. It took until this point, for example, for serfdom to disappear from the scene in most of Europe, while the long-established demographic pattern of high birth rates and high death rates did not begin to change, except in France, until the so-called 'demographic transition' of the decades after 1850. On the other hand, industrialization was a marginal process confined to small pockets of the European economy until the same period. Some historians, indeed – notably Arno Mayer in his book *The Persistence of the Ancien Régime* (1981) – have argued that the dominance of traditional aristocratic elites remained all the way up to the First World War, so that not much of significance changed in the political sphere either, despite all the surface turmoil of the era. But Mayer's view has not been widely accepted by historians: change there certainly was in nineteenth-century Europe, not just in politics but in other spheres of life as well.

Some, indeed, have decided that the most meaningful period to study is the *Age of Revolution*, to quote the title of the first volume of Eric Hobsbawm's survey of the years 1789 to 1914, published in 1962. Hobsbawm's periodization was followed by Jonathan Sperber in his *Revolutionary Europe* (2000), covering the years 1789–1848, the same period as Hobsbawm's first volume. Yet there is a price to pay for choosing these years, for what came after was a very different Europe, one much less easy to conceptualize in a single framework. Not by chance, Sperber's follow-up volume has a wordy title that conveys, no doubt unconsciously, the difficulty he encountered in finding a unifying theme: *Europe 1850–1914: Progress, Participation and Apprehension* (2008). Hobsbawm went on to write two more volumes, *The Age of Capital* (1975) covering the years 1848 to 1875, and *The Age of Empire* (1987), taking the story up to the First World War. Anyone who attempts to write a history of nineteenth-century Europe has to confront these three magnificent books, which tower over the literature on the period. And, with his uncanny gift for conceptual innovation, Hobsbawm went on to characterize the whole period covered by his trilogy as 'the long nineteenth century', a model followed by many textbooks and primers, for example William Simpson and Martin Jones's *Europe 1783–1914* (2000). The long nineteenth century is, however, a broken-backed century, divided into two very different halves by the 1848 Revolutions. Not surprisingly, like Sperber, many historians covering the period from the French Revolution or the defeat of Napoleon to the First World War have given up the attempt to find any kind of conceptual unity, and have chosen anodyne titles such as *Europe's Uncertain Path* (2012), to quote R. S. Alexander's recent political narrative.

Through most of the twentieth century, historians regarded the rise of nation states and the conflicts between them as the central features of European history in the nineteenth century. The triumph of nationalism forged new political and cultural entities and inspired revolts against large and, it seemed, outmoded multinational empires, revolts against oppression by other nationalities or ambitions to achieve dominance over them. This model of the nation state was exported across the globe in the twentieth century, making its emergence in Europe in the nineteenth seem even more important. Historians once saw this process in positive terms, putting celebratory accounts of the unification of Italy and Germany, the growth of Czech and Polish national consciousness, and other products of the age of nationalism at the centre of their narrative. As national and ethnic rivalries spilled over into the vast conflagration of the Second World

War, however, the rise of nationalism appeared in a darker light, a view underlined by the Balkan wars of the 1990s. But since then we have come increasingly to live in an age of globalization, as the barriers created by the Cold War have crumbled, international institutions, worldwide means of communication, multinational companies, and many other influences have eroded national boundaries and begun to bind us all together as a global human community. Since the turn of the century, this has also altered our vision of the past, which historians have come to see increasingly in a global perspective. The call for the writing of global history is not in itself new: it was issued as long ago as the 1970s by the French historian Marc Ferro and was present in the concept of *Universalgeschichte* (universal history) as practised by Leopold von Ranke in the nineteenth century or Arnold Toynbee and William H. McNeill in the twentieth. But a global history that links the different parts of the world rather than telling their discrete stories has emerged only recently, as historians have begun to examine subjects such as the effects of empire on European economies, societies, cultures and political systems, notably but not exclusively those of Britain; the global economic ties that bound Europe to other parts of the world in a nexus of mutual interaction; and the rise of worldwide empire as a common European process rather than one specific to any particular European nation. Historians have also been busy rewriting the history of individual European nations in a global context, emphasizing the effects of European diasporas – the millions of Europeans who emigrated to other parts of the globe – on the 'mother country', the infusion of European nationalism with elements of racial theory derived from the experience of colonization in Africa or Asia, and the emergence of global geopolitics as a key factor in relations between European states.

A particular influence on my own approach here has been exerted by the German historian Jürgen Osterhammel, whose *The Transformation of the World: A Global History of the Nineteenth Century* (2009) is indeed a truly global history, not a Eurocentric one such as Hobsbawm's trilogy. Covering the nineteenth century, his chapters deal with an astonishing variety of topics, including memory and self-observation, time, space, mobility, living standards, cities, frontiers, power, revolution, the state, energy, work, communications, hierarchies, knowledge, civilization, religion and many more. Osterhammel deliberately picks out common themes, connections between different parts of the globe, shared developments and global processes. Yet the author's argumentative and reflective presence generally eclipses that of the people who lived in the era about which he is writing. Often, too, historical surveys spend all their time establishing the broad contours of interpretation without attempting to convey how they could be discerned in the lives and experiences of contemporaries. This is perhaps understandable in a brief textbook, whose ultimate purpose is to prepare students for examinations, but a more extensive work such as the present one, aimed in the first place at the general reader, fortunately has the space to provide the detail that conveys the flavour of the period, in its mixture of strangeness and familiarity, and as far as possible to allow contemporaries to speak for themselves.

Other, no less ambitious works of global history written around the same time as Osterhammel's have offered a rather different approach to the nineteenth century, based on the perception that this was the period above all others when Europe led the world and came to exercise dominion over other parts of the globe. Historians like the late Chris Bayly, in his impressive *The Birth of the Modern World* (2004), and John Darwin, in his masterly survey of global empires, *After Tamerlane* (2007), have established with a wealth of comparative evidence the approximate equality in almost every respect, from living standards to cultural achievements, of a whole range of civilizations across the world in the early eighteenth century. The Mughal Empire in India, the Qing Empire in China, the great pre-colonial empires of Benin and its neighbours in Africa, the Ottoman Empire and other states were roughly on a par with Europe around 1700. By 1815 this was no longer the case; Europe had forged ahead, not, as some historians, notably Niall Ferguson in his sweeping survey of *Civilization* (2011), have maintained, because of its intrinsic superiority, but because of quite specific historical circumstances. Europe maintained and extended its advantage on many fronts right up to the early years of the twentieth century, though by then, as we shall see, that advantage was increasingly coming under attack. The First World War called it into question; the Second World War destroyed it, bringing down the global European empires in its aftermath. This global hegemony is the main justification for taking the years 1815 to 1914 as a distinct and meaningful period of European history. Throughout this book, the global context will be repeatedly emphasized, and events and processes on other continents will be brought into the narrative as a way of helping to explain what was happening in Europe during these decades.

Global history also means *transnational* history. Many histories of Europe have consisted of largely separate narratives of different national histories. Arthur Grant and Harold Temperley's *Europe in the Nineteenth Century* (1927) falls into this category; William Simpson and Martin Jones's *Europe 1783–1914* is in the same mould, with separate chapters on France, Germany, Italy, Russia and the Habsburg Empire. The German historian Michael Salewski's *History of Europe* (2000) is subtitled *States and Nations from the Ancient World to the Present* and presents a series of histories of its individual countries and the relations between them. This means that the reader largely loses sight of what, if anything, bound Europe together as a whole, what these countries had in common, or what wider processes affected them. The long-established and still incomplete *Oxford History of Modern Europe* takes a similar approach, with every volume devoted to a single country except for the four volumes that cover the relations between them over different periods. And yet, as well as being an evolving assemblage of individual states, Europe, as this book hopes to demonstrate, also had a definable existence as a collective entity. This was not as a geographical area: Europe's eastern boundaries in particular were vague and hard to define, and Europe's social and cultural limits became blurred in the course of mass emigration to other parts of the world. Rather, with these provisos, Europe is best seen as a social, economic, political and cultural region sharing many common characteristics and stretching from Britain and Ireland in the west to Russia and the Balkans in the east.

In taking an approach that as far as possible is transnational, I am consciously following in the footsteps of Lord Acton, the founder of the *Cambridge Modern History* at the end of the nineteenth century. In his plan for this ambitious enterprise, Acton told his contributors that:

> Universal history is not the sum of all particular histories, and ought to be contemplated, first, in its distinctive essence, as Renaissance, Reformation, Religious Wars, Absolute Monarchy, Revolution &c. The several countries may or may not contribute to feed the main stream . . . [but] attention ought not to be dispersed, by putting Portugal, Transylvania, Iceland, side by side with France and Germany . . . My plan is to break through the mere juxtaposition of national histories and to take in, as far as may be, what is extra-territorial and universal.

In the event Acton died before he could realize this ambitious project, and when it was eventually published under the more efficient but less imaginative editorship of Sir Adolphus Ward, the *Cambridge Modern History* did indeed largely adopt a country-by-country approach, reflecting very much the nation-based vision of a younger generation of historians in the changed political and cultural atmosphere of the Europe they inhabited. It was only with the fall of communism, the extension of the European Union to much of Eastern Europe, and the renewed onward march of globalization, that the possibility of writing a real European history re-emerged. It is no longer possible to equate it, however, as Grant and

Temperley and their counterparts elsewhere tried to do, with the history of national politics and international relations. Since the 1970s at the latest, historical investigation has expanded its field of vision until it encompasses almost every aspect of human activity in the past. Already in the early 1960s, Hobsbawm's *Age of Revolution* contained chapters on religion, ideology, science, the arts, the economy and much else besides. Subsequently historical research has extended its range even further, as Osterhammel's list of topics suggests, most recently into the history of landscape and environment. Hobsbawm was able to bind his themes together through an overarching master-narrative that placed the development and determining influence of capitalism at its core. But the historians of the early twenty-first century, a time when grand master-narratives have fallen into disrepute, can no longer enjoy this advantage: the most we can do, as Tim Blanning says, is to trace 'lines of development'.

Two of the main lines of development Blanning identifies for the years 1648 to 1815, what he calls 'the relentless march of the state to hegemony' and 'the emergence of a new kind of cultural space – the public sphere', continued through the nineteenth century. They achieved an expansion and a dominance that were almost unthinkable in the eighteenth century. The state structures of the Restoration Europe that emerged in 1815 would in some respects still have been familiar to the continent's inhabitants of thirty years before, even though appearances in many ways were deceptive. The power and intrusiveness of the state were still relatively limited. Popular participation in politics was still minimal, despite the recent, vivid example of the events of the French Revolution. The public sphere was still confined mostly to a small stratum of the educated and the literate and their institutions, from the periodical publication to the coffee house or the reading club. But by 1914 the state had been transformed. On the one hand there was universal male and in some parts of the continent even female suffrage, and direct popular participation in the shaping of national, regional and local policy, not least through organized political parties. On the other hand there was a vast expansion in the control that the state could exercise over its citizens, in areas ranging from education to health, military service to social work.

The linked processes of the improvement of communications and the growth of the economy delineated by Blanning accelerated faster in the nineteenth century than anyone in the eighteenth century could have imagined. In 1815 the railway, the telegraph, the steamship and the photograph were barely visible over the historical horizon. By 1914 Europe was entering the age of the telephone, the motor car, radio and cinema. In 1815 we are still in the age of the Newtonian understanding of the universe, of representational art and classical music. By 1914 Einstein had propounded his Theory of Relativity, Picasso had painted his Cubist works, Schoenberg had composed his first atonal pieces. Europe was also in an even more immediate sense entering the age of the machine gun, the tank, the submarine and the fighter plane. The first aerial bombardment of an enemy was recorded in 1911, during the Italian invasion of Libya, and the first European concentration camps were opened in South Africa by the British and in South-West Africa (Namibia) by the Germans. Such developments, foreshadowing the immense violence and destructiveness of the first half of the twentieth century, stand as a warning against treating the nineteenth century as most of its inhabitants treated it, as an age of linear progress and open-ended improvement. Progress had its price, and in the succeeding period, between 1914 and 1949 – as Ian Kershaw shows in *To Hell and Back*, the next volume in this series – Europe paid it in full measure.

Blanning's volume ends on a gloomy note as far as the condition of life of the vast majority of Europeans was concerned, with the beginnings of industry and the effects of rapid population growth bringing 'a new kind of poverty . . . not a sudden affliction by famine, plague or war but a permanent state of malnutrition and underemployment'. The nineteenth century, indeed, as this suggests, was relatively free of major European famines, plagues and wars, and one task of this book will be to explain why. As in so many other aspects of this period, the changed relationship of Europe with the rest of the world was an important determining factor here. Famines there were, notably in Ireland, Scandinavia and Russia, and plagues too, in the form of periodic outbreaks of cholera that swept the continent, but these too were neither so frequent nor so devastating as in some previous eras, and by the end of the century they had largely vanished from Europe.

This did not mean, however, that social, economic and other forms of inequality vanished along with them. Running through this book is the representation of the shifting contours of inequality in the nineteenth century, with its older forms, such as serfdom on the land, giving way to newer ones, such as wage labour in the factory. The nineteenth century can be seen as the age par excellence of emancipation, with millions of people being given greater equality of status, including in key respects the majority of the rural population, women, and religious minorities, notably the Jews, and this book will explore in detail these enormous changes and how they came about. But equality and emancipation were only ever partial and conditional, as the years after 1914 were to show, and describing the limitations people experienced in this process of liberation is also a central task for the historian of nineteenth-century Europe.

Arguments and disputes about inequality were at the centre of nineteenth-century European politics. Building on the legacy of ideas bequeathed by the French Revolution, increasing numbers of political thinkers and actors began to conceive and tried to implement ways and means of overcoming the inequalities they witnessed. The spectrum of solutions ranged from aristocratic paternalism and the sense of *noblesse oblige* at one extreme to the anarchist attempt to destroy the state at the other. Socialism, liberalism, communism, nationalism and many other doctrines prioritized one method or another of freeing people from the yoke of oppression and exploitation according to how they defined it. Those who put stability and hierarchy first recognized they could not survive simply by clinging to the old order, or at least, most of them did; and so they too became participants in the great debate on inequality. Religions offered a variety of answers to problems rooted in the temporal world, or advocated escape from it altogether. What all these many different strands of thought had in common was a desire to acquire and wield power so that they could put their ideas into action. Thus while Tim Blanning calls his history of Europe from 1648 to 1815 *The Pursuit of Glory*, signifying the priorities of the dominant political elites of the age, this book has the title *The Pursuit of Power*.

The pursuit of power permeated European society in the nineteenth century. States grasped for world power, governments reached out for imperial power, armies built up their military power, revolutionaries plotted to grab power, political parties campaigned to come to power, bankers and industrialists strove for economic power, serfs and sharecroppers were gradually liberated from the arbitrary power exercised over them by landowning aristocrats. The central social process of the century, the emancipation of vast sections of the oppressed from the power of their oppressors, found its most widespread manifestation in the emancipation of women from their imprisonment in a nexus of laws, customs and conventions that subordinated them to the power of men. Just as feminists fought for equality before the law, so too in the new world of industry, labour unions went on strike for more power over wages and conditions of work, modernist artists challenged the power of the Academies, and novelists organized their work around struggles for power within the family and other social institutions.

Nineteenth-century society increased its power over nature: governments gained the power to avert or alleviate hunger and natural disasters such as fires and floods; medical researchers reached out in their laboratories for power over disease; engineers and planners channelled rivers, drained marshes, drove out wild animals and levelled forests, they built towns and cities, railway and sewer networks, ships and bridges, to extend humankind's power over the natural world; and in a different sense, scientists and mechanics devised and exploited new sources of power, from steam to electricity, from the power loom to the internal combustion engine. Power could be formal or informal, it could be exercised through violence or persuasion, it could be consensual or majoritarian, it might take economic, social, cultural, political, religious, organizational or a host of other forms. But as the nineteenth century progressed, people increasingly prioritized power over glory, honour and comparable values that had been dominant through most centuries before 1815. By the end of the century, too, power was being reconceptualized in racial terms, as Europeans came to regard their hegemony over much of the rest of the world as evidence of their superiority over its inhabitants. How and why all this came to be, and how power relations within Europe affected and were affected by the rapidly changing power relations between Europe, Asia, Africa and other parts of the globe, are the themes that stand at the centre of this book.

The book is divided into eight chapters, each of which is subdivided into ten sections. Chapters 1, 3, 7 and 8 deal primarily with political history, Chapters 2 and 4 with social and economic history, and Chapters 5 and 6 with what might broadly be called cultural history. The first chapter takes the story of European politics from the final defeat of Napoleon in 1815 to the last aftershocks of the 1830 Revolutions; the third chapter takes the story up to the 1848 Revolutions and follows their aftermath in the conflict-ridden and unstable years up to the early 1870s; the seventh chapter examines how European states responded to the growing challenge of democracy between 1871 and 1914; and the eighth and final chapter turns to Europe's subjugation, however partially realized, of most other parts of the globe in the age of imperialism, and its ultimately devastating effects on Europe itself with the coming of the First World War. In between the first two of these chronologically defined narratives there is a chapter on the development of European economy and society from 1815 to 1848 – though full coverage of the key change of the period, the emancipation of the serfs in many parts of the Continent, demands that some strands of development in the rural world have to be followed all the way up to 1914. The fourth chapter deals with the major structures of Europe's society and economy from mid-century onwards and the massive changes they underwent during these years. Chapter 5 ranges over the whole period in a discussion of society's attempt to impose order and control over nature, from the wild forests, rivers and mountains of the Continent to the struggle for mastery over human nature in its many forms of expression. The sixth chapter contrasts the century as an age of emotion with the age of reason that preceded it, dealing with the various manifestations of the human spirit, religion, belief, culture, education, and ideas of humanity itself, that shared this fundamental characteristic.

To underscore the human dimension of this history, each chapter begins with the life story of an individual whose beliefs and experiences raise many of the topics the chapter discusses. Each of the eight individuals comes from a different country, and there are four men and four women. This balance is quite deliberate. Women formed over half the population of Europe during this period, as in almost every other period in history. Just as important is another fundamental feature of the period, namely that the overwhelming majority of Europeans, even on the eve of the First World War, lived in and off the countryside. Peasants, farmers and landowners often get pushed to the margins in histories of nineteenth-century Europe, particularly those structured around the rise of industrial society, but to consign these millions to a category labelled by Karl Marx as 'the idiocy of rural life' or to portray them as nothing more than the victims of historical change seems to me to be fundamentally misguided.

The book is designed to be read through from start to finish; those who wish to use it as a work of reference are advised to consult the index. In conformity with the overall format of the series, there are no footnote or endnote references. As in any synthetic work of this nature, the author is reliant principally on the work of others; such originality as it possesses is to be found in the arguments and interpretations that the book advances, and in the range and juxtaposition of the themes it treats. I hope the many other historians whose specialized research and writing I have plundered will forgive me for not crediting their work explicitly. At least, however, I may be permitted to reference the sources for the biographies that open each chapter (full details in the Further Reading on pp. 717–26): *The Diary of a Napoleonic Foot Soldier*, ed. Marc Raeff (New York, 1991), for pp. 1–3; *A Life under Russian Serfdom*, transl. and ed. Boris B. Gorshkov (Budapest, 2005), for pp. 85–8; Máire Cross and Tim Gray, *The Feminism of Flora Tristan* (Oxford, 1992) and *The London Journal of Flora Tristan*, transl. and ed. Jean Hawkes (London, 1992), for pp. 169–71; Hermynia zur Mühlen, *The End and the Beginning*, transl. and ed. Lionel Gossman (Cambridge, 2010), for pp. 274–7; Wendy Bracewell, *Orientations* (Budapest, 2009), for pp. 355–8, also for pp. 143 and 489; Brita K. Stendhal, *The Education of a Self-Made Woman* (Lewiston, NY, 1994), for pp. 444–7; Martin Pugh, *The Pankhursts* (London, 2001), for pp. 537–40; and Ivor N. Hume, *Belzoni* (Charlottesville, VA), for pp. 626–9. Other lengthy quotations are taken from original sources, except for pp. 426 (Dirk Blasius, *Der verwaltete Wahnsinn* [Frankfurt, 1980]); 429–31 (Andrew Scull, *The Most Solitary of Afflictions* [London, 1993]); 437 (John A. Davis, *Conflict and Control* [London, 1988]); 576–7 (F. S. L. Lyons, *Charles Stewart Parnell* [London, 1977]); 605 (Hartmut Pogge-von Strandmann, 'Domestic Origins of Germany's Colonial Expansion under Bismarck', *Past and Present*, February 1969); 612 (Franco Venturi, *Roots of Revolution* [London, 1960]); 614 (Edvard Radzinsky, *Alexander II* [New York, 2005]); and 663 (Adam Hochschild, *King Leopold's Ghost* [New York, 1998]).

I began writing this book in 2009, but its origins go back much further, to the decades I spent teaching the history of nineteenth-century Europe at a number of universities before my interests shifted to the twentieth century with my move to Cambridge in 1998. I have been fortunate to be able to draw on the many lectures I have given on the history of nineteenth-century Europe over the years, at the University of Stirling in Scotland, at Columbia University in the City of New York, at the University of East Anglia at Norwich, at Birkbeck, University of London, and most recently at Gresham College in the City of London. I am grateful to the students who listened patiently to my ideas in lectures and seminars in all these institutions and helped firm up, or change, my arguments and my general approach with their comments. A project as wide-ranging as this one could not have been completed in so short a time without research assistance, and I am especially grateful to my former students Daniel Cowling, Niamh Gallagher, Rachel Hoffman, Susie Lada and Georgie Williams for supplying me with material. Cambridge University's History Faculty and Wolfson College provided invaluable time to write by granting me sabbatical leave in 2012, and the University Library's inexhaustible resources and helpful staff made it the first port of call for information on many subjects.

Many friends and colleagues have read all or part of this book, suggested improvements and corrected my errors. Simon Winder at Penguin Books, a prince among editors, has suggested many improvements. I owe a huge debt to Rachel Hoffman for her careful and detailed reading of Chapters 1, 3 and 6, to David Motadel for the many corrections he made to Chapters 2, 4–5, 7–8, to Joanna Bourke for commenting incisively on Chapter 5, and to Tim Blanning, Lucy Riall and Astrid Swenson for their very helpful reading of the entire manuscript. Any remaining mistakes are entirely my own responsibility. Cecilia Mackay provided invaluable help with the illustrations, which have been chosen to offer additional insights on the topics discussed, and selected to follow the sequence of the chapters. The paintings and photographs referred to in the text can easily be located on the Internet, if so desired. Andras Bereznay, as ever, proved a learned and stimulating cartographer. Richard Mason has been a meticulous copy-editor; he corrected many errors and helped materially improve the readability of the text at a number of points. Christine Shuttleworth produced a splendidly comprehensive index. Richard Duguid has put me in his debt by overseeing the process of production. Several knotty problems of orthography had in the end to remain unresolved, most notably the transliteration of Russian names: we opted for the traditional forms, since the modern Library of Congress system is still unfamiliar to the majority of readers. As far as possible, people's original names are used – thus for example Wilhelm rather than William, or Franz rather than Francis – but in a few exceptional cases, notably those of the Russian tsars, this would seem strange, so the English forms have been preferred. In the case of place names, the most widely used contemporary appellations have been used, with their modern equivalents provided in the Index.

Finally I am, as always, deeply indebted to Christine Corton for taking time off from her own work to check the proofs, and, with our sons Matthew and Nicholas, for sustaining me throughout the long process of gestation.

Richard J. Evans
Cambridge, May 2016

I

The Legacies of Revolution

THE AFTERMATH OF WAR

At some time in the late 1820s or early 1830s – the date is uncertain – in the town of Ellwangen in the south-west German state of Württemberg, the stonemason Jakob Walter (1788–1864) sat down to write his memoirs. He had been conscripted into the Grand Army of French Emperor Napoleon Bonaparte (1769–1821) as a common foot soldier and marched with it all the way to Moscow and back. In stark, simple prose, Walter recorded the terrible sufferings he had experienced during the army's retreat in the last months of 1812. Constantly harassed by Cossacks, scavenging for food, cold, dirty and hungry, robbed by bandits, and narrowly escaping death on numerous occasions, Walter somehow survived the ordeal. On finding regular quarters, for the first time in many weeks, in a Polish town, he gave himself a wash:

> The washing of my hands and face proceeded very slowly because the crusts on my hands, ears, and nose had grown like fir-bark, with cracks and coal-black scales. My face resembled that of a heavily bearded Russian peasant; and, when I looked into the mirror, I was astonished myself at the strange appearance of my face. I washed, then, for an hour with hot water and soap.

All attempts to rid himself and his clothing of lice ('my "sovereigns"') proved futile, however. Tramping further westwards with his unit, he began to suffer from a fever, most probably typhus, and had to be carried on a cart the rest of the way. Some 100 out of the 175 men in his convoy of wagons did not survive the journey. When, still lice-ridden, Walter reached his homeland, he did not think his relatives would recognize him: 'I made my entrance with a sooty Russian coat, an old round hat, and, under and in my clothing, countless travelling companions, among which were Russians, Poles, Prussians, and Saxons.' Finally he was able to wash properly, dispose of his lice-infested clothes, and begin the slow recovery of his health. Local people started to greet him 'as a "Russian" – as everyone who had been there was called at the time'.

Like the vast majority of ordinary Europeans of the era, Walter had little or no interest in, or indeed knowledge of, politics. He had been conscripted by the authorities in the French puppet state of Württemberg in 1806, and recalled to arms in 1809 and 1812. He had no more choice about this than did the many hundreds of thousands of other conscript soldiers of the time. His diary shows no sense of commitment to the French or indeed the Württemberg cause, no interest in the outcome of the war, no hatred of the Russians or desire to kill them. As an ordinary foot soldier he showed little awareness of the strategic issues behind the campaigns in which he took part. All Walter was really interested in was surviving the ordeal to which he had been unwillingly subjected. The elan of the French troops who had surged victoriously towards the counter-revolutionary Austrian armies in the early 1790s singing the *Marseillaise* had long since disappeared. Only a small number of Napoleon's soldiers, such as the elite Imperial Guard, were still motivated and committed to his cause by this time. The war-weariness that makes itself felt throughout Walter's diaries was experienced more generally across Europe, and for good reason: almost a quarter of a century of more or less continuous war had left everyone numb with suffering and despair. If Jakob Walter had any kind of commitment, it was to the strong Catholic faith that sustained him during his experience, but this did not prevent him from portraying in graphic detail the increasingly dehumanizing effects of the conflict on its participants.

After his return to his homeland, Jakob Walter settled down once more to an unremarkable life as a stonemason. He married in 1817 and the couple had ten children. Five of them survived to 1856, when Jakob, now a relatively prosperous building contractor and overseer, wrote a letter with news about the family to his son, who had emigrated to America and was living in Kansas. The following year the young man travelled back to Germany to visit his parents, and married a local girl, the daughter of the mayor of a village near Ellwangen. According to family tradition, he took the manuscript memoirs of his father back with him on his return to Kansas in 1858. Here the memoirs remained in the family's possession until they were made available to scholarship in the early 1930s. Jakob Walter himself lived on in Ellwangen for another few years, dying in 1864; his wife survived him and died in 1873. Almost everything about him remains hidden from us, like the lives of countless other villagers in the nineteenth century: only his experiences in the Grand Army's fateful expedition to Moscow, the fact that, unlike most of those who took part in it, Walter survived the ordeal, and the chance circumstances, whatever they were, that led him to put down these experiences in writing, raise him above the common obscurity in which the vast majority of Europeans led their lives.

On the way back from Moscow, Jakob Walter had at one point caught a glimpse of Napoleon himself, sitting down for an al fresco meal near the Berezina river. He was not impressed:

> He watched his army pass by in the most wretched condition. What he may have felt in his heart is impossible to surmise. His outward appearance seemed indifferent and unconcerned over the wretchedness of his soldiers; only ambition and lost honour may have made themselves felt in his heart; and, although the French and Allies shouted into his ears many oaths and curses about his own guilty person, he was still able to listen to them unmoved.

By this stage of the disastrous retreat from Moscow, the majority of Napoleon's surviving troops had nothing but hatred and contempt for him. Ripped from their domestic lives by the insatiable engine of the French Empire's military recruiting machine, 685,000 troops from Germany, Poland, Italy and France – the last named supplying fewer than half the total – had marched on Russia; fewer than 70,000 had returned, leaving 400,000 dead and more than 100,000 prisoners of the Russians, with an unknown number of stragglers and deserters making their way back unrecorded. Further battles, in which Napoleon was driven back relentlessly westwards by a coalition of European armies led by the British, the Prussians, the Austrians and the Russians, had caused further carnage. Finally, in 1814, the Allies had occupied Paris, forcing Napoleon into exile on the Mediterranean Isle of Elba.

It used to be thought that the damage inflicted by the French Revolutionary and Napoleonic Wars was relatively light compared to the devastation wrought by later conflicts. Yet altogether, in twenty-three years of more or less continuous warfare that had swept back and forth across Europe in the wake of the French Revolution, an estimated five million people had died; compared to Europe's population as a whole, this was proportionately as many as, if not more than, those who died during the First World War. One in five Frenchmen born between 1790 and 1795 had perished during the conflicts. Napoleon's armies had lost anything up to one and a half million men in all. Moscow had been burned to the ground by the Russians to deny its resources to the enemy for overwintering. For three days, one observer had noted, 'the whole city was on fire, thick sheaves of flame of various colours rose up on all sides to the heavens, blotting out the horizon, sending in all directions a blinding light and a burning heat'. In the chaos, French soldiers had looted everything they could lay their hands on, joined in the pillaging by peasants who descended upon the city from the surrounding countryside. After the fires had died down, the charred ruins of the burnt-out city had offered little in the way of food and shelter to sustain Napoleon's army through the winter. Nearly 7,000 out of just over 9,000 houses, more than 8,000 shops and warehouses, and over a third of the city's 329 churches had been totally destroyed. Some 270 million roubles' worth of private property had been lost without any possibility of compensation. Many civilians had already fled, and most of the rest had subsequently left the city, facing a life of vagabondage and destitution. Only 2 per cent of the population had remained, and a large proportion of these, including many soldiers, did not survive. When the Russians had eventually reoccupied Moscow, they had been forced to pile up 12,000 corpses on huge pyres and burn them. The reconstruction of the city only began properly in 1814, with parks and gardens springing up where once there had been a jumble of narrow streets, and a grand new palace for the tsar. For more than a generation Moscow remained a building site; the commission established to oversee the city's reconstruction was only wound up in 1842, and even then, Moscow still had far to go before it could regain its former splendour.

In Spain meanwhile, pitched battles and sieges had devastated numerous towns and villages. Puerto Real, occupied by the French during a two-year siege of Cádiz between 1810 and 1812, had lost half its population of 6,000; 40 per cent of its buildings had been destroyed, along with three-quarters of its olive trees and most of the surrounding pine forests. Many towns in Spain never recovered. Everywhere, the depredations of the French had caused a precipitous drop in the numbers of cattle, horses, pigs and sheep. Extremadura had lost nearly 15 per cent of its pre-war population. Francisco de Goya (1746–1828) captured the realities of the conflict in eighty-two engravings known by the title *The Disasters of War*. Unpublished until the 1860s, they showed horrific scenes of rape, pillage, mutilation and butchery. In one of the engravings, a corpse is depicted rising from a coffin holding a sheet of paper inscribed with the word *Nada*, 'Nothing', the word that the painter chose to summarize the end result of the bitter years of conflict.

In the Rhineland, the repeated rampages of French troops over the years had stripped the fields of their produce, the farms of their livestock, and the towns and villages of their supplies. Ferocious financial levies imposed by the French on the inhabitants of the region had added to the general picture of rapacity and greed. The damage had been done early on in the conflict, with lasting effect. Returning from the area in 1792, a French agent had reported that 'not even the most vital means of subsistence – nothing for the animals or the seed – have been left behind, and other objects in the villages have also been stolen'. Bands of robbers had roamed the countryside, dressed as French soldiers to deceive their victims, signalling by so doing that local inhabitants were habituated to the rape, pillage and destruction being carried out by the occupying military. Indeed, when the French armies had arrived at Aachen, they had immediately denuded the town and the surrounding countryside of grain, forage, clothing, livestock, and almost anything that could be moved; hundreds of local inhabitants had died of starvation as winter began to bite.

Not only the French but other armies too had lived off the land, looting and plundering as they went. All of them had made heroic efforts to organize essential supplies, and in the period 1812–14 at least, growing patriotic sentiment among the Allied nations had ensured that nobles, merchants and ordinary farmers had made extensive voluntary contributions of many kinds to the war effort. But this had seldom been enough, given the enormous scale of the fighting. The Russian army had organized basic supplies of food for itself, transported across long communication lines that had become stretched almost to breaking point as it marched westwards in 1813–14. However, these supplies had consisted of little more than black bread and the basic ingredients of gruel or porridge, and the troops had been forced to find more varied and palatable things to eat by stealing them, sometimes from their own allies. Feeding the hundreds of thousands of horses that carried cavalrymen, pulled field artillery or dragged supply wagons had posed a particular problem for all the armies involved in the war, and foraging parties had ranged far and wide in search of oats and other fodder. As the Russians had moved into France, whole villages had been devastated by the fighting. Peasants had fled to the forests, as they were already used to doing to evade Napoleon's conscription agents, emerging every now and then to waylay Allied supply trains along the roads. After the Battle of Waterloo, some 900,000 foreign troops occupied France, causing widespread economic hardship by their exactions.

Nature did not help the process of recovery. In April 1815 a massive eruption of the Tambora volcano, the largest known in history, on the island of Sumbawa in present-day Indonesia, sent a vast dust cloud up to twenty-seven miles high. The noise of the explosion was heard 1,250 miles away. Huge masses of sulphur were ejected into the stratosphere, where the minute particles lingered for more than two years, darkening the skies and creating spectacular orange sunsets. 'Morn came and went,' wrote George Gordon, Lord Byron (1788–1824), '– and came, and brought no day.' In Hungary brown-coloured snow fell in January 1816, and whole houses were said to have disappeared beneath snowdrifts. The eruption occurred in the middle of a decade of cold summers that had already begun in 1811, caused by changes in the sun's output and the circulation of weather systems around the earth, and by an earlier major volcanic eruption that had taken place in Colombia in 1808. By the end of 1816 it was clear that crop yields had declined in many areas to little more than a quarter of their normal levels, and the harvest, such as it was, came in over a month later than usual. In the Netherlands violent summer storms inflicted further damage on crops. 'Melancholy accounts have been received from all parts of the Continent of the unusual wetness of the season,' reported a British newspaper in July 1816: 'In several provinces of Holland, the rich grass lands are all under water, and scarcity and high prices are naturally apprehended and dreaded. In France the interior of the country has suffered greatly from the floods and heavy rains.' The Paris Observatory recorded summer temperatures that would turn out to be 5.4 degrees Fahrenheit below the mean for the period 1740–1870, and in some areas the grapes failed to ripen before winter set in.

'Every storm of the past summer', stated a yearbook compiled in Württemberg in 1817, 'was followed by the most severe cold, so that it regularly felt like November.' The Lower Rhine flooded for five whole months, and in Lombardy-Venetia snow was still lying on the ground in May. Early frost during the autumn did further damage. Carinthian farmers were unable to sow winter grains for the third year in succession, and 1817's grain yield in the south-west German state of Baden was said to be the poorest within living memory. In south-eastern Europe the harsh winter of 1815–16 killed more than 24,000 sheep in the county of Bács, in the Vojvodina, it was reported, while continuous rains in the early spring led to 'extensive flood, mostly because of the Danube', as the chroniclers of the Franciscan monastery of Šarengrad recorded. 'Nobody, not even old men remember such a flood happening before. It flooded many villages on this and on that side of the Danube, arable land and hayfields . . . The water rose as high as man's height.' The parish priest in the Croatian village of Zminj called 1816 a year that was 'fatal':

> because of frequent rain and other bad weather [it] was so sterile that many citizens could not prepare enough cereals to last them for half a year, and some not even for two months . . . As early as the month of March, these people began to be affected by Black Famine; yet they supported each other

as long as they had anything to eat ... But this was of short duration ...
Reduced to the uttermost misery they were walking around and falling
dead, some at home, some along roads, some in the forests etc.

For Croatia, 1816 and above all 1817 was the time of the 'great famine'.
Grain prices were between two and three times higher than they were five
years later. War had disrupted communications, so relief was hard to
organize. This global climatic calamity thus resulted in the worst harvests
to be seen in Europe for more than a century; and it happened when
Europe was struggling to recover its trade and industry after the disrup-
tions of the French Revolutionary and Napoleonic Wars. The British
blockade and the Napoleonic counter-blockade known as the Continental
System had ruined commerce on the Continent and in the United Kingdom
too, cutting off markets and throwing thousands out of work. By the end
of 1816 there were said to be between 20,000 and 30,000 unemployed
weavers in the London district of Spitalfields, and similar conditions were
observed in textile towns in Saxony, Switzerland and the Low Countries.
Hundreds of thousands of soldiers like Jakob Walter were demobilized at
the end of the war, adding to the already numerous armies of the
unemployed.

At the same time as people were suffering a severe loss of income, the
catastrophically bad harvest of 1816 caused grain prices to rise precipi-
tously. Bread was the staple of most people's diet, and in Paris it cost more
than twice as much in 1817 as it had done a year before. Touring the
Rhineland in 1817, the Prussian army officer and military theorist Carl
von Clausewitz (1780–1831) noted 'a complete harvest failure in all of
southern and western Germany', which was resulting in 'a true famine'.
Clausewitz 'saw ruined figures, scarcely resembling men, prowling around
the fields searching for food among the unharvested and already half-rotten
potatoes that never grew to maturity'. In the uplands of Habsburg-ruled
Lombardy, the poor were living off roots and herbs. In Transylvania and
the eastern provinces of Hungary, deaths from starvation were estimated
at more than 20,000. The Habsburg Emperor Franz I (1768–1835) complained that in one part of Lombardy 'the distress had become so severe
that the population was reduced to a diet of lettuce and soup made from
herbs, and on very many days had nothing to eat at all'.

In these dire circumstances, the poorest were reduced to begging, stealing, or fleeing to the towns in search of food. In Munich, wrote one
observer towards the end of 1816, 'beggars appeared from all directions,
as if they had crawled out of the ground'. Hungary was said to be 'overrun
with bands of beggars', while in Rome and Vienna the police began to

conduct regular raids to take them off the streets and put them into public works projects. 'The number of beggars,' wrote one visitor to the Swiss canton of Appenzell in June 1816, 'mostly women and children, is perfectly shocking.' They had, as another observer noted, 'the paleness of death in their cheeks'. Many of the poor took the drastic decision to leave Europe altogether, assisted by local authorities who were only too glad to get rid of them: more than 2,000 people left Baden for Rio de Janeiro in 1818; 20,000 German and 30,000 French people were said to have left for the United States in 1817; more than 9,000 impoverished inhabitants of Württemberg made the long trek eastwards to the Russian Empire in 1817, in response to promises of support from Tsar Alexander I (1777–1825). The movement of masses of human beings across large areas of territory brought with it epidemic disease, especially in the unhygienic conditions in which armies and bands of destitute migrants and beggars subsisted during an age before hygienic precautions or antibiotic remedies. Deaths from smallpox nearly quadrupled in Paris between 1816 and 1818, with a major epidemic breaking out in the Low Countries as well. Malnutrition weakened people's resistance and made them susceptible to diarrhoea, dysentery and oedema; in the northern Italian town of Brescia, the hospitals admitted nearly 300 cases of scurvy in the first half of 1816 alone. Typhus, carried by the human body louse, spread with particular rapidity, affecting almost every town in England and Wales, Scotland and Ireland – in 1818 alone some 32,000 cases and 3,500 deaths from the disease were recorded in Glasgow, a city of 130,000 inhabitants. Famine relief measures only helped the disease to spread more quickly. A physician in Ireland considered, accurately enough, 'the contagion to have been rapidly spread by the numbers wandering about in search of subsistence, and also by the establishments for the distribution of soup and other provisions among the poor where multitudes were gathered together'.

Bubonic plague spread rapidly across the Balkans, reaching Italy in 1815, killing one-seventh of the population of the Italian town of Noja, near Bari on the Adriatic; when it reached the Balearic islands it devastated the population, causing a total of 12,000 deaths in 1820. Large numbers of people died of the plague in Bosnia, perhaps a third or more of the townsfolk and a quarter of the peasantry. Driven desperate by hunger, people flocked from the countryside to infected towns in search of food, evading quarantines and cordons sanitaires. The population of the Dalmatian city of Makarska fell from 1,575 to 1,025 as a result of the epidemic, while the village of Tucepi lost 363 of its 806 inhabitants. The Ottoman administration, which still ruled over the greater part of the Balkans, was incapable of dealing with these calamities. This was the last major outbreak of the plague in Europe, and it was a severe one. One historical study of the epidemic has concluded that 'the sanitary and demographic catastrophe which befell Bosnia in the years 1815–18 had no parallel in other European countries since the Black Death in the years 1347–1351'. In the western Mediterranean, seaports hastily improvised quarantine arrangements for incoming ships, while the province known as the Military Frontier of the Habsburg Monarchy, the heavily garrisoned border with the Ottoman Empire, posed another barrier to communication. These institutions mostly proved effective, stopping the plague from spreading to the north and west. Nevertheless, the combined effect of all these factors, particularly harvest failure and epidemic disease, was to increase the number of deaths across Europe. In most of western Europe death rates rose by 8 or 9 per cent, but some areas were particularly badly affected; for example, mortality rates doubled in eastern Switzerland over the same period.

Beginning in 1816, Europe experienced the most widespread and violent series of grain riots since the French Revolution. Starving crowds in East Anglia wielding cudgels studded with iron spikes and carrying a banner inscribed with the words 'Bread or Blood' trashed the houses of suspected profiteers, demanding a lowering of the price of bread and meat. In northern England and Scotland, crowds seized grain stores and attacked the homes of millers, tradesmen and corn merchants. In many parts of France, groups of people prevented the movement of grain outside their own area, while in Italy granaries and bakeries were looted, and there were grain riots in Augsburg and Munich. As cereal prices reached unprecedented levels in the Low Countries in June 1817, mobs attacked and looted bakeries, and used the second anniversary of the Battle of Waterloo to protest against the price of bread. Crowds raided farms in eastern France and were so numerous that some people were reminded of the mass peasant mobilization known as the Great Fear in 1789. In many cases these disturbances took on a distinctively political tone, most notably in a mass uprising at Lyon in 1817, sparked by rumours of Napoleon's impending return. In Manchester, on 10 March 1817, several hundred weavers (the 'Blanketeers') resolved to march on London to demand measures to relieve the crisis in the cotton industry. In June politics played some part in the abortive uprising in Nottingham known as the Pentrich Revolution, and in the Breslau insurrection of 23 August when conscripts refused to take the Prussian militia oath. Looking at these disturbances on a Europe-wide basis makes it clear that they were fundamentally caused not by local or national political factors but by the subsistence crisis, by mass unemployment and destitution, and in many cases by fear of worse to come. Of the 2,280 prosecutions undertaken in France during the so-called 'White Terror' of the post-Napoleonic years in France, the vast majority concerned offences such as enforcing lower grain prices, preventing shipments of grain, resisting tax collectors, or cutting down trees in privately owned forests. Counter-revolutionary politics played only a marginal role.

Even as the crisis began to subside, in 1819, rioting continued. A mass public protest meeting in August of up to 60,000 people at St Peter's Fields in Manchester was shot down by the military in an action popularly dubbed 'the Peterloo Massacre', an ironic reference to the Battle of Waterloo; fifteen protesters were killed. In the same year antisemitic riots spread across western and central Europe under the name of the 'Hep-Hep' movement, ascribed by nervous authorities to the machinations of secret societies. In all likelihood they emerged from popular resentment against the perceived commercial success of Jewish businessmen at a time of economic distress. Enraged artisans, encouraged in university towns by radical students, physically attacked Jews, destroyed their property, and forced many to flee. The riots spread from Würzburg to Karlsruhe and Heidelberg, down the Rhine to Frankfurt, north as far as Copenhagen and nearby communities, where sailors joined with local citizens to throw stones at Jewish houses, east to Cracow, Danzig, Prague and Riga, and west into the French departments of the Upper and Lower Rhine and the Moselle. Since property was being attacked, the authorities moved in everywhere to suppress the disturbances, and by 1820 the wave of unrest was over. Here too, the participation in some towns of better-off citizens and university students gave the riots a political element that was profoundly alarming to governments.

The post-Napoleonic crisis and the accompanying Europe-wide unrest, unevenly distributed though they both were in their incidence and impact, impelled governments to adopt welfare and relief measures, creating a general acceptance of the state's obligation to take steps to alleviate the distress of the most impoverished sectors of the population. In 1815–19 the ability of European states to implement this idea was often very limited. The frequent border changes of the previous decades, the fact that newly created states were still putting together their administrative machines and extending them to far-flung areas, and the difficulties of getting grain to the afflicted parts of the country – in an era when roads were often still rudimentary, railways yet to exist, canals few in number and rivers difficult to navigate – all meant that people in more remote regions were doomed to starve unless they migrated closer to the centres of power. But the disturbances also added to the general fear among elites that unrest could lead to revolution as it had done in 1789, with all the consequences that followed. As a result, the post-Napoleonic settlement paid as much attention to preventing revolution, and repressing it where it seemed to be taking place, as it did to curbing whatever the military and political ambitions of France might threaten to be in the future.

AFTER NAPOLEON

Before the victorious European powers could get very far in drawing a line under the French Revolutionary and Napoleonic past, they were confronted by the sudden return of Napoleon from his enforced exile on the Mediterranean island of Elba. The restored French monarchy under Louis XVIII (1755–1824), brother of the executed Louis XVI (1754–93), had run into trouble almost immediately, overwhelmed by the need to pay for the legacy of the war. It retained the unpopular taxes imposed by Napoleon, imposed cutbacks in expenditure on the army, and reimposed censorship after decades of impassioned debate. The proclamation of a militant Catholicism as the state religion alienated many educated Frenchmen. There were widespread fears that the king would try to restore lands confiscated by the Revolution to their original clerical and aristocratic owners. Napoleon's return thus triggered an outburst of popular sentiment in favour of preserving the legacy of the Revolution. 'The people of the countryside,' reported a local official in central France, 'are manifesting an extraordinary sense of enthusiasm [for Napoleon]; fires are lit every evening on elevated positions, and there are public celebrations in many communes.' And, he concluded, 'It is commonly asserted that if the emperor had not returned to put the aristocrats in their place they would have been massacred by the peasants.'

Such outbursts, compounded by demonstrations of support from Parisian workers, alienated many bourgeois notables, and the former emperor faced serious hostility among the clergy. In areas such as the Vendée, the Midi and Brittany, traditionally favourable to the royalists, he was unable to win much support. It was above all among his former soldiers, angered by the mass dismissals and economic measures imposed by the restored monarchy, that Napoleon was popular. 'I only have the people and the Army up to captain level for me,' he remarked: 'The rest are scared of me but I cannot rely on them.' His arrival exposed the deep divisions in French society left by a quarter of a century of revolutionary change. However, within weeks of landing in France on 1 March 1815, he was able to muster 100,000 men, as the provincial administrators, mostly appointed by him, did their job of recruitment as before, and veterans rallied to the imperial flag. Breaking off their peace negotiations, the Allies acted swiftly, fearing that if he remained in power the ex-emperor would quickly resume his career of conquest and the pursuit of glory. Within a few weeks they too managed to raise a formidable military force, consisting of 112,000 British, Dutch and German troops under Arthur Wellesley, Duke of Wellington (1769–1852). They held back Napoleon's army at the village of Waterloo on 18 June 1815 until 116,000 Prussians under the veteran General Leberecht von Blücher (1742–1819), whom Napoleon wrongly thought he had disposed of at the Battle of Ligny two days before, arrived at 4 o'clock in the afternoon. Blücher rescued the British and joined with them in a final assault that drove the French from the battlefield and Napoleon into another enforced exile, this time safely on the remote Atlantic island of St Helena, where he died on 5 May 1821.

Napoleon left behind a political legend that quickly developed into a potent myth among liberal writers, politicians, army officers and students, who were encouraged by his own turn (whether genuine or not) to liberal ideas during the 'Hundred Days' before Waterloo in an attempt to broaden his support. Very much aware of the weakness of his situation, Napoleon had gone to some lengths to reassure the world that his dreams of conquest were over, and the French that he would respect the rights and liberties of the citizen and no longer behave like an imperial dictator. He continued in the same vein in his writings in exile before his death. In subsequent decades the legend of the 'liberal Emperor' gained still further in potency. 'During his life,' remarked the writer François-René de Chateaubriand (1768–1848), 'the world slipped from his grasp, but in death he possesses it.' In France, 'Bonapartism' came to stand for patriotism, universal manhood suffrage, the sovereignty of the nation, the institutions of an efficient, centralized, bureaucratic administration that dealt equally with all citizens, the periodic consultation of the people by its government through plebiscites and referendums, and an implicit contract between Frenchmen and the state that provided social order and political stability, national pride, and military glory. Not so far removed from Republicanism, Bonapartism differed from it by its greater emphasis on strong leadership and military prowess. But like Republicanism, it struck deep roots in significant parts of the French population.

Former soldiers of Napoleon's armies propagated their ideas among them for some decades following his final defeat in 1815, after they had resumed their peacetime lives in town or country. Most potent of all was the political inspiration of Napoleon's military coup d'état on 18 Brumaire (9 November) 1799, which had overthrown the revolutionary Directory, brought him to power as First Consul, and led to his establishment of the First French Empire in 1804. Particularly during the 1820s, radical officers all across Europe considered that this was the quickest and most effective way to destroy the repressive regimes of the Restoration and bring about a liberal transformation of the political system wherever they were. Meanwhile, the image of Napoleon was celebrated in countless popular stories and cheap pamphlets, folk songs, paintings and sculptures, old imperial coins, tobacco boxes and trinkets, scarves and caps, even in children's sweets, with chocolates or boiled sugar confections made in the shape of the emperor or cheap bonbons with wrappings displaying Napoleonic symbols. Men cultivated extravagant moustaches to advertise their admiration for the Grand Army's magnificently bewhiskered Old Guard, and wore violets or red carnations in their buttonholes in defiance of the ban imposed on these imperial colours by the restored French monarchy. For many people outside France, too, the cult of Napoleon stood for the achievements of the Revolution, translated into purposeful reform after the excesses of the Terror in the early 1790s. Irish republicans and Polish nationalists looked to Napoleon for inspiration in their political struggles. The Venezuelan liberator of large swathes of South America from Spanish rule, Simón Bolívar (1783–1830), admired Napoleon so much that he had made the journey to Milan to see his hero crowned King of Italy. In China and Madagascar, Napoleon was worshipped by some as a god.

Retrospectively, in France itself, even the Battle of Waterloo became a kind of victory for the French, a celebration of courage in the face of overwhelming odds, of patriotism and self-sacrifice for the 'Great Nation' – 'The Old Guard dies,' General Pierre Cambronne (1770–1842) was supposed to have said at Waterloo, 'it never surrenders.' No matter that the quotation was most probably a later invention, and that Cambronne eventually surrendered anyway: his defiance exerted a powerful fascination for later generations. In *The Charterhouse of Parma* (1839) by Stendhal (the pen name of Marie-Henri Beyle, 1783–1842), the novel's hero, Fabrice del Dongo, joins up with Napoleon out of pure idealism, while in the same author's *The Red and the Black* (1830) the post-Napoleonic France portrayed is one of hypocrisy, snobbery and complacency. Another French novelist, Victor Hugo (1802–85), devoted more than forty pages of his novel *Les Misérables* (1862) to refighting the Battle of Waterloo, speculating at many points on how easily it might have gone the other way. Napoleon's plan of battle had been 'masterly', but it had been frustrated by rain ('a few drops of water') that delayed the initial movement of his artillery, by the lie of the land, by luck, and by Wellington's textbook tactics ('Wellington was the technician of war, Napoleon was its

Michelangelo ... genius was vanquished by rule-of-thumb ... Waterloo was a battle of the first importance won by a commander of the second rank'). Had Napoleon won, things would have been very different. 'Waterloo was not a battle but a change in the direction of the world.'

In reality, the ultimate defeat of Napoleon had never been in doubt; even if Wellington, as seemed not unlikely at more than one point, had been driven from the battlefield before Blücher and his Prussians arrived, Napoleon would have been vanquished in the end by sheer weight of Allied numbers. A large army led by the Austrians was encamped on the eastern bank of the Rhine further south, and a huge Russian force was marching westward, having already reached Germany by the time of Waterloo. Napoleon was simply unable to raise enough troops to match either of these forces, let alone both. Nevertheless, the spectre, raised by Napoleon's return, of a renewal of the upheavals of the past quarter of a century, had been alarming in the extreme. It had prompted the sovereigns of Britain, Austria, Prussia, Russia and numerous other, smaller European states to undertake a concerted intervention in the affairs of another, sovereign country. This had happened before, in the early 1790s, but then there was at least the excuse that the revolutionaries in France were threatening the lives of the king and his wife Marie-Antoinette, sister of the Austrian Emperor. Beyond that, they had threatened to spread the democratic principles of the Revolution to other parts of Europe. What was striking about the intervention of 1815 was its wholly preventive nature. It set the scene for further actions of this kind in the following years. Wherever the threat of revolution seemed imminent, the great powers of Europe were now clearly prepared to join forces to quash it before it became a reality.

Putting the genie of revolutionary change back into the bottle of history was not easy. For the destructiveness of the wars fought by Napoleon and his predecessors since the early 1790s was not merely physical. Napoleon had redrawn the map of Europe several times, annexing large swathes of it to France, from the Hanseatic cities in the north through the Low Countries to north-west Italy in the south, creating a French Empire that at its height covered 290,000 square miles and counted 44 million people as its inhabitants. He had surrounded this with a ring of satellite states, often ruled by his relatives, including the Grand Duchy of Warsaw, the Kingdom of Italy and the Kingdom of Westphalia. The Holy Roman Empire of the German Nation, created by Charlemagne in 800, had come to an inglorious end in 1806. Many of these changes would have been reversed in 1815, but Napoleon had shown that borders were not immutable. There were other changes too. The power of the Church had been reduced, with vast swathes of land secularized and ecclesiastical states swept off the map. The registration of births, marriages and deaths had been assigned to secular authorities. Monasteries had been dissolved, and the power of the Church had been further reduced in many areas by the introduction of freedom of religion, civil marriage and divorce, secular education and the state appointment of clergy. The Church had also been pressured into introducing freedom of worship and a measure of equal rights for non-Christians, notably Jews.

Everywhere that Napoleon ruled he had replaced encrusted custom and privilege with rationality and uniformity. While the emperor's armies rampaged across Europe, his bureaucrats had moved in silently behind, reorganizing, systematizing, standardizing. In the areas that France annexed and the borderlands where it established its client states, notably western Germany, northern Italy and the Low Countries, a new generation of professional administrators had emerged to run things while Napoleon was away waging his never-ending military campaigns. Local and regional jurisdictions, such as those exercised by hundreds of imperial knights in the Holy Roman Empire, and by Church and seigneurial courts, had been supplanted by a system of centralized uniformity administered by a judicial bureaucracy. In all these areas, the Napoleonic Law Code had disposed of existing, often tradition-bound laws and ordinances, introducing a key element of equality before the law, even if in some respects this central principle of the French Revolution had been modified by Napoleon's more conservative outlook on issues such as the rights and duties of women. Property rights were guaranteed wherever the Code applied, as they had not been in many areas before. The Code adhered to many of the key ideas of the French Revolution, including the freedom of the individual, and, as Napoleon himself proclaimed in his testament, equality of opportunity, 'career open to talent', and 'the rule of reason'. Weights and measures had been at least to some extent standardized, internal customs tolls abolished, guilds and other restrictions on the free movement of labour swept away, serfs freed (including in Poland). Everywhere Napoleon had brought change, and as he departed for his final exile on St Helena in 1815, it was clear that much of it could not be reversed.

Napoleon's legacy was even more far-reaching than this. The wars of the late eighteenth and early nineteenth century had been not merely European but global in scale. They had shattered existing global empires and paved the way for a new relationship between Europe and the rest of the world. British rule in much of North America had already been destroyed in the American War of Independence. In their turn, however, the British had broken what remained of French power in Canada and India, and had taken over Dutch and Spanish colonies in the Caribbean as well as annexing Mauritius, the Cape of Good Hope, Singapore and Ceylon. Republican movements, inspired by the French Revolution and backed by the British, sprang up all over Latin America. Their leading figure, Simón Bolívar, raised a series of irregular armies from the mixed-race and Native American population to defeat the royalists and establish a set of independent states corresponding to the old Spanish provinces – Venezuela, Colombia, Bolivia, Ecuador and Peru – while similar events further south had led to the creation of Chile and Argentina, Uruguay and Paraguay as independent or autonomous states. Between 1811 and 1824 the Spanish Empire in the Americas was destroyed. Spain had been weakened too much by the devastating Peninsular War (1807–14) to be able to raise enough troops to assert itself: and in any case, of the 42,000 soldiers it did send between 1811 and 1819, only 23,000 were left by 1820, the rest having succumbed to disease and desertion. Spain's fleet, destroyed at the Battle of Trafalgar (1805), was unable to blockade rebel ports or defeat the rebel fleet commanded by the radical British ex-naval officer Lord Thomas Cochrane (1775–1860). Sea power was vital to the South American independence movement, and it was British sea power that tipped the balance.

The British government, while remaining ostensibly neutral, turned a blind eye to men like Cochrane and their securing of supplies from Britain. It was very much in its interest to open up Latin America to free trade, and when Britain recognized the new states in 1823, the Monroe Doctrine proclaimed by the US government, which opposed any European intervention in the Americas, put an end to any further action. In 1826 the British Foreign Secretary George Canning (1770–1827) justified the long years of British support for Bolívar: 'I resolved that if France had Spain, it should not be Spain with the Indies. I called the New World into existence to redress the balance of the Old.' By this time, Brazil had also become independent from Portugal, again as a result of the Napoleonic Wars. When the French conquered Portugal in 1807, the regent Dom João (1767–1826), acting for Queen Maria the Mad (1734–1816), sailed to Rio de Janeiro and set up court there, proclaiming Brazil a full sovereign state with all the rights and privileges that went with it. This reduced Portugal to the status of a province of Brazil, especially when Dom João, becoming king after Maria's death in 1816, decided to stay on in Rio. In 1820, Dom João was forced by political upheavals in Portugal to return to Lisbon as king. He was also obliged to accept the policy of reimposing mercantilist restrictions on trade with Brazil. This in turn led his son Dom Pedro (1798–1834), now regent in Rio, to bow to Brazilian mercantile pressure and become king of an independent constitutional monarchy in Brazil in 1822.

Portuguese interference was defeated by Admiral Cochrane's fleet, and the British recognized Brazilian sovereignty in 1825.

The end of the European empires in the Americas was thus bound up inextricably with events in Europe: the ferment of ideas generated by the French Revolution; the assertion of British sea power in the drive to open up mercantilist-controlled areas of South America to free trade; the severing of connections between the Americas and European colonial metropoles by war; and the insistence of European states on imposing tight and in some cases new economic regulations and taxes on increasingly prosperous and autonomous American colonies. At the same time, events in the Americas also had a profound effect on Europe. For European liberals, radicals and revolutionaries, Latin America (with the exception of Brazil, where slavery continued virtually unchanged through the following decades) became a classic example of the success of movements of emancipation and liberation. Bolívar's wars of liberation provided a new model of heroism that in due course was to find further embodiment in the charismatic figure of Giuseppe Garibaldi (1807–82), who was to return from exile in Uruguay and Brazil to lead the popular struggle for Italian unification.

The connections between Spanish American and European liberals were many and close. Latin American revolutionaries eagerly published justifications of their actions in Europe and corresponded with an astonishing variety of European thinkers. The father of Guatemalan independence, José Cecilio del Valle (1780–1834), for example, regularly exchanged letters with Jeremy Bentham (1748–1832) and Alexander von Humboldt (1769–1859), who had himself travelled extensively in South and Central America. At the same time, Italian exiles such as Giuseppe Pecchio (1785–1835), forced to leave Italy for England after a failed uprising in 1821, advised Latin American liberals like del Valle, while a group of Italian émigrés including Claudio Linati (1790–1832) took an active part in the politics of the Mexican revolution's struggles between the factions of *Yorkinos* and *Escoceses*, named after respective Masonic lodges. The example of Latin America was particularly potent in southern Europe, where the linguistic distance was smaller than it was for Germans, Poles or Russians. The liberals and revolutionaries driven into exile by the reactionary regimes of the Restoration formed a kind of radical international whose connections spanned the Atlantic.

The events of the Revolutionary and Napoleonic era changed the balance of forces between the different parts of the globe. This was not the outcome of some long-term process whereby Europe was becoming superior to other parts of the world in terms of competitiveness, religious dedication, or culture. Far-flung, pre-industrial empires were nothing unusual in the seventeenth- and eighteenth-century world. The Chinese Empire in particular still dwarfed European empires in size. The Ottoman Empire, though it had reached its apogee by around 1700, following the failure of its siege of Vienna in 1683, still covered a huge swathe of territory from south-eastern Europe through north-west Africa to the Indian Ocean and the Middle East. Until the 1750s Islamic states still ruled India and most of south-east Asia. In Africa large states such as Oyo or Benin controlled a diverse range of territories and peoples. But Napoleon's invasion of Egypt had undermined the hold of the Ottoman Empire on the region and threatened the empire's leadership of the Muslim world with its seizure of the teaching centre of the Al Azhar mosque in Cairo. A series of fundamentalist movements had posed an additional challenge to Ottoman legitimacy. The British had arrested the Mughal Emperor in India, and invaded royal palaces in Java. In China the expedition led by Lord George, Earl Macartney (1737–1806) to Beijing in 1793 had inaugurated a long and increasingly problematic relationship with the European states, while the death of the Qian Long emperor in 1799 had undermined the legitimacy of the Qing dynasty more directly, as factional squabbles broke out and revolts against the corruption of the regime flared up in one province after another.

The global wars that ended in 1815 undermined the legitimacy of rulers everywhere, not just in Europe. By the time they were over, the relationship between Europe and the rest of the world had shifted fundamentally. Other states across the globe had managed to increase economic production and prosperity through much of the eighteenth century, largely keeping pace with European economic development; but by 1815 they had fallen behind, under the impact of European competition. China was preoccupied with its own internal affairs, as were Russia and the United States; none of these looked for a global role in the nineteenth century, though all of them would have been capable of exercising it. France was exhausted by continuous war while the French economy, on the road to industrialization in the eighteenth century, was shattered by 1815. Along with Spain and Portugal, France had lost most of its overseas empire. The British had no serious rival by 1815. None the less, the prolonged conflicts of the period had stimulated European states to reform themselves root and branch; many, indeed, had been forced to adopt some of the principles advocated by the French, in order to beat Napoleon at his own game.

The Kingdom of Prussia, for instance, had been compelled to free the country's serfs from the most onerous dues and obligations to which they had been subjected, to modernize its army, and to reform bureaucratic administration of the state to make it more effective. Tsar Alexander I's

reforming minister, Mikhail Speransky (1772–1839), a brilliant administrator of humble origin, had led the centralization of Russia's ramshackle
state apparatus, drastically reducing the power of the aristocracy over the
direction of the country's affairs and rationalizing administration through
a system of functional Ministries headed by a Council of State charged
with scrutinizing imperial legislation. However, his wider plans for reform,
including the introduction of representative institutions, were frustrated
and led to his dismissal in 1812. By this time, nevertheless, Speransky had
pushed through a major reform of education, with a new system of secondary schools and new universities founded in a number of major towns.
In many parts of Europe, the influence of Napoleon had created greater
efficiency in administration and the vital arts of troop recruitment and
tax-gathering that went hand in hand with measures to stimulate economic production, allowing entrepreneurs to accumulate wealth for
themselves and their families so long as they paid their dues to the state.
Military efficiency was thus linked productively to economic growth in
ways that the restrictive and rapacious state economic policies of China
or the Ottoman Empire did not allow.

Above all, perhaps, it was European, and as a result of the wars, overwhelmingly British command of the seas that provided the basis for the
new, dominant relationship of Europe with the rest of the world after 1815.
It allowed Europeans to colonize further parts of the globe, like Australia
or much of Africa, where the state was weak, non-existent or less well
equipped with military technology. It provided Europeans with the means
to throttle rival manufacturing centres through their control of seaborne
trade. Driving this expansion was a set of ideologies, given concrete
expression in the French Revolution and the international wars that followed it, which legitimized the conviction that European ideas and beliefs
were superior to the great majority of those held by the rest of the world,
except where, as in America, they had already taken hold. The ideas of
liberty, equality and fraternity propagated by the French Revolution and
claimed retrospectively by Napoleon had no immediate purchase here.
Even Napoleon reintroduced slavery into Haiti after its abolition by
the rebel leader Toussaint L'Ouverture (c.1743–1803), who was himself inspired by the ideals of the French Revolution. The assumption of
European superiority in terms of power politics and economic and technological strength over the rest of the world had been widespread before
1789; for the century after 1815, it had for the first time a recogniza-
ble basis in reality. And crucially, in the longer term, the assault on the
hereditary principle, beginning in America and spreading from France
throughout Europe, fatally undermined the legitimacy of institutions such

as monarchy, aristocracy, slavery and serfdom. The consequences of this assault were to become ever more momentous as the century progressed.

THE CONGRESS OF VIENNA

On 1 November 1814, following a lengthy series of preparatory meetings, the heads of state and representatives of the major European powers met in Vienna to decide how to put Europe back together again. With a brief and panic-stricken interruption for the duration of Napoleon's return and defeat at Waterloo, the Congress continued in session until 8 June the following year, and was followed by further negotiations that led to the final settlement in the Second Treaty of Paris on 20 November 1815. The Congress quickly became legendary for its many parties, entertainments and balls. Many of these were astonishingly extravagant. Estimates of the number of candles at the opening ball in this pre-electrical age varied from 12,000 to 16,000, amplified by mirrors that had one participant 'blinded and almost dizzy' as she paused at the top of the stairs. The occasion was marred only by the reported theft of a quarter of the 10,000 silver teaspoons provided for the occasion. At another ball, held in the Austrian riding school, some of the court ladies appeared dressed as the Elements. According to Anna Eynard-Lullin (1793–1868), the young wife of a wealthy Swiss participant in the proceedings, 'the prettiest of this whole masquerade was without question the Earth', represented by young women who 'wore dresses of silver cloth, their breasts were covered with diamonds, their neatly brushed hair framed their faces in the most modest manner, and this was topped by baskets of diamonds of a delightful shape, which encircled their heads and out of which cascaded quantities of flowers'. Alongside the music and dancing there was a magnificent buffet, offering, as Eynard-Lullin commented, 'a thousand good things to eat, ices, punch, broths, sweets of all sorts, and the finest delicacies'. On 6 December 1814 a ball thrown by Tsar Alexander in the Razumovsky Palace was accompanied by a thirty-six-course dinner served on twenty large tables. Shortly afterwards, the whole palace was burned to the ground in a fire caused by a malfunction in the recently installed heating system, destroying Prince Razumovsky's entire library along with his art collection, furniture, and much else besides. Many of the participants in the Congress, including the tsar, turned up to watch the spectacle as the blaze reached the roof and brought it crashing down on what was left of the contents.

With several thousand members of the aristocracy, major and minor royals, army officers, diplomats and hangers-on of various kinds staying in the city for months on end, the opportunities for intrigue, flirtation and seduction were almost limitless, and the diaries of many of the participants are filled with details of the social whirl that accompanied the negotiations. The lead in the bargaining that went on at Vienna, and during the various meetings that took place before and after the Congress, was taken by Count (later Prince) Klemens von Metternich (1777–1859), a Rhenish nobleman now in his early forties. As a diplomatic official he had risen up the ranks during the Napoleonic era, playing the principal role in arranging the marriage of a Habsburg princess to Napoleon in 1810. By this time, Metternich, handsome, elegant, charming and vain, and also intelligent, energetic and very hard-working, had become Austrian Foreign Minister. He was to guide the foreign policy of the Habsburg Empire for over three decades; and he did so in the spirit of the *ancien régime* in which he had grown up and come of age. From his diplomatic experience in a variety of European courts, he had gained a wide-ranging knowledge of international affairs; and having lived through the Revolutionary and Napoleonic cataclysms, he was determined that upheavals of this kind would never happen again.

Metternich gained much of his influence from the power of the state he represented. The Congress was not held in Vienna simply for its geographical convenience, located at the centre of Europe. It was held there above all because Austria had taken the lead in putting together one coalition of European powers after another to fight the French Emperor. It had triumphed at last alongside Russia, Prussia and – deserting Napoleon at the crucial moment – smaller states such as Saxony and Württemberg in the stupendous four-day Battle of the Nations at Leipzig in 1813. With France shattered and defeated, the Austrian Empire was the most powerful state in Europe. Numbering around 23 million inhabitants at the beginning of the century, it was a force to be reckoned with, easily standing comparison with France (28 million) and Russia (around 30 million), while dwarfing Britain (11 million), Spain (11 million), and Prussia (16 million in 1815). Population strength did not automatically translate into political influence, but in an age still dominated by mass, infantry-based armies, it certainly counted for a very great deal. Much depended on the state's ability to mobilize its resources in time of war. Unlike many other states, Austria had not reformed itself root and branch during the Revolutionary and Napoleonic eras, and many leading Austrian politicians regarded the final victory as a vindication of traditional structures and methods. As much as any other of the major powers, therefore, Austria looked for a restoration of the state of affairs as it had been before 1789, a vision gaudily symbolized in the revival of pre-Revolutionary aristocratic sociability in the balls and banquets that went on at the margins of the Congress of Vienna.

Certainly, in terms of population, Russia led the states of Europe, though not, at this stage, by very much, since it had yet to extend its domination over large parts of Central and Eastern Asia, and had only just, in 1813, seized the Caucasus from the Qajar dynasty of Persia. Tsar Alexander I, who had come to the throne in 1801 when his father, Pavel I (1754–1801), was murdered by Guards officers who resented his Prussian military style, was an enigmatic figure, dubbed by Napoleon 'the Northern Sphinx'. Initially liberal in inclination, Alexander granted a constitution to the Grand Duchy of Warsaw, ruled by Russia from 1815 as the Kingdom of Poland or 'Congress Poland', and took some steps towards improving the educational system in Russia. However, not least as a result of Napoleon's invasion of 1812, he became steadily more religious and reactionary, and insisted on keeping legislative and administrative power in Russia to himself. Victory in 1815 seemed to confirm the viability of tsarist institutions, of autocracy and serfdom, underpinned by modest administrative and military reforms. It set Alexander's face against any further change. A Russian army had marched through Europe and was occupying Paris. This not only set the seal on Alexander's belief in the validity of his own mission, it also signalled that Russia had moved into the centre of European politics.

Thus it was Alexander who took the lead in 1815 in forming, with Austria and Prussia, a Holy Alliance, committing the three powers to mutual assistance if religion, peace or justice was threatened at any future point. Later joined by other, smaller states, the signatories agreed to rule in accordance with the principles of the Christian Gospel, so that war would henceforth be banished from Europe. The treaty reflected Alexander's strong tendency towards idealism, and in effect bound him, along with the two leading German powers, to achieving their aims by co-operation, rather than by fomenting discord among their rivals within the triumvirate. The British Foreign Secretary Lord Castlereagh (1769–1822) dismissed the Holy Alliance privately as 'a piece of sublime mysticism and nonsense'. But he was convinced enough of its utility in practice to get the Prince Regent (1762–1830, from 1820 King George IV) to subscribe to the Holy Alliance while at the same time avoiding any formal commitment on the part of the British government itself. The spectre of democracy raised by the French Revolution was as alarming to conservative British statesmen like Castlereagh as it was to the Prussian bureaucratic regime established after the cataclysmic defeat of the Prussian armies by Napoleon at the battles of Jena and Auerstedt or to the reactionary administration led by Metternich in Vienna. The Holy Alliance held out the prospect of Russian intervention to suppress revolution in other parts of Europe, giving Russia a role it retained until the middle of the century, and then did not regain before the end of the Second World War; but it did so also by ensuring that Russia would not act alone, rather, in concert with the other major victorious powers.

Terrified of any renewal of war or violence, not least on the part of France, the negotiators at Vienna were concerned not only to restore and bolster the legitimacy of sovereigns but also to reconcile real and potential opposing interests as far as they could. This meant binding France into the new network of international relations. With a remarkable lack of national hatred or recrimination, the Austrians, Prussians, British and Russians included a representative of the French in the negotiations – Prince Charles-Maurice de Talleyrand-Périgord (1754–1838), who had been Napoleon's Foreign Minister but had switched sides at the right moment and now served the restored French monarchy. The wars, in the end, were seen as being fought not between nations but between regimes, even, in a way, between ideologies, which led a separate existence from nations and peoples. After Napoleon's 'Hundred Days', however, sentiment in the chancelleries of Europe turned against the French, who were now forced to restore looted artworks, pay an indemnity, and put up with the presence of nearly a million Allied soldiers, many of them German, and all of them living off the land, for a period of several months. Negotiations over territorial adjustments turned against France. The Second Treaty of Paris was a good deal harsher than the first one, which had been concluded before the Battle of Waterloo. Unable to prevent this, Talleyrand resigned his position in protest. Meanwhile Austria, Prussia, Russia and the United Kingdom agreed to declare war on France if any member of the Bonaparte family should return to power at any time in the next twenty years.

The Congress of Vienna and the negotiations that followed in the autumn of 1815 redrew the map of Europe one more time after all the many boundary changes of the previous quarter-century. The Austrians lost their part of the Netherlands, which went to the Dutch, but regained all their other territories, and established control over Lombardy and Venetia in northern Italy, as well as a large swathe of the Dalmatian coast. Austria was also given the Chair of the body representing the member states of a new 'German Confederation'. This had much the same borders as the old Holy Roman Empire, but consisted now of thirty-nine states instead of more than a thousand, as it had in the eighteenth century. It was not a national state. Some of its members were ruled by foreign

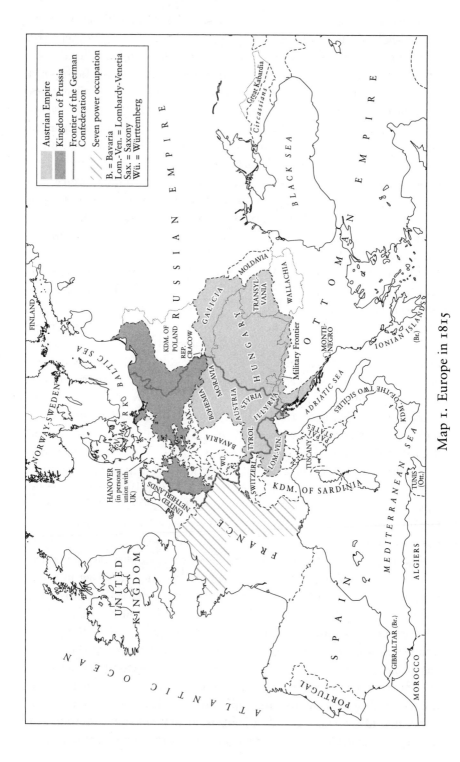

Map 1. Europe in 1815

monarchs, like the Kingdom of Hanover, whose king was the British monarch; others had extensive territories outside the Confederation, like the Habsburg Monarchy, which extended to the south and east of the Confederation, or the Kingdom of Prussia, whose territories ranged far beyond its borders to the boundaries of Russia. A number of the smaller states were completely surrounded by larger ones, with corresponding results for their freedom of action (indeed, by 1866, the thirty-nine member states had been further whittled down to thirty-four). At the Vienna Settlement, the Prussians gained territory in the Rhineland, including the Ruhr valley, as part of a series of buffer states intended to contain any future French expansion, including the Kingdom of the Netherlands; in the long run, the economic and later industrial resources of the Ruhr were to provide a major boost for Prussian economic and military power. Prussian strength was augmented by the acquisition of the former Swedish Pomerania, northern Saxony, Posen and Danzig, to counterbalance Russian control of 'Congress Poland'. All of this made Prussia one of the major winners. For its part, Russia gained huge swathes of territory, not only in Poland but also in Finland and Bessarabia. The ring of buffer states around France, stretching from an enlarged Kingdom of the Netherlands round by the Prussian Rhineland and through a reconstituted Swiss Confederation, was completed by the Kingdom of Piedmont-Sardinia, enlarged to include Genoa, Nice and part of Savoy.

The peace settlement also had to deal with the imperial possessions of the European powers involved in the conflicts of the previous decades. The British consolidated their empire while the Spanish and Portuguese would soon lose most of theirs; Malta gave the British another key point in the Mediterranean, while Ceylon, the Cape of Good Hope and Mauritius further secured sea routes to India. Underlining the moral principles that the powers claimed had infused the Vienna Settlement, the Congress formally outlawed the slave trade. In general, however, it excluded consideration of extra-European affairs; the idea, briefly mooted in the period immediately following the Congress of Vienna, of intervening in Latin America to save the colonial empires of the Spanish and Portuguese, was torpedoed by the promulgation in the United States in December 1823 of the Monroe Doctrine, which committed the USA to preventing European intervention in the affairs of the Americas. The British war on the United States of America, which had led to the burning down of the White House by a British expeditionary force in 1812, had been finally brought to an end in 1814, with disputes over the border with Canada, over fishing rights, and other relatively minor matters, settled or silently shelved. The exclusion of global political issues from the Vienna Settlement implicitly allowed imperial rivalries, such as they were, to proceed without affecting intra-European politics. This was a startling change from the wars and conflicts of the previous century.

Through most of the nineteenth century, European states had little option but to acquiesce in British dominance of world trade and shipping, and British control of the high seas. The British did not try to exclude other nations from trading, as had been the custom in the age of mercantilism up to the late eighteenth century, but promoted free international trade, in a competition that their economic and industrial advantage would ensure for the ensuing decades that they would almost always win. It was not to be until the last quarter of the century that this advantage began to be challenged, and that extra-European conflicts between the major European powers began to have an effect on relations between states in Europe once again. Within Europe itself, the Vienna Settlement was as comprehensive as it could be. Nagging secondary problems such as relations between the Scandinavian states were resolved by recognizing Sweden's de facto suzerainty over Norway. Sweden was able to establish a tradition of neutrality in European politics that has lasted to the present day. An enlarged Switzerland was also guaranteed neutral status in return for an international guarantee of the Swiss Constitution, which was intended to bring to an end the internal conflicts that had caused inter-cantonal violence on a number of occasions in the past. The sheer destructiveness of the Revolutionary and Napoleonic Wars was a lesson that the leaders of all the powers, including ultimately France itself, were determined to learn.

Warfare had been a way of life in Europe for centuries by the time the Napoleonic Wars came to an end in 1815. At times it was truly devastating in its impact. The Thirty Years War, lasting from 1618 to 1648, is estimated directly or indirectly to have caused the deaths of anything up to a third of the entire population of Germany, for example, and in some areas such as Württemberg the proportion was even higher. The eighteenth century saw repeated and often prolonged wars ranging from the War of the Spanish Succession (1701–14) through the War of the Austrian Succession (1740–8) and the Seven Years War (1756–63) to the French Revolutionary and Napoleonic Wars that lasted from 1792 to 1815, involving virtually every European state at one time or another. By contrast, the century between the Congress of Vienna, which met between 1814 and 1815, and the outbreak of the First World War in 1914, witnessed only a small number of wars in Europe, and these were relatively limited in impact and duration and did not involve more than a handful of European states. Some of them were bilateral conflicts. They included the

Crimean War in 1854–6 between Britain, France, Turkey and Russia; the Wars of Italian Unification involving France, Austria and Piedmont-Sardinia; and the Wars of German Unification in 1864 between Austria, Prussia and Denmark, in 1866 between Prussia and Austria, and in 1870–1 between the German states and France. There were brief conflicts between Russia and the Ottoman Empire in 1828–9 and 1877–8, but these contrasted with the seven wars between the two states that had taken place in the eighteenth century and up to 1815, lasting nearly a quarter of a century between them. Altogether, the death rate of men in battle between 1815 and 1914 was seven times less than that of the previous century.

How can we explain this startling contrast? It has been most persuasively explained by the abandonment on the part of the European states of the traditional emphasis on the Balance of Power, the doctrine according to which no single state should be allowed to become so strong that it dominated all the rest, and its replacement by a network of collaborative institutions, summed up in the idea of the 'Concert of Europe', whose main purpose was the maintenance of peace. Leading members of European states, including after a brief hiatus, crucially, France, became used to meeting on a frequent basis to thrash out their differences, and managed to take common action on a number of occasions, despite their opposing interests. What lay behind this powerful desire for co-operation was, of course, fear of revolution and upheaval, which, on the evidence of the 1790s and 1800s, could, it was believed, very easily cause international instability and conflict. When the Great Powers collaborated, therefore, from the 1820s to the 1840s, it was as often as not in order to put down liberal revolutions of one kind or another. But there was more to it than that. To begin with, the balance of power still in fact counted for a good deal. Ever since the time of Louis XIV, the main contender for European domination had been France, in wealth and population and military organization by far the greatest of the European powers. But the prospect of French hegemony was destroyed forever by the Revolutionary and Napoleonic Wars. The other European states remained deeply apprehensive about French ambitions for decades to come, but in fact the defeat of Napoleon was decisive. France's population growth was beginning to stagnate, and the country was unable to make good the loss of nearly one and a half million men on the battlefield. France's share of the European population became steadily smaller. For the rest of the nineteenth century, there was more or less an equilibrium of power between the major continental European states, and on a larger scale, European colonial rivalries, so disruptive in the previous century, were now settled by international agreement, building on the experience of the Congress system and the Concert of Europe.

Some historians have claimed that it was the *ancien régime* that ultimately triumphed over Napoleon in 1814–15, and certainly there were many notable continuities across the Revolutionary and Napoleonic divide. In the manner in which it was negotiated, the peace settlement seemed in some respects to hark back to earlier habits of cabinet diplomacy in the eighteenth century, when territories were transferred from one sovereign to another without any regard for the wishes of their inhabitants. 'I spent the day carving up Europe like a piece of cheese,' wrote Metternich to his mistress at one point during the Congress. Nobody asked the Rhinelanders whether they wanted to be part of Prussia, or the people of northern Italy what they felt about being ruled from Vienna. But in fact, the French Revolution had among other things fundamentally changed the nature of sovereignty in Europe. In the seventeenth and eighteenth centuries, a major, perhaps the major cause of European wars had been dynastic disputes arising on the death of a sovereign – the War of the Spanish Succession, for example, or the War of the Austrian Succession. This was no longer the case after 1815. For all the insistence of monarchs like Louis XVIII or Alexander I on their Divine Right to rule, the basis of sovereignty had shifted perceptibly from individuals and families to nations and states. Before 1815, all international treaties were considered to have been rendered invalid on the death of a sovereign, and had to be immediately renewed with the signature of the new sovereign if they were not to lapse. After 1815, this rule no longer applied. Treaties like those of 1814–15 were concluded between states, not between individual monarchs, and retained their validity unless and until one or other party deliberately abrogated them. The prince or ruler became, in effect, the executor of national or state sovereignty guaranteed by international agreement with the virtual force of law. Of course, there were to be succession disputes in the nineteenth century too, notably over Spain and Schleswig-Holstein, but they gained their potency largely from their exploitation by state governments for national purposes, and had no real impact of their own. Dynastic marriages dwindled to mere symbols of amity between nations. Similarly, armies now owed their allegiance to states rather than to individual sovereigns; the old eighteenth-century system of mercenary armies and soldiers selling themselves to the highest bidder had gone forever. The newly restored sovereigns had to adapt or perish. The 1820s were to show that many of them had failed to learn this lesson.

REFORGING THE CHAIN OF TIME

Nowhere was the changed nature of the relationship between rulers and ruled brought about by the French Revolution more obvious than in France itself. On his restoration to the throne, Louis XVIII's allegiance to the *ancien régime* was symbolized by his replacement of the *tricolor* with the royal *fleur de lys* as the official flag of France, his refusal to recognize the Legion of Honour instituted by Napoleon, and his official announcement that 1814 was the nineteenth year of his reign. When a courtier told him in 1814 of Napoleon's abdication: 'Sire, you are King of France', he replied: 'Have I ever ceased to be?' The court rituals, titles and ceremonies of the *ancien régime* came back in their full pomp. Louis XVIII rejected the constitution voted through by Napoleon's last Senate after it had formally deposed the emperor, because he did not accept that his royal authority derived from an implicit contract between king and people. It came, he said, from Divine Right, and in the Declaration of Ouen, which served as the basis for the French constitution under the restored monarchy, he made it clear that he was granting the French people their rights of his own free will, as 'Louis, by the Grace of God King of France and Navarre'.

Yet for all his deep-rooted belief in the legitimacy of the *ancien régime*, Louis recognized, especially after the alarms of the 'Hundred Days', that he could not entirely turn the clock of history back to 1788. He agreed not to initiate any restoration of land confiscated during the Revolution to the Church, the nobility or the Crown. Half a million people had purchased this property, and it was politically impracticable to force them, or the people to whom they had sold it on, to disgorge it. The Napoleonic Law Code was retained. The rights of hereditary nobles to posts in the military and the civil administration, abolished by the introduction of the 'career open to the talents' during the Revolution, were not restored. Freedom of religious practice remained in force despite the regime's proclamation of Catholicism as the state religion. The Revolution's division of the country into *départements* was left intact, as was its organization of Paris into *arrondissements*, both originally introduced in 1790. Summing up these measures, the king declared that it was his intention to 'reforge the chain of time', portraying these changes as part of a long series of reforms granted by the French monarchy since the days of Louis the Fat in the Middle Ages (a king whom Louis XVIII resembled in more than one respect). At the insistence of the Duke of Wellington, he appointed two of Napoleon's chief aides to leading positions – Talleyrand as Foreign Minister and head of the government, and Joseph Fouché (1759–1820) as

Minister of Police – 'vice leaning on the arm of crime', as Chateaubriand put it. Louis also realized that the Estates General could not be revived, and that the pressure on the restored French monarchy from the victorious Allies to avoid a repetition of the problems that had contributed to the Revolution necessitated the creation of some element of constitutional rule. So he established a bicameral legislature, consisting of a Chamber of Peers and a Chamber of Deputies. Their consent was required for all taxes to be levied, although he reserved to the Crown the right to initiate legislation.

The new constitutionalism was undermined, however, by the fact that Louis XVIII could dissolve the Chamber of Deputies and call new elections at any time, overriding the provision that each year one-fifth of its members were to submit themselves for re-election. He alone possessed the right to declare war, ministers were appointed by and responsible to him and not to the legislature, and, crucially, he could issue 'regulations and ordinances necessary for the safety of the state', which in effect gave him the power to abrogate the constitution should he choose. This, then, was not really a constitutional monarchy; it was an absolute monarchy limited by constitutional provisos that could be dispensed with at any time. Moreover, the Upper House was nominated by the king, and the Chamber of Deputies was elected by men over forty who paid 300 francs or more in taxes per year. This had the effect of creating a very small electorate, numbering no more than 90,000 from a population of 28 million. In Britain, by comparison, with a population less than half this size, the electorate numbered 440,000 even before the 1832 Reform Act, which added another 216,000. Moreover, the narrowness of the franchise for the new French legislature led to the election of a Chamber composed of 'Ultras', hard-line royalists who ousted Talleyrand's government and initiated a purge of former revolutionaries and Bonapartists. The new Chamber of Peers, acting as a court, sentenced some of these men to death, and drove others into exile, including both Fouché and Talleyrand.

If they were going to preserve the monarchy in the face of such intransigence, Louis XVIII's ministers, led by Élie Decazes (1780–1860), a former aide to Napoleon and his family, knew that the regime needed a broader base in society. Merchants, lawyers and others were turning to the liberal ideas of the early phase of the 1789 Revolution, outraged at the domination of politics and administration by the restored aristocracy. Attempting 'to nationalize the royalty and to royalize France', Decazes got Louis to dissolve the Chamber of Deputies. A new one was elected, consisting mainly of large landowners and higher state officials, many of whom had served under Napoleon. But before Decazes could get very far, the Duc de Berry (1778–1820), second son of Louis' younger brother the Comte d'Artois (1757–1836) and thus (since Louis had no children) third in line to the throne, was stabbed to death as he was leaving the Paris Opera on 13 February 1820 by a disgruntled saddler. 'We are all assassinated!' was Decazes' despairing comment.

In the ensuing reaction, Decazes was dismissed, and his immediate predecessor the Duc de Richelieu (1766–1822), a conservative who had spent his years of exile before 1815 in the service of the tsar, was reinstated. Before long, he too had been ousted to make way for a royal favourite, the Comte de Villèle (1773–1854), an ultra-reactionary whose aim was to restore the monarchy of pre-revolutionary times in undiluted form. When Louis died on 16 September 1824 of morbid obesity, the throne went to the Comte d'Artois, who took the title of Charles X (1757–1836). In his late sixties, socialized under the *ancien régime*, and fiercely conservative, the new monarch had made common cause with the Ultras, to the dismay even of his elder brother, and he persuaded Villèle to push through a law against sacrilege, criminalizing offences against the Church: the profanation of sacred vessels was made punishable by life imprisonment, and the desecration of the Host by death. He followed this with a law providing financial compensation to the nobles who had lost their lands during the Revolution. Symbolizing his hard-line stance in a magnificently traditional coronation ceremony, Charles tightened press censorship and increased the power of the Church, which in 1824 was given control over the appointment of all primary-school teachers.

These reactionary moves, continuing the policies of the Ultras led by Villèle and before him Richelieu, were almost calculated to arouse opposition from liberals. This was articulated partly through critical newspapers and magazines, two of which were founded in 1817–18 by the writer Benjamin Constant (1767–1830), and partly through political campaigning. This resulted in Constant being elected to the Chamber of Deputies in 1819 and the Marquis de Lafayette (1757–1834), veteran of the French and American Revolutions, elected the previous year. The liberals were funded by bankers like Jacques Laffitte (1767–1844) and Casimir Perier (1777–1832), who felt excluded from social and political influence by the Restoration aristocracy; Laffitte had been ousted as Governor of the Bank of France in 1817 for defending the freedom of the press. The debate on the legacy of the Revolution was fuelled by young journalists and historians such as Adolphe Thiers (1797–1877), whose multi-volume history of the Revolution, published between 1823 and 1827, justified the constitutional monarchy as an inevitable outcome of the human desire for freedom, but argued that the 'excesses of the multitude' had perverted the

Revolution. In similar vein, François Guizot (1787–1874), who had been appointed professor of history at the Sorbonne in 1812 at the age of twenty-five, taught that the essence of the Revolution lay in its early constitutional reformism, not in the Terror, and during the period when his lectures were banned by the government (1822–8), he put forward his cautious liberal arguments in the press. These two men were to play pivotal roles in French politics during the decades that followed.

Alongside this moderate and respectable liberal opposition there also emerged a wide variety of secret societies, some disguised as drinking clubs (where political songs were sung), some working under the cover of businesses, some operating as Masonic lodges, some adopting more explicit titles such as the Knights of Liberty. These spanned Europe and had connections with Latin America in a kind of radical liberal international that transcended political boundaries and was driven on by political exiles whose life took them from place to place in pursuit of their ideals. The most radical and the most active was the collection of small clandestine groups known as the *charbonnerie*, or association of charcoal-burners, inspired by similar organizations in Italy. They brought together unemployed Napoleonic civil servants, frustrated university students, and officers and NCOs from the imperial armies forced to eke out a meagre existence on half-pay. Napoleon's late propagation of an image as a defender of constitutional liberty helped unite the Republicans and Bonapartists among them. The conspirators attempted to foment military uprisings in garrisons, including Paris in 1820, Belfort and Saumur in 1821, and Strasbourg and La Rochelle in 1822; none succeeded, and the last-named led to the public execution of four sergeants. The event was witnessed among others by the student Auguste Blanqui (1805–81), who was inspired to join the revolutionary movement by the widespread belief that the men had died as 'martyrs for liberty'. Altogether in this period twelve members of the secret societies were put to death. The failure of their enterprises led to internal dissension, and the *charbonnerie* had more or less ceased to exist by the middle of the 1820s. Blanqui himself was put out of action for a while by injuries received in a street brawl in 1827. It was not therefore military insurrection but liberal parliamentarism that offered the main threat to the rule of the Ultras in France by the late 1820s. The return of an increased number of liberal deputies in the elections of 1827 led to the resignation of Villèle, and when his successor the Vicomte de Martignac (1778–1832) tried to negotiate with them, he was dismissed in favour of Jules de Polignac (1780–1847), who had been imprisoned by Napoleon for twelve years and was fully committed to the king's belief in the idea of absolute monarchy. Neither revolution nor reform seemed to be making any progress in France in the face of royal intransigence, and the prospects for change in a liberal direction seemed remote as the decade drew to a close.

A similar picture can be drawn of post-Napoleonic politics in Germany. Here too, in most of the states of the German Confederation, not everything had been restored. Between 1815 and 1819 a whole swathe of south German states adopted constitutions with representative assemblies, designed not least to lend them an aura of popular legitimacy in their efforts to revise the boundaries established in the peace settlement to their own advantage and to the disadvantage of their rivals. Quarrels such as these prevented the south German states from combining effectively against Austrian and Prussian domination of the Confederation. As a result, Metternich, provided he obtained the agreement of the Prussian government, was able to push through most of the measures he wanted in the Diet of the Confederation (where representatives of the member states met). His task was made easier by disputes between the leading Prussian reformers that let in a more conservative set of ministers who persuaded King Friedrich Wilhelm III (1770–1840) to renege on his earlier promise to grant a constitution.

Volunteers returning from the war against Napoleon were often disappointed by the hegemony exercised by the princes over the German Confederation. They had fought to liberate not just Prussia or Hesse or Saxony from French domination but also, and in the eyes of some, even more, Germany as a whole. A few, like the educational reformer Wilhelm von Humboldt (1767–1835), who had founded Berlin University in 1810, thought that the Confederation might provide the basis for stronger national institutions, but others, particularly the young students who formed the *Burschenschaft* movement at Jena in 1815, thought that only when its individual, overwhelmingly authoritarian member states were swept away and replaced by a single national constitution could true unity be achieved. They drew their inspiration from the writer Ernst Moritz Arndt (1769–1860), who had been born in Swedish Pomerania and studied theology at Greifswald and Jena. Arndt had developed a strong sense of linguistically based German nationality after being driven into exile following Napoleon's occupation of his homeland in 1806. A gifted publicist, Arndt called in 1814 for the unification of Germany under a constitutional monarchy with its capital in Berlin (Vienna was too multinational for him), and stressed the underlying unity of the German people, which he wanted to see expressed in a common language, common rituals and symbols, and even a common style of dress; the mobilization of patriotic volunteers against Napoleon in 1812–13 had shown the way.

Such ideas inspired the students of the *Burschenschaft*, who wore the black, red and gold colours of the volunteers. In October 1817 they celebrated the anniversary of Martin Luther's Reformation at the Wartburg castle, where Luther had translated the Bible into vernacular German, by listening to fiery speeches extolling their Germanness. The festival earned subsequent notoriety through the burning of more than two dozen books and magazines, including the Napoleonic Law Code, German tracts from the Napoleonic period urging collaboration with the French, and contemporary pamphlets criticizing the students' aims and activities. To procure real books would have been too expensive for them, poor as they were; instead, the students threw labelled balls of waste paper onto the flames. The event was condemned by the young poet Heinrich Heine (1797–1856) as ignorant and medieval. However, his famous pronouncement, 'That was only a Prologue: where books are burned, in the end people will be burned as well', referred to the burning of the Qur'an by the Spanish Inquisition during the conquest of Granada in 1499, not to the Wartburg event.

Among the books consigned to the flames at the Wartburg was a *History of the German Empire* by the popular and extremely prolific playwright and journalist August von Kotzebue (1761–1819), who had angered the *Burschenschaft* by pouring scorn upon their ideas and activities in his magazine. Kotzebue had lived in exile in Russia and joined the Russian foreign service, in which capacity he returned to Germany on the fall of Napoleon and reported on German affairs to the tsar. He was hardly in a position to be the spy that some believed he was, but he did support the conservative ideals of Alexander I. Together with his ridiculing of the *Burschenschaft* this persuaded the twenty-three-year-old Karl Sand (1795–1820), a theology student and member of the organization's radical wing, that Kotzebue deserved to die. Visiting the playwright in his home on 23 March 1819, Sand stabbed him repeatedly before rushing out into the street and stabbing himself in the chest, crying out 'Long live the German Fatherland!' He survived, to be tried and publicly beheaded the following year. While many commentators, even supporters of the nationalist movement, viewed the deed with revulsion, others regarded Sand as a hero and a martyr; the executioner, who sympathized with the ideals of the nationalists, dismantled the bloodstained scaffold after the event and used the wood to build a secret summer house in a nearby vineyard, placing it at the disposal of members of the *Burschenschaft* for their meetings.

Metternich seized on this event, and an unsuccessful assassination attempt against the Nassau government official Karl von Ibell (1780–1834) by the apothecary and *Burschenschaft* member Karl Löning (1791–1819), as the pretext to introduce a drastic package of repressive measures. These were formulated by representatives of ten German states at the spa town of Karlsbad in August 1819 and ratified by the German Diet in Frankfurt the following month. They obliged the member states to exercise a close control over universities, dismissing any teacher who advocated 'harmful doctrines hostile to public order or subversive of existing governmental institutions' and ensuring that he would not be re-employed in any other institution of higher learning. Students found to be members of secret societies like the *Burschenschaft* were to be banned from all universities and debarred from entering public employment. All periodicals had to be subject to censorship by a central body before publication. A special commission was set up to investigate the revolutionary movement and take action against it. The *Burschenschaft* disintegrated – members had numbered only 500 even at its height – and organized nationalism more or less ceased to operate. The police forces of individual states exchanged information about alleged subversives, engaged in the close surveillance of clubs, coffee houses and other meeting places, and looked with suspicion on any kind of voluntary association. Cheap pamphlets and broadsheets were rigorously censored or banned altogether, so that it was difficult for anyone not in government to exchange ideas or keep up with the political news, such as it was. The few who favoured constitutional reform and national unity began to call themselves 'liberals', picking up a term already used by reformers in Spain, but they were unable to agree on any kind of common programme.

The triumph of reaction in Germany was embodied in the constitution of the Confederation, which was revised in July 1820 to provide for any member state to intervene in the affairs of another to preserve order. Previous references to Jewish emancipation and religious toleration were dropped. Governments in the member states of the Confederation moved to ensure that legislative assemblies, where they existed, did not become vehicles of liberal protest. They refused to allow the publication of parliamentary debates, and forced deputies to sit in pre-assigned seats so that they could not group themselves together into factions. Everywhere, elections were indirect. Censorship restricted campaigning so tightly that there was little chance of public debate. As in France and indeed everywhere in the 1820s where elections were held, property qualifications, often very elaborately drafted, ensured that only the wealthy could be elected. The result was widespread indifference even among those who did have the vote; in 1816, for example, only 5 per cent of the (in any case, very small) electorate bothered to turn up to local elections in Königsberg. In some areas representative assemblies consisted of old-style Estates, limited to the nobility; in Prussia, these institutions, set up in 1823, were intended to advise the government rather than engage in debate, and often met in a room of one of the royal palaces. Nevertheless, the fact remained that representative institutions, however limited and circumscribed they might have been in their constitution and their powers, did exist in most German states in the 1820s. The idea of 'Enlightened Despotism' had died in the French Revolution and could not be revived. Government was more broadly based; German states were run bureaucratically, not autocratically, and a rule-bound system of administration was widely regarded as a more effective limitation on the arbitrary power of the sovereign than representative assemblies were ever likely to be. Often, in any case, the same men belonged to both. As the young Otto von Bismarck (1815–98), who did not enjoy his early experience as a civil servant, remarked in 1838, 'in order to take part in public life, one must be a salaried and dependent servant of the state, one must belong completely to the bureaucratic caste'.

REVOLT AND REPRESSION

The widespread desire among European governments to build secure collective defences against the possibility of any recurrence of the devastating wars of the previous decades found its expression not only in the idea of the 'Holy Alliance' but also in a wide range of other measures designed to foster co-operation between the victorious powers. These included especially the Quadruple Alliance, urged by the British Foreign Secretary Lord Castlereagh, in which diplomatic representatives of Britain, Austria, Prussia and Russia, and, later, France as well, would meet on a regular basis in general conferences to maintain international co-operation. Meetings between representatives of these Great Powers brokered, and enforced, a series of deals, including the rejection of a Bavarian claim on part of the territory of the Grand Duchy of Baden at the Congress of Aachen in 1819, and a downward revision of the amount of compensation to the Allies required of France for the destruction caused by the Revolutionary and Napoleonic Wars. They also brought the Allied occupation of France to an end, admitting the French informally to the Concert of Europe. Monarchy was to be the foundation of order, and in principle it was to be absolute, tempered only where unavoidable by traditional legislatures such as Estates or assemblies of notables, or by representative assemblies whose powers were strictly limited. These principles were not fully shared by the British, whose own constitution contained a powerful elected legislature, and through the 1820s the differences between the British and the

Austrian understandings of these arrangements repeatedly surfaced to make common action more difficult.

Already by this time, however, it was becoming clear that liberal constitutionalism, inspired by the legacy of French Revolutionary and Napoleonic rule, and by the ideals of popular sovereignty expressed in practical terms by widespread uprisings against the French in the last years of their European domination, was not dead. Its supporters in many parts of Europe grew increasingly dissatisfied with the authoritarian policies of the Restoration. In Spain, King Fernando VII (1784–1833), restored by Napoleon to the throne after the defeat of the French armies in the Peninsular War, rejected the liberal constitution passed in 1812 and brought back the previous absolutist regime. He readmitted the previously banned Jesuits, imposed strict censorship, and restored to the aristocracy and the Church the land seized during the Napoleonic occupation. Ministers were made individually and directly responsible to the king, and barred from discussing policy collectively. Fernando hired and fired them at will, resulting in an average tenure of ministerial office between 1814 and 1820 of no more than six months. To last any length of time government ministers had to demonstrate their allegiance to reactionary principles in the most open ways possible. The War Minister General Francisco de Eguia (1750–1827) signalled his adherence to the *ancien régime* by wearing an eighteenth-century wig. The king regressed even further by banning the Freemasons and reintroducing the Inquisition, which immediately began hunting down heretics.

All this made it difficult for the government to respond coherently or effectively to the insurrections in Spanish America, the more so since Fernando's government adopted an intransigent line and refused to make any concessions to the rebels. Financial troubles caused by the legacy of the French occupation and the post-war economic depression were made worse by the costs of sending military expeditions across the Atlantic in a vain attempt to defeat the independence movement and restore control. By 1820 the Spanish state was effectively bankrupt, unable even to pay the army it was mustering for another expedition to Latin America. In January 1820 junior army officers 'pronounced' publicly in favour of the 1812 constitution, inaugurating a tradition of the military *pronunciamiento* that lasted for well over a century. Fernando had bypassed many of the military men and guerrilla leaders who had fought against Napoleon, driving them even further towards liberalism. They were joined by disgruntled civilian politicians, many of whom had been arrested or exiled, or were frustrated by the royal clampdown on public life and free discussion. The shambolic inefficiency of the Spanish police allowed these men to put together a whole series of conspiracies, mainly based on Masonic lodges which of course continued to meet in secret despite the police ban on their activities. These conspiracies all failed, including one plan to kill the king as he was visiting a brothel. But in 1820 the conspirators were backed by the army rank and file, who were appalled at the thought of being taken off on yet another futile expedition to the Americas. The uprising gained strength in the provinces, and was carried to victory by street demonstrations outside the royal palace, expressing popular detestation of the heavy taxation imposed by the government in order to try and rescue its crumbling finances. Fernando was forced to recognize the 1812 constitution, to summon a *Cortes* (legislative assembly), and to make way for a liberal government for the next three years. However, he consistently vetoed all the resolutions of the *Cortes*, and did everything he could to frustrate the actions of the constitutionalists. Amid growing chaos and disorder, accompanied by escalating violence in town and country, the king appealed for international intervention. By 1823 the *Cortes* had deposed the recalcitrant monarch, and radicals were beginning to threaten a repeat of the September Massacres of Revolutionary Paris. One of them, the Jacobin Juan Romero Alpuente (1762–1835) – 'ugly, dirty, and badly dressed', as one of his critics disdainfully called him – alluded to the massacres and reminded his audience menacingly that 'fourteen thousand were executed in one night'.

From the point of view of the Holy Alliance, the growing chaos and the revolutionary threat in Spain could not be tolerated. The crisis there was compounded by similar events in Italy. Here, the ultimate symbol of restoration, the eighteenth-century wig, was also worn by King Vittorio Emanuele I (1759–1824) when he returned from exile in 1814 to rule the Kingdom of Piedmont-Sardinia. He also restored the pre-Napoleonic legal system, except in formerly independent Genoa where local objections were too strong. He reinstated the privileges of the aristocracy (including its sole right to occupy boxes in opera houses, a matter of some cultural importance in Italy), and he allowed feudalism to continue on the island of Sardinia. Jews and Protestants lost the rights they had gained under French rule. Vittorio Emanuele handed control over censorship and education to the Jesuits. In the Duchy of Modena, Napoleon's reforms were abolished, as they were, unsurprisingly, in the central Italian states ruled by Pope Pius VII (1742–1823). Among other things the Pope got rid of street lighting and vaccination against smallpox as objectionable modern innovations. In some other parts of the peninsula many of Napoleon's judicial and administrative reforms were retained. Such was the case, for example, in the Bourbon-ruled Kingdom of the Two Sicilies. Most liberal of all was the Grand Duchy of Tuscany in the north, where Enlightenment values had long informed the practice of government. Austrian influence, cemented by armed garrisons in the Papal States, was present to deter any dangerous recrudescence of liberalism.

Here too, however, discontent began to emerge among the educated men who had been rudely expelled from the posts they had occupied in the Napoleonic era to make way for returning aristocrats, while in the Kingdom of the Two Sicilies, where a good number of them were allowed to stay in office, there were not enough administrative jobs to go round. The centralizing policies of the Kingdom were resented by local notables, who saw their autonomy being reduced. Conscription caused opposition among the lower classes. The Kingdom of Lombardy-Venetia retained most of Napoleon's reforms, yielding a Habsburg-ruled centralized administration, state control over senior Church appointments, no restoration of confiscated lands, and the retention in office of the great majority of the civil servants appointed in the Napoleonic era. Nevertheless, the fact that the administration of the Habsburg Monarchy was centralized in Vienna gave these civil servants a sense of impotence, underlined by the fact that promotion was available only to German-speakers in the Habsburg capital. Military conscription, which now lasted for eight years instead of four, was made more comprehensive, and Italian recruits were likely to find themselves serving in far-flung parts of the Monarchy, north and east of the Alps. Successive governors of the Kingdom warned Metternich not to repeat the mistake of the reforming eighteenth-century Habsburg monarch Joseph II (1741–90), who had tried to impose uniformity and central control over the entire empire. 'The Lombards,' one of them declared, 'have been and always will be unable to get used to the Germanic forms imprinted on the government of their country.'

The frustration of local notables in the face of state centralization was shared by the men who had been involved in the resistance to Napoleon. In southern Italy they had organized themselves from about 1806, in Masonic-style secret societies known as the *carbonari*, the model for their French counterparts (the *charbonnerie*) after 1815. These groups had been encouraged by the British to conspire against Napoleonic rule. Opposition to absolutism was a key element in the movement, and after the fall of Napoleon its members found a new object for their activities in what they regarded as the tyranny of the restored governments that had taken power in many parts of the peninsula. Inspired by the example of the Spanish liberals, the *carbonari* rose in revolt. Joined by discontented soldiers, they marched through Naples and forced King Ferdinando I (1751–1825) of the Two Sicilies, popularly known as *Re Nasone* (Conky

King, from his unusually large nose), to adopt the Spanish constitution of 1812. The unrest spread up the peninsula, and liberals in Piedmont started to plan a rising against the reactionary monarch. In March 1821 the tricolor was raised by discontented officers in a number of Piedmontese garrisons, and the frightened Vittorio Emanuele abdicated, to be succeeded by his intransigently reactionary brother Carlo Felice (1765–1831), who issued a stern warning from his safe retreat outside the Kingdom, in Modena, that he would not tolerate anything that diminished 'the plenitude of royal authority'. Meanwhile, the leader of the Piedmontese insurrection, Count Santorre di Santarosa (1783–1825), was appointed Minister of War by the regent, the young and supposedly liberal Carlo Alberto (1798–1849), and began to prepare an invasion of Austrian-controlled Lombardy.

These events in Italy and Spain posed a collective challenge of major proportions to the conservative programme adopted at Vienna. Initially, though the Russian tsar urged intervention, the Austrians and the British did not take the Spanish situation very seriously, but when the liberal movement spread to Italy, the Austrians felt threatened. At a Congress held towards the end of 1820 in Troppau, Austrian Silesia, the Holy Alliance agreed to take action, despite the objections of the British. These decisions were reinforced at another Congress in Laibach early in 1821, attended by Ferdinando, who had been released from captivity in Naples after promising to respect the constitution – a promise he repudiated as soon as he reached safety. The Austrians sent an army into the Papal States and down to Naples, which they reached in the face of minimal resistance on 23 March. Divided between supporters of the democratic *carbonari* and the moderate liberal adherents of the former Napoleonic ruler Joachim Murat (1767–1815), many of whom had served in his administration, the revolutionaries could offer only minimal resistance. In Sicily news of the uprising in Naples had sparked a popular revolt with riots in the streets, crowds storming the prisons in Palermo, and bands of artisans beheading two of the leading constitutional liberals. The artisan guilds refused to give their support to the liberals. These events reflected among other things the depths of the post-war economic depression in the region, but they frightened the local notables, and outside Palermo the rebels had few supporters, so that they were unable to defeat the Neapolitan army on the island, and with the arrival of the Austrians the uprising came to an end.

Meanwhile the Austrians also sent an army into northern Italy, where they also easily defeated the rebels, forcing more than a thousand into exile. They included Santarosa, who lived for a time under an assumed name in Paris before he was discovered by the police and expelled again, ending up in Nottingham, where he eked out a living teaching French and Italian. The plight of the refugees inspired the fifteen-year-old Genoese student Giuseppe Mazzini (1805–72), who encountered them on the quayside at Genoa in April 1821 looking for a ship to take them to Spain and begging for money 'for the exiles of Italy'. 'That day,' Mazzini later recalled, 'was the first on which there took shape confusedly in my mind . . . the thought that we Italians *could* and therefore *ought* to struggle for the liberty of our fatherland.' In the wake of the Austrian victories, ninety-seven *carbonari* and other rebels were sentenced to death (though all but seven had fled and were sentenced *in absentia*). The sentences of the rest were commuted to imprisonment. In the Kingdom of the Two Sicilies the restored King Ferdinando I was not so lenient, and under his Minister of Police, Antonio Minutolo, Prince of Canosa (1768–1838), there were mass arrests and trials, with several members of the *carbonari* being executed in public and many others sentenced to long terms of imprisonment. This was too much even for Metternich, who successfully put pressure on the vengeful monarch to dismiss his minister. Authoritarian reaction was now the order of the day. In the Papal States, the new Pope, Leo XII (1760–1829), banned Jews from owning property and strengthened the power of the Jesuits over education. Everywhere in Italy there were mass dismissals of civil servants thought to have participated in, or been sympathetic to, the revolts. As Carlo Felice, the new King of Piedmont, put it, as far as the mass of ordinary citizens were concerned, 'the bad are all educated and the good are all ignorant'; so only the army and the Church could be trusted.

The Congress Powers found it more difficult to decide what to do about the situation in Spain. Eventually, in April 1823, the French sent in an army to restore Fernando VII to the throne, much to the disapproval of Metternich. Although the Spanish revolutionaries inevitably recalled the resistance against Napoleon and 'the energy and decision that had astonished the world in 1808', the 100,000 French troops were careful to avoid looting and paid for their food and supplies. They met with no serious resistance either from the Spanish people or from the Spanish army, whose generals quickly made their peace with the monarch. Fernando had spent the last days of his captivity in Seville throwing paper darts from the roof of his lodgings as the French army approached. He now emerged to dismiss the liberal ministers and reinstitute a royal despotism, purging the army and clamping down on freedom of thought at every level. The army was reformed, on the basis of files drawn up on the political sympathies of every single officer. None of this was much to the liking of the French occupying forces, who urged reconciliation. Some royalist officers also

considered Fernando's purge went too far; the Captain-General of Catalonia, for example, allowed liberal professors to take home suspect books
from the university library before sending in a delegation of royalist 'puri-
fiers'. In general, however, the repression succeeded, and the few further
attempts at liberal uprisings were easily swept aside in the absence of
popular support.

The example of the Spanish liberals was an inspiration not only in Italy
but also in Portugal. The complex cross-currents of the era were illustrated
by the brief career of the liberal Portuguese army officer Gomes Freire de
Andrade (1757–1817), who had served in Napoleon's Portuguese Legion
and become imperial governor of Dresden. Grandmaster of the Freemasons in Lisbon, Freire had been arrested for his involvement in an alleged
plot to overthrow the British military authority under Viscount Beresford
(1768–1854), a British general who had been appointed head of the Portuguese army with the title of Marshal. The transnational careers of both
men, characteristic of the immediate post-Napoleonic years, ended in
failure: Freire was convicted of treason and executed in 1817, while a
motley crew of middle-class professionals and army officers, inspired by
the January uprising in Spain, 'pronounced' against the British in August
1820. Beresford, who had gone to Brazil to obtain more powers from the
king, was prevented from disembarking when he returned, and retired to
Britain to take up a new and politically less hazardous post in 1821, as
Governor of Jersey. After lengthy negotiations, the Portuguese revolutionaries implemented a radical constitution in 1822. A parliament was elected,
restoring the monarchy but according it only limited powers, broadening
civil rights, and abolishing feudal restrictions on free enterprise within
Portugal, while attempting at the same time to reimpose mercantilist regulations on trade with Brazil. This prompted, as we have seen, the separation
of Brazil from Portugal. However, the French intervention in Spain led in
1823 to a military coup in which a young brigadier, João Saldanha (1790–
1876), raised a small army and marched on Lisbon, dissolved the
parliament, and promulgated a new constitution that gave increased
powers to the king, João VI (1767–1826). This settled nothing, however,
since the king aroused widespread resentment among the liberals by
inviting Beresford back to serve as his personal adviser, while Saldanha's attempts at a compromise failed to satisfy the conservatives, who
regarded him with suspicion as a leading figure in the Freemasons. Saldanha's coup was enough to forestall a French invasion, but it stoked the fires
of conflict in Portugal, which were to break out in open civil war a few
years later in a conflict that was ostensibly dynastic in character but which
in fact had much deeper roots.

In Russia, a younger generation of army officers had imbibed French Revolutionary ideas during the wars and the occupation of France in 1815. As in other countries, Freemasonry exerted an influence in Russia, with its emphasis on humanity and philanthropy and the possibilities of open discussion behind closed doors. Some European liberals were well known to the Russian elite, and a number of Russian army officers had taken up contact with the Swiss *carbonari*. In February 1816 a group of them formed a 'Union of Salvation', in which young Guards officers from noble families discussed ideas like the abolition of serfdom and public trial in open court instead of the secret proceedings customary in Russia. In February 1817 the Union became the Union of Welfare and set up an elaborate organization, some of whose members composed drafts of a new constitution for Russia loosely based on the Constitution of the USA. A few, notably Pavel Pestel (1793–1826), a young colonel who had been wounded in 1812 at the Battle of Borodino during the Napoleonic invasion, went further and advocated the removal of titles and privileges from the nobility and the abolition of poverty by the nationalization of land. Pestel wanted a Russian republic headed by a unicameral legislature and administered centrally. His liberalism did not extend to non-Russian parts of the tsar's dominions, including Finland, the Baltic states, Georgia, the Caucasus, Belarus and the Ukraine; all subject nationalities, he believed, should be merged into the Russian nation apart from the Poles, who were entitled to a limited degree of independence. (Indeed, the autonomous, constitutional status of Congress Poland was one of the factors influencing the group, for if Poland could be granted a constitution, then why not Russia?)

By 1823 the group had been joined by another radical secret organization, the Society of United Slavs, whose twenty-five members were also mostly aristocratic and upper-class army officers. They laid plans to arrest or even assassinate the tsar as a prelude to revolution. But on 19 November 1825 Alexander I died, leaving no legitimate son. To the consternation of the revolutionaries, he was not succeeded by his brother the Grand Duke Konstantin Pavlovich (1779–1831), who was next in line to the throne and enjoyed – with how much justification is uncertain – a liberal reputation. Konstantin had married a Polish countess and decided to stay in Poland, renouncing his claim to the Russian throne. The succession thus passed to the youngest of the three brothers, Nicholas, who also had a son and therefore promised a continuation of the Romanov dynasty. Nicholas I (1796–1855) had a well-deserved reputation as a reactionary, which strengthened the conspirators' determination to act. Made aware by an informer of the conspiracy, he hurriedly had himself proclaimed tsar, on

14 December 1825, thus trumping the revolutionaries' attempt to forestall his succession by staging a coup. Mustering 3,000 troops on the Senate Square in Moscow, the revolutionaries shot dead an intermediary sent by the tsar, who then ordered his own troops, some 9,000 in number, to open fire. The revolutionary forces fled the scene. Another, smaller uprising further south was dispersed on 3 January 1826. The so-called 'revolt' was over. Nicholas set up a commission of inquiry, which examined 600 people and put 121 on trial, condemning five of them to death, including Pestel, thirty-one to exile with hard labour in Siberia, and eighty-five to shorter terms of imprisonment.

The rebels went down in history as the 'Decembrists'. Like similar groups in other European countries in the 1820s, they were young army officers drawn from the upper classes. They aimed at a military coup, but they were also intellectuals, influenced by their experience of the French Revolutionary and Napoleonic Wars, and inspired by democratic and egalitarian ideas. As in other countries, too, secret societies derived from, or inspired by, Freemasonry were the preferred means of discussing and preparing a revolt. They caused a huge amount of alarm in Europe's chancelleries. Metternich called them 'a real power, all the more danger-ous as it works in the dark, undermining all parts of the social body, and depositing everywhere the seeds of a moral gangrene which is not slow to develop and increase'. Only close co-operation between the Great Powers of Europe, Metternich told Alexander I in December 1820, could ward off the threat. Conservative writers blamed the revolution of 1789 on secret societies such as the *carbonari*. 'Among peoples which are sick,' remarked one of them in 1815, 'you find conspiracies.' The Habsburg government required all civil servants to swear an oath that they did not belong to any secret society. Paranoia was rife. In 1814 the Habsburg Emperor Franz I even asked for a report on tiepins he had seen men wear-ing during his visit to Florence, fearing they were some kind of secret sign of Freemasonry. His agents tried to collect information from all over Europe, and built up an alarming picture of a vast international network of subversives. The fact that some of them used names – Masons, *carbonari* – that transcended national boundaries seemed to confirm these suspicions. At the century's mid-point, the English politician and novelist Benjamin Disraeli (1804–81) could still put forward the view that the secret societies 'cover Europe like a network': 'Acting in unison with a great popular movement they may destroy society, as they did at the end of the last century', he warned in his usual melodramatic manner.

These views were exaggerated in the extreme. Nineteenth-century states had less to fear from revolutionary conspiracies than they did from fear itself. These anxieties reflected, among other things, Metternich's desire to find a justification for internationally co-ordinated repression, and Disraeli's incurable tendency to romanticism. True, there were contacts between some individuals involved in the secret societies in various countries, but they did not amount to anything by way of a coherent or co-ordinated organization. The wave of military revolutionary conspiracies had receded in most of Europe by 1823; the revolt of the Decembrists in 1825 was a kind of coda. Nevertheless, the secret societies were in some ways the first, halting, embryonic example of an international revolutionary movement, inspired by similar ideas and committed to similar methods, derived from the French Revolution and the rule of Napoleon, the feeble mirror image of the international conservatism propagated by Metternich and the Holy Alliance. Politics had become internationalized by 1815 as a result of the upheavals of the previous decades. Virtually every European country had been invaded and occupied by foreign armies, and had in turn sent its troops to invade and occupy others. This development was to emerge again and again, in increasingly stronger and more coherent forms, as the century progressed.

Of course, there were national peculiarities as well. In Britain it was not junior officers who conspired to overthrow the government but a group of Jacobins who called themselves the Spencean Philanthropists, after Thomas Spence (1750–1814), an opponent of the enclosure of common land who advocated universal male suffrage and the end of the landed aristocracy. Led by Arthur Thistlewood (1774–1820), who had been involved in the Spa Fields riots in 1816, when the Spenceans had planned to use a mass meeting to storm the Tower of London, they tried to use the death of George III (1738–1820) to stage an uprising, rather as the Decembrists were to do with the death of the tsar a few years later. Their intention was to interrupt a Cabinet dinner and kill everyone present; one of the conspirators boasted that he would decapitate them all and exhibit two of their heads on Westminster Bridge. This would, the conspirators imagined, spark a general uprising against the government, and they would go on to establish a Committee of Public Safety on the lines of the French revolutionaries of the early 1790s. However, the mass assassination had in fact been concocted by a member of the group, George Edwards (1788–1843), who had turned police spy and was acting as an *agent provocateur*. He betrayed the plot to the Home Office, who raided the conspirators' headquarters in Cato Street. In the ensuing fight, Thistlewood put one of the police officers to the sword, but while a few of the conspirators escaped, most were arrested, and ten were tried for treason. Five of them were transported for life, while on 1 May 1820 the other five, including Thistlewood, were publicly hanged then cut down and beheaded (an act that called forth loud boos from the vast crowd of onlookers).

The Cato Street conspirators were unusual in the sense that they were civilians rather than military men, but in other respects they were typical of the revolutionary groups of the early 1820s. Even more than their counterparts in Britain, Spain or Italy, the Russian Decembrists, for all their egalitarian ideals, were largely cut off from the rest of society, aristocratic in origin but democratic in spirit, looking to broaden the basis of politics but unable to gain the support that would enable them to do so. The absence of a genuine civil society in Russia condemned the Decembrists to using the traditional means of a military coup to try and put their ideas into practice. Elsewhere in Europe, a military coup was also the favoured means of deposing Restoration regimes. But where a public sphere had emerged in the course of the late eighteenth and early nineteenth centuries, the involvement of civilian members of the educated classes – lawyers, doctors, teachers, merchants – in revolutionary activity was greater than in Russia. Where, as in Sicily, they were threatened by the revolt of the masses, they quickly turned back from radical action. The example of the Jacobins in the French Revolution of 1789–94, whose alliance with the plebeian forces of the *sans-culottes* had ended by plunging the country into the Reign of Terror, was sufficient to deter educated liberal groups from enlisting the common people in their support after 1815, unless they had no choice in the matter. The most widespread rioting of the Restoration years, the 'Hep-Hep' disturbances of 1819, had, it is true, involved members of the educated classes as well as artisans and other members of the lower classes, but the antisemitic focus of these disturbances repelled many liberals, and the rioters' attacks on property alarmed Metternich, who saw them as a serious threat to public order: wherever they broke out, he wrote in 1819, 'no security exists, for the same thing could arise again at any moment over any other matter'. Middle-class liberals largely shared this view. Their fear of the unruly masses was to reappear later in the century, with serious repercussions for revolutionaries.

THE GENDARME OF EUROPE

Of all the regimes established or re-established in the post-1815 Restoration, the most conservative was undoubtedly that of Tsar Nicholas I in Russia. A professional soldier, with a reputation as a stern disciplinarian, he was married to a Prussian princess and admired the institutions of the country from which she came. He spoke a number of foreign languages, and had visited England, France and Scotland, but he rejected the political and legal systems of these countries as unsuited for emulation in his own. Liberal intellectuals saw him as a sinister figure, and certainly the revolt of the Decembrists with which his reign began coloured Nicholas's attitudes towards reform for the rest of his life. Even more than his predecessor Alexander I, he was determined to nip any revolutionary conspiracy in the bud. Nicholas's hero was Peter the Great (1672–1725), whose bust he kept on his desk, telling an official: 'Here is the model which I intend to follow for the whole of my reign.'

As soon as he acceded to the throne, the new tsar reshaped his administration, centralizing power in his personal Imperial Chancery, of which the First Department was his own secretariat; the Second codified the law under the leadership of Speransky; and the Fourth dealt with aspects of education. Count Sergei Semyonovich Uvarov (1786–1855), Nicholas's Education Minister for sixteen years, wanted universities to curb 'excessive impulses towards the abstract, in the misty field of politics and philosophy' and to train students to resist 'so-called European ideas'. The aim of education was, he said, to provide a 'deep conviction and warm faith in the truly Russian saving principles of Autocracy, Orthodoxy and the National Principle, which constitute the sheet-anchor of our salvation and the most faithful pledge of the strength and greatness of our country'. At the same time, Uvarov expanded the universities and oversaw a modest growth in the school system. He reformed university administration and encouraged the study of both the sciences and the ancient Classics. Uvarov might have been reactionary, but he was not obscurantist; his higher education policy laid the foundations for the emergence of that peculiarly Russian social stratum, the intelligentsia, in the 1840s and 1850s.

The Third Department of the Imperial Chancery, responsible for state security, was run by the former cavalry general Count Alexander von Benckendorff (1781–1844), a Baltic German nobleman and brother of the international socialite Dorothea von Lieven (1785–1857), who had once enjoyed notoriety in a much-publicized affair with Metternich. (Princess Lieven ran a celebrated *salon* in London for twenty-two years while her husband served as Russian ambassador.) Benckendorff was also head of the gendarmerie, so that the Third Department, in effect, was responsible for the police. It was armed with the power to collect 'reports on all events without exception', to carry out surveillance of politically suspect persons – two thousand a year on average in the 1840s – and banish them to Siberia, and to supervise all foreigners who came to the country. Frequently officials in the Third Department fabricated cases or acted uncritically on false denunciations. It employed an army of informers, one of whom reported complaints from the public about its intrusiveness: 'Do you not know,' one bureaucrat was reported as asking the informer menacingly, 'how General Benckendorff treats people and what measures he adopts to unearth family secrets?'

The Third Department was charged with uncovering corruption in the bureaucracy; one bureaucrat described it disapprovingly as a 'black cloud' that 'rose over Russia and . . . lay on her horizon for many years'. For its part, the Third Department reported in 1827 that among officials, 'honest people are seldom met. Plunder, fraud, perverse interpretation of the laws – these are their trade.' Benckendorff's deputy and effective successor, Leonid Vasilievich Dubbelt (1792–1862), another veteran of the Napoleonic Wars, struck terror into all who came within his orbit, not least because of the elaborate courtesy with which he treated his victims. When the writer and critic Alexander Ivanovich Herzen (1812–70) complained to him of the mess the gendarmes had made when they searched his house, Dubbelt exclaimed, 'Oh, my goodness, how unpleasant! How clumsy they all are!' His politeness did not stop him informing Herzen that he was being exiled to Vyatka, a small town in north-eastern Russia, for his involvement in criticism of the government. While the Third Department kept a tight rein on political dissidents, however, it failed altogether to eliminate inefficiency and corruption, not least because they went to the very heart of government. Count Pyotr Alexandrovich Tolstoy (1761–1844), the head of the military department of the Council of State, was described by the Council's Imperial Secretary as 'combining an indescribable indifference to all official business with an exemplary, legendary laziness'. The Governor of St Petersburg, Pyotr Kirillovich Essen (1772–1844), neglected his office so much that he did not notice his Head of Chancery was taking bribes and embezzling public funds until the scandal came to light in 1843. The Third Department also exercised censorship over the theatre. In 1836, when Nikolai Vasilievich Gogol (1809–52) presented his satirical play *The Government Inspector*, focusing on the mayor of a provincial town who mistakes a chance visitor for a government inspector and tries both to cover up his own corruption and placate the visitor with massive 'loans', the tsar personally overruled the censors and had it staged as a warning to officialdom. Censorship was enshrined in a statute promulgated in 1826 and revised in 1828, backed by the Holy Synod of the Orthodox Church. Although the effects of the statute were mitigated because some of the officials were closet liberals, the tsar or some other senior figure was always liable to intervene to demand the closure of a magazine or the arrest of a writer. Arbitrariness always accompanies despotism, and Russia was no exception. But for all its inefficiency, Nicholas I's regime managed to keep the lid on dissent, for which there was no institutional outlet such as an elected legislature, only novels, drama and poetry, which were easily muzzled. Nicholas I, as Queen Victoria remarked, was 'sincere even in his most despotic acts, from a sense that is the only way to govern'. It would not be until his death in 1855 that the permafrost of Russian politics would begin to thaw.

Extending Russian power, as Peter the Great had done, was one of Nicholas I's primary aims. He pursued it not least in the interests of order. The tsar was as determined as Peter had been to use Russia's military might to suppress revolution in other parts of Europe. He upheld the ideals of the Holy Alliance and continued to participate in the Congress system. In his zeal to prevent revolution, Nicholas soon became known as the 'gendarme of Europe'. He justified this sobriquet not least as a result of the way he dealt with the events that unfolded in Poland. His predecessor Alexander I, influenced by his friendship with the Polish grandee Adam Czartoryski (1770–1861), had left intact many of the reforms introduced by Napoleon through his creation of the Grand Duchy of Warsaw, hoping that these would placate Polish opinion. (Some 85,000 Poles had served in Napoleon's Grand Army in 1812, and the establishment of the Grand Duchy had excited many Polish aristocrats who saw in it the chance to recover their country's sovereignty, lost as recently as 1795.) 'Congress Poland' had a constitution of its own with its Diet and administration, its own taxes, and even its own army. One Russian official called it disapprovingly 'a snake spouting its venom at us', clearly fearing that the poison of democracy might infect the Russian body politic.

After Alexander's death in 1825, Nicholas I put increasing pressure on the Russian viceroy in Poland, his brother the Grand Duke Konstantin, to curtail what he regarded as these excessive liberties. He was strengthened in his resolve by the discovery that the Decembrists had been in contact with a secret society in Warsaw, one of many that had sprung up in the early 1820s, closely connected to the Freemasons who already had thirty-two lodges in Congress Poland in 1815. The tsarist police broke up some of the early groups, which had names such as the National Patriotic Society or the League of Free Poles, though their support came almost entirely from junior officers in the Polish army, and from students. At the University of Vilna, once part of the old Kingdom of Poland-Lithuania but now in Russia, beyond the Polish border, a nationalist conspiracy was broken up by the police in 1823 and its leader Adam Mickiewicz (1798–1855) exiled to central Russia. Five years later, the tsar's enquiries prompted the trial for treason of leading figures in the Patriotic Society, and when the judges declared them not guilty (apart from Lieutenant-Colonel Seweryn Krzyzanowski [1787–1839], who had carried on dealings with the Decembrists), Konstantin had the judges arrested while Nicholas I ordered the conspirators to be transported to Siberia in chains. Matters were made worse by the requirement of all officers in the Polish army to renew their oath of allegiance to the tsar.

Following the Decembrist revolt a small group of liberal army officers came together in 1830 at the infantry officers' school in Warsaw, with a view to seizing power. They were galvanized into action by Nicholas I's orders to mobilize Russian forces to stop the overthrow of the monarchy in France. As the conspirators gained more adherents, a group of them burst into the viceroy's palace on the night of 28–29 November 1830. Finding a gaudily uniformed man at the entrance to the Grand Duke's suite, they stabbed him to death, then rushed into the streets shouting 'The Grand Duke is dead!' They were mistaken: they had in fact killed the Governor of Warsaw – the Grand Duke had been hiding in his wife's bedroom. As senior officers tried to restore order, calling the conspirators 'ignorant murderers', they were shot dead, and the conspirators seized control of the town and its munitions depots. Instead of using his troops to crush the conspiracy, the Grand Duke withdrew from the city in panic, taking with him the prisoners whom the tsar had ordered to be transported after the fiasco of the 1828 show trial. 'The Poles have started this disturbance,' he declared, 'and it's Poles that must stop it.' Attempts by moderates to negotiate with the tsar met with a predictable, blanket refusal to make any concessions, driving the rebellion into the hands of the most radical faction in the Diet. After commemorating the memory of the Decembrists on 24 January 1831, they persuaded the Diet to depose the tsar the next day and issue a declaration of independence.

Afraid of compromising their own social and economic position, the mainly aristocratic radicals rejected the idea of rousing the peasantry to back their cause by introducing agrarian reform. Meanwhile, the tsar had already mobilized an army 120,000 strong to crush the uprising. They were dealing not only with professional and well-organized Polish forces, however, but also with a raging cholera epidemic they had brought with them from further east. In the fierce fighting that ensued, the Poles won several significant victories. But they failed to follow them up. Despite their imaginative deployment of rockets, the Poles were decisively defeated at Ostrołęka on 26 May 1831, and divisions among the leading Poles hastened the disintegration of the revolt. Their principal commander, General Jan Skrzynecki (1787–1860) met with bitter criticism for his dilatory tactics. Failing to persuade the Diet to make him dictator, he arrested his critics and several military rivals and put them on trial. On 15 August the Diet deposed him amid chaotic scenes in Warsaw, where a crowd broke into the prisons and massacred thirty-four inmates, including four generals. The Polish army responded by taking control of the streets, shooting the alleged ringleaders and breaking down the barricades thrown up by the rebels across the streets. While the Poles were tearing themselves apart, the Russian army arrived at the gates of Warsaw, where the defenders had thrown up earthworks and assembled a defensive force of 40,000. It was all to no avail. In two days of fierce fighting the vastly superior Russian force overwhelmed the defences and entered the city at the Wola church-yard, where the corpse of the local Polish commander, General Józef Sowiński (1777–1831), a veteran of the Napoleonic Wars, was later found, riddled with bayonet wounds, propped upright against a gun carriage by his wooden leg. The revolt was over, the last remnants of the rebellion surrendering on 21 October.

The tsar now exacted his retribution. All Polish officers involved in the uprising were cashiered and transported to central Russia while the rank and file were marched off to serve in the Caucasus. About 100,000 men were punished in this way. Another 80,000 Polish citizens who had supported the revolt were also transported. Some 254 men were condemned to death. More than 5,000 landed properties were sequestered in Poland and Lithuania. 'Order a search to be made in Warsaw,' commanded Tsar Nicholas, 'for all the flags and standards of our former Polish Army and send them to me . . . Remove everything that has historical or national value, and deliver it here.' Nicholas abolished the Polish constitution, along with the Diet and the army, brought Russians in to run the administration, and ruled henceforth by military decree. The universities were closed down and the library was seized. From 1839 study abroad was banned, the publication of books on history and social studies was halted, the works of national poets were suppressed. So angry was the tsar at the uprising that at one stage he even proposed to wash his hands of the Poles by ceding all their territory to Austria and Prussia. Although his ministers calmed him down, the legacy of the conflict was a new bitterness in relations between Poland and Russia, equally vehement on both sides. Nicholas eventually contented himself with abolishing the provincial administrative structure of the Kingdom. He replaced the Polish złoty with the Russian rouble, and, in 1849, causing enormous confusion, he introduced Russian weights and measures in place of Polish ones. The imprisoned rebels were not forgiven, and many were still in jail or exile in Siberia a quarter of a century later. Despite the massive repression, Polish nationalism survived, to resurface on many occasions later in the century.

The Poles lost because of their isolation from the masses. A small group of army officers, supported by students and intellectuals, had attempted to seize power. Unlike the Decembrists they had managed to win the support of large numbers of ordinary soldiers, and a part of the artisan class, driven to revolt by poor economic conditions and the feeling that these owed a lot to Russian exactions. What the rebels really needed was to rouse the peasantry, that is, the overwhelming mass of the population. Some of them realized this. But an attempt to introduce land reform into the legislature disappeared without trace in the face of the indifference of the landowning majority. The peasants remained quiescent, and the uprising a purely urban phenomenon. This had been an essentially internal affair as far as the tsar was concerned. There was no involvement on the part of the other European Powers, although the Polish conspirators had tried to get Austria to intervene. The repercussions of the revolt within Europe, however, were at a different level. Liberal opinion everywhere was outraged. The events of 1830–1 inaugurated a long period of Russophobia in Britain. The House of Commons passed a unanimous vote of censure on the tsar. In Germany popular songs condemning the enslavement of Poland were in vogue for a time. The Russian poet Alexander Sergeyevich Pushkin (1799–1837) responded with a diatribe against 'the slanderers of Russia', accusing critics abroad of feelings of envy because they had done less than the Russians to overthrow Napoleon. It was, he declared, a quarrel between Slavs. That was not the way it was seen in the rest of Europe, where anything up to 7,000 Poles fled during or after the uprising. One of them was the composer Fryderyk Chopin (1810–49), who had left Warsaw just before the rebellion and was never to return. From Stuttgart he wrote helplessly to his father after the fall of Warsaw: 'The enemy must have reached our home. The suburbs must have been stormed and burned … Oh, why could I not kill a single Muscovite!'

In crushing the Polish uprising, Tsar Nicholas I had flagrantly defied the Vienna Settlement, which had granted Congress Poland a substantial degree of autonomy. But in another sense he was upholding the Settlement: its central thrust, against the threat of revolution, implied that anyone who acted to maintain order was acting in the spirit that had inspired it. Although Russia had acted alone in the case of Poland, however, the tsar strongly preferred to act in concert with other European states in time of trouble, especially in cases where the problems did not arise in his own backyard. Yet Russian collaboration and co-operation in the maintenance of the post-1815 European order could run up against the divergent interests of even the most conservative states elsewhere on the Continent. This was to become abundantly clear over the most serious issue to confront the Concert of Europe in the 1820s, the question of Greek independence from the Ottoman Empire.

GREEK INDEPENDENCE

Like so many other European rulers of the period, the Ottoman Sultan Mahmud II (1785–1839) had observed with admiration the effectiveness of Napoleon's rule in France. At the beginning of the nineteenth century, the Ottoman Empire still controlled a large swathe of territory in south-eastern Europe, stretching from the principalities of Moldavia and Wallachia across to Bosnia, Serbia and Montenegro, and down through Bulgaria and Albania to Greece and the islands of the Aegean. Also controlling Anatolia, Iraq, Syria, Palestine, the Arabian peninsula, Egypt, and the north coast of Africa as far west as Tunis, the Ottoman Empire remained a force to be reckoned with in European politics. It was still not much more than a century since Ottoman armies had laid siege to Vienna (1683). However, the reorientation of European trade from the Middle East to the Atlantic, and the acceleration of economic growth in western Europe towards the end of the eighteenth century, were beginning to leave the Ottoman economy behind. Organizational and technological improvements in western armies and navies meant they were starting to outperform Ottoman forces. The corruption characteristic of eighteenth-century government and administration had been curtailed in most of Europe, but it continued among the Ottomans. In Constantinople (Istanbul), the Ottoman capital, the sultans found it increasingly difficult to impose their authority. Local and regional leaders were gaining increasing autonomy in many parts of the empire.

One such was Tepedelenli Ali Pasha (1740–1822), a retired Muslim brigand who controlled a large area of territory stretching from the Peloponnese and mainland Greece across Macedonia into Albania (from where he originally hailed). Appointed 'Pasha', or Ottoman administrator, in 1788, he levied taxes on his own account and ruled by violence and extortion. Famously avaricious and sybaritic, by 1819 he had become so fat that he could no longer sit in the traditional fashion cross-legged on the floor. However, the pasha had come to enjoy more autonomy than Mahmud was prepared to tolerate. By 1820 some 20,000 Ottoman troops were besieging his headquarters at Ioannina, where his resistance proved so stubborn that reinforcements had to be sent from garrisons in the Peloponnese. Looking around for allies, the pasha established contact with the secret 'Society of Friends' founded in 1814 by Greek merchants and seeking 'the liberation of the Motherland'. Its President, Alexander Ypsilantis (1792–1828), an officer in the Russian army, invaded the Danubian Principalities of Moldavia and Wallachia with a small force raised by the society, with the ultimate aim of provoking a war between Russia and Turkey that would liberate Greeks everywhere by destroying the Ottoman Empire.

But the tsar repudiated Ypsilantis's action and refused to support this dangerous attack on state authority, instead sending troops into Moldavia with the claim that the Holy Alliance sanctioned intervention of this kind. Ypsilantis managed to persuade a minor Romanian boyar (landowner) called Tudor Vladimirescu (1780–1821) to lead an uprising with the aid of a band of mercenaries, and soon Vladimirescu's promise of land reforms had roused the Wallachian peasants, enabling his force to occupy Bucharest. Despite his efforts, however, they burned and sacked indiscriminately, attacking the property even of Greek landowners who supported the cause of independence. This cut the ground from underneath Ypsilantis's plan of using the Greek landowners in the region to provide a basis for destroying Ottoman power there. When a Turkish army arrived, Vladimirescu switched sides in desperation, but it was too late. His own officers betrayed him to the Greeks, who had Vladimirescu tortured to death and then threw his mutilated body into a latrine, while Ypsilantis fled to Austria and died in exile. However, Ypsilantis had succeeded in winning the support of the Greek Orthodox hierarchy, which encouraged armed peasant uprisings in the Peloponnese. Greek officers in the Ottoman army joined in, angered by Turkish executions of alleged Greek nationalist plotters. Eager to throw off the authority of the Ottomans, armed bands of brigands were soon roaming the countryside, attacking local officials and massacring Muslims, while in the Aegean, islanders became pirates and harried the Ottomans by sea. By April 1821 some 15,000 out of 40,000 Turkish inhabitants of the Peloponnese had been killed.

On 27 January 1822, meeting at Epidaurus in the Peloponnese, a self-styled Greek National Assembly issued a ringing declaration of independence from 'the cruel yoke of Ottoman power'. The Greeks, it proclaimed, were fighting a 'holy war, a war the object of which is to reconquer the rights of individual liberty, of property and honour – rights which the civilized peoples of Europe, our neighbours, enjoy today'. Yet despite the ideological proclamations of the Assembly, which provided the formal leadership of the rebel movement, the uprising remained uncoordinated, internally divided and chaotic, a huge gulf separating the educated professional elements from the rough-and-ready and often barely politically aware fighters on the ground. Nobody was able to establish central control or ensure order in those places where the rebels were successful. Witnessing their seizure of Tripolitsa in the Peloponnese, the British observer George Finlay (1799–1875) exclaimed in despair at the Greek Christians' massacre of the local Muslim population:

Women and children were frequently tortured before they were murdered. After the Greeks had been in possession of the city for forty-eight hours, they deliberately collected together about two thousand persons of every age and sex, but principally women and children, and led them to a ravine in the nearest mountain where they murdered every soul.

The Ottoman reaction was scarcely less brutal. The sultan had the Orthodox Patriarch of Constantinople hanged from his cathedral gate, despite the fact that he had tried to calm the situation by excommunicating the rebels. Muslim crowds were let loose on the Christian population in a number of towns. Ottoman troops burned villages and destroyed crops. In Salonica the deputy pasha instigated a series of massacres of the Christian population. The city's mullah recorded in shocked disbelief how the air was filled with the 'shouts, wails, screams' of the victims: 'Salonica, that beautiful city,' he wrote to the sultan, 'which shines like an emerald in Your honoured crown, was turned into a boundless slaughterhouse.' Local Christian notables, including the city's Orthodox metropolitan, were brought in chains to the flour market, tortured and executed, and their heads taken to the deputy pasha, who had them put up on the city's western gates. Numerous Christians were sold off as slaves.

Ottoman troops overran Ali Pasha's fiefdom and he fled to an island on Lake Pamvotis, where he refused to accede to their request to surrender for beheading ('My head will not be surrendered . . . like the head of a slave'). Leading the resistance from an upper floor of his refuge, he was shot dead from below, and as if to disprove his prediction, his head was severed from his dead body and sent to the sultan. International opinion was aroused most powerfully, however, by events on the island of Chios, just off the Turkish coast, where Greek rebels laid siege to the local Ottoman garrison. There were many wealthy Greek merchants on the island, who had made their fortune cultivating and harvesting mastic resin, an early form of chewing gum (for 'mastication'); on sighting an Ottoman relief fleet, the garrison troops massacred the hostages they had taken, and forced their servants to reveal where they kept their fortunes (after which they strangled them). So impressive were the confiscated goods brought to the mainland that many Turks came over to Chios to take part in the plunder, expecting to find unbounded riches for the taking. A

French-language newspaper based in Smyrna described how the streets of the main town on the island were littered with corpses as the buildings burned to the ground around them. Between 25,000 and 30,000 Christians were massacred, and many more fled or were sold into slavery. The island's population fell dramatically, from 120,000 before 1822 to no more than 30,000 a year later.

As news of the killings reached western Europe, public opinion reacted with outrage. In France, Eugène Delacroix (1798–1863) painted *The Massacre at Chios* (1824), depicting a turbaned Turkish cavalryman rearing his horse above dead and dying Greek women and children, contributing to the wave of sympathy that swept through the educated classes everywhere. More practical support was lent by the former Piedmontese revolutionary Santorre di Santarosa, who left his exile in Nottingham to fight alongside the Greek rebels on November 1824 and was killed by Ottoman imperial Egyptian troops on the island of Sphacteria on 8 May 1825. The cause of Greek independence was interpreted by many Italian exiles and *carbonari* as parallel to their own, involving the recovery of a glorious Classical past now submerged by foreign domination, and the expression of solidarity with a Mediterranean sister nation. Committees were formed in the capital cities of many European states to organize aid for the insurgents and put pressure on their own governments. Public opinion in the United Kingdom in particular was overwhelmingly on the side of the Greeks. In 1823 the government was pressured into agreeing not to interfere with the naval blockade imposed on Turkey by the island-based Greek 'fleet' (essentially pirate ships), which was making it difficult for the Ottomans to supply their troops. Adventurous Englishmen demonstrated their enthusiasm by travelling to the region to lend their support to the rebels. Often they were shocked by what they found. 'All came expecting to find the Peloponnesus filled with Plutarch's men,' noted one of them, 'and all returned thinking the inhabitants of Newgate [the main London prison] more moral.'

The most prominent of the philhellenes who sailed to the assistance of the Greek rebels was the English Romantic poet Lord Byron. Living in Genoa, he travelled to Greece in July 1823. His fame made Byron the object of bids for support from the warring factions of the rebellion, which gave him a soberly realistic understanding of the situation on the ground. His death from fever, possibly sepsis, at Missolonghi in April 1824 transformed him into a martyr for the cause and led to still more volunteers making their way to Greece from many different European countries. Meanwhile committed supporters of the political principles of the French Revolution also backed the Greeks, including, most notably, the ex-slaves

running the Caribbean republic of Haiti, who had already formally recognized Greek independence in 1821. A hundred volunteers sailed from
the island to help the Greeks, but were captured by pirates on the way
and, tragically, returned to the slavery from which they had formerly
escaped. Unable to raise money in the Greeks' support, the Haitian republic instead sent twenty-five tons of coffee beans with instructions to the
rebels to sell them for cash with which to buy arms and ammunition.
Meanwhile philhellenes in New York collected money for the insurgents,
and a number of volunteers from the United States joined the uprising.
They included George Jarvis (1798–1828), son of an American diplomat
based in Germany, who learned Greek, donned the costume of the Greek
troops, and served as 'Capetan Zervos' with the rebel forces on land and
at sea until his death from typhus. The promulgation of the Monroe Doctrine prevented philhellenes in Congress from securing any official
government intervention, but the cause was widely supported within
American public opinion.

None of this, however, helped very much. The different factions of the
uprising, based on shifting alliances of pirates, brigands, educated indigenous nationalists and returning expatriates – there were Greek
communities all over the Mediterranean and south-eastern Europe – began
to fight among themselves. The Ottomans dispatched a strong force of
Egyptian troops supplied by the sultan's nominal vassal Muhammad Ali
(1769–1849), who had agreed to put down the rebellion in return for the
addition of Syria to his fiefdom. His troops soon began advancing up the
Peloponnese, leaving a bloody trail behind them. Public pressure in western Europe mounted, but serious differences opened up between the
Russians, who sought to exploit the weakness of the Ottomans for their
own purposes, and the British, who distrusted Russian ambitions. Alexander I had initially shrunk from unilateral action since he knew this
would undermine the Holy Alliance, which after all had largely been his
own creation. But the continued deterioration of the situation made
this policy difficult for his successor Nicholas I to continue without serious damage to Russian influence and prestige. Soon the tsar felt forced to
act. A chance for him to intervene was supplied by serious internal disturbances within the Ottoman capital of Constantinople, resulting from
military reforms introduced by Mahmud II, who was understandably
concerned by the multiple threats now emerging towards his rule over
south-eastern Europe.

The disturbances started with the Janissaries, created in the fourteenth
century as an elite military corps of slaves recruited from young Christian
boys but which had evolved into a largely hereditary body by the early

modern period, becoming corrupt and undisciplined. In 1826 the sultan, recognizing that they had become largely useless for military purposes, ordered that the Janissaries be disbanded. In the past they had on more than one occasion deposed sultans who attempted reform, and in 1826 too, most of the 135,000 members of the corps refused to obey the command. But as well as the Janissaries, Mahmud II had been recruiting a modern army on European lines, consisting of free Turks, so that when the Janissaries began fighting their way towards the sultan's palace, they were quickly forced back into their barracks. The sultan's new troops bombarded the barracks, killing at least 4,000 of the mutineers; the rest fled or were imprisoned. At least 2,000 of them were taken to Thessaloniki and beheaded in what became known as the 'blood fort'. These disturbances provided the opportunity for the Russians in 1826 to impose on the sultan the Convention of Ackerman, which forced the Turks to evacuate the Romanian Principalities. In July 1827 the British, French and Russians managed to patch up their disagreements in the Treaty of London to work together for an armistice between the Greeks and the Ottomans without committing themselves to either side, and dispatched their fleets to the area. The commander of the joint fleet, the British Vice-Admiral Sir Edward Codrington (1770–1851), was less than impressed by the town of Nafplio ('the filthiest town, with the worst streets and most wretched houses, I ever saw'), the capital of the provisional Greek government in the Peloponnese, and still less by the gunfire that echoed round the streets as the different Greek factions tried to pick each other off with small-arms fire. But when the sultan refused to accept the Treaty of London, Codrington, encouraged by the British consul in Istanbul, the philhellene Stratford Canning (1786–1880), ordered his ships in October 1827 to open fire on the Turkish fleet lying at anchor in the sheltered bay of Navarino in the south-western corner of the Peloponnese. There was nowhere for the Turkish ships to escape apart from a narrow channel leading to the waiting British fleet. In three and a half hours of relentless bombardment, the Turkish fleet was sunk and Ottoman naval power destroyed.

Both Canning and Codrington had exceeded their brief. The Duke of Wellington, commander-in-chief of the British Army at the time, was furious and publicly disavowed the action. It was not in the British national interest to weaken the Ottoman Empire, because this would simply open the door to an extension of Russian power in the area. His perception was correct, but he was unwise to give it public expression. The Ottoman Sultan saw Wellington's statement as an encouragement to repudiate the Ackerman Convention and continue with his efforts to suppress the Greeks; the tsar responded by declaring war on the Ottoman Empire.

Initially the campaign did not go well – Frederick the Great of Prussia (1712–86) had described wars between Russia and Turkey as the one-eyed fighting the blind – but by August 1829 a Russian army was threatening Constantinople and the Ottoman Empire seemed on the verge of collapse. Paradoxically, this provided the stimulus needed to patch up the Concert of Europe that had come so badly unstuck over the Greek rebellion. It was in nobody's interests at this stage to replace the Ottoman Empire in Europe with a disorderly collection of weak and unstable states run by bandits and revolutionaries. A conference held in London between November 1829 and February 1830 decided to establish by European agreement a small independent Greek state under a constitutional monarchy, assigned the Romanian Principalities to Russia's sphere of influence, and committed the participants, including Russia, to abandoning any further claims on Ottoman territory in the Balkans. The Greek revolt had posed the most serious threat to the Concert of Europe so far. In the end, the Concert had held together.

A key figure in these events, and one with a wider European significance, was Ioannis Kapodistrias (1776–1831). Kapodistrias belonged, like Simón Bolívar or Toussaint L'Ouverture or any number of political leaders who came of age around the end of the eighteenth century, to a generation whose ideals were inspired by the moderate constitutionalism of the early French Revolution and whose belief in the possibility of their practical implementation was grounded in the example of Napoleon. Born on the island of Corfu at a time when it was still ruled by Venice, Kapodistrias had studied medicine, philosophy and the law at the University of Padua before returning to Corfu to work as a doctor. In 1797 the Ionian islands, including Corfu, had fallen to the French following Napoleon's conquests in Italy. Two years later they had been occupied jointly by the Russians and the Turks, who organized them in the so-called Septinsular Republic. By this time Kapodistrias had already begun to imbibe some of the key ideas of the French Revolution. He was soon to put them into action. As a leading medical man Kapodistrias had been appointed the first director of the military hospital and then one of the two ministers of the Septinsular Republic, standing in for his father. He had persuaded the envoy of the occupying powers to accept liberal amendments to the oligarchical constitution they had imposed. He had managed to bring the most influential groups on the islands to accept the reforms, and organized elections to a Senate, which had duly voted through a new, liberal constitution and appointed him Chief Minister. However, in 1807 the French had reoccupied the islands and Kapodistrias had been forced to flee to Russia, where he had entered the foreign service (a move made possible by the currency of French as the language of international diplomacy and of the Russian court). Charged in 1813 with sorting out the boundaries and constitution of Switzerland, he had achieved such success, ending with securing the neutrality of the country by international guarantee, that Alexander I had made him joint Foreign Minister. At the Congress of Vienna (1814–15), Kapodistrias had become the advocate of a liberal approach diametrically opposed to the cabinet diplomacy of Metternich and his party. 'They have forgotten,' he complained, 'that this war was won not by sovereigns but by nations.' Metternich, for his part, described Kapodistrias as 'a complete and utter fool, a miracle of wrong-headedness . . . He lives in a world to which our minds are often transported by a bad nightmare.'

By 1818, Kapodistrias had begun to hope for Greek independence, although he was initially unsuccessful in his attempts to win the tsar's support for this cause. He took a leave of absence from his post as Russian Foreign Minister in 1822 and went to live in Geneva. He lobbied European governments in support of the Greek revolt and organized material assistance for the rebels. By now he was by far the best-known Greek politician in Europe, and together with his close Russian connections this secured him the appointment as 'Governor' of Greece by a National Assembly elected in 1827. Returning to the capital at Nafplio in 1828, Kapodistrias introduced a new currency and implemented educational reforms, as he had done on Corfu more than two decades earlier, setting up schools, establishing a university, and using his medical knowledge to establish a quarantine system against infectious diseases such as the plague. Among other things, he also introduced the potato into Greece in an effort to improve people's diet. At first, this met with deep scepticism among the peasantry, who refused to take up his offer of free distribution of seed potatoes to anyone who would plant them. Trying a new tactic, Kapodistrias had the potatoes piled up on the waterfront at Nafplio and surrounded by armed guards. This convinced local people and visitors from the countryside that these new vegetables were precious objects, and thus worth stealing. Before long, as the guards turned a blind eye, virtually all the potatoes had been taken – and their future in Greece was assured. But Kapodistrias did not take such a subtle approach in his dealings with the warring factions whose internecine rivalries were proving such an obstacle to the creation of a viable Greek state. His attempts to centralize military administration and recruitment, taxation and customs revenues, met with determined opposition from the fiercely independent leading families of the Mani peninsula, where an uprising was quelled with the aid of Russian troops. Further trouble was caused by the piratical merchant-shipowners of the islands of Hydra, Spetses and Psara, who captured the ineffectual Greek national fleet, but were themselves defeated by the French navy and scuttled their own ships rather than be incorporated into a new Greek navy under central government control.

The most dangerous opposition to Kapodistrias came from the Mavromichalis family, one of the turbulent and powerful clans based on the Mani peninsula. In an attempt to bring the clan to heel, Kapodistrias imprisoned its leading figure, Petrobey Mavromichalis (1765–1848), formerly governor of the peninsula under the Ottomans. Outraged at this insult to their honour, Petrobey's two brothers decided to follow local tradition and assassinate Kapodistrias. They were waiting for him as he went to church on 9 October 1831. As Kapodistrias made to enter the building, one of the brothers shot him in the head, while the other stabbed him through the lungs. After this, the situation in Greece descended into violent anarchy. It was eventually overcome in May 1832 when the British, French and Russians, after some years of trying to find someone willing to take on the thankless task, finally imposed the seventeen-year-old Bavarian Prince Otto von Wittelsbach (1815–67) on Greece as king, under the terms of the Treaty of London. He was recognized by the Ottomans in exchange for a hefty subsidy (or, to put it more starkly, bribe). As a good Classicist, Otto moved the capital from Nafplio to Athens, but he imported so many of his fellow countrymen into government and administration that his reign was popularly known in Greece as the *Bavarokratia*, the rule of the Bavarians. In the following years Otto was to struggle vainly to retain control over events, though he won some support by backing Greek nationalist attempts to enlarge Greece's borders so as to include many Greeks who were still under Ottoman rule, a policy that itself was hardly designed to bring stability to the region.

That stability seemed to be crumbling fast as the example of the Greeks spread to another part of the Ottoman Empire inhabited mainly by Orthodox Christians: Serbia. Following the defeat of a major uprising of Orthodox Serbs led by Djordje Petrović (1768–1817), known as Karadjordje (Black George), 1815 witnessed a second uprising led by Miloš Obrenović (1780–1860), an illiterate pig-farmer who was nevertheless cunning enough to avoid direct military confrontation with Ottoman forces. His aim was to get Serbian autonomy tolerated by the sultan. When Karadjordje returned in secret as an agent of the Greek rebels, charged with the task of destabilizing Ottoman rule in Serbia, Obrenović, fearful of his influence, had him hacked to death in his sleep, inaugurating more than a century of murderous rivalry between the two families. Both men were effectively guerrilla leaders; their forces were armed bands of peasants, not regular troops. Skilfully building up close relations with Orthodox Russia, Obrenović exploited the difficulties of the Ottomans caused by the Russo-Turkish War of 1828–9 to take full control. Over the years, he had built up a large personal fortune from his livestock business, using it to bribe officials in Constantinople to give him the right to collect taxes. This increased his wealth to such a degree that in 1830 he actually bought the right to hereditary rule for his family in perpetuity, as Princes of Serbia. So severe were his financial exactions by this time that the Serbian peasantry were constantly staging armed local uprisings, invariably defeated by Obrenović's well-armed and centrally directed troops.

In 1830, most likely under pressure from Obrenović, Sultan Mahmud II decided to cede six Bosnian municipalities to the Principality of Serbia. Outraged at their loss of autonomy, fearful of Mahmud's centralizing drive in the administration of the empire, and apprehensive about losing ground to Serbia's Christian population, the Bosnian Muslim elites organized a convention early in 1831 and raised a rebel army that drove the vizier out of Bosnia. In September an all-Bosnian assembly in Sarajevo effectively declared Bosnian autonomy within the Ottoman Empire. Supported by at least some Christian subjects in the area, this can be seen effectively as the first real declaration of Bosnian national identity. The rebellion was crushed by the Ottoman authorities in 1832. Concerned though the European powers (with the exception of Russia) were about the stability and durability of the Ottoman Empire, it still clearly had the muscle in the early 1830s to assert itself over rebels and revolutionaries who did not have the international support that had brought the Greeks their independence. Nevertheless, unrest continued, and Obrenović's hold on his dominions became steadily shakier. In 1838 the sultan, noting that discontent was reaching fresh heights, forced him to accept a constitution with a legislature. This in turn made Obrenović abdicate in favour of his young son Mihailo (1823–68), who was soon forced into exile after doing nothing to moderate the hated policies of his father. He was replaced by Alexander Karadjordjević (1806–85), the son of the rebel leader murdered in 1817. Ottoman efforts to bring stability to the region were not much helped by this intervention, which merely stoked the fires of what was fast becoming the most extreme of nineteenth-century dynastic rivalries.

In the end, however, the European powers still needed the Ottoman Empire at this juncture. Greek independence was very much an exception. Britain was especially worried by the prospect of Russia moving into the space left vacant by a possible disintegration of the Ottoman Empire. The fate of Ioannis Kapodistrias illustrated both the power and the limitations of the influence of the French Revolution and Napoleon, their ideas and their example, on European politics in the years after Waterloo. On the one hand, a generation of political figures from the educated elites and the younger echelons of the military officer class, inspired by ideals of liberty and national sovereignty, had taken the lead in movements of national liberation and liberal reform, refusing to accept the conservative and restorationist aspects of the 1815 settlement. They managed to win enough support to shake the edifice constructed at the Congress of Vienna to its very foundations in almost every part of Europe. On the other hand, it was clear that these men represented only a minority of the educated classes and lacked real popular support. Where ordinary people in town and country did rise up against established authority, it was usually in their own interests, and they seldom shared the ideals of national freedom and liberal reform proclaimed by the educated revolutionaries. The Napoleonic inspiration that lay behind the conspiracies of the revolutionaries involved a strong belief in a rational, centralized state administration that sometimes sat uneasily with their campaign for representative government. Moreover, the nervousness their activities caused in the chancelleries of Europe was a significant factor in keeping the Concert of Europe together, for all the rivalries and differences between its leading powers. By the end of the 1820s, the settlement reached in Vienna in 1815 had been dented in a number of places, but fundamentally it was still intact.

THE JULY REVOLUTION

The first really serious crack in the European edifice constructed at Vienna occurred in 1830, when the reactionary regime of Charles X in France crumbled virtually overnight. With the appointment of Jules de Polignac to head the government in August 1829, a confrontation with the liberals in the Chamber of Deputies elected in 1827 became inevitable. Remembering his role in the last Ministry of his brother Louis XIV in July 1789, the king told his government that 'the first concession that my unhappy brother made was the signal for his fall'. The liberals, he ranted, wanted to overthrow the monarchy: 'in attacking the ministry, it is at the monarchy that they are really aiming'. Addressing the assembled deputies on 2 March 1830, Charles declared that if they opposed him, he would take the steps necessary to maintain public order. So agitated was he that in waving his arms about to lend emphasis to his words, the king accidentally knocked off his own hat, which rolled across the floor and ended at the feet of his cousin Louis-Philippe, Duke of Orléans (1773–1850). Over the years Louis-Philippe had acquired a reputation as a liberal, following in the footsteps of his father, whose sympathy with the Revolution in 1789 had earned him the sobriquet of 'Philippe-Égalité'. The symbolism was not lost on those present.

From this point, the crisis accelerated rapidly. Alarmed by Charles's threat, 221 deputies voted for an address to him rejecting Polignac's Ministry because it had no support in the Chamber. The king responded by bringing even more intransigent conservatives into the government, dissolving the Chamber and holding fresh elections. But these produced a stunning victory for the liberals, who won 274 seats to the government's 143 (with 11 undecided). In the meantime, Charles sought to bolster his prestige by declaring war on Algeria, nominally a part of the Ottoman Empire, where the governor had caused a diplomatic incident by hitting the French ambassador with a fly-whisk in a fit of pique. Not for the last time, a French sovereign was attempting to shore up his position at home by emulating Napoleon abroad. The bulk of the French overseas empire, in India and America, had been lost by 1815, but the dream had lived on, together with the hope of profit. A start had already been made in Senegal and Madagascar; an even more promising acquisition beckoned on the north African coast. In three weeks, an expeditionary force succeeded in occupying Algiers and laying the foundations there for a new French colonial empire. News reached Paris in the second week of July and emboldened the king to take action against his internal opponents.

On 25 July, Charles X and Polignac issued four ordinances, imposing strict official censorship, dissolving the newly elected Chamber of Deputies, reducing the electorate to the richest 25 per cent of existing voters, and initiating fresh elections. Thiers and the advocates of a constitutional monarchy issued a public call to resist such a coup. This in turn provoked an uprising on the streets of Paris, led by printworkers whose livelihoods were threatened by the new censorship decree, students, veterans of Napoleon's army, and ordinary working people made mutinous by three years of high grain and bread prices as a result of a series of poor harvests. Crowds roamed the streets smashing street-lanterns and shouting 'Down with the Bourbons!' Polignac's carriage was stoned as it went past. Charles ordered the garrison of Paris to restore order, but the man in charge, Auguste-Fréderic Marmont (1774–1852), one of Napoleon's marshals, had only about 13,000 men at his disposal, since 40,000 of the best troops were on campaign in Algeria. The king and Polignac had stripped their regime of its defences just when they needed them most. On 27 July 1830 Marmont's troops fired on demonstrators gathered in front of the Palais Royal, killing several of them; the corpses were paraded round the city to advertise their martyrdom, and even larger crowds assembled the following day. 'This is no longer a riot,' Marmont wrote to the king, echoing, perhaps deliberately, the words addressed to Louis XVI on the fall of the Bastille: 'this is a revolution.'

On 29 July, Marmont mustered his troops and began to march towards the insurrection. But the crowds responded with a new tactic that was to become standard in all Parisian uprisings of the century: the barricade. Ripping up cobbles from the streets, they piled them up across the streets, adding furniture, upturned carts, and anything else they could find, to a height of anything up to ten feet. As Marmont's troops moved in, their avenue of retreat was blocked by trees felled behind them, while supporters of the revolution pelted them with all kinds of objects from above in a 'war of the chamber-pots'. Napoleonic veterans took the lead in organizing the defence; many of them had kept their arms at home after demobilization, and the royal troops were forced to withdraw under heavy musket-fire. Reluctant to fire on crowds including women and children, Marmont regrouped his forces in defence of the Tuileries and the Louvre. But their morale was low, they were poorly equipped, and they had had nothing to eat since breakfast. Harangued by the liberal politician Casimir Perier, two whole regiments went over to the insurrection, causing the rest to flee in disorder. Most public buildings now fell to the insurgents. Observing the scene from an upstairs window, Talleyrand, who had returned from exile some time before to aid Louis-Philippe's cause, took out his pocket-watch and announced: 'Twenty-ninth July, five minutes past midday, the elder branch of the house of Bourbon has ceased to reign.' As Marmont withdrew his remaining forces from Paris, Thiers and the liberal deputies, notably the banker Jacques Laffitte, alarmed by the news that the crowds had been shouting 'Vive Napoléon!', printed and distributed a manifesto declaring Charles X deposed and urging the offer of the crown to Louis-Philippe as the only person who could be trusted to respect the constitution agreed by Louis XVIII at his restoration. Making his way out of Paris, Thiers persuaded Louis-Philippe to accept, a decision endorsed by the advice of Talleyrand. Greeted on his return to the capital by a large crowd chanting 'Vive la République!' Louis-Philippe was rescued by the Marquis de Lafayette, the veteran of 1789, who took him onto the balcony of the Hôtel de Ville to wave the tricolor. As more of his troops deserted, Charles threw in the towel, wrote out his formal abdication, and departed for England and subsequently Austria. He died in Görz, a Habsburg possession on the Mediterranean coast, of cholera in 1836.

As revolutions go, the 1830 Revolution in France was neither particularly bloody nor especially dramatic. It happened only in Paris, and its outcome was meekly accepted in the rest of the country. Its results were rather less than spectacular. They included the revision of the constitution of Louis XVIII to provide for the abolition of the hereditary element in the nominated Chamber of Peers; the removal of the preamble stating that sovereignty lay solely with the monarch; the deletion of the clause allowing the king to suspend or block laws; the extension of the right to propose legislation to both Chambers; the abolition of censorship; and the downgrading of Catholicism from the official religion of the state to 'the religion of the majority of Frenchmen'. The electoral law was liberalized, lowering the qualifications for the vote and for standing for election sufficiently as almost to double the size of the electorate, though it still included no more than 5 per cent of the adult male population. Louis-Philippe and his advisers made a conscious effort to include Bonapartists and Republicans in the post-revolutionary settlement. Four of Napoleon's marshals officiated at his swearing-in ceremony (there was no formal coronation) and the royal palace was thrown open to the public, whom the new monarch greeted in person, joining in their singing of the hymn of the French Revolution, the *Marseillaise*.

Louis-Philippe's first ministry included Lafayette, symbolically representing the Revolution, General Étienne Gérard (1773–1852), representing the empire, and François Guizot, who had served under Louis XVIII, as well as Orléanists like Thiers and Casimir Perier. Napoleon's former marshal, Jean-de-Dieu Soult (1769–1851), was also a leading figure in the government. The effort at national reconciliation was palpable. Popular attempts to have the reactionary ministers of Charles X's last months executed were thwarted, and Polignac and his colleagues were only briefly imprisoned before being allowed to go into exile. At the same time, the surviving signatories of the warrant for Louis XVI's execution, revolutionaries who had been exiled in 1816, were amnestied and allowed to return home. For all its unspectacular moderation, this was indeed a revolution. Over half the senior administrators of the Council of State were dismissed, along with 76 regional prefects, 196 sub-prefects and 393 mayors or deputies. Sixty-five generals were forcibly retired, and most of the diplomatic corps lost their jobs. Louis-Philippe adopted the tricolor as the official flag of France, declared that 'the will of the nation has called me', and styled himself King Louis-Philippe rather than Louis XIX or Philippe VII. He took the title 'King of the French', as Louis XVI had been forced to do in 1789, and as Napoleon had echoed in his own title of 'Emperor of the French', rather than the traditional 'King of France'. This was a new kind of monarchy, modelled at least in part on the English constitutional system, whose supposed origins in the civil wars of the seventeenth century Guizot devoted himself to chronicling in his major historical work of these years. Although

Louis-Philippe retained the right to appoint ministers, he was always careful to do so only if they had the support of the legislature. Fresh elections in 1830 brought a liberal majority.

But at the same time, the new regime was in some ways as committed to the maintenance of order as the old one had been. In Lyon, where the silk industry employed 50,000 people, the introduction of Jacquard looms and the dismissal, at the behest of local manufacturers and merchants, of a prefect who had guaranteed minimum prices for the weavers' products, led to a mass insurrection in 1831. Armed bands of weavers stormed the police barracks, routed the military garrison in a battle that left 169 dead and more than 400 wounded, and took over the town. After several days, an army of 20,000 troops under Soult reconquered the city without bloodshed. Three years later, however, during a boom, an attempt by local businessmen to reduce the weavers' pay led to a series of strikes, culminating in the arrest and trial of alleged ringleaders and the occupation of the town by the army. The weavers put up barricades in the streets and raided the arsenal. During the ensuing battles, around 200 were killed and 10,000 insurgents arrested and condemned to prison or exile. Predictably, the authorities in Paris suspected the involvement of Republicans, and indeed the insurgents did issue decrees using the old Revolutionary calendar, dating from 1792 as Year I. The government also severely repressed attempted uprisings by Republicans in Paris in June 1832 and again in April 1834. After the latter revolt, led by the quasi-Jacobin Society of the Rights of Man, Thiers ordered mass treason trials, which ended in dozens being found guilty and imprisoned or deported.

Chronic instability continued to mark Louis-Philippe's reign during the 1830s. The first assassination attempt on the king, in 1832, was a failure, but in 1835 there was a more serious attempt to assassinate him by the Corsican Giuseppe Fleschi (1790–1836). Together with two other extreme democrats, Fleschi devised an 'infernal machine' that could fire twenty gun barrels simultaneously. He aimed it at the king from an upper-storey window as he passed along the Boulevard du Temple in Paris on 28 July 1835; one ball grazed Louis-Philippe's forehead, his horse was killed, and eighteen people, including Marshal Édouard Mortier (1768–1835), were shot dead. The machine also injured the assassin when it went off; surgeons tended him until he was ready to stand trial and face the guillotine. The police discovered six other plots to kill the king in 1835 alone. The following year, the Republican soldier Louis Alibeaud (1810–36) aimed a shot at the king with a musket disguised as a walking stick; Louis-Philippe was saved only by the fact that he had bowed deeply to acknowledge the guards on the street presenting arms as the shot was

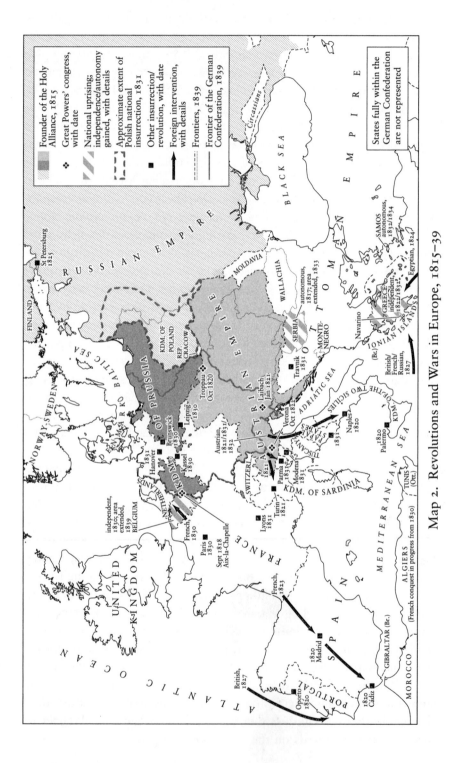

Map 2. Revolutions and Wars in Europe, 1815–39

fired (it went into the woodwork of his coach, three inches above his head). Another attempt a few months later failed because an onlooker hit the would-be assassin as he was firing the shot. In 1840 another attempt was made, but the weapon blew up in the assassin's hands. In 1835 the hyperactive Louis-Napoleon Bonaparte (1808–73), nephew of the great emperor, attempted a coup by suborning the garrison in Strasbourg in 1835 (he was quickly arrested and the attempt came to nought). In 1840 he landed with a small party of followers at Boulogne, accompanied by an eagle (or, some alleged, a vulture) as a symbol of the imperial cause; fired on by the National Guard, the group gave up and were apprehended. The previous year, Auguste Blanqui and 600 radical Republicans had tried to storm the Palais de Justice and the Town Hall in Paris; shots were exchanged, and twenty-eight soldiers and thirty to forty insurgents were killed before order was restored. Governments seemed unable to establish political stability. During the seventeen years of the July Monarchy there were seventeen successive Ministries, sometimes with substantial gaps between them. The 1830 Revolution in France seemed to have settled little, as Republicans, Bonapartists, Orléanists and Legitimists continued to fight each other for the right to rule.

EUROPEAN REPERCUSSIONS

The French Revolution of 1830 dismayed Metternich, though in the longer run it became clear that it brought some stability to the international system by quashing Charles X's ambitiously conceived and unilaterally pursued policy of overseas imperial aggrandizement and replacing it with a more cautious and modest conception of French interests abroad. Metternich attempted to rouse the Holy Alliance against Louis-Philippe, and Tsar Nicholas I of Russia duly obliged with a ringing denunciation of the revolution's violation of the sacred principle of monarchical legitimacy. However, by early October 1830 all the Great Powers, including Russia, recognizing a fait accompli, had extended formal recognition to Louis-Philippe. But this did not settle the matter. In the 1790s the French had carried their Revolution to the rest of Europe, where it had initially met with a positive reception only from tiny and often isolated minorities of radicals. Four decades on, the number of educated liberals who sympathized with the ideals of moderate constitutionalism and national self-determination had grown sufficiently in parts of western and central Europe for the events in Paris almost immediately to spark similar upheavals elsewhere.

For Metternich, the fall of the French monarchy represented 'the collapse of the dam in Europe', opening the floodgates of revolution. The first indications that the 1830 Revolution would not remain confined to France came on 25 August, during a performance in Brussels of an opera whose action centred on an uprising of Italians against Spanish rule in Naples during the seventeenth century. As the celebrated young tenor Adolphe Nourrit (1802–39) sang *Amour sacré de la patrie* ('Sacred love of the Fatherland'), the audience erupted, carrying their enthusiasm into the streets after the performance. Here they were joined by crowds of discontented artisans, thrown into poverty by a sharp economic crisis that had begun some months before. The authorities had cancelled a firework display at short notice, fearing disturbances, but their action proved to be a self-fulfilling prophecy. Robbed of their promised entertainment, the artisans put up barricades, and middle-class militias from outside Brussels soon arrived to lend armed backing to the uprising. Underlying this upsurge of discontent was bitter resentment among the largely French-speaking inhabitants of the city against rule from Holland, imposed by the Congress of Vienna. While the diplomats had intended the union of the Kingdom of the Netherlands with the former Austrian territory to its south as a peaceful buffer state co-operating with the Concert of European Powers to constrict any renewed drive to expansion by the French, King Willem I of the Netherlands (1772–1843) had other ideas. Seeking to create a coherent and centralized medium-sized European state, Willem discriminated against the Catholics who formed the majority in Brussels and most other parts of the region, forcing them to pay higher taxes, making them contribute to the upkeep of Protestant schools, and denying them proper representation in the central administration. Nobody had asked people in Brussels whether they wanted to be ruled by the Dutch; now they were making their views felt, and their answer was clearly no.

Faced with the uprising in Brussels, Willem first sought international intervention, which only met with delaying tactics on the part of the British in particular. He then convoked the States-General, which issued some minor but unsatisfactory concessions, and finally, when the revolt showed no signs of dying down, he sent his younger son Prince Frederik (1797–1881) to Brussels at the head of an army of 14,000 men. In a few days of confused fighting the young, inexperienced Dutch troops were overawed by the barricaded defenders of the city and panicked. On 27 September 1830, Frederik withdrew. The uprising rapidly spread to Antwerp, where another Dutch army began bombarding the city, driving its mainly Flemish and Protestant inhabitants into the arms of the revolutionaries. The formation of a provisional national government on 26 September was followed on 4 October by a Belgian declaration of independence and then by the calling of a national Congress. Demonstrating the enduring influence of the American Revolution in European political thought, the Congress issued a ringing condemnation of the Dutch government for reducing Belgium to the status of a colony, accompanied by 'the despotic imposition of a privileged language' and 'taxes, overwhelming in their amount, and still more in the manner in which they were apportioned'. The Congress declared its intention 'of founding, on the broad and solid basis of liberty, the edifice of the new social order which will be the beginning and guarantee of durable happiness to Belgium'.

The reactions of the Great Powers to this imbroglio were contradictory and confused. The Russians issued sabre-rattling declarations and mobilized their troops, while the south German states argued for non-intervention. The French, despite powerful voices urging a partition of Belgium, with the southern, French-speaking part falling to themselves, eventually took a back seat in view of the precarious situation of their own newly established government. Advised by Talleyrand, who emerged yet again at a moment of crisis, this time as ambassador to London, the French government put its own stability above everything else, and this meant going along with whatever the British wanted to do. Besides, an independent Belgium would be a weaker anti-French buffer state than a powerful united Netherlands. Metternich, realizing that the Belgians could not be stopped in the long run, sent an ambassador to the inevitable conference in London with instructions to mobilize the Concert of Europe in favour of a moderate, monarchical and independent Belgium. Skilfully led by the newly appointed British Foreign Secretary Lord Palmerston (1784–1865), the conference met on 4 November 1830 and quickly settled the main issues, establishing a constitutional monarchy with a bicameral legislature on a restricted property franchise. The only issue that remained to be settled was the question of who was to be king of the new state.

After extensive discussion, and the rejection of many candidates as unacceptable to one participating nation or the other, the choice fell, as in the case of so many small nations later in the century, on a minor German prince, Leopold of Sachsen-Coburg-Gotha (1790–1865), who was by far the most internationally acceptable candidate. Leopold had spent most of his life as an officer in the Imperial Russian Army, leading his cavalry with distinction against Napoleon's forces at the Battle of Kulm in 1813 and ending his career just two years later at the age of twenty-five as a lieutenant-general. Although German, he was actually a British subject, having married the Prince Regent's only legitimate offspring, Princess Charlotte (1796–1817), in 1816, an alliance that brought him British citizenship and the rank of field-marshal in the British Army and, some time later, official membership in the British Royal Family with the title of Royal Highness. Charlotte had died giving birth to a stillborn child in 1817, however, so to perfect his appeal to the 1830 Belgian conference Leopold declared himself willing to placate the French by marrying a French princess if one was available. There was, to be sure, a minor obstacle, in the form of his marriage in 1829 to a young German actress, Caroline Bauer (1807–77), but the relationship ended two years later, and Leopold was able to persuade everybody that the marriage, which was by private contract only, had never been valid. Overcoming all these obstacles, Leopold was crowned King of Belgium in July 1831, marrying Louis-Philippe's eldest daughter Louise-Marie the following year.

This did not quite end the affair, since King Willem of the Netherlands proved obdurate and tried to involve the German Confederation early in 1831 when the Belgians invaded the Grand Duchy of Luxembourg, a member state of which he was titular head. The Great Powers accepted the incorporation of the Grand Duchy, however, and the Confederation did nothing. Resentment in Holland boiled over, and Willem invaded Belgium on 2 August 1831. Leopold quickly called in a French army, which expelled the Dutch forces, leaving them still in charge of the fortress garrison in Antwerp. European pressure now turned on the French, who were proving suspiciously reluctant to withdraw. On 30 September 1831 they finally pulled out, and a new treaty made some small adjustments to the previously agreed boundaries and terms, dividing Luxembourg between the two rival states. The stubborn Dutch were still refusing to leave Antwerp a year later, however, so in November 1832 the French invaded again and besieged the town, while the British Navy blockaded the river Scheldt to coerce the Dutch into surrender, which they did in December 1832. It was to take until 1839 before the outstanding issues were finally settled. Luxembourg, or rather its German-speaking eastern half, remained under the Dutch king until the succession of Queen Wilhelmina (1880–1962) to the Dutch throne in 1890 caused it to pass to the nearest male heir, since the Grand Duchy was governed by the Salic Law, which banned succession through the female hire. In previous or possibly subsequent times, the convoluted and often intractable Belgian issue would have been too important to France, Prussia, or Britain for a conflict to be avoided. Yet despite recurring divisions between the Great Powers, and the barely contained anger of Nicholas I of Russia, who saw the settlement as a direct violation of the principles of the Holy Alliance, the issue had been settled peacefully and without military conflict, except between the Dutch and the Belgians.

The French invasions had been backed by general European consensus. As the London conference declared in its protocol issued on 19 February 1831, Europe's rights, derived from its obligation to preserve the international order, took precedence over those of individual states. Even Nicholas I was only prepared to take action as part of a general European intervention. This proved to be a major reason why the revolutions of 1830 did not develop into major conflicts or pose a serious threat to the social order.

At the same time, however, there could be no doubt about the seriousness of these upheavals, nor about their pan-European spread. Events in France sparked uprisings not just in neighbouring Belgium but in other countries too. French remained the common language of educated elites, still used as the lingua franca of European diplomacy, and news spread by travellers, journalists, diplomats and traders. In Portugal a long-running dispute between Dom Pedro, Emperor of Brazil, and his younger brother Miguel (1802–66), was settled on the death in 1826 of Dom João, the Portuguese king. Dom Pedro now renounced all rights to the Portuguese throne in favour of his seven-year-old daughter Dona Maria de Glória (1819–53). But the arrangement was torpedoed by Miguel's usurpation of the throne two years later. Miguel was backed by the British Tories, who hoped to use him to reassert British influence, and by the Portuguese absolutist party of landowning grandees, who resented the liberal constitution of 1822 and the continuation of laws introduced in the 1800s by Napoleon. Portuguese liberals reacted to Miguel's annulment of many of these laws in a rebellion that was forcefully put down by the Miguelists. A reign of terror ensued, with arrests, imprisonments and executions. But in 1831, in the wake of the revolutionary tide sweeping across Europe, Pedro handed over the imperial throne of Brazil to his son, sailed for Europe, obtained British and French backing, and captured Porto, where he was besieged by the Miguelists for over a year. His officers, it was reported, were amply wined and dined by English port merchants, but their men suffered badly from malnutrition and the effects of a cholera epidemic. Pedro and his supporters obtained the assistance of the liberal English Admiral Sir Charles Napier (1786–1860), who under the pseudonym 'Carlos da Ponza' took command of the rebel ships and inflicted a crushing defeat on the Miguelist fleet at Cape St Vincent. This enabled the rebels to occupy Lisbon, where jubilant crowds expelled the Miguelist garrison, captured the arsenal, and opened the prisons. Breaking the siege of Porto, Pedro moved to the capital. The liberals now proclaimed Maria de Glória queen and marched southwards, defeating a large Miguelist force of 18,000 at the Battle of Asseiceira in May 1824.

Miguel was obliged to agree to go into exile (with a large pension, agreed at the time), while Pedro restored the liberal reforms and constitution, confiscated the Miguelists' property, and paid back the Church for its support for his brother by dissolving the monasteries and seizing their buildings and assets. Dom Pedro died in September 1834, and his daughter Maria de Glória, now fifteen, took up her duties as Queen Maria II. She had become the ruler of a country that years of conflict had plunged into deep indebtedness and renewed subservience, this time economic, to the British.

Meanwhile in Spain, the repressive regime of King Fernando VII continued unchanged into the early 1830s until the monarch succumbed to a fatal attack of gout in September 1833. With his infant daughter enthroned as Queen Isabella II (1830–1904), steered from behind the scenes by Fernando's widow Maria Cristina (1806–78), the liberals were able to take advantage of the government's weakness by forcing through a moderate liberal constitution in 1834. It enshrined the power of aristocratic oligarchs, and looked back to pre-revolutionary constitutionalism, with its many limitations, and its symbolic links to the old idea of representational Estates or orders. When the government met, indeed, the deputies had to wear medieval dress to underline their difference from modern elected representatives. Three years later, however, continual agitation by the more radical deputies forced through a new constitution that rested on popular sovereignty, though with restrictions imposed by the reservation of extensive powers to the Crown. The essential basis for their triumph lay in a series of revolutionary outbreaks in Spanish towns and cities. These were powered by violent crowd disturbances and demonstrations by the urban poor, especially in times of high wheat prices, that were brought under control by liberal committees prepared to make concessions. The revolutionary leaders, 'bloody parodies of Robespierre', took their cue from the French Jacobins of the early 1790s, burning convents, massacring the inmates of the local prisons, and attacking notoriously conservative aristocrats. After one encounter, a defeated general's 'severed hand was passed round the tables of the *Café Nuevo*', as a historian later reported. Memories of the French Revolution continued to condition the behaviour of revolutionary activists and revolutionary crowds across Europe some forty years on.

In Italy such memories inspired the *carbonari* to rise up against both the Austrians in the north and papal rule in the centre of the peninsula. Encouraged by Francis IV, Duke of Modena (1779–1846), who was looking to extend his territory, they had begun preparations in the late 1820s, but the Parisian revolution both spurred them to action and prompted the duke to withdraw his support out of fear of social upheaval. The *carbonari* raised the Italian tricolor across the Papal States and in the Duchy of Parma. The ageing revolutionary Filippo Buonarroti (1761–1837), who had followed Robespierre in the early 1790s and been imprisoned for his part in Babeuf's egalitarian conspiracy against the post-Jacobin rule of the Directory, had been hyperactive in spearheading conspiratorial societies in exile, with names like 'The World' or 'The Militia of the Condemned' or, less melodramatically, 'The Society of the Friends of the People'. Buonarroti formed a 'liberating Italian junta' to co-ordinate the uprisings, but its members quarrelled over his strict Jacobin principles and were rightly suspicious of his demand for a 'transitional' dictatorship once power had been seized. The various Italian cities now under the control of the *carbonari* proved unable to abandon their centuries-old rivalries and failed to respond to a call for a unity conference in Rome; in Bologna they even refused to admit revolutionary troops from Modena, under the command of the former Napoleonic general Carlo Zucchi (1777–1863). 'Citizens,' the insurrectionaries proclaimed, 'Remember the Modenese circumstances are not ours!' The insurgents failed to interest the peasantry in their cause, though they attracted a number of European adventurers, including Louis-Napoleon Bonaparte. While living in Italy, Louis-Napoleon had joined the *carbonari* and taken part in a plot to seize power in Rome, easily unmasked by the authorities. The Austrians sent in an army with the tacit support of the Great Powers and quickly crushed the rebellions. Zucchi was betrayed and clapped in irons by the Austrians; he remained in prison under harsh conditions until released by revolutionaries in 1848. Buonarroti continued his life's work of building conspiracies in exile; his account of Babeuf's insurrection, published in 1828, became a kind of practical handbook for revolutionaries, and was much admired later in the century by anarchists.

Events in Paris also had a profound effect in Germany. In Aachen (Aix-la-Chapelle), on the north-western edge of the German Confederation, people wore the tricolor cockade to symbolize their solidarity with the revolution in France. The economic downturn that so affected artisans in Belgium also brought unemployed and discontented craftsmen onto the streets in a whole variety of cities, including not only Cologne, Frankfurt and Munich but also Vienna and Berlin. In Leipzig, as the political artisan Wilhelm Weitling (1808–71) wrote, 'in one night the people were master of the city and its environs'. Crowds demolished the houses of unpopular merchants, lawyers and officials, but had little idea how to channel their discontent into particular demands. The liberal writer Karl von Rotteck (1775–1840) called such actions 'crimes against the community without concern for the fatherland and the constitution – which have as their impulse and expression the mob's personal passions, crude energy, irrationality, and larcenous desires'. Such views were common among the middle classes, and made it easy for the authorities to stamp out the unrest. Two thousand heavily armed Prussian troops arrived in Aachen to restore order, and in many other parts of Germany the crowds were quickly dispersed.

In some small and medium-sized German states, however, the liberals were bold enough to play on government fears of 'the mob' to extract significant reforms. In Brunswick a state official, Wilhelm Bode (1779– 1854), took the lead, securing the replacement of the unpopular Duke Carl (1804–73), who had abrogated the constitution in 1827, with his more liberal brother Wilhelm (1806–84), thus destroying the principle of strict legitimacy so sacred to the ideologues of the Restoration. Middle-class minds had been concentrated by the burning down of the Ducal Castle and the flight of the terrified Duke Carl into exile, leaving the citizens' militia to restore order. Wilhelm obliged in 1832 by introducing a representative constitution. In Hesse-Kassel the Elector Wilhelm II (1777–1847) alienated middle-class opinion by his attempt to give his live-in mistress the title of princess. As rioters mobilized in protest against high taxes, over-zealous policing, high customs duties and the payment by peasants of feudal dues to rural landlords, the middle-class citizens' assembly in Kassel demanded a constitution in order to prevent 'the war threatened by the poor against the propertied'. While Wilhelm II left the city, with his mistress in tow, the liberals forced through a new constitution with a unicameral legislature based on a wide franchise including even elements of the peasantry, and gave it powers that included the right to file lawsuits against the king's ministers (whom the king, rather than the legislature, continued to appoint). In Saxony a similar wave of unrest among artisans and workers, extending into rural centres of the textile industry, prompted concerned middle-class citizens to form militias, while senior officials forced the government to concede a new constitution, promulgated in 1831. Hanover, still ruled by the British monarch, saw an uprising of students and professors in the university town of Göttingen against the hated, arch-conservative leading minister Count Münster (1766–1839). Münster was duly dismissed, and after much wrangling a moderately liberal constitution was finally passed in 1833.

Everywhere in Germany liberal opponents of the Restoration were emboldened not only by events in Paris but even more, perhaps, by the revolution in Poland. In some states, such as Baden and Bavaria, they brought about changes in the composition of the government and reforms in the press law. The climax of this upsurge of liberal reformism in the German states culminated in a massive festival held around a ruined castle near the town of Hambach in the Palatinate. Modelled, like the Wartburg Festival before it, on the great popular festivals of the French Revolution in the early 1790s, it brought an estimated twenty to thirty thousand people together under the leadership of a campaigner for press freedom, the journalist Johann Georg Wirth (1798–1848), to listen to demands for reform. Among those present, professional men, businessmen, craftsmen and students predominated, but the crowds, vigorously waving revolutionary black, red and gold flags and in many cases wearing the Phrygian red caps of the French Revolution, heard a variety of speeches advocating unity and freedom for Germany. Revolution here brought together different levels of the social order: it had left the smoke-filled rooms of Freemasons and conspirators, come out into the open, and was taking the road of legal and constitutional reform, not that of violent upheaval. The speaker's rostrum and the journalist's desk were at the centre of the events in Hambach, not the guillotine or the lamp post. A variety of smaller festivals followed in other places.

For Metternich these events provided the signal for a crackdown. 'Liberalism has given way to radicalism,' he declared. He persuaded the Federal Diet to introduce new laws (the notorious 'Six Articles' and 'Ten Articles') sharpening censorship, banning political parties, festivals and demonstrations, forbidding regional legislatures from rejecting government budgets or passing motions critical of the monarch, and much more. As armed forces marched into Germany's towns to drive the crowds off the streets, liberal reforms were rescinded almost everywhere, and a blanket of reaction seemed to descend over the land. In 1833 the Confederation set up a central political police organization to co-ordinate the fight against political unrest. Leading officials from Austria, Prussia and Russia met to resolve on joint action against revolution. Liberal writers such as the poet Heinrich Heine were driven into exile, while others, including Wirth and other Hambach speakers, were arrested and imprisoned. Time would reveal that the triumph of reaction was more fragile and short-lived in Germany than it had been when the Carlsbad Decrees were issued in 1819.

In Switzerland an ideology of freedom had provided legitimacy for the self-assertion of a Confederation of autonomous cantons in defiance of the Holy Roman Empire since the sixteenth century; this sense of a separate national identity was cemented by resistance to Napoleon's curbing of independence and the enforced conscription of young Swiss men for his armies. Inspiration was provided among others by the semi-mythical figure of Wilhelm Tell, the medieval Swiss archer who is said to have proved both his nerve and his accuracy by shooting an arrow through an apple placed on his son's head when ordered to do so by the Austrian authorities. The story was celebrated in 1804 in a play by the German poet Friedrich Schiller (1759–1805), and then in 1829 by the fashionable Italian composer Gioachino Rossini (1792–1868) in an immensely popular opera infused with the liberal and romantic sentiments of the day. Swiss independence had been re-established by the Congress of Vienna along with the Confederation's traditional liberties. By 1823, however, these liberties had become irksome to Metternich and the Holy Alliance because they led a number of cantons to offer a haven to unsuccessful but potentially still dangerous foreign revolutionaries. The Congress Powers forced the Swiss Confederation to curb the rights of the exiles and impose restrictions on press freedom. Chafing under this interference, a coalition of middle-class professionals and educated men, artisans and shopkeepers, and substantial peasant farmers reacted to the 1830 revolution in France by pushing through the Federal Diet a series of reforms. These included, in ten of the cantons, universal male suffrage and guaranteed freedom of expression. In Zürich, the most liberal of the Swiss cities, universal schooling from six to sixteen was introduced, with fee waivers for the less well-off, and significant changes were made to the city's administration.

A similarly peaceful process of reform brought about major changes in the political system in Great Britain. The riots and disturbances of the post-Waterloo years had subsided as the economy improved and state repression began to bite – in the form of the Six Acts, which banned protest gatherings, censored the press, and suspended habeas corpus, allowing imprisonment without trial. At the end of the 1820s, however, the economy suffered a downturn again, as in the rest of Europe, one of the factors that underlay the grievances of the artisans who played such an important part in the events of 1830. The political class's fear of revolution, already renewed by the post-Napoleonic disturbances, grew more acute as popular unrest spread once more. Huge crowds sporting tricolor ribbons and cockades attended meetings in London addressed by radical politicians such as Sir Francis Burdett (1770–1844). A large gathering of workers in Manchester began a campaign to stop the reduction of wages during the economic depression. Angry farm labourers, reacting to the introduction of threshing machines which threw many people into unemployment in the winter months, burned hayricks and barns and smashed machinery across the southern counties and into East Anglia. In the capital in 1830, crowds objecting to the creation of the new, uniformed Metropolitan Police the previous year – itself a sign of increased anxieties about law and order – shouted slogans such as 'No police! No Polignac!' 'Men,' complained the conservative Prime Minister, the Duke of Wellington, victor of Waterloo, 'fancied that they had only to follow the examples of Paris and Bruxelles, and that they would acquire all that their imaginations had suggested as the summit of public happiness and prosperity.' 'The country,' he complained, 'was in a state of insanity about Reform.'

Wellington's intransigence brought his government down. A reforming ministry, led by the aristocratic Whigs, came into office towards the end of 1830, determined to defuse the escalating crisis before it caused an explosion. The issues at stake were comparable to those that had convulsed the political system in France, Belgium and Switzerland: middle-class reformers and artisans and small farmers all wanted a liberalization of the laws of assembly and association, freedom of the press, and above all a widening of political participation. The new British government introduced a Reform Bill to get rid of scandals such as 'rotten boroughs', where depopulated villages sent one or even two deputies to the House of Commons, 'pocket boroughs' where the local grandee nominated the member, the effective lack of representation for new industrial towns such as Manchester or Birmingham, and the widespread corruption resulting from the public nature of voting and its continuation over a period of several days. When the Bill was rejected by the hereditary aristocracy and senior clergy in the House of Lords, the seriousness of the revolutionary threat became quickly apparent: riots broke out in many parts of the country, with Nottingham castle razed to the ground and the Bishop's Palace destroyed by fire in Bristol, along with forty-five private houses and the local prison, resulting in twelve deaths. The country, thought one Member of Parliament, was 'in a state little short of insurrection', while the political elite, according to the writer Sydney Smith (1771–1845), was in a 'hand-shaking, bowel-disturbing passion of fear'. As radical orators stoked the fires of popular outrage, the king agreed reluctantly to create enough new Whig peers to overcome the Lords' resistance, and Wellington and his supporters caved in.

The Bill was passed by both Houses of Parliament and became law in 1832, eliminating anomalies and abuses, but only extending the electorate by about 45 per cent, to just under 5 per cent of the population, in a reform comparable to parallel changes in the political systems of France and Belgium. The debates on the extension of the franchise gave birth to a new concept: 'the middle classes', as Earl Grey (1764–1845) the Prime Minister, put it, 'who have made wonderful advances in property and intelligence', and who 'form the real and efficient mass of public opinion, and without whom the power of the gentry is nothing'. As on the Continent, so too in Britain, radicals intent upon extending the vote to all adult males railed

against the limitations of the reform, 'the most illiberal, the most tyran-
nical, the most hellish measure', as the *Poor Man's Guardian* put it, 'that
ever could or can be proposed'. These ideas were not to go away. But for
the moment, the Reform Act did enough to defuse popular outrage and,
with further reforms in local government and other areas of administration, stabilized the British political system on a new, moderately liberal
basis. The outcome of the great struggle over reform was in the end a
constitution and political system not so very different from those of other
European states that had experienced a successful transition in 1830.
Unlike them, however, it was, in the short-to-medium term at least, to be
more durable and to prove more resistant to further attempts at changing
the status quo. The main proponent of the Bill, Lord John Russell (1792–
1878), declared firmly that this reform was 'final'.

THE CHANGING SHAPE OF POLITICS

'My most secret thought,' wrote Prince Metternich in 1829, 'is that old
Europe is at the beginning of the end. Determined to go down with it, I
will know how to do my duty.' The year 1830 seemed initially to prove
him correct. Yet as the wave of revolution receded, it became clear that
the revolutionaries and reformers had scored only very modest successes.
In many centres their initial gains had been reversed. Moreover, east of
the Rhine there had been relatively little serious revolutionary activity,
with the important exception of Poland, and the power of existing state
structures remained virtually untouched. But though the Vienna Settlement had largely survived the storm, the old Europe that Metternich had
known in his childhood and adolescence – he was sixteen when the French
Revolution broke out in 1789 – was no longer really there. 'The French
Revolution and the doings of Napoleon,' a Greek bandit was heard to say,
'opened the eyes of the world.' They made it 'more difficult to rule the
people'. In the 1820s the Turin chamber of commerce summed up the
change by noting that the French Revolution had caused 'a total confusion
among the different classes' in society: 'Everyone dresses in the same manner, the noble cannot be distinguished from the plebeian, the merchant
from the magistrate, the proprietor from the craftsman, the master from
the servant; at least in appearances, the woeful principle that created the
revolutions is regrettably maintained.' The genie was out of the bottle,
and it was impossible to put it back.

The monarchs and statesmen who returned to power in 1815 knew this.
Although the symbols and trappings of the *ancien régime* were frequently

invoked by the restored monarchies in 1815, they masked, perhaps deliberately, the fact that the conservatism of the age was something essentially
new. Thinkers and politicians alike thought of 1815 as a new start, marking the end of an era of rationalistic excess. Religious faith, human instinct
and emotion, tradition, morality, and a new, self-consciously historical
sense of the past, were to replace Enlightenment rationalism as the basis
of the social and political order. Thinkers like Joseph de Maistre (1753–
1821), building on the critique of the French Revolution by the Irish politician
Edmund Burke (1729–97), argued that stability could only come from the
general recognition that monarchy wielded an absolute power ordained
by God. People thus had to obey or face the consequences. 'The first servant of the crown,' declared de Maistre, 'should be the executioner.' In this
conservative view, a society governed by traditional hierarchies was the
only guarantor of order. Reason was the enemy: only faith and feeling
could be relied upon. 'When monarchy and Christianity are both attacked,'
wrote the French émigré Louis de Bonald (1754–1840), 'society returns to
savagery.' Civilization depended on the suppression not just of subversive
thought but of all thought. As Metternich's secretary Friedrich Gentz
(1764–1832) wrote in 1819: 'I continue to defend the proposition: "In order
that the press may not be abused, nothing whatever shall be printed in the
next . . . years. Period." If this principle were to be applied as a binding
rule . . . we should within a brief time find our way back to God and
Truth.' Thinkers like Chateaubriand, who had been prompted by the
excesses of the revolutionary era to convert back to Catholicism after
initially sharing in the rational scepticism of the Enlightenment, saw in
Christianity the faith that alone could guarantee contentment and subservience to authority.

Yet figures like de Bonald and de Maistre were in fact marginal extrem-
ists. During the 1820s writers and thinkers began to move towards a more
liberal point of view. Victor Hugo, who in 1824 declared that literature
should be 'the expression of a religious and monarchical society', was by
1830 propounding the principle that 'Romanticism, taken as a whole, is
only liberalism in literature . . . Freedom in art and liberty in society are
the twin goals to which all consistent and logical thinkers should march
in step.' In 1827 the French art critic August Jal (1795–1873) declared that
Romanticism was 'the echo of the cannon shot of 1789', and as if to prove
his point, Eugène Delacroix produced in 1830 what is probably the most
famous representation of revolution in any artwork, *Liberty Leading the
People*. For many Romantic poets and writers, the Greek uprising was a
turning point, symbolized by Byron's death at Missolonghi. The opera
that launched the Belgian revolution in 1830 was only one example of a

new trend, begun in Italy, of portraying ancient struggles for liberty in words and music in such a way that their contemporary relevance was unmistakeable.

If liberal views in many respects looked back to the ideals of the moderate first phase of the French Revolution of 1789, with its ringing declarations of freedom and popular sovereignty, representative government and constitutional rule, in the 1820s they also began to take on a new tone, increasingly infused with the ideals of nationalism. By spreading the principle of popular sovereignty across Europe while at the same time bringing repression, extortion and alien rule, Napoleon had stimulated among educated elites the belief that freedom from oppression could only be achieved on the basis of national self-determination. By the 1820s liberals from Belgium to Greece were articulating this potent idea. It was to become ever more powerful as the century progressed. As yet, liberals and revolutionaries generally regarded themselves as engaged in a common European struggle, a point of view symbolized through the international networks of the *carbonari* and the Freemasons, whose effectiveness was no doubt much exaggerated by Metternich and his political police. Even the Greek uprising was very much an international affair, at least as far as its leadership was concerned. From 1830 onwards, however, nationalist movements began to go their separate ways, with effects that were already apparent in the mid-century revolutions.

These revolutions, and those that swept across Europe in 1830, were the aftershocks of the great political earthquake of 1789. Yet there were differences too. In some ways the social forces that underpinned the upheavals of 1830 were the same as those that had driven on the French Revolution: the educated and professional middle classes pushing for more rights and greater freedoms, artisans and craftsmen desperate for bread and work. Yet the relationship between the two had changed. The Jacobin Terror of 1793–4 loomed large in people's memory and sometimes inspired radical action, as in the Spanish municipal revolutions of the early 1830s. Jacobin tactics of open-air assemblies, demonstrations and riots, reinforced now by the creation of barricades to block the forces of order, were still the primary means by which the urban masses sought to articulate their views. But only in exceptional cases, most notably in Belgium, did the bourgeois professional classes join forces with them. Almost everywhere, the latter were too scared of the rowdy violence of 'the mob'. In one country after another, they mobilized citizens' militias to restore order, or watched with anxious passivity while the old authorities brought in the troops. In most places, this limited the results of revolutionary upheavals to moderate liberal constitutional reforms. The principle of monarchy was left generally untouched. What was destroyed almost every-where, apart from in the great imperial states of central and eastern Europe, was the principle of absolutism.

The legacy of two and a half decades of war, and the example of Napoleon, had brought to the fore a new social force not much in evidence in 1789: the officer corps, or to be more precise, the junior and middle ranks of the officer corps, a social grouping that was also to play a major role in 'Third-World' revolutions in the second half of the twentieth century. Young army officers who had served in the Napoleonic Wars had been politicized by the experience, and felt sidelined by the hierarchical restorations of 1815. In many countries they took the lead in fomenting revolution, reinforced by the spread of conspiratorial organizations of one kind and another. Sometimes, as in Poland or Spain, they were able to recruit sufficient numbers of rank-and-file troops to their cause to make a fight of it. More generally, however, in the early to mid-1820s, in the immediate aftermath of the Napoleonic Wars, junior officers mostly failed to win enough support among the civilian population to succeed in stirring up a revolution. If, however, they did win such backing, they were dependent on middle-class and artisanal forces that were too weak to bring them victory despite the emergence of discontented groups of educated men who had benefited from employment in Napoleonic bureaucracies and now found themselves removed from the centres of power. In the early to mid-1820s, finally, the Holy Alliance and the Concert of Europe were still too nervous about a revival of the devastating conflicts of the revolutionary era to stand idly by, and mobilized international intervention if things seemed to them to be getting out of hand.

By 1830 this situation had changed. New social developments were pushing the junior and middle-ranking army officers out of the political mainstream and bringing the middle classes and the urban crowd, still dominated by the Jacobin forces of artisans and craftsmen, to the fore. The Concert of Europe was still functioning, but the statesmen who dominated it, including even Metternich, had become less paranoid about the dangers of revolutionary upheavals, and less willing to act. For this change the widespread European enthusiasm for the Greek uprising bore some responsibility. Here, in any case, the revolt was against an established power, the Ottoman Empire, that was itself marginal to the Concert of Europe, and owed its allegiance to another religion than the Christianity espoused by the Holy Alliance. More generally, however, it had become clear that absolutism allied to inefficiency was no recipe for political order. By 1830 revolutions no longer seemed to threaten mayhem, disorder, violence and war; everywhere, they brought moderate liberal constitutional reform, and even if conservative statesmen like Metternich did not like this, the fact that they had stopped short of giving power to the crowd offered enough reassurance to make international intervention seem a step too far.

Above all, however, there was one major social force that was almost entirely absent from the revolutionary stage in 1830: the peasantry. The great French Revolution of 1789 had gained its power not least from the fact that it spread through the countryside. It had attracted to its cause desperate and discontented farmers and rural labourers, and it had destroyed much of the political power of the aristocracy by sweeping away its foundations in the feudal order that had hitherto dominated social relations and economic structures in the rural world. In 1830 the countryside was almost universally quiescent. Yet it formed the context for the real lives of the overwhelming majority of Europeans at this time. It is to that context, and those lives, that we now turn.

2

The Paradoxes of Freedom

LORDS AND SERFS

Savva Dmitrievich Purlevsky (1800–68), born in the village of Velikoe in central Russia, had few good words to say about the system of obligations and impositions under which he had grown up, the system of serfdom. 'Our peasant dependence,' he complained, 'was bitter!' His village belonged to a small estate owned by a lieutenant-colonel, and consisted of around 3,000 acres of arable land, 432 acres of forest, and 1,620 acres of meadow and pasture. Dissolute and undisciplined, the colonel spent his life in St Petersburg, drinking, gambling and womanizing, and never visited his estate, which was run for him by a steward who creamed off much of the income for himself. Although most of the peasants on the estate were illiterate, Purlevsky learned to read with the aid of an ABC given him by the parish priest. He began to collect books with the small sums of money relatives gave him on his birthday and other occasions. This was to prove more than useful as he grew up.

The villagers, around 1,300 in number, had to pay the seigneur an annual rent. They were able to afford this without too much trouble, however, since besides the agricultural produce they farmed for their own subsistence, they also grew flax and other products which they traded on the market. The villagers knew they were better off than most. 'The common folk of the northern provinces lived almost entirely on rye bread and grey vegetable soup,' wrote Purlevsky. 'Everything the peasant household produced – dairy products, beef, lamb, eggs, and so on – was sold out of necessity. People lived on peas, oats, and steamed turnips. Our village was an exception. Trade and crafts brought us money and made us richer than other villages.' Nevertheless, the villagers of Velikoe had to suffer repeated additional demands from their seigneur, who periodically sent down orders from St Petersburg to be read out in the village assembly. On one occasion, for example, he commanded his steward 'to select four tall men no older than twenty, who would be suitable to stand on the footboard at the back of his carriage, as well as four beautiful eighteen-year-old girls [for purposes that he left unspecified but which can be guessed at]. All these people were to be taken personally to the landlord in St Petersburg.'

Russian noble landowners frequently lived away from their estates. They spent much of their time and money in St Petersburg or in French resorts and central European spas, running up enormous debts at the gambling table. Even if they were not indebted or mortgaged up to the hilt, they often saw their estates as little more than sources of income to sustain their lifestyle in the big city. So it was with the village of Velikoe. After the colonel's death in 1817, his daughter and her husband, a general in the Russian Army, arrived in the village and demanded the immediate payment of 200,000 roubles, a vast sum, as an advance on the next ten years' rent. The peasants refused point blank. Rebuffed, the general and his wife climbed into their coach and left for St Petersburg. But this was far from being the end of the affair. Soon after, fresh orders were read out to the village assembly. The new seigneurs had mortgaged the estate as security for a twenty-five-year loan, and required the villagers to pay the interest, calculated at 30,000 roubles a year, on top of their existing annual rent of 20,000. Those who failed to pay their share were to be conscripted into the army or taken off to Siberia to work in the seigneurs' metallurgical factories. The villagers received this fresh demand in shocked silence. 'At that very moment, for the first time in my life,' Purlevsky wrote later, 'I tasted the sorrow of my status as a serf.' What mattered indeed was the powerlessness of the enserfed. There were estates where peasants were beaten or whipped by their lord, or put in an iron collar if they disobeyed his orders. Purlevsky had even heard of a seigneur who punished a peasant boy for throwing a stone at one of his hunting dogs by stripping the lad of his clothes, which he showed to his borzois to sniff, then putting him in a field and loosing the dogs from their leads to hunt him down. (Fortunately the dogs did not harm him, and the emperor, on hearing this story, had the landlord arrested; there were limits even under serfdom, and he had clearly transgressed them.) Nevertheless, the serfs, not just educated ones like Purlevsky, keenly felt their overwhelming impotence in the face of seigneurial demands.

In the 1820s the situation of the serfs in Velikoe began to deteriorate even further. A new German steward started to interfere in who married whom, flogged those who disobeyed, forced serfs to work in the manorial textile factory, and had troops sent in when they complained. A hundred men were publicly whipped in front of all the serfs on the estate. Although the steward was replaced by another one who was less brutal, the peasants continued to complain about mismanagement until Purlevsky, almost the only man in the village able to read and write, was himself appointed steward in a bid by the seigneur to quell the discontent. He began to improve the administration of the estate and persuaded the seigneur to establish a school and a medical centre in the village. But Purlevsky's assistants started embezzling money behind his back, and the seigneur, blaming him for the financial irregularities when they came to light, summoned Purlevsky to St Petersburg, where he gave him a severe dressing-down. Terrified that he would be whipped as a punishment, Purlevsky absconded, making his way first to Moscow and subsequently Kiev. Then, building a raft for himself out of reeds, he floated down the river Dnieper all the way to Moldova, some 330 miles away. Arriving in 'Yassakh, exhausted, ragged, hungry and without money', he was taken in by Russian exiles belonging to the 'Old Believer' religious sect known as the Skoptsy. The German traveller Baron August von Haxthausen (1792–1866) came across them on his travels in 1843, and described their 'strange secret ceremonies', mostly held at night, where 'their shrill voices, dismal fervour, and wild enthusiasm made an indelible and painful impression on me'. They practised not only celibacy but also, alarmingly, self-castration.

The Skoptsy made a living as carters, and soon Purlevsky proved his worth to them by his honesty and hard work. One night, however, he overheard two of them talking about him. 'He is a good fellow, we need to convert him to our faith.' As Haxthausen had observed, the Skoptsy were 'very zealous in making converts to their doctrines, and in performing the operation alluded to upon their disciples'. Forced conversions, Purlevsky had learned, were far from uncommon. Terrified, he fled again, this time westwards for over 600 miles before reaching the Danube, where he fell in with another group of sectarian Russian exiles, with whom he stayed a further two years, working in the fisheries. In 1834, however, he discovered that Nicholas I had amnestied runaway serfs, so he left for Odessa some 800 miles to the east, where they were now allowed to settle legally, and began working as a waiter in a bar. Before long, he had become the manager, and then, with the help of a regular customer, he went into business as a sugar merchant, re-establishing contact with his family back in Velikoe. By 1856 he had saved enough to buy freedom from serfdom for his son. He died in 1868. All in all, Purlevsky's life was a lucky one for a serf. His village was prosperous. Like many others in central Russia, where agriculture was less intensively developed than in other areas, it was slowly turning itself into an industrial town centred on textile production and trading. The nature of the village economy meant that the serfs

frequently travelled on business, possessed a considerable degree of freedom of action, and could in no way be described as backward or isolated
from the world outside. They had no difficulty in standing up for their
rights when these were threatened, though this did not always meet
with success. Yet these developments were slowly undermining the institution of serfdom. Purlevsky saw it as exacting and burdensome in
financial terms, but more importantly, he bitterly resented the humiliations
and injustices it imposed, so much so that in the end he ran away from it
altogether.

By Purlevsky's time, European Russia contained the vast majority of
serfs who lived on the Continent. Across many western and central parts
of Europe the formal institution of serfdom had come to an end under the
egalitarian impact of the French Revolution of 1789, including Baden,
Bavaria, Denmark, France, the Netherlands, Schleswig-Holstein, Swedish
Pomerania and Switzerland. In Württemberg, and in Latvia and Estonia,
it was abolished in 1817. But in other areas it remained in force, including
the Kingdoms of Hanover and Saxony, where the institution of serfdom
was not abolished until the early 1830s; in Austria, Croatia and Hungary;
in Prussia, where it continued in a weakened form until 1848 or shortly
thereafter, following the rolling-back in 1816 of more radical reforms
introduced five years before; and in Russia and Poland, where it remained
in force until the 1860s. In Bulgaria serfdom was not abrogated in practice
until 1880, and in remote Iceland, where about a quarter of the population
worked in effect as serfs, it lasted until the legal compulsion for anyone
without land to provide labour for a farmer was formally ended in 1894.
Only in Bosnia, seized by Austria-Hungary from the Ottomans in 1878 and
formally annexed in 1908, did serfdom remain until the First World War;
serfs could buy their freedom, but it was expensive, and only 41,500 managed to do so by the time the war broke out. Popular resentment in the
Bosnian countryside at this failure to end serfdom stored up a legacy of
bitterness that was to find dramatic expression in 1914. Standing trial for
the murder of Archduke Franz Ferdinand (1863–1914), heir to the Austrian
throne, the young Bosnian Serb Gavrilo Princip (1894–1918) declared: 'I
have seen our people being steadily ruined. I am a peasant's son and know
what goes on in the villages. This is why I meant to take my revenge and
I regret nothing.' The shadow cast by serfdom across nineteenth- and early
twentieth-century Europe was long indeed.

Serfs were not slaves (although there were slaves in Europe, notably the
gypsies of Romania, who were treated as chattels and bought and sold on
the open market until their emancipation by both Church and state in the

1840s, and altogether in 1848); serfs had rights as well as duties. But neither were they free agents. Because serfdom had evolved gradually over the centuries and depended for its implementation on local or regional custom, it appeared in many thousands of variants that make it difficult to generalize about the way it functioned. Fundamentally, however, it obliged the peasant farmer to work without pay on certain tasks, or for a specific number of days per week, on the estate of the local landowning aristocrat, the seigneur, and to carry out particular duties such as assisting in hunts, repairing the seigneur's buildings, carrying messages for him, and performing various other menial tasks. The serf's wife might have to spin for the seigneur and his family or do light manual work, and his children might be made to guard his sheep or goats, or serve in the manor house. In some areas, further obligations were imposed by the state, which could require serfs to keep the local roads and bridges in good order, pay heavy taxes, provide horses for messengers, or make the younger men in the family available for military service. In some areas, like the village of Velikoe, these obligations had been commuted into an annual rent, but this did not free the serfs from having to do things such as work in the village textile factory, obey the dictates of the steward as to who should marry whom, or submit to physical punishments if they were considered refractory by the seigneur or his steward. Whatever the nature of their obligations, their servile status was always clear.

For most serfs, work on the seigneur's estate generally included the provision of draught animals to pull ploughs, but it could also involve labour such as threshing and winnowing, as well as bringing in the harvest. The amount of labour was usually tied to the amount of land held by the peasant. Thus in Lithuania, for example, where peasant landholdings had been divided up over the decades, a farmer with a quarter-holding was usually obliged to provide the seigneur with two workers, one male, one female, for three days a week each, a day being counted from sunrise to sunset. A three-day norm was also common in Russia, thanks to a ruling laid down by Tsar Pavel in 1797. The serf frequently had to provide produce to the seigneur, such as eggs or milk, nuts or vegetables. In western Europe, where peasant holdings were usually hereditary and labour services had often been commuted into money payments, the serf frequently had to pay the seigneur a fee in cash or kind when he transferred his holding by selling it or bequeathing it to his heirs. In addition the peasant had to pay a tithe, usually levied in produce, to the seigneur and the local priest or pastor. Across most of eastern Europe, a peasant needed the permission of his seigneur to leave his village and had to pay a fee if he moved (hence the danger of becoming, like Purlevsky, a 'runaway serf' if he failed to do so).

Added together, all these obligations could amount to a major burden on the peasant family. In the 1840s, for example, a substantial peasant family in Austrian Silesia owning around 42 acres of land was obliged to provide the local seigneur regular labour service with two draught animals for up to 144 days a year, plus twenty-eight days of manual labour, three days of hunting assistance, and two days of herding sheep or cattle. In addition the family had to supply 36 cubic yards of wood, a large quantity of spun yarn, sixty eggs, six hens and a goose. The annual tax on the family holding came to just over 23 florins a year, and there were additional payments and tithes adding up to another 15 florins. In the Habsburg Monarchy it was estimated that the average serf farmer paid 17 per cent of his income to the state and 24 per cent to the seigneur in money, labour or produce, totalling over 40 per cent altogether. This left very little room for keeping the family going even in good times, and almost none at all for improving its lot; for all of this prevented the peasant and his family for a large part of the week from doing work on their own farm, work that was essential to keep them alive, and deprived them of a very large proportion of the income they could have earned from the sale of their own produce had they been free to do so. The power of the serfs to determine their own fate was further restricted by the many rights and monopolies that the seigneurs possessed. In many parts of Europe serfs were only allowed to buy produce such as salt, tobacco, herring or alcohol from their seigneur, and were compelled by law and custom to bring their grain to the seigneur's mill for grinding. Only the seigneurs were allowed to hunt, a privilege that not only deprived peasants of access to important sources of food and clothing but also caused serious damage to their crops. Deer and wild boar could roam unchecked across their land, and noble hunts sometimes charged through the fields in pursuit of their quarry, trampling on the crops in the process. In some areas peasants could not fence off their crops in case the wooden stakes injured fleeing game or impeded the hunt; they had to feed the seigneur's hunting dogs and keep their own dogs chained up in case they ran after game. Only seigneurs could keep pigeons, which caused further damage to peasant crops, and seigneurs frequently had a monopoly over fishing rights in the local rivers and streams.

These rights and restrictions were enforced in most parts of Europe by seigneurial courts, where the local lord sat in judgement over his own refractory subjects. The powers of these courts were underwritten by the state and enforced by seigneurial police, in other words by the lord's own servants. Peasants caught snaring game or shooting game birds, or failing to pay their dues, could be hauled before the courts and punished. Many seigneurs had their own prisons or possessed the right to administer corporal punishment, usually whipping, but more serious offences had to be referred to higher state courts, and most states, such as Russia, imposed restrictions on the degree of punishment that could be ordered. The power of these courts was not limitless but was bound by state law. Most seigneurs summoned a trained lawyer or judge to preside over the court when it sat, and the involvement of the law also meant that peasants could bring lawsuits against the seigneur if his exactions exceeded what was allowable. The growing intrusion of state law into seigneurial justice, indeed, increasingly persuaded poorer landlords to pass over their judicial powers to the owners of nearby large estates, or to suggest the abolition of seigneurial justice altogether, as the Estates of Lower Austria did in 1833. Even where peasants did bring their cases before the courts, however, they were disadvantaged in a system that across much of Europe was characterized by widespread corruption and inequality. 'How can you expect the peasant to obtain justice,' remarked a wealthy Russian landowner to a traveller in the 1840s, 'when he only gives the judge an egg, while we give him a silver rouble?' Of course, serfdom had two sides to it. Law and custom required the seigneur to provide for his serfs in hard times, to care for the sick, the elderly and the feeble-minded if their families were unable to look after them, and to feed the serfs and their draught animals while they were working for him. In many areas the serfs had the right to graze their animals on the seigneur's pastures, to glean the pickings from harvested fields on his estate, to send their pigs to root in the lord's forest, and to enter his forest to cut wood. In turn, the seigneur usually had the right to graze his animals on the village common land and make use of the common forests.

Encompassed as they were by a web of rights and duties, serfs could still be bought and sold along with the land they rented or owned. If the seigneur sold an estate, the serfs on it passed to the new owner. The state often gave tacit approval to the practice of selling serfs on their own without land, as implied in a Russian law that banned the use of the hammer at public auctions of serfs, or in a regulation of 1841 that made it illegal to sell parents and their unmarried children separately from one another. In Russia serfs were not just tillers of the soil; increasingly they were enrolled as domestic servants, footmen, coachmen, cooks and much more besides. The aristocrat-turned-anarchist Pyotr Alexeyevich Kropotkin (1842–1921) noted that his father had possessed 1,200 serfs in the mid-nineteenth century: 'Fifty servants in Moscow and sixty or so in the

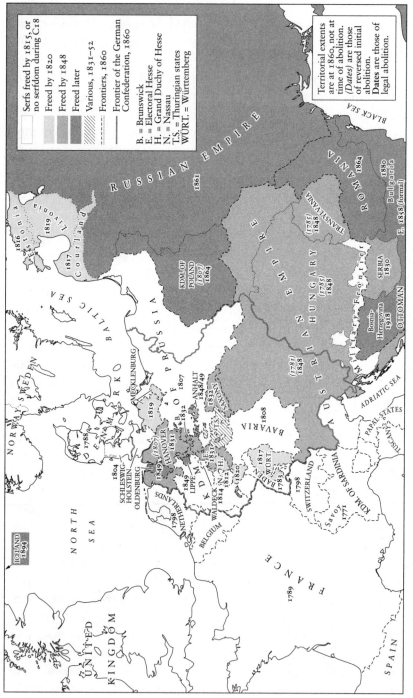

Map 3. The Abolition of Serfdom

country did not seem too many . . . The dearest wish of every landowner was to have all his requirements supplied by his own serfs . . . so that if a guest should ask, "What a beautifully-tuned piano: did you get it tuned by Schimmel's?" the landowner could reply: "I have my own piano-tuner." ' Even educated serfs could be bought and sold, however, and sometimes gambled away on the gaming tables in Moscow or St Petersburg. For serfs such as Purlevsky, an educated man performing clerical functions but living in constant fear of the knout, and also for many who were much worse off than he was, the humiliation of belonging to someone else was among the worst features of the servile system.

THE GREAT EMANCIPATION

Several pressures came together over a period of time to bring about the ending of serfdom in Europe. The first and most important of these was the growing discontent of the serfs themselves. Especially during times of hardship they found the exactions imposed on them unbearable. Officials in many areas expressed the fear that peasant soldiers returning from the wars against Napoleon would now turn their arms against their landlords. In Russia historians have counted nearly 2,000 violent peasant disturbances between 1826 and 1840, with troops called out to restore order in 381 of these cases. The number of disturbances increased dramatically after the Crimean War (1854–6), as serfs began to anticipate a measure of emancipation, with riots spreading rapidly between 1857 and 1861, necessitating the use of troops on 903 occasions. Even in areas where serfdom had been formally abolished, as in Russian-ruled Estonia in 1816, residual obligations requiring the provision of unpaid labour on specific occasions could still arouse bitter resentment; a major revolt on an estate near Tallinn in 1858 saw an army of 800 peasants confronted by regular troops, involving deaths and injuries and a mass trial resulting in large numbers of the peasants being sentenced to death by the courts or transported to Siberia. Serf revolts could take many forms. At their most basic, they involved serfs taking everyday matters into their own hands, as in 1834 when the inhabitants of four villages in Lower Austria drove the seigneurial flocks from the village pastures, remaining obdurate until troops arrived to enforce the lord's grazing rights. Peasant resistance could also be expressed more mundanely, keeping it within the letter of the law. By the 1830s seigneurs in Silesia were complaining that the peasants were sending their youngest son, often a child, to perform labour service, while in Austria they were paying dues late, sending stringy chickens, addled eggs and mouldy honey as tribute, working slowly and with reluctance, and in some areas keeping an especially old and decrepit horse for work on the seigneur's demesne. In Poland and Russia, when a serf decided to take his time over a job, he said he was going to 'work as you work on the demesne'. In addition, increasing numbers of serfs (like Savva Purlevsky) were abandoning their villages and fleeing to the cities or to regions where they could conceal their servile status and find work as free men. In 1856 it was reported that more than 100,000 servile Romanian peasant families had abandoned their holdings and left for Bulgaria, Serbia and Transylvania since 1832 in search of freedom. By the 1860s some 300,000 runaway Russian and Ukrainian serfs were said to be living in Bessarabia, where serfdom had recently been abolished.

But some serf protests were far more violent, and far more dangerous in the eyes of the authorities. When the Russian Tsar Nicholas I imposed a formal, legal system of serfdom in the Danubian Principalities through the so-called Organic Statutes of July 1831, Hungarian rural colonists, angry that the privileges they had been promised were being abrogated, were joined by Romanian serfs in an armed uprising of more than 60,000 peasants. Cossack regiments soon arrived, arrested the ringleaders, and sent them off to the salt mines of Siberia. Many of the others were each punished by fifty blows of the cudgel. But repression, it was increasingly recognized, would not solve the problem. 'I have closely observed the spirit of the peasant classes and, in general, of the lowest ranks of the population,' wrote a Russian government inspector in 1832, 'and have noticed a vast change in their attitude. They have grown bolder, more independent, less submissive, and at the same time poorer. They have stopped revering, as they once did, officials and the representatives of constituted authority.' Nicholas's son and successor Alexander II (1818–81) drew radical conclusions from the increasingly refractory behaviour of the serfs. 'It is better to abolish serfdom from above,' he declared in 1856, 'than to wait until the serfs begin to liberate themselves from below.' Defeat in the Crimean War that year led him to embark on a wholesale reform of the Russian state and Russian society. The military commander in the later part of the war, Prince Mikhail Gorchakov (1793–1861), had urged emancipation as a means of building greater loyalty and commitment among the troops, who consisted overwhelmingly of conscripted serfs. 'The first thing,' he was reported as saying, 'is that we must emancipate the serfs, because this is the knot which binds together all the things that are evil in Russia.' But there were longer-term processes at work in the ending of serfdom in Europe. Many landlords seeking improvements to the system felt that the

inefficiencies of servile labour impeded agrarian reform. Servile obligations, noted the declaration of emancipation in Saxony the following year,
'hinder the free development of agricultural activity and damage one of
the chief sources of national wealth'. The heavy burden of obligations
prevented peasants from investing in better methods and materials, just
as the forced reliance of seigneurs on inefficient servile labour and easy
income from servile dues made them reluctant to improve working standards. The open-field system, where large fields were divided up into strips
each farmed by an individual serf family, made it hard to achieve economies of scale by consolidating holdings. Serfs could not invest in better
livestock or afford fertilizers. Landlords who sought improvements by
hoping to imitate the achievements of the 'agricultural revolution' in England grew increasingly frustrated.

International factors could also play a role. Thus, for example, the
Treaty of Paris that ended the Crimean War in 1856 led to the emancipation of the serfs in the Danubian Principalities not least because Britain
and France wanted a viable state – Romania, created by the unification of
the two Principalities in 1858 – to act as a buffer against Russian expansion-
ism. The objections of seigneurs had to be overridden by an international
convention in 1858 that required laws to be introduced to end serfdom
and thus to give all Romanians a stake in the country's future. The new
sovereign, elected by assemblies convened in the two Principalities, overcame further landowner resistance by seizing full power in 1864, and
immediately issued an emancipation decree, thus cementing his own
domination over the nobility as well as carrying out the wishes of the
international community. Although the ending of servile status and
the introduction of the equality of all citizens before the law was one of
the central demands of liberals in the first half of the nineteenth century,
for conservative governments, cementing the loyalty of the peasantry
became a major tool in the battle to stave off the drive to power of the
liberals. The peasants, it was generally if rather inaccurately assumed,
were conservative, pious, monarchist, anti-liberal, anti-capitalist, and
would form the ultimate bulwark of order in the face of the liberal advance.
Therefore, acceding to their demands for the ending of serfdom could be
seen as constituting a vital element in the preservation of the existing
political order. So there were political forces of many kinds acting in
favour of emancipation.

Everywhere, the abolition of serfdom became the subject of complicated
political manoeuvrings between the major interested parties. The serfs
themselves were seldom formally consulted, but legislators knew well

enough that if the terms on which they were freed proved too restrictive, popular uprisings would probably follow. The accession of a new monarch or government frequently provided the opportunity, most notably with Alexander II in Russia, but also with lesser sovereigns such as King Friedrich Augustus of Saxony (1797–1854). His nomination in 1830 as co-ruler with his elderly uncle, the reigning monarch, resulted in major agrarian reforms. Meanwhile in Hanover, the revolutionary upheavals of 1830–1 led a new government to introduce sweeping changes in the system of serfdom, as also happened in Hesse-Kassel. Revolution, as these examples suggest, could also prompt action. In 1848 remaining feudal dues and obligations were abolished across much of Europe by revolutionary legislatures in measures that traditional state authorities found no difficulty in subsequently ratifying. Men such as the Habsburg Emperor Franz Joseph I (1830–1916) and his advisers in effect regarded abolition as inevitable and were broadly convinced of its advantages for the state.

The abolition of serfdom usually involved legal instruments of daunting complexity, made more convoluted by previous mitigations of servile obligations by Enlightened monarchs in the eighteenth and early nineteenth centuries. The Prussian edict of 2 March 1850, which finally abolished the last vestiges of serfdom in the kingdom, listed thirty-three previous laws passed between 1811 and 1849 that it superseded. Grand statements declaring peasants to be free men were followed by a maze of legal technicalities that often heavily qualified the principle on which the legislation rested. The revolutionary declaration of abolition in Hungary on 11 April 1848 had to be supplemented over the next five years by a series of detailed measures implementing abolition in each of the counties separately. Between the announcement of the principle and its application in practice there was often room for hard bargaining between the seigneurs and the government. The key issue here was the level of compensation the lords were given for the loss of peasant dues and services. In Hungary, for example, as in many other parts of Europe, the original revolutionary decree ended serfdom without compensation for the seigneurs, but by the time it came to be implemented, compensation had become a central part of the deal.

In most places the lords received no indemnification for the loss of noble privileges that stemmed from the peasants' servile status itself, such as seigneurial jurisdiction, since all serfs were now declared to be free men. Rights such as freedom of movement, inheritance, labour and so on were also granted without charge. But agreement had to be reached on compensating the seigneurs for the loss of labour services and the payments in kind and other dues that the peasants had paid as rent. Officials delved into the files and came up with elaborate calculations of what this all meant in monetary terms. In the Habsburg Monarchy the value of servile labour was set at one-third of that of hired wage labour, an indication of how little effort serfs were thought to put into their work. In addition a third was deducted to account for the money that the seigneurs had spent in administering the servile system. In some areas, such as Württemberg, Baden, Romania or the Habsburg Monarchy, the state helped the peasants with their redemption payments, even meeting them in full in Habsburg-ruled Hungary and Bukovina. Usually, however, the former serfs had to bear the entire burden themselves. In Romania the instalments had to be paid over a period of fifteen years, in Saxony twenty-five, in Russia forty-nine, so that redemption payments to the tsarist authorities resulting from the Emancipation Edict of 1861 were not scheduled to end until the year 1910. Often special banks were set up to manage the payments, especially in the German states. Just as important were the arrangements made for the distribution of land. As a general principle, the emancipation deal allowed the peasants to carry on farming the land they had occupied before emancipation, but there were, inevitably, variations in this pattern. Romania lay at one extreme, where the seigneurs could seize the best land for themselves provided they compensated their peasants with the same acreage elsewhere, usually on inferior soil or even broken up into smaller plots miles apart. Poland was at the other extreme, where the hostility of the Russian government to the nobility added two and a half million acres to the peasants' land, or 8 per cent of the entire area of Congress Poland.

A more difficult situation confronted the many serfs who held no land, including 1.5 million household serfs in Russia. Worried about the possibility of unrest among cottagers, smallholders and landless peasants, tsarist administrators in Congress Poland distributed 130,000 smallholdings of government land to these people. In Romania similarly the Crown, in its determination to create a loyal peasantry as a counterweight to the nobility, promised every former serf some land, though the promise was never fully honoured. In Russia peasants on state land were given limited title to it, later converted into freehold in return for a redemption fee payable according to a schedule that envisaged payments on an annual basis all the way up to 1931. In parts of Germany, peasants were still making redemption payments in the early 1920s. Payments in rent could sometimes be little different in practical terms from feudal obligations, as in Denmark, where serfdom had been abolished in the eighteenth century but redemption payments continued to impose a heavy burden on the peasantry through much of the first half of the nineteenth century. If a landlord preferred payment in work rather than in cash, it was frequently easy enough for him to put his wishes into effect.

The scale of these measures was vast. In East-Elbian Prussia, 480,000 peasants became free proprietors in the wake of the emancipation edicts of the early nineteenth century. Even in a small country such as Romania, more than 400,000 peasants received ownership of their land, and another 51,000 households were given land enough for a house and garden. Nearly 700,000 peasants in Poland became landowners. In the German and Slav provinces of the Habsburg Empire, the emancipation involved more than two and a half million peasant households indemnifying nearly 55,000 landowners for the loss of 39 million days of labour services without animals and 30,000 days with them, plus over 10 million florins' worth of annual fees and tithes and nearly 4 million bushels of dues in kind. In Russia the emancipation was even more gargantuan in its effects, with some 10 million peasants on private estates receiving title to nearly 100 million acres of land, quite apart from the similar measures already enacted for the even larger number of serfs on state demesnes. Nevertheless, everywhere the measures were put into effect relatively quickly, with a minimum of fuss. In principle this was the greatest single act of emancipation and reform in Europe during the whole of the nineteenth century. A huge class of people who had hitherto been bound to the land in a form of neo-feudal servitude had been emancipated from its chains and given equal rights as full citizens. Legally prescribed social distinctions now came to an effective end. Encrusted status and privilege had been swept away and every adult male was now in almost every respect equal before the law and free to dispose over his person and his property. The last significant legal vestiges of the society of social orders assailed by the French Revolution of 1789 had now left the stage of history.

WINNERS AND LOSERS

Who gained most from the emancipation of the serfs, and what were its overall effects? Much depended on the terms on which land was redistributed and the level at which compensation was set. The lords lost their exclusive hunting and fishing rights, and were no longer able to hunt on other people's land. Seigneurial monopolies were ended, though the sole right to distil and sell liquor was retained in the Habsburg Monarchy until the end of the 1860s. The feudal status of the lords came to an end, though not the social deference that came with it. The remaining formal patri-monial juridical and police powers in Prussia were only ended by laws passed in 1872 and 1891, though the former seigneur usually occupied the position of local administrator (*Landrat*), so in effect he could exercise similar powers on behalf of the state. This power was particularly marked in East Prussia and the traditional lands of the *Junker* noblemen to the south of the Baltic. In the lands of the Baltic German nobility, under Rus-sian suzerainty but to a considerable extent self-governing, manorial justice continued even longer, if in a diluted form. But in general, eman-cipation completed the process of the removal of juridical rights from seigneurs, even though it was delayed in some areas. In some parts of Europe judicial power was partially devolved onto local village councils or courts, as in Austria (after 1862), Russia, Saxony and Switzerland. Where a lord had previously taken matters into his own hands, he now had to go through an elaborate procedure of judicial enforcement. As a local judicial official in Königsberg noted, previously, when a peasant had been caught stealing fruit from the seigneurial orchards:

> the seigneur took several of his men to the thief's orchard and harvested all the fruit on his trees for himself. The tears of the peasant's wife and children failed to move him, and he harvested perhaps three times more fruit than the quantity he had lost, and his action was unanimously approved by his fellow lords.

Now this would itself be regarded by the state as a breach of the law. 'The nobleman,' complained one Austrian aristocrat 'with thirty-two or sixty-four ancestors, has to bow to that vulgar local council . . . The ignorant peasant who often cannot write . . . becomes the superior of his cultured and wealthy lord.'

As this indignant exclamation suggests, many of the seigneurs objected strongly to the emancipation on a variety of grounds. Aristocratic Russian officials complained bitterly about what they saw as a disastrous increase in crime and disorder in the countryside. 'In earlier times,' a marshal of the nobility declared, 'estate owners supervised their peasants' morality and therefore . . . legal order was maintained.' But now, he went on, 'our peasants – or at least 99 per cent of them – are not aware that a person is obliged to be honest and to recognize his duty to obey government orders and lead a patriarchal family life.' Prince Alfred zu Windischgrätz (1787–1862), a large landowner and leading military figure in the Habsburg Monarchy, protested to Emperor Franz Joseph about the emancipation in 1850. 'The most outstanding of communists,' he declared, 'has not yet dared to demand what Your Majesty's government has carried through.'

Such extreme views were less common in areas where large landowners already farmed for profit. On the Hungarian plains, estate owners could plough their monetary compensation into agricultural improvement and sell all of their produce on the market. In Austria and Bohemia large landowners, faced with huge quantities of cheap cereals coming in from Hungary, converted their farms to cash crops like sugar beet and abandoned marginal and unprofitable land altogether. In France the expropriation of noble and Church land and the emancipation of the serfs in the late eighteenth century meant that the number of small peasant farmers increased by more than 50 per cent in the decades after 1790. By 1851, 68 per cent of French peasants were independent farmers. In the plains around Bologna in northern Italy, the end of feudalism in the aftermath of the French Revolution reduced the value of noble lands from 78 per cent of the total in 1789 to 51 per cent in 1835, many of them bought up not by peasants but by middle-class entrepreneurs eager to share in the profits of a successful agricultural region. By contrast, 90 per cent of land in Sicily stayed in noble hands until well into the second half of the century.

Landowners who had survived the vagaries of war and revolution often did very well out of the emancipation. They remained a dominant force in areas of Europe where grain could be grown on a large scale for the market: on the baking-hot plains of Spain, in northern France, in the flatlands extending southwards from the Baltic, in the fertile soil of Hungary and Bohemia, and in 'Europe's breadbasket' – Ukraine. In Bohemia redemption payments for the ninety-three biggest estates totalled nearly 16 million florins. Such payments enabled landowners, and others like them elsewhere, to buy up a lot of the land that poorer estate owners were forced to sell to make ends meet. Thus between 1867 and 1914, estates of over 14,300 acres increased from 8.5 per cent to 19.4 per cent of the area occupied by landed estates in Hungary. By and large, these belonged to major noble families, as was also the case in Austria and East-Elbian Prussia. In general, therefore, except in the special case of Poland, the landowners did reasonably well out of the emancipation of the serfs. Whether they were able to capitalize effectively on the gains they made in a rapidly changing economic climate was, however, another matter altogether.

What was the effect of the emancipation on the peasantry? In the Habsburg Monarchy commentators waxed lyrical about the effects they imagined emancipation would have on the improvement of the rural economy. 'The ex-villein,' wrote one of them, 'now become freehold owner of his land, is able to devote his whole labour to the cultivation and profitable exploitation of his land, while the woodlands formerly owned by him, which had been deteriorating progressively, are now preserved and rationally exploited.' In practice, however, this applied mainly to market-oriented peasants with substantial farms; many smaller peasants, lacking familiarity with monetary transactions, continued farming just for their own subsistence, quickly ran into debt, and had to go back to working for the local lord so they could pay their taxes and meet their redemption payments. In East-Elbian Prussia some 7,000 large peasant holdings and more than 14,000 smallholdings were bought out by the larger noble estates between 1816 and 1859, furthering the creation of a landless rural proletariat. By mid-century there were more than two million people in Prussia and Mecklenburg earning a living either in part or in whole as farmhands; also by this time, 30 per cent of the agrarian population in Austria were wage-labourers; in Bohemia the proportion was 36 per cent.

Many better-off peasants now found themselves in a position to purchase extra land or rent it from middle-class proprietors. The land owned by Russia's peasants increased by a quarter from 1877 to 1905. Much of the increase was funded by a Peasant Land Bank set up by the state in 1882. Yet such a surge did not keep pace with population growth. By the end of the nineteenth century, nearly 40 per cent of landholdings in France consisted of less than 2.5 acres; in Denmark the proportion of holdings under 1.2 acres had reached 27 per cent, in Germany 33 per cent. These were little more than gardens, and their owners had to work for a living in some area other than farming to keep their families alive. The rural poor with no land had to hire themselves out as farm labourers. From 1750 to 1870 landless or semi-landless labourers and their families in Sweden increased from around a quarter to a half of the population, a class extremely vulnerable to dearth and economic crisis. These people had to purchase their food and most other necessities of life since they were unable to produce enough to feed themselves and their families. All over Europe the growing integration of agriculture into the capitalist economy created increasing numbers of people who only had their labour to sell. In some parts of the continent, indeed, a kind of quasi-serfdom was maintained by legal restrictions on the freedom of manoeuvre of rural labourers. The Prussian Statute of Farm Servants, passed in 1810 and valid up to the end of the First World War, denied permanently employed rural labourers many of the rights enjoyed by urban workers, and allowed their employers to administer corporal punishment if they so desired. Similar provisions obtained in Denmark. The Hungarian Farm Servants Act of 1907 forbade workers who lived on an estate to leave it or even to see anyone from outside it without their employers' permission, and allowed them to be whipped if they were under the age of sixteen; those who urged strikes could be imprisoned. It was only the growing preference of land-lords for casual labour hired for a few weeks at a time during the harvest or sowing season that began to release these rural workers from the restrictions under which they suffered, and allowed them to begin looking for work elsewhere.

PEASANT REVOLTS

Even at the outset, emancipation disappointed many of those it affected. In Russia peasants were outraged by the provisions for compensation accorded to the seigneurs, believing, in a popular phrase, that 'we are yours, but the land is ours'. The intrusion of government inspectors and agents into their lives was another source of dismay. In many parts of Russia the peasants simply wanted to be able to govern themselves without interference from anyone else. A wave of uprisings and revolts had already swept the country in the years leading up to emancipation. In the short run at least, the promulgation of the Emancipation Edict intensified this process rather than bringing it to an end. In one village, in the department of Perm, the peasants said that the Edict, read out by the local policeman, was a fake, since the real one would surely have been written in gold. They objected violently to 'a kind of liberty that leaves us just as before under the authority of the Count, our landlord'. Troops were sent in to restore order. By early 1863, the wave of protest had run its course. It indicated a strong and widespread feeling of dissatisfaction with the terms of eman-cipation, a feeling that was to grow rather than diminish over time.

The main problem was that emancipation did little to improve agricul-tural production in Russia. Over the decades following emancipation, to be sure, grain production per capita did rise, even after grain exports were deducted from the total, but not everywhere, and livestock farming was getting into serious difficulties. The number of pigs, horses and cattle in Russia fell almost continuously between 1880 and 1914. Population growth, especially in the rich 'black-earth' region, led to a shrinkage of farm sizes, and much of the land was still held communally, portioned out among an increasing number of families. After emancipation the peas-ants were barred from the landowners' forests and meadows: 'even chickens could not find a place to roost,' they complained in one petition. Peasants everywhere considered that unfarmed land was communal prop-erty, so they paid no attention to the landlords' enclosure of forests. As a result, wood theft and illegal tree-cutting in Russia increased from 14 per cent of all crimes brought before the criminal courts in the years 1834–60 to 27 per cent in the years 1861–8, with an average of 20,000 cases tried each year. (A similar phenomenon can be observed in Prussia from 1815 up to 1848, where wood theft made up the great majority of all cases of theft, and was often accompanied by individual or even mass violence against foresters on the part of the peasants.)

The aftershocks of emancipation continued through the rest of the century and into the next. Land prices and rents rose in Russia in the 1890s as a result of population pressure, which also kept rural wages down. Redemption payments continued to exact a heavy burden. As so often, a crisis of the state gave the opportunity for protest. In 1905 news of the military defeats in the war with Japan sparked strikes and revolutionary uprisings in the cities. Helped by local teachers and officials, peasants held mass meetings, drew up petitions, and articulated their demands. Where there were large estates and landless labourers, as in the west of the empire, strikes were the favoured medium of protest, but more traditional methods prevailed elsewhere. In the central black-earth region, the Volga and Ukraine, peasants stormed noble estates and sacked manor houses, particularly where there were no alternative means of earning a living apart from the land, and where landlords had been particularly harsh in the terms they exacted for leasing land or setting the terms for sharecropping. In many areas, peasants attacked and burned down noble residences, along with their records, and seized the land in an attempt to ensure the landlords would never return – tactics seen in peasant *jacqueries* all over Europe since the Middle Ages.

Altogether between 1905 and 1907 there were 979 cases of arson in Russia, almost all of them involving manor houses; 809 cases of illicit wood-cutting; 573 instances of the seizure of pasturage; 216 instances of the seizure and tillage of arable land; and 316 cases of the seizure of foodstuffs and fodder. Predictably, a subsequent government inquiry blamed many of these events on 'the intoxication of the people by agitators, Jews, and students', 'psalm-readers' and even 'railway guards', but few concrete examples were provided, and the key role was usually played by peasants who had a degree of literacy and some experience of the world outside the village, along with peasant soldiers and sailors returning from military service holding the strong conviction that they should be rewarded for their sufferings. The Russian peasant uprisings of 1905–7 were brutally put down by the police and army, but led directly to government measures to defuse rural discontent in an attempt to restore order and stability after the unsuccessful revolution in the cities. These included the final cancellation of redemption payments, the freeing-up of the peasant land market to allow individual farmers greater flexibility in buying and selling land outside the commune, and the extension of the Peasant Land Bank. Encouraged by the leading minister Pyotr Arkadyevich Stolypin (1862–1911), a new class of substantial peasant farmers began to emerge in the following years, the famous *kulaks* later so reviled and persecuted under Stalin. But Stolypin's intention of destroying the influence of the peasant commune was widely frustrated by peasant resistance, reflecting widespread attachment to collective methods of exploiting the land.

In Romania post-emancipation peasant discontent ran as deep as it did in Russia. State officials colluded with obstinate landowners to slow down the process of land redistribution, so that the peasants were granted land too slowly to meet the very tight, fifteen-year deadline to pay the compensation they owed, and ten years on, in 1874, the state had to cancel the unpaid compensation payments altogether. The peasant holdings were usually very small – nearly eight out of ten peasants possessed fewer than 12 acres at the end of the century – and after the fifteen years were up, the lords took advantage of the clause in the 1864 emancipation statute that abrogated the rights the peasants had to exploit seigneurial pastures and forests. Some 38 per cent of the arable land was owned by 1,500 large estates at the turn of the century. By 1882 a commentator could note that 'the misery in which most of the Romanian peasantry live beggars all description'. Under these circumstances, the landlords were able to force the peasants into a state of dependency not far from serfdom by demanding that rent be paid in labour rather than cash. As late as 1900, the landlords' estates were worked mainly by the peasantry, who owned nearly 95 per cent of all draught animals in the country and were obliged to use them when tilling the landlord's fields. A steep property qualification ensured that the vast majority of them lacked the right to vote and thus to express their grievances in political form.

The scene was set for the last great peasant *jacquerie* in European history, as a confrontation between the administrator of a 30,000-acre estate in Moldavia, who increased his demands over those of the previous year, and an angry assembly of villagers, spilled over into violence as he was assaulted and beaten. 'We are poor people,' said the peasants in a petition to the regional prefect, 'all we do is till the fields . . . We have come to the end of our tether as we can find no piece of land to provide food for us and our children this spring, and so we are threatened with starvation.' If they were not granted better prices for their crops, and allowed to pay rent in cash rather than in work on the estate, they threatened 'we will take the estate by force'. As their demands were ignored, Romanian peasants began to occupy noble forests and estates. Manors were destroyed, and bands of peasants marched on the towns, attacking the offices of merchants and dealers (many of them Jewish). In some places they forced state administrators to order a redistribution of land. As the government sent in troops, peasants armed 'with poles, clubs, stones, and even weapons' rushed the soldiers 'with unspeakable rage' and drove them into their barracks. The revolt spread southwards across Moldavia, and manor houses were burned to the ground, archives destroyed, and clerks beaten up. Everywhere the peasants demanded lower rents, and more grazing and wood-gathering rights. At Negresti they wrecked the estate office, seized the books, and 'divided the cattle amongst themselves and took possession of the mill too'. The revolt spread south to Wallachia, where in some towns apprentices and shop assistants joined in the mayhem as bands of peasants invaded the towns.

Government repression was savage. The prefect of one district reported on 15 March that:

Baielesti village was shelled by the artillery, and when the 5th Mountain Corps Battalion arrived in the commune to inquire into the prevailing state of mind, the rebels, who were in their houses, began to fire revolvers, wounding two officers and ten soldiers, then the Mountain Corps shot ten salvoes, killing forty-two rebels and wounding over one hundred. Half the village was on fire.

As the revolt was quelled, thousands of arrests followed, while troops, egged on by landlords, attacked and devastated peasant cottages and farms. 'Ringleaders' were brutally beaten, and there were complaints about torture in the overcrowded prisons. Long sentences were meted out to many of the participants. In all, an estimated 11,000 people were killed in what was the largest and most violent peasant uprising in Europe anywhere in the period between 1815 and 1914. Ionel Bratianu (1864–1927), Minister of the Interior in a new Liberal government, pushed through legal maxima for rents and minima for wages, and created a Peasant Bank, the Casa Rurală, to provide loans for the purchase or leasing of estates to be divided into peasant lots. But these measures were seldom put into practice. The compulsory sale of 440,000 acres of pasturage by landlords to create communal grazing lands in no way met the needs of the 725,000 households who still held under 12 acres of land.

Similar if less dramatic events took place in southern Europe. In Portugal serfdom had come to an end in the Middle Ages, but seigneurial and ecclesiastical rights and privileges continued to weigh heavily on tenant farmers, especially in the Crown lands, which made up a quarter of the

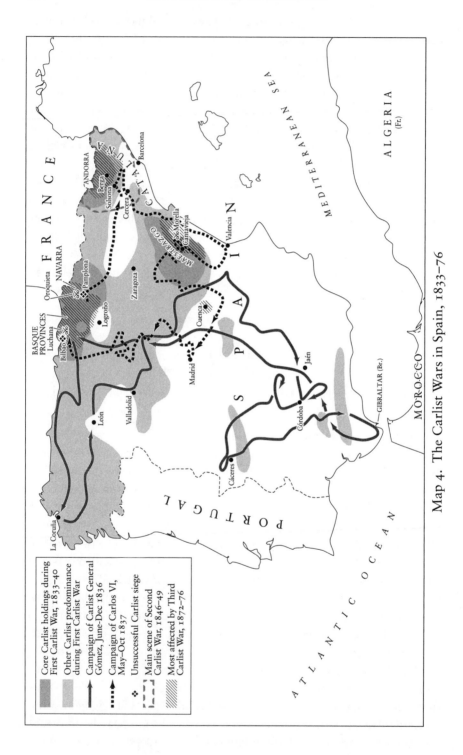

Map 4. The Carlist Wars in Spain, 1833–76

national territory. One church estate in the early 1830s owned 6,000 home-
steads and had a monopoly of all the mills, olive presses and granaries in
the area. Tenant farmers had to pay it a tribute of the first-born livestock,
an eighth of the linen woven, and duties on bread, wine and fruit. In other
estates the landlords charged a threshing fee and demanded rent for the
use of ploughs and oxen. These obligations were heavy enough, but in
1846 liberal reforms aimed at registering land ownership and privatizing
the commons triggered a revolt led by Maria da Fonte (dates unknown),
a peasant woman of the north. Claiming that the government planned to
sell the land to 'the bogeymen of northern Portugal, the English', the rebels
burned down registry offices and invaded the towns. The government had
also tried in the name of health and safety to abolish the custom of leaving
dead bodies in charnel houses until the bones could be recovered and
buried in family vaults, ordering their immediate burial outside town
perimeters instead. Armed bands attacked funerals and carried the bodies
off to their traditional resting places, increasing the disorder. In the end
the uprising, which destabilized the political system, was crushed by a
British seaborne invasion, sanctioned by the Great Powers. The peasant
grievances remained.

In Spain the ending of feudal obligations in the mid-1830s put more
power above all in the hands of landowners operating the sharecropping
system. Under this system, families contracted with landowners to work
their fields and receive pay in the form of a share in the crop. Since disentailment and agrarian reform, including the sale of common lands, were
carried out by liberal administrations, protest tended to be anti-liberal,
distinguishing it from uprisings and revolts in other parts of Europe. Peasant revolts in Spain also took on a political hue, as they were joined by
local notables and priests who provided them with leadership. In 1822–3
the royalists managed to gather widespread peasant support in the conflicts centred on King Fernando VII; the Governor of Valencia reported
that peasants were raiding grain stores and forcing tithe administrators
to return the taxes they had collected 'under threats of murder'. In 1827
a royalist uprising known as the War of the Malcontents engaged many
peasants who had earned their spurs in the guerrilla wars against Napoleon. At the height of the revolt there were said to be 30,000 men in arms,
above all impoverished small farmers, sharecroppers and labourers.

Rural protest coalesced around the figure of King Fernando's younger
brother Carlos (1788–1855), who rejected the 1830 abolition of the Salic
Law and the accession of Fernando's daughter Isabella II (1830–1904), a
mere infant, in 1833. The First Carlist War lasted from 1832 to 1839 and
spread across the Basque Country, Aragon, Catalonia and Valencia. Many

of the liberal generals had fought in the wars of independence in Latin America, and their experience gradually told. In 1847 a Second Carlist War, also known as the War of the Early Risers (from the rebels' habit of mounting their attacks before dawn), expressed the hatred of the rural poor for the liberals who had taken power in the 1830s. A Third Carlist War lasted from 1872 to 1876, sparked by the accession of Amadeo I (1845–90), whose right to the throne the Carlists also disputed. Carlism aimed above all at abrogating the agrarian reforms of the liberals. Extreme cruelty, torture, rape and massacre characterized the conflict, as with many peasant uprisings, despite an agreement on the orderly treatment of prisoners brokered by the British ambassador Lord Eliot (1798–1877) in 1835. Capitalizing on divisions within the royal family and the political elite, the Carlist uprisings acquired sufficient political significance to engage foreign supporters, including monarchists from Belgium, Britain, Germany, Italy and Portugal; active fighters included leading members of the Habsburg Monarchy's aristocratic conservative Schwarzenberg and Lichnowsky families.

A very different form of peasant protest took hold in areas further south in Spain, dominated by *latifundia* and landless labourers. After 1848, as the liberals failed to deliver improvements to their lot, landless labourers in the south turned to anarchist ideas, which exercised a strong appeal to people who felt the state, with its taxation, military conscription and de facto support of the landowning class, was a hostile and alien institution that had to be swept away. A wave of arson and banditry swept southern Spain in the 1860s, as unemployed labourers stole crops and uprooted trees to sell them for firewood, and discontent spilled over into an uprising in Seville in June 1857 put down by government forces, who executed ninety-five of the rebels. A more thoroughgoing liberal revolution in 1868, bringing about the deposition of Queen Isabella II and the proclamation of a republic in 1875 after the brief interlude of Amadeo I's unsuccessful reign, was the signal for peasants across the south to occupy and divide seigneurial and common lands. Illegal grazing, occupations, theft, and all kinds of low-level agrarian protest rumbled on in parts of Spain beyond the end of the century.

The sharecropping system existed in Italy as well as in Spain, and aroused a similar level of discontent, though one with fewer political repercussions. In Tuscany contracts imposed strict limits on the amount of land any given family worked, allowing them just enough to survive after the landowner had taken his 50 per cent of the harvest. Landowners in this region of Italy customarily demanded the right to give permission for members of the sharecropper's family to get married, keeping an eye on their moral conduct, and they could even order members of the family to move elsewhere if they were surplus to labour requirements. If a sharecropper left the farm without permission, he was in breach of contract and guilty of a criminal offence. The bailiff inspected the harvest to make sure the sharecroppers did not take more than their contracted portion of the harvest. Sharecroppers in the Italian region of Emilia-Romagna had to provide the landlord with chicken, eggs and hams free of charge. In some areas they had to dig ditches and perform other labour services without payment. They were not allowed to work for others or use the farm cart to help other families. They could be dismissed and evicted simply for disobeying the proprietor's orders. The portion of the harvest the sharecropper was allowed to keep was intended for his family's subsistence; all the cash crops had to be made over to the landlord, who would sell them and make over half the proceeds. In bad harvest years, the sharecroppers usually had to take out loans from the proprietor, and this deepened their dependency on him still further.

Peasant protest in Italy was sparked by the liberal reforms that accompanied unification in the 1860s. The most frequent form of protest was the occupation of enclosed former common land, but banditry and brigandage were also rife in southern Italy, Sicily and Sardinia for much of the century. In 1847, for example, a mountain villager in Sardinia justified raids on the farms of the plains to the Bishop of Sassari in the following terms:

> Monsignore: until now we did not believe that we were offending against the law of God when we took the lambs, ewes, cattle and swine that we needed. Since the providence of Almighty God offers pity for all his creatures, how could he suffer that the shepherds of the Galkura plains should possess in some cases 500, in others 800 or even 1000 sheep, while we possess only tiny flocks numbering less than a hundred each?

Brigandage was such a major problem in the 1860s that the newly created Italian state sent a large military force to the south, making up at one point two-thirds of the entire Italian Army, during the so-called 'brigand wars'. The Napoleonic land reforms still needed to be implemented in many respects, and peasant land hunger had not been appeased. Kidnapping, murder, cattle-rustling, highway robbery and other crimes were met with thousands of arrests – 12,000 in the second half of 1863 alone. By this time more than 2,500 insurgents had been shot. Eventually order was restored by what was virtually an army of occupation, numbering 120,000 troops. 'This is our fate!' one brigand leader exclaimed to a military tribunal, blaming landowners for the disturbances: 'The *signori* are the root of this evil business, but we are the ones who pay the price: but what does it matter anyway, since that was why we were born.'

Banditry was a common phenomenon in the wake of the abolition of serfdom. Travelling in Spain in the mid-1840s, the Romanian historian and politician Mihail Kogălniceanu (1817–91) remarked that 'nobody dares show himself on the open plain unarmed ... The roads are still not safe and looting occurs up to the gates of Madrid and the *Gacetilla de provincias* rubric of the newspapers is filled daily with paragraphs entitled *Ladrones* [bandits].' There were even bolder brigands in other parts of Europe. The Hungarian rebel Sándor Rózsa (1813–78) began his career as a bandit in his teens, and was caught and imprisoned in 1837. He managed to escape, however, and lived for the following years as a highwayman, waylaying travellers on the sparsely populated Hungarian plain. He took advantage of the revolutionary upheavals and the effective ending of serfdom in the middle years of the century to form a band of robbers, acting under the pretext that they were defending the Hungarian revolution against the Habsburgs. Captured and sentenced to prison, he was released by the Emperor Franz Joseph as part of an amnesty of a thousand prisoners issued to celebrate his coronation in Hungary, and joined another gang of bandits who derailed the Szeged-Pest railway train, shooting the drivers. Several of the passengers were armed, however, and after a gun battle the gang withdrew, having failed to collect any booty. Rózsa was finally captured in January 1869 and died in prison in November 1878.

Such men inspired many legends and stories, along the lines of the medieval English outlaw Robin Hood, providing the rural poor with outlets for their fantasies and desires about living freely. The Calabrian bandit Giuseppe Musolino (1876–1956) was said, for example, to give money to churches and monasteries and wrote frequently to the king complaining of the misdeeds of the rich in Calabria. Greek bandits, called *klephts* from the word for 'thief' (as in 'kleptomania'), were the subject of a whole genre of songs and ballads, though their most durable invention was probably 'lamb klephtiko', a meat dish roasted slowly in a pit to avoid giving off suspicious-looking smoke. In Bulgaria and other parts of Ottoman territory in the Balkans, the bandits known as *Haiduks*, despite their notorious cruelty, served as the symbolic vehicle of the resentment of rural Christians against their Turkish overlords. At least some bandits, especially in Italy, retained their close connections to settled rural society: young unmarried men, shepherds and goatherds guiding their flocks through mountain pastures, casually employed farmhands, were all able to escape the forces of the law with relative ease, while poverty and immiseration frequently drove them to a life of crime. Only rarely did banditry take on a political hue, as with the activities of the Greek-Macedonian Kota Christo (1880–1904), who collaborated with Bulgarian irridentists in the fight against Ottoman rule: 'Let's kill the bear', he is said to have told them, referring to the Turks, 'and we'll manage easily to share the skin.' Following a victorious pitched battle against an Ottoman force in 1902, however, his Bulgarian allies deserted him and his career, like that of many bandits, ended in betrayal, in his case by the Church authorities: he was handed over to the Ottoman governor in 1904 and beheaded.

As the example of Sándor Rózsa showed, it was especially in moments of political crisis that the rural poor were able to assert themselves. In Sicily, on the slopes of Mount Etna, the miserably poor estate of Bronte, which had been given to the British Admiral Horatio Nelson (1758–1805) by the king, along with the title Duke of Bronte, as a reward for defending him against Napoleon, was still ruled by the admiral's family in mid-century. The arrival of Giuseppe Garibaldi and his volunteer army in 1860 plunged the Kingdom of the Two Sicilies into terminal crisis and prompted the peasants to rise in open revolt. Thousands marched on the town of Bronte, burned the archives to the ground, looted the houses of town officials, and stabbed a notary to death before throwing his body onto a bonfire in front of his son's house. One man stuck a knife into the body and licked the bloodstained blade; another was said to have cut out the notary's liver and eaten it with a piece of bread. More murders followed: the objects of the peasants' fury in Bronte were the same as in other parts of Europe; legal documents and their authors, the instruments of their dispossession, were targeted in the belief that the natural right to common land outweighed the letter of the law that had assigned it to the former feudal landowners as their private property. Conscious of his need to win the support of the local landowners, Garibaldi quickly had the revolt put down.

Sicily was brought under control, but peasant discontent was considerably more widespread than this, and far from appeased; it found expression in the revolt of the Siclian *Fasci* at the beginning of the 1890s. Numbering 300,000 sharecroppers, agricultural labourers and small farmers, they named themselves *Fasci*, 'bundles', because while anyone can break a single stick nobody can snap a whole bundle. They mingled socialist ideas with religious millenarianism, wore red rosettes, and carried religious symbols and portraits of the king as well as pictures of Garibaldi. The targets of their protest meetings and processions were rising rents and food prices, high taxes, and discriminatory sharecropping contracts. Peasants began to seize land and occupy tax offices, burning mills and government buildings. The Italian government responded in 1894 by declaring a state of siege and drafting in 40,000 troops. Hundreds of insurgents were shot or subjected to summary executions, a thousand were sent to a penal colony without trial, and many others were arrested.

By this time, however, sharecropping and its attendant discontents were in decline. Several factors began to undermine the sharecropping system in southern Europe towards the end of the century. Import tariffs protected Italian agriculture against foreign competition; by 1885 Italy had the highest grain duties in Europe. This did not stop prices from falling, as wheat sold on the Italian market dropped from 33 lire per quintal in 1880 to less than 23 lire five years later, hemp from 103 to 75. Grain yields in Italy were poor (6.4 quintals per hectare in the south, 11 on average across the country, compared to 32 in Britain) – largely a result of the dominance of sharecropping. In Tuscany, as late as 1901, half the rural workers were sharecroppers, whose short-term priority was keeping the family fed. This led to over-exploitation of the land. The vine disease phylloxera, which reached Chianti in 1890, devastated the vineyards. Tax increases, especially on essentials like salt and sugar, and the failure to improve harvest yields, led to increasing destitution, and sharecroppers began to steal or conceal produce, and to engage in demonstrations and protests, often involving violence – fifty-four in Tuscany between 6 and 13 May 1898 alone, following a particularly bad harvest the previous year.

Landlords responded to these crises by switching to more profitable crops like sugar beet, and by mechanizing production to reduce labour costs. This accelerated the decline of sharecropping, especially in more commercially viable agricultural regions. As early as 1883 one conservative commentator in Bologna complained, in terms that bore a striking resemblance to similar complaints by landlords in the last decades of serfdom in northern Europe, that:

> The sharecropping families of today are breaking up and dividing due to the lack of respect, obedience and subordination towards the household heads, whose virtues provided the cement that bound together old families and gave them their well-being. The sons of the family, just as soon as they are able to do all the farm work, begin to want to take part in the direction of the farm, and want money to pay for their habits and vices. They want clothes with better materials than those made at home, and they want much more spending money than was ever requested in the old families.

Not only was the sharecropping system disintegrating as a result of changing economic, social and cultural influences in the wider society, it was also increasingly being replaced by a more modern economy of wage labour. As markets expanded from the mid-nineteenth century, landlords began to prefer employing labourers who could be taken on and laid off as needed, and who had every incentive to work hard. From the 1880s onwards, trade unions and socialist parties began to recruit rural labourers, harnessing sharecropper discontent with their harsh contractual conditions into strikes and protests, but these remained sporadic and largely unsuccessful. Meanwhile the labourers lived in miserable conditions, often, according to an Italian inquiry of 1881, crammed hundreds at a time into decaying brick apartment blocks in nearby towns, with bare clay floors and minimal hygienic and sanitary facilities. Nearly three-quarters of their income went on food, even though they were often supplied with some basic form of sustenance while they worked, and customarily sent their children round the local farms to beg for bread. By the time of the First World War, much of southern Europe too had evolved into a rural wage-labour economy; but poverty and exploitation had already driven hundreds of thousands to emigrate to the New World.

FEEDING THE PEOPLE

The emancipation of the serfs and its consequences, and the decline of the sharecropping system, were of such enormous importance in nineteenth-century Europe not least because right through the century, the overwhelming majority of people lived on the land and depended on it for their survival. Almost everywhere, towns were few and far between, urban islands in a rural sea. As late as 1850 only 20 per cent of Italians lived in towns, 17 per cent of Spaniards, 15 per cent of French people, 11 per cent of Germans, 9 per cent of Poles, and 8 per cent of Austrians and Bohemians. The relatively high rates of urbanism in Italy and Spain reflected old patterns of settlement rather than the newer influences of industrialization, and the same can be said of the Netherlands, where 30 per cent of the population lived in towns at this time. The great exception was Britain, where fully 50 per cent of people lived in towns in 1850, the consequence of the rapid growth of the industrial economy. The proportion of the adult male population in Britain employed in agriculture, which stood at 41 per cent in 1800, had declined to 29 per cent by 1840, in sharp contrast to other parts of Europe. Even by the end of the century, relatively few European states could boast that more of their citizens lived in towns than in the countryside – Belgium and Germany certainly, but not France or Spain and certainly not Russia. Urbanization had barely begun in eastern Europe. The typical European for most of the century was a peasant living on and from the land.

During this time, despite the wars and famines of the early years of the century, Europe's population was on the rise, growing in total from around 205 million in 1800 to some 275 million fifty years later. The rise in population was uneven in pace and extent, but it was happening across the whole Continent, and it took place under what historians have called the demographic *ancien régime*, where birth and death rates were both extremely high; typically there were around forty-five live births per 1,000 population at this time, and thirty to forty deaths. The main reason for the rising population was the disappearance of the great epidemics that had swept across Europe in the past, such as the bubonic plague, which had killed between a third and a half of the entire population of Europe in the mid-fourteenth century but had retreated eastwards during the eighteenth. Medical intervention was also important, for example the widespread campaign to promote breastfeeding, the clearing of swamps (reducing the incidence of malaria, common throughout southern Europe and all the way up into the Rhine valley), and the improvement of public hygiene, at least in major European capital cities. The decline of smallpox, a major killer before the development of effective vaccination by Edward Jenner in 1798, also played a role, as did the relative absence of wars in Europe after the Battle of Waterloo. Birth rates also began to rise as a result of women marrying younger, increasing the excess of births over deaths that created population growth.

The annual percentage rate of population growth was striking. Between 1800 and 1850 it measured 1.3 per cent in England and Wales, around 0.9 in Russia, Norway, Finland and Denmark, 0.8 in Sweden, the Netherlands and Belgium, and 0.6 to 0.7 almost everywhere else apart from France, Bulgaria and Portugal. There was, to be sure, an east-west contrast, with life expectancy at birth in mid-century a mere twenty-four years in Russia compared to forty in western Europe, the consequence above all of very high rates of infant mortality, but Russia compensated by high birth rates, of around fifty per thousand, reflecting a much lower average age at first marriage. The part played in bringing about this population growth by falling death rates at a time when birth rates remained very high can be neatly illustrated with the case of Sweden, where early demographic records are particularly good. After two massive crises of mortality in the 1770s and again in the famine of 1815–16, with death rates soaring respectively to more than fifty and just under forty per thousand, before the late 1840s Sweden experienced no more major peaks in the death rate, which declined unevenly but steadily from just under thirty per thousand in a normal year in the late eighteenth century to just over twenty per thousand by 1840.

In the late eighteenth century the Reverend Thomas Malthus (1766–1834) had warned that in an agrarian society, population tended to grow beyond the capacity of the land to sustain it. Dearth and famine would be the result. In Britain this threat was averted not merely by agricultural improvement but also by the increasing ability to use income from the export of industrial goods to import foodstuffs, above all following the abolition in 1846 of grain duties. Governments everywhere increasingly made efforts to improve the efficiency of agriculture, with the Russians establishing a Ministry of State Domains in 1837 to build and run model farms and set up training schools for state peasants. Local agricultural improvement societies formed by progressive-minded landowners had some influence in distributing information. But most effective of all was the profit motive, which only really took hold after the emancipation of the serfs. Even before this, landowners had begun to import British-made tools and machines such as threshers, and new improved breeds of sheep and cattle onto the Continent. By the middle of the century, a quarter of the 44 million sheep kept in European Russia were fine-wool varieties like the merino. Good profits were to be had farming sheep for the market: while in 1816 fewer than ten in every hundred of the 8 million sheep grazing on Prussian soil were fine-wool breeds, more than a quarter of the 16 million there in 1849 were merinos. The rest of Germany already exported nearly 3 million pounds of wool to Britain in 1816; by the mid-1830s this number had increased more than tenfold. Only by this point, however, did competition from overseas wool, particularly from the southern hemisphere, begin to undercut European producers and prompt a turn to pig-rearing instead.

It was normal in the early nineteenth century for peasants to leave a substantial part of their fields untilled in rotation every year to allow the soil to recover from the previous years' crops, but increasingly this practice was declining, under the influence of English agricultural writings whose message filtered down from landlords seeking a change in methods and greater efficiency. Instead, small farmers began to plant root crops that tapped deeper layers of the soil than wheat could do, or clover, which restored its value when ploughed back in. Even before emancipation, too, enterprising peasant communities had begun to consolidate holdings, overcoming the diseconomies associated with the strip-field system. Stock-breeding improved the quality of sheep, pigs and cattle, while crop rotation – changing the crops planted in any given field year by year so as not to exhaust the soil – further reduced the amount of fallow land and made animal fodder available during the winter, when previously many animals had to be slaughtered.

Perhaps the most dramatic transformation of agriculture, in the areas where larger farms produced for a wider market and were thus able to invest, was in the use of fertilizers to replenish exhausted soil and improve crop yields. By far the most important fertilizer in the first half of the century was guano, or seabird dung, which had accumulated over millennia in enormous mountains on the Chincha islands off the coast of Peru, where the arid climate prevented the nitrates they contained from being dissolved by rainwater. Alexander von Humboldt had confirmed the effectiveness of guano as a fertilizer, and the German chemist Justus von Liebig (1803–73) also advocated its use. After achieving independence from Spain in the 1820s, Peru needed new sources of income, and guano exports started to provide it from the early 1840s onwards. Chinese coolies were imported to excavate the mountainous deposits, while Peruvian merchants signed export contracts with British shippers. This inaugurated something of an economic boom in Peru, the so-called Guano Age, which only came to an end in the 1870s as artificial fertilizers began to take over. In Europe it helped achieve a sharp increase in productivity in market-oriented agriculture.

Despite Malthus's gloomy predictions, in general, agricultural production in Europe grew over the decades to keep pace, more or less, with the growth of the population. This was largely because a greater amount of land was being brought under cultivation. It has been estimated that the cultivated land of the Continent as a whole increased from 270 million acres in 1800 to 378 million in 1910. In the Netherlands, where many new agricultural techniques had been pioneered, huge areas of marshland were drained and polders and dykes assisted the reclamation of more low-lying land from the sea. In all, nearly 123,000 acres of land were brought under cultivation with the help of the state between 1833 and 1911. Most Dutch farmers were small producers, and they were unusual in farming for the market, increasingly in specialized produce such as cheese. Slowly, peasant farmers in some other parts of Europe followed suit. Particularly important was wine-growing, an activity carried on by small producers just as much as by capitalist agribusiness. In France wine production grew from 25 to 60 million hectolitres between the 1780s and the 1870s. Fruit, hemp, tobacco and olives gradually helped free peasants from the tyranny of subsistence farming in areas where it was possible to grow them.

In some parts of Europe agriculture remained stubbornly traditional well into the nineteenth century. This was not least because governments frequently hid its inefficiencies behind protective import tariffs. Like many other European governments, for example, the Spanish authorities imposed severe restrictions on the import of grain, which was only allowed in from other countries when prices for Spanish grain reached exceptionally high levels. This only happened four times before the abrogation of the measure in 1869. Spanish peasants and labourers tilled the soil using the same methods as they had done for centuries, and although the grain-producing *latifundia* of the plains began to use machinery and fertilizers to boost profits from exports later in the century, even their methods remained relatively primitive for many decades. Successive Spanish governments made repeated attempts to free up a market in land and remove restrictions on production. Even where change came to agriculture, it was often seriously disadvantageous to the peasantry. In Hungary, for instance, the agricultural depression of the 1820s and 1830s caused widespread indebtedness among the nobility and gentry, which they tried to remedy by converting their lands from arable to pasturage, enclosing large areas of common land for sheep to graze on.

Although increasing numbers of small farmers produced for the market, to a very large extent peasant life in rural Europe was self-sufficient. Economists grew impatient with 'the narrow spirit that makes every family, even locality, every *pays* live on its own resources, asking nothing of trade'. Peasants were unused to outsiders; a middle-class traveller near Saint-Agrève in southern France noted around the middle of the century: 'The peasant is extremely suspicious, a stranger can expect no help from him even for money, and the most insignificant questions seldom receive an answer.' When this traveller drew a map, he was arrested by a group of armed men and charged with sorcery. Further east, Russian and Ukrainian peasants might greet strangers with traditional offers of bread and salt, but they might just as easily set on them and drive them away, suspecting they were coming to collect taxes. Yet however self-sufficient they might be, peasants always had to purchase at least some goods from tinkers and travellers or from the nearest town, especially metal and ceramic goods. In times of hardship, harvest failure or economic crisis, however, rural communities often had to fend for themselves, with predictably disastrous results. Even in normal times, poverty and destitution were never far away. As the numbers of the landless poor grew, as a result both of population increase and dispossession following the emancipation of the serfs, the question of how they were to be supported became rapidly more urgent. Many took to the roads or sought refuge in the towns in time of hardship, begging for alms or throwing themselves on the mercy of government poor relief and charitable institutions as the traditional patterns of family support broke down.

Visiting western Europe in the late 1830s, the Polish poet Zygmunt Krasiński (1812–59) found the streets of Messina, in Sicily, 'populated by masses of beggars, children on crutches, crippled in legs and arms'. Poverty was everywhere, even in the towns he visited in England, where he thought attitudes towards it far harsher than on the Continent. In Bavaria it was calculated in 1818 that 6.2 per cent of the population depended on poor relief to survive, but these were only sedentary poor, and the figures did not include itinerant beggars or the recipients of private charity; an additional 19 per cent of the population were thought to be living on the verge of poverty. There was no welfare state in the modern sense anywhere; no state benefits, no national insurance, no unemployment support, no old people's homes. Poor relief traditionally depended on the Church. Especially in Catholic areas, giving was thought to ennoble and sanctify the soul. Christian charity provided alms for the destitute, and professional beggars, asking for support, ritually gesturing to the passer-by, and calling down God's blessing on those who gave them money, were ubiquitous.

In view of the Church's inability to deal with the mounting problem of pauperism, secular voluntary associations across Europe were playing a growing role in poor relief. In Russia, where the institutions of civil society were weak in the extreme, it was not surprising that the most important of the voluntary poor-relief organizations, the Imperial Philanthropic Society, was founded in 1816 on the initiative of Tsar Alexander I, who supplied it with an annual grant to increase the income it received from membership fees and private donations. Branches opened in many cities, and the number of people it assisted increased from just over 4,000 in the 1820s to more than 25,000 in the early 1840s and nearly 38,000 in 1857. Some twenty new charitable societies were granted licences in Russia between 1826 and 1855. Typical was the house of industry opened in 1833 by Anatoly Nikolayevich Demidov (1813–70), the son of a rich industrialist, providing soup and work to the needy. On a visit to the main prison in St Petersburg in 1837, Tsar Nicholas I was shocked to find beggars mingling with common criminals, and he set up a Supreme Committee for Differentiation and Care of Beggars in St Petersburg, as well as a similar institution in Moscow. The Committee took beggars arrested by the police, sent those thought to be the deserving poor unable to work through no fault of their own to the Imperial Philanthropic Society, and referred the able-bodied to employers. Allegedly idle professional beggars were returned by the Committee to the police and then sent on to labour colonies in Siberia, while those in temporary difficulty were helped out with funds or documents.

The relative centralization of poor relief in Russia was unusual. In most parts of Europe it was localized. In 1816, for example, a new poor law devolved poor relief onto Bavarian municipalities, granting it on the basis of birth or marriage in the community or long years of work there. The system, which lasted for exactly a century, required local administrations to register paupers and provide them with food, clothes and shelter. Help also included the provision of free medical services, for which local doctors were paid from poor-law funds; pharmacies had to sell medicaments at a two-thirds discount. It was only a safety net and it proved entirely inadequate to deal with the growing immiseration of the working population during the 1820s or at times of crisis. All European relief systems had been designed above all to help the rural poor, in a society in which the overwhelming majority of people lived on and from the land. They were vulnerable not only to agrarian crises but also to the changing nature of poverty as Europe began to become more urban. In most countries, municipalities and parishes were obliged to provide relief for the sick, the elderly, the disabled, and the orphaned, but the Church continued to provide for the vast majority of the poor. In the Netherlands food, shelter, fuel and funds were made available by local authorities in limited quantities, mainly to the elderly, widows and the disabled. In the period 1829 to 1854 an average of 25 per cent of the entire population of Amsterdam was in receipt of poor relief on a regular basis. Some 90 per cent of the relief consisted of work. Three out of every four paupers were still supported by the Reformed Church, as was also the case in the bustling port of Rotterdam, where in 1859 some seventeen out of every hundred people were in receipt of poor relief.

All across Europe, the growth of pauperism was highly alarming to middle-class urban elites, who increasingly thought that the Church was encouraging it. Poverty in this view was the result of idleness, breeding an underclass whose lack of property made it a potential social and political threat. In Castile the political upheavals of the 1820s brought liberal programmes of welfare reform to the forefront of politics, in which municipalities waged an aggressive campaign against Church welfare foundations, expropriated their property (in the Welfare Law of 1822), and placed welfare institutions under the control of local councils. However, it was in Britain, the first country to experience industrialization and the rapid and uncontrolled urban growth evolving from it, that a new way was found to try and grapple with pauperism and reduce the burden of expense it imposed. Like other European states, Britain operated a system of relief in which those capable of work were provided with it, unless they refused, in which case they were imprisoned or whipped. But this system, the so-called Old Poor Law, under which – as in other countries – local authorities, in this case parishes, were responsible for supporting the destitute, began to impose impossible burdens on ratepayers during and after the economic crisis of 1815–16. Parishes were mostly too small to deal with the growing numbers of the rural poor dispossessed by the enclosure of common lands and the conversion of arable to pasture. Malthus and others thought the system of allowances for the poor based on the price of bread and the size of their family – the so-called Speenhamland system – encouraged irresponsible breeding and wanted the Old Poor Law abolished altogether. It 'spread pauperism and improvidence', as one commentator complained in 1831.

By the early 1830s, with a reforming government in power, the time had come in the eyes of most British politicians to apply the new principles of political economy to the relief of the poor. In 1834 the British Parliament passed a New Poor Law designed to push the able-bodied poor into work. The 1,500 parishes of England and Wales were grouped into 600 Poor Law Unions, run by Boards of Guardians elected by ratepayers (with larger landowners having plural votes). Outdoor relief – the provision of work for the poor – was abolished. If any able-bodied man wanted relief he had to find it in a workhouse, where the conditions were deliberately made unpleasant, with strict discipline, miserable food, spartan living conditions and no social amenities. As one of the new assistant commissioners remarked, the workhouse was a deterrent, with its 'prison-like appearance' intended to 'torment the poor' and inspire 'a salutary dread', while the work the inmates had to do was, as the Act itself put it, to be made as 'disagreeable' as possible. 'Every penny bestowed that tends to render the condition of the pauper more eligible than that of the independent labourer,' said the report that led to the passage of the New Poor Law, 'is a bounty on indolence and vice.' If a pauper found life in the workhouse really unpleasant then he would expend all his energies in finding paid work, 'he begs for a job, he will not take a denial'.

This principle of 'less eligibility' was applied to all. Orphans and the elderly and infirm were expected to be cared for by their families, or by more distant relations. The workhouse, with its minimal level of support, its harsh discipline, its uniforms, its degrading delousing sessions, and its social stigma, was popularly regarded as something to be avoided if at all possible. Its reputation was made even worse by the 1832 Anatomy Act. This was a response to the growing price of corpses supplied to the Anatomy Schools, which encouraged 'resurrection men' to dig up newly interred bodies to sell them to the medical schools, and the grisly Burke and Hare murders in 1829, in which two criminals in Edinburgh, William Burke (1792–1829) and William Hare (1807–1829) killed people in order to make money by selling their corpses to the anatomists. From 1832 the bodies of paupers were assigned free of charge to the medical schools if they were unclaimed by relatives. In a religious age when most people believed in the physical resurrection of the body, this was probably even more disturbing than the workhouse itself.

Not surprisingly, the New Poor Law was widely criticized as a denial of traditional English rights. It separated husbands from wives in the workhouse, and subjected to its harsh discipline children, orphans, the sick and the elderly – some 80 per cent of inmates in the 1850s and 1860s – none of whom was likely to obtain paid employment in society outside, as well as the able-bodied poor to whom it was directed. Its mean-spiritedness and its potential for corruption were memorably pilloried in the early novel by Charles Dickens (1812–70), *Oliver Twist*, where the eponymous orphaned boy creates an uproar in the workhouse by asking on behalf of the starving inmates for a second helping of gruel. Written in 1837–9, the novel caricatured the pomposity and hypocrisy of the parish board members responsible for running the workhouse, described the painful and pointless work the inmates had to perform, and condemned the ineffectiveness and cruelty of the system.

While some 350 workhouses had been built by 1839, the Act's failure to provide a specific timetable meant that more than 170,000 paupers were still receiving outdoor relief in 1849, as against 28,000 'able-bodied' adult inmates of the workhouses. Nevertheless, by the end of the 1830s British expenditure on poor relief had been halved, doubtless to the satisfaction of ratepayers. The Act's harsh spirit of utilitarianism, in which ideals of charity and benevolence were replaced with a rational calculation of rewards and (more obviously) punishments as incentives to work, could be seen increasingly in other countries too. In Germany the 'Elberfeld System' of poor-law administration, involving the division of a municipality into districts each with a volunteer poor-law overseer who applied stringent conditions for relief and reviewed cases on a regular basis, began to spread following Prussian municipal administrative reforms in 1823. In the eyes of Political Economy and its followers, there was no reason for anyone to starve except in the most extreme cases of illness or decrepitude: if the able-bodied were destitute, it was because they were idle. This doctrine was to have calamitous consequences, above all in Ireland, in the economic crisis of the late 1840s.

THE HUNGRY FORTIES AND BEYOND

If European agriculture managed to adapt to support a rapidly growing
population, despite the alarming rise of pauperism, it was not least because
farmers in many parts of the Continent showed themselves more than willing to introduce new crops. Maize proved so popular in the Danubian
Principalities (later Romania), where it had been grown since the seventeenth century, that by the 1830s it occupied 70 per cent of the arable land
in Wallachia and provided the basis for the peasants' diet there. Tobacco
and tomatoes were increasingly grown in the warmer parts of Europe,
and the cultivation of sunflowers, like them another American import,
went to meet the growing demand for cooking oil. New crops allowed
landowners and peasants to diversify into more industrial kinds of production, and here sugar beets registered particularly impressive results. Although
their yield could compete with colonially produced cane sugar neither
in quantity nor in quality, improvements in the refining process in the
1820s, coupled with new government incentives, allowed an expansion, so
that the number of sugar refineries in the Russian Empire, for example,
increased from seven in 1825 to 448 by 1861, most of them located in
Ukraine.

By far the most important of the new crops imported into Europe after
the colonization of America, however, was the potato. It took a long time
to find acceptance among the European peasantry. In Russia in the 1830s,
peasants called potatoes 'apples of the Devil', and government attempts
to make state serfs plant them sparked a series of violent disturbances
known as the 'potato revolts'. In 1834 the English radical William Cobbett
(1763–1835) dubbed the potato 'this nasty, filthy hog feed', while in one
French district, the Sologne, it was reported ten years later that the local
inhabitants 'would consider themselves disgraced if they ate potatoes'.
Nevertheless, in most parts of Europe, the potato had found acceptance
by this time, not least as a consequence of the post-Napoleonic famine,
when, notably in hard-hit areas of Hungary and Poland, it proved an
indispensable foodstuff in the absence of adequate supplies of grain. It
was easy to grow, it was nutritious, it gave high yields, and it required
nothing more than washing and cooking to make it edible. Almost everywhere in northern Europe, the acreage devoted to potato cultivation
increased dramatically during the early decades of the nineteenth century,
reaching more than half a million acres in the Russian provinces of Belarus
by the early 1840s, and reportedly increasing twentyfold in Estonia during the 1820s alone. Large areas of land were planted with potatoes in

Bohemia, Moravia, Silesia and Galicia by the 1840s, and potato cultivation spread rapidly across Scandinavia, northern France and the British Isles. Potatoes gained a particular importance in Ireland, where rural overpopulation made their intensive cultivation irresistibly attractive. By the early 1840s, nearly a third of arable land on the island was devoted to growing potatoes, a proportion more than twice that of the next most potato-friendly country, Belgium. Daily per capita consumption of potatoes in Ireland was estimated at more than two kilos, meaning that many people were effectively using it as their only means of nutrition.

In the summer of 1845 warm and humid weather conditions across Europe caused the infection of potatoes everywhere by a fungal blight that turned them into a foul-smelling, soggy brown mess in the ground. The blight was worst where winters were mild and summers wet, as in Ireland and the west of Scotland, but it affected almost all of Europe in one way or another. In 1845 potato crops collapsed by a catastrophic 87 per cent in Belgium, 71 per cent in the Netherlands, 50 per cent or more in Denmark and the south-west German state of Württemberg, and 30 per cent in Ireland. The blight continued into 1846, but although crops recovered slightly in most parts of Europe, they experienced a further sharp fall in Ireland, where the yield was now 88 per cent below normal. And after a brief recovery in 1847, the blight hit hard again in 1848–9. In Prussian Silesia, where dependency on the potato was almost as great as in Ireland, people in the winter of 1846–7 were said to have 'nothing to eat except grass and nettles, coltsfoot, or a mess concocted of chaff, clover and blood'.

In Holland, Belgium and Prussia, the problems caused by the potato blight were exacerbated by the loss in 1846 of almost half of the rye harvest and a large portion of the wheat harvest as well. This was a catastrophic collapse, unparalleled since 1816–17, and hit these regions hard because of their heavy dependence on bread made from rye and wheat. Population growth in Germany, France, Belgium and the Netherlands came to a standstill in the late 1840s, as people died from malnutrition-related diseases, succumbed to epidemics (notably cholera in 1849, and malaria on the Dutch coast), fled to the towns, and stopped having children. Governments moved swiftly to limit the damage, with the Prussian authorities organizing the purchase of massive quantities of Russian grain, the Danish government abolishing import duties on corn, and the French government also buying up Russian grain. By 1840, Belgians were consuming an average of 1.5 kilos of potatoes a day, but in 1846, 95 per cent of the potato crop in Flanders was destroyed by blight. Moreover, the rural flax industry, which employed nearly a third of a million people by the 1840s, fell into crisis as well, undercut by mechanized cotton production and damaged by falling demand. The Belgian government poured in 2.5 million francs in subsidies, lifted duties on food and grain imports in September 1845, purchased 5.5 million kilos of healthy seed potatoes from abroad in 1846, and spent 14.7 million francs on public works. Municipalities immediately organized massive relief efforts, supported by the Church; in the town of Bruges, for example, the winter of 1846–7 saw the distribution of a quarter of a million kilos of coal, 247,000 litres of soup, bread coupons to the value of 64,000 francs, and 40,000 francs in direct support to the poor. Local and national elites in Belgium had a strong interest in overcoming the crisis, especially in view of the very recent advent of national independence.

In the Scottish Highlands and the Western Isles over three-quarters of crofting parishes reported a total failure of the potato crop in 1845. Starving and malnourished crofters and their families began succumbing to diseases of the digestive organs; mortality rates in the Ross of Mull increased threefold in the winter of 1846–7. Yet the disaster was mainly confined to areas where the population depended on the potato, so that the Scottish Lowlands largely escaped despite the continuation of the blight into the 1850s. Around 200,000 people in the Highlands and islands were affected. By the end of 1846, the government had moored two ships off Mull and Skye to sell cheap grain, and public works were starting to provide wages for the distressed. Roads were laid, walls built, piers constructed, drainage ditches excavated. Religious and secular charities formed a relief board early in 1846 to supply grain to the stricken areas, and raised nearly £210,000, an enormous sum that has been described as probably the largest amount ever raised in nineteenth-century Scotland for a single cause. Local committees organized the distribution of grain and meal.

Acting in the spirit of the New Poor Law, the authorities insisted that only those who worked were entitled to relief. A bureaucracy sprang up to enforce this principle with work-books, inspectors and meal-tickets. The Assistant Secretary to the British Treasury, Sir Charles Trevelyan (1807–86), who was in charge of relief in both Scotland and Ireland, insisted that 'next to allowing the people to die of hunger, the greatest evil that could happen would be their being habituated to depend upon public charity'. What saved the day was the intervention of the landowning elite. By the 1840s, 75 per cent of Highland estates had been bought up by businessmen seeking hunting preserves and looking to acquire status and power. Coming from an urban-industrial, trading and financial background in Glasgow, Edinburgh and the Lowlands, these men had the financial muscle to provide relief for their starving tenants, and most of them did so. Drawing on the resources of Jardine Matheson, the powerful and immensely successful merchant enterprise that dominated the tea and opium trades with China in this period, Sir James Matheson (1796–1878) pumped £107,000 into the island of Lewis, which he had previously bought, between 1845 and 1850, some £68,000 more than he earned in revenues from the estate in these years. In these various ways, catastrophe was averted. Such measures mitigated, but did not prevent, a real crisis of mortality in Europe in the late 1840s. Mortality in Belgium was nearly a third higher than average in 1847, with a total of up to 50,000 deaths attributable directly or indirectly to the harvest failure; in the flax-growing areas of Flanders excess death rates doubled in places. As in all famines, many deaths were caused by people crowding together in towns in search of relief, and succumbing to diseases that spread easily in unhygienic and overcrowded conditions, notably typhus. In the Netherlands excess mortality in 1847 reached 32 per cent, with 60 per cent in some areas, and in Prussia there were 42,000 more deaths than in a normal year, an increase of 40 per cent; conditions were worst in proto-industrial areas like Upper Silesia. Elsewhere, deaths were only about 5 to 10 per cent higher than usual and mostly the consequence of epidemic disease.

The situation was far worse in Ireland, for a variety of reasons in addition to the population's uniquely heavy dependency on the potato. Poor relief was not decentralized as it was in Belgium. Moreover, unlike in Scotland, absentee landlords had little direct contact with their tenants and were not bound to them by ties of nationality, nor were they able to call on industrial and financial wealth to underpin any charitable activities. During the crisis, mortality rose in Ireland by a staggering 330 per cent, compared to a more modest but still grim rise of 40 per cent in Flanders. Distressing reports of the rapidly deteriorating situation in Ireland were already beginning to reach England in the autumn of 1845. Action had to be taken. But there were political obstacles in the way. The most important of these were the Corn Laws, which protected British agriculture by favouring exports while imposing extremely steep import duties on grain from outside the country. Their existence reflected the domination of landowning, grain-producing aristocrats in British politics, and they were not going to abandon them without a fight. They made it difficult if not impossible to import food to relieve the situation in Ireland. In November 1845 the Mansion House Committee, consisting of a number of important figures including Augustus Fitzgerald, Duke of Leinster

(1791–1874), and the Lord Mayor of Dublin, condemned 'the culpable conduct of the present administration' for the 'crime of keeping the ports closed against the importation of foreign provisions', which drove up prices 'for the benefit of a selfish class who derive at the present awful crisis pecuniary advantages to themselves by the maintenance of the oppressive Corn Laws'. Worse still, the ports remained open for the export of Irish grain, in 'a quantity nearly adequate to feed the entire people of Ireland'. The government of Sir Robert Peel (1788–1850) in London announced in January 1846 its intention to repeal the Corn Laws, a triumph for a lengthy campaign waged by the liberal, mostly middle-class proponents of free trade; but the passage of the Bill in June 1846 came too late for Ireland, since it only provided for a gradual reduction of import duties until their final abolition in 1849. By this time the damage had been done.

Aware of the dimensions of the crisis, the British government mobilized public works projects to provide the destitute with wages, and introduced strict controls on the price of potatoes. Grain imports were organized, with Indian meal distributed from central depots. But these measures were patchy, often incomplete, and above all slow to be implemented. It was not until 1847, for instance, that soup kitchens were operating on any scale, and even these were inadequate. Starving Irish families crowded into the workhouses, which contained 135,000 inmates at the beginning of 1848 and 215,000 eighteen months later, all looking for food and sustenance. Yet poor relief was legally unavailable to anyone with more than a quarter-acre of land. In the end, private relief operations were more important, though landlords were both less willing and less able to dole out relief to their tenants than were their counterparts in hard-hit Scotland. Underlying the whole crisis in Ireland was a widespread feeling in the British political and social elite that the Irish had brought their fate upon themselves by being lazy and having too many children (precisely the complaint made by Malthus about the supposed effects of the Old Poor Law). They had a fatal tendency, one critic declared, to 'loiter about upon the land', doing nothing.

By the end of 1846, crisis had become catastrophe. The secretary to the Relief Committee for Clonlolan told the *Sheffield Independent* on 26 December that he had received applications from 1,400 families. On his travels through the barony he was everywhere:

> attended by crowds of famishing wretches, – gaunt with hunger. Men who ought to be comfortable farmers were clothed in rags, and bore all the appearance of the most abject want. Women were to be seen with hardly

enough of clothes to preserve decency; but the aspect of the children struck me most painfully of all, – pinched, sallow, wrinkled, like little old men and women.

A magistrate in Cork, writing to the Duke of Wellington, described a village near Skibbereen 'apparently deserted', but on entering 'some of the hovels' he found no fewer than two hundred 'famished and ghastly skeletons, to all appearance dead', most of them 'delirious, either from famine or from fever'. In one house the police had found 'two frozen corpses . . . half devoured by rats'. The scenes, he wrote despairingly, were 'such as no tongue or pen can convey'. Soup kitchens had been opened by this time, but they were in no way adequate to the task. 'It is the very maximum if two out of any ten that are absolutely starving get relief in this way,' it was reported on 4 March 1847.

Altogether the Irish potato famine killed a million people, or around a fifth of the entire population of the island. This made it the greatest of all European famines in the nineteenth century. In absolute terms it stood with the famine of 1816–17, but most deaths then had been from epidemic diseases, notably bubonic plague in the Balkans, which can best be seen as a side effect of the harvest failure. In the late 1840s the same holds true for most other European countries, where the majority of the 400,000 excess deaths were caused by cholera. In Ireland, uniquely, most deaths occurred as a result of actual starvation. And this was not the end of it. There were longer-term effects as well. Many children and adolescents who survived suffered from stunted growth: in the Netherlands, for instance, the proportion of army recruits under 5 feet 2 inches tall increased by 20 per cent in the years after 1847. Births fell by a third in Ireland, a fifth in Flanders, and an eighth in Prussia compared to a normal year, as people proved either unwilling or unable to conceive children during the crisis. The marriage rate fell by 40 per cent in Flanders and even in France it dropped by 11 per cent in 1847. In Ireland more than anywhere else, survivors responded by emigrating. By the mid-1850s, a quarter of all survivors born in Ireland had moved abroad. Helped by assisted passage schemes and driven out by land clearances, a third to a half of the population of some parts of the Scottish Highlands emigrated as well, either to England or overseas, between 1841 and 1861. A million people left Germany in the decade after the crisis, but legal restrictions, both in Europe (notably the limitations placed on the free movement of serfs and sharecroppers) and in the United States, where farmland in the Midwest did not become legally available until the 1860s, prevented most from people in other parts of the continent leaving.

The Irish famine was not the last to occur in Europe. Russia and Scandinavia, with their long winters and harsh climates that made agriculture vulnerable to the vagaries of the weather, were badly hit on several more occasions in the middle decades of the nineteenth century. Where communications were difficult, it proved impossible to get relief to stricken areas. In Russian-ruled Finland there was an almost complete crop failure in 1856. By the spring of 1857, the poor were eating bread made of bark and straw mixed with a small amount of barley or rye meal, and bands of starving people were flocking to the cities in search of food. A series of poor or mediocre harvests every year from 1862 onwards, culminating in a total harvest failure in 1867, caused not least by a severe frost in September, before the barley, oats and potatoes had been harvested, resulted in yields only 25 per cent of normal rates. The country was plunged once more into a calamitous famine. The government, worried about balancing the budget, left it too late to buy in foreign grain supplies. By the early spring of 1868, people were starving.

Poorhouses fed migrants arriving from the countryside – over 100,000 of them in Finland as a whole, according to one estimate – on bark, straw, roots and lichens. In the municipality of Uusikaupunki in Turku province, migrants coming in from Ostrobothnia 'were so hungry that they immediately went to the slop bucket and ate the food that was reserved for the pigs'. One man remembered begging, but 'they didn't want to give me anything, only scraps of food ... one boy was sitting beside the road, eating horse manure'. Beggars were buried in mass graves all over the country. Some 90,000 deaths were reported from March to August 1868, nearly twice as many as in a whole year in normal times, while reported deaths from dysentery, a sure sign of malnutrition, rose from 1,038 in 1867 to 7,855 the following year. Travellers commented on 'the black, empty windows in villages where all the inhabitants have either starved or emigrated'. The famine of the mid-1860s also hit Sweden, where meteorologists recorded average temperatures between 3 and 6 degrees lower than normal in April and May, and snow was still covering the ground in many areas at a time when the summer seed had to be planted. The governor of Jämtland instructed his local officials to provide lessons to the peasants on how to make bread from lichens and pea stalks, a policy that earned him the nickname *Lav-Kungen*, the Lichen King, in his district; many people fell ill as a result of taking his advice, and not a few died. Other officials encouraged people to eat mushrooms, which were generally considered fit only for cattle fodder. All these efforts had only limited effect: mortality in Westrobothnia reached eighty-four deaths per thousand population by 1868, far above normal levels. The famine extended to the Baltic coast of Poland, Courland, Livonia and Estonia, and along the shores of the Gulf of Bothnia; a report from St Petersburg pictured 'villages depopulated; private houses turned into hospitals; fever-parched skeletons tottering from the doors of overcrowded places of refuge'.

By the end of the 1870s, improved transportation and greater governmental and administrative vigilance ensured that bad harvests seldom led to famine anymore. The spread of the railways to rural areas made it possible to transport food supplies to districts affected by poor harvests, and so stave off the public disorders that officials so feared as an accompaniment to famine. Already in 1854 when the harvest failed in the French department of Maine-et-Loire, the prefect reported with satisfaction that 'for the first time . . . a calamitous year will have passed without sedition and almost without muttering'. The spectre of famine continued to stalk nineteenth-century Europe, especially in areas that were difficult of access. In March 1897 a newspaper reported a regional famine in León, a province of Spain:

> where agriculture is almost the only source of wealth, [and] the inhabitants are on the verge of starvation; nearly all their flocks and herds have died either of disease or want of food. As for the crops, they were practically destroyed by the late storms and floods and by the drought of a few months ago, and all the horrors of famine threaten the already sorely tried peasants. Those who can do so emigrate to Brazil in hundreds, and those who cannot are reduced to eating acorns.

The government rushed food supplies to the area, and averted total disaster, as it did again when famine threatened in 1905 following a drought in Andalusia. Over a million people were affected, children were reported to be eating cactus leaves and fir cones, and infant mortality rates rocketed. Angered by the slow response of the government, bands of armed farm labourers roamed the countryside and entered the towns looking for food. Emigration was the response of many. An Irish potato failure in 1879 had similar effects. Overall, however, for all their dilatoriness, governments managed to prevent the worst from happening in these later episodes of dearth.

The most striking exception was Russia, where vast distances and poor communications, ill-advised fiscal reforms, and the long-term effects of the emancipation conditions led to disaster at the beginning of the 1890s. An early frost in October 1890 destroyed the seedlings for the following year's crops, sown late because of unusually dry autumn weather. Winter was exceptionally long, and followed by another lengthy dry spell. The grain harvest of 1891 in European Russia was 26 per cent below normal, while the rye crop fell by an average of 30 per cent overall, and 75 per cent in the black-earth province of Voronezh. During the 1880s the government had tried to work towards the convertibility of the rouble into gold by stimulating grain exports while racking up taxation at home. But these policies squeezed the peasantry, already suffering from the loss of land as a consequence of the emancipation of 1861 and the rising population in the countryside. Peasant farmers had also taken advantage of the new market for corn by converting pasturage to arable, cutting down forests to turn into fields, and reducing their livestock, which deprived them of their major source of fertilizers. Over-intensive farming and the droughts of 1890 and 1891 did the rest.

Travelling through the stricken regions towards the end of 1891, Brayley Hodgetts (1859–1932), Reuters' news agency correspondent in Berlin, encountered starving peasants everywhere he went. 'We have no bread,' people told him as they huddled round the stove in one peasant cottage: ' "We have had nothing to eat for three days, by God", they all sang in a kind of chorus . . . They looked as if they had not eaten anything for weeks – not days.' They had consumed or sold almost everything they had. Hodgetts wrote that 'some of the food of these poor peasants was terrible to see. Broken bits of bread, collected through begging; some mildewed, others foul with dirt, lay together in the peasants' bread-basket.' In another village he found people eating soup 'little better than dirty, hot water. The men were wretched-looking, with hollow eyes, some in the last stages of fever, all huddled up on their double stoves, whither they had crawled to die. People were eating only every other day.' As so often, epidemics swept across the starving countryside, carrying off thousands of people already weakened by malnutrition. In another area, a Tolstoyan Swede, Jonas Stadling (1837–1945), who thought the Russian government was deliberately keeping the peasants ignorant and crushing any sense of initiative they might try to develop, saw families taking the straw off their thatched houses and feeding it to their cattle or using it for winter fuel.

By the autumn of 1891, the need for full-scale relief operations was clear. But State Secretary Alexander Alexandrovich Polovtsov (1832–1909) thought everyone in authority was 'weighed down with despair . . . no-one [had] a clear idea what to do but all . . . [vie] with each other in proposing the most wild-eyed schemes'. Grain exports were banned, but although money was released, the relief effort was hampered by poor communications and lack of information from the provinces. The railway network was effectively non-existent in many of the areas worst affected, different lines were managed by different companies and different state agencies, and there was a bitter personal feud between the two ministers responsible for running them. Public works and food loans to peasants were organized, but the schemes took a long time to get off the ground and were too limited in scope to be wholly effective. Even in August 1891 only 200,000 people were receiving food loans. By the time the programme was fully operational, in March 1892, the number exceeded 11 million, but most of the damage had already been done. By the end of 1892, death rates had increased by around 55 per cent in Samara and Saratov, 50 per cent in Ufa and Voronezh, 40 per cent in Orenburg, 36 per cent in Kazan and Simbirsk, and 30 per cent in Penza and Tambov. A total of 406,643 more people had died in the provinces most seriously affected by famine than in a normal year; 103,364 of these deaths can be attributed to the cholera epidemic that broke out in the summer, so that the figure of famine deaths is most likely to have been around 300,000, among which there were also many deaths from typhus, spread by starving peasants crowding together in relief centres in the towns.

The halting aid effort of 1891–2, even if partially successful, brought down massive criticism on the head of the tsarist administration. 'The famine is a great lesson,' commented one newspaper: it should galvanize the government into reform. This did not happen. There was no effective intensification of liaison and co-operation between the tsar's central administration in St Petersburg and the local administrative bodies, the mainly liberal and professional *zemstva* in the provinces. Mutual suspicions were too great. In 1899 dearth struck Russia again, after bad harvests in the two preceding years. Some 10,000 cases of scurvy were reported by the medical authorities in the Kazan province alone by May 1899, and in one district 5,588 people out of a total population of 8,659 were in receipt of poor relief. The tsar's Minister of Finance, Sergei Yulyevich Witte (1849–1915), commented that the Russian peasant 'seems unable in any way to provide for the future, and by a single bad harvest is plunged into an abyss of misery from which he can only be extricated by external help'. Witte blamed the situation not on the burden of taxation, which he said did not fall on necessities and was generally very light, even when it included annual redemption payments, but on the peasants' ignorance of their rights and duties within the rural community, and their reliance on custom and tradition. Witte was supposed to be a modernizer, but opinions such as these indicated a deep lack of understanding of Russian society that was to prove fatal in the end for the regime he served.

By 1914, famine had been banished from the greater part of the Continent. The 'hungry forties' had seen the deepest and most devastating crisis of subsistence. In some areas at least, notably in Flanders, the crisis had gained its depth from a combination of a simultaneous collapse of agriculture and proto-industry, the old economy and the new: just as had happened periodically for centuries, a poor harvest pushed up the price of grain, so that people in the countryside as well as in the towns had to use a greater part of their income to pay for bread and other foodstuffs, reducing demand for clothes, utensils and other manufactured goods. This caused a crisis in urban factories and workshops, which therefore had to lay off their workers, throwing them into destitution just at the moment when they most needed an income to survive. By the 1840s, however, a new dimension to such crises was emerging in the shape of the spread of modern industrial production across Europe, beginning in Britain.

THE TEXTILE REVOLUTION

Industrial production on the European Continent in the early nineteenth century was overwhelmingly small-scale, concentrated in individual workshops rather than in large factories, and driven by human or horse power, woodfires, water-mills or (especially in Holland) windmills. Artisanal workshops produced a whole variety of goods, ranging from glassware and silverware to clocks and furniture, often to high specifications for sale to the better-off. Agricultural workers and small farmers in areas like Switzerland or south-west Germany supplemented their meagre incomes with a handloom or spinning wheel in their home, selling their product to a middleman under the so-called 'putting-out' system, a highly seasonal and unreliable source of income, dependent on the labour of women and children in the family. During the French Revolutionary and Napoleonic Wars, Britain had forged ahead economically, leaving the European Continent far behind. Per capita industrial production in Britain in 1830 was almost twice that of Switzerland or Belgium, more than twice that of France, and three times that of the Habsburg Empire, Spain, Italy, Norway, Sweden, Denmark or the Netherlands.

Linen and wool had long formed the basis of the textile industry. What was new in the late eighteenth century was the arrival of cotton, previously used mainly for printed fabric or calico, for mass consumption. By this time, England was mass-producing cloth from raw cotton grown with cheap labour in India and then exporting finished cotton products back to the subcontinent. In the American south, cotton was farmed by slaves, making it cheaper still. Soon cotton in Europe was replacing the more expensive linen and wool, which did not undergo mechanization until the 1820s or later, as the basic fabric used in clothing. Imports of raw cotton into Britain rose from 11 million pounds in weight in 1785 to 588 million in 1850, all used to manufacture cloth. India, meanwhile, was sent head-long into industrial decline, to be followed by Egypt, where the attempts of the local pasha, Muhammad Ali, to develop a cotton industry were undermined by the Anglo-Ottoman Convention of 1838. The British inter-vened the following year, after the pasha defeated an Ottoman army in battle and threatened to march on Constantinople. His monopoly on trade was forcibly abolished, and as Egypt was flooded with cheap British cotton products, the domestic industry collapsed. Britain's industrial advantage over the rest of the world was not the product of British ingenuity or inven-tiveness or other domestic factors. More than anything else, the explosion of cotton production in Britain was driven by world trade. In 1814, Britain was already exporting more cotton cloth than it sold at home; by 1850 the disparity had increased, with thirteen yards sold abroad for every eight in the UK. In 1820, 128 million yards of cotton cloth were sold to the Euro-pean Continent, with 80 million going to the Americas (apart from the USA), Africa and Asia: by 1840 the comparable figures were 200 million and 529 million. British domination of the seas guaranteed a virtual monopoly for cotton sales to Latin America, which took a quarter more cotton cloth than the European Continent in 1820 and nearly half as much again twenty years later. Exports to India rose from 11 million yards in 1820 to 145 million in 1840. Cotton products made up nearly half the value of all British exports between 1816 and 1850. The growth of a new industrial economy in Britain after 1815 was not just the product of sci-entific or technological superiority, it was also the product of global empire.

The boom in mechanized cotton production in Britain was concen-trated overwhelmingly in Lancashire, Yorkshire, Derbyshire and Cheshire, in the north of England, where fast-flowing mountain streams turned the water-wheels that powered the machinery through a system of shafts operating a large number of looms weaving cloth under the same factory roof. Machinery had been introduced because labour costs were high, whereas elsewhere in Europe labour costs were low and so did not justify the substantial capital outlay needed to install the new machines. By 1829 there were 55,000 power looms in England; five years later their number had almost doubled, to 100,000. Power looms gradually drove handlooms out of business. In 1820 there were 240,000 handloom weavers in Britain. Increasing demand could still not be entirely satisfied by power looms. But the handloom weavers were becoming increasingly impover-ished. Mechanization was driving down prices for the average piece of printed cotton: 3 shillings and 7 pence in 1818, 2 shillings and 11 pence in 1824, just over 2 shillings by the end of the decade. The handloom weavers could not compete. By the mid-1840s, their number had fallen to a mere 60,000. By the end of the decade, there were 250,000 power looms in operation in Britain, up from 100,000 in 1833. And the increase in numbers was not all. Continual improvements in technology meant that spinning machines were growing steadily in capacity, with machines of 300 spindles by the 1830s doing, in other words, the work of 300 individual women each sat at a hand-operated spinning wheel. In 1830, moreover, the 'self-acting mule' came into operation, invented by Richard Roberts (1789–1864) after factory owners had approached him in an effort to procure a technological means of dealing with the problem of strikes by reducing the number of workers. His invention incorporated many more aspects of spinning into machine operation, including for example the reversing of the spindle to 'back off' the yarn, an operation that previously had to be carried out by hand. Mechanization drastically lowered prices while producing a better-quality, finer and more even yarn, though where labour costs were low, as for example in Germany, the expensive self-acting mules were not adopted until the late 1850s.

Technological innovation also took place on the Continent. The French Jacquard loom, for example, invented in the late eighteenth century, revolutionized silk weaving and had an application to fancy cotton products as well; the number of looms in Lyon doubled between 1788 and 1833, by which time two-thirds of them were Jacquard models. And one of the most significant innovations in textiles came in 1845 when the Alsatian engineer Josué Heilmann (1796–1848), in Mulhouse, invented a machine that could be used for worsted wool yarn as well as fine cotton. He had previously developed an embroidery machine, and in 1832, Philippe de Girard (1775–1845) produced a machine for combing flax (or 'heckling' as it was known). Another French engineer, Benoît Fourneyron (1802–67), developed a new, highly efficient way of using water power in 1827 by turning a water-wheel on its side. He called it a turbine, and over the following years he built increasingly effective models, producing in 1837 a 60-horsepower turbine that could rotate 2,300 times a minute and operate at 80 per cent efficiency. Most remarkably of all, the wheel was only a foot in diameter and it weighed a mere 40 pounds. By 1843 his turbines were at work in 129 factories in France, Germany, Austria, Italy and Poland. But the most powerful means of introducing technological innovation into the textile industries on the Continent was through the export of British machinery, either directly or at second hand. After the war with France ended in 1815, the export of cotton to the Continent became possible again, and soon it was conquering one country after another as entrepreneurs saw the advantages of the new material and the new techniques.

Not surprisingly, after the war was over, the textile industry grew very rapidly once more in northern France. The first spinning machine was set up in Reims in 1815, while in Roubaix the woollen industry introduced the first power loom in 1844. Power-loom weaving began further east, with the installation of a steam-driven cotton mill in Elberfeld in 1821; by 1834 there were ten engines in the Wupper valley. The spread of the new industrial production across Europe was as uneven as its driving forces were diverse. The Spanish textile industry increased only very slowly in the first decades of the century; although there were fourteen water-powered textile mills in 1808, this number had only grown to thirty-six by 1836. The loss of the American colonies had cut off Spain's major export market, and it was only after the import of cotton goods was banned in 1832 that the industry began to mechanize and to flourish. By contrast, there were 225,000 cotton spindles in Lower Austria by 1828 and 118,000 in Bohemia; weaving continued to be done by hand, except in the Vorarlberg, where there were 466 power looms by the early 1840s. The nascent cotton industry of Italy in the 1830s was dominated from the beginning by Swiss and German immigrants, and even at the end of the century the world of the industrialists in Lombardy, as one commentator reported, 'abounded in guttural sounds and harsh terminations'. Despite a few improvements in the machines in the 1830s and 1840s, this was not a fully industrialized branch of the economy by any means; yet silk accounted for a third of the value of all Italian exports right through the nineteenth century and beyond. Still, by 1848 there were sixty cotton mills in Piedmont and Lombardy, with 200,000 spindles, giving an average of just over 3,000 spindles per mill.

Government initiative was responsible for the early mechanization of the textile industry in Poland. Rajmund Rembieliński (1774–1841), the Prefect of Mazovia, a low-lying district in east-central Congress Poland, was an Anglophile Polish nationalist whose publications included a play entitled *Lord Salisbury*; he succeeded in getting two Saxon manufacturers to set up a mechanized cotton mill in Łódź, powered by water. Meanwhile, the woollen and linen industries had revived in Białystok and Żyrardów, where a factory set up by a French engineer managed to obtain a monopoly of linen production from the Russian authorities. Yet the industrialization of Congress Poland was frequently retarded by government policies as well. From 1823 to 1825 a tariff barrier with Prussia made contacts with western Europe more difficult, while from 1832 to 1850, in the wake of the failed uprising of 1830, Congress Poland was excluded from the Russian customs area so that Polish industrial goods found it hard to secure a market to the east. In Russia itself, British machinery was imported into the state-owned Alexandrovsk factory in St Petersburg and already in the 1840s Russian firms had stopped importing finished cotton cloth from Britain, and were buying raw cotton direct from the United States instead. After mid-century, domestic machine-building firms quickly began to supply most of the wants of the textile industry in Russia: by mid-century there were fifty-eight cotton mills in Vladimir, with 900 looms and 5,800 workers on the premises, but also 45,000 handlooms and 65,000 workers processing the cotton at home in the surrounding villages.

The most important centre of the new textile production in Europe was in northern France and southern Belgium, where the industrial mills exemplified the new world of work and discipline that was now being established. Here the flat land and sluggishly flowing rivers meant that steam power was used from the outset, since watermills were impractical. In the early industrial town and port of Ghent there were already 250,000 spinning jennies by 1815. The largest mill in the town, owned by the Voortman family, signed a contract in 1821 with two English businessmen to import and set up 100 power looms, ten dressing machines, a steam engine and a washing machine, at a total cost of £5,000. This was an enormous sum in the currency of the day, funded by the profits the firm had made during the Napoleonic Wars. By 1824 the mill was employing sixty workers, but such was demand that the business was still contracting out work to 800 handloom weavers. Other enterprises followed suit, and by 1830 the town's cotton mills were employing 10,000 workers in spinning and printing cotton, with a further 20,300 handloom weavers working to commission at home outside the city. Access to markets and imported raw materials was improved by the construction of canals linking the town to the coalfields of Wallonia, lowering the costs of operating the machines. By 1830 there were 700 steam-driven power looms in Ghent, increasing to 3,600 by 1840 and 5,000 by 1846.

The annual profits of the Voortman factory had tripled by 1830, largely on the basis of new contracts to export finished textiles to the Dutch colonies, but there was a crisis following the revolution of that year and the mill closed temporarily. The Voortmans were originally Dutch and the company had an office in Amsterdam; the family was known to be Orangist. Moreover, the firm was unpopular not only because of its introduction of machinery but also because it had responded to a strike in November 1829 by locking the workers out, hiring twenty-five spinners from France, and getting several of the strikers sent to prison. In 1831 the workers spread a rumour that the company was concealing weapons on its premises; they broke in and during their search they also, not coincidentally, smashed the factory machines. Somewhat tactlessly, the owner told workers demanding the reopening of the factory 'Go and eat your freedom tree if you are hungry!' The workers broke into his house, beat him badly, and forced him to kiss the Freedom Tree, though they did not make him eat it. When he recovered and reopened the factory, in 1832, wages were lowered, only twenty-seven of the previously employed 132 workers were re-hired, and the police were called in to protect him from the workers yet again.

Discipline in Voortman's mill was harsh; wages were docked for arriving late for work, being drunk, going to the toilet too often, submitting a sub-standard finished product, or even suspending work briefly to fetch tools or oil the machinery. Fines were a cause of bitter resentment and contributed further to worker discontent. There were further strikes in July and September 1834. Working conditions in the new factories elsewhere shared many of these characteristics. The factory as an institution introduced a ferocious new time-discipline for those it employed. Hand-loom weavers might be forced to sit at their looms for fourteen hours a day to make ends meet, but they could choose when to start, when to finish, and when to take a break. Workers had to arrive on time to hear the bell sounding the start of the day's work, and a long list of rules and regulations docked their wages for any perceived or supposed slackness. A description of regulations in a spinning factory at Tyldesley, near Manchester, handed out by the workers during a strike in 1823, noted that the temperature in the factory was normally around 27 or 28 degrees Celsius, the working day was fourteen hours 'including the nominal hour for dinner; the door is locked in working hours, except half an hour at tea time; the workpeople are not allowed to send for water to drink, in the hot factory'. A fine of a shilling, a not inconsiderable sum, was levied on any worker who was five minutes late for work, 'found with his window open', 'found washing himself', or 'heard whistling'. 'Any spinner being sick and cannot find another spinner to give satisfaction must pay for steam per day 6 s[hillings].' Such harsh new rules and regulations were widely resented by workers wherever they were imposed.

Early industrial cotton mills were dangerous places. Workers suffered from bronchitis, indigestion, varicose veins and deafness, caused respectively by working long hours in an environment filled with fluff and dust, by standing for lengthy periods of time, and by spending their days amid the enormous noise of machinery. Some weavers had the task of threading the 'kissing shuttle', placing their lips to the threading hole and sucking in, making respiratory diseases a certainty. Hair or clothing could be caught between belt and shaft, pulling a worker in and twirling her around the shaft until she was beaten to death; shuttles could fly off the loom, spiking a worker in the face. Workers could be caught in machinery, like the young 'scavenger' Patrick Noon of Stalybridge, whose job was to clean the floor underneath a spinning mule; in March 1846 his head became trapped in a space only four inches wide, and the whirling machinery flayed the skin from his head, revealing the bone. Over a period of six months in 1840, the English and Scottish Factory Commissions reported 1,114 accidents in cotton mills caused by machinery, along with another 907 of various kinds, all resulting in 22 deaths and 109 amputations. There were few provisions for compensation, though some companies did put funds into charities set up for this purpose. Workers were widely assumed to be engaged in their chosen occupation out of free choice and at their own risk. Employers frequently accused injured workers of negligence.

A high proportion of the workers in the mills was female. In 1843 two physicians in Ghent commented that 'the tendency to replace men with women and children exists here as in other manufacturing districts' because of the mill-owners' desire to 'economise'. The more new machines were installed, the more women were employed. In 1829 over 40 per cent of employees in Ghent cotton mills were female, a figure that increased to 48 per cent in the highly mechanized Voortman mill. Male workers in the mill actually went on strike in 1832 in an unsuccessful attempt to prevent a further increase in the employment of women. Even more than women, young children were thought to be dexterous and known to be cheap. Employing them would keep them off the streets and contribute to family income. There were no Belgian child-labour protection laws until 1889. The number of children aged five to nine employed in the Voortman textile factory increased from 1 per cent of the workforce in 1842 to 9 per cent in 1879, and the number of those aged ten to fourteen rose from 6 per cent in 1842 to 34 per cent in 1859. Many of these were girls working in the carding room, or on spinning or weaving machines. Almost all of them were relatives of people who already worked there; more than three-quarters of the workers in the mill had been born in the town. A family income was especially necessary in bad times such as the late 1840s, when food prices increased by 20 per cent and food expenditure accounted for 76.2 per cent of the total expenditure of Ghent cotton workers (normally it was around 66 per cent). A typical family of workers in Ghent, the Bauters, tied up their entire lives with the Voortman factory. Louis Bauters

(1801–?) worked as a weaver in the factory from 1840 to 1850, while his wife, whom he married in 1829, was employed as a weaver there from 1835. The couple had twelve children. Those who survived infancy started work in the factory when they were thirteen: there were three wage-earners in the family in 1845, and five in 1849. Yet this was a family living precariously on the very margin of existence. Only one of the Bauters' twelve children lived beyond the age of twenty-five; four died in infancy, and seven died between the ages of twenty and twenty-five. According to a survey of 1845, food for the Voortman factory's workers consisted mostly of bread and potatoes, eked out with meat four times a week for 20 per cent of them, twice a week for 35 per cent, once a week for 26 per cent, and not at all for 18 per cent, and otherwise a thin gruel of buttermilk or leeks and potatoes. Poverty, malnutrition, disease and infant mortality were not newly created by the industrial revolution, but the new world of the factory did nothing to alleviate them and in some respects made them worse.

COAL AND IRON

There could be no doubt of the significance of steam technology, even when it powered only a minority of industrial enterprises. Its introduction was rightly described as an 'industrial revolution', a term first used in France in the 1820s to denote a momentous change in production, in which, as the economist Jérôme-Adolphe Blanqui (1798–1854) wrote in 1831, 'industrial conditions were more profoundly transformed than at any time since the beginnings of social life'. What was momentous was not so much the organization of production into large factories where hundreds or even thousands of people laboured to make standardized products; these enterprises had existed already in the eighteenth century. The difference was that in those earlier 'manufactories' the workers had each been working essentially by hand, using their own muscle-power. Natural sources of power – human beings for operating handlooms, horses for pulling carts, wind for operating windmills, above all, water for driving water-wheels – each played a part in the first stage of the industrial revolution. But very quickly steam became the key source of power. This was the decisive breakthrough. From now on, society was free from the tyranny of the elements and the limitations of human, elemental and animal strength in the creation of industrial power.

The industrial revolution was not confined to textile manufacture, but was in the longer run of even greater significance in the production of coal and iron. Here what marked out Britain from the rest of Europe in the industrial sphere was above all its early use of coal as a source of energy and its continued domination of coal production well into the second half of the century. Between 1815 and 1830 coal output in Britain virtually doubled, from 16 million tons a year to 30 million. As late as 1860, Britain was still producing more than twice as much coal as the whole of the rest of Europe put together. As demand grew, so mines had to be sunk deeper to access coal seams hundreds of feet below the surface. Water had to be pumped out of the mine, air circulated along the pits and galleries, gallery roofs held up with timber props, coal hauled to the surface and taken away by specially built canals or, in the 1840s increasingly, by rail. The need to pump water out of coalmines was a key factor in the development and refinement of the steam engine, but the actual cutting of coal from the seam was done by hand. Production could only be increased by bringing ever more miners to the coalfields, and areas where there were rich seams of coal, for example in south Wales, saw increasing numbers of immigrants drawn by the prospect of steady work.

The work was dirty, difficult and dangerous. Spectacular colliery disasters were frequent. At the Wallsend pit near Newcastle, for example, it was reported on 23 October 1821:

> At around 8:00am the new pit shaft called New Belcher Seam, in Wallsend Colliery, on the river Tyne, blew up with a most tremendous explosion, which was heard at the distance of several miles around. It is not known with any certainty how the accident originated, but it is thought to be by the ignition of the hydrogen gas. The report of the explosion having alarmed the people belonging to the collieries in the neighbourhood, hundreds instantly came running to the fatal spot, wishful to ascertain the extent of the calamity . . . In the pit, out of fifty-six men, it was found only two had escaped unhurt – four men got out alive, but in a very weak state, two of whom are since dead. The rest, to the amount of fifty souls, had all perished.

On 18 June 1835 people working above ground at the same pit heard 'a considerable report, which they spoke of as being like an earthquake, accompanied by a rushing of choke damp to the mouth of the shaft, bringing up with it some of the pitmen's clothes and other light articles from the bottom'. A huge gas explosion had killed twenty-six men and seventy-five boys working underground. Crowds of distraught relatives gathered at the pithead as the bodies were brought up over the following days. Gas explosions were the cause of the greatest disasters such as these, but day in, day out, miners suffered injuries and sometimes death from less spectacular causes: broken arms or legs from runaway wagons, bodies scarred by falling rock, drowned by a sudden onrush of water, trapped by rock falls, or injured in many other ways. Pregnant women working underground pulling heavy coal wagons were frequently reported to suffer miscarriages.

Flooding became more common as mines sank deeper shafts to reach more remote seams, often disregarding the geology of the area. In 1838, for example, it was reported:

> A dreadful accident occurred at Mr Hughes' colliery near Begelly Pembrokeshire on Saturday last in consequence of a very thoughtless . . . cutting in of water; by which means 6 poor men . . . were drowned. The quantity of water cut in was so great as to take the constant working of persons, night and day, at two pits, with the assistance of a steam engine at a third pit, from the day the accident happened, to Thursday morning.

Unusually, the father of one of the men killed prosecuted the manager for manslaughter, though he failed to get his case through a grand jury. On 14 February 1844 the Garden Pit in Pembrokeshire, which went some 197 feet beneath the estuaries of the rivers Cleddau and Daucleddau, and produced 10,000 tons of coal a year, suffered one of the decade's worst disasters. An unusually high tide put heavy pressure on the relatively shallow workings, sending the sea roaring through the mine and drowning forty workers who had no chance of escape.

There were no formal rules of compensation in such cases, though employers sometimes made *ex gratia* payments. In the mid-1840s the mine-owners of South Staffordshire mines were reported to be giving 6 shillings a week to men off work because of injuries, one shilling and sixpence to widows of miners killed in the pit, and an extra shilling a week for every child under ten. Such generosity was more forthcoming after great disasters, when the newspapers sometimes organized public subscriptions for the bereaved, though it was only directed at the 'deserving poor'. Following the 1821 explosion in Wallsend, the mine-owners buried the dead in the local churchyard at their own expense and gave the bereaved families money for food and fuel as long as they needed it. However, many employers were commonly critical of the workers' 'recklessness in dangerous occupations, their neglect of cleanliness, their refusal to adopt preventive measures against evident evils, and above all, their widespread habit of intemperance', as the hygiene expert John Thomas Arlidge (1822–99) put it. Workers often set up their own collections or 'gatherings' to help injured comrades, but, rather than depend on unsystematic and intermittent charity, many miners went back to their job as soon as they recovered. William Morrow (1836–?) lost his leg in 1844 at the age of eight when he was run over by a coal wagon, but he was reported working at the pit six years later, now sporting a wooden leg. Miners and their families often treated their mishaps as mere bad luck, or acts of God, or the fault of the injured worker. Safety improvements were slow to come. The covered Davy Lamp, introduced in 1816, gradually replaced the far more dangerous candles, but also encouraged the exploitation of deeper, more remote and more difficult seams, leading to an increase in the number of accidents. The expansion of coalmining in Britain during the first half of the nineteenth century was achieved at a high price, paid by the workers.

The growth of the coal industry was paralleled by rapid expansion and technological change in ironmaking. Here, innovation was driven by the high cost of charcoal in the absence of abundant supplies of wood. In Britain, too many trees had been felled to build the ships of the Royal Navy and provide land for ploughing and pasturage, so a new method had to be found. By 1790 almost all pig iron (basic smelted iron) was being smelted using coke, a concentrated form of coal that could be heated to very high temperatures. New techniques of purifying pig iron and turning it into wrought or bar iron ('puddling' and 'rolling') developed in the 1780s and fuelled a massive boom in iron production in Britain. In 1750, France and Sweden had dominated European iron production, while the British imported much of what they needed. By 1860, Britain was producing 60 per cent of all pig iron manufactured in Europe, basing the industry around iron ore and coal mines in Nottinghamshire, Derbyshire and Yorkshire, and other areas of the country.

The only part of the Continent to follow suit in the first half of the century was the region located on large coal and iron-ore deposits stretching from Belgium into northern France and western Germany. The long capitalist industrial tradition of the region, its rich natural resources, the lack of a strong agrarian political interest, and the concentration of banking and financial resources, strengthened by heavy government investment, all made Ghent and the southern part of Belgium the pioneering centre of industrialization on the Continent, not only in textiles but also in coal and iron. By 1838, British-made steam-pumps were routinely used in all the deeper Belgian pits – and the average depth of pits in Belgium was 689 feet at this point. By the 1820s coke blast furnaces and puddling and rolling mills were being constructed around Liège and Charleroi, using technology imported from Britain. Import duties protected the industry from British competition, and the reduction of costs undercut traditional means of production. By the 1830s, coked pig iron made up virtually 100 per cent of all pig iron produced in Belgium, as it did in Britain, whereas in Germany and France traditional charcoal-based methods continued to dominate. Charcoal continued to be used in Sweden for refining pig iron in an adaptation of the British puddling technique until the 1860s. Alpine pig iron continued to be smelted exclusively by charcoal up to the 1860s, and the Vítkovice ironworks in the north of the Habsburg Empire, which introduced coke smelting in 1836, remained the only one to use coke in the entire Empire until 1854, probably because it had been set up by two ironmasters brought over from Wales.

Much of the innovation that took place on the European Continent was a direct result of the importation of British men and machinery. British governments tried to prevent the export of technical know-how by passing laws forbidding the export of machinery and the emigration of artisans in the 1780s. But these regulations were completely unenforceable. Already in 1798 the Belgian (at the time, French) engineer Liévin Bauwens (1769–1822) had smuggled a disassembled spinning jenny packed into sugar crates out of Manchester to Ghent via Hamburg, despite the fact that the export of machinery was punishable by death. Count István Széchenyi (1791–1860), a Hungarian aristocrat who visited England in 1815, succeeded in obtaining:

> a model of the gas-driven engine, which cost me a deal in both money and effort and was obtained only by dint of sheer will-power and persistence . . . Several acquaintances mocked me for my preoccupation with machines, especially the light-generating one to which I devoted so much time while in England. Of course, it is indeed odd for a captain of the hussars to take three hours of instruction from not just mechanics but their assistants, in both theory and practice, and to be covered in wood oil in the morning and eau du Rasumovsky in the evening.

Nevertheless, while he considered steam engines useless and dangerous ('We have no factories, and thank God that we do not'), the count thought that machines which made light out of coal gas had many potential uses, and he was prepared to pay 2 pounds for the model and a further sum to bribe a 'proud Englishman guised as a customs official', who 'for a potage of four ducats sold the soul of his nation: a gas machine'. Such subterfuges were common enough in the period immediately after the end of the Napoleonic Wars.

In the mid-1820s, Britain's export ban was replaced by a licensing system and in 1843 it was done away with altogether. Foreign entrepreneurs eager to acquire the latest techniques came over to England to work, and took plans and blueprints back with them, or hired British experts to modernize their workshops. A case in point was the celebrated German iron and steel firm Krupp, whose owner Alfred Krupp (1812–87) (his English first name was a deliberate homage to English industrial superiority) travelled to England in 1838 (lightly disguised as 'Herr Schropp'). He returned to Germany but every now and then sent agents over to England to learn the latest factory designs and industrial techniques. Sometimes the state took a hand in bringing the new methods into its domains. On the vast Zamoyski estates in Congress Poland the Physiocrat Stanisław Staszic (1755–1826), an official in the Russian administration responsible for trade and industry, began to encourage mines, steel mills, textile processing and canal-building, based on the English example. In Dąbrowa Górnicza he discovered coal deposits and founded a coalmine, and he modernized the blast furnaces of the Staropolskie Basin so that they used coke instead of charcoal.

But in most of Europe private enterprise played the major role, and initially too this frequently involved entrepreneurs from Britain, such as the Irish engineer William Thomas Mulvany (1806–85). A civil servant in charge of job-creation schemes in Ireland, mainly in canal and road building, after the famine Mulvany had found himself without a job when the schemes were wound up, and began to search for new opportunities to make a living. Visiting the Ruhr area with a group of potential investors, he found what he was looking for :

> As a result of a short visit to the Head Mining Office and examination of the geological map, I immediately realised what wonderfully extensive riches were hidden under the earth. I had seen how inadequate in those days were your railways and how insufficiently your canals and transport facilities were used. I said to myself on the spot: these people do not understand what they possess here.

The coalmines he founded were named *Hibernia*, *Shamrock* and *Erin*, and remain so to this day; Mulvany was eventually made an honorary citizen of Gelsenkirchen, and died in old age in Düsseldorf, where he spent the last part of his life.

Yet the state remained important in providing the legal, institutional and economic framework for industrialization. In Britain in particular it undertook limited reforms of working conditions. The Cotton Mills and Factories Act of 1819 banned the employment of children under the age of nine, and restricted the hours of work for those under sixteen years of age to sixteen hours a day. Such legislation was difficult to enforce, but in 1833 a new Factory Act not only further limited the hours of work for children and required them to have at least two hours of education a day, it also set up a Factory Inspectorate. Often the legislation was introduced after a public outcry resulting from an industrial disaster. People became aware of conditions in the country's collieries in 1838 after a freak accident at Huskar Colliery, near Barnsley. A stream overflowed into the ventilation system after violent thunderstorms, causing the death by drowning of twenty-six children – eleven girls aged from eight to sixteen and fifteen boys aged from nine to twelve. The reading public was appalled by the revelation of the widespread use of child labour. The disaster came to the attention of Queen Victoria (1819–1901), who ordered an inquiry. The Christian philanthropist Lord Ashley (1801–85, later Earl of Shaftesbury) led the Commission in its visits to collieries and mining communities, gathering information sometimes against the wishes of mine-owners. The report, illustrated by engraved illustrations and the personal accounts of mineworkers, was published in May 1842. Victorian society was shocked to discover that children as young as five or six worked as 'trappers', opening and shutting ventilation doors down the mine, before becoming 'hurriers', pushing coal tubs along the underground tunnels. Lord Ashley deliberately appealed to early Victorian prudery, focusing on girls and women wearing trousers and working bare-breasted in the presence of boys and men, a practice that 'made girls unsuitable for marriage and unfit to be mothers'. The resulting Coal Mines Act of 1842 and the Factory Act of 1844 established an inspectorate and banned women and children from working underground, continuing initiatives begun in the previous decade. The 1844 legislation reduced the limit to nine hours a day for nine-to-thirteen-year-olds. It required guard rails to be put around equipment. Owners could be fined if a worker was injured by unsafe machinery.

These reforms had few parallels elsewhere in Europe. Far more important was the state's involvement in the expansion of industry and above all in transportation. The construction of roads and canals was overwhelmingly funded by governments, which also invested heavily in railway-building. The state was a key source of investment capital, as well as legislation making it easier for banks to provide loans to business. Just as important perhaps were the activities of men such as Peter Beuth (1781–1853), head of the Prussian Department of Trade and Industry, who in 1821 set up a Technical Institute in Berlin, and visited Britain in 1823 and 1836 to gather information about the new industrial techniques and machines. More significant still was the lead taken by Prussia in dismantling onerous tariff barriers, first through a reform passed in 1818 and then through the German Customs Union founded in 1834, soon to be joined by South German states such as Baden, though not by Austria. The Customs Union brought together a range of earlier, smaller tariff agreements on the basis of a uniform import duty based on the Prussian one. A major and often neglected effect of the Customs Union was to protect German industry from British competition; in 1844, for example, it was charging an import duty on pig iron of a pound a ton.

Free trade was initially championed in Germany by the British economist John Prince-Smith (1809–74), a schoolmaster who taught in the Baltic port of Elbing and set up a Free Trade Association in Berlin in 1847. The cause made little headway before mid-century as far as Germany's relations with the rest of Europe were concerned. The breaking-down of internal tariff barriers was, however, vital for economic progress. A case in point was the river Rhine, the main artery connecting central Europe with the North Sea and the Atlantic. In the mid-eighteenth century there had been a customs barrier on average every ten miles of the length of the Rhine, which abutted on numerous different states. Free traffic all along the length of the river was actually ordained by the Congress of Vienna in 1815 but proved so fiendishly complicated to implement that it did not come into effect until 1831. Up to that point, among other things, all boats had been legally obliged to offload their cargo in Cologne and again in Mainz, and offer it for sale there. The reform of 1831 led to a temporary crisis in the two cities, as most boats and barges now just bypassed them; tonnage passing through Cologne harbour fell by a half between 1834 and 1840, in Mainz by a third between 1829 and 1832, and only slowly recovered with the coming of the railways. But in the long run the creation of free trade along the river drastically lowered costs for the goods it was used to transport.

There were other respects in which a reduction of state interference in the economy played a significant role in freeing it up for technical innovation. Surviving from the mercantilism of an earlier age, the state in Prussia for example regulated by law the number of workshops to prevent economic distress, enforcing the restriction with particular vigour in times of crisis like the late 1840s. The Prussian state of the time owned twenty coalmines, mostly in the Saar and Silesia, producing more than 20 per cent of all coal mined in the kingdom in 1850. Nationalized ironworks were producing 150,000 tons of pig iron a year at this time, and the state exercised a total monopoly over the production of salt. The Prussian Overseas Trading Corporation (known as the *Seehandlung*) owned and ran textile mills in Silesia, as well as chemical works and machine-building factories. It made loans to struggling industrial companies, but its activities in subsidizing loss-making enterprises with taxpayers' money got it into trouble. In 1845 the king ordered the Corporation not to undertake any new ventures, and in the late 1840s it was forced to start selling off most of its enterprises. Similar conditions existed in Bavaria, where the state also owned the salt mines, along with coal and iron-ore mines, the Royal Bavarian Bank, three health spas, and the largest beer cellar in the world, the Hofbräuhaus in Munich. Christian von Rother (1778–1849), head of the *Seehandlung*, roundly condemned 'the familiar cry that a civil servant cannot compare with the private citizen when it comes to running an industry successfully'. The phrase 'familiar cry', however, was a sign of the times; critics pointed out that civil servants had no interest in fostering industrial growth – Rother, for example, had declared that there was no future in railways – and liberal economists and politicians gradually brought about the withdrawal of the state and agencies such as the *Seehandlung* from direct involvement in industry, except, notably, in the railways, where strategic considerations were often more important than economic ones.

Yet despite the influence of the state in financing industrialization, determining tariffs and subsidies, constructing roads, railways and canals, and collecting and publishing economic statistics, it is important to remember that the distribution of natural resources and markets did not follow state boundaries. Rather, it determined that industrialization would take place in regions that in many cases cut across them. A case in point is the north-west European coalfield, stretching from southern Belgium and northern France across to the Ruhr in western Germany. Elsewhere industry was concentrated near coal and iron-ore deposits in the Scottish Lowlands, in north-east and north-west England, in south Wales, in east-central France, in Silesia on the borders of Prussia and Austria-Hungary, in the Saar on the German-French border, or in Liegnitz and Zwickau in Saxony. Early industrialization in Europe was no respecter of borders; it was characterized above all by the borrowing of techniques, the migration of labour, and the spread of investment and expertise from country to country. In no area of the industrial economy was this more obviously so than in the case of the railways.

RAIL, STEAM AND SPEED

Industrial growth depended not least on cheap, rapid and effective means of communication, carrying raw materials to the factories and finished goods to the markets. In the course of the eighteenth and early nineteenth centuries, major improvements had been made to Europe's roads and waterways, though their impact was uneven. Napoleon's road-building

programme had been based on the need to move troops around strategically; it was patched up in the 1820s until popular disturbances in
1832 prompted the July Monarchy to make bridges and highways usable
by troops in every kind of weather; over 800 miles of new roads of various
grades, most of them not metalled, were constructed every year in the
1830s and 1840s. In 1824 nearly 60 per cent of national roads in France
were in bad need of repair; by 1845 almost all main arteries were service-
able all the year round, though the actual size of the network of metalled
roads barely increased at all – from just under 21,000 miles in 1824 to
almost 23,600 miles in 1914.

In the Habsburg Empire the road-building budget increased from
420,000 thalers in 1821 to 3 million two decades later. Up to 15,000 workers were employed on road-construction schemes, and the network grew
from 1,965 miles in 1816 to 6,864 miles in 1846. Getting from place to
place became easier and faster as a result of these projects. A post-chaise
could cover 18 to 25 miles a day on a good road in the early nineteenth
century; a small 'diligence' could reach speeds of 9 miles an hour, reducing
the journey time from Frankfurt to Stuttgart from forty to twenty-five
hours when it was introduced in 1821. In the earlier part of the century
it was reckoned that a stagecoach could achieve about 6 miles per hour
on a good road, travelling some 50 miles a day in summer and half that
distance in autumn and winter, when roads were muddy and weather
conditions bad. A journey from Buda in Hungary to Vienna took a mere
thirty-one hours by the 1830s, where it had required two whole days
half a century before; the state road system within Hungary itself had
expanded from 435 miles in 1790 to 1,100 miles in 1848, though a carriage provided by the national transportation company, complained one
traveller in 1830, was 'dirty and uncomfortable' and resembled 'a covered
wagon of gypsies'.

Metalled roads remained an extreme rarity in the Russian Empire, which
had none before 1831, only 3,000 miles of these *chaussées* in 1850, and
just 10,000 fifty years later. In *Eugene Onegin* the poet Alexander Pushkin
described in unflattering terms a journey undertaken by road from a
country estate to Moscow by the Larin family: 'Our roads are bad.
Neglected bridges rot. At post-stations you can't get a minute's sleep for
bugs and fleas.' In summer the roads were covered in choking dust, in
autumn and spring they turned to mud and slush in which coaches frequently got stuck fast. Many Russians found travel by land easiest in
winter, when the ground was covered in a thick layer of snow and ice, and
large horse-drawn sledges took their passengers gliding along a route
marked by tall posts sticking up above the surface. Open to the elements,

the sledges exposed their passengers to strong winds and blizzards. The richer and more important the passengers, the faster the journey: Tsar Alexander I took forty-two hours to travel from St Petersburg to Moscow in the winter of 1810, while Nicholas I lowered the record to thirty-eight hours in December 1833. Most travellers would take far longer.

Beyond this system of turnpikes, highways and arterial roads, European travel was much more difficult. Carts and carriages, horses, mules, flocks of sheep and herds of cattle, and individual human beings making their way on foot, had to find their direction as best they could along unmapped and unmade trails, across fords and along causeways, or down tracks and paths that could barely be discerned in bad weather. Some of these served specialized uses, such as pilgrimage routes or drovers' trails, others connected villages to local markets, or linked mines, quarries and factories to major arteries of communication, but the overwhelming majority of trails were purely local, at most regional. Mountain passes were treacherous in all weathers, and had to be traversed on horseback or by mule, using the services of a local guide. On the plains, peasant farmers ploughed over the unmade roads, turned them to mud by driving cattle over them, and neglected to restore roads when they were washed away by floods. Fords, far more common than bridges, were impassable after it had rained. Wheeled traffic was not possible on the overwhelming majority of roads and was not seen in many areas until the dawn of the twentieth century. Farmers often carried produce to market on their backs, especially if they could not afford a mule. In 1840 a regional primary-school inspector in one part of France reported that the peasants in his district divided the local roads into three kinds: *rabid* where the horse sank to the level of its breast, *perishing* where the rider sank to his eyes, and *desperate* where horse and rider both disappeared into the morass without trace.

For the transport of bulk goods, industrial raw materials and goods for export, waterways were by far the most efficient means of communication in the first half of the century. The seventeenth and eighteenth centuries had been an age of canal-building, and this continued after 1815. Some canals were dug to link rivers, such as those joining the Rhône and the Rhine in 1832, the Marne and the Aisne, or the Saône and the Yonne. Others were constructed for specifically industrial or trading purposes, like the Oise canal, dug in 1836 in order to facilitate the transport of coal from northern French mines to Paris. Governments were active sponsors of these projects, and the Restoration authorities in France even drew up plans in 1820 for 6,200 miles of new canals, though curbs on government spending meant that only 1,900 were completed by the end of the 1840s in addition to the 1,240 already in existence. The Prussians built a network of canals around Berlin, notably the Oranienburg canal in the 1830s and the Landwehr and Louisenstadt canal in the late 1840s, enabling cheap British coal to be transported to the city. In Britain most canals had been short waterways linking collieries, quarries or iron foundries to the sea, or to the market, and they had been built mainly as industrialization was already under way.

However, steam power was rapidly revolutionizing travel and transport by river, canal and sea. Steamboats were already operating on the Clyde and the Thames in 1815, and their use – mainly for carrying passengers – quickly spread to the Continent. By the 1840s, for example, the Austrian Royal and Imperial Steamboat Company already had a fleet of 224 ships transporting over 200,000 passengers on the Danube every year, and it had extended its operations to the Black Sea. Its rivals, including the Hungarian Danube Steamship Company, the Kulpa Navigation Company, and others, covered the demand for local transportation. By the 1820s it was possible to travel by water between the Black Sea, the Caspian and the Baltic, and barges with up to 700 tons of cargo could make their way along 2,500 miles of water from Astrakhan to St Petersburg in under two months. In 1815 the first steamboat appeared on the Neva at St Petersburg, and by the 1820s steamboats could be seen on the Volga and Dnieper, but they remained uncommon until around 1900, and most barges were pulled by horses on a riverbank towpath, or indeed by teams of men (the source of the famous 'Song of the Volga Boatmen', which became popular across Europe). The great advantage of the paddle steamer was its ability to travel upstream against a river current, but this innovation was slow to come in Russia, where labour was cheap. Continuous improvements led to over 100,000 miles of navigable inland waterways in Russia by the end of the century, and the tonnage of freight carried on them increased from 6 million in 1861 to 30 million by 1900, more than half of it timber and firewood.

Short railway lines designed to serve mines and quarries, with wagons pulled by men or by horses, had been around for many centuries; what transformed them was, first, the use of iron for rails from the mid-eighteenth century onwards, and second and most important, the invention of the self-propelled steam-powered locomotive, devised in the early nineteenth century by Richard Trevithick (1771–1833) and made fully viable by George Stephenson (1781–1848) and his son Robert (1803–59). In September 1830 the Liverpool and Manchester line was opened in a ceremony attended by the Duke of Wellington and 'immense crowds' of people who 'lined almost every inch of the road, and flags and banners, booths and scaffoldings, and gorgeous tents', according to a contemporary newspaper report. Once the 30-mile Liverpool to Manchester line was in operation – carrying not only large quantities of raw cotton and coal but also half a million passengers in its first year – it was soon followed by others. Within twenty years there were 7,000 miles of railway line extending across many parts of the British mainland. Railway companies earned huge profits and fuelled speculation. At the height of the British railway mania, in 1847, no fewer than a quarter of a million men were engaged in railway construction, and the demand for iron rails, steam engines, rolling stock, signals and other equipment took up 33 per cent of brick production and 18 per cent of iron production. Railways consumed all these things voraciously, along with gravel for the permanent way and coal for the engines. Soon their profitability was exerting an appeal for investors on the Continent as well, where horse-railways were already in existence but steam technology was as yet unused. Indeed the Austrians actually boasted the world's longest horse-railway, begun in 1825 and eventually covering 90 miles from Linz to Budweis; it kept going up to the mid-1850s, with over a thousand light, wooden-wheeled trucks and ninety-six passenger cars, carrying nearly 200,000 people a year and travelling an average of 40 miles in a day through the period of its operation. But the future, as was apparent well before the last horse-drawn train made its way from Budweis to Linz in December 1872, lay with steam.

Perhaps unexpectedly, steam railways, originally designed to carry goods, turned out to be immensely profitable because of their passenger traffic, and soon they were spreading not only across Britain but to the Continent as well. The first French railway was opened at Saint-Étienne in 1828 to carry coal, but when the horses that pulled the wagons were replaced with steam locomotives four years later and the line was extended to Lyon, the railway began to attract passengers, who travelled on double-decker trains, with the more expensive seats on the lower deck protected at least to some degree against inclement weather. In 1835 the first line was opened in Belgium, and another in Bavaria, with the Russians opening a short line from St Petersburg to the royal palace at Tsarskoe Seloe in 1837, and the Netherlands following in 1839. In 1847 it was the turn of Denmark and Switzerland. In Italy the first two railways, from Naples to Portici and Milan to Monza, were opened in 1839–40, in each case to connect the king's palace with the capital city. Railway development in Italy was slow before unification, with fewer than 1,100 miles built by the end of the 1850s, though it was later boosted by politicians in the more prosperous parts of the north, especially Piedmont, who clearly saw its economic advantages. Railway construction was held up in part by opposition from Pope Gregory XVI (1765–1846), an inveterate enemy of modern technology who had also blocked the introduction of gas lighting on the streets of Rome. After his death, the city's inhabitants joked that when he complained to St Peter on the way to the Pearly Gates that his legs were getting tired, and asked how far he had to go, St Peter told him: 'If only you had built a railway, you would be in paradise by now!'

When George Stephenson visited Spain in 1845 to investigate the potential for building railways there, he commented gloomily: 'I have been a whole month in the country, but I have not seen during the whole of that time enough people of the right sort to fill a single train.' Only 283 miles of track had been laid by 1855. In areas lacking in resources and low in population density, railways came even later: the first lines were not opened in Norway until 1854, Sweden in 1856 and Finland in 1862. Romania and Greece opened their first lines in 1869, leaving only Albania without railways. This was partly because railway construction required heavy initial investment. Private capital was available in Britain because industrialization was already in progress and the need was to provide cheap and quick means of transport for industrial goods and raw materials. But on the Continent railway-building preceded industrialization, and so either the investment had to come from the British or it had to be provided by the state.

In Belgium the government regarded the railways as a means of unifying the newly created country as well as assisting industrialization. So it issued government bonds to finance construction. King Leopold I also sought to use the railway network to provide an alternative means of importing goods to the country's main waterways, all of which went through potentially hostile territory, namely the Netherlands. The first lines, approved in 1834, linked Antwerp, Brussels and Mons with Aachen and Cologne, and Ostend with Liège. This meant that Belgian trade could either bypass the Rhine completely or avoid the Dutch part of it and so make it impossible for the Dutch to impose a blockade in the event of a dispute. German states also saw railways as a way of expressing their statehood, centring the network on their respective capital cities and ignoring links with the outside world; in the Grand Duchy of Baden, indeed, the state-built and state-run railways operated on a broad gauge and only converted it to standard gauge in 1853. Even with state investment, the costs of building networks far exceeded the capacity of most states to finance them, so the majority of railways, particularly those in France, were financed from Britain. Many of the Belgian government railway bonds, for example, were bought up by British investors. Even so, the scale of the national financial investment required for railway construction was staggering. By mid-century the French were investing more than 13 per cent of their gross domestic capital formation in railways, while the railway shares issued in Prussia from 1845 to 1849 amounted to the equivalent of a third of the national budget each year. This had become, in other words, the leading sector of the economy. Speculators like George Hudson (1800–71) in Britain put huge sums of other people's money into railway projects, many of which turned out to exist on paper only; he was disgraced after he was found to have defrauded investors and bribed Members of Parliament. Yet Hudson soon found his counterparts in other countries, notably Bethel Henry Strousberg (1823–84), whose dizzying speculations in Germany were founded on a similarly shaky basis and brought many investors to ruin when his schemes eventually crashed. And just as the British initially supplied much of the capital, so they also initially supplied the rails, the wagons, the locomotives and the equipment. In 1841 only one of the fifty-one locomotives used in Prussia was not British, and it did not work.

The personnel were usually also British. The Paris-Rouen line was not only financed and run by the British, but it used locomotives built at a local workshop staffed entirely by British workmen. The Leipzig to Dresden line was constructed, perhaps unusually, with native capital raised in Saxony in 1835, but a Scottish engineer, James Walker (1781–1862), who had worked on the Liverpool to Manchester line, was brought in to survey the route, the first sixteen locomotives were shipped over from Britain in boxes and assembled by British engineers, drivers and mechanics, and on the first journey the train was driven by a British engine-driver. The coaches were designed by Thomas Worsdell (1788–1862), tempted over from his position in the Liverpool and Manchester Railway. Belgian railways too were built with British expertise; George Stephenson produced the first locomotives, travelled incognito on the first train with the king and his advisers, repaired the engine when it broke down, and was knighted by the monarch for his services. This pattern was entirely typical of early railway construction on the European Continent, so it was not surprising that most states adopted the British standard gauge of 4 foot 8½ inches for their lines; apart from Baden, only Spain, with a 5 foot 6 inch gauge, and Russia, where an American engineer called in to advise on railway construction recommended a 5 foot gauge, went down a different route, thus making it impossible for trains to come through from other countries and storing up considerable problems for the future.

While local labourers were often used – the first Russian railways were largely constructed by serfs – British labourers predominated here too in most parts of Europe in the early years. The railways everywhere were built by gangs of 'navvies' – short for 'navigators' – casual manual labourers who lived at the railhead or lodged in nearby villages if there were any, and stayed on the job until the line was finished. They built embankments and carved out cuttings, blasted tunnels, threw up bridges, and laid thousands of miles of permanent way, all by hand. Accidents were common, explosions went off prematurely, embankments and tunnels collapsed, wagons broke loose and crushed navvies to death; there was no health and safety legislation to protect their lives and prevent them from being injured. Matters were made worse by the fact that they were often drunk; gangmasters were paid a commission by brewers to supply beer to their men, and even one British contractor who refused to allow the sale of beer at the workings conceded that 'a man has a right to bring a gallon with him if he likes in the morning'. Fatalities were frequent. More than a hundred men were killed during the construction of the Box Hill tunnel on the Great Western Line from London to Bristol between 1836 and 1841. At Ashton-under-Lyne in 1845 a nine-arch viaduct collapsed, burying the men working on it under the rubble; a crowd estimated at 20,000 gathered to watch the rescue operation, and troops were called to hold them back. Fifteen men were killed, and only two were brought out alive; an inspector's report concluded that poor workmanship had caused the disaster. Such accidents were often preventable, and they multiplied as railway-building spread across Europe.

The railway navvies were hired in enormous numbers; in 1845 there were said to be 200,000 working on around 3,000 miles of new railway lines in Britain, and at any one site several hundreds would be toiling away, if not thousands. Often the railway-builders paid scant attention to the ownership of the land on which they built the permanent way. 'In some cases,' wrote one commentator, 'large bodies of navvies were collected for the defence of the surveyors [against local landowners]; and being liberally provided with liquor, and paid well for the task, they intimidated the rightful owners.' A minority of the navvies were Irish, and violent clashes with the resentful local English workers were not uncommon, sometimes involving hundreds of men on either side. Five thousand British navvies worked on the Paris-Rouen railway in the early 1840s, shipped over by an entrepreneur from Southampton; in Rouen they spent liberally on drink, and, after every pay day, construction had to stop for three days until the navvies had been collected from the bars and cabarets and sobered up. This made them popular with the local bar-owners though not with their employers. A British engineer, Robert Rawlinson (1810–98), said that 'they labour like degraded brutes; they feed and lodge like savages; they are enveloped in vice as with an atmosphere'. In 1842, when a large part of the city of Hamburg burned to the ground, some of the inhabitants blamed the British and Irish navvies working on the construction of a nearby railway line, there were protest meetings and riots, and Englishmen were attacked in the streets.

From their earliest days, the railways were known above all for the speed with which they conveyed passengers and goods from one place to another. George Stephenson called his first locomotive *Rocket*, while the two engines that pulled trains on the first German steam railway, from Nuremberg to Fürth, were called the *Eagle* and the *Arrow*. Travelling by train at night in the late 1830s, Thomas Carlyle (1795–1881) thought it the 'likest thing to a Faust's flight on the Devil's mantle; or as if some huge steam night-bird had flung you on its back, and was sweeping through some unknown space with you'. In 1840, taking his first train trip, the future historian Jacob Burckhardt (1818–97), then a student in Berlin, noted with astonishment that the 'train . . . glides in 33 or 35 minutes to five-hours' distant Potsdam . . . It really flies there like a bird.' In 1844 the painter J. M. W. Turner (1775–1851) tried to capture these novel sensations in his *Rain, Steam and Speed: The Great Western Railway*. 'These steam-train journeys,' noted the poet Joseph von Eichendorff (1788–1857) in 1850, 'tirelessly shake up the world, which actually only now consists of railway stations, like a kaleidoscope, in which the passing landscape continually takes on new shapes.'

As railway traffic increased, the inevitable accidents began to occur. The first actually happened at the opening of the Liverpool to Manchester railway in September 1830, when the President of the Board of Trade, William Huskisson (1770–1830), was run over by Stephenson's *Rocket*, coming up slowly and silently behind him to take on water as he conversed with the railway's promoters. As a newspaper report sagely noted, since 'no engine can move off the rail, any person who stands clear of it, is perfectly safe from danger. Unfortunately,' the paper continued, 'in the hurry and agitation of the moment, Mr. Huskisson did not pursue this advice.' Instead, he ran *along* the track, and then when he tried to climb into a carriage on an adjacent rail, was knocked back into the path of the oncoming locomotive by a swinging door and was run over, 'uttering a shriek of agony, which none who heard it will ever forget'. He died in hospital shortly afterwards. In May 1842 newspapers across Europe carried lengthy reports of a crash on the Paris-St Germain line in which fifty people were killed and more than a hundred injured: a long train of eighteen carriages pulled by two engines came to grief when the axle of the first locomotive snapped, causing it to derail; the second engine, still going at full speed, smashed into it, causing it to burst into flames, and as the whole train went off the line, the fire spread to the carriages, which had just been painted. The doors were locked on the outside, and, as a newspaper correspondent reported, 'the flames were 30 yards high, and as a smart wind was blowing, the wagons and their living contents were instantly consumed, amidst heart-rending screams for aid'.

And yet, 'the safest place in which a man could put himself,' declared the British politician John Bright (1811–89), 'was inside a first-class railroad carriage of a train in full motion'. First-class carriages had buffers, padded seats and stout wooden frames holding up the roof, and would have been a better protection for their passengers in such a situation. Travelling third-class in the early 1840s was not a pleasant experience. 'I took a train to Rochdale,' reported one early traveller. 'We were put into a truck worse and more exposed than cattle trucks. There were seats, or forms to sit on, but they were swimming with rain.' In 1844 an Act of Parliament required all railway carriages to offer protection from the weather, an example quickly followed on the Continent. This encouraged many more people to travel by train. However, the major economic effect of the railways was achieved through the transportation of bulk goods. By carrying large quantities of goods over longer distances at faster speeds, the railway reduced costs sharply. According to one estimate, one ton of goods cost an average of 64 pfennigs a mile to transport by road in Germany in 1800, falling to 43 pfennigs in 1875, but in 1850 the cost of transporting it by rail was a mere 16 pfennigs per mile. Lower transport costs boosted the production of heavy and bulk industrial goods, providing further income for the railways and an incentive to build new lines. Continental countries soon stopped importing railway-building materials and began using their own, further stimulating production. After buying 51 British-made locomotives up to 1841, the Prussian railways bought another 124 engines in 1842–5, but 40 per cent of these were German-made, and by the 1850s almost all of the new railway engines were built in Germany. In France 88 out of 146 locomotives at work in 1842 were British, but by 1854 the French were already producing 500 a year. The largest ironworks on the Continent, in Belgium, was producing 30,000 tons of rails a year by the mid-1840s.

This was a classic case of industrial substitution, and it further advanced industrialization on the Continent as well as stimulating demand for local labour. In Germany most of the 178,500 men working on the lines in 1846 were not British but German. Once the initial lines had been constructed, the same development occurred elsewhere. The full impact was to be felt in the decades after the middle of the century, but already by the late 1840s railways and railway-building were beginning to transform

European economies and societies. The German firm of Krupp really got under way in the 1840s, when it began to supply axles and crankshafts for railway engines and rails for them to run on. A few years later his business had expanded so fast that Krupp's ambitions had become global in scale: his ultimate vision encompassed the supply of railway equipment to the whole world, with railway lines 'linking and crossing the great continents of Africa, America and Asia so that they will come to the status of civilized countries and with connecting and branch lines will keep industry busy until the end of the world – as long as some windbag does not destroy this expectation by developing air transport'.

Railways made communication faster and easier, carrying letters, documents and other vehicles of information speedily from place to place. So too did the aerial telegraph, using stations equipped with semaphore signals and carrying messages by visual contact. Systems were reported working in Prussia in 1832, Austria in 1835 and Russia in 1839. The French system played a role in *The Count of Monte Cristo* (1844), by Alexandre Dumas (1802–70), as the count altered signals to cause a financial disaster in Paris. But the semaphore was only visible a third of the time because of the weather and the night, and the cost of operating it was considerable – £3,300 a year in the case of the London to Portsmouth line around mid-century, for example. Electromagnetic telegraphs began to replace them after the American Samuel Morse (1791–1872) patented the first fully functioning one in 1837. It only required a single wire, and was cheap to operate. In 1846 the Electric Telegraph Company was established to begin its commercial exploitation. Many people were mystified by its operation, 'Some,' it was reported, 'firmly believe that the paper on which the message is written actually passes through the interior of the wire itself.' Morse's code of long and short impulses initially had to compete with a variety of other codes, but in due course it became standard. By 1850 there were 620 miles of telegraph wires in France, with a further 899 under construction. Where they were above ground, they were mostly suspended from telegraph poles placed alongside railway lines for convenience.

The Prussians preferred to coat the wires in gutta-percha and bury them underground: 2,468 miles of wires were set up in this way, out of a total of 4,000 altogether. Later on, lead tubing was used, as a more solid and reliable casing. Governments were seriously worried about the subversive potential of telegraph communication, and in France and Prussia all despatches had to be submitted to government agents at the stations before being transmitted. Private individuals were not allowed to send messages themselves anywhere. By 1850 it was being reported that 'Calais may send news to the city of the Magyar in the Danube; and ere long intelligence will be flashed without interruption from St Petersburg to the Pyrenees.' Such novel means of communication began the process whereby ideas and information could spread quickly across the Continent, encouraging the formation of new political movements and a new political consciousness that transcended boundaries. This was a vital development that was to provide an essential communicative basis for the revolutionary outbreaks of 1848, which would not have occurred in so many countries virtually simultaneously without it.

THE MAKING OF THE EUROPEAN
WORKING CLASS

Before the coming of industrial manufacture, the production of goods such as cutlery, textiles, furniture, pottery, wine and beer and the like was regulated across much of Europe by guilds, formally incorporated institutions that aimed to maintain high standards of production and ensure a decent living for all the workers in the trade by limiting the amount produced. Over the centuries guilds had come to exert an enormous influence over the affairs of many towns and cities in Europe, which often depended heavily on their reputation for producing high-quality goods for sale on the market. Guildsmen frequently had seats on town councils, and were able to use their influence to punish anyone who tried to ply their trade without being a member. These restrictions were made easier by the fact that many if not most European towns still had outer walls in 1815, required guildsmen to live within them, and closed the town gates at dusk, obliging strangers to depart unless they had legitimate business in the town extending over more than one day. Guildsmen had a large range of ceremonies and 'mysteries' with which they cemented their corporate identity; frequently they wore a particular kind of clothing, amounting almost to a uniform, that could distinguish a mason from a carpenter, a draper from a haberdasher. The guilds formed strong bonds between their members, which frequently provided a basis for collective action. Among their services were pensions for widows and orphans. By training up and promoting young men in the business, guilds ensured that everyone earned a living and would eventually be well enough off to get married and found a family (something the guild rules did not permit for those below the rank of master).

The guilds were controlled by master craftsmen, tried and tested in their skills, and these in turn employed young apprentices to whom they taught the basics of their trade. When he had satisfied the master that he could make a good-quality product, the apprentice was given a letter or certificate from his guild that advanced him to the grade of journeyman, in which he was obliged to travel for up to three years, seeking work from masters in other towns and gaining as wide a range of technical experience as he could. Finally, the journeyman would be obliged to produce a 'masterpiece', a complicated product demanding advanced skills in his trade. He would then be admitted as a master providing his masterpiece satisfied the demanding standards set by the guild. While they may have ensured that high standards were maintained, however, the guilds' ingrained respect for tradition meant that they had no interest in pioneering new methods, least of all if these pointed towards producing for a mass market. By keeping out interlopers they prevented the development of free trade and free enterprise.

In 1853, Otto von Bismarck enumerated the disadvantages of the guilds in Frankfurt, where he was based as Prussian envoy to the German Confederation: 'excessive prices for manufactured articles, indifference to customers and therefore careless workmanship, long delays in orders, late beginning, early stopping, and protracted lunch hours when work is done at home, little choice in ready-made wares, backwardness in technical training, and many other deficiencies'. Conservative though he was, even Bismarck did not fail to recognize that things had to change. Not surprisingly, already in eighteenth-century England the guilds had largely ceased to have any real influence, and absolutist regimes on the Continent had launched a determined campaign to reduce their privileges. The decisive blow had come with the French Revolution, when guilds had been formally abolished in France. The influential textile guilds of Flanders had been destroyed when the French invaded, as they had also been in western Germany. Reforming administrations in Germany abolished guild privileges and gave everyone the freedom to choose their own trade without any restrictions, unless they required a very high level of expert knowledge (such as was needed for apothecaries, for instance). Guilds continued in existence after 1815, even in France, but in most parts of Europe they entered the post-Napoleonic world in a severely weakened condition.

Even where economic growth was slow and the market in industrial goods arrived relatively late, as in Sardinia or Sicily, the growing financial problems of guild members – here, as in some other parts of southern Europe, responsible for putting on elaborate and expensive religious festivals and processions – led state officials to allow craftsmen exemption from membership in 1841. The involvement of guilds in the uprising of 1821 in Palermo led to their abolition by the Crown the following year, but, as in Naples, where the same measures were implemented, associations such as friendly societies and co-operatives continued to organize artisanal workers long afterwards, both reflecting and perpetuating the weakness of market competition. In Spain the government abolished the privileges of the guilds in 1831 and introduced complete freedom of enterprise three years later. They collapsed rapidly – the Holy Thursday procession in Gerona was cancelled in 1836 because the guilds could not afford to take part, and those in Seville were described as being in a state of 'general calamity' around the same time. Not only legislative but also economic developments further undermined their influence. Guilds routinely expelled any member found working in a factory, but as factory production gathered pace after the coming of peace in 1815, the guilds were increasingly bypassed by the new methods. They showered governments and legislative assemblies with petitions complaining about declining standards of workmanship and the effects of increased competition from new centres of production. In Bavaria guildsmen complained that a law of 1825 had created 'an increase in destitution and complete impoverishment, which are in turn further aggravated by the creation of new master artisans which the industrial law facilitates'.

But none of this could stop the onward march of mass industrial production. In 1826 there were no non-guild master plasterers in Berlin at all; by 1845 they made up 65 per cent of masters in the trade. Non-guild master bakers increased from 5 per cent to 19 per cent in Berlin over the same period, non-guild master shoemakers from 35 per cent to 82 per cent. Only in luxury goods did guilds retain any influence. 'Free' craftsmen in the villages and the countryside, far away from guild controls in the town, were able to use new methods, and already in 1816 some 75 per cent of masters and journeymen in Bavaria were located in the countryside. In areas like textiles and the production of finished iron and steel goods, masters and guildsmen either had to lower their prices to compete, or abandon their old methods and embrace the new technology of mass production. The crisis of the guilds was expressed in the breakdown of the promotion system. In 1816 there were 259,000 masters and 145,000 journeymen and apprentices in Prussia; by 1846 their numbers had increased to 457,000 and 385,000 respectively, signifying the growing difficulty of journeymen and apprentices in obtaining a mastership. This, not the peasantry or the landless labourer class, was the reservoir of labour that early industrialization tapped.

The more the numbers of guild artisans grew, the poorer they became, and the more the primary purpose of the guilds, to ensure a decent living for all their members, was undermined. By 1840 three-quarters of all master artisans in Berlin had an income so low that they were no longer charged even the basic rate of business tax. The situation of journeymen was even worse. Brockhaus's encyclopedia of 1839 confessed: 'The journeyman is also regarded by the master only as his wage-labourer, and the master is only interested in him insofar as he wants to earn money with his labour.' The Prussian authorities responded in 1845 by extending the freedom of production first introduced in 1810, but implemented unevenly, across the whole state. Some trades disappeared entirely through changes in fashion (the wigmakers' guild was a prime example) while others were decisively undercut by factory production, such as furniture-makers. Some were able to make the transition: locksmiths, for example, found a new source of income in the machine-tool industry. A very small number succeeded in building an expanding business, but only by flouting the guild rules and becoming industrial producers themselves. For the vast majority, the choices were becoming increasingly stark: become a pauper and subsist off poor relief, or join the swelling ranks of the new factory proletariat.

The artisans, however, did not give up without a fight. If the guilds were increasingly ineffective, then there were other institutions they could use to articulate their interests. In France apprentices and journeymen had long been involved in the *compagnonnage*, a system of secret societies with initiation rites, passwords and the like, through which they sought to ease their journeymen years on the *tour de France* by providing work and accommodation, and put pressure on masters to provide a living wage. When they left the *compagnonnage* artisans frequently set up friendly societies into which they paid money to support themselves and other members in their old age, or if they were unemployed. It was estimated that around 100,000 young workers passed through the *compagnonnage* every three years in the 1830s. But while the institution possessed some of the attributes of a trade union, it was riven by internal disputes, often based on petty rivalries and struggles over status. Blacksmiths agreed to admit wheelwrights to their *compagnonnage* on condition they wore their ribbons in their bottom buttonhole, but the wheelwrights insisted on wearing them in a buttonhole as high as that of the blacksmiths. Farriers refused to admit harness-makers at all. If two groups of journeymen encountered each other on the road, they would shout the ritual greeting 'Tope!' after which they would ask each other's trade; if it was the same, they would share a drink; if not, and one journeyman considered himself to be of superior status, he would demand that the other give way. Fights would often ensue, and be continued in revenge attacks in town. Serious injuries and sometimes deaths were the result. The institution was already in decline in the 1830s, as a new generation of workers entered their trade with a sceptical attitude towards tradition. Apprentices rebelled against the tyranny of the journeymen, while the journeymen themselves began to abandon the *tour de France* as railways robbed it of its excitement and industrialization undermined what was left of the guilds. An attempt was to be made to unite the rival groups in 1848, but it came to nothing, and the *compagnonnages* were unable to represent workers effectively in the dawning industrial age.

The future lay with trade unions. But these existed only in Great Britain, and even here their development was severely curtailed by the Combination Laws, originally designed to combat Jacobinism during the years of conflict with Revolutionary France. Already before this, organized strikes for higher wages and better working conditions had occurred from time to time, above all in the cotton-spinning industry, but they had frequently been suppressed and their leaders imprisoned. A fresh wave of strikes that broke out after the repeal of the Combination Laws in 1824 (when post-war unrest had subsided) prompted the founding of a number of trade unions to represent the workers' collective interests, but all proved short-lived. Frustrated by their inability to convey their demands effectively, Lancashire cotton handloom weavers engaged in attacks on power looms in the mid-1820s, continuing a machine-breaking movement supposedly led by the mythical 'King Ludd' during the Napoleonic Wars. Machine-breaking was restricted to small towns where there were few opportunities for alternative employment. A period of high inflation led to numerous strikes for higher wages, and in 1825 new Combination Laws were passed, but at least they legalized trade unions, despite placing severe restrictions on their activities. Local unions began to form, but like the guilds on the Continent, they frequently aimed above all to restrict the influx of new workers into their trade. Many, too, used quasi-Masonic titles, rituals, regalia and language to underscore their links with older traditions, but they were soon bypassed by more modern organizations.

The law in Britain still discriminated heavily against workers' unions, and when in 1834 a group of farmhands in Tolpuddle, near Dorchester, formed a Friendly Society and went on strike to stop employers lowering wages as a general economic depression began to deepen, they were prosecuted under a 1797 Act forbidding seditious oaths, and sentenced to transportation to Australia. A national outcry followed and the 'Tolpuddle Martyrs' were allowed to return home after the remittance of their sentences in 1836. Trade unions only emerged on a wider, more permanent basis among highly skilled workers whose withdrawal of labour could prove damaging to employers. Rivalries between different trades that had limited the prospects of collective action in the 1820s were overcome at the start of the next decade with the formation of the nationwide Amalgamated Society of Engineers, Machinists, Millwrights and Patternmakers, which levied a high subscription (a shilling a week) and aimed to provide sickness, unemployment, retirement and burial benefits. It survived an unsuccessful strike and lasted through the following decade, though its membership of 12,000 in 1831 was not always sustained. Most unions were highly regionalized, and where they were able to form a national association, this often failed to endure, as with the National Typographical Association, founded in 1844, which split into three regional bodies four years later because the London printers felt they were subsidizing their northern comrades and gaining little in return. During a long economic downturn that lasted until mid-century, trade unions were defeated in labour disputes time and again as employers forced lower wages on their members, leading to the rapid disintegration of national associations like the Grand General Union of Cotton Spinners or the National Association for the Protection of Labour.

A typical example of the difficulties of securing effective worker representation may be seen in the case of the Miners' Association of Great Britain and Ireland, formed by an alliance of coalminers in Durham and Yorkshire in 1842–3. By 1844 it had 70,000 members, or 30 per cent of all miners in the region, along with a general secretary, a national executive and a newspaper. Its clearly stated aim was to keep prices and wages from falling by restricting output. In that year the inevitable strike was quickly defeated when the employers brought in substitute labour and sacked the leading activists. By 1848 the union had collapsed. Strikes and labour actions were confined to local or at most regional disputes. A politically driven attempt to form a Grand National Consolidated Trade Union in 1833–4 had done nothing except hold a much-publicized Congress before it too broke up in disarray. The lesson that increasing numbers of leading trade unionists drew from all this was that trade unionism and the improvement of the workers' bargaining power stood little chance of success without political action.

Although union activism could potentially lead to political activism in the United Kingdom, police repression and the relative backwardness of the industrial economy ensured that this was far more difficult for workers on the Continent. In France a Combination Law passed in 1834 made any association of more than five people potentially illegal. The 1830s and 1840s witnessed a growing crescendo of protest across those parts of Europe most affected by the penetration of the market in industrial goods and the calamitous effects on the life of the urban artisan of harvest failures and the potato famine, which forced up food prices and left people with little money with which to purchase finished goods, thus severely reducing demand. Everywhere, protests were led by skilled and literate artisans, using their traditions of solidarity and mutuality to articulate demands that could not be satisfied by the political system. Industrial strikes certainly took place but they were confined to a relatively small number of factories and addressed immediate practical issues such as wage cuts. During industrial depressions, fear of unemployment kept workers quiet; in Rouen sackings for insubordination fell by 75 per cent during the depression of 1845–6. More than a third of the textile employees in the town were women, and a fifth were children; they lacked the tradition of activism common among male artisans. Strikes among miners, predominantly men, were more common, and were mounted in Anzin in the Nord department in 1834 and 1846 for higher wages, but during these decades worker protest was articulated above all by the artisans and guildsmen.

The majority of protests were backward-looking in nature, aiming to establish a 'fair price' or 'fair wages' for the workers' products, and above all a 'just price' for food. Riots and public protests centred on bread-and-butter issues; guildsmen tried to protect their rights and privileges, and crowds of men, women and children articulated demands for a ceiling on food prices. There were an estimated 186 examples of machine-breaking and attacks on power looms in the German Confederation between 1816 and 1848. This was not an attempt to stop the march of technological progress so much as a drastic form of bargaining for better wages. After the largest outbreak of wrecking in Bohemia, in 1844, the workers marched on Prague to ask for help, only to be met with a hail of bullets from the police and the military. Yet protest of this kind, for all the notoriety of 'King Ludd' in England, was unusual. A study of 'social protest' in north German towns between 1815 and 1848 has estimated that forty-one incidents of violent collective action arose from economic issues, sixty-three from clashes with authority, nineteen from quarrels between guilds, and thirty-five from struggles over political rights. In the south German state of Baden over the same period, research has uncovered over a hundred violent collective protests, seventy-five of them directed at trying to protect the privileged status of guildsmen. Protest expressed not the despair of uprooted landless labourers or a new urban underclass, but the community spirit of specific groups of craft workers or villagers attacking outsiders whom they blamed for their plight, whether bailiffs, merchants, gamekeepers, foreigners or, as in Germany, Jews. Harsh actions by the police could sometimes spark violent incidents, as in Cologne in 1846 when several young people were arrested for letting off fireworks during a religious festival and rioted in protest.

Yet such actions were also beginning to express the new consciousness of the nascent working class. A particularly significant uprising took place in Silesia in 1844. Here the handloom weavers, originally independent craftsmen, had declined in both status and income as the merchants who supplied them with the yarn and bought their cloth were forced to reduce their prices in the face of competition from the power-loom industry. On 4 June a crowd stormed the opulent residence of the Zwanziger family, merchants who had refused the weavers' demand for increased compensation for their labour. Troops were sent in and shot eleven of the protesters, arousing denunciations from appalled journalists and writers across Germany. The incident was characteristic of the transitional nature of protest in this period of working-class formation. On the one hand, it was an attempt to secure higher wages, not a bid to restore guild privileges. On the other, the workers, though acting as workers, directed their ire against particular individuals and did not seek to generalize it. Contemporary commentators reacted with dire warnings about the emergence of a new class, the proletariat, 'a large class [that] can subsist only as the result of the most intensive labour', as Brockhaus's encyclopedia put it in 1846. In English and French the terms 'worker' and 'working class' gradually came into use to describe the poor single master, the factory worker, the miner and the urban wage labourer, indeed all those who lacked property and were forced to live entirely off their own physical labour and that of their families. The differences between guildsmen and wage labourers were being eroded, and a new social class was being born. In some areas and trades, indeed, there were signs of the formation of a hereditary working class. 'Our peculiar race of pitmen,' said the mining engineer John Buddle (1773–1843) in 1842, ' . . . can only be kept up by *breeding* – it never could be recruited from an *adult population*.' The process of creating a hereditary proletariat in this and in other parts of the new industrial world had not gone very far by the middle of the century, but it was clearly under way.

MAPPING THE 'SOCIAL QUESTION'

'A new epoch of world history is beginning,' noted the poet Heinrich Heine on the occasion of the opening of the railway line from Orléans to Paris in 1843, 'and our generation can be proud to say it was there.' Not everyone saw things in such a positive light. By this time, thinking Europeans were aware that society was beginning to change with unprecedented rapidity. The conservative German writer Wilhelm Heinrich Riehl (1823–97) complained of a 'confusion of concepts', in which 'new things emerge daily, and with them new words, and if a new word can't be found right away, then an old one changes its meaning'. Already in 1835 another German writer, the jurist Robert von Mohl (1799–1875), was warning of the potential social damage that industrialization could cause. The factory worker, unlike the apprentice, he said, could never hope for advancement; he was destined to remain 'a serf, chained . . . to his wheel', 'like the machinery' he operated, 'that belongs to a third party'. His desperate situation created 'every sort of immorality', especially when men were taken from home and family. Voluntary associations were the cure, von Mohl advised, especially those devoted to improving the educational standards of the working class.

The 'social question' of the era was dramatized in a number of 'social novels', of which one of the most influential was *Sybil: Or the Two Nations*, published in 1845 by the Tory politician and future British Prime Minister Benjamin Disraeli. Like many other observers, Disraeli was shocked by the living conditions of the new industrial poor, who inhabited 'wretched tenements . . . with the water streaming down the walls, the light distinguished through the roof, with no hearth even in winter', fronted by 'open drains full of animal and vegetable refuse' or 'spreading into stagnant pools'. Lamenting the death of traditional paternalistic relations between the classes, Disraeli saw British society disintegrating into 'two nations; between whom there is no intercourse and no sympathy . . . THE RICH AND THE POOR'. An irresponsible, self-aggrandizing aristocracy confronted an exploited people led by agitators with 'wild ambitions and sinister and selfish ends', and at the climax of the novel the alienation between the classes breaks out into open violence and the destruction of property. Social criticism permeated the popular novels of Charles Dickens, most notably *Oliver Twist*, with its portrayal of the neglected pauper boy drifting into the sinister London criminal underworld, while the German novelist Ernst Willkomm (1810–86) entitled his novel about factory workers, published in 1845, *White Slaves*, underlining the power of anti-slavery rhetoric to stimulate radical ideas. In 1843, Bettina von Arnim (1785–1859), who was active in literary and cultural circles, published *This Book Belongs to the King*, passionately pleading with the Prussian monarch to establish a 'social monarchy' dedicated to overcoming the social crisis that threatened to overwhelm the country. It exerted a widespread influence and fuelled an impassioned debate about the growing pattern of 'pauperism'.

In the first half of the century, the most popular of all the books written about poverty was, however, not an earnest social tract, but *The Mysteries of Paris*. It was written by Eugène Sue (1804–57), who served as a military surgeon in the French invasion of Spain in 1823, and was present at the Battle of Navarino in 1827 during the Greek War of Independence. Sue wrote Romantic, sensationalist stories with subjects featuring pirates and bandits, and in his novel *Mathilde* (1841) coined the saying 'revenge is a dish best served cold'. Serialized in ninety parts during 1842–3, *The Mysteries of Paris* featured a Parisian worker, a prostitute, a doctor, a freed black slave, and many other figures from the common people. The worker was of course a German nobleman in disguise, one of many 'mysteries' that permeated the story; the novel pilloried the indifference of the upper classes to the plight of the workers. The book found imitators across Europe, notably *The Mysteries of London* by George Reynolds (1814–79), a 'penny-dreadful' that sold 40,000 copies in instalments in 1844 and was translated into numerous European languages. It featured characters such as hump-backed dwarfs, libertine clergymen, grave-robbers and violated maidens, but expressed underneath it all a strong sympathy for the urban poor. Similarly, in *The Mysteries of Berlin*, also published in 1844, the author August Brass (1818–76) insisted that the 'mysteries' of lower-class existence in the Prussian capital were there for all to see, 'if we took the trouble to cast off the convenient veil of selfish comforts and turned our gaze outside our usual circles'.

All this literature signified a deep anxiety about the advent of a new social world whose future was freighted with conflict and danger. The social novel of the period did not, however, extend to portrayals of rural life, even though the vast majority of Europeans in every country continued to live there. Frustrated by the resistance to change they frequently encountered in the countryside, agricultural reformers often regarded the peasants as little better than animals. The peasant in Moldavia, wrote a local administrator who served in the province during the 1830s and 1840s, was 'reduced almost to the abject status of a beast, abandoned to the rapacity of all who use him'. The French novelist Léon Cladel (1834–92) called the peasants 'quadrupeds on two feet . . . Greedy, envious, hypocritical, crafty, cynical, cowardly, and brutal'. Russian literature is full of complaints about the dullness of the *muzhik*, mired in drink and superstition, hostile to any kind of agricultural improvement, stubbornly sticking to tried and tested methods of cultivation and suspicious of anything newfangled. Most nineteenth-century novelists stuck to writing about the bourgeoisie, the aristocracy and the urban poor, and ignored the peasants except as objects of schemes of improvement. Honoré de

Balzac (1799–1850) called one of his novels *Les Paysans* (*The Peasants*, written is 1844 and published in 1855), but on opening the pages it becomes clear that it is an indictment of the rural habit of gleaning or scrounging, collecting leftovers from the landlords' fields after the harvest. Yet, given the overwhelming numerical dominance of country-dwellers in nineteenth-century Europe, the behaviour of the peasantry, small farmers and landless labourers in times of political upheaval was crucial. A peasant revolt had underpinned the French Revolution of 1789, the rural uprisings that swept across Russia in 1905–7 shook the tsarist regime to its core, and an even greater rebellion of the countryside was to be a vital component of the Russian Revolution in 1917. The stance of the peasantry in the upheavals that convulsed Europe in 1848–9 would play a large part in determining the outcome of the dramatic events that brought the 'hungry forties' to an end.

3

The European Spring

VISIONS OF THE MACHINE AGE

On her visits to England during the 1830s the writer and revolutionary
Flora Tristan (1803–44) was shocked by the condition of the factory workers she encountered:

> Since I have known the English proletariat, I no longer think that slavery
> is the greatest human misfortune: the slave is *sure of his bread all his life*,
> and of care when he is sick; whereas there exists no bond between the
> worker and the English master. If the latter has no work to give out, the
> worker dies of hunger; if he is sick, he succumbs, on the straw of his pal-
> let . . . If he grows old, or is crippled as the result of an accident, he is fired,
> and he turns to begging furtively for fear of being arrested.

For women, unemployment meant a fate even more diabolical, Flora noted,
as she observed the prostitutes crowding the pavements along Waterloo
Road. 'In London,' she wrote, 'all classes are badly corrupted.' To try and
find out something of the system of government that presided over these
horrors, she shocked a Tory Member of Parliament by asking him to lend
her his clothes so she could sit in the public gallery (women were not admitted). Eventually she gained admission dressed as a young Turk; though this
fooled nobody, the custodians let her in anyway. She listened to a speech
by the Duke of Wellington ('cold, tame, drawling') but found no enlightenment. The machinery of the new factories impressed her, but she found the
damage they inflicted on human beings appalling.

Born on 7 April 1803 to a French mother and a Peruvian father who
had met in Spain, where her mother had gone 'to escape from the horrors
of the revolution', Flora Tristan led an eventful life between the old world
and the new. Her father, a landowner and friend of Simón Bolívar who
claimed to be a descendant of Montezuma, served in the Spanish Army
but died in 1807, leaving his widow and small child in serious financial

difficulties. Her mother had married him in a church ceremony, which was not recognized in France, where only civil ceremonies had legal validity, so Flora was technically illegitimate. Living in a poor part of Paris, she became a wage-labourer, colouring engravings for an artisan, André Chazal (1796–1860), who owned a workshop in Montmartre. He fell in love with her and in 1821 they married. She was seventeen, he twenty-four. The marriage was not a success. She found him boorish, uneducated and irresponsible, prone to gambling and always in debt. He thought she 'gave herself airs'. In 1825, pregnant with their third child, she left the marital home, claiming her mother had forced her into a marriage that had been nothing but 'endless torture'.

Divorce was illegal in France; as a wife, Flora was a legal minor, with no rights and no property. In 1828, Chazal agreed to a legal separation of their property. Three years later, he began to look for her with the aim of getting back his children – two boys and a girl, Aline, – over whom he had by law the sole right of guardianship. While Flora went to Peru to try and recover her family property, Chazal tracked down Aline at a boarding school and kidnapped her. He began publishing defamatory pamphlets about Flora. 'She possesses none of the virtues which bring esteem to the *daughter*, the *wife*, the *kinswoman* or the *woman of quality*,' he complained: 'For her, *family ties*, the *duties of society*, and the *principles of religion*, are useless impedimenta, from which she frees herself with an audacity which is fortunately quite rare.' Ominously, he designed a gravestone for Flora, bought a pair of pistols, and started shooting practice. He became a regular in a wine bar opposite her apartment in Paris. On 10 September 1838 he spotted her walking along the street, approached her from behind, and shot her at point-blank range. The bullet entered the left side of her body, but failed to kill her. Doctors treated her, and she recovered, though the bullet was never removed. Chazal was arrested, found guilty of attempted murder, and sentenced to twenty years' hard labour.

For Flora Tristan, the situation of a wife trapped in an unhappy marriage, like that of an operative in an English factory, was no better than that of a slave. In November 1837, in *Peregrinations of a Pariah*, she pilloried her husband, and told every woman trapped in an unhappy marriage: 'Feel the weight of the chain which makes you his slave and see if . . . you can break it!' She began to petition the Chamber of Deputies for the legalization of divorce. 'Up to now,' she wrote in 1843, 'woman has counted for nothing in human society . . . The priest, the lawmaker, and the philosopher, have treated her as a *true pariah*. Woman (half of humanity) has been excluded from the Church, from the law, from society.' Searching for ideas with which to justify her increasingly radical stance,

Flora began to read the works of the Utopian socialists, mainly French writers such as Charles Fourier (1772–1837), who since the Revolution of 1789 had been attempting to sketch the contours of the ideal society. She was not impressed with what she found. 'Many people,' she wrote in 1836, 'among whom I count myself, find the science of M. Fourier very obscure.' Utopianism also 'paralysed all action' in the workers, she thought. She was frequently assisted by the *compagnonnages* on her travels through France, and came to be regarded by them as their 'mother', but her dismay at their internal divisions and quarrels was another spur to her to create a unified workers' movement. 'Divided,' she told them, 'you are weak, and you fall, crushed underfoot by all sorts of misery! Union creates power. You have numbers in your favour, and numbers mean a great deal.'

Her critics resented the very fact that she was challenging masculine supremacy through her melodramatic pronouncements and her assertive independence. Even more shocking was her advocacy of the communal upbringing of children and her acceptance of Fourier's belief that permanent sexual relationships were contrary to human nature. Moreover, her appalling experience at the hands of her husband led her to reject relationships with men, and she took refuge in intimate friendships with other women, where power relations, she thought, would not be involved. Women, she declared, should have the vote, along with all adult men, as well as the right to work and education. The emancipation of women was closely bound up with the emancipation of the workers; both, in the end, would triumph together. She urged workers to declare the rights of woman, just as their fathers had declared the rights of man in 1791. Equal wages for equal work would follow if inequalities in power between men and women were done away with. This would only be a recognition of the fact that 'in all the trades where skill and dexterity are required, the women do almost twice as much work as the men'. Flora did not live to see her ideas put into practice. She caught typhoid on a visit to Bordeaux in 1844 and she died on 14 November, aged just forty-one. Her memory was kept alive by the workers and resurfaced in 1848. Her daughter Aline married Clovis Gauguin, a republican journalist, in 1846, but he died en route to Peru three years later. Their son Paul Gauguin (1848–1903), who stayed with Aline in Peru for seven years, supported by her family, later became an artist whose own global peregrinations perhaps owed something to his upbringing in two continents.

For the most part, Flora Tristan was right to criticize the Utopians' lack of realism. But this did not mean that they failed to think about how to translate their ideas into reality. Central to many of them was the belief that by establishing perfect human communities, they would show the way to the future, a way so rational and so harmonious that people everywhere would quickly choose to go down it. Charles Fourier, for instance, proposed in his tract *The New Industrial and Social World*, published in 1829, the foundation of what he called *phalansteries*, or phalanxes, where around 1,600 people, men, women and children, would live a communal life based on shared social facilities. An architect, statistician and man of independent means, Fourier set up a community of this kind just outside Paris in 1832, though its inhabitants quickly quarrelled among themselves and departed increasingly from the ideas of its founder. His disciples eventually established communities in the United States. Perhaps inevitably, most of them only lasted a handful of years, or were transformed into more conventional settlements based on principles far removed from those of their founder.

Similar ideas were propounded by the lawyer and journalist Étienne Cabet (1788–1856), a man of humble origins who had taken part in the 1830 Revolution and served as an oppositional deputy in the early 1830s. More determinedly egalitarian than Fourier, he envisaged in his famous *Voyage to Icaria* (1840) a community where everyone worked equally and received the same rewards, everyone would have the vote, and all property would be held in common. This was 'communism', a word he invented. The downside of his Utopian prescription was that everyone would have to obey the community's laws, and there would only be one newspaper, whose function was to express the common opinion of the community's members. The desire for liberty, he warned, was 'an error, a vice, a grave evil' born of 'violent hatred'. In 1848, despairing at ever being able to put his plans into operation in Europe, he sailed with a multinational group of followers, mostly artisans, to the United States, where they founded a number of Icarian communes. Most of them were short-lived. Their rules, which included a ban on smoking, were too strict for many of their members; even Cabet himself was expelled from one of them shortly before his death in 1856. It seemed that merely establishing Utopian communities was not enough by itself to convince humankind of their utility. Something more was needed.

One means of making an impact was developed by another group of Utopian socialists, the Saint-Simonians, founded by Claude-Henri de Rouvroy, Comte de Saint-Simon (1760–1825), who had had a career more adventurous than most: he had served under Washington at Yorktown in 1781, narrowly escaped the guillotine during the Revolution of 1789, and been incarcerated as a lunatic with the Marquis de Sade (1740–1814) at the asylum in Charenton. He continued to live a troubled life thereafter, even attempting suicide in 1823 by shooting himself. His central concern was with developing a rational form of religion in which people would obtain eternal life 'by working with all their might to ameliorate the condition of their fellows'. He attracted a number of followers, including not only *carbonari* but many highly trained, educated and talented people, particularly those associated with the coming world of industry, such as engineers, technologists, bankers and the like. Saint-Simon's secretary was Auguste Comte (1798–1857), later the founder of sociology, author of *Industry* (1816–18) and *Of the Industrial System* (1821–2). Comte too was a troubled man; he was admitted to a lunatic asylum briefly and tried to commit suicide in 1827 by jumping off a bridge into the river Seine. He was no more successful in doing away with himself than his master had been, and survived for another thirty years, following Saint-Simon in devising a new 'religion of humanity' and coining the word 'altruism'. His six-volume *Course of Positive Philosophy*, published between 1830 and 1842, was to have a major impact not only in France but in other countries too through the sociological doctrine of 'positivism'.

Saint-Simon's movement survived his death in 1825. He was succeeded as its leader by the bank cashier Prosper Enfantin (1796–1864), who had led a group of Napoleonic enthusiasts in armed resistance to the Allies as they invaded Paris in 1814 and subsequently joined the *carbonari*. Enfantin declared the improvement of 'the poorest and most numerous class' to be the will of God. But the lead in this task would be taken by scientists, engineers and industrialists. One Saint-Simonian, the former *carbonaro* and printer Pierre Leroux (1797–1871), introduced the term 'socialism' into French political vocabulary in 1834 (he also invented the word 'solidarity'). Enfantin subsequently became a director of the Paris and Lyons Railway. Many of Saint-Simon's disciples played a significant role in French industrial, economic and academic life in the 1850s and 1860s. His ideas also informed the writings of Louis Blanc (1811–82), tutor to the son of an ironmaster. In 1839, Blanc published an immensely popular book, *The Organization of Labour*, which proposed factories based on profit-sharing among the workers, financed initially by loans. Blanc rejected the hierarchical aspects of Saint-Simon's philosophy and replaced his slogan 'To each according to his works' with a new one: 'To each according to his needs'.

Among the Utopians it was above all Fourier who propounded the identity of women's emancipation and general human emancipation, a belief shared by Flora Tristan: 'The extension of privileges to women,' he wrote, 'is the general principle of all social progress.' He too compared women to slaves: marriage for them was 'conjugal slavery'. In the phalanstery, women would have fully equal rights and would be free to marry and divorce as they wished. Just as Cabet invented the word 'communism', so Fourier invented the word 'feminism'. The Saint-Simonians were equally preoccupied with women's place in society. Enfantin proclaimed 'the emancipation of women' as a central goal of a new Church that he would lead. He included in this concept, however, the 'rehabilitation of the flesh', and his advocacy of the sexual emancipation of women brought a conviction for offending public morality in 1832. Far more conventional was Cabet, who, perhaps surprisingly, thought that the main constituent unit of communist society would not be the individual but the heterosexual married couple and their children, so that shared childrearing did not come into his vision. Every woman should be educated, but the aim of her education should be to make her 'a good girl, a good sister, a good wife, a good mother, a good housekeeper, a good citizen'.

Utopian socialism was not confined to French thinkers. The Welshman Robert Owen (1771–1858), born in humble circumstances, rose to become a factory manager and assumed control of the New Lanark cotton mill in Glasgow after marrying the owner's daughter and organizing a consortium to buy him out. Owen found the workers dissolute and degraded, so he set up schools for the children and opened the first ever co-operative store, selling goods cheaply to the workers and sharing out the profits with them. New Lanark became famous as a model factory community, and led Owen to declare in 1827 that it could become the basis for the establishment of co-operatives across the industrial world. His mission was to overcome industry's 'individualization' of the human being and replace this atomized society with what he called a 'socialist' one – the first time the term had been used in English. He invested heavily in communitarian experiments in the United States, most notably 'New Harmony', which flourished briefly between 1824 and 1829. His ideas had a considerable influence among the new industrial workers in Britain. But he eventually withdrew into another obsession of the Utopians, the foundation of a new Church. Owen became the self-styled 'Social Father of the Society of Rational Religionists', before converting to Spiritualism and enjoying conversations with the shades of Benjamin Franklin and Thomas Jefferson until he too passed over to the other side, in 1858.

Owen, Fourier, Cabet and other Utopian thinkers spread their ideas to workers like the German tailor Wilhelm Weitling (1808–71), who in works such as *Humanity: As it is and as it should be* (1838) and *The Gospel of Poor Sinners* (1845) traced back communism to the doctrines of early Christianity and proposed to force it onto society by a millenarian uprising of 40,000 convicted criminals. However, few of the Utopians had roots in the artisanal world, let alone the world of the new industrial working class. When they did, like the French artisan Pierre-Joseph Proudhon (1809–65), who grew up as the son of an impoverished cooper and himself trained as a compositor, their ideas were very different from those of theorists such as Enfantin. Thrown out of work in 1830, Proudhon embarked on a career as a writer, putting forward in a long series of books and pamphlets what he called 'a people's philosophy'. In his book *What is Property?*, published in 1840, he famously answered the question posed in the title by declaring: 'Property is theft'. By this phrase, he did not intend to dismiss all private property; rather, he wanted society to own all property but to lease it all out to prevent profiteering and unfair distribution. Nevertheless, his declaration resonated across the century as a slogan for socialists, communists and anarchists alike. Proudhon was vehemently opposed to female equality. If women obtained equal political rights, he declared, men would find them 'odious and ugly', and it would bring about 'the end of the institution of marriage, the death of love and the ruin of the human race'. 'Between harlot or housewife,' he concluded, 'there is no halfway point.'

In this, as in other respects, Proudhon's ideas differed from those of most Utopian socialists. What they had in common with them, however, was a determination to deal with the new political world made by the French Revolution of 1789, and the new economic and social world in the throes of being created across Europe by the advance of industrialism. This determination was shared by some variants of Hegelianism, another, more academic tradition of radical thought in the first half of the nineteenth century. Georg Friedrich Wilhelm Hegel (1770–1831), who grew up in south-west Germany under the influence of the Enlightenment, was an admirer of the French Revolution, and of Napoleon, whom he witnessed entering Jena after winning the battle of 1806. Following a variety of teaching positions, Hegel was appointed to the Chair of Philosophy in Berlin in 1818, where he remained until his death from cholera in 1831. An atheist, he replaced the concept of God with the idea of the 'World-Spirit' of rationality, which he believed was working out its purposes through history in a process he called 'dialectical', in which one historical condition would be replaced by its antithesis, and then the two would combine to create a final synthesis. As he became more conservative, Hegel began to regard the state of Prussia after 1815 as a 'synthesis' requiring no further alteration. Not surprisingly, he was soon known as 'the Prussian state philosopher'. But his core idea of ineluctable historical progress held a considerable appeal for radicals in many parts of Europe. In Poland the art historian Józef Kremer (1806–75) propagated Hegel's ideas in his *Letters from Cracow*, the first volume of which was published in 1843. The

French philosopher Victor Cousin (1792–1867) made a pilgrimage to see Hegel in 1817. 'Hegel, tell me the truth,' he demanded: 'I shall pass on to my country as much as it can understand.' The great man, having worked his way through Cousin's *Philosophical Fragments*, was not impressed: 'M. Cousin,' he wrote scornfully, 'has taken a few fish from me, but he has well and truly drowned them in his sauce.'

In the emerging world of the intelligentsia in Russia during the 1830s and 1840s, as Alexander Herzen, author of *Who is to Blame?* (1845–6), one of the first Russian social novels, later remembered, Hegel's writings were discussed deep into the night. 'Every insignificant pamphlet . . . in which there was a mere mention of Hegel was ordered and read until it was tattered, smudged, and fell apart in a few days.' Hegel's dialectic sharpened vague perceptions of the differences between East and West and forced Russian intellectuals to take sides. The literary critic Ivan Kireyevsky (1806–56), whose religious father was so vehemently hostile to the atheism of Voltaire that he bought multiple copies of the Frenchman's books solely in order to burn them in huge piles in his garden, attended Hegel's lectures in Berlin and concluded that Russia was destined to belong to the East, founding its society on collectivism rather than individualism, and building its moral character on the doctrines of the Orthodox Church. However, Hegel's philosophy of history convinced others that Russia was on a preordained trajectory towards a liberated future by acquiring the freedoms common in the West. The young literary critic Vissarion Belinsky (1811–48) began labelling everything he thought backward in the culture and politics of his native land 'Chinese'. Herzen drew similar consequences from a reading of Hegel, but stopped short of advocating violent revolution in order to achieve them.

That step was taken by the most radical of the Russian Hegelians, Mikhail Bakunin (1814–76), who imbibed the works of the German philosopher while studying in Moscow. Bakunin was a man of violent, volcanic temperament, described by his friend Belinsky as 'a deep, primitive, leonine nature', also notable, however, for 'his demands, his childishness, his braggadocio, his unscrupulousness, his disingenuousness'. In 1842, by now in Paris, Bakunin published a lengthy article urging 'the realization of freedom' and attacking 'the rotted and withered remains of conventionality'. The article breathed a spirit of Hegelianism so abstract that for long stretches it was almost incomprehensible. But it ended with a chilling prophecy of the violent, anarchist extremism of which Bakunin was the founding father: 'The passion for destruction is also a creative passion.' These sentiments expressed the influence of a group of German philosophers known as the Young Hegelians, whose atheism led to their expulsion by the pious King of Prussia, Friedrich Wilhelm IV (1795–1861), soon after he came to the throne in 1840. Bakunin met them in Paris, publishing his article in one of their short-lived magazines, edited by Arnold Ruge (1802–80). It was also in Paris that Bakunin met another Hegelian, Karl Marx (1818–83), who was to be his rival in the small and intense world of revolutionary activists and thinkers for most of the rest of his life. The two men disliked each other on first sight. Marx, as Bakunin later recalled, 'called me a sentimental idealist, and he was right. I called him morose, vain and treacherous; and I too was right.'

In the longer run, it was Marx who was to prove the more influential. Born on the western fringes of Germany, in the small, declining provincial town of Trier, in the Rhineland, Karl Marx gravitated towards the Young Hegelians at the University of Berlin, one of whom, Ludwig Feuerbach (1804–72), was the source of Marx's famous statement 'Philosophers have hitherto only interpreted the world: the point is to change it.' Marx became a freelance writer, penning articles for a recently founded radical paper based in Cologne, the *Rheinische Zeitung*. The paper was soon closed by the authorities in April 1843, and three months later Marx moved to Paris. His reading of the English political economists made him pessimistic about the economic prospects of the working class. His reading of the French socialists led him to see in the abolition of private property and the establishment of communal and collective forms of labour the way to overcome the alienation of the workers' labour through the appropriation of its products by the employers. Socializing with radicals in Paris also brought Marx for the first time into contact with Friedrich Engels (1820–95), who became his lifelong collaborator. Marx wrote a number of polemics in the 1840s that reflected the fractious mood of the émigré circles among whom he now moved. It was socialists like Proudhon who were making the running, a situation which Marx's vehement critique of the Frenchman's ideas, *The Poverty of Philosophy* (1847), had no real chance of changing. Still, all of these ideas, building on the legacy of the eighteenth-century Enlightenment and the French Revolution, were to play a part in the revolutionary events that brought the decade to a close.

NATIONALISM AND LIBERALISM

More immediately, however, in the 1830s and 1840s, it was the ideas of nationalism that had the greatest and most disruptive impact. It is common to define nationalism as the demand for a state respondent to the sovereign will of a particular people, but many nationalists in the first half of the nineteenth century stopped well short of embracing this radical principle. Some sought to free their own nation from a foreign yoke. Most persistent here were the Poles, who sought independence from tsarist Russia, the Habsburg Empire and the Kingdom of Prussia, which had carved up the dysfunctional Polish state between them in the eighteenth century. But most other nationalists of this type only wanted greater autonomy within a larger political structure, or simply the official recognition of their language and culture. In the Habsburg Monarchy, distinctive national groups like the Czechs and Hungarians fell into this category; none actively campaigned for the dissolution of the monarchy itself. In Finland the Fennoman movement, led by Johan Vilhelm Snelmann (1806–81), a teacher and philosopher who advocated the use of Finnish rather than Swedish in the schools (although he himself only spoke the latter), did not raise any demand for independence from Russia. A second type of nationalism sought to bring together a single nation split into a number of different independent states – notably German and Italian – and here, the demand from the beginning was for complete sovereignty. Of course, these categories were not entirely separate from one another. Uniting Italy meant throwing off the Austrian yoke in the north of the peninsula; uniting Germany meant coming to an arrangement with Denmark and in particular the Habsburg Monarchy, both of which covered a part of the German Confederation but had most of their territory and inhabitants outside it. Still, it is important not to read back later demands for independence into the nascent nationalism of the 1830s and 1840s. Before mid-century, indeed, nationalism for many was as much a means to an end as an end in itself, a means to bring about liberal political and constitutional reform in the face of the conservative order enforced by the Holy Alliance and the police regime of the German Confederation under Prince Metternich.

It would also be unwise to read back into the 1830s and 1840s too much of the later aggressiveness and egoism of European nationalism. Giuseppe Mazzini, the best-known European nationalist of his age, believed in a United States of Europe, composed of free and independent peoples in a voluntary association with each other. The disunity of the 1831 urban insurrections in northern Italy and their easy suppression by the Austrians convinced him that the *carbonari*, to which he belonged, had to be replaced by a truly national organization, dedicated above all to organizing the expulsion of the Austrians from the peninsula. Living secretly in Marseille, he founded an association called Young Italy, possibly in imitation of the literary movement Young Germany founded shortly before. Despite its conspiratorial trappings, Young Italy had a clear programme – Italian unification on a democratic and republican basis. It also compiled membership lists, charged subscriptions, and employed a courier service to keep members in various towns and cities in touch with one another. Soon the members of Young Italy numbered thousands, inspired by Mazzini's tireless campaigning, his incessant pamphleteering, and the fact that he was apparently the 'most beautiful being, male or female' that people who encountered him said they had ever seen. Metternich declared membership punishable by death. Carlo Alberto, the King of Piedmont-Sardinia, had twelve army officers who were involved in a plot to stage a military uprising under Mazzini's influence early in 1833 publicly executed. Mazzini himself was condemned to death *in absentia* and the sentence read out in front of his family home in Genoa. Metternich succeeded in getting him expelled from France, but Mazzini continued to run Young Italy from Switzerland. He now focused his numerous plots on Piedmont: one of them, like so many betrayed to the Piedmontese authorities, involved a young naval officer, Giuseppe Garibaldi, who had joined Young Italy after meeting a member on a trading expedition to the Black Sea. Also condemned to death *in absentia*, Garibaldi fled to South America, where he took part in the 'War of the Ragamuffins' in Brazil before fighting in the Uruguayan Civil War.

Working through correspondence, conducted after 1837 from London, Mazzini created individual national movements under the aegis of Young Italy: Young Austria, Young Bohemia, Young Ukraine, Young Tyrol and even Young Argentina came briefly into being. Young Poland played a significant role in the 1830 uprising. The most enduring and important organization of this kind was Young Ireland, a term mockingly attached by the English press to a movement founded in 1840 by Daniel O'Connell (1775–1847); it had nothing to do with Mazzini, who did not think that Ireland should be independent; it eschewed violence and insurrection, and it dedicated itself not to the creation of a new nation but to the repeal of the Act of Union with England passed in 1800. But through the organizations he actually did found, Mazzini had changed the terms and tactics of nationalism. Nationalists had learned to co-ordinate their efforts within each particular country, and a strong dose of realism had entered their discourse, causing all but the Poles to recognize that insurrections were unlikely to succeed by themselves, and that the formation of secret societies was not leading anywhere: nationalists needed a programme and a formal organization, equipped with a propaganda apparatus and aimed at securing democratic support.

Under the leadership of Metternich, the Habsburg Empire continued indeed to be the major obstacle that lay in the path of nationalist movements – in Italy, Bohemia, Germany, Hungary and – along with Russia and Prussia – in Poland. Austria had led the European states in the overthrow of Napoleon; for thirty years, from 1815 to 1845, Austrian dominance in Europe was unquestionable. Following Napoleon I's abolition of traditional legislatures such as feudal Estates, few outlets remained for popular discontent. The Emperor Franz I refused to introduce any new constitutional arrangements to his domains in northern Italy. 'My Empire,' he remarked, 'resembles a ramshackle house. If one wishes to demolish a bit of it one does not know how much will collapse.' In central Italy, Gregory XVI, who was elected pope in 1831, ruled the Papal States through a militia of 'centurions' who suppressed all criticism of the corruption and inefficiency of his administration. So chaotic was the state of affairs in his dominions that the papal government did not even manage to prepare a state budget for the last ten years of his pontificate. In Piedmont-Sardinia throughout the 1830s and the first half or more of the 1840s, the fear of conspiracy and revolution kept Carlo Alberto of Piedmont on the Austrians' side in northern Italy. Yet he was pessimistic in the longer run. 'The great crisis,' he wrote in 1834, 'can only be more or less delayed, but it will undoubtedly arrive.'

Avoiding it was one of the aims of the moderate liberal reformers who arrived on the political scene in the 1840s. As with similar figures elsewhere in Europe, they looked above all to Britain as an example. The Milanese reformer Carlo Cattaneo (1801–69), an ex-*carbonaro* who had turned to more moderate ways, thought that 'peoples should act as a permanent mirror to each other, because the interests of civilization are mutually dependent and common'. In Piedmont, the most influential of the moderates in the long run was Camillo Benso, Count of Cavour (1810–61), a Protestant who had travelled widely in Britain and France and supported economic progress, railway-building and the separation of Church and State. As liberal sentiment spread among the educated classes, above all in northern Italy, the British Foreign Secretary Lord Palmerston warned the Austrian ambassador in London that it was time to make concessions: 'We think ourselves conservative in preaching and advising everywhere concessions, reforms, and improvements, where public opinion demands them; you on the contrary refuse them.' But change in Italy seemed to be heralded by the election of Giovanni Maria Mastai-Ferretti (1792–1878) as Pope Pius IX on 16 June 1846. The new Supreme Pontiff amnestied political prisoners, relaxed the censorship rules, and appointed commissions to improve the Papal States' administration, laws and educational provision. His summoning of a consultative assembly sent shock waves through the Italian states. Others followed suit. In Tuscany censorship was partially abolished in May 1847, a legislature was convened following demonstrations in a number of cities, and in September 1847 the Grand Duke Leopold II (1797–1870) appointed a moderate liberal government. In Piedmont, Carlo Alberto granted elected communal councils and limitations on censorship in October 1847. In the Habsburg Monarchy, Metternich's refusal to relax the censorship rules in 1845 had no effect since nationalist and liberal literature poured in from outside, including French, English and German newspapers. The crisis seemed to be coming. 'We are now,' warned the former civil servant Viktor Baron von Andrian-Werburg (1813–58), author of an influential, pessimistic book on the future of the multinational monarchy, 'where France was in 1788.'

This seemed to be particularly the case in the Hungarian provinces of the Habsburg Empire. The leading reformer István Széchenyi's Anglophilia made him a gradualist, desiring 'to change the condition of the fatherland with as little fanfare as possible'. He believed in bringing different social classes together in harmony, a purpose he thought could be fostered by horse-racing, for which he had conceived a passion following a visit to Newmarket – he founded the Hungarian Derby to this end in 1826. Following the Polish uprising and a devastating cholera epidemic in 1831, the Hungarian Diet met in 1832 with a programme of reform, but the emperor vetoed even the modest measures that got through. In 1837 the lawyer and journalist Lajos Kossuth (1802–94), who published Hungary's first parliamentary reports, was arrested for sedition. This sparked a serious crisis, as Kossuth's supporters in the Diet forced Metternich to climb down and release him and other imprisoned liberals in May 1840. The same Diet removed legal barriers to the establishment of factories, approved the building of the country's first railway line, and relaxed restrictions on the occupation and residence of Hungary's Jews. Further reforms gave Protestants civil and legal equality with Catholics and legitimated mixed-religion marriages. But this did not satisfy the liberals. Kossuth was joined by the leading moderate Ferenc Deák (1803–76), and together they produced a statement of their aims. In the new Diet of 1847, to which Kossuth was elected by a triumphant majority, Metternich felt obliged to make concessions, including the abolition of customs barriers on the Austrian border with Hungary. But it was too late: these measures altogether failed to appease the growing nationalist opposition, and divisions between the Hungarian liberals and the Monarchy's leadership in Vienna continued to deepen until they became irreconcilable. Within only a few months they had broken out into open conflict.

In Switzerland, reforms passed by moderate liberals whose strength was in the towns and cities of the Protestant cantons ran into fierce objections from the largely Catholic, more rural parts of the Confederation. When the liberals passed a centralist constitution and began closing Catholic monasteries, the conservative cantons reacted by forming a 'special league' in 1843, the *Sonderbund*, in violation of the Federal Treaty of 1815. Both sides began to mobilize, and in November 1847 hostilities commenced. Federal troops captured the *Sonderbund* stronghold of Fribourg and installed a liberal government, which promptly expelled the Jesuits, as liberal and reforming governments everywhere were wont to do. In the Battle of Gislikon, the last pitched battle ever to involve the Swiss Army, thirty-seven soldiers were killed and one hundred wounded. For the first time in military history, horse-drawn ambulances arrived on a battlefield and took away the wounded. Further skirmishes led to the surrender of the *Sonderbund* on 29 November 1847. A new, more liberal constitution was passed a few weeks later.

The Swiss Civil War was a foretaste of conflicts to come in other parts of Europe. The revolutions of the early 1830s had only been partially negated by the repressive measures undertaken by Metternich in most parts of the German Confederation, and a good number of the states now had elected legislative assemblies that provided a forum for liberal politicians. Conservative rulers did not appreciate this change in the political climate. In 1837, when Queen Victoria acceded to the British throne, the Salic Law prevented her from doing the same in Hanover, and her uncle, Ernest August, Duke of Cumberland (1771–1851), already notorious for the extreme conservative views he was in the habit of expressing in the British House of Lords, ascended the Hanoverian throne and immediately abrogated the constitution of 1833, demanding an oath of loyalty from all the state's employees. Seven professors at Göttingen University, including the brothers Jacob Grimm (1785–1863) and Wilhelm Grimm (1786–1859), compilers of the famous folk tales, refused to swear the oath and were dismissed from their posts. Their action achieved nothing in the short run – the constitution stayed abrogated – but aroused liberal sympathies all over Germany. In 1840 the accession of Friedrich Wilhelm IV as King of Prussia prompted liberal hopes of reform. Oppositional clubs and societies sprang up everywhere, and liberals got themselves elected to previously dormant city councils, which began petitioning the king to summon a constituent assembly. In an attempt to defuse the situation, Friedrich Wilhelm summoned the provincial Estates to a United Diet in 1847, prompted not least by the need to raise more taxes in the middle of the economic crisis of the late 1840s. When he spurned calls for a constitution, the majority rejected his request for tax reform. The king dissolved the Diet, but its potential role as a focus for constitutional reform had become clear.

In Bavaria, King Ludwig I (1786–1868) was becoming increasingly unpopular in view of the repressive, pro-clerical policies of his minister Karl von Abel (1788–1859) – nearly a thousand political trials were held during Ludwig's reign, which began in 1825. What really undermined the king's authority, however, was the arrival in Munich of the Spanish dancer Lola Montez (1821–61). Famous for her erotic 'Spider Dance', at the climax of which she lifted her costume to reveal that she was not wearing any undergarments, Lola was a veteran of previous affairs with the virtuoso pianist and composer Franz Liszt (1811–86) and (possibly) the novelist Alexandre Dumas. Despite her exotic-looking, dark beauty, Lola was not actually Spanish at all. Her real name was Eliza Gilbert and she was Irish, the daughter of the county sheriff of Cork. She made an instant impression on King Ludwig: when he met her, overwhelmed by her shapely form, he felt emboldened to ask whether her bosom was real, upon which she is said to have ripped off her bodice to prove that indeed it was. Soon she had become the king's mistress. He showered her with gifts, gave her a generous annuity, and ennobled her as Countess of Landsfeld. When Abel objected ('all those who plot rebellion rejoice,' he warned the king), she had him dismissed. The pillorying of Ludwig in popular pamphlets and broadsheets reminded many of the scurrilous attacks on the French King Louis XVI and Queen Marie-Antoinette that had done so much to discredit the French monarchy in 1789. A similar loss of legitimacy, though without the additional element of farce, undermined other monarchs in Germany too. The refusal of Wilhelm I of Württemberg (1801–64) to grant reforms led to the formation of an energetic liberal opposition, while the stubborn conservatism of the Grand Duke of Hesse-Darmstadt, Ludwig II (1777–1848), led to the victory of an organized liberal movement under the lawyer and former *Burschenschaft* member Heinrich von Gagern (1799–1880) in the elections to the state Diet in 1847.

The model polity that inspired such men was the liberal state in Britain, according to the German encyclopedist Carl Welcker (1790–1869) 'the most glorious creation of God and nature and simultaneously humanity's most admirable work of art'. What impressed European liberals was the ability of the British political system to avoid revolution through timely concessions to liberal demands. In power from 1832 to 1841, the Whigs passed legislation reforming the Poor Law (1834), reshaping the criminal law, and creating a new, uniform system of municipal government based on elected councils (the Municipal Corporations Act of 1835). Over a hundred Royal Commissions were set up between 1832 and 1849, with experts being examined, information compiled, and their reports, published as 'Blue Books', selling thousands of copies across the land and providing a detailed factual basis for public debate. When the Whigs were finally ousted in the General Election of 1841, a new kind of Tory came to power as Prime Minister – the efficient, hard-working Sir Robert Peel, who as Home Secretary under both Lord Liverpool (1770–1828) and the Duke of Wellington had simplified the criminal law and famously, in 1829, established London's blue-uniformed Metropolitan Police Force, popularly dubbed 'Bobbies' or 'Peelers'. Reticent, undemonstrative, upright and rationalist in character and approach, Peel was nonetheless animated by a powerful Evangelical conscience – one which, for example, had caused him to oppose equal rights for Catholics in the 1820s. Peel's administration set up a uniform currency with notes issued by the Bank of England. The Companies Act of 1844 required companies to be registered and to publish their balance sheets, a necessary measure in an age of manic railway speculation. Peel also put the national finances in order by introducing an income tax, grudgingly accepted by the political class.

If both Whigs and Tories were, in European terms, moderate liberals, then there were also the equivalents in Britain of the radicals and democrats who had emerged on the Continent. Many forms of working-class self-help organizations emerged in the new industrial districts of the country in the 1830s and 1840s, notably friendly societies such as the Rochdale Equitable Pioneers' Society, founded in 1844, which set up co-operative stores where members could buy goods cheaply. But the most overtly political of these groups was the Chartist movement, so called because it centred on a document called the Working Men's Charter, drawn up in May 1838 by a group of radical Members of Parliament. Unlike the Jacobins or the Cato Street conspirators or the Utopian Socialists, the Chartists believed in the parliamentary system, but they wanted the House of Commons to be elected on a democratic vote with a secret ballot and equal electoral districts. They found a powerful orator in the Irishman Feargus O'Connor (1794–1855), a sometime MP and advocate of the repeal of the Act of Irish Union. Over six feet tall, with a ready wit, O'Connor appealed to 'unshaven chins, blistered hands, and fustian jackets' rather than the respectable classes. At a series of huge meetings, he addressed tens of thousands of Chartists in his booming voice, winning them over with his powerful rhetoric.

The climax of the Chartists' agitation came with the London convention in February 1839 at which quarrels between moderates and radicals (some of whom wore Phrygian bonnets) revealed a serious split within the movement. When a petition adorned with 1,283,000 signatures, urging the House of Commons to adopt the Charter, was rejected in July 1839, the radical wing became more extreme in its rhetoric, and a number of its leaders were arrested for seditious libel and sent to prison. In Newport, Monmouthshire, the Chartist John Frost (1784–1877) organized a protest demonstration that turned into an uprising when several thousand miners, equipped with bludgeons and firearms, marched on the local jail to free fellow Chartists who had been arrested. Troops were summoned and fired on the crowd, killing more than twenty. Altogether 500 Chartists were in jail by 1840. After a second petition, with more than 3,250,000 signatures, was rejected by the House of Commons in 1842, Chartism died down, and O'Connor turned his energies to land reform. The mantle of the country's leading pressure group fell on the Anti-Corn-Law League, which enjoyed strong middle-class backing for the ending of import tariffs on corn, and mounted a sophisticated and well-organized campaign that ended in success in 1846. The aristocratic Whigs voted with Peel, recognizing the need for a concession despite their identification with the landowning interest, but a strong minority of Tory MPs, led by the opportunistic young novelist-politician Benjamin Disraeli and counting among its number many gentry farmers, voted to support the Corn Laws and split the party, with the result that the Whigs were returned to office. Chartism was undercut by an improvement in the economy and by Peel's demonstration through his reforms of the integrity of the political Establishment. Moderate liberals, incorporated both in the English Whigs and in Peel's reformist Tories, had clearly seen off the democrats and radicals for the time being.

The dilemmas of moderate liberalism were nowhere better illustrated than in France, where its representatives had come to power in the 1830 Revolution. Overcoming the chronic political instability of the 1830s, François Guizot, a Protestant historian whose father had been guillotined during the Reign of Terror, managed to establish a stable ministry in 1840, which lasted until 1848. He became more conservative over time. 'Not to be a republican at 20 is proof of a want of heart,' he remarked: 'to be one at 30 is proof of a want of head.' An Anglophile who translated Shakespeare and published a collection of English historical documents in thirty-one volumes, Guizot was the arch-apostle of English-style constitutional monarchy. His commitment to the established order was unquestionable. His ambition, one critic said, was 'to be incorporated into the Metternich clique of every country'. His response to those who complained at not having a vote because they did not have the

1,000 francs a year needed as a qualification, laid bare the materialism at the heart of the July Monarchy: 'Enrich yourselves!' The restrictive franchise remained unaltered until the regime's end. In Britain, by contrast, the electorate was already proportionately larger even before the reform of 1832 (3.2 per cent of the British population as against 0.5 per cent of the French), and the fear of revolution, sparked in London by events in Paris two years before, had brought about a substantial widening of the electorate that for many years defused the campaign for democracy.

Guizot's main achievement was in the sphere of education, where he laid down the principle that every commune, or group of communes, had to have a teacher-training college and a primary school, with a secondary school in each town containing over 6,000 inhabitants. Yet he encountered criticism for his restrictions on press freedom, imposed in 1835, which resulted in over 2,000 arrests and led to a show trial of 164 seditious journalists. Demands for social reform, he said, were 'chimerical and disastrous'. The Factory Act of 1841, which forbade the employment of children under the age of eight in factories with machinery, remained the only law of its kind until 1874 and was far from effective. On the other hand, laws were passed to facilitate railway-building, which gathered pace in the 1840s. No wonder that Balzac described the July Monarchy as an 'insurance contract drawn up between the rich against the poor'. Guizot's government was beset by scandal, especially in 1847, when it emerged that the Minister of Public Works, Jean-Baptiste Teste (1780–1852), had accepted 100,000 francs from an ex-Minister, General Amédée Despans-Cubières (1786–1853), as a bribe for allowing him to renew a salt-mining concession. Corruption of this kind increasingly called the July Monarchy into question as the decade neared its end.

THE SPECTRE OF 1789

The first sign of a renewal of revolutionary violence was in Poland. The crushing of Polish autonomy by Russia in the early 1830s had driven many Polish nationalists abroad, where the national-democratic ideologies and secret societies of the post-Napoleonic era focused their energies and gave them a purpose. Typical was the Paris-born poet Ludwik Mierosławski (1814–78), whose godfather was one of Napoleon I's marshals. Mierosławski had fought in the 1830 uprising, and belonged not only to Young Poland but also to the *carbonari*. After lengthy preparations, his plans for a simultaneous insurrection in Prussia, Cracow and Galicia finally reached maturity in 1846. But the Prussian police got wind of the conspiracy and arrested the ringleaders in their part of the partitioned land. The Austrian governor of Galicia felt too weak to oppose the armed noble rebels of the province and enlisted a local peasant leader, Jakub Szela (1787–1866), who rashly promised an end to serfdom for all who joined his forces. Matters got out of hand as a classic *jacquerie* of major proportions developed. Armed bands of peasants burned 500 manor houses, butchering their inhabitants and offering the severed heads of the aristocratic landlords to the Austrian authorities, who rewarded them with bags of salt. Altogether nearly 2,000 noble estate owners were massacred. Eventually the Austrian Army arrived to restore order. Szela was rewarded with a medal and a plot of land, and while serfdom, predictably, was not abolished, the revolt had sounded its death knell. An Austro-Russian Treaty signed on 16 November 1846 abolished the status of Cracow, the centre of the revolt, as a free city and merged it into Galicia.

The Galician uprising might have failed, but it sent shock waves across the Continent. Moderate liberals everywhere were spurred into action, fearing that without serious constitutional reform social revolution would overwhelm them. Democrats and socialists saw their chance. Authoritarian governments were shaken out of their complacency and started to make concessions. Underpinning all this were the catastrophic crop failure and potato blight that plunged the European economy into depression from 1846 onwards. Starving and desperate people flocked to the towns in huge numbers. Artisans were thrown into destitution, their income slashed just as food prices were soaring. Compounding this disastrous situation was a massive increase in the number of university students, from 9,000 in Germany during the 1820s to around 16,000 in the 1840s; they too found themselves on the breadline and, just as bad, without a prospect of a job after graduating. The crisis of the late 1840s was also a crisis of the industrial age. The centres of the events of 1848 were all in areas affected by British industrial competition, which was undercutting continental manufactures. The collapse of demand for manufactured goods caused the Borsig railway and engineering works in Berlin to lay off a third of its workforce at the beginning of March 1848, while a wave of bankruptcies swept over the textile industry in Bohemia. Capital cities in Europe were the fulcrum of revolution in 1848, but they were also major centres of industry. Here the formation of a new working class was as advanced as anywhere, and the street demonstrations that drove on the revolution were influenced by the ideas of the Utopian socialists of one variety or another.

Monarchs and princes and their leading ministers expected revolution – some of them had prophesied it for many years – and the expectation all too easily became self-fulfilling. The year 1848 marked the temporary displacement on the European Continent of English gradualism by French insurrectionism. Many people expected 1789 to happen all over again. In conformity with this script, it was in France that the revolution began. Middle-class opponents of Guizot and Louis-Philippe began holding a series of huge banquets, seventy in all during the year 1847, mostly in Paris but also in twenty-eight *départements* in the provinces, at which speeches were made demanding the reduction of the tax threshold for the right to vote. At one such banquet a large but peaceful crowd sang the *Marseillaise* outside, while 1,200 electors sat down to a candlelit dinner of cold veal, turkey and suckling pig inside a series of vast tents at twelve tables, each with a hundred places set for the participants, in what a contemporary newspaper described as a 'truly magical spectacle'. A seventy-piece orchestra played 'patriotic airs'. Toasts were raised 'To national sovereignty!', 'To democratic and parliamentary reform!', 'To the deputies of the Opposition!' and 'To the improvement of the lot of the labouring classes!'. 'What taste!' exclaimed the writer Gustave Flaubert (1821–80): 'What cuisine! What wines and what conversation!' One speaker after another mounted a tribune to deliver speeches denouncing the government. A supporter of the movement made a pointed distinction between the cold veal (*veau froid*) eaten at the banquet and the golden calf (*veau d'or*) worshipped by the elite supporters of Guizot's regime. A satirical broadside imagined conservatives holding their own version of the banquets with beefsteak – a reference to Guizot's Anglophilia – and brie, an allusion to his own constituency in Normandy. They were clearly not going to consume 'reformist veal' or 'Jacobin asparagus'.

As the campaign gathered pace, its threat to the stability of the July Monarchy became obvious. The political writer and historian Alexis de Tocqueville (1805–59), already well known for his two-volume study of *Democracy in America* (1835), asked the Chamber of Deputies on 27 January 1848 'Do you not smell . . . a whiff of revolution in the air?' The influence of Cabet and the socialists, he thought, had been increasing rapidly. Ignoring this warning, Guizot's government decided to outlaw the banqueting campaign. The organizers riposted by calling for a huge procession to precede the next banquet, openly defying the ban on public demonstrations. As the demonstration went ahead, the troops defending the Foreign Ministry, under heavy pressure from the crowd, panicked and opened fire, killing more than eighty of the demonstrators. Within a few hours more than 1,500 barricades had gone up all over Paris. Adolphe Thiers was appointed Prime Minister; but soldiers of the National Guard greeted the king's attempt to rally them with cries of 'Long live reform! Down with the ministers!' The paralysis of the regime was complete. Louis-Philippe went back to his chambers in the Tuileries Palace, slumped into an armchair, with his head in his hands, as Thiers, sunk in gloom, exclaimed repeatedly: 'The sea is rising! The sea is rising!' Louis-Philippe gave in. 'I abdicate,' he mumbled from his armchair, repeating the words more loudly a few minutes later. Accompanied by loyal troops, the king and his family and a few retainers decamped to the coast, where they were taken in hand by the British consul in Le Havre, George Featherstonhaugh. His whiskers shaved off, his face disguised in spectacles, his body muffled in a thick scarf and a heavy jacket, Louis-Philippe, following the consul's plan, boarded a ferry, where Featherstonhough greeted him in English in an elaborate pantomime of deception that bordered on the farcical ('Well, uncle! How are you?' 'Quite well, I thank you, George.') On 3 March 1848 the boat landed at Newhaven, and 'Mr. Smith', soon to be followed by other members of his family, began his life in exile. The July Monarchy was over; France's 1848 Revolution had begun.

While 1789 was in everybody's minds during these events, the revolution of 1848 differed from its predecessor in many respects. Most obvious was its European dimension. In the 1790s the French revolutionaries had spread their ideas across large swathes of the Continent by force of arms. In 1848 they did not need to do this; revolutions broke out in many different countries almost simultaneously. A large part of the reason for this lay in the vastly improved state that communications had reached by the middle of the nineteenth century. Although still in its infancy, Europe's railway network, assisted by better roads and faster, steam-powered ships, was sufficiently well developed to make the distribution of news far more rapid than it had been in the 1790s. Improved rates of literacy went along with a huge increase in the number of urban-industrial workers to provide a ready market for revolutionary ideas. Industrialization and the spread of capitalist institutions, compounding the Continent-wide economic crisis of the late 1840s, meant that distress and discontent impacted on the whole of Europe, not just on relatively isolated areas. Thus the French revolution of 1848 was paralleled by similar upheavals elsewhere.

In Italy trouble started on New Year's Day in 1848, when the inhabitants of Milan, under Austrian rule, followed the principle of the Boston Tea Party by giving up smoking in order to stop the Austrians obtaining revenue from a tax on tobacco. On 3 January a participant in the boycott knocked a cigar out of the mouth of an Austrian soldier. Scuffles ensued and turned into a full-scale riot. In Sicily the official celebrations of the birthday of the king, Ferdinando Carlo (1810–59), on 12 January 1848 were met by crowds building barricades and flying the Italian tricolour amid cries of 'Long Live Italy, the Sicilian Constitution and Pius IX!' Peasants armed with rustic weapons streamed in and braved the grapeshot fired from the garrison at the fortress of Castellamare to drive the troops out of the city. All over Sicily, peasants stormed government offices and burned tax records and land registers. Liberals and democrats joined forces to establish a provisional government and call for elections. Ferdinando Carlo shipped 5,000 troops across to the island, stripping the mainland of its defences. The impoverished slum-dwellers of Naples rose in revolt, inspired by the example of the Sicilians. Terrified of what might happen if no concessions were granted, the liberals organized a demonstration of some 25,000 people in front of the royal palace. The royal troops were persuaded to stand down, and Ferdinando Carlo reluctantly issued a constitution that led to the formation of a moderate liberal government. As the unrest spread northwards, Pope Pius IX, faced with crowds shouting 'Death to the cardinals!', promised a part-lay government for the Papal States. Leopold II of Tuscany granted a constitution on 12 February 1848 and Carlo Alberto of Piedmont on 4 March 1848.

Although these events in Italy were already in progress, it was the fall of the July Monarchy that really marked the start of the 1848 revolutions. As the news spread across the Continent, 'it fell', in the words of William H. Stiles (1808–65), the American chargé d'affaires in Vienna, 'like a bomb amid the states and kingdoms of the Continent; and, like reluctant debtors threatened with legal terrors, the various monarchs hastened to pay their subjects the constitutions which they owed them.' In Mannheim huge crowds led by the radical lawyer Gustav Struve (1805–70) demonstrated in favour of the acceptance by Grand Duke Leopold I (1790–1852) of Baden of a petition he had drawn up, demanding freedom of the press, trial by jury, a militia with elected officers, constitutions for all the German states, and, crucially, elections to be held for an all-German parliament. As the petition was reprinted and circulated across the land, its items becoming known as the 'March Demands', constitutions were granted in Baden, Württemberg and Hesse-Nassau; Grand Duke Ludwig II (1777–1848) of Hesse-Darmstadt handed over his office to his son Ludwig III (1806–77) in protest, but a constitution was issued there too. King Ludwig I of Bavaria, already in deep trouble because of his affair with Lola Montez, was forced to grant the March Demands when irate crowds stormed the royal armoury on 4 February 1848, but the situation only calmed down when he agreed to abdicate in favour of his son Maximilian II (1811–64). On 6 March, King Friedrich Augustus II (1797–1854) of Saxony was obliged to enact constitutional reforms and dismiss his

conservative chief minister. By 5 March delegates from the newly liberalized states were meeting in Heidelberg to organize a 'pre-parliament' that
would stage elections for a German constituent assembly.

Events were now moving with dizzying speed. Remarkably, the revolutionary wave now spread across to the Habsburg Empire, which had
remained relatively unaffected by the French Revolution of 1789. When
the news of the Parisian revolution reached the Hungarian Diet in Press-
burg, Kossuth immediately demanded self-rule for Hungary under a
reformed Habsburg Monarchy. Copies of the speech circulated in Vienna
and students petitioned the government for liberal reforms including the
participation of the German areas of the monarchy in a new united German state. Four thousand marched with a petition to the centre of the city
and tore up the Estates' own, very mild petition for changes amid cries of
'No half measures!' and 'Constitution!' Large numbers of workers armed
with their work tools marched in from the suburbs, pulling up lamp posts
with which to smash the city gates, which had been prudently closed by
the authorities. On the main square, the Ballhausplatz, troops were met
with a hail of stones and opened fire. Barricades went up and as the workers finally broke through, alarmed members of the bourgeoisie demanded
Metternich's resignation. On 13 March 1848 the Chancellor finally gave
in, announcing his resignation in a lengthy speech of self-justification. He
left the city the next day with his third wife in a horse-drawn fiacre and
made his way in stages to Brighton, on the south coast of England, consol-
ing himself with the thought that at least his reputation had not been
sullied by having been forced to cross the English Channel on the same
ship as Lola Montez. Meanwhile, in Vienna, the abolition of censorship
and the convening of a constitutional assembly were announced by
Emperor Ferdinand I (1793–1875) on 15 March.

The ousting of Metternich, perhaps more than any other event, signalled the profound breadth and depth of the upheaval. He had succeeded,
more or less, in keeping the lid on protest and revolution for more than
thirty years. Now the lid had been blown off in an explosion of popular
rage. There was no going back. Governments everywhere buckled then
gave way under the strain. The first to react was Archduke Stefan (1817–
67), Palatine (i.e. governor) of Hungary, who had been born in Buda and
was generally pro-Hungarian. On hearing the news of Metternich's downfall he summoned an emergency meeting of the Upper House of the
Estates. It agreed to demand a new, liberal constitution. Kossuth, Széchenyi and the liberal reformer Count Lajos Batthyáni (1807–49) travelled by
steamboat upstream to Vienna in a delegation of 150 to present their

demands. Stefan extracted an Imperial Rescript from Emperor Ferdinand on 17 March 1848, agreeing to an autonomous Hungarian government with Batthyáni as Prime Minister. Kossuth pushed events forward by organizing a twelve-point petition demanding parliamentary sovereignty, trial by jury, the end of serfdom, and the evacuation of all non-Hungarian troops. Swollen by a stream of fresh recruits, a 20,000-strong crowd marched on the Palatine's castle at Buda, where the troops guarding the Vice-Regal Council melted away and the Council accepted the twelve points in full. In April these were ratified in a lightly amended form by the Diet, making Hungary an autonomous constitutional monarchy, with a widened franchise and parliamentary sovereignty, but still with the Habsburg Emperor as monarch.

The Habsburg Empire was now in serious trouble. As in other parts of Europe, a combination of middle-class discontent, popular desperation, liberal ideologies and revolutionary anger provoked an almost irresistible wave of uprisings that rocked an already nervous and pessimistic civil and military establishment to its foundations. In the Austrian-ruled provinces of northern Italy, the news of Metternich's fall and the end of royal abso-lutism in Piedmont spurred the liberals into action. As disorder broke out across Milan, with barricades going up all over the city, paving stones torn up and the vice-governor kidnapped, the commander of the Austrian forces in Italy, Marshal Joseph Radetzky von Radetz (1766–1858), a vet-eran of the Napoleonic Wars, deployed his troops at key points and stationed snipers on the cathedral spires. Fighting broke out; insurgents clambered onto the rooftops and began firing at Austrian – mostly Croa-tian and Hungarian – troops below. As his strongholds fell, Radetzky was forced to withdraw, laying siege to Milan from outside. In Piedmont, Cattaneo's improvised republican administration was pushed aside by the moderates, who persuaded Carlo Alberto to march on the city (he was keen to incorporate it into a new Kingdom of Northern Italy under his rule, and afraid that republicans would overthrow him if he failed to act). While Lombard artisans and farmers rounded up the smaller Austrian garrisons across the land, the Milanese broke Radetzky's siege in a bloody, five-day battle, and the Austrians withdrew after a last, vengeful bombard-ment. The victory was symbolized a few days later by the arrival in Milan of none other than Giuseppe Mazzini, ready to take up in person the cause of Italian unity.

The upheavals spread to other parts of Austrian-ruled northern Italy with lightning speed. In Venice, Daniele Manin (1804–57), a liberal nationalist imprisoned by the Austrians for treason the previous year, was released by jubilant crowds as the news of Metternich's fall reached the city, and immediately organized a citizens' militia to counter the violence of the occupying Austrian forces, who had opened fire on the crowds on 18 March 1848. On 22 March, at his prompting, workers in the naval dockyards, angered by the Austrian commander's refusal to give them a pay increase, rose in revolt, beat him to death, and took over the entire area. Manin declared a republic, and the Austrian (mostly Croatian) troops, withdrew rather than damage the city's beautiful buildings. Habsburg flags were torn down everywhere and thrown into the canals. These events put enormous pressure on Pope Pius IX to join the war against Austria. The Pope sent an armed force to the northern border of the Papal States, where it was joined by 10,000 young Roman men, inflamed by nationalist passion. Grand Duke Leopold of Tuscany was forced to contribute 8,000 troops, and King Ferdinando Carlo of Naples reluctantly sent a naval force to break the Austrian blockade of Venice, while a Neapolitan detachment of 14,000 men marched slowly northwards to join the other armies. In late May, 560,000 Milanese voted for incorporation into Piedmont, with fewer than 700 votes against, a result soon replicated in Parma and Modena. On 4 July, brushing aside Manin and the intransigent republicans, the Venetian Constituent Assembly agreed to 'fusion' with Piedmont as well. Italian unification suddenly began to look like more than a nationalist dream.

However, the revolutionaries did not have everything their own way. As northern Italy erupted, the violence spilled over into the Kingdom of the Two Sicilies, where a liberal government forced on King Ferdinando Carlo had formed a citizens' militia that proved wholly unequal to the task of restoring order. Elections held on 15 May 1848 on a low turnout returned a largely moderate liberal parliament from which Ferdinando Carlo demanded an oath to support the existing constitution. Enraged republicans threw up barricades in Naples, which were assaulted by 12,000 royal troops. In fierce hand-to-hand fighting, 200 soldiers were killed and a larger number of insurgents died as Ferdinando Carlo defeated the rebels. The troops shot many of their prisoners, and extorted money from others, while the urban poor took advantage of the situation to rampage through the city, looting and pillaging amid cries of 'Long live the King!' and 'Death to the Nation!' Ordered to return to Naples, the Sicilian naval force sent to relieve the Venetians obeyed, along with the bulk of the troops. A minority under General Guglielmo Pepe (1783–1855), a former *carbonaro* who had fought on Napoleon's side after the emperor's escape from Elba, remained, and found their way eventually to Venice to join the forces fighting the Austrians. Yet the republicans had met with a decisive defeat. Worse was to come. Radetzky was told by the government in Vienna 'to end the costly war in Italy', but he refused to negotiate. He was encouraged behind the scenes by hardliners in Vienna, led by Count Theodor Franz Baillet von Latour (1780–1848), Minister of War, a soldier descended from a Walloon family in the former Austrian Netherlands. Radetzky advanced his 33,000 troops against Carlo Alberto's 22,000 at Custoza, a small hill town near Verona. On 24 and 25 July 1848 the Austrian troops drove the Piedmontese down the hill in fierce hand-to-hand fighting. It was the end of Carlo Alberto's attempt to unite northern Italy. He was forced to sign an armistice. 'The city of Milan is ours,' Radetzky crowed: 'no enemy remains on Lombard soil.' Mazzini took a different view. 'The royal war is over,' he declared in a proclamation issued in August 1848: 'The war of the people begins.'

Much still depended on what happened in Vienna. Here, events had been moving fast since the fall of Metternich on 13 March 1848. Four days later a constitutional ministry was formed, the imperial police force was restructured, and police spies were dismissed. Food taxes were lowered, a political amnesty was declared, and job-creation schemes were established. But the granting of a constitution by Ferdinand on 25 April outraged the radical democrats, because it still reserved decisive powers to the emperor. By 4 May mass demonstrations, joined by many workers, had forced the head of the new government to resign. When a restricted franchise was announced on 11 May, the radicals' anger knew no bounds. Impatiently pushing forward the demand for the election by universal male suffrage of a democratic constitutional assembly, the students formed an Academic Legion that soon numbered 5,000 men, while the moderate liberals' militia, the National Guard, counted 7,000 in its ranks. On the night of 14–15 May 1848, led by the students, a massive crowd marched on the royal residence to demand the revision of the constitution and the immediate holding of democratic elections. Ferdinand and his entourage panicked and gave in. The Cabinet resigned in protest. Two days later the emperor and his family left Vienna at night for Innsbruck. The parallel with Louis XIV and Marie Antoinette's ill-fated flight to Varennes was lost on no one.

Safely away from the capital, Ferdinand issued a proclamation condemning the actions of an 'anarchical faction' and calling for resistance; or rather, it was issued for him, since, though not unintelligent, he was incapable of ruling. He had a severe speech impediment, and suffered up to twenty epileptic fits a day (he had five when he tried to consummate his marriage, and not surprisingly, had no children). One of his few known coherent remarks was a reply to his cook, who had told him that he could not have apricot dumplings because apricots were out of season: 'I'm the

Emperor,' Ferdinand was said to have replied, 'and I want dumplings!' On 24 May 1848 his advisers closed the university in Vienna, then, the next day, they ordered the disarming and disbanding of the Academic Legion. But the National Guard went over to the side of the students, while hundreds of workers descended on the city centre. Tearing up paving stones and carrying furniture out of the houses, the students put up 160 barricades at key points, some of them rising up to the second floor of the houses on either side of the street and topped by red and black flags. The government forces were too weak to assert themselves, and were withdrawn, while Ferdinand and his entourage acceded on 12 August to the students' demands for his return. Driving from the quayside at Nussdorf to the centre of the city in an open carriage, he was greeted with hisses mingled with barely audible shouts of welcome from the crowds lining the streets. The emperor 'stared at his knees', as an observer reported, while 'the Empress had evidently been weeping'. The serried ranks of the National Guard let them pass without a salute, and the band of the Academic Legion played Arndt's *What is the German's Fatherland* as they passed, instead of the Austrian national anthem. The democrats in Vienna had, for the moment at least, gained the upper hand.

What happened in Vienna was closely bound up with what happened in the rest of the German Confederation, where one state after another had been forced to grant a constitution with full parliamentary rights. The pressure on the largest of the member states, Prussia, was growing daily. On 16 March 1848, when news of Metternich's fall reached Berlin, panic broke out in the ruling clique. While Friedrich Wilhelm IV's adjutant-general, Leopold von Gerlach (1790–1861), and the king's brother and heir, Prince Wilhelm (1797–1888), urged the use of force, the king decided to make concessions, announcing the abolition of censorship and the summoning of the United Diet, in abeyance since the previous year. It would consider strengthening the German Confederation with a national law code, a flag and a navy. But this was not enough. As the demonstrators shouted for the troops to be withdrawn, shots were fired, and soon barricades were going up all over the city and men began to sound the tocsin on the bells of the city churches. On 18 March the Prussian troops mounted a full-frontal attack on the barricades with infantry and artillery, and soon, as an eyewitness reported, the streets were running with blood. By the end of the day 800 demonstrators, the vast majority of them impoverished artisans and unskilled workers, members of the new working class, were dead.

Rather than spelling the end of the revolution, however, the March events only drove it on. The king had not sanctioned the use of firearms, and was appalled by the bloodshed. On 19 March, as crowds bearing the bodies of many of those killed the previous day broke into the Palace yard, demanding to see the king, Friedrich Wilhelm appeared, 'white and trembling', and removed his hat amid mocking shouts from the crowd. The scene inevitably reminded people of the crowds that had stormed the royal palace in France in 1789 and forced Louis XVI to bow to their will. 'Now only the guillotine is left,' the queen is said to have remarked. But the king's gesture restored calm. Two days later Friedrich Wilhelm gained further popularity by riding through the streets wearing the German national colours of black, red and gold, and accompanied by numerous officers bedecked in the same insignia. On 22 March he was forced to attend the elaborate funeral of the victims of four days before, again removing his helmet in a gesture of reverence to the dead and submission to the masses. Friedrich Wilhelm gained huge popularity by these gestures; privately, however, he experienced them as a deep humiliation. Towards the end of the month he ordered his troops to withdraw from Berlin, against further protests from the hardliners in his entourage. The city was now in the hands of the revolutionaries.

At this point, however, serious divisions began to open up between the moderate liberals and the hard-line democrats. In the Prussian Diet, elected by indirect though ultimately universal adult male suffrage, the conservatives mustered 120 delegates out of 395, enough to block the policies of the moderate liberal, Gottfried Camphausen (1803–90), a banker appointed head of the Council of State on 29 March 1848. On 14 June violence broke out in Berlin when democratic demonstrators, including many workers carrying red flags, looted the royal armoury. Helpless in the face of continued disorder, Camphausen resigned on 20 June. The diehards were thoroughly alarmed by the Diet's presentation on 26 July of a draft constitution removing virtually all power from the king and the army and abolishing all aristocratic titles. On 9 August the deputies demanded that all soldiers should swear an oath of loyalty not to the king but to the constitution. As Camphausen was followed by a succession of weak ministers, the outraged monarch began making plans with Gerlach and the conservatives to take back the initiative. Similar cleavages soon became apparent in the national pre-parliament that met at Mannheim on 31 March 1848, in this case between moderate liberal deputies such as Heinrich von Gagern, who envisioned a united Germany as a federation of monarchies, and radical democrats such as Gustav Struve and Friedrich Hecker (1811–81), both from Baden, who demanded a single unitary German republic and the abolition of the existing German states along with their sovereigns. Outvoted in the pre-parliament, the two democratic leaders proclaimed a republic on 12 April 1848, and began raising an army. They were joined by a band of German emigrants from Paris under the leadership of the radical poet Georg Herwegh (1817–75), but they were no match for the 30,000 disciplined and well-armed troops mustered in Baden, Württemberg and Bavaria by the German Confederation, who defeated them at Kandern on 20 April and in a few subsequent minor skirmishes.

Meanwhile, the slow and cumbersome process of creating a national German state continued. The pre-parliament had ordered elections to a National Assembly that met in Frankfurt on 18 May 1848. Each state was left to organize the process the way it wanted, but almost all of them used a system of indirect elections based on a property qualification. This was fairly low, so that some three-quarters of all adult males had the right to vote at one stage or another. The 812 deputies included few out-and-out conservatives, since most of them had boycotted the elections on principle; around half of them were moderate liberals, constitutional monarchists; the rest were mostly democrats, of whom some were more radical than others. Three-quarters of the deputies had a university education, but actual professors numbered only 15 per cent. Fewer than 10 per cent were businessmen, and there was a sprinkling of professionals such as doctors, journalists and the like. In true revolutionary fashion the deputies debated at great length a declaration of rights, finally passed on 27 December, which included freedom of religion, speech, trade, assembly and education, as well as the abolition of capital punishment. It also appointed a Provisional Central Power on 24 June, under Archduke Johann of Austria (1782–1859) as head of state, which began to establish ministries and a national bureaucracy. The road to German unification seemed to be open.

These events made clear the cataclysmic impact of the events of 1848. Europe's thrones had been shaken to their foundations. Figures like Metternich and Louis-Philippe, who had long dominated the political world had been ousted. Monarchs had been pressured into abdicating, abjuring a large part of their powers, or surrendering their claim to rule by Divine Right and undergoing the humiliating experience of bowing before enraged crowds of their citizens. Representative assemblies had come into being across Europe, and where they had existed already, gained significant new powers. The principle of national self-determination had been successfully asserted in one country after another. Vast and far-reaching social and economic reforms had been put in train in a dramatic expression of the principle of equality before the law. The 1848 Revolutions have

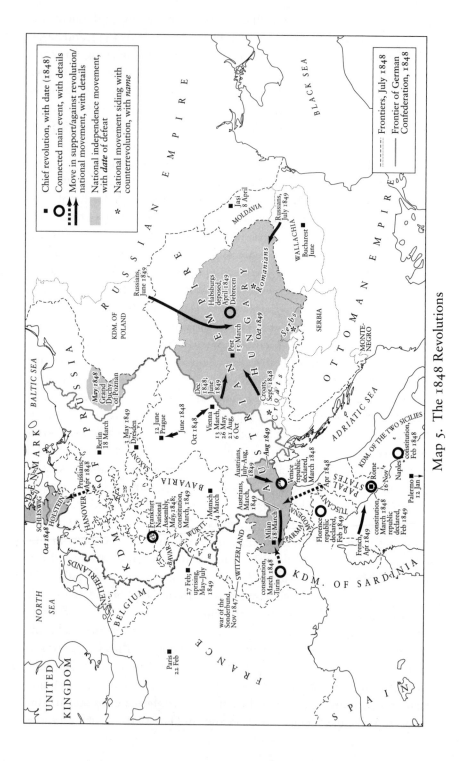

Map 5. The 1848 Revolutions

often been dismissed in retrospect as half-hearted failures, but that is not how they seemed at the time. Nothing in Europe would ever be the same again after the events of January to July 1848. True, there had been setbacks. But in the summer of 'the crazy year', as it was later called in Germany, or, more optimistically, 'the springtime of peoples', there still seemed everything to play for.

THE REVOLUTION FALLS APART

Already by this point, however, it is clear in retrospect that the 1848 Revolutions were beginning to implode under the weight of their own contradictions. The real state of power in Germany was dramatically revealed by events on the German-Danish border, where the Duchy of Schleswig, with a Danish-speaking majority, had been joined to the German Duchy of Holstein, within the German Confederation, since the Middle Ages, under the personal rule of the Danish king. By a lucky chance for Danish liberals, the absolutist King Christian VIII (1786–1848) died in January. His successor Frederik VII (1808–63) was in no position to reject moderate liberal demands for a constitution. Huge demonstrations in Copenhagen forced Frederik to abandon the last remnants of absolutism and appoint a liberal Ministry, abolish the vestiges of serfdom, and declare the union of Schleswig with Denmark on 5 June 1848 with all parts of the Kingdom voting for a national parliament on a broad franchise. All men in Schleswig were to be liable for service in the Danish Army. German landowners in the Duchy declared independence in protest, and German nationalists, above all students, flocked to their support. The Diet of the German Confederation called in the Prussian Army, which marched into Denmark. Diplomatic pressure from Britain, Russia and Sweden forced the Prussians to sign an armistice at Malmö on 26 August 1848, followed by the withdrawal of German troops and the establishment of a joint Danish-Prussian administration in Schleswig.

These events caused a storm of indignation among the nationalists gathered in Frankfurt. Radical democrats told a meeting of 12,000 supporters in front of the Paulskirche, where the parliament was meeting, that the war against Denmark had to continue. The situation now began to turn ugly. On 18 September Archduke Johann's new first minister, Anton von Schmerling (1805–93), summoned 2,000 troops from Hesse-Darmstadt, Austria and Prussia stationed nearby, and they opened fire on the crowds, driving them away. Sixty people were killed, including the conservative deputy Felix Lichnowsky (1814–48), who was beaten to death by the crowd, his body tied to a tree with a placard hung round his neck proclaiming him to be an 'outlaw'. An attempt by Struve to revive the radical democratic cause by marching across the Swiss border into the town of Lörrach, where he proclaimed a German republic on 21 September 1848, was crushed by Badenese troops at Staufen. As Struve was taken away to prison, Frankfurt was placed under martial law, the national parliament now depending on Prussian and Hessian arms for its existence. It was all very well for the Frankfurt Parliament to issue laws and proclamations, but the brutal truth was that without armed force to back them, they counted for little or nothing in the end.

The revolution went through a similar trajectory in France, where, following the departure of Louis-Philippe, the poet Alphonse de Lamartine (1790–1869), who had served in the Foreign Ministry in the 1820s, was chosen by the triumphant liberals to proclaim a Republic on 26 February 1848. He was appointed President, and led a coalition government that included Louis Blanc, the socialist, and a man only ever known as Albert the Worker (1815–95). On 2 March the government declared that all adult males would have the right to vote for the Constituent Assembly due to be elected on 23 April. Meanwhile, Louis Blanc pushed through a measure setting up National Workshops, which were employing 100,000 destitute workers by the end of May in activities such as building roads and planting trees, at a cost of 70,000 livres a day in wages paid by the state. Blanc and Albert set up a labour commission at the Luxembourg Palace to consider demands for wage increases, a reduction of the working day, the abolition of subcontracting and putting-out, restrictions on machinery, and similar, typically artisanal demands. Here was a striking mixture of the new socialist thinking, exemplified by Blanc, with traditional artisan politics reminiscent of the economic controls introduced during the French Revolution of 1789.

On 23 April 1848, alarmed by the turmoil in Paris, and alienated by the new land taxes levied to pay for the National Workshops, the largely rural electorate returned a Constituent Assembly dominated by moderates and conservatives. On 15 May hundreds of demonstrators, including many employees of the National Workshops, invaded the National Assembly to protest. After clearing the Chamber, the Executive Commission closed down the Luxemburg Commission, condemning it as socialist, and then on 20 June abolished the National Workshops. Outraged by this precipitate action, crowds of workers, now deprived of an income, began to gather and march through the streets, where shouts of 'Napoleon for ever!' could be heard among the demands for work. Thoroughly alarmed, the Executive Commission asked the Minister of War, Louis-Eugène

Cavaignac (1802–57), a professional soldier who had fought in the Greek War of Independence and had moderate Republican views, to take action. While he prepared, the crowds built barricades amid cries of 'Liberty or Death!' and choruses of the *Marseillaise*. Cavaignac rightly mistrusted the National Guard, the vast majority of whom failed to respond to his order to mobilize, and some of whom defected to the insurgents. On 23 June, deploying his 25,000 troops in three columns against some 50,000 insurgents, Cavaignac brought his artillery to bear on the barricades one by one, blasting them to pieces amid heavy carnage. The following day, as the city continued to echo to the sound of cannonades, the Assembly passed a vote of no confidence in the Executive Commission and appointed Cavaignac dictator. Even the most determined Republicans like Alexandre Ledru-Rollin (1807–74), whose violent rhetoric had helped turn the 1847 banqueting campaign against the July Monarchy, backed the general. The Parisian clubs were thrown into confusion. None of them supported the uprising; neither did Louis Blanc, nor Pierre-Joseph Proudhon, who had been elected to the Assembly by Parisian workers. Prisoners were summarily shot on both sides. Altogether some 1,500 of the insurgents were killed, at least 2,500 wounded, and 11,727 arrested, mostly to be released over the coming months, with 468 transported to Algeria. Louis Blanc, his standing with the workers destroyed by his opposition to the rebellion, left for London. Paris remained under martial law until October 1848.

What happened in Paris in June had a major impact on events elsewhere in Europe, emboldening moderate liberals and diehard conservatives alike and bringing them closer together in a shared fear of the masses. Everyone remembered how the popular uprisings of 1789–93 had plunged France into the abyss of the Reign of Terror. Nervous liberals were becoming increasingly worried that such events might occur again. But class contradictions were not the only rock on which the Revolution was to founder. Already in the 1840s rival nationalisms were beginning to rub up against one another. This was above all the case in east-central Europe, where the revolutions in Berlin and Vienna gave a powerful stimulus to movements for national unity and autonomy. These movements in turn were to have a major effect on the further development of the revolutions in Germany and Austria, opening up massive contradictions between liberalism and nationalism and giving conservatives and reactionaries the opportunity to recover the initiative. These contradictions were at their most obvious in Hungary, where Croats, Serbs, Slovaks, German-speaking Saxons and Romanians, all present in significant numbers in the lands of the Crown of St Stephen, could not speak or read Magyar. Hungarian nationalists began to advocate the complete Magyarization of these minorities. As one of them put it: 'Our country, from the point of view of language, is a true Babel. If we cannot change the course of things, and the country cannot be united through Magyarization, sooner or later the German or Slav elements will assimilate our nation, and even our name will be forgotten.' Rival nationalisms like that of the Croats began to emerge as counterweights to those who sought to impose Magyar as the dominant language, a development that was to store up serious trouble for the future. In the Hungarian Diet of 1843–4, as the law replaced Latin, finally, with Magyar as the official language of government and administration, and enforced its teaching in all secondary schools, the Croatian deputies still insisted on addressing the legislature in Latin, the only form of protest they could engage in and still be understood.

These tensions played a decisive role in the events of 1848–9 within the Habsburg Monarchy. When they were told by Magyar nationalists in revolutionary Budapest that they should 'consider it an honour to be allowed to become Magyar' within a liberal Hungary, young Romanian intellectuals in Transylvania organized a National Petition, presented to a crowd of 40,000 on the 'Field of Liberty' outside Blaj on 15–17 May 1848. They turned to Vienna for help against the Magyars. The Austrian military commander in the province, General Anton von Puchner (1779–1852), another veteran of the Napoleonic Wars, called on all loyal Transylvanians to rise up against the government in Budapest. Peasants launched a traditional *jacquerie*, killing Maygar and German landlords and officials. On their side, the Transylvanian Magyars raised a force of 30,000, including border regiments in the army, and began to retaliate, shooting Romanian peasants in mass executions and razing 230 villages to the ground. Puchner's troops established control gradually, but were beaten back by a strong Hungarian military force when they tried to push on towards Budapest. Altogether the number of deaths was estimated at 40,000.

The revolutionary upheavals of 1848 spread even further east, to Moldavia and Wallachia, the two predominantly Romanian-speaking principalities adjoining Transylvania on the eastern side. The principalities were nominally under joint Ottoman and Russian control, ratified in the Organic Statute of 1831, which had imposed the rule of the princes, or *hospodars*, from outside. Liberal students and Romanian nationalists, influenced by the radical ideas many of them had imbibed in Paris, formed a secret society called 'The Brotherhood' in 1843 to prepare for revolution. On 9 April 1848, following a mass meeting at the Petersburg Hotel in Iaşi, liberal demonstrators issued a list of thirty-five demands for liberalization to the currently reigning prince of Moldavia, Mihail Sturdza (1795–1884). He brought in the army, arrested 300 protesters, had them 'beaten like dogs' and deported them across the Turkish border. To back him up, the Russians moved troops into the province. The revolution succeeded in Wallachia, however, where on 13 June large demonstrations toppled the *hospodar* Gheorghe Bibescu (1804–73) and issued the Proclamation of Islaz. It announced a series of classic liberal principles including the abolition of civil ranks, the ending of capital punishment, and the formation of a provisional government. Acting under Russian pressure, the Ottoman government sent in a military force to the Wallachian capital of Bucharest on 25 September, occupying the city after a brief exchange of fire; two days later, not trusting the Ottomans to finish the job, the Russians moved in as well. Ninety-one revolutionaries were arrested and sent into exile, and many more fled to Paris or across the border into Bulgaria. Britain and France had refused to intervene, the conservative landowners in Moldavia and Wallachia had recoiled in alarm at the liberals' proposals for the ending of serfdom, and the ultimate objective of the revolutionaries – the unification of the two provinces to form an independent Romania – seemed as far off as ever.

Similar clashes quickly developed in the Habsburg Empire. Slovak nationalists' demand for the use of Slovak as an educational and official language was rebuffed by the Magyars, and the nationalists' anger spilled over into a series of violent conflicts starting in September 1848 that ended in the Slovak leaders going over to the Habsburg side. The Austrians roused Ruthenian (that is, Ukrainian) peasants in eastern Galicia against their Polish nationalist landlords by freeing them from serfdom, allowing them a representative Ruthenian Council and permitting the publication of the first-ever periodical in the province written in Ukrainian. Polish nationalists staged an uprising in the Prussian province of Posen in late April and early May 1848, led by Ludwik Mierosławski again, like its predecessor two years before. After a series of minor skirmishes with a large Prussian force sent at the request of the province's German inhabitants, the Polish insurgents abandoned the struggle, whose only result was the abolition of the Grand Duchy of Posen and its reduction to the status of an ordinary Prussian province. At Frankfurt the moderate liberal Wilhelm Jordan (1819–94) asked pointedly whether the Germans in Posen should live in 'a nation of lesser cultural content than themselves'.

Other national minorities were not slow to stake their own claims. Nationalist Serbs living in the southern area of the Kingdom of Hungary, encouraged by the neighbouring Principality of Serbia, proclaimed the autonomy of their province, the Vojvodina, in March 1848. Magyar troops crushed the rebellion, massacring some 300 Serbs in the town of Bečej, then marched slowly through the province during the late autumn and winter months, torching Serb villages as they went, and hanging many of their inhabitants, while the Serbs responded with ambushes and surprise attacks. Meanwhile, in Croatia, debates on of national unity with the Serbs led to the calling of a Croatian national congress in Zagreb on 25 March, which proclaimed the abolition of serfdom and called for Croatian autonomy. Conservative Croatian landlords were unhappy about the abolition of serfdom, which the Magyar liberals were advocating. A talented Croatian officer, Count Josip Jelačić (1801–59), an individual with strong monarchist and conservative views, seemed to the hardliners in Vienna to be the man to bring the weight of the Serbs and Croats to bear against the Hungarians. Appointed Ban, or governor, of Croatia, and given command of the Military Frontier, the series of defences against the now faded threat once posed by the Ottomans, Jelačić tried to unite the Serbs and Croats (publicly praying, for example, in both Serbian Orthodox and Croatian Catholic churches). If, he warned the Croatian parliament, 'the Hungarians continue to prove themselves to act not as brothers . . . but as oppressors, let them know . . . that we are ready with sword in hand!' On 4 September he led 50,000 troops across the river Drava into the core territory of the Magyars in support of the Serbs.

What happened in the Habsburg Monarchy also had serious repercussions for German unity. For one thing, the Austrian authorities were in the end not prepared to see the German-speaking part of their empire lopped off and attached to a unified Germany ruled from Frankfurt. For another, problems were also caused by the assumption of German nationalists that because Bohemia was part of the German Confederation and had many inhabitants who spoke German, it would become part of a united Germany. When the German Pre-Parliament at Mannheim invited the eminent Czech historian František Palacký (1798–1876) to join its members and help prepare all-German elections, he responded on 11 April 1848 by declaring that he had no interest in German affairs. 'I am a Czech of Slavonic blood,' he declared defiantly. Outraged, the German deputies threatened to use force to bring Bohemia into a united Germany. Meanwhile, Czech and German nationalists began to form separate Czech and German militias in Prague, and the middle classes, many of whose members were bilingual, began to take sides. At this point, the leading hardliner in Vienna, Count Latour, decided to intervene. Like a number of the leading Austrian generals, he had fought in the struggle against Napoleon, and regarded all liberals and revolutionaries as enemies of the state. The man Latour chose to seize control of events in Prague was Field Marshal

Alfred Prince zu Windischgrätz, a veteran of the Battle of the Nations at Leipzig in 1813 and an arch-conservative who had opposed all the concessions made by the emperor and his advisers. Windischgrätz placed his 10,000 troops in strategic positions around Prague, sparking a protest march on 12 June 1848 led by Czech militia, students, bourgeois National Guards and some 2,500 workers. When they encountered members of the German militias, fighting broke out, and soon barricades went up all over the city, 400 of them in all. German and Czech militias shot wildly at each other, and when a stray bullet killed Windischgrätz's wife, the Field Marshal withdrew his troops and bombarded the city from the surrounding hills until the insurgents surrendered on 17 June. A committee of the Frankfurt Parliament gave full support to Windischgrätz. Yet the Field Marshal's conquest of Prague was in fact the first stage of the counter-revolution that in due course would sweep all these revolutionary institutions away.

Windischgrätz had already established communications with Marshal Radetzky and the Habsburg court even before Ferdinand I's return to Vienna. Jelačić's army, repulsed by the Hungarians, was now encamped not far from the Austrian capital. After Radetzky's victory at Custoza in July 1848, Latour and the hardliners at court envisaged a pincer movement of the loyal armies, converging on Vienna and Budapest. They were able to exploit not only the national divisions among the revolutionaries but also the gulf that had opened up between moderate constitutional liberals on the one hand and radical republican democrats on the other. When the government announced a sharp cut in wages, the men employed on earthworks at the Prater made a clay and straw effigy of the Minister of Public Works and set it on a donkey with a kreutzer coin in his mouth and a placard labelling it 'The Kreutzer Minister'. On 23 August they began a mock funeral procession into the city centre. It quickly clashed with loyal units of the National Guard. Eighteen workers were killed and more than 150 seriously wounded as the demonstration was dispersed. The government followed this victory by immediately abolishing the public-works scheme, though it did make an effort to find alternative employment in the private sector for those thrown out of a job.

This was class war. Terrified middle-class Viennese liberals now began to turn to the monarchy and the army for protection. Taking advantage of the situation, the government arrested leading student journalists and suppressed republican newspapers. It now moved against Budapest, where Jelačić's invasion in early September had brought Kossuth to power as Batthyáni dithered and Széchenyi, his attempts at a peaceful solution to the crisis brought to nothing, had a nervous breakdown, tried to commit suicide, and was put in an asylum. Caught in an impossible conflict of interests, the Archduke Stefan resigned as Palatine, and the Court sent Field Marshal Franz von Lamberg (1791–1848), yet another veteran of the Napoleonic Wars, to Budapest to replace him. However, on his arrival, on 28 September 1848, Lamberg was beaten to death by an irate crowd as his coach crossed the Danube; his mutilated body was carried in triumph, impaled on scythes, through the streets. This turned Court opinion decisively against Budapest. On 3 October the government in Vienna felt bold enough to issue a decree abolishing the Hungarian Parliament and placing the country under martial law, with Jelačić as imperial commissioner and commander-in-chief. As Latour sent a battalion of troops to Vienna's railway station to make their way to join forces with him, angry crowds of workers, joined by democrats still sympathetic to the Hungarian cause, tore up the railway lines and blocked their way. Reinforcements arrived and opened fire on the crowd, but the officer in command was killed and the imperial troops were forced to withdraw. There were exchanges of fire on St Stephen's Square, but the government forces were unable to master the situation.

Seeking to avoid further violence, Latour ordered the gates of the Ministry of War opened and his troops not to fire on the crowd. The hostile demonstrators outside burst into the building, seized him, knocked his hat off, then beat him to death, stabbing and trampling the body as it lay on the floor. Latour's clothes were removed, and his naked corpse was hanged from a lamp post and used for target practice. The imperial arsenal was bombarded and looted, though only after its defenders had killed many of the besiegers with grapeshot. On 7 October 1848 the terrified emperor and his family fled the city for the Moravian town of Olmütz, leaving Vienna in a state of chaos as the Parliament (whose Czech deputies had decamped to Prague), the clubs, the student committee, the city council and the bureaucracy issued and countermanded orders on a daily basis: for the rest of October, as one observer commented, the Viennese were 'ruled with placards'.

The end in Vienna came quickly. On 16 October 1848, after Windischgrätz arrived in Olmütz, a new proclamation from Emperor Ferdinand condemned the 'reign of terror' in Vienna, in a deliberate reference to the events of 1793–4 in Paris, and gave Windischgrätz, who helped draft the document, full powers to restore order. An imperial army numbering 70,000 surrounded the city and cut off its food supplies. On 28 October it began a sustained bombardment, and started clearing the barricades, while Windischgrätz's Croatian troops went from house to house, looting and torturing the inhabitants. Meanwhile, 28,000 loyal soldiers, led by

Jelačić, also entered the city and quickly cleared thirty barricades in hand-to-hand combat, led by Montenegrin troops clenching their scimitars between their teeth as they climbed over the obstructions. In a few hours of bloody fighting, the city was retaken. Windischgrätz declared martial law, abolished the Academic Legion and the National Guard, banned public meetings, and imposed a strict censorship of the press. More than 2,000 radicals and democrats were arrested; nine were executed, including Wenzel Messenhauser (1813–48), a former officer who had commanded the National Guard throughout the conflict. Another victim was Robert Blum (1807–48), a worker from Cologne who had been employed as a gardener, a goldsmith and an operative in a lamp factory. Blum's talent for oratory had won him a seat in the Frankfurt Parliament, which had sent him to Vienna to support the revolution; he was arrested for treason and executed on 9 November (the first but far from the last time that this date marked a major turning point in German history).

The resurgence of Habsburg power demonstrated not only the Austrian government's determination to keep its domains intact in the face of the revolutionary and nationalist tide, but also its utter ruthlessness in going about the business of re-establishing its authority. In Vienna a new government was appointed under Prince Felix zu Schwarzenberg (1800–52), Windischgrätz's brother-in-law and a military adviser to Radetzky. As a first step in ensuring the Monarchy's future, his government persuaded the hapless Ferdinand to abdicate his throne on 2 December 1848 in favour of his eighteen-year-old nephew, Franz Joseph. 'The affair,' Ferdinand wrote in his diary, 'ended with the new Emperor kneeling before his old Emperor and Lord, that is to say, me, and asking for a blessing, which I gave him, laying both hands on his head and making the sign of the Holy Cross . . . After that I and my dear wife packed our bags.' He lived out the rest of his life, which lasted until 1875, in the Hradčany Castle in Prague. With order restored in Vienna, the new government turned its attention to Budapest, where in the face of the Habsburg declaration of war on 3 October 1848 and the rampages of Jelačić's Croatian troops and their Serbian and Romanian allies, who murdered, looted and burned their way across the land, radicals and moderates had united to form a National Defence Committee under Kossuth's leadership.

Windischgrätz now led 52,000 men slowly down the Danube, defeating a small and poorly equipped Hungarian force and entering Budapest on 15 January 1849. Batthyáni, attempting to mediate, was arrested and imprisoned by the Habsburg general, tried for treason, and after many months in prison, shot by firing squad on 6 October 1849. But the Habsburg armies did not have everything their own way. The Hungarian

National Defence Committee removed itself to Debrecen, to the east of the capital. Conscription boosted the strength of the Hungarian Army to 170,000 by June 1849, Hungarian munitions factories turned out large quantities of arms and ammunition, and Kossuth managed to purchase and smuggle in further military materiel from abroad. Insurgents from non-Magyar minorities were arrested and tried; 122 were sentenced to death. Inevitably, the situation played into the hands of the radicals, and as the newly replenished Hungarian Army, now in the hands of competent commanders, began to push the Habsburg forces back, Kossuth declared complete independence on 14 April 1849 and was elected President by acclamation. On 23 April 1849 the Hungarians retook Budapest. The Austrians had left a garrison in Buda Castle, however, towering high above the Danube. Some 40,000 Hungarian troops, armed with heavy artillery, spent two weeks besieging it before storming the heights on the night of 20–21 May 1849, giving no quarter and putting more than a thousand Austrian soldiers to the sword in the course of a few hours. After this humiliating reverse, Windischgrätz was relieved of his command.

The fate of the Habsburg Monarchy hung in the balance. In this desperate situation, Franz Joseph and the government in Vienna took the radical step of going to meet Tsar Nicholas I of Russia in Warsaw on 21 May 1849 to ask for support in 'the holy struggle of the social order against anarchy'. This was a brief resurrection of the largely moribund principles of the Holy Alliance. The tsar was flattered by the young Franz Joseph's gesture of falling to his knees and kissing his hand in supplication. More pragmatically, he feared the effect of Hungarian independence on his Polish subjects, a number of whom were serving in the Hungarian Army, some of them in senior positions. The new Austrian commander, the hot-tempered Julius von Haynau (1786–1853), another veteran of the Napoleonic Wars, threw 83,000 men and 330 guns into the fray in the west, while Jelačić's 44,000 troops, equipped with 190 artillery pieces, advanced from the south. Fully occupied with resisting these invasions, the Hungarians were unable to prevent an enormous force of 200,000 Russians, equipped with 600 pieces of artillery, pushing forward into Transylvania in support of the 48,000 Habsburg and Romanian fighters there. By 13 July 1849, Haynau had retaken Budapest, while the Hungarian government and Diet fled to Szeged in the south. Hungarian appeals for international protection fell on deaf ears. Desperate for allies, the government in Budapest issued a belated guarantee on 28 July that minority languages and cultures would be protected.

It was too late. Haynau's force soon reached Temesvár, the principal town in the Banat. Here, on 9 August 1849, it crushed a Hungarian army led by the Polish soldier József Bem (1794–1850), who had served in Napoleon's Grand Army and taken part in the 1830 uprising in Poland and in the Portuguese Civil War. Ever on the lookout for liberal causes, he went to Vienna in 1848 and next to Transylvania. Unlike his commander-in-chief, the gifted military tactician Artúr Görgei (1818–1916), Bem had a record in battle of almost unrelieved failure. He spoke no Hungarian, and at Temesvár he fell off his horse and was unable to command his forces at the crucial moment. Escaping once more, he made his way across the border to the Ottoman Empire, converted to Islam, and died under the name of Murat Pasha as governor of Aleppo. This was the last battle of the war. Kossuth resigned and, shaving off his whiskers, went to Constantinople, from where, after a period of house arrest, he took a ship to England, arriving in 1851 to the applause of tumultuous crowds. His English, learned from reading Shakespeare with the aid of a dictionary, was described as 'wonderfully archaic and theatrical'. After visiting America, where he addressed a joint session of Congress, he returned to Europe, ending his days in Turin; his voice, captured on an Edison phonograph in 1890, is the first recording made in the Hungarian language.

On 13 August 1849, Görgei surrendered to the Russians. Disregarding the tsar's pleas for clemency, Haynau had 4,600 Hungarians arrested, 1,500 imprisoned for periods between ten and twenty years, served by many of them in irons, and 500 sentenced to death. While many of the death sentences were commuted to long terms of imprisonment, 120 were carried out, mostly by hanging. Kossuth and other leading escapees were tried *in absentia* and their names nailed to the gallows in a kind of mock-execution. Görgei himself, as the signatory of the surrender, was spared. In the end, the Hungarians had been defeated partly by the overwhelming numerical superiority of the Russian Army, which inflicted on them the final, decisive defeat, partly by the depredations of the Romanians, Croats and Serbs, which forced them to divide their forces, and most of all by the superior discipline, organization and equipment of Haynau's troops, which were able to draw on financial and industrial resources not available to the Hungarians.

RADICALS AND REACTIONARIES

The recovery of nerve by the Habsburg Monarchy and the reconquest of Vienna and Prague in the summer and autumn of 1848 had profoundly negative effects on the prospects of German unification. On 20 December the Frankfurt Parliament, after many months of discussion, finally promulgated the Basic Rights of the German People, guaranteeing all the liberal freedoms, secularizing marriage, abolishing aristocratic titles and privileges, introducing trial by jury in open court, and abolishing the death penalty. Yet these would prove impossible to enforce. Since Austria and Bohemia had definitively rejected inclusion in a unitary German nation state, the Parliament was left with no choice but to go for a smaller Germany, with the King of Prussia as hereditary sovereign, able to delay legislation but not reject it. Sufficient numbers of democrats were persuaded to support the idea with the inclusion of the vote for all men over the age of twenty-five in the Constitution, which narrowly passed on 27 March 1849. Twenty-eight German states adopted the Constitution, including Prussia, where the newly elected, largely liberal Parliament endorsed it on 21 April. Immediately, however, Friedrich Wilhelm IV, who referred to the imperial crown as a 'dog-collar with which people want to chain me to the 1848 Revolution', dissolved the Parliament, shortly afterwards declaring that he would never accept an office given him by election rather than Divine Right. This severely undermined the political position of the moderate constitutionalists and played into the hands of the radical democrats and republicans, who now seized the initiative. However, it was striking that they were able to do so only in relatively peripheral regions of Germany, in Saxony and the Rhineland, where the last stand of the radical democrats now took place.

The King of Prussia's decision to reject the constitution of a united Germany emboldened other monarchs to do the same. But they were not all equally well equipped to back it with force. On 30 April 1849, sending the liberal deputies in Dresden back home, King Friedrich Augustus II of Saxony appointed a hard-line government that sanctioned the use of force to restore order. By 3 May demonstrators had put up 108 barricades across the city, the civil guard had begun to desert the government, and the king and his ministers fled to the impregnable fortress of Königstein, just outside Dresden, from where they called upon the Prussians to restore order. The dismissed democratic deputies now formed a new Saxon government, and revolutionaries flocked to its defence from outside the city. Among those who mounted the barricades was the Court music director Richard Wagner (1813–83), who had come under the influence of the ideas of Proudhon and Feuerbach and saw revolution as a way of creating the ideal conditions in which to achieve his mission as a universal artistic genius. Enthused by the uprising, he declared optimistically: 'The old world is in ruins from which a new world will arise; for the sublime goddess REVO-LUTION comes rushing and roaring on the wings of the storm.' More radical still was the anarchist Mikhail Bakunin. He had arrived in Dresden in March 1849 after first having taken part in the revolution in Paris, then being expelled from Berlin, and finally telling the delegates at the Pan-Slav Congress in Prague in June that they should 'overthrow from top to bottom this effete social world which has become impotent and sterile'. Bakunin had no sympathy with the aims of the Saxon liberals; he was in Dresden simply because he liked a good revolution.

While Wagner busied himself making hand grenades and looking out for the Prussian army from the top of the Frauenkirche, Bakunin helped build the barricades. It was all to no avail. The Prussian government acted with lightning rapidity, sending its troops to the Saxon capital by train. Some 5,000 Prussian and Saxon soldiers marched in on 9 May 1849, demolished the barricades, and overcame the resistance of the 3,000 poorly organized revolutionaries defending them; 250 of the insurgents were killed in the action, 400 were wounded, and 869 others were arrested. No fewer than 6,000 were prosecuted for offences going back to March 1848, and 727 received prison sentences, many of them lengthy. Ninety-seven per cent of them were native Saxons; outsiders, blamed for the revolt by the authorities, were in fact an extreme rarity. Nearly 2,000 insurgents fled to Switzerland, among them Wagner. He reported that Bakunin 'had to submit his huge beard and bushy hair to the tender mercies of the razor and shears ... A small group of friends watched the operation, which had to be executed with a dull razor, causing no little pain, under which none but the victim himself remained passive. We bade farewell to Bakunin,' he added, 'with the firm conviction that we should never see him again alive.' Despite his disguise, Bakunin was arrested, and had the distinction of being sentenced to death twice, first by the Saxons for his part in the uprising, then by the Austrians for his inflammatory rhetoric at the Pan-Slav Congress in Prague. As a Russian citizen, however, he was extradited to St Petersburg, where he was sentenced to a lengthy period of imprisonment in the Peter and Paul fortress, followed by exile in Siberia.

The uprising in Saxony was part of a wave of protest and rebellion against the Prussian decision to reject German unity. In most other parts of Germany it was more easily dispersed. At Frankfurt, the titular head of state, Archduke Johann, refused to condemn the Prussians' action in Dresden, and Heinrich von Gagern resigned as a minister, leading sixty deputies out of the Parliament on 20 May 1849. The Austrian and Prussian delegates were recalled by their respective governments, and those of the other two states that had rejected the Constitution, Saxony and Hanover, followed suit. The remaining 104 deputies left for Stuttgart to escape the Prussian troops in Frankfurt, but under pressure from Berlin,

Württemberg troops broke up the meeting on 17 June, trashing the Stuttgart assembly chamber and tearing up the black, red and gold colours with which it was adorned. In the Rhineland, meetings organized by the democratic clubs and associations demanded the acceptance of the Constitution by the Prussian and Bavarian governments. On the Lower Rhine, barricades went up in Düsseldorf, Elberfeld and Solingen in early May 1849, with machine-breaking a notable part of the insurrection. As crowds released prisoners from the local jails, citizens and militia commanders formed Committees of Public Safety. Prussian troops began bombarding the barricades in Düsseldorf, and, realizing the hopelessness of their situation, the poorly organized insurgents in Elberfeld and Solingen dismantled theirs and went home, while other insurgent forces in the area, including many peasants, also disbanded.

The revolutionaries and democrats were not so easily cowed further upriver. On the Upper Rhine, democratic clubs met in a ferment of excitement on 2 May 1849, establishing a 'Provisional Government' in the Bavarian Palatinate after King Maximilian II had rejected the Frankfurt Constitution. Two columns of armed workers and citizens, mobilized by the democrats in Rhine-Hessen, marched to their aid. Soldiers sent to restore order mutinied and joined the rebels. Red republican flags and ribbons were everywhere. Further upstream, the armed forces of Baden mutinied in support of the democrats and forced the Grand Duke to flee to France on 13 May. Declaring Baden to be a republic, the democrat leaders joined forces with the insurgents in Hessen and the Palatinate to try and rescue what was left of the Frankfurt Parliament. The troops were commanded by the veteran Polish revolutionary nationalist Ludwik Mierosławski, aided by Gustav Struve, whom the rebels had released from his imprisonment. Struve raised an impromptu force of students and returned exiles, including Friedrich Engels; they were poorly equipped and ill-disciplined (Engels reported that one regiment broke into a wine cellar and got completely drunk). A force of 30,000 Prussian, Hessian and Württemberg troops invaded the Palatinate on 12 June, brushing aside resistance with their artillery, and reached Baden a week later, defeating Mierosławski's forces at the Battle of Waghäusel. The last town to resist was Rastatt, where 6,000 democrats surrendered on 23 July 1849. The prisoners were decimated and the 600 bodies of those executed thrown into common graves. Engels escaped to Switzerland along with many others. Mierosławski made his way to Paris. In the following months, no fewer than 80,000 people left Baden for America.

A dialectic of radicalization on the left and military reaction on the right had emerged in many parts of Europe by the later stages of the revolution. In contrast to 1830, popular uprisings all over Europe had been powerful, persistent, and violent enough to shake the foundations of authority to their core. Many democratic revolutionaries were former *carbonari*, but by the late 1840s they had abandoned their old conspiratorial habits and put themselves at the head of the insurgent masses, just as the Jacobins had done in the French Revolution. But by the later stages of the 1848–9 revolution this was increasingly an act of desperation. And the more the democrats turned to the masses for backing, the more the moderate liberals were driven to invoke the military support of established authority. There was desperation too on the other side: as they recovered their nerve, monarchs and conservatives realized that in some cases they could not turn the tide without outside help. Just as the Russians had intervened with military force to rescue the Habsburgs in Hungary, so too the French, for very different reasons, would intervene to stabilize the situation in Rome. Dramatic events were to occur in both France and Italy before this happened.

These divisions were especially stark in the Papal States. Pope Pius IX had appointed as Minister of Justice the moderate liberal Count Pellegrino Rossi (1787–1848), a former supporter of the Napoleonic regime in Italy in 1815 who had lived in exile in France, taking French citizenship and being sent to Rome by Guizot as French ambassador. Rossi soon became in effect the head of the government and had leading radicals, exiles from Naples, arrested. On 15 November 1848 he was surrounded by demobilized soldiers on the steps of the Parliament and stabbed to death. A crowd gathered outside his widow's house, chanting 'Blessed be the hand that stabbed Rossi.' Thousands of people assembled in front of the papal residence at the Quirinal Palace demanding a republic. Some started firing weapons. The Pope's secretary was shot by a bullet entering through his office window, and a cannon was pointed at the palace gate. Thoroughly terrified, Pius IX fled to Naples in a carriage, disguised as a parish priest. He withdrew his troops from northern Italy, alarmed by the nationalists' declaration of the war as a holy crusade: the Austrians, after all, were good Catholics as well.

In Tuscany, moderate liberals tried to hold the ring against a popular insurrection in Livorno, where democrats assumed power following a popular occupation of the arsenal on 23 August 1848. A huge demonstration in Florence forced the Tuscan authorities to agree to elect thirty-seven delegates to the Constituent Assembly on the basis of one man, one vote. Grand Duke Leopold fled, calling upon Marshal Radetzky to help him restore order. Rioters tore down the Grand Duke's insignia from buildings and Tuscany was proclaimed an independent republic. In Piedmont, democrats pressured Carlo Alberto into repudiating the truce declared with the Austrians after his defeat at Custoza in July 1848 and mobilizing his forces against the Austrians. In a battle lasting all day on 22 March 1849 and until the following dawn, Carlo Alberto's army of 85,000 poorly trained and badly equipped men was routed by 72,000 well-disciplined soldiers under Radetzky at Novara, north-east of Milan. For Carlo Alberto this was the last straw. After trying, and failing, to die in battle ('even death has cast me off,' he complained), he abdicated in favour of his son, Vittorio Emanuele II (1820–78), and left for Portugal, where he died an embittered man a few months later. Radetzky forced a large indemnity on Piedmont, and amnestied all except a hundred of the Tuscan and Lombard revolutionaries. Democrats in Genoa tried to rescue the situation but were overcome by Radetzky's army, which bombarded their city into submission. For his part, Vittorio Emanuele warded off further domestic pressure by adhering publicly to Piedmont's liberal constitution and declaring his allegiance to Italian unity ('I will hold the tricolor high and firm'). This was to pay handsome dividends a decade later.

In the south of the peninsula, continuing social unrest in Naples and Sicily played into the hands of King Ferdinando Carlo. Even after crushing the democratic revolt in Naples in May 1848, he was still faced with a rebellion in Sicily. In classic style, the moderates there created a National Guard to try and restore order, but it was poorly trained and no match for the 10,000 regular troops dispatched by the king in August 1848 across the Straits of Messina. They retook Messina in a six-day bombardment that destroyed two-thirds of the city and earned Ferdinando Carlo the nickname 'King Bomba'. In Sicily the revolutionary government had chosen the ubiquitous Ludwik Mierosławski to command its small force of 7,000 men, but it was no match for Ferdinando Carlo's trained troops. Moreover, Mierosławski could not speak Italian and so was unable to give proper commands to his troops. As a Neapolitan fleet sailed towards Palermo, barricades went up, adorned with red flags, but the rebels were divided, and there was little serious resistance: as the young lawyer Francesco Crispi (1818–1901), a radical member of the Sicilian Parliament, complained, 'the moderates were more afraid of the people's victory than that of the Bourbon troops'. On 11 May 1849 the king completed his seizure of Palermo, dissolved the Parliament, and re-established his ramshackle autocracy on the island. In Naples he dissolved the Parliament and arrested the deputies.

As far as the remaining revolutionaries across Italy were concerned, this left no immediate option except a republic. As the Tuscan republican movement fell apart in disarray, a force of 15,000 Austrian troops marched in on 26 April 1849 and restored Grand Duke Leopold to the throne. Only Rome now remained. The Pope's flight led to the proclamation of the Roman Republic, in which Mazzini, elected an honorary citizen by a unanimous vote of the democratic Assembly, played the leading role. Mazzini proved to be an unexpectedly competent administrator, winning general approval for his modest way of life, his probity and his effectiveness. He closed down the Inquisition and made over its premises for the accommodation of the poor, scrapped the censorship and abolished the death penalty, introduced public courts run by lay judges, set up a progressive taxation system and introduced religious toleration. His commissioner in Ancona, a town on the Adriatic coast of the Papal States, Felice Orsini (1819–58), a former *carbonaro*, restored order in the midst of a crime wave. The American writer Margaret Fuller (1810–50), visiting Rome at this time, called Mazzini 'a man of genius, an elevated thinker' and compared him to Julius Caesar.

However, the Pope's appeal to the international community, now led again by the resurgent monarchies of Europe, did not fall on deaf ears. Surprisingly, perhaps, it was the French who responded. Following the defeat of the Parisian workers and radicals in the 'June Days' of 1848, the moderate liberals were desperately looking for a figure who would maintain order while preserving the political achievements of the revolution. They found one in the inveterate plotter Louis-Napoleon Bonaparte, whose last escapade had been a botched landing in Boulogne, where he had been arrested on the beach with his armed followers. Sentenced to life imprisonment, he had escaped in 1846 dressed as a builder during restoration work on the fortress where he was incarcerated, and was living in exile in London. In 1844 he had won support from the workers by publishing a book, written in prison, advocating the elimination of poverty by the creation of state-subsidised savings schemes and labour colonies. He also won over the moderates: 'I desire order,' he proclaimed. Unprepossessing, dismissed by many as a 'cretin', to use the term applied to him by Thiers, and a stranger to France (he spoke French with a German accent as a result of his education in exile in Germany), Louis-Napoleon seemed to be so marginal a figure that the Assembly, on Lamartine's prompting, had no qualms about passing a Constitution that provided for a popularly elected President even though it was clear he would be a candidate. Yet, skilfully exploiting the Napoleonic legend for his own benefit, Louis-Napoleon, in the elections held on 10–11 December 1848, won by a landslide against the unpopular general who had put down the June insurrection, Cavaignac, and a motley collection of fringe candidates, including Lamartine himself.

The new Prince-President, as he styled himself, of the Second Republic was aware of the need to win over conservatives and monarchists in France to his support, as well as to turn popular hostility to Austria to his own advantage. A French expedition to Rome to restore the Pope to his throne would win Catholic support in France and satisfy liberals and leftists by pre-empting the Austrian threat to do the same. In March 1849 the Assembly approved the sending of an expedition, and on 24 April, 6,000 French troops led by Charles Oudinot (1791–1863), who had fought with the first Napoleon from 1809 to 1814, landed on the Italian coast and moved towards Rome. Mazzini had been joined in Rome by Garibaldi, who had come back from exile in South America the previous August and taken part with his band of 500 volunteers in the fighting in northern Italy. Mazzini put him in charge of military affairs in Rome. Eight thousand troops of the Roman Republic surprised the French on 30 April and drove them back with heavy losses in a fierce bayonet charge, led by Garibaldi himself brandishing a sabre. Further republican victories followed against a Neapolitan army approaching from the south. Louis-Napoleon knew that the humiliation of Oudinot's initial defeat had to be avenged if he was to continue to associate himself plausibly with the military legend of his uncle. Oudinot moved heavy artillery up to the heights around the Eternal City and began a systematic bombardment.

On 3–4 June 1849 an assault on Italian positions allowed the French to move further forward, and by 22 June they had captured the outer walls of the city. With their ceaseless cannonades causing huge destruction and loss of life, the French entered the city on the night of 29–30 June, beating back Garibaldi's volunteers, who had now begun to wear the red shirts that later made them famous. Recognizing defeat, Garibaldi told Mazzini the game was up. The veteran revolutionary left for renewed exile in Switzerland, while Garibaldi led his volunteers out of Rome on an epic march across the mountains towards Venice, during which his wife Anita died and most of his followers were captured by the Austrians. They were not treated leniently. The Austrians stripped the skin off the forehead of the renegade priest Ugo Bassi (1800–49), where he had been anointed during his consecration, before putting him in front of a firing squad: 'I am guilty of no crime save that of being an Italian like yourself,' he told a papal official before his death. Garibaldi himself managed to make his way to the coast and sail to the Americas, where he eked out a living in a variety of countries over the next few years. In Rome, Pius IX, having by now thoroughly cast off his earlier reputation as a liberal reformer, disregarded Louis-Napoleon's advice to respect the liberties of his subjects, re-established the Inquisition, forced the Jews back into the old ghetto, and refused to amnesty the majority of the Republic's officials.

In northern Italy, Radetzky's victory over Piedmont at the Battle of Custoza a year earlier had left only Venice still in the hands of the revolutionaries. The enforced withdrawal of Piedmont from the struggle played into the hands of the republicans, where Daniele Manin restored order, held elections, and became effective dictator by popular acclaim in March 1849. Some 12,000 troops and volunteers from across Italy joined 10,000 Venetian soldiers in manning more than fifty fortified emplacements that defended the island city from attack by the Austrians massing on the mainland. Manin's 21,000 Venetian troops were commanded by the Neapolitan General Guglielmo Pepe, whose support enabled Manin to suppress the radical Mazzinian Italian Club in the city and deport most of its leading figures. As the siege went on, however, the Venetians began to run out of food and munitions. Rationing was introduced. Manin tried to get outside support, but only Kossuth and the Hungarians responded, and their forces were in the end unable to penetrate to the Dalmatian coast. Typhus, malaria and cholera began to take their toll on the citizens, 4,000 of whom died in the spring and summer of 1849. Over three weeks in May a massive bombardment of 60,000 shells rained down on Fort Marghera, on the causeway to the mainland, until the defenders were forced to abandon it. Moving their heavy artillery slowly into position, the Austrians fired a thousand cannonballs into the city on 29 July 1849. Recognizing the inevitable, Venice surrendered to Radetzky on 22 August, on relatively generous terms that allowed Manin and the other leaders to embark on a steamer to take them into exile. About 8,000 Austrian troops had died in the conflict, from enemy action or disease, and almost as many Venetians. As in other parts of the Habsburg domains, the ruthless determination and military superiority of the Austrian and allied forces had preserved the integrity of the empire. Few would have thought at the time that these events in fact spelled the beginning of a long crisis that within twenty years was to destroy the Habsburgs' position not only in Germany but in Italy as well.

By September 1849 the revolutions everywhere were over. Only in France was there a coda. After his election as President of the Second Republic in December 1848, Louis-Napoleon Bonaparte dissolved the National Assembly and secured a conservative majority in the elections of May 1849, building on the right-wing inclinations of the countryside. Packing his administration with former Orléanists, he rode the storm of democratic protest, led by the indefatigable Ledru-Rollin, that broke over him when his troops crushed the Roman Republic at the end of June 1849. On 11 June a crowd of 25,000 people singing the *Marseillaise* and including both Karl Marx and Alexander Herzen marched on the Assembly but was dispersed by cavalry. Only in Lyon, where artillery was used to destroy barricades put up by silk weavers, was there serious violence, involving fifty deaths and 1,200 arrests. Louis-Napoleon responded by introducing curbs on the press and on clubs, and introduced a law requiring three years' domicile as a qualification for voting, thus disenfranchising many electors in the often migratory urban working class. Two-thirds of Parisian electors lost their right to vote, and nearly three million across the country as a whole. Ledru-Rollin fled to England, while Republican deputies were arrested and imprisoned in France.

Travelling round the country from 8 August to 12 November 1850 rallying support for himself, Louis-Napoleon declared that 'the name of Napoleon is in itself a programme. At home it means order, authority, religion and the welfare of the people; and abroad it means national self-respect.' A petition with 1.5 million signatures demanding the revision of the Constitution to extend his term of office as President failed to win the required two-thirds majority in the Assembly, so Louis-Napoleon began preparing a coup d'état, buoyed by shouts of *Vive l'Empereur!* that had greeted him on his travels. On the night of 1–2 December 1851 he had opposition leaders including Thiers arrested, and the Assembly dissolved. Uprisings all over south-eastern and central France followed, and were effectively put down by the army; they justified Louis-Napoleon's pose as the guarantor of order. His propaganda condemned Republicans for instigating the violence and his police arrested 27,000 protesters, 3,000 of whom were imprisoned, 9,530 exiled to Algeria, and 239 sent to the penal colony of Devil's Island in French Guiana. Louis-Napoleon issued a proclamation condemning the Assembly for factionalism and corruption while at the same time appealing to democrats by restoring universal male suffrage. On 20 December 1851 a plebiscite resulted in 7.5 million votes approving his actions and only 640,000 against. Some 1.5 million electors had not voted, however, and the opposition was undoubtedly hamstrung by the imposition of martial law in most of the French departments. Another plebiscite in November 1852 approved his inauguration as Napoleon III, Emperor of the French (the numbering reflected the fiction that Napoleon I's son had reigned after his father's death until his own untimely demise in 1832). Victor Hugo referred to him sarcastically as 'Napoleon the Little' and was forced to flee to Brussels for his pains, going eventually to the Channel Islands, where he completed his great novel *Les Misérables* (1862). The new emperor had chosen for his self-crowning the anniversary of his uncle's victory at Austerlitz and his own coup the year before. Comparing the events of 1851 with Napoleon I's coup against the First Republic in 1799, Karl Marx commented caustically that history was repeating itself, 'the first time as tragedy, the second as farce'. This was neither the first nor the last time that Napoleon III's critics underestimated his singular abilities.

THE LIMITS OF CHANGE

Almost everywhere, the bourgeois liberals who led the revolution took their inspiration from British parliamentarianism, which underpinned Britain's world hegemony and industrial growth, while radicals and democrats were inspired by the ideals of the French Revolution of 1789–93. Moderate liberals sought the destruction of inherited authoritarian constitutions and the end of traditional, legally inscribed social hierarchies, while more radical spirits wanted a democratic republic. At the beginning, whatever their constitutional beliefs, revolutionaries everywhere thought of themselves as enrolled in the same causes. Some, like Bakunin or Mierosławski, even moved from country to country, taking part in several revolutionary events in the course of a few months. In many parts of Europe, too, veterans of the Napoleonic Wars re-emerged, to fight for or against the revolution according to their personal history and ideological past. The 1848 Revolutions broke out in the middle of a deep and widespread period of economic malaise that drove the impoverished masses to desperation and created a massive crisis of confidence in government in one state after another. The crisis hit Europe at a time when monarchs, from the weary Louis-Philippe in France to the nervous Friedrich Wilhelm IV in Prussia, from the epileptic Ferdinand I in Austria to the irresponsible Ludwig I in Bavaria, were peculiarly unfit to deal with it. Governments everywhere were paralysed by the memories of 1789. Revolution seemed inevitable and so they bowed to its historical force.

After decades in which they had made concessions to reform too slowly and too reluctantly, failing to address the key issues of economic distress and political participation, established governments were overwhelmed by the twin forces of moderate liberalism and democratic republicanism. Mass demonstrations, mounted by hundreds of thousands of disaffected workers and the urban poor, drove on the revolution in the major cities, just as they had in Paris in 1789–93. Everywhere, the moderate liberals established citizens' militias to carry out the twin tasks of replacing the trained armed forces of absolutist monarchs and to restore and maintain order on the streets. Inspired by the constitutional monarchist political model of the United Kingdom, the most politically powerful and economically advanced nation in the world, they sought to harness the forces of revolution for the politics of reform. Many of the reforms they tried to implement – trial by jury in open court, the abolition of the death penalty, parliamentary sovereignty, popular representation, free trade, the removal of import tariffs – were generally acceptable to the population at large; others were not. The liberals' ambivalent attitude towards state intervention to provide jobs for the unemployed and cheap food for the masses did not go unnoticed and helped fuel the anger of demonstrators. The creation everywhere of a National Guard or citizens' militia proved a double-edged sword, with the men enrolled in its service wavering in their allegiances between the forces of order and the fighters on the streets.

Strikingly, the demonstrators did not on the whole call for a return to the days of guild regulations and restrictions. Their demands for state intervention in society looked forward to a new democratic world rather than back to the old society of ordered social hierarchies and legally demarcated economic functions. Most of the statistics we possess on the composition of the crowds strongly suggest a powerful element of the new working class in them. The great majority of the 727 people condemned for their part in the revolution in Saxony, for example, belonged to the nascent working class: 19 per cent were master artisans, 26 per cent journeymen, 12 per cent 'artisans' and 12 per cent 'workers'; almost all of these in practice would have been factory workers. Saxony was the most industrially advanced part of Germany at this time, and the revolution there was more radical than most; the commitment of these workers to republican and democratic revolution was testimony to the depth of the economic crisis that had overtaken them. The rioters of the June Days in Paris were a similar random mixture of impoverished artisans and factory workers, most of them unemployed. All over Europe the disenfranchised built barricades to assert their claim to authority over urban space, establishing their power not just over the streets but also over the state, represented by the buildings ranged along them. In one city after another, barricades proved perhaps the most successful means of asserting popular sovereignty in a world where moderate liberals, restricting the franchise to a minority of the propertied wherever they could, denied it.

In the end, hastily assembled and poorly trained citizen militias proved no match for the disciplined and well-equipped forces of the professional armies, whose loyalty to the established state remained overwhelmingly intact. The monarchs recovered their nerve, having lost confidence in the liberals to maintain order. They were pushed to reassert their authority by a determined minority of diehard army officers and bureaucrats who regarded compromise as weakness and undermined it behind the backs of newly appointed liberal governments. There was little the revolutionaries could do to stop them regaining power. The revolutions of 1848 have sometimes been dismissed by historians as half-hearted, timid affairs, but the violence of the crowds, the lynching of hated royal officers, ministers and bureaucrats, and the storming of palaces and offices all over Europe, showed little evidence of reluctance to use force. Yet the ruthlessness and lack of inhibition shown by the armed forces of the old order far outweighed the violence of the crowds, in the face of which moderate liberals in most parts of Europe, with the notable exception of Hungary, gravitated towards the traditional forces of order. Democrats' attempts to ride the tiger of popular insurrection only pushed moderate liberals further in the direction of counter-revolution. Memories of the Reign of Terror exercised by Robespierre in 1793–4 were simply too strong.

The revolutionaries were also undermined by the failure of the peasantry in most parts of Europe to lend their support to them. In many countries, most notably France, serfdom had long since been abolished or, as in Prussia and Austria, watered down by attrition until only its last vestiges remained. The peasants did not harbour the overwhelming sense of grievance that powered them during the great French Revolution of 1789 or the Russian Revolution of 1917. Most of the Prussian troops who crushed the revolution of 1849 in the Rhineland came from rural backgrounds. In Italy, Garibaldi found no support from the peasantry in his attempt to wage a guerrilla war against the Austrians after the defeat at Custoza: 'I saw,' he later wrote, 'how little the national cause inspired the local inhabitants of the countryside.' It was Tuscan peasants who crushed the republican movement in Florence, called in by moderate liberals seeking to restore Grand Duke Leopold in April 1849. In France the peasantry, accorded the vote by the Second Republic's introduction of universal adult male suffrage, backed the forces of order and voted for Louis-Napoleon. In Poland the peasants massacred the nationalist landowners in 1846 and refused to support them two years later. In Habsburg central Europe the Monarchy's emancipation orders left peasants with nothing further to fight for. By 1848, moreover, landownership was no longer identified exclusively with aristocracy as it had been in the eighteenth century. Many estates had been bought up by newly wealthy bourgeois, blurring the contours of social hierarchy. Moderate liberals, including landowners, were keen to privatize the countryside, abolishing common grazing rights and introducing a free market to override customary practice. This did not endear them to the peasantry either. Peasant revolts broke out in 1848 in the areas where grievances still remained to be remedied, but they failed by and large to connect with the revolutionaries of the liberal middle class.

Most serious of all were the divisions that so quickly opened up in the revolutionary camp: not merely between liberals and democrats, or constitutional monarchists and republicans, but above all between rival nationalisms. The principle of national self-determination ran up against the confusion of national boundaries in many parts of Europe. An historic entity such as the lands of the Crown of St Stephen clashed with the existence of linguistic groups like the Serbs or the Romanians that both lived within it and crossed its borders. Germans and Magyars considered themselves superior to smaller and, as they thought, less advanced nations like the Czechs or the Croats. The Habsburgs in particular were able to exploit these cleavages to their own advantage. The core of the European resistance to nationalism, democracy and parliamentarianism was indeed located in Vienna; and the Habsburg Monarchy came out of the conflicts of 1848–9 with its integrity intact and its position as Europe's hegemonic power restored. Yet the revolutions contained the seeds of the empire's decay. For it had become clear to many German nationalists in particular that a German nation state would have to be constructed outside the empire, without Austria or Bohemia. This would require strong action to expel these Habsburg lands from the German Confederation, and that in turn would require the leadership of Prussia. In a similar way, Italian unification had been frustrated largely by the intransigence of the Habsburgs; the peninsula's wealthiest and most advanced state, Piedmont, remained the obvious leader of the unification process, but it had proved incapable of expelling the Austrians from northern Italy, and foreign aid, most obviously from France, would be required if the process were to succeed. For the moment, however, both German and Italian unification were off the European agenda.

The spirit of 1848 affected some parts of Europe in different ways and with a different chronology from the main course of events. In Spain, periodically racked by the Carlist Wars, moderate liberal hegemony had become imperilled by the authoritarian habits of General Ramón Narváez (1800–68), who presided over a constitutional reform in 1845 that limited the vote to the propertied classes, centralized the administration, reformed state finances and embarked on colonial wars in north Africa. Terrified that the 1848 Revolutions might spread to Spain, he muzzled the press, made frequent use of police spies, and ruled by decree. When asked on his deathbed whether he wished to forgive his enemies, he replied: 'I have no enemies: I have shot them all.' In February 1854, however, as economic depression hit the country, street protests began in Zaragoza and spread to other parts of Spain. More than 500 barricades were erected in Madrid, and Barcelona was similarly in uproar. In the south, General Leopoldo O'Donnell (1809–67), a descendant of Irish Catholic immigrants, 'pronounced' against the government, declaring 'that we wish to lift from the populations the centralization that is devouring them.' The political power of the military, significantly greater than in most other parts of Europe, ensured his success, sweeping him to power together with another progressive liberal general, Baldomero Espartero (1793–1879), victor in the First Carlist War. However, Queen Isabella's continual vacillation between progressives and moderates gradually turned the military leadership against her. The collapse of the railway boom that had sustained O'Donnell's leadership prompted another military revolution, backed by popular uprisings. In 1869 the victorious democrats pushed through a new Constitution – the sixth to be passed in Spain in the course of the nineteenth century – providing for universal male suffrage and all the classic liberal freedoms. They stopped short of introducing a Republic, but as one of the leading democrats remarked, 'to find a democratic king in Europe is as hard as to find an atheist in Heaven!' The search, perhaps unexpectedly, was to lead within a few months to the outbreak of a major European war.

Elsewhere in southern Europe, Greece had already experienced its liberal revolution in 1843, when a conspiracy of leading civilian politicians and army veterans of the War of Independence in the 1820s staged a bloodless coup against the 'Bavarocracy' of German officials brought in by King Otto when he had been imposed on the country by the Great Powers in 1832. Storming out of their barracks, the soldiers gathered below Otto's palace window, shouting 'Long live the Constitution!' Reluctantly, the king yielded, appointing one of the leading conspirators, Andreas Metaxas (1790–1860), Prime Minister in what was now a constitutional monarchy with a restored legislative assembly elected by universal male suffrage. Otto never fully accepted the Constitution, and his continued intrigues against it, combined with his failure to produce an heir, eventually led to another conspiracy that overthrew him in 1863. Told to accept this fait accompli by Britain and France, who had called the shots in Greece throughout his reign, Otto went back to Munich, where he would regularly appear in the Bavarian Court in traditional Greek dress until his death in 1867.

Greek independence was guaranteed by the Great Powers, but remaining European parts of the Ottoman Empire were beginning to experience disturbances, notably Albania. Here the Ottoman reform programme known as the *Tanzimat*, begun in 1839, imposed new taxes and centralized the administration, disempowering local feudal magnates and introducing Anatolian administrators who had no connection with the country and did not even speak the language. Huge resentment was caused by the Ottoman administrators' attempts to disarm the population, almost all of whom were used to carrying guns, and to recruit young men into the Ottoman Army. The arrest of refractory Albanian leaders led to an uprising in 1843 that drove Ottoman officials from most of the major towns. After three weeks of fierce fighting, the town of Kalkandelen fell to the rebels and became the headquarters of the Albanian Great Council, which demanded the rescinding of the reforms. The sultan sent an armed force to bring the Albanians to heel, commanded by Omer Pasha (1806–71), an ethnic Serb, originally called Mihajlo Latas, who had served in the Austrian Army on the Military Frontier but fled to Bosnia when he and his father were charged with embezzlement. He was described by his enemies as a 'careerist, with the zeal of the mercenary'. Omer Pasha brought together a force of 30,000 men, shelled Kalkandelen for several weeks, arrested the rebel leaders, and ended the uprising. This was anything but a liberal revolution, and it does not even seem to have provoked the development of a nationalist ideology among the Albanians, who possessed neither a functioning state nor an education system, and could not even agree on a common alphabet. Most disputes in Albania continued to be settled not by the law but by blood feuds.

This was a rather different situation to that of Bosnia, despite the similar origins of revolt in the resentment of Muslim landowners at the introduction of the *Tanzimat* and the imposition of military conscription. Here a Bosnian Muslim national identity had begun to emerge after the uprising of 1831, powerfully boosted by the resistance movement led by the Vizier of Herzegovina, Ali Rizvanbegović (1783–1851), who now declared that if the reforms were imposed, 'Bosnia would cease to be Bosnian in thirty years.' 'Mostar,' he announced to the Bosniaks, 'is your Istanbul.' Here too the Ottomans sent Omer Pasha to crush the rebellion. He entered Sarajevo in May 1850 at the head of an army of 8,000 men, including many Islamicized Poles and Hungarians who had fled to Istanbul in 1849, accompanied by 2,000 Albanian irregulars and armed with thirty-four modern cannon. Fierce but uncoordinated resistance from the local Bosnian magnates followed, over two years of brutal civil war, in which Omer Pasha reduced one rebel stronghold after another. So fierce was the fighting that Omer Pasha advised a friend to avoid eating fish from the river Sava, 'for they have been feeding on Bosniak flesh which I drove into the river'. As his troops plundered and pillaged their way across the country, imposing huge fines on rebel towns, Omer Pasha turned his headquarters at Travnik into 'one enormous prison'. 'Not a single office of state is now held by a Bosniak', it was reported. Rizvanbegović, who was in his late sixties, was forced to walk in chains for over ninety miles before being shot dead. Heavy taxes and billeting of troops reduced Bosnia to a state of destitution. 'Sarajevo,' one commentator noted after Omer Pasha's victory, 'is dead.'

Some countries remained relatively little affected by the events and ideas of 1848. In Sweden there were riots on the streets of Stockholm in 1848, but the crisis was partly defused by the fact that King Oscar I (1799–1859), who had acceded to the throne in 1844, was himself known to have liberal inclinations; his proposals for introducing a parliamentary system were rebuffed by the traditional Estates, however, and it was not until the early 1860s that the measure was successfully introduced, by Oscar's son Karl XV (1826–72), transforming Sweden into a constitutional monarchy. In Norway, which fell under the Swedish Crown, a largely peasant society enjoyed considerable autonomy following the constitutional changes of 1814 and their confirmation after the 'Battle of the Square' in 1829, and avoided the upheavals of 1848. The opposite situation obtained in Russia, where Nicholas I tightened the censorship and called up extra troops on hearing of the outbreak of revolution in Paris in 1848; in any case, however, the development of civil society in Russia had not reached a stage where a mass insurrection or a bourgeois liberal revolt was possible. In the realm of ideas, matters were different, and a number of Russian radicals – most notoriously, of course, Bakunin – took inspiration from the revolution as well as some of the ideas that circulated on its fringes.

In Britain the economic crisis of the late 1840s prompted a revival of the Chartist movement, which staged a series of massive demonstrations in Glasgow and London, with railings being torn up and shop windows smashed. Rioters in Manchester attacked a workhouse, and a national Chartist Convention staged a demonstration in South London in April 1848 attended by an estimated 150,000 people. Alarmed by the possibility that the marchers might try to emulate their counterparts in Paris, the government recruited 100,000 special constables (including Louis-Napoleon Bonaparte, just before his return to France) to prevent the demonstrators moving across the river. But the demonstration ended peacefully, and the movement was publicly ridiculed when it was revealed that many of the two million names on the petition it presented to Parliament were fakes, including 'Queen Victoria' and 'Mr. Punch'. Nevertheless, the government passed new legislation banning public meetings and strengthening the law on treason, and a group of ultra-radicals around the mixed-race tailor William Cuffay (1788–1870), a descendant of slaves, were arrested after a police spy revealed their plans to stage an insurrection. Cuffay was transported to Tasmania, taking with him a volume of Byron's poetry presented to him by London Chartists 'as a token of their sincere regard and affection for his genuine patriotism and moral worth'.

The British governments of the period, anxious not to impose extra tax burdens on the population at a time of economic hardship and potentially rising discontent, cut back sharply on expenditure on the large armed forces kept in the colonies, and stopped subsidising colonial planters and sugar growers at the expense of domestic consumers by an extension of free trade to the colonies. This in turn caused widespread unrest in the colonies, with Jamaican planters refusing to pay taxes and the governor of Canada pelted with eggs, while rebellious Anglo Loyalists burned down the parliament building in Montreal. The British colonial power's imposition of fresh taxes in Ceylon, again to avoid extra burdens at home, sparked a massive rebellion, in which 20,000 armed Buddhists tried to impose the indigenous Kandian monarchy and were crushed by colonial troops; their leader was shot in full robes and his body left hanging from a tree for four days. In Malta and the Ionian islands, both ruled by Britain, governors prudently introduced liberal constitutional reforms to prevent the revolution spreading from the mainland. Further afield, Boer farmers in Natal, encouraged by their 'observance of the state of affairs in Europe', as the governor of Cape Town, Sir Harry Smith (1787–1860), noted, rose in rebellion in 1848 against the introduction of English settlers into the area; when he defeated them, Smith observed complacently that Britain was more capable of uniting its various territories than Germany was.

Moderate liberals across Europe continued after 1848, indeed, to point to Britain's gradualist reforms as the way to defuse social tension. For mid-Victorian Britons, the idea of progress legitimized the nation's global hegemony and informed the politics of improvement. Lord Palmerston, a leading figure in the Whig governments of the late 1840s and 1850s, and Prime Minister (with a short break in the middle) from 1855 to 1865, encouraged liberal movements on the European Continent in the belief that the British model of society and politics was the way to be followed by all. 'We have shown the example,' he declared,

of a nation, in which every class of society accepts with cheerfulness the lot which Providence has assigned to it; while at the same time every individual of each class is constantly striving to raise himself in the social scale – not by injustice and wrong, not by violence and illegality, but by preserving good conduct, and by the steady and energetic execution of the moral and intellectual faculties with which his creator has endowed him.

The class warfare waged by the Chartists in the 1840s was indeed replaced in the 1850s by the steady pressure exercised by the new model trade unions such as the Amalgamated Society of Engineers, founded in 1851, which avoided strikes and focused on encouraging thrift among their members with a view to building up insurance funds to be dispensed in time of hardship. The 'Junta' of new, moderate union leaders based in London insisted that 'the riots of the rough population have but very little bearing on the claims of such societies as the Amalgamated Engineers or the Amalgamated Carpenters'. The fundamental principle of the age was individual advancement, and its Bible was *Self-Help: with Illustrations of Character and Conduct* (1859) by the Scottish journalist, railway administrator and ex-Chartist Samuel Smiles (1812–1904). 'Every human being,' declared Smiles, 'has a great mission to perform, noble faculties to cultivate, a vast destiny to accomplish. He should have the means of education, and of exerting freely all the powers of his godlike nature.' The book sold 20,000 copies in its first year of publication, and 250,000 by the time of its author's death.

The social harmony and liberal individualism of the 1850s and 1860s in Britain were reflected in the relative stability of the political system, in which the Whigs were largely dominant following the split in the Tory Party over the Corn Laws in 1846, though internal divisions and frequent dependence on the radicals weakened their effectiveness. Parliamentary sovereignty, celebrated in the treatise *The English Constitution* (1867) by the businessman and journalist Walter Bagehot (1826–77), was unchallenged, and so the improvement of the parliamentary system proceeded at a steady pace, cementing the dominance of the House of Commons in public life. Corrupt practices during elections were reduced by the outlawing of bribery in elections in 1854 (though it was not until 1883 that it was eliminated altogether), while the secret ballot was introduced in 1872 and the uneven distribution of seats according to population rectified in 1867. Party allegiances were shifting and unclear, but minority Tory administrations never lasted very long. After the death of Sir Robert Peel in 1850, his followers slowly gravitated towards the Whigs, but it was really Palmerston's popularity in the country that counted for most. The relative weakness of British governments in these decades reflected a wider scepticism about the role of government in a society based on freedom of enterprise, a scepticism underlined by the rigorous financial policies of the Chancellor of the Exchequer from 1852 to 1855 and again from 1859 to 1866, William Ewart Gladstone (1809–98), who had come over to the Whigs with the Peelites. Over this long period, he abolished hundreds of tariffs and excise duties and reduced income tax to four pence in the pound. Money, he believed, should not be handed over to the state to waste, but should be allowed to 'fructify in the pockets of the people'. Further reforms included the liberation of the press through the abolition of stamp duty on newspapers (1855) and the ending of paper duty (1861), measures that hugely increased the circulation of the dailies, and in 1857 the imposition of duties on inherited estates. All of this made Gladstone a popular figure among the working classes and their representatives and paved the way for his electoral successes after he became leader of the Liberal Party (as the Whigs were rechristened in 1859) two years after the death of Palmerston in 1865.

By this time, the central political rivalry of the period had emerged, between Gladstone and the Tory leader Benjamin Disraeli, a novelist of Jewish origin whose rise to fame owed an enormous amount to his oratorical abilities and to the fact that he had taken the lead in the opposition to Sir Robert Peel within his own party. As Tory governments were led from the House of Lords by the sickly Earl of Derby, Disraeli came to be the party's effective leader in the House of Commons. As such, he steered through a second Parliamentary Reform Bill in 1867, which increased the electorate by 88 per cent, from just over one to just under two million adult men, and abolished many remaining abuses. Vast but peaceful crowds demonstrated in favour of the Bill, whose provisions were widened beyond its original scope in a series of amendments designed to appease the demands of a working class that politicians in both parties now regarded as 'respectable'. In securing the approval of the Bill, Disraeli aimed to enfranchise a sizeable sector of men who were not well off but earned enough to give them a stake in the country and, as he hoped, vote Conservative. Similar considerations motivated the new French President, Louis-Napoleon Bonaparte, in retaining the universal male suffrage introduced in 1848. They were to inform other conservative regimes later in the century too, which realized belatedly that they could no longer maintain their supremacy in the modern world by using methods that belonged to the eighteenth century.

THE CRIMEAN WAR

The regimes that came to power in the wake of the failure of the 1848 Revolutions looked to new methods to cement their hard-regained authority. All of them recognized that economic distress had been at the root of the revolutions of 1848, so each focused with a new vigour on economic development. In Portugal, indeed, the regime of the Duke of Saldanha, a veteran of the Miguelist wars who came to power in 1851 in a coup (one of no fewer than seven that he led over the course of his life), described his government as one of 'regeneration', introduced a new constitution with direct elections, abolished the death penalty, and devoted government funds to improving the infrastructure by building a road, rail and telegraph network across the country. In Spain a new Ministry of Commerce, Education and Public Works was founded in the same year. In Piedmont the government of Cavour did the same. Restored princely regimes in the German states borrowed heavily to build railways, bridges, canals and schools. Everywhere on the Continent the state took over the central direction of railway-building, the major source of the economic boom of the 1850s. Governments set up statistical bureaux to assess the state of society and the economy, not only as an adjunct to police repression but also as a basis for economic, social and administrative reform. 'The people,' purred Saldanha in 1854, 'are renouncing politics in order to busy themselves with their own affairs.' Urban improvement was undertaken everywhere. Press censorship shifted from the futile pre-revolutionary attempt to stop critical articles being published to surveillance of those who wrote them, coupled with the increasing willingness of governments to use the press for their own propaganda.

Whatever was restored in 1850, it was not the Europe of the Vienna Settlement. Symbolized by the departure of Metternich (in 1848), the new Europe was very different from the Europe of the Restoration. After a lengthy period in which the Great Powers had worked together to maintain the status quo, 1850 inaugurated two decades of rapid change and violent upheaval on the international scene, led by a new generation of intelligent and flexible conservative politicians who emerged in the post-revolutionary situation. Men like Cavour, Bismarck, Napoleon III or Disraeli recognized that the preservation of order and stability required radical measures to co-opt the masses into support for the state. They also realized that nationalism was becoming increasingly powerful, indeed unstoppable, and in their different ways they were determined to exploit it for their own purposes. All of them were more than willing to use foreign policy to help achieve these ends. This introduced a powerful new element of instability into European politics. The man who did more than anyone else to inaugurate it was Emperor Napoleon III of France.

Napoleon III has some claim to be the first modern dictator. He realized that his legitimacy depended on popular support, not on some old-established religious or secular principle or tradition. Thus his coup and later the Senate resolution declaring him emperor were both put to a national vote. Other votes followed on other issues. This was, in other words, a plebiscitary dictatorship. Behind the scenes, the emperor managed and manipulated elections and referendums by a mixture of bribery and intimidation in order to get the right result, whether a yes vote for his policies, or an obliging, pro-government majority in the legislature. Meanwhile, he too invested heavily in economic development to keep the people happy. He encouraged the creation of new banks, which helped finance a huge boom in railway construction during the 1850s – by the end of the decade, the total length of railway lines in France was three times what it had been at the beginning. This stimulated the iron, steel and engineering industries, and the emperor was also careful to ensure full employment by embarking on a major programme of public works, much of it privately financed. Still, not everything was new. The similarities between Bonapartism and Orléanism were expressed in the emperor's appointment of former stalwarts of the July Monarchy to positions of importance in government. Some of them were members of his own family, on whom he relied closely. They included his Interior Minister, the Duc de Morny (1811–65), son of Napoleon I's stepdaughter (the estranged wife of one of Napoleon's brothers), and his Foreign Minister, Count Alexandre Walewski (1810–68), an illegitimate son of the first Emperor Napoleon. The role of the legislature was seriously diminished, with only 260 elected members as against 750 under the Second Republic, and the ability to initiate bills was taken away from it. It only met for three months every year.

There was no organized Bonapartist Party as such: the third Napoleon ruled above all through the bureaucracy. The real power was held by the Council of State, presided over by the emperor, and an upper Senate that was packed with government appointees. Napoleon III made sure that the departmental prefects, mayors and other officials in the provinces did as they were told by the Council of State, undercutting the influence of local oligarchies and massively increasing the power of central government. The regime was bolstered by a huge increase in the police force – tenfold in Paris, with the reforms of 1854. The number of police commissioners was doubled, and the rural *gendarmerie*, 14,000 strong under Louis-Philippe, was strengthened until it had 25,000 officers all told. The police hounded opponents of the regime and imprisoned those who dared publish attacks on it, sometimes after trials in which the critics could gain valuable publicity, sometimes without any kind of trial at all. Above all, the army, which had demonstrated its importance as a force for order with the failure of the National Guard during the revolutionary months of 1848, became a central bulwark of the regime, its prestige, pay and conditions raised, its new importance symbolized by the flamboyant uniforms of the new Imperial Guard. De Tocqueville's choleric dismissal of the regime as a 'bureaucratic and military despotism' was not far off the mark. But more was needed than prosperity and order, the suppression of opposition and the manufacture of the appearance of consent. Real popularity was required too. Napoleon III felt he had an important myth to live up to – the myth of his uncle, the great Napoleon I. He had made liberal use of the Napoleonic legend in gaining support: he loudly proclaimed that the restoration of French glory and prestige was a central part of his mission. Now he sought to live up to this propaganda on the international stage. This suddenly made France an unpredictable and destabilizing factor in European politics. For the last time, indeed, the French were attempting to regain the position of European hegemony they had enjoyed in the seventeenth and eighteenth centuries. There were other reasons too why Napoleon III was determined to cut a dashing figure in Europe. Military conspiracies had not entirely disappeared from the political arena. 'Serious plots are afoot in the army,' he wrote privately towards the end of 1852: 'I am keeping my eye on all this, and I reckon that by one means or another, I can prevent any outbreak: perhaps by means of a war.'

In addition, Napoleon also relied heavily for the generation and maintenance of internal political support on the French Catholic Church, which perhaps more than any other institution had seen itself threatened by the revolutionary outbreak of 1848. An opportunity soon presented itself. For much of the nineteenth century there had been a simmering conflict between Russia and the Ottoman Empire. Russia desired to expand its influence in the Balkans, most of which was still ruled by the Ottomans, and to gain an ice-free port in the Mediterranean. The increasingly rickety Ottoman Empire, dubbed by Tsar Nicholas I 'the sick man of Europe', still controlled much of the region, as well as the Middle East. Nicholas was well aware, of course, of the dangers of pushing too far or too fast; the last thing he wanted was the Ottoman Empire to disappear altogether; paradoxically, perhaps, in view of his actions, he saw it as a bulwark of stability in the region and was willing on occasion to prop it up. His solution to the dilemma was to try to assert Russian influence

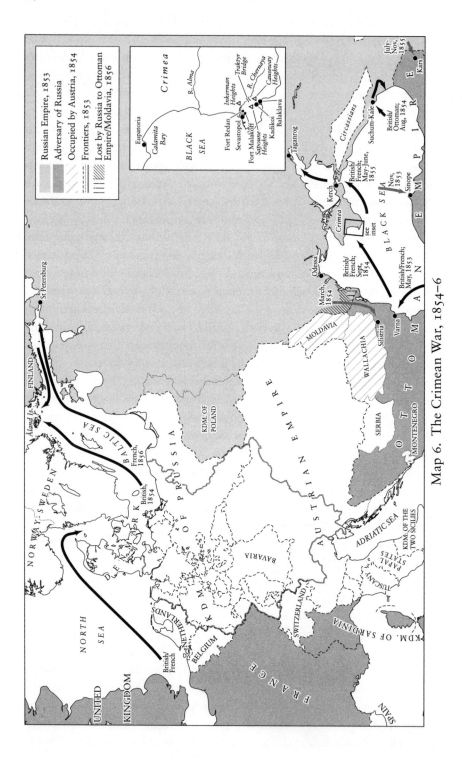

Map 6. The Crimean War, 1854–6

over the empire. Correspondingly, he tried to stop other powers from doing the same thing. The competition for influence soon became serious. In 1852, Napoleon III sought to win Catholic support by backing the claim of Catholic monks to a small area of the floor in the Church of the Holy Sepulchre in Jerusalem, then a half-forgotten backwater in the Middle Eastern territories of the Ottoman Empire. Orthodox monks had enlarged their share of the Church over the previous few years when nobody had been paying much attention. Nicholas backed them; and the issue quickly became a proxy for the rival ambitions of the two powers in the Middle East, where Napoleon III was keen to clear the way for the construction of a canal across the isthmus of Suez, still nominally under Ottoman control.

The Ottoman Sultan, faced with these rival claims, dithered; and in the summer of 1853, losing patience with him, the tsar invaded the Danubian principalities of Moldavia and Wallachia, nominally under Ottoman suzerainty. The Russian navy destroyed the Ottoman fleet at the Battle of Sinope in November 1853. The British were now seriously concerned about the growth of Russian naval power in the Mediterranean and the potential threat to the route to India, and indeed in the long run India itself. They were also alarmed about what they regarded as an upset of the balance of power in Europe through the Russian intervention in Austria-Hungary in 1848–9. So the British joined the French in sending a naval expedition to the Black Sea. Nicholas was not intimidated, and on 30 March 1854, Britain and France joined the Ottomans by declaring war on Russia. Fearing a land invasion, and mistrusting the Austrians, Nicholas withdrew his troops from the Danubian principalities in order to deploy them in defensive positions elsewhere. The Austrians duly moved in jointly to the principalities with the Ottoman forces, enraging the tsar by what he saw as their ingratitude after he had saved the Habsburg Empire from disintegration a few years before by invading Hungary and then, in 1850, helping them scotch Prussian plans for a union of German states in the treaty known as the Punctation of Olmütz.

Meanwhile there were military actions between the British and French allies on the one hand, and the Russians on the other, in the Baltic and on the Pacific coast at Kamchatka, while the Russians advanced across Ottoman territory in the Caucasus. None of these encounters was particularly important, still less decisive, but they did tie up large numbers of Russian troops – 200,000 in the Baltic alone, for example – and so prevented Tsar Nicholas from concentrating his forces at the main point of attack. Napoleon for his part was aware of the fatal consequences of staging a full-scale land invasion of Russia, in view of his uncle's disastrous experience in 1812. So together with the British, he decided on an invasion of the Crimea, where troops could easily be supplied by sea instead of having to cover vast distances over land. A joint expeditionary force set up its headquarters at Varna, on the Bulgarian coast, and then landed in the Crimea, where 35,000 Allied troops defeated a Russian force of 57,000 at the Battle of the Alma in September 1854, thus threatening the Crimean city of Sevastopol. The Russians strengthened the city's fortifications and in October launched a counter-attack at Balaklava, leading to the famous Charge of the Light Brigade, when British cavalry, misled by a mistransmitted and misunderstood order, charged the wrong way, into a furious Russian cannonade. As the French general present observing the event noted, '*C'est magnifique, mais ce n'est pas la guerre*' ('It's magnificent, but it's not war').

By this time the Russians had called up more than 100,000 reserves, but at the confused Battle of Inkerman in November 1854 they failed to use them against an inferior Allied force, which was thus able to beat back the Russian attack. After this, the war settled down into a prolonged siege of Sevastopol. The incompetence of the British leadership quickly became notorious. The commanding general, Lord Raglan (1788–1855), who had spent years fighting against Napoleon and lost an arm at the Battle of Waterloo, kept on referring to the enemy as 'the French', much to the annoyance of the French officers sitting on their horses at his side. The mostly aristocratic officers paid more attention to discipline than to fighting. An extreme though far from untypical example was that of Lord Cardigan (1797–1868), who led the fatal Charge of the Light Brigade. A wealthy man, he had purchased the command of the 11th Hussars in 1835 for the vast sum of £40,000 – the purchase of commissions was how posts were filled in the British Army – and soon transformed the regiment into the famous 'cherry-pickers', turned out smartly in tight-fitting maroon-coloured uniforms. Cardigan was married to the sister of his commanding officer Lord Lucan, but the marriage had ended in 1844 in a divorce that turned the men's friendship into mortal enmity. Later, appropriately enough for a cavalry officer, he married the cigarette-smoking Lady Adeline de Horsey (1824–1915), who married a Portuguese nobleman after Cardigan's death and subsequently wrote a scandalous set of memoirs. 'Two bigger fools could not be pulled out of the British army,' noted a captain in his diary. Neither Cardigan nor Lucan had experience of command in battle. Their incompetence and mutual hatred played a fatal role in the misunderstandings that led to the disastrous Charge of the Light Brigade.

Conditions among the troops soon deteriorated sharply, and lack of proper hygiene and sanitation in their camps led to disease and death. The British military hospital at Scutari, on the Bosphorus opposite Istanbul, was soon overcrowded with the sick, the wounded and the dying all crammed together in filthy conditions. The London *Times* began a campaign to improve the situation, spurred on by its local correspondent Thomas Chenery (1826–84), who wrote: 'The worn-out pensioners who were brought out as an ambulance corps are totally useless, and not only are surgeons not to be had, but there are no dressers or nurses to carry out the surgeons' directions.' Matters became worse when cholera broke out, brought over with the troops from France. As in all other wars of the time, and long before, more soldiers died from disease than from enemy fire, a point noted by the English nurse Florence Nightingale (1820–1910), whose achievements in improving medical care and treatment made her famous. Altogether on all sides, a high proportion of the men who died in the war died of disease: 16,000 out of 21,000 British fatalities, 60,000 out of 95,000 French, and 72,000 out of 143,000 Russian.

As these figures suggest, if the Anglo-French conduct of the war was incompetent, the Russian conduct of the war was even more so. Cholera and other diseases were rife in Sevastopol and the Russian encampments, and here too there was eventually a real effort, led by the Grand Duchess Elena Pavlovna (1807–73), a German princess who escaped from her unhappy marriage through good works, to establish a modern nursing service and improve hygiene and nursing care. Russian military command was no better than the French or British. Afraid that an invasion might be staged to the north-west of the Crimea by the Austrians, who signed an alliance with the British and the French in December 1854, the elderly and indecisive Russian commander-in-chief, General Ivan Fyodorovich Paskevich (1782–1856), who had led the Russian armies in Poland in 1831, persistently prevented the sending of further reinforcements to the Crimea. He was thus unable to relieve Sevastopol, where the Allies had launched a poorly co-ordinated attack on the Malakov redoubt in June 1855. A sizeable technological gap had opened up between the Russian forces and those of the Allies. The Russian Black Sea fleet, for example, had easily defeated the Ottoman navy, but its ships were mostly made of softwood from Russia's vast coniferous forests and were unseaworthy, they were poorly armed, very few of them were steam-driven, and their crews were badly trained. As soon as the French and British navies arrived on the scene, the Russians were clearly outsailed and outgunned. Russian troops still had flintlock muskets with a range of 200 yards, compared to that of 1,000 yards covered by Allied rifles. The Russian cavalrymen were mostly mounted on parade-ground horses that found it difficult to withstand the rigours of campaigning and were woefully slow at the charge. The Russian swords were blunt and easily broken, and were no match for the industrially produced Sheffield steel of their British counterparts, which could slice through enemy greatcoats with ease, whereas the Russian sabres simply bounced off them.

Russian troops were drafted for twenty-five years from the serf population, so that many of them were in their forties, and there was no proper reserve army; 400,000 of the new recruits drafted during the war had received no training because there were no officers available to train them. Similarly, many of the officers were middle-aged or elderly, over-cautious and uninspired. General Eduard Ivanovich Totleben (1818–84), the engineer who organized the construction of Sevastopol's formidable defences, was the great exception to this rule. Since there were no railways south of Moscow, it took up to three months for troops from central and northern Russia to reach the Crimea. And when they arrived, they encountered a calamitous shortage of supplies, partly because of the difficulties in getting them there, partly because the absence of industrial plant in Russia meant manufacture was so slow that by the end of 1855 there were only 90,000 guns and just over 250 field artillery pieces in the stockpile of weapons. By contrast, the British and French were constantly replenishing their equipment by sea. Above all, perhaps, the Russian state was unable to finance the war effort, so that at the beginning of 1856 the State Council issued a warning to the new tsar, Alexander II, that state bankruptcy was likely unless he called a halt to the conflict.

Helped by the death of Tsar Nicholas I on 2 March 1855 and the appointment of Palmerston as British Prime Minister on 6 February, negotiations to end the war had already begun. After a relief attempt on Sevastopol had been beaten back in August 1855, the Russians now negotiated in earnest, and the Treaty of Paris was signed in April 1856. It neutralized the Black Sea, preventing Russia from stationing warships there, and gave independence to the Danubian principalities. These soon united to form Romania along with the former Ottoman territory of southern Bessarabia, which was removed from Russia, to which it had belonged since 1812. The peace settlement was therefore seriously damaging to Russia's influence in the region but also affected the Ottoman Empire adversely. The Crimean War proved to be the most destructive European war Since Napoleon's day, with around half a million killed in action or dying from wounds or disease. Yet it was very limited in geographical scope. It involved a very small proportion of the forces available to the belligerent powers, and it was fought for strictly limited aims. No state, neither tsarist Russia nor the Ottoman Empire, was threatened with destruction. The war was old-fashioned in another sense too. It was not only the generals, or some of them, who were leftovers from the Battle of Waterloo. The battles were still fought between gaudily uniformed masses of troops, firing rifle volleys, attacking the enemy on foot, or engaging in cavalry charges that were little different from those of half a century before.

If the results of the Crimean War were very limited in terms of direct outcomes, then the broader effects of the Russian defeat on international politics in Europe were more profound. Russia was beaten back to the margins from the central position it had taken in European politics in 1815. France re-entered European politics, its power and prestige greatly enhanced. The Ottoman Empire survived more or less intact, with the loss only of the Danubian principalities. Nevertheless, the sultan had to confirm in an official *firman* the rights of the Christians in his realms, and especially in Jerusalem. It slowly became clear that the empire's institutions required serious reorganization. As the tough-talking and long-serving British ambassador, Stratford Canning, told the sultan: 'Your present administrative system . . . is leading you only to destruction.' Sultan Abdülaziz (1830–76) and his successor Abdülhamid II (1842–1918), who came to the throne in 1876 following Abdülaziz's assassination and the rapid deposition of his mentally unstable successor Murad V (1840–1904), realized the need for reform, but were unable to meet it. Before long, the Ottoman Empire was the sick man of Europe again, defaulting on its debts and presenting easy pickings for Russian aggression when it resumed two decades later.

The inadequacies of the respective performances of the various armies led to far-reaching reforms in military organization and supply both in Russia and the United Kingdom. In Britain the absence of a system of conscription meant the army was relatively small and had few reserves. Public disquiet at the conduct of the war was fuelled by critical reports from the correspondent of *The Times* in the Crimea, William Howard Russell (1820–1907). A debate began about the best way to finance, organize and supply the armed forces, and a Royal Commission was established. But it was not until the late 1860s and early 1870s that reforms came into effect, increasing expenditure on the army and abolishing the system through which wealthy and mostly aristocratic young men had been able to purchase commissions instead of training for them and acquiring them by merit. In Russia, Tsar Alexander II, who was a grandson of Friedrich Wilhelm III of Prussia and thus, like many if not most European monarchs of the nineteenth century, part-German, reacted to the defeat by embarking on a series of fundamental reforms. The most significant of these was the emancipation of the serfs, carried out after lengthy preparations in 1861. Creating an army whose soldiers had a positive stake in Russia's military success was one of the motivations for the emancipation, which was followed by a reorganization of government in the provinces. The abolition of serfdom had significant implications for rural Russian administration.

Ending the landlords' police powers meant introducing a centralized system of policing, while on the other hand a sense of loyalty to the regime was to be encouraged by establishing locally elected assemblies, introduced in 1864. The assemblies, or zemstva, existed at district and provincial levels and were elected separately by nobles, townsmen and peasants (the last-named indirectly). At the provincial level, nobles predominated, a factor that dissuaded liberal reformers from pressing for a national assembly; the idea was opposed by conservatives in the tsar's entourage anyway. Thus the autocracy continued. Alexander made efforts to reform the judicial system, introducing western European-style courts and public trials in 1865, with irremovable judges and jury trials for criminal offences. The police retained powers of 'administrative arrest' and exile to Siberia without trial for political offenders, but the reform was still a significant one: in due course, the courts became major centres for the free expression of opinion. In 1862 preventive censorship was replaced by prosecutions after publication. Universities were given greater autonomy, with the professors free to teach what they wanted, and the school system was restructured and extended. Serious attempts were made to purge corrupt bureaucrats and improve the standard of administration. The decentralization of many functions of government to the zemstva undoubtedly helped this process.

Alexander II appointed the liberal Dmitry Alexeyevich Milyutin (1816–1912) as Minister of War in 1861 with the task of reforming the army. Between 1861 and 1881 Milyutin streamlined the administration, reducing the volume of correspondence by 45 per cent, divided the empire into fifteen military districts, integrated the various branches of the army, reorganized and professionalized the military schools and training centres, and increased the available reserve from 210,000 in 1862 to 553,000 by 1870. After tremendous struggles with conservatives at Court who wanted nobles to remain exempt from military service, Milyutin finally succeeded in persuading the tsar to introduce universal conscription in 1874, with a six-year period of service followed by nine in the reserve. Milyutin was also concerned by the low level of literacy among recruits – a mere 7 per cent in the 1860s – and set up educational schemes within the army that resulted in a swift increase in the literacy rate among soldiers, half of whom were able to read by 1870 and a quarter of whom could write as well. Thus Russia entered the second half of the 1870s far better prepared for war than it had been two decades before.

The blow dealt to Russia's position in Europe by defeat in 1856 was only temporary, though it lasted for a crucial period of almost two decades. The consequences for Austria, paradoxically, were far more serious, even though the Habsburg Empire had not fought in the Crimea. The Habsburgs had alienated Russia by supporting the Allied side, destroying the partnership that had been at the core of the Holy Alliance after 1815. But Austria's contribution to the Allied war effort had been brief, hesitant and half-hearted, so that the Habsburgs became relatively friendless, with fatal consequences for their position in Europe. Of all the combatant powers, France came out the best. Most of the major victories in the war were largely due to the French, and Napoleon III emerged from the conflict with his power and status enhanced. The French triumph was sealed by the symbolic decision to hold the peace conference in Paris. The emperor was allowed to continue his quest for glory above all by the effective end of the Concert of Europe in the Crimean War and the final demise of the idea of monarchical solidarity. Looking for another foreign success, the emperor's eyes lighted next upon Italy.

SUCCESS AND FAILURE OF THE
NATIONAL CAUSE

France felt no particular obligation to Austria as a result of the war; a far more significant alliance was formed between France and the Kingdom of Piedmont-Sardinia, now in the hands of moderate liberal reformers led by Cavour. Towards the end of the Crimean conflict, Cavour had supplied a small contingent of 15,000 troops to the Allied war effort, and begun to cultivate the friendship of Napoleon III; he even obligingly supplied him with a mistress in the shape of Virginia Castiglione (1837–99), the wife of the Piedmontese ambassador in Paris. Cavour knew that the best way to preserve the institutions of the Piedmontese state from the threat posed by democratic-nationalist revolutionaries led by Giuseppe Mazzini was to go with the tide of nationalism but ensure it took a moderate course. The representative institutions of Piedmont, a constitutional monarchy based in classic moderate liberal style on a legislature with substantial powers elected by a limited property franchise, would not survive the re-emergence of democratic nationalism. Cavour therefore prepared to pre-empt the revolutionaries by putting Piedmont at the head of the movement for Italian unity so cruelly aborted in 1848–9.

The first step had to be the expulsion of Austria from northern Italy. In the wake of the successful counter-revolution, the government of Emperor Franz Joseph's domains was in the hands of Prince Felix zu Schwarzenberg, a scion of one of the richest landowning families in Europe. His affair with the Englishwoman Jane Digby (1807–81) while in London in the 1820s had earned him the sobriquet 'Prince of Cadland' in London's clubland. By the 1850s, Schwarzenberg had left the world of the Regency dandy behind and developed into an astute politician, 'the greatest minister I ever had at my side', as Franz Joseph called him. For Nicholas I of Russia he was 'Palmerston in a white uniform'; even Metternich sang his praises, calling him 'a pupil of my diplomatic school'. Schwarzenberg began the process of imposing a regime of almost perfect reaction with the New Year's Eve Patent of 1851, issued by Franz Jose and cancelling virtually all previous concessions and constitutions. Justice was integrated into government, abolishing the independence of the courts. The Patent restricted the legislature to a single-chamber *Reichsrat* with all the deputies appointed by the emperor. German-speaking Austrian bureaucrats imposed a uniform administration on the entire empire, obliterating national autonomy not merely in Italy and Hungary but also in Transylvania, Bukovina, Croatia and the Banat (the inconveniently independent Jelačić was sacked in 1853). Censorship was re-introduced, and the police were made directly responsible to the emperor.

To the emperor's dismay, Schwarzenberg died from a sudden stroke on 5 April 1852. The disconcerted Franz Joseph assumed power himself, unable to nominate a successor. He also became Minister of War, and conducted his own foreign policy. Young and inexperienced (he was only twenty-one), he was hardly the right person for these jobs. Not surprisingly, his mother and his former tutor were the key influences on his policies. The reactionary political course continued unabated as a result, with a Concordat signed by the Austrian government and Pope Pius IX in 1855 giving wide powers over education and censorship to the Church and guaranteeing ecclesiastical property and jurisdiction over marriage. Meanwhile, however, Franz Joseph's ministers encouraged railway-building, concluded an agreement reducing tariff barriers between Austria and Prussia, and, perhaps most importantly of all, emancipated the serfs in Hungary and Croatia, Galicia and Bukovina, Transylvania and all the rest of the Hereditary and Bohemian lands within the empire, concluding agreements in 1853 that implemented the bold but empty declarations of emancipation issued by the revolutionaries five years before. In 1854,

Franz Joseph sealed the establishment of the neo-absolutist system by finally lifting martial law in Hungary, by marrying the seventeen-year-old Princess Elizabeth of Bavaria, whose beauty and vivacity had bowled him over on their first encounter, and by issuing an amnesty. But his attempt to establish an a-national rather than a multinational state met with sullen resentment almost everywhere. And the imposition of a uniform administration across the empire proved very expensive indeed. In addition, armed neutrality in the Crimean War caused government indebtedness to rocket. To try and deal with this situation, railway lines were privatized and taxes raised, but in 1857 a general European financial crisis hit the banks in Vienna particularly hard and required further economies. Under severe financial pressure, the government was forced to make savage cutbacks in expenditure on the army.

By the late 1850s, nationalism was beginning slowly and cautiously to revive. It was clear to Cavour that for all its problems, neo-absolutist Austria was still too strong for Piedmont to defeat on its own. He needed a powerful ally. France under the Second Empire was the obvious candidate. As a young man, Napoleon III had fought with the *carbonari* against the Austrians in the uprisings of 1831. He had long supported the idea of Italian unity. Intervention offered the prospect of further military glory and political advantage. And, decisively, the revolutionary Italian republican Felice Orsini, who had been briefly in charge of Ancona during the Roman Republic, became convinced that Napoleon III constituted in his very person the chief obstacle to Italian unity. After imprisonment at Mantua, which he had escaped in classic manner by sawing through the bars of his cell and descending a hundred feet from the window by means of bedsheets twisted into a rope, Orsini designed a bomb, had six casts made in Birmingham and tested in Sheffield, then transported them to Brussels and thence to Paris. Here on 14 January 1858, he and his accomplices threw three of the bombs at Napoleon III as he passed in his carriage on his way to the opera to hear Rossini's *William Tell*. The bombs hit the carriage and the cavalcade, killing eight people and wounding 142, but the emperor was unhurt and in a characteristically flamboyant gesture proceeded to the opera as if nothing had happened. The incident convinced Napoleon that revolutionary Italian nationalism had to be neutralized by achieving national unity without revolution. A letter purportedly written by Orsini to Napoleon from prison indeed urged him to support the cause of Italian unification; it was rumoured that parts of it were actually written by the emperor himself. Orsini was guillotined on 13 March 1858; one of his accomplices was also executed and two were sentenced to lengthy terms of imprisonment. One of these two, Carlo Di Rudio (1832–1910), eventually escaped from the penal colony on Devil's Island, emigrated to America, and joined the Seventh Cavalry under General George Custer (1839–76), managing somehow also to survive its massacre by Native American braves at the Battle of the Little Bighorn in 1876.

Spurred into action by the assassination attempt, Napoleon III met Cavour secretly at the French spa town of Plombières in 1858, where they agreed on a war against Austria that would restructure Italy into a new confederation, reduce the power of the Pope, extend the Kingdom of Piedmont eastwards and rename it the Kingdom of Northern Italy. As a reward, France would receive Nice and Savoy. Napoleon III would contribute 200,000 soldiers, Cavour 100,000. At a New Year's Day reception in 1859 the emperor loudly told the Austrian ambassador: 'I regret that our relations with your Government are not so good as in the past.' In the highly constrained diplomatic language of the day this amounted virtually to an insult. It caused a sensation. Cavour added fuel to the fire by getting King Vittorio Emanuele of Piedmont to open Parliament with the words: 'We are not insensitive to the cry of pain which rises up to us from so many parts of Italy.' The Russians were kept happy with the promise of a revision of the treaty of 1856 that had ended the Crimean War; and in any case they were not disposed to help the Austrians after the Habsburgs' failure to come to their aid in 1854.

When the Austrians began drafting Italians into the imperial army, Piedmont mobilized. Nationalist associations sprang up all over Italy in a fervour of excitement. After Vittorio Emanuele refused to stand down his troops, Franz Joseph foolishly declared war, making Austria appear the aggressor and entirely losing the sympathy of Britain and Prussia. Hostilities were duly opened, and a largely French force outflanked a superior Austrian army at Magenta, forcing it to retreat, and then defeating it in June 1859 at the decisive Battle of Solferino, which involved a total of nearly 300,000 troops, the largest number to engage in a battle since the days of the first Napoleon. Casualties, however, were relatively light, with around 3,000 killed on either side. This was the last battle in world history in which the opposing forces were commanded by their respective sovereigns: Napoleon III proved a better general than the inexperienced Franz Joseph, who afterwards refrained from any more direct involvement in armed conflict. The Austrians retreated further to the east and effectively lost their grip on northern Italy. So far, things had gone according to plan for both Napoleon III and Cavour. At this stage, however, the situation began to escape their control. Cavour had sought to weaken the Austrians, and undermine the Papal States, by encouraging nationalist uprisings in central and north-eastern Italy. These forced the

Austrian-backed rulers of Bologna, Tuscany, Modena and Parma to flee, leaving the Piedmontese to take over. Napoleon III began to fear that Cavour was becoming too successful and that the Prussians and other German states might intervene on Austria's behalf. So he concluded a peace at Villafranca in July 1859, without consulting his Piedmontese allies. Much to the disgust of the Piedmontese, this left Austria in possession of the substantial territory of Venetia, in the north-east. Nevertheless, Cavour had no option but to consent, and subsequently ceded Nice and Savoy to the French as agreed.

But this was by no means the end. In Sicily, King Fernando Carlo had earned European disapproval by his harsh policies of repression, incarcerating some 2,000 dissidents in his mouldering jails. Gladstone's condemnation of his rule ('the negation of God erected to a system of government') helped isolate his regime internationally, and the British and French governments both withdrew their ambassadors in 1856 after the king refused to follow their advice to reform. The defeat of Austria isolated him still further. At a crucial moment, on 22 May 1859, Fernando Carlo died, probably from the long-term effects of an assassination attempt three years before, when a soldier had stabbed him with a bayonet. His successor was Francesco II (1836–94), who had married the younger sister of the Empress of Austria in February 1859. The Sicilian government had made itself deeply unpopular by raising taxes and driving up the price of bread, and instead of making concessions to secure his position, Francesco rejected the demand for reform. This unwise act was to prove his undoing.

The war in the north had caused immense excitement among the revolutionary nationalists, whose leading active figure, Giuseppe Garibaldi, had lived as a sea captain following the defeat of the Roman Republic. After travelling to China, South America and Britain, he had returned to Genoa in 1854 and lived quietly on the island of Caprera, north of Sardinia. When the conflict began, he raised an army of volunteers who dressed themselves in red shirts, imitated in various colours by fascist movements all over Europe after the First World War. Dubbed 'the Thousand', they were mostly from northern Italy but also included thirty-three foreigners, among them four Hungarians. The rebels quickly mounted an expedition against Sicily, where Garibaldi landed in early May 1860 and declared himself dictator. Joined by local rebels and using the mobile tactics he had learned in guerrilla warfare in South America, Garibaldi defeated the royal army and took Palermo in three days of street fighting, made more desperate by a naval bombardment from the royal ships in the bay. After his victory in Palermo, Garibaldi crossed to Naples, which the king had been persuaded to abandon in order to regroup his forces. With

Map 7. The Unification of Italy, 1815–70

every success, Garibaldi won new followers, including 600 men from Britain who joined his forces in Naples. There, he was welcomed by ecstatic crowds, with 'waving hats and handkerchiefs, hands raised in salute, and a deafening frenzy of shouts and cries'. In a two-day battle at Volturno that began at the end of September 1860, Garibaldi's army of 20,000 defeated a Neapolitan force of more than twice its strength.

His actions had made Garibaldi a European hero. Bolstered by the many speeches he delivered during his triumphant progress through Sicily and Naples, and by stories, not always exaggerated, of his bravery in battle, he became an international icon of liberal nationalism. His carefully tailored letters, and many written by his soldiers, were published in translation in many languages; there were newspaper stories, magazine articles, novels and countless illustrations of his deeds. The London *Times* called him 'the Washington of Italy'. Biographies began to appear in America, France, Germany and many other countries; Alexandre Dumas produced a French version of his memoirs; Charles Dickens and Florence Nightingale among many others sent him donations; money in large quantities arrived from North and South America to finance his cause; and later, when he visited England, he was mobbed by enthusiastic crowds, celebrated in specially written songs and verses, commemorated in porcelain figures, and elevated into a fashion icon. His cult knew no bounds; it paralleled but exceeded by far the celebrations held for the exiled Kossuth, and marked a first high point in the hero-worship that was to become such a marked feature of European politics and culture in the later nineteenth century.

Yet Garibaldi had to recognize the political realities of the situation, and after defeating the Neapolitan army he agreed to hold plebiscites in Naples and Sicily on their annexation by Piedmont. After an almost unanimous vote of approval in both cases, Garibaldi resigned his command and returned to Caprera. In March 1861, Vittorio Emanuele declared himself King of Italy. The end result was the effective extension of Piedmontese institutions to the rest of Italy. No sooner had this been achieved than Cavour died, probably of malaria, at the age of fifty-one. His achievement was to have preserved social stability by harnessing nationalist enthusiasm to the cause of the established social and political order. But he had done this at a price. Napoleon III was incensed. Italian unification had not been what he had agreed at Plombières. He had conjured up a new and potentially threatening Kingdom of Italy on his doorstep. His standing with the Catholic Church had been seriously damaged, potentially losing him significant support at home, and he quickly sent troops to protect the Pope in Rome, mollifying him as far as he could by providing him with a private train for his personal use, though the distances he could travel in it were now very limited indeed. The French troops were to remain in Rome, keeping it out of the unified Kingdom of Italy, until they were needed for other purposes in 1870, when the Italians promptly moved into the city themselves. The Pope and his successors were left walled up in the Vatican until the papacy finally conceded the legitimacy of the Italian state with the signing of the Lateran Treaty in 1929.

The defeat of Austria prompted Franz Joseph to accelerate his retreat from the policy of neo-absolutism. He was forced to agree to an elected element in the *Reichsrat* by the desperate situation of the imperial finances after the war. The leading minister, Anton von Schmerling, succeeded in introducing a constitution in the western half of the Monarchy in 1862, but when faced with the opposition of resurgent Hungarian and Croatian nationalists to a unitary political system covering the whole empire, he mortally offended them by declaring that Hungary could wait for its own political institutions. In 1865, getting nowhere, he was dismissed. Revived the same year, the Hungarian Diet was not likely to satisfy the renewed demands of the exiled Kossuth and the radical nationalists. Increasingly, the Austrian Empire seemed to be in a cul-de-sac. Meanwhile, the Austrian government failed to learn the lesson of its military defeat and reform its increasingly outdated army.

The consequences of the Italian war, for all its limited scope and duration, were decisive and Europe-wide. All over the Continent, Italian unification gave a tremendous boost to the idea of the nation state, which had been so badly defeated only a decade before. New nationalist associations and pressure groups began to form in one country after another. It was not only in Hungary that the example of Italy inspired a rebirth of the nationalist movement: a similar development took place in Poland too. In the 'Congress' part of Poland, Tsar Alexander II's reform programme, begun in the wake of the Crimean War, included defusing the simmering discontent of the nationalist nobility by restoring the right of assembly, granting an amnesty to the former participants in the 1831 uprising still in exile in Siberia, and involving Polish landowners in discussions about the terms of servile emancipation. A Polish Agricultural Society was founded in 1858; with 4,000 members, it quickly became the vehicle for nationalist aspirations, as did a City Delegation formed in Warsaw in 1861. Secret societies re-emerged, discussion groups started to meet, and there was a demonstration in the streets on the thirtieth anniversary of the 1831 uprising. To stem the flood, the tsar appointed a conservative aristocrat, Count Alexander Wielopolski (1803–77), as head of the civil administration. 'You can't do much *with* the Poles,' he was reported as saying, 'but with luck you might do something *for* them.' In pursuit of this somewhat paternalistic aim, Wielopolski dissolved the Agricultural Society and the City Delegation. Mass protest demonstrations followed: on 8 April 1861, when Cossack troops opened fire on the demonstrators, killing a hundred, Wielopolski rushed in front of the troops and commanded them to stop, at considerable risk to his own life. This did not stop the crisis escalating, however, and mass arrests and deportations only made matters worse.

The conscription of 30,000 young Poles into military service was the spark that lit the flame of revolt. In guerrilla actions across Congress Poland, groups of armed rebels acting on a plan devised by the clandestine successor organization to the City Delegation in Warsaw spirited potential recruits away into the forest, so that only 1,400 were actually conscripted into the Russian Army. The organization had over 200,000 adherents. Its organizers were middle-class citizens, bank clerks, postal officials, merchants and the like, and they set up a shadow government, with five permanent Ministries, a system of couriers, an intelligence network and a security apparatus. Yet the movement remained entirely secret, and its membership utterly obscure, so that all kinds of people were suspected of belonging to it. As Field Marshal Fyodor Berg (1793–1874), a Baltic German who had been Governor General of Finland, and was appointed military governor to replace Wielopolski, ironically commented to the Grand Duke Konstantin Konstantinovich (1827–92), the new viceroy: 'I have reached the conclusion that I do not belong to it myself, and nor does your Imperial Highness.' In more than 1,200 small-scale military engagements fought across Poland, Lithuania, Belarus and the Ukraine, groups of nationalist guerrillas attacked Russian garrisons and troop units. Both sides promised the abolition of serfdom. The Polish nationalists learned from experience, and the landed nobility were much less prominent in the movement than in 1846. Significant groups of peasants were co-opted into the uprising, taking part in military actions such as the Battle of Małogoszcz on 24 February 1863, where 3,000 of them wielding scythes bravely attempted to defeat a well-armed unit of the Russian Army.

Yet the nationalists were bitterly divided between 'Whites' and 'Reds', liberals and revolutionaries. In October 1863, in desperation, both groups ceded power to Romuald Traugutt (1826–64), a Polish nobleman and Russian officer who led a small guerrilla unit and then travelled to Paris to try, in vain, to enlist the French in support of his cause. Traugutt was appointed dictator, reshaped the administration of the nationalist movement, introduced army ranks and hierarchies to the guerrilla bands, levied a tax on Polish exiles, and purged the movement of 'private firebrands' by threatening to denounce them to the police. All the leading figures in the nationalist movement now had pseudonyms; fewer than twenty people were aware of Traugutt's real identity, and only six had permission to visit him. But on 8 April 1864 one of the revolutionaries broke under interrogation and revealed everything he knew. (Traugutt, he said, could be recognized by his 'medium height, large head, swarthy complexion, dark hair, large black sideburns and small beard, ordinary white spectacles'.) On 10 April 1864, at one in the morning, a squad of armed police burst into his Warsaw lodging and took Traugutt away to the Pawiak Prison. A mass trial followed. Traugutt and five of his companions were publicly hanged in Warsaw on 5 August on a specially built multi-person gallows. The insurrection was over.

As the guerrilla bands melted away following the smashing of the central co-ordinating body, Field Marshal Berg rescinded Wielopolski's reforms, closed down all the Congress Kingdom's autonomous institutions, subordinated the administration directly to St Petersburg, and inaugurated a ruthless programme of Russification. A Russian university replaced its Polish equivalent, and most towns lost their municipal rights. Thousands of Poles were arrested and sent to Siberia. Even the name Poland was wiped off the map; it became the Vistula Land. In Lithuania a military occupation razed recalcitrant villages to the ground, confiscated estates, and tortured and killed suspected rebels. Polish intellectual life was crushed; an entire generation of nationalists was taken out of circulation. Across the rest of Europe, these draconian measures caused shock and outrage and confirmed liberal opinion, not least in Britain, in its hatred and suspicion of the Russian colossus. Indeed, from the outset, the Polish uprising attracted sympathy from across Europe.

Volunteers rushed to its aid, including François Rochebrune (1830–70), a French teacher and ex-soldier living in Warsaw who had taken part in a military expedition to China in 1857. As a sideline Rochebrune also ran a fencing school, and he enlisted some of his students in a unit he called the 'Zouaves of Death', clad in baggy trousers and fez caps. At the Battle of Grochowiska in March 1863, seeing Polish insurgents flee in panic, he grabbed them and pushed them back into the line at gunpoint, shouting repeatedly: '*Psiakrew! Która godzina?*' – 'Damn it! What time is it?' – which was the only Polish he knew. Enthusiasm for the Polish cause in France led to Rochebrune being awarded the Legion of Honour when he eventually returned to his native land. Most volunteers, however, never managed to reach the scene of the conflict. The steamship *Ward Jackson*, sailing with 200 foreign volunteers from Gravesend, came to grief on a sandbank in the Baltic on the way. Writers and left-wing figures as varied as Garibaldi and Marx polemicized against the Russians. But the bitter truth was that no major power had any interest in helping the Poles. Britain, France and Austria sent two joint diplomatic notes requesting the tsar to make concessions, but they got nowhere. The Prussians even suggested joint action with the Russians against the rebels, though eventually thought better of it. Intervention was in any case logistically difficult. Unlike the Italians, the Poles were on their own, and they paid the price.

STEERING A COURSE ON THE STREAM OF TIME

By the second half of the 1860s, Napoleon III was beginning to face increasing opposition to his dictatorship from the growing economic and financial power of the middle classes. He was forced into granting a series of reforms that inaugurated the final phase of his rule, the so-called Liberal Empire. His foreign adventures, outside Europe as well as within, had proved extremely costly, and further expense was incurred by military reforms approved in the Army Law of 1868. His public works required massive loans for which the retrospective approval of the legislature was required. Elections in 1869 led to an increase of 1.5 million in the opposition vote, which stood at 3.5 million compared to 4.4 million for the government. Forced to dismiss his chief ministers and appoint a liberal Prime Minister, Émile Ollivier (1825–1913), a former moderate Republican who had won a reputation as a charismatic public speaker, the emperor had to grant a new constitution in April 1870, ratifying the liberalization that had taken place over the previous few years of the 'liberal Empire'. It was approved by a vote of more than 80 per cent in a plebiscite, but this electoral triumph could not conceal the fact that the central pillars of the dictatorship had finally begun to crumble.

Yet the emperor had not abandoned his ceaseless quest for popularity and sought it once again in military glory. Soon a new opportunity to win the support of French patriots was to emerge in the shape of the looming threat to the east, a united Germany. Here the ferment of nationalist activity inspired by the unification of Italy found its expression in the *Nationalverein*, the National Association, established in 1859. It rapidly won adherents among middle-class liberals. Two years later the revivified liberals founded the Progressive Party, whose aims included the election rather than appointment of governments and administrative bodies; the guarantee of civil and religious freedoms; and, crucially, the effective replacement of the tradition-bound Prussian Army, with its reactionary officer corps and its independence from legislative supervision as an institution answerable to the king alone, by a people's militia, along the lines of the National Guard so popular with the moderate liberals in 1848. The militia would be placed under the budgetary and supervisory control of the elected legislature. Liberal nationalists knew that a major reason for their defeat in 1848 had been the failure of the national parliament assembled at Frankfurt to establish control over the armies of Prussia, Austria and the other states, and they were determined not to make the same mistake again.

The experience of 1848 had taught them in addition that the idea of a unified Germany coinciding with the boundaries of the German Confederation was not a viable one. The Confederation had been resurrected by the so-called Punctation of Olmütz on 29 November 1850, and Austrian hegemony had been reasserted. The travails of the Frankfurt Parliament had made it clear that the Czechs in Bohemia would not be absorbed into a state dominated by German-speakers. And just as important, the Habsburgs, as the reassertion of their authority in 1849 had shown, were not going to allow the parts of their empire that fell within the borders of the German Confederation simply to be lopped off and assigned to a new German nation state. If Germany was going to be unified, it would have to be without Austria and Bohemia, without the Habsburgs, and without the German Confederation. This meant it would have to be led by Prussia. The problem was that Prussia was not a liberal state. In almost a decade of power the leading minister, Otto von Manteuffel (1805–82), had modernized the public administration and deregulated the economy, but he had also promoted the police as a positive, formative influence in society, and protected the central place of the professional army in the state.

Manteuffel was dismissed in 1858 when the reactionary Prince Wilhelm (1797–1888) became regent, following the incapacitation of Friedrich Wilhelm IV by a major stroke (he died in 1861, at which point Wilhelm acceded to the throne). Surprisingly, Wilhelm appointed a relatively liberal cabinet, and proclaimed a 'New Era' in Prussian politics in an attempt to defuse the growing agitation from the liberal nationalists in the legislature. He met with little success. Enthused by the success of Italian unification, the Prussian Progressives began a major offensive to try to gain control over the army and put their militia plan into effect. By 1862, a year after their formation, when the limited franchise secured the middle-class Progressives a controlling position in the legislature, they had got nowhere. To make matters worse, the military introduced a new system of universal conscription and increased the length of service from two to three years, thus enormously boosting the size and influence of the army under its existing administration. So the Progressives exercised one of the few real powers of the legislature, the right to approve the state budget, and voted it down. Without parliamentary approval it would be illegal to collect taxes or spend money on keeping the government and administration going. And they were not prepared to grant it until they won the argument over the replacement of the army by a militia.

In this stalemate Wilhelm I turned to the toughest and most conservative politician he knew: Otto von Bismarck. Bismarck's family background was in the Prussian landed and service aristocracy. Neurotic, hypochondriac, frequently ill, Bismarck was nevertheless a man of enormous energy and gargantuan appetites. In 1880 a visitor to his estate noted that after a lunch consisting of 'roast beef or beef steak with potatoes, cold roast venison, fieldfare, fried pudding etc.' he consumed a dinner of 'six heavy courses plus dessert', then another meal called 'tea' eaten just before midnight. He drank wine with every meal including breakfast, and took beer with his afternoon ride – it was hardly surprising that he fell off his horse, according to his own account, more than fifty times. After a misspent youth, during which he fought many duels, Bismarck settled down to a pious married life. From early on he was frank about his ambition, which, he wrote in 1838, 'strives more to command than to obey'. A poor speaker with a squeaky voice, he was never a particularly charismatic figure, and he was unable to move crowds in the way that someone like Gladstone could. But he was a ruthless and calculating politician who had no scruples about using force to gain his ends.

Throughout his life Bismarck was a passionate advocate of Prussian independence and Prussian power. Impressed by his ultra-conservatism in 1847–8, Friedrich Wilhelm IV had appointed him in 1851 as Prussia's representative to the general meetings of the German Confederation to defend Prussian interests. It was during his eight years in this post that Bismarck came to accept that, as he said, 'politics is the art of the possible'. Later in life he reflected on the nature of statesmanship: 'People,' he mused, 'can't create or divert the stream of time, they can only travel on it and steer with more or less experience and skill, in order to avoid shipwreck.' The stream of time in the 1860s, following the enormous boost given to the movement for German unification by events in Italy, was, he recognized, flowing swiftly and unstoppably in the direction of a united Germany. Bismarck was determined that it would not lead the Prussian ship of state onto the rocks of liberalism. Prussia had to be kept intact, with its key institutions, a strong, professional, independent army, an authoritarian monarchy, and a dominant landed and service aristocracy.

On 23 September 1862 the king appointed him Prussian Minister-President and Foreign Minister. A week later Bismarck confronted the budgetary committee head-on. He did not mince his words: 'Prussia,' he declared, 'must concentrate and maintain its power for the favourable moment which has already slipped by several times. Prussia's boundaries according to the Vienna treaties are not favourable to a healthy state life. The great questions of the time will not be resolved by speeches and majority decisions – that was the great mistake of 1848 and 1849 – but by iron and blood.' Nothing can have been more calculated to strike terror into the Prussian liberals. But what exactly did Bismarck's dramatic and chilling phrases mean? In the first place, it was clear from the map that Prussia was indeed something of a ramshackle creation. While the core areas of the old Prussian state, East and West Prussia, lay outside the German Confederation, the newest part of the Kingdom, Rhineland-Westphalia, added by the Congress of Vienna, was separated from the rest of Prussia by the Kingdom of Hanover. These western areas were by the middle of the century proving to be a huge advantage to Prussia: traditionally a centre of manufacture and commerce, they were now undergoing rapid industrialization on a large scale. But they had to be governed separately, they had a different set of laws and administrative arrangements, and communication with the rest of the Kingdom was understandably difficult. The Kingdom of Hanover had been ruled by the kings of Britain until 1837, but fortuitously the accession of Queen Victoria, who as a woman was debarred from becoming a German monarch by the Salic Law, effectively severed Hanover's ties with the world's leading commercial and naval power. Bismarck thus saw the opportunity to join up the different bits of Prussia into a single state.

The key, Bismarck realized, lay in engineering the destruction of the German Confederation. The route to this lay through the notorious Schleswig-Holstein question, which was so complicated that Palmerston once declared: 'Only three people have ever really understood the Schleswig-Holstein business – the Prince Consort, who is dead – a German professor, who has gone mad – and I, who have forgotten all about it.' The question, which had already come to the fore in 1848, boiled up again in 1863, when King Frederik VII of Denmark died without an heir. Since the rules allowed succession through the female line in Denmark but not, because of the Salic Law, in the German Confederation, to which the duchies belonged, the new king, Christian IX, who did indeed inherit through the female line, could not become Duke of Schleswig and Holstein, which would have to come under a relative who inherited through the male line. Behind this rather arcane dispute there was a clash between

German and Danish nationalisms, with one side backing a candidate who was Danish, the other a candidate who was German. In addition, the Danes passed a new constitution that undermined the traditional power of the German-speaking landed aristocracy in Schleswig, the northern of the two Duchies and the one bordering on Denmark proper. Bismarck demanded it be withdrawn, and the Danes refused. The dispute escalated until Bismarck persuaded Austria, in the name of the German Confederation, to join in forcing the Danes to give up their claim to the Duchies.

On 1 February 1864, 38,000 Prussian troops (eventually reinforced by 20,000 more) and 23,000 Austrian troops marched through Holstein and crossed the border into Schleswig. In the midst of a snowstorm the Danish Army was forced to retreat from its defensive positions on the border to the key fortress of Dybbøl, which was besieged and eventually stormed by 10,000 Prussian troops on 18 April with heavy losses on both sides. As negotiations in London ran into the sands, the German forces pressed on, expelling the last Danish troops from both Duchies by the end of June. When the Prussians advanced deep into Denmark itself, the Danes caved in. On 30 October they were forced to abandon both Duchies, which were now ruled respectively by Austria and Prussia; Denmark lost about a quarter of its population, including 200,000 Danish-speakers, in the process. Given the enthusiasm among German nationalists in 1848 for the German cause in the Duchies, there was no question that the Prussian liberals supported these actions.

Bismarck's next step, however, was more controversial. The war against Denmark had introduced yet another geopolitical anomaly into north Germany in the form of Austria's administration of the southern Duchy of Holstein, agreed with Prussia in the Gastein Convention of 1865. It was in Prussia's interest to incorporate it into its own territory along with Schleswig, and Bismarck saw in the continuing disputes between the two states over the administration of the Duchies the opportunity for launching a war against Austria that would finally lead to the expulsion of the Habsburgs from Germany. When Austria appealed to the German Confederation to mediate in the dispute, Bismarck declared the Gastein Convention void and invaded Holstein. Austria persuaded the German Confederation to mobilize against the Prussians, winning the support of south German states such as Bavaria, which feared the consequences for their independence of Prussian domination. Bismarck responded by declaring that the Confederation no longer existed. He had prepared the ground by securing an alliance with the Italians, who still needed to expel Austria from Venetia, which was still under the control of the Habsburgs, and the benevolent neutrality of the French, arranged in a meeting with

Napoleon III at Biarritz. Russia had remained alienated from the Austrians over their behaviour during the Crimean War, and saw in a strong Prussia a bulwark against an independent Poland. Britain did not regard the conflict as relevant to its interests. So the way was clear.

Most observers predicted a victory for the Austrian-led Confederation. The Prussian commander was Helmuth von Moltke (1800–91), an intellectual soldier who had published a novel and translated Edward Gibbon's *Decline and Fall of the Roman Empire* into German (or at least, most of it). Moltke had a cosmopolitan background: his wife was English, and during the 1830s he had served with the Ottoman Army in Egypt. A student of the Prussian military theorist Carl von Clausewitz, he was fascinated by the use of railways in battle (and indeed was director of a railway company). He believed in swift and decisive aggression as the best way to win a war, and broke up the massed Prussian infantry columns into smaller, more mobile and tactically responsive units, leaving much of the initiative in their deployment to their individual commanders, to the derision of many military commentators. By contrast, Austrian military doctrine regarded an emphasis on attack as a mistaken principle that had led the first Napoleon to disaster, and put its faith in a defensive strategy based on military strongpoints and fortresses. The leading Austrian military man, General Ludwig von Benedek (1804–81), who owed his rise to the courage he had shown in the war with Italy in 1859, boasted that he never read books on military strategy and observed that 'the only talents required in a chief of staff are a strong stomach and good digestion'. He persuaded Franz Joseph to put strategic planning in the hands of his best friend General Alfred von Henikstein (1810–82), whom he valued not as a strategist but as a 'paterfamilias, gigolo, gourmand, gambler and stag-hunter'. The bulwark of imperial power in 1848 and again through the neo-absolutist 1850s, the Austrian Army was lavishly rewarded with funds, but spent them on luxuries, uniforms, and extra, largely useless administrative posts rather than on modernizing its armaments and equipment. Many of the ordinary soldiers were poorly educated, badly prepared, weedy and stunted, unlike their Prussian counterparts.

Benedek decided to mass his forces around the fortress at Königgrätz (or Sadowa), to block any Prussian southward invasion from Silesia. Moltke quickly moved the three Prussian armies through Bohemia's mountain passes towards the positions of the Austrians, who failed to respond and stayed put. After a series of minor encounters the two main forces met at Sadowa on 3 July 1866. Wilhelm I was nominally in command, but in practice it was Moltke who called the shots. Not everything went smoothly for him. Problems with telegraph communication and the last-minute improvisation of railway transport meant that only two of the three Prussian armies had arrived by the time the battle began. Thus some 240,000 Austrian and Saxon troops faced a Prussian force of only 135,000. The odds were decidedly in Benedek's favour as hostilities commenced.

The Austrians might have been even stronger had they not had to deploy 75,000 troops to deal with an attack by a Piedmontese army a week earlier, when the Kingdom of Italy had decided to take advantage of the outbreak of war to invade Venetia. The Italians were poorly prepared: the leading general, Alfonso La Marmora (1804–78), admitted that of the 200,000 men who were mustered, 'only half might actually be considered "soldiers", Austrian spies reported that 'chaos reigns along the entire front . . . Italian troops have nowhere to sleep and are famished'. There was no strategic planning system and there had been six different Ministers of War since unification five years before. The king summoned Garibaldi to raise an army of volunteers, but these 'revolutionary *canaille*', as Vittorio Emanuele described them in private, were 'handled like pigherds' by regular officers. Discontent was rife, and 'a royal major was knifed by his own men', as the Austrian spy gleefully reported. When the two armies met in June 1866 at the Second Battle of Custoza, superior Austrian firepower prevailed, and the Italians fled in confusion. The roads were 'jammed with Italian troops, wagon trains and disbanded stragglers', as one officer reported. Yet the Austrian commander, the Archduke Albrecht (1817–95), dismayed by his heavy losses, refused to pursue the defeated enemy. His outraged officers expressed 'astonishment'. Albrecht had abandoned any chance of making his victory a decisive one.

At Sadowa, meanwhile, the fate of the conflict seemed in the balance. The Prussian centre was pinned down by superior Austrian artillery fire. 'Moltke,' King Wilhelm moaned, 'we are losing this battle.' But to the chagrin of some of his officers, Benedek refused to counter-attack. Indecisive and confused, he had no idea which direction to choose for an advance, and dithered despite his massive numerical advantage. Amidst heavy rain, the Prussian Third Army, with 100,000 men under the Crown Prince, struggled along a twenty-five-mile front to reach the battlefield, its guns and equipment bogged down in the mud. At 2.30 in the afternoon, however, it finally arrived, charging into the Austrian right flank. While Benedek had failed to act, Moltke had devised a classic envelopment strategy, and poured men and guns into a hole in the Austrian centre, beginning to roll up the flanks from both sides. Described by one officer later as 'apathetic, fatalistic', Benedek joined the retreat, which from 3 o'clock onwards, as the Prussians poured fire into the Austrian ranks, became a rout. Thousands of men fled in what a later court of inquiry described as

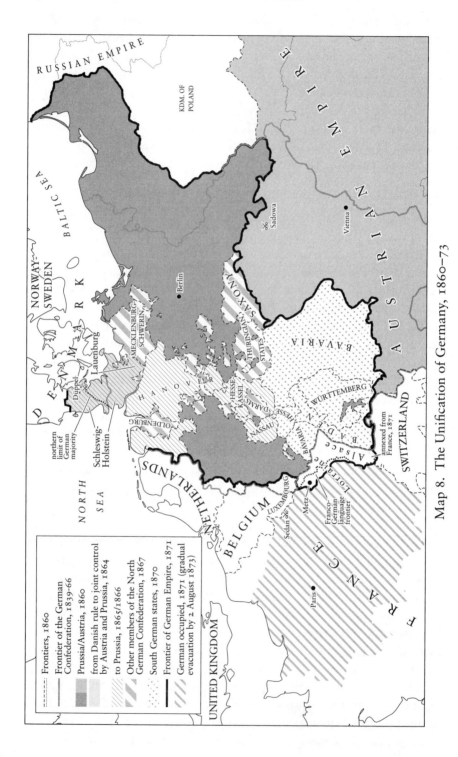

Map 8. The Unification of Germany, 1860–73

RUSSIAN EMPIRE

KDM. OF POLAND

AUSTRIAN EMPIRE

BALTIC SEA

Sadowa

Vienna

NORWAY

SWEDEN

D · E · N · M · A · R · K

Berlin

MECKLENBURG-SCHWERIN

Lauenburg

Düppel

northern limit of German majority

Schleswig-Holstein

HANOVER

OLDENBURG

SAXONY

THURINGIAN STATES

HESSE-KASSEL

HESSE-DARMSTADT

NASSAU

BAVARIA

WÜRTTEMBERG

BADEN

BAVARIAN PALATINATE

ALSACE

annexed from France, 1871

SWITZERLAND

NETHERLANDS

NORTH SEA

BELGIUM

LUXEMBOURG

Metz

Lorraine

Franco-German language frontier

Sedan

FRANCE

Paris

UNITED KINGDOM

Frontiers, 1860

Frontier of the German Confederation, 1839–66

Prussia/Austria, 1860

from Danish rule to joint control by Austria and Prussia, 1864

to Prussia, 1865/1866

Other members of the North German Confederation, 1867

South German states, 1870

Frontier of German Empire, 1871

German occupied, 1871 (gradual evacuation by 2 August 1873)

'wild panic', pursued by Prussian hussars slashing at them with their sabres. Hundreds of Austrian soldiers drowned trying to cross the river Elbe. The Prussians lost 9,000 men in the fighting, killed, wounded, captured or missing, whereas the Habsburg army's losses totalled over 40,000, more than half of them taken prisoner. The Austrians and their allies had no more forces to counter the Prussian attack. Moltke occupied Prague and advanced on Vienna. In a short time his requisitioning columns reduced Lower Austria north of the Danube to 'a vast desert'. His morale broken, Franz Joseph sued for peace. On 26 July 1866 an armistice signed at Prague brought the war to an end.

King Wilhelm and the generals wanted to push on and take the Austrian capital before imposing harsh terms on the defeated Habsburgs. But Bismarck, who had been present on the battlefield, knew that this would only lead to fresh resistance from the Austrians, and leave them bitter and resentful, ready to join in any future alliance against Prussia. From Bismarck's point of view the main, and clearly articulated, aims of the war had been achieved. Austria had been expelled from Germany. Demonstrating his ruthless disrespect for tradition and legitimacy, Bismarck ousted the King of Hanover and turned his kingdom into a Prussian province, thus bridging the gap between the two halves of the Prussian state. For good measure Bismarck also grabbed other German territories, notably the previously self-governing city of Frankfurt, Germany's financial centre, which like Hanover had backed the wrong side in the war. Bismarck might have seized the opportunity to reduce the power of the Prussian Parliament. But he knew that a modern government needed the support of the liberal middle classes in the long run. So he recognized the legitimacy of the Prussian legislature by introducing an Indemnity Bill, which invited the deputies to approve retrospectively the breach of the law he had committed in collecting taxes without parliamentary approval since 1862. As Bismarck intended, this divided the liberals, with a minority refusing to agree; but the measure was passed, among other things successfully sidelining the hard-line Prussian conservatives who had pushed for the introduction of a more authoritarian constitution. Even more shockingly for conservatives, Bismarck now created a new union of twenty-two German states, naming it the North German Confederation. This was halfway to being a German nation state, with a parliament, the Reichstag, which, astonishingly, was elected by universal male suffrage, in contrast to the property qualifications that governed voting rights in Prussia itself. Here Bismarck was taking a leaf from Napoleon III's book, bypassing the liberal middle classes to appeal to what he assumed were the loyal and conservative masses in the countryside.

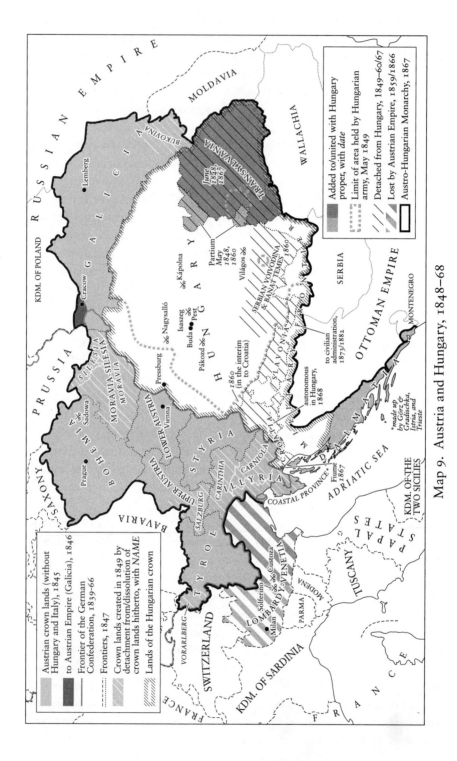

Map 9. Austria and Hungary, 1848–68

Bismarck made sure that the Reichstag's powers were limited; it had the right to approve legislation but not to introduce it, and it could neither appoint nor dismiss governments and ministers, which remained the prerogative of the President of the Confederation, who was none other than King Wilhelm I of Prussia himself. Prussia's dominance was sealed in the executive organ of the North German Confederation, the Bundesrat or Federal Council, where it could always effectively outvote the representatives of the other member states. The President also commanded the joint army of the Confederation, and could summon and dissolve the Reichstag. Below the President was the Federal Chancellor, who was also to be by custom, though not by law, the Minister-President of Prussia, or in other words Bismarck himself. The effect of these arrangements was to ensure the continued survival of Prussia and Prussian institutions, above all the army, into the new era of the emerging German nation state. At the same time Prussian rule meant liberalization in many respects in backward, ramshackle states like Hanover, winning over many liberals to the new arrangements.

The events of 1866 had major repercussions in the rest of Europe. After their defeat by Prussia, the Austrians realized they could not continue to fight the Italians, despite the victory of Custoza, and capitulated, leaving the peace settlement to cede the rest of northern Italy to the Italian state – an outcome which led to the jibe of a Russian diplomat at a peace conference later in the century, that since the Italians were demanding more territory, he supposed they must have lost another battle. The Habsburg monarchy was thrown into a deep crisis. The deposed Emperor Ferdinand is said to have remarked: 'I don't know why they appointed Franz Joseph; I could have been just as good at losing battles.' There was immediate trouble from the Hungarians. The Diet elected in 1865 had a majority of moderate liberal nationalists, led by Ferenc Deák. Assisted by Count Gyula Andrássy, recently returned from exile under an amnesty, Deák seized the opportunity provided by the monarchy's expulsion from the now-defunct German Confederation and the consequent change in the balance of forces within the Habsburg domains. Concerned that moves towards complete independence would encourage their other nationalities, notably the Slavs, to follow suit, the Hungarians began to negotiate with Franz Joseph for the restructuring of the empire as a Dual Monarchy, divided into an Austrian and a Hungarian half, each with its own government, legislature, laws and administration.

The deal reserved control over the armed forces and foreign policy and their finances to the central authority in Vienna, and put it in the hands of common ministers, though each half of the Monarchy had to be consulted on major actions such as the conclusion of international treaties. The respective Austrian and Hungarian legislatures were to negotiate via 'delegations', with the final power resting in the Monarch. Franz Joseph was crowned King of Hungary on 8 June 1867 and signed the law, known as the *Ausgleich* or Compromise, on 28 July. The Czech nationalists led by František Palacký objected and boycotted the Austrian legislature, under whose purview they fell, for eight years. The Croatians were appeased by the concession of the use of Serbo-Croat as an official language and generous provisions for the retention of tax revenues. Other nationalities – Slovaks, Serbs, Romanians, Italians, Saxons – were covered by a Nationalities Law passed in 1865 with significant concessions on the use of their languages in schools. The monarchy, now in control of a central administration named *kaiserlich und königlich*, 'Imperial and Royal', for the two halves of the Dual Monarchy, retained most of its key powers. The fact that these arrangements lasted for another half a century demonstrates that they were a reasonably effective solution to the problems that had been dogging the Habsburgs since 1848.

In Germany the Prussian victory marginalized the separatist politicians of the south German states, led by Bavaria, where the National Liberals were now generating an almost unstoppable enthusiasm for a final act of unification through the extension of the North German Confederation to the south. But France stood in the way. Following the Prussian victory, Napoleon III began to search for ways of limiting the threat to France that he saw in the emergence of a new strong power on the right bank of the Rhine. But he was unable to find any allies to back him up; the Italians were irritated by the continuing French military defence of the Pope's remaining territories in and around Rome, Britain stood aloof, and Russia still valued the Prussians' role in Poland. Nevertheless, war fever began to grip the French political elite. As early as February 1869 the Minister of War told the Council of Ministers in Paris that 'war with Prussia is inevitable and imminent. We are armed as never before.' Thus the French emperor felt unable to remain inactive when on 2 July 1870 a member of a cadet branch of the Prussian royal family, Prince Leopold of Hohenzollern-Sigmaringen (1835–1905), was offered the throne of Spain, which had become vacant through the enforced abdication of Queen Isabella. France considered Spain part of its own sphere of influence, and thought that Bismarck and Wilhelm were behind the candidacy. The result, French public opinion feared, would be a Prussian threat from the south as well as the east.

Bismarck won international sympathy by claiming at the time, and later, that Prince Leopold's candidature had come as a complete surprise to him. It was not until after the Second World War that documents from the Sigmaringen archive came to light showing that Leopold's father had consulted Wilhelm I as soon as the first tentative approach was made from Spain, and that Bismarck had advised the king to encourage the candidacy. This was not because Bismarck wanted a war; it was for him just another lever of diplomatic pressure. Indeed, when the French ambassador Count Vincent Benedetti (1817–1900) met Wilhelm at his spa retreat in Bad Ems, the king agreed to withdraw his support for Leopold, who retired to his estate and never did become a monarch, although his brother and his son both became rulers of Romania. The matter seemed to be settled. However, the Prussian king was waylaid by the French ambassador during a walk and confronted with fresh demands. Wilhelm 'sternly' rejected Benedetti's 'importunate' demand that Prussia should support a candidature like Leopold's neither in the present nor at any time in the future, and he sent his aide-de-camp to tell Benedetti that he was not willing to receive him again. Wilhelm's staff sent a telegram to Bismarck reporting the outcome. Bismarck's published brief summary of the telegram left out the polite phrases with which Wilhelm had gilded his conversation with Benedetti. But the key lay in the mistranslation of the French term aide-de-camp as 'adjutant of the day', which made it seem as if a very lowly non-commissioned officer, not a close personal assistant, had been sent to give Benedetti the brush-off. This apparent insult was enough for Napoleon III, already seeking another foreign success to bolster his fading popularity, to issue a declaration of war.

What were the reasons for Bismarck's aggressive and underhand behaviour? First, the ousting of the pro-Prussian Ministry in Bavaria in February 1870 and its replacement by a government of the 'Patriot Party', Catholic, anti-Prussian, and pro-French, threatened to derail the progress of unification. Bismarck feared this development could well be repeated in other south German states. Secondly, military reforms in France, though incomplete, meant that in the near future French military strength would be even more formidable than it already was. Thirdly, the French, currently on their own, might also gain allies in the near future; indeed, Napoleon III gambled on the Austrians and the Danes choosing this moment to take their revenge. Fourthly, it seemed to Bismarck that at this point Napoleon III could easily be made to appear the aggressor and thus international intervention be avoided. Both sides proceeded to mobilize their forces. Most people expected the French to win as they had expected the Austrians to win in 1866. While Moltke allowed his officers wide latitude in taking tactical decisions, however, the rigid French chain of command bound Napoleon's officers into slow-moving, largely defensive manoeuvres. The chain of command through the Prussian General Staff – the only General Staff in Europe at the time – was far more decisive and effective. By the time of the first encounters, the French had brought 250,000 men to the front, many of them inadequately armed and supplied, whereas the Prussians and their allies deployed 320,000 battle-ready troops on the border. French intelligence was poor, and the seizure of the town of Wissembourg by 80,000 Prussian and Bavarian troops on 4 August 1870 came as a complete surprise to the French general who had inspected the town the day before. Poorly trained French recruits fired aimlessly and without co-ordination and were no match for the disciplined Prussians. At Froeschwiller and Spicheren the French armies, dug into defensive positions, were out-manoeuvred by the Germans. These initial victories opened the way for the Prussians to advance across France; they came as an enormous shock to public opinion across Europe, dissuading the Austrians, Danes and Italians from intervening, causing the overthrow of the French government, and leading to increasingly vehement criticism of the emperor by Republican journalists and politicians. Ill with gout and kidney problems, his face 'stamped with suffering' according to one account, Napoleon III finally passed over command to Marshal Achille Bazaine (1811–88), a rough soldier who had risen through the ranks and fought in Mexico and the Crimea.

But Bazaine dithered, absorbed in quarrels with his fellow commanders, with the emperor, and with the Empress Eugénie, who was in charge of affairs back in Paris. Without orders from Moltke, 30,000 Prussian troops dashed forward to encounter 150,000 French troops ensconced in defensive positions at Mars-la-Tour in north-eastern France. In the gathering gloom Prussian hussars charged, deceiving the French infantry with shouts of '*Vive la France! Vive l'Empereur!*' before skewering them on their lances. Bazaine had failed to exploit his superior numbers by ordering an advance. Under heavy fire from Prussian artillery, and worried by his massive expenditure of ammunition and supplies, Bazaine retreated towards Metz, leading to the first major set-piece battle of the war, at Gravelotte on 18 August 1870, where 200,000 German troops with 730 guns faced 160,000 French troops with 520 cannon. Bazaine again stayed put, allowing his line to be outflanked. As his subordinates raged at him to move his troops to face the enemy, Bazaine remained inactive, until he was forced to pull his men back. The war now moved rapidly to a climax. As Bazaine retreated with 140,000 troops into the fortress at Metz, Moltke deployed an army of 150,000 to surround it, beating back the one French attempt at a sortie. A new French army put together by Napoleon III and Marshal Patrice de MacMahon (1808–93), whose Irish ancestors had emigrated to France after the defeat of King James II (1633–1701) in 1688, moved forward to relieve Metz. But this force was blocked at Beaumont and then surrounded by the German armies, now at a strength of 200,000, near the fortress of Sedan. 'We are in the chamber-pot,' commented the French general Auguste-Alexandre Ducrot (1817–82), who assumed command when MacMahon was wounded 'and about to be shat upon'. Under a relentless artillery bombardment, the French army disintegrated and began to flee in panic and disorder, leaving 17,000 dead and wounded on the battlefield (the Germans lost 9,000).

Seeing the game was up, Napoleon III sent a message of surrender to Wilhelm, Moltke and Bismarck. Offered a flask of brandy, Bismarck toasted everyone in English, 'Here's to the unification of Germany', and drank the entire flask. In an attempt to gain mild terms, Napoleon III rode out in person from Sedan, and was met by Bismarck, who sat him down on a bench by an inn. The conversation was held in the German the emperor had learned as a child. Bismarck informed Napoleon that the entire French army would be taken into captivity, and the siege of Metz would continue. 'Then everything is lost,' the emperor mumbled. 'Yes, quite right,' replied Bismarck brutally: 'everything really is lost.' Some 100,000 French troops were made to lay down their arms and were taken to prison camps. As the news reached Paris, on 3 September 1870, riots broke out. About 60,000 people gathered on the Place de la Concorde, shouting 'Death to the Bonapartes! Long live the nation!' On 4 September the Assembly proclaimed the deposition of the dynasty and the creation of the Third Republic. Napoleon III was taken to Kassel, from where he was eventually allowed to go into exile in England.

But the war was not yet over. 'There is much bloody work ahead of us,' King Wilhelm told his officers. Holed up in the fortress of Metz, Bazaine and his troops began to starve; by 30 September 1870 they had slaughtered half their horses for food. Two huge foraging columns of 40,000 men each were repulsed by Prussian artillery fire and shot to pieces with the *chassepots* the Germans had captured at Sedan. Bazaine surrendered his 133,000 troops and 600 guns to the Germans on 29 October 1870. As the soldiers trudged into captivity, the Prussians were taken aback by their desperate need for food: 'all the French did from 29–31 October,' commented one of them, 'was eat and talk about food'. In France a provisional Republican Government of National Defence was formed under Léon Gambetta (1838–82), a long-term opponent of the empire. Dedicated to continuing the fight, Gambetta, escaping from Paris by hot-air balloon, raised 250,000 more troops, as the German armies completed their encirclement. In a series of bloody encounters, the French armies recaptured

Orléans in early November, but an attack by 60,000 French troops on Beaune-la-Rolande was beaten back in heavy fighting, and a sortie from Paris planned to coincide with the attack never happened because the balloon carrying the message from Beaune was blown off course, eventually landing in Norway. Demoralized, and plagued by desertions, the remaining French armies disintegrated. All that was left were the 400,000 troops garrisoning Paris.

Surrounded on all sides by the German armies, Paris soon ran out of food, and the increasingly desperate inhabitants were subsisting on bread and not much else by the end of the year. An attempted breakout with 100,000 troops was repulsed with losses of 12,000 men in a three-day battle at Villiers and Champigny at the end of November 1870. Two more large-scale sorties fared no better. The Prussians began bombarding the city, but the losses the shells caused were far outweighed by deaths from starvation in the besieged city, which were running at 3,000 a week by January 1871. On 10–11 January a surviving French army dug in at Le Mans was destroyed by a surprise attack, losing 25,000 dead and wounded and 50,000 deserters. Another French army of 110,000 men fell to pieces in the south; men and horses were dying of sickness or malnutrition, and even the arrival of Giuseppe Garibaldi, who quickly assembled 25,000 volunteer troops to fight for the new French Republic, was unable to redress the balance. Meanwhile the conflict had become increasingly bitter, as the Germans looted everything in sight, focusing especially on wine cellars. ('All the way down from Sedan,' reported an American observer of the German advance, 'there were two almost continuous lines of broken bottles along the roadsides.')

When armed French civilians and deserters, quickly dubbed *francs-tireurs*, or 'free sharpshooters', ambushed their foraging parties and patrols, the Germans responded with heavy reprisals, summarily executing any armed civilians they encountered. Garibaldi and his men did not help by threatening to cut the ears off fourteen Prussian prisoners if the Germans continued with their reprisals. Bismarck ordered villages that resisted demands for supplies to be burned to the ground and all the male inhabitants hanged. There should be no 'laziness in killing,' he said. Their inhabitants suspected of aiding the *francs-tireurs*, the villages of Varice, Ourcelle and Ablis, near Orléans, were burned to the ground, while Prussian troops attacking *francs-tireurs* near Fontenoy-sur-Moselle set the buildings alight, bayoneted the inhabitants and threw them, still living, onto the flames. The situation was finally resolved when long-postponed elections were held in France, with the co-operation of the Germans, on 8 February 1871. They brought victory to anti-war conservative monarchists. The new Assembly appointed the seventy-three-year-old Adolphe Thiers as President. In bad-tempered peace negotiations, Thiers was browbeaten by Bismarck and Moltke until he agreed to sign a treaty on 26 February 1871, ceding Alsace-Lorraine to the new united Germany, reluctantly approving the payment of an indemnity of 5 billion francs, and sanctioning a German victory parade through the streets of Paris.

Altogether in the war, the French lost 140,000 killed and roughly the same number wounded, the Germans 45,000 killed and twice as many wounded. The peace terms imposed by Bismarck aroused lasting resentments that were to find their eventual outlet in 1914. To add insult to injury, Bismarck organized the proclamation of the German Empire, extended to include the now helpless south German states as well, in the Hall of Mirrors in the Palace of Versailles, on 18 January 1871. The political significance of the war was immediately recognized by Disraeli, who declared on 9 February 1871:

> This war represents the German revolution, a greater political event than the French revolution of last century . . . Not a single principle in the management of our foreign affairs, accepted by all statesmen for guidance up to six months ago, any longer exists. There is not a diplomatic tradition which has not been swept away . . . The balance of power has been entirely destroyed, and the country which suffers most, and feels the effects of this great change most, is England.

ECHOES OF REVOLUTION

In little over two decades, from 1848 to 1871, Europe had been transformed. Both Italy and Germany, despite the dashing of the nationalists' hopes in 1848–9, had been united, though on the basis of a conservatively designed constitutional monarchy rather than a democratic republic. In Germany's case the liberals had to make do with a parliamentary system in which the powers of the monarchy and the army were far greater than they had wished them to be. Universal male suffrage was also very far from what the moderate liberals wanted; they were more comfortable with the situation in Italy, where a limited property franchise still applied. Gambling on the loyalty and conservatism of the rural masses, bold and imaginative statesmen like Napoleon III, Bismarck and Disraeli had sought to outflank the liberals and deliver mass support to their new conservative ideology. Reaction, rampant almost everywhere in 1850, had failed by the end of the decade, even in Russia, despite its attempts to adapt to the new circumstances of the post-revolutionary era. The Vienna Settlement had been torn up, Metternich's immobile conservatism brushed aside, and a new political order born. It was to last, though with perceptible shifts and changes, almost all the way up to 1914. After a short burst of rapid boundary changes and the formation of new geopolitical entities, the major states of Europe – Britain, France, Germany, Austria-Hungary, Russia, the Ottoman Empire – and many of the minor ones, from the Balkans to Scandinavia, remained within more or less stable borders for over four decades after 1870.

The dramatic changes of the 1850s and 1860s were set in motion by the 1848 Revolutions, even if they were not exactly what any of the revolutionaries had envisaged. The year 1848 put a whole range of political forces on the European agenda, from constitutional monarchy to democratic republicanism. From 1848 onwards, nationalism was a major driving force in European politics. The old world of the secret societies and Jacobin-style revolutionary clubs gave way almost everywhere, though not in Russia, Poland, or the Balkans, to the new world of organized political parties, the political press (used by government as well as by opposition), single-issue pressure groups, and increasingly as time went on, mass communications. Revolutionary activism bifurcated into organized Marxist movements on the one hand, and increasingly violent anarchist plots on the other. The old politics of Metternich's stubborn resistance to the forces of change was superseded by a new, more flexible politics espoused by conservative statesmen who saw that these forces had to be embraced and turned to their own advantage if the society they wished to preserve could be saved. Even the most reactionary regimes of the 1850s recognized the need for economic deregulation, educational improvement and judicial reform, all of which can be counted major results of the 1848 Revolutions. The relations of governments with the public everywhere, even in Russia, were no longer shrouded in secrecy and mystery or dependent on assumed habits of deference, but were based far more on an openly propagandistic appeal to the loyalty of the masses. In many respects it makes sense to see the whole period from 1848 to 1871 as a single period of revolutionary change, rather than focusing individually on each of the short-term upheavals that followed one another with such breathtaking speed during these years.

Seen in a global context, the most notable achievement of the 1848 Revolutions was the abolition of slavery in a number of Europe's overseas colonies. Here, as in many other respects, the running was made by the British, who had already abolished slavery in their colonies in the 1830s and used the power of the Royal Navy to suppress the trade in slaves from Africa to the New World. The Second Republic in France brought the committed anti-slavery campaigner Victor Schœlcher (1804–93) into government, and on 27 April 1848 it issued a decree freeing the slaves in the remaining French colonies in the West Indies – Guadeloupe, where 87,000 people became free men and women and French citizens, and 74,000 in Martinique. His action, however, was pre-empted by a slave revolt on the island of Martinique on 20 May, following protests at the arrest of a recalcitrant slave, two weeks before the news of the decree arrived on the island. The island's authorities, anxious to quell the revolt, formally emancipated the slaves on 22 May. When the decree was announced in Guadeloupe in early June, the slaves fled the plantations, as they had done in Martinique, and by the end of the year Indian indentured labourers were being imported to get the sugar plantations going again. A slave rebellion that broke out on the island of St Croix in the Danish Virgin Islands in 1848 was also the trigger for the emancipation decree issued by Governor-General Peter von Scholten (1784–1854) on 3 July 1848; the slaves on the Swedish Caribbean island of St Barthélemy had already been freed the previous year.

The ideas of 1848 and the broader ideology of anti-slavery were all the more persuasive because pressures had long been growing for the abolition of the slave trade. The Evangelical Revival in late eighteenth- and early nineteenth-century Britain brought to slave-owning areas radical missionaries who soon began to champion slaves' rights. Thus in Demerara, part of British Guiana, acquired by Britain from the Netherlands in 1815, the arrival of one John Smith (1790–1824), sent by the London Missionary Society two years later, soon sparked discontent as he began to fight plantation owners for the slaves' right to attend chapel services. Smith encouraged the slaves to educate and improve themselves and made a number of them deacons of his ministry. Yet conditions were so harsh that 10,000 slaves rose in rebellion in 1823. An even larger uprising, involving 60,000 slaves, took place in Barbados in 1831. A great slave revolt in Bahia province, Brazil, in 1835, like the West Indian uprisings, was in part inspired by the Haitian Revolution (1791–1804), with the rebels carrying pictures of the Haitian leaders, and led by Muslim preachers who were able to mobilize slaves transported from Islamic states in west Africa. This was a more violent rebellion, and it was put down with considerable force by the Brazilian Army. These revolts caused growing alarm among European colonists, plantation owners and governments. The Brazilian slave trade was formally ended shortly after the great revolt. The British Parliament abolished slavery in British-controlled areas of the world two years earlier, in 1833, in a law that came fully into effect in 1838. In the 1850s and 1860s, including in North and South America, slavery was formally abolished almost everywhere, and international treaties were negotiated for the suppression of the slave trade. On the Caribbean island of St Martin, in the Antilles, divided between the French and Dutch, the French emancipation decree sparked a slave rebellion in the Dutch half, but slavery in the rest of the islands, including Curaçao, was not ended until 1863; in the Dutch colony of Suriname, on the north-eastern coast of South America, the slaves were forced to continue working, for meagre pay, for another decade, and in all these areas the ensuing labour shortage was made good by the import of indentured labour from the Dutch East Indies. The Spanish colony of Cuba did not outlaw the slave trade until 1867 and slavery itself in 1886, while it took the French another decade to abolish slavery in Madagascar.

The immediate or eventual emancipation of the slaves in the European overseas colonies where it remained could be seen as one of the wider consequences of the 1848 Revolutions, expressing liberal and democratic ideals of human equality and equal rights that had other corollaries in the parallel moves to end serfdom in the parts of Europe where it still remained. But these principles emphatically did not extend to at least half the population of the Continent, namely the female sex. The vast majority of revolutionaries of all political persuasions were of one mind in considering politics a matter for men; women's place was in the home. Women might participate in revolutionary uprisings, help build barricades, defiantly fly revolutionary flags, as they did in Paris, in the face of oncoming troops, or prepare and carry supplies to the fighters: none of this was thought by men to entitle them to a say in politics. Nevertheless, in raising the question of the rights of man, the Revolutions of 1848 also by implication raised the question of the rights of woman, and some women at least spoke out in favour of female emancipation. The Czech writer Božena Němcová (1820–62) urged improvements in women's education ('We women have remained far behind the age, behind the banner of freedom and culture'), while the German social novelist Louise Otto-Peters (1819–95) founded the *Frauen-Zeitung* (*Women's Newspaper*) to publicize the demand for votes for women and urge the formation of women's societies.

As revolutionary clubs, meetings and demonstrations multiplied, women increasingly took part, and where they were not permitted to join, they sometimes formed their own, most notably the Club for the Emancipation of Women, established in Paris by Eugénie Niboyet (1796–1883), a former Saint-Simonian and veteran journalist whose *salon* had been frequented by Flora Tristan. Backed by her 'socialist and feminist' journal *La Voix des Femmes* (*The Voice of Women*), the Club raised the demand for the legalization of divorce and the right of married women to control their own property. Most notably, it also urged the extension of the franchise to women, proposing the celebrated writer George Sand (the pseudonym of Amantine Dupand, 1804–76) for the Constituent Assembly in 1848 (Sand declined). The former seamstress and teacher Jeanne Deroin (1805–94), a Saint-Simonian who brought up Flora Tristan's children and edited a number of short-lived feminist newspapers, stood for election to the Legislative Assembly in 1849, but her candidacy was disallowed by the government. In Prague a Club of Slavic Women was founded to encourage women's education, while patriotic women's associations emerged in many parts of Germany. Few of these initiatives, which at their most radical, in France, reflected the feminism of the Utopian socialists, received the support of male radicals, democrats and republicans. They were denounced by the incorrigibly misogynistic Proudhon, and as the revolution disintegrated, the newly resurgent monarchical authorities banned women's participation in political meetings (notably in Austria and Prussia and indeed almost all the German states) and closed any remaining feminist newspapers. Deroin was arrested in 1850 and not released from prison until the following year. Nevertheless, a number of the feminists who had spoken out in 1848–9 re-emerged with the resurgence of liberalism a decade or so later to form feminist associations and publications that would ultimately have a much greater effect and a more lasting influence.

Feminism was in the end marginal to the ideas and events of the 1848 Revolutions. So too, in the larger scheme of things, was socialism. At the beginning of the revolutionary year the socialists were in disarray, many of them in exile, without any mass following. If socialist principles such as state workshops were popular, they paled before the mass attraction of democratic ideas such as universal male suffrage. Socialists' attempts to turn the revolutionary course of events to their advantage had little success. In exile in London, Karl Marx had already engineered the transformation of the League of the Just, a small group of exiled German artisans, into the League of Communists, shifting its focus from revolutionary conspiracy to open propaganda. As the revolutionary atmosphere intensified, Marx published its statement of aims in February 1848, drawing on previous drafts by Engels. This was the *Communist Manifesto*. Many of its pithy phrases have become famous: 'the idiocy of rural life'; 'the ruling ideas of an age are the ideas of its ruling class'; 'the proletarians have nothing to lose but their chains'; 'workers of the world, unite!' Capitalism, argued the *Manifesto*, was expanding relentlessly, creating an ever-growing, ever more exploited working class that would eventually come together under socialist leadership and overthrow it: the bourgeoisie 'produces above all its own gravedigger. Its decline and the victory of the proletariat are both equally inevitable.'

For all the force of its rhetoric, however, the *Manifesto* met with only a limited response. Returning to Cologne in 1848, Marx joined forces with the democrats to polemicize against the moderate liberals and above all against Prussia. Expelled from the city, he travelled around the insurgent centres in 1849 with Engels, but they were disappointed with their 'petty-bourgeois' hesitancy. Marx revived the *New Rhenish News* with the subtitle *Review of Political Economy*. In 1850 it carried his brilliant essay, *Class Struggles in France, 1848 to 1850*. This recounted the defeat of the revolutionary forces but predicted a fresh outbreak in which the proletariat would come to power. The periodical was not a success, however. The Communist League became mired in ideological quarrels and personal animosities, and its members in Cologne were arrested and subjected to a mass show trial. Naively forgetting their assertion in the *Manifesto* that the law was just an instrument of class interests, Marx and Engels expected their exposure of forged evidence to produce an acquittal, but the jury found several of the defendants guilty. Driven to despair, Marx brought about the dissolution of the Communist League. In his pamphlet, *The Eighteenth Brumaire of Louis Bonaparte* (1852), he was forced to conclude that capitalism had yet to develop to the point where a revolution would become inevitable.

None of this stopped Marx from engaging with the newly founded General German Workers' Association. This had been created by the charismatic Hegelian Ferdinand Lassalle (1825–64), who had established the Association in meetings held as he travelled the length and breadth of the land in the months preceding his death in a duel at the hands of a rival in love on 31 August 1864. Marx also attracted considerable attention in London when his backing for the Polish nationalist revolt against Russian rule in 1863 led to a public meeting at which the organizers founded a new International Working Men's Association. The Association was not a tightly knit group as the League of Communists had been, but a loose confederation of already existing trade unions, mutual benefit societies and educational associations, and it soon won adherents in France as well as Austria, Belgium, Italy and Spain. Marx exerted his influence on the Workers' International largely from behind the scenes, advocating reformist aims such as a shorter working day and labour actions such as persuading workers of one nationality not to break strikes in another country, in order to expand the movement and create a favourable basis for revolution when the moment came.

The Workers' International now played a key role in the dramatic coda to the Franco-Prussian War that took place in Paris in 1871. On 18 March 1871, following repeated popular disturbances and struggles over the control of weapons, the government of the Third Republic, its bureaucrats and its troops decamped from the city along with much of the Parisian bourgeoisie. The Central Committee of the National Guard organized an election to create an independent municipal authority, the Commune, which they dominated along with the Proudhonians. The Workers' International won only four seats. However, most of the Commune's representatives had acquired their experience in the International's sections, in the democratic clubs, or in the National Guard, and there was a high proportion of workers among them, alongside petty-bourgeois and artisans. The Commune spent most of its time organizing food and other supplies, but it also set up work schemes, laid down a minimum wage, decreed the separation of Church and State, abolished fines in factories, outlawed night work for bakers, and set up some schools on Fourierist lines. It seems reasonable enough to call such policies socialist. As the writer Edmond de Goncourt (1822–96) remarked, 'what is happening is very simply the conquest of France by the workers'. Yet the ferment of radical ideas in the clubs had little practical effect, and led to massive disagreements within the Commune: 'The best day of my life,' one member was heard to say to another, 'will be the one on which I arrest you.' The Commune established a Committee of Public Safety and imposed a censorship. For many, this was 1792 all over again, though in reality the politics of the Commune were very different from those of the *sans-culottes* of the late eighteenth century.

The obvious dominance of the Jacobins did not prevent the government of the Republic, led from Versailles by Thiers, from claiming they were in reality communists acting under the orders of Karl Marx, who was accused of being the 'head of a vast conspiracy' operating through the Workers' International. Elated at his new notoriety, Marx fired off his classic polemic *The Civil War in France* (1871), condemning Thiers, 'that monstrous gnome', and hailing the Commune as a new form of state created by working men, 'the glorious harbinger of a new society'. The pamphlet was lauded by socialists across Europe and featured in newspapers and magazines everywhere. Yet the Commune did not last long. Communes proclaimed in other French towns were quickly suppressed. Thiers ordered the regular army into Paris to re-establish the authority of his government. The release from German captivity of French prisoners of war swelled the Versailles forces from an initial 55,000 to 120,000 by the end of May. The bombardment began on 2 April 1871. There was no co-ordinated defence, and no attempt to prevent the troops from entering the city; each quarter of the city set up its own barricades.

The breakthrough of Thiers' forces at the Porte de Saint-Cloud on 21 May 1871 inaugurated the *semaine sanglante*, in which his troops rushed into the houses abutting the barricades and shot the people manning the defences until they were either all dead or had abandoned the obstruction. Hostages were killed on both sides, including the Archbishop of Paris, taken by the Communards in an attempted exchange for Auguste Blanqui, who had been seized on Thiers' orders on 18 March 1871 but was subsequently elected President of the Commune *in absentia*. A recent investigation based on contemporary documents, including hospital and burial records, puts the number of dead at between 5,700 and 7,400, perhaps 1,400 of them executed in cold blood on capture. After Thiers re-established control over the city, 38,578 supporters of the Commune were arrested, imprisoned and brought to trial over the next two years; 10,137 were convicted, nearly half of whom were deported to the tropical penal colony of New Caledonia. This was the last gasp of the Parisian insurrectionary tradition, the final paroxysm of more than eighty years of Jacobinism. It polarized French politics and society. But it also changed the nature of socialism.

The suppression of the Commune opened up fresh divisions and recriminations in the Workers' International, above all between the followers of Marx and those of Bakunin, who had escaped from his Siberian exile while on parole and reached London via Japan and the United States. After staying with Alexander Herzen, Bakunin moved to Italy, where he found disciples among the younger generation of political radicals in Naples. Moving next to Switzerland, he began again to spin revolutionary conspiracies, proclaiming his faith in the revolutionary potential of the dispossessed rural masses. In September 1867 he appeared with Garibaldi on the podium at a meeting of a new, largely liberal League for Peace and Freedom (also attended by Victor Hugo and John Stuart Mill), but after failing to persuade it to take a revolutionary course, he resigned and joined the Workers' International. Here, however, he formed his own sub-group, incurring the wrath of Marx, who rejected the idea of insurrectionary secret societies in favour of organized, open political parties. As the polemics flew, Marx outmanoeuvred Bakunin's supporters on the General Council of the International at the 1872 Hague Congress, which he attended in person. Armed with a clear majority, Marx dropped a bombshell: the seat of the Council would move to New York. The delegates duly obeyed. Behind this startling move was Marx's belief that the new era of political reaction and police repression following the suppression of the Paris Commune would make the International's work impossible, his fear that his own failing health might open the way to the Bakuninists once more, and his desire to clear the deck so he could make progress with his own economic writings at his customary seat in the British Museum reading room.

From now on, there was to be a clear distinction on the far left between the socialists, mostly followers of Marx, who eschewed the bullet for the ballot box, trusting in the inexorable growth of the proletariat to deliver, in the end, a democratic majority for a peaceful revolution, and the anarchists, mostly followers of Bakunin, who relied on violence, assassination and insurrection to destroy the state and open the way for the naturally egalitarian instincts of the rural masses to express themselves. Both these doctrines won millions of adherents in the last decades of the nineteenth century and the first decade of the twentieth century. To see why this was so, we now have to turn to examining the ways in which European societies and economies developed over the years between 1850 and 1914.

4

The Social Revolution

THE DECLINE OF THE ARISTOCRACY

In 1907 the twenty-four-year-old Hermynia Isabella Maria, Countess Folliot de Crenneville (1883–1951), the only child of an Austro-Hungarian diplomat descended from an émigré French aristocrat, married the twenty-eight-year-old Viktor von Zur Mühlen (1879–1950), a nobleman from a prominent family of Baltic Germans. Viktor was good-looking and charming, and had cultured relations (one of them a well-known singer and friend of Johannes Brahms). For her part, Hermynia was obviously not unattractive, but she had, not merely in her own mind, been cursed with a rather large nose. 'With that nose, child,' her Uncle Anton told her, 'you absolutely have to become a very cultivated and clever woman.' Taking this advice to heart, Hermynia grew up bookish, restless and intellectually ambitious: by her early twenties she had mastered several languages, most notably English, during her stays in the foreign cities where her father's diplomatic postings took the family. In her memoirs, written in the mid-1930s, Hermynia described the incorrigible arrogance of many of her relatives, who treated middle-class people, 'even when they were millionaires', with high-handed disdain. Her great-uncle's wife said to her one day: 'The bourgeois, you know, are perfectly fine, and I know that before God we are all alike, but I just can't see them as people like ourselves.' Seeking to get away from mounting pressure from her father to marry into Viennese high society, she saw in Viktor von Zur Mühlen a means of escape and a passport to independence from her family. The two met at a ball in the resort of Merano in the Austrian Alps while her parents were away, and were instantly attracted to one another. Three weeks later they were engaged to be married.

Her father, returning from his trip, did not approve. The young man was a Protestant German Balt; she should have married a Catholic Viennese aristocrat. 'Has it occurred to you,' he asked Hermynia, 'that your sons can never become chamberlains or your daughters ladies of the Order of the Star and Cross?' But this was not Hermynia's ambition. In her romantic imagination she was going to live on a rich estate set in a magical Baltic landscape. The couple wed quietly in Frankfurt and set off for Russia. Hermynia did not think that marriage would constrict her life any more than her parents had done. But she was wrong. On arriving at the von zur Mühlen estate in Estonia, she found only two books in her husband's country house, 'the Bible and a pornographic work, *The Memoirs of a Singer*'. Imported magazines and newspapers were routinely censored by the tsarist authorities, who blacked out almost everything apart from the Court Circular. 'Even in my encyclopedia,' she wrote, 'which was sent after me along with other books, whole sections of "Russia: History" had been blacked out.' She was shocked by the ignorance of the Baltic German aristocracy in Estonia, who referred to middle-class people, whatever they did, as *literati*. 'When I went to Dorpat for the first time,' Hermynia later remembered, 'and bought four hundred roubles' worth of books, and subscribed, on top of that, to magazines in various languages, my husband was genuinely dumbfounded, and my mother-in-law asked in astonishment: "What do you need all those books for? A good housewife has so much to do taking care of the house that she hardly has time to read."' Further scandal was caused by her habit of taking two baths a day ('No decent woman does that!' exclaimed her mother-in-law) and wearing clothes made of coloured fabrics: ' "Why don't you wear black instead?" my mother-in-law asked me when I appeared in one of my prettiest Paris dresses. "You are a married woman now, for goodness' sake!" '

Relations between the Baltic German nobility and the Estonian peasants and farm workers were not good. Hermynia's husband gave her a Browning revolver as a wedding present, warning her to carry it every time she went out for a walk on her own. There was no knowing what 'these animals' might do, Viktor said. And indeed, 'whenever one encountered a little farm cart on a country road, the peasant would shout angrily *"kurrati-sax!"* (German devil)!' But they soon got used to her and said: 'The master has married a blonde gypsy; she is crazy, but a good sort.' Hermynia even became popular when she began to use the medical knowledge she had gained while helping out at the infirmary of the Sisters of Mercy in Florence, treating minor ailments and even assisting a peasant woman in childbirth, to the consternation of the local doctor who lived three hours' ride away and put hunting before his professional duties. She was appalled by the squalor and ignorance she found, and taken aback by the habitual drunkenness of the peasantry, who were not satisfied with vodka but would even get hold of ether to fulfil their craving for oblivion.

The Baltic nobles with whom she now mixed, Hermynia observed, 'truly believed in aristocracy and in their own place among the elect. It never occurred to them, at any moment in their lives, that other people were also human.' When her husband came home one day with his cane broken in two, and

> I asked him in astonishment what had happened, he replied: 'I broke it over the back of one of the labourers.' He could not understand when I cried, half-weeping, half in anger: 'Have the carriage hitched. I am leaving. I am getting a divorce!'

When Viktor reported on another occasion that he had given another worker 'the hiding of his life' because he had 'dared to whistle the Marseillaise', Hermynia 'went to the piano, which was by the open window, and played the Marseillaise over and over again the whole day long. The workers laughed: "The master can't handle that gypsy".' And indeed he could not. She was not interested in bearing and bringing up children, her main purpose in life in the eyes of her husband's parents ('What, not yet? You should ride less and above all not bathe so much'). For his part, Viktor was not interested in anything apart from managing his estate and going on elk-hunting expeditions (on one of which, when she was supposed to be looking after the estate, Hermynia allowed the peasants to steal large quantities of goods from the barns because she thought it would alleviate their poverty).

Hermynia's marriage was unusual in a number of respects, not merely because it was so clearly a marriage of opposites. Marriage within the closed circle of Baltic German families was still the norm in Estonia: 58 per cent of the 2,060 marriages contracted by noblemen between 1860 and 1914 were within the corporate nobility, 20 per cent were sealed with non-noble local women (*literati* and burghers), and 22 per cent with Russian women. Marriage to a foreigner was so rare that such liaisons did not figure in the general statistics at all. The Baltic German nobility in Estonia still owned 58 per cent of the total land surface of the province in 1914. Nevertheless, by 1902 the corporate nobility, owning 401 manors, had been forced to witness seventy-nine of them falling into the hands of commoners. Some nobles tried going down the legally tricky route of entailing their manors, but the trade in manors could not be stopped. Others began using imported fertilizers, switched from traditional cultivation to a multi-field system, exploited their timber commercially, shifted to dairy production, and started to employ machinery. Overall in the three decades leading up to 1914, agricultural productivity in the three provinces of Estonia, Livonia and Courland increased by 20 to 30 per cent as a result, though this required investment which increased noble indebtedness. The geologist Alexander von Keyserling (1815–91) commented in his diary in 1889 on how 'hard it was to be a manor lord in Estonia', because 'one does not become rich'.

Hermynia's marriage did not last. The couple's political differences multiplied until 'my husband and I were no longer good-humouredly scornful of each other's opinions or hopeful of bringing the other around to our own position'. They took politically opposed newspapers, Hermynia left-wing, Viktor right-wing: 'When the mail bag arrived whoever opened it handed the other his newspaper with the fire-tongs so as not to dirty his hands on it. More and more frequently I heard the words: "I will not allow such a thing to be said in my house!"' Hermynia's father-in-law tried to intervene: 'He would stare at me as though he thought I had lost my mind, then he would roar louder than ever: "If I were your husband I should beat you to a pulp." "If you were my husband," she replied, "I should either have murdered you a long time ago, or else you would have learned how to behave like a gentleman."' Hermynia fell ill with tuberculosis and had to spend many months recuperating at a sanatorium in Davos in Switzerland, where she was still staying in 1914 when the war broke out. She did not return. The Russian Revolution allowed her to obtain a divorce. By 1919 she was in Germany, where she joined the Communist Party and earned her living by translating more than 150 novels from French and English into German, including the entire output of the American writer Upton Sinclair. She lived with the Jewish writer Stefan Isidor Klein (1889–1960) in Frankfurt and wrote many novels and short stories of her own, several of which became best-sellers. In 1933, when the Nazis took over, she left, after publishing a letter condemning the new regime, and eventually made her way to England, where in 1951 she died in poverty and obscurity in Radlett, Hertfordshire, her works entirely forgotten. Viktor, meanwhile, organized an anti-Bolshevik militia after the 1917 revolution, joined the Nazi stormtroopers in the 1930s, and died in 1950, shortly before his ex-wife.

The two worlds inhabited by Hermynia von Zur Mühlen before the First World War could hardly have been more different from one another: on the one hand, the cosmopolitan, sophisticated, literate and cultured world of the Austrian service nobility, on the other the impoverished, philistine, brutal and provincial world of the Baltic German landowning aristocracy. Yet both were recognizably part of the upper echelons of European society at the beginning of the twentieth century: both, in their very different ways, were holding out against the tides of modernity that had been flowing across Europe for many years. The Baltic German nobility were exceptional only in the extreme nature of their situation. They were not just a small hereditary caste, constituting less than 7 per cent of the population of Livonia, Estonia and Courland, they were also an autonomous feudal corporation whose rights and privileges had only gradually been undermined in the course of the nineteenth century. It was not until the 1890s that their ancient judicial system was replaced with modern Russian courts introduced under Alexander II's reforms in 1864, though even then the nobles retained some manorial police rights. They ignored the Russification policies of the government in St Petersburg for as long as they could, obstinately celebrating their German culture and Protestant faith despite Russian being made the official language and Orthodoxy the official religion. Moreover, the Baltic German nobility stubbornly resisted conceding any administrative or political power to the local indigenous population. This was a major reason why they were so disliked by the native peasantry. In the course of the 1905 Revolution this hatred broke out into open hostility, when 184 manors were burned in Courland and Estonia and 90 German landowners killed. Reprisals by troops sent from St Petersburg, including Cossacks, were still continuing in some parts as late as 1908, supported by local landowner militias. Altogether 2,000 alleged insurgents from the provinces were sent to Siberia, and at least 900 were executed.

Noble landowners of modest means, like those who made up the majority of the Baltic German community, existed in many parts of Europe. In Russia, where all the children inherited their father's title and property, princes and princesses abounded; some 890,000 people were legally defined as of noble status in the late nineteenth century; their number virtually doubled between 1858 and 1897. In Hungary, where comparable arrangements obtained, the nobility made up around 5 per cent of the population during the same period. Nobility in parts of the Continent, notably in pre-Revolutionary France, had been conferred by the possession of a state office, and if the office did not generate substantial revenues, the office-holder's son inherited the noble title without having the resources to sustain the lifestyle that was conventionally supposed to go with it. This system did not exist in England, where until 1871 even army officers had to buy their commissions, while the navy was a socially egalitarian institution where promotion was obtained on merit; indeed, there were almost no poor aristocrats in England, where primogeniture limited the numbers of men with titles, and the legally defined privileges of the nobility, apart from membership in the House of Lords, had vanished well before the nineteenth century. Nobles in some parts of Europe could also lose their titles. Tsar Nicholas I reduced some 64,000 Polish nobles to commoner status as a punishment for their rebelliousness, and by 1864 around 80 per cent of the hereditary noble caste of *szlachta* had lost their titles and privileges. Prince, later King, Nikola I of Montenegro (1841–1921) had no scruples about removing noble titles from disloyal subjects (of whom there were many), as he did with the *Vojvoda* (warlord) Duke Marko Miljanov Popović (1833–1901), who lost his title after a quarrel with the prince in 1882. Sometimes titles simply fell into disuse, as with the boyars of Romania, who lost their noble status with the ending of serfdom and were just known thereafter as large landowners. In Sweden no new noble titles were granted after 1902, the last one being given to the explorer Sven Hedin (1865–1952).

Despite the popularity in castle and palace reading rooms of the *Almanach de Gotha*, the bible of noble genealogy, the aristocracy in most parts of Europe was not always of ancient lineage. In Prussia there were 1,129 ennoblements in the period 1871–1918 alone, all by definition of individuals of bourgeois origins. In France there were no more titles of nobility created after 1848, but attempts to abolish titles by law all failed, apart from during the brief interlude of the 1848 Revolution. A law passed under Napoleon III in 1858 allowed *ancien régime* nobles to obtain an official confirmation of their title for a substantial sum – 5,000 francs for a duke and 2,000 for a marquis. The relative value of a new imperial title even under the Second Empire was illustrated by the charge made for the confirmation of a Napoleonic dukedom, which came in at a mere 200 francs. Bourgeois pretensions were catered for in France by a law which allowed people to add the noble 'de' prefix to their names, so that for example a certain Laurent Delattre (dates unknown) had his name legally changed in 1829 to Lattre de Tassigny, after a small estate he owned. This in turn allowed his descendant, Jean Joseph Marie Gabriel de Lattre de Tassigny (1889–1952), a celebrated general, to obtain a coat of arms and claim noble ancestry. In Spain, Queen Isabella gave noble titles to many leading generals and politicians. But she also ennobled a number of wealthy bankers and industrialists. Between 1886 and 1914, 210 Spaniards received noble titles, most of them from the world of business and politics.

Increasingly, the new nobility married into the old, a transaction that brought status to the former and wealth to the latter. A prime example was the family of the Spanish banker and industrialist Eusebi Güell i Bacigalupi (1846–1918). In 1871 he married the daughter of Antonio López, Marquis of Comillas (1817–83), a shipping magnate. Their son Juan Antoni Güell López (1874–1958) had two sisters, both of whom married into old aristocratic families, one of which, the Castelldosirus family, possessed a title dating back to 1148. In this new marriage market, American heiresses were a particularly sought-after prize. French noblemen entered the lists with gusto; the Duc Decazes (1864–1912), for instance, married Isabelle-Blanche Singer (1869–96), one of the heiresses to the Singer sewing-machine fortune, who brought him a dowry of two million dollars. In Britain the Dukes of Marlborough, who had been obliged to sell off some of their art collection in the 1880s to make ends meet, became past masters at discovering willing American heiresses. The eighth duke, George Spencer-Churchill (1844–92), married an American millionairess, Jane Warren Price (1854–1909), widow of a New York realtor, while his son the ninth duke, Charles Spencer-Churchill (1871–1934), married Consuelo Vanderbilt (1877–1964), who owned $4.2 million of railway stock in the USA; their marriage, conducted for purely mercenary reasons on his part and maternal social ambition on hers, ended in divorce. Altogether, between 1870 and 1914 there were more than a hundred marriages solemnized between the sons of English peers and wealthy American women.

Aristocrats continued to play the major role at Court, supplying monarchs and their spouses with personnel for exotically titled offices like (in Britain, for instance) Lady of the Bedchamber or Silver Stick in Waiting. But these were mainly ceremonial positions with little political significance. Armies underwent a steady process of *embourgeoisement*. In the Habsburg Monarchy, only two out of the thirty-seven generals active in 1804 were bourgeois; by 1908, twenty out of thirty-nine were. In the Prussian Army in 1806, under 10 per cent of the officers were non-noble; by 1913 the proportion had climbed to 70 per cent, including nearly half the generals and colonels. Similar developments took place in the rapidly expanding bureaucracies of European states. In some states with a bicameral Parliament, the hereditary aristocracy possessed its own rights in the Upper Chamber, such as the Prussian *Herrenhaus* or the British House of Lords, but these steadily lost legitimacy in comparison with elected Lower Chambers; in Britain the powers of the House of Lords were severely circumscribed by an Act of Parliament in 1910, which the government of the day forced through by persuading the king to agree to swamp the Lords with new creations should they fail to agree. The number of landowners in the House of Commons fell from 209 in 1874 to 78 in 1885. While landowners outnumbered all other members of the British Cabinet in 1868 (twelve against eight), new men joining the Cabinet between 1868 and 1886 included fifteen business and professional men but only nine landowners. After the turn of the century, prime ministers such as

Robert Gascoyne-Cecil, 3rd Marquess of Salisbury (1830–1903), a member of one of Britain's oldest landed families, and his nephew Arthur Balfour (1848–1930), gave way to new men from a different social background like Herbert Henry Asquith (1852–1928), son of a wool merchant, and Sir Henry Campbell-Bannerman (1836–1908), son of a clothier. Meanwhile new politicians from humble or even poor backgrounds such as David Lloyd George (1863–1945), who was brought up by his widowed mother and her brother, a shoemaker, in straitened circumstances in a north Wales cottage, were rising to dominate the political scene.

The power of the 'landed interest' in British politics was weakened steadily by extensions of the franchise, in 1832, 1867 and 1884, and by the ongoing processes of industrialization and urbanization. Social change forced aristocrats to engage in parliamentary politics. Adapting to the new political climate in their own country, Russian aristocrats began to engage in the party politics that emerged with the creation of an elected Duma after 1905, with Prince Georgy Yevgenyenich Lvov (1861–1925) heading up the moderate liberal Cadet Party. In Prussia the splendidly named Elard Kurt Maria Fürchtegott von Oldenburg-Januschau (1855–1937), an arch-conservative *Junker*, publicly branded the German socialists a 'mob of pigs' and became notorious for saying: 'The King of Prussia and German Emperor must always be able to say to a lieutenant: take ten men and lock up the Reichstag'; but he still felt obliged to stand for election to the Prussian Parliament in 1901 and the German Reichstag the following year. Aristocratic landowners such as Oldenburg-Januschau now had to campaign for their seat; they could no longer rely on the habits of deference of the peasants and labourers who lived on and around their landed estates. Secret ballots were introduced by law in England in 1872, and most European countries thereafter (they had existed in France since the 1790s). In Germany it became steadily more difficult to apply coercion and intimidation as the ballot became more secret: Oldenburg-Januschau lost his seat in 1912. Nor did the nobility as such wield much political power in liberal Spain; titled politicians, of whom there were many, did not generally acquire political power because of their titles, but acquired titles because of their political power.

More important still in the decline of aristocratic power was the growing might of the state, which over the course of the century abrogated noble rights of self-governance in feudal corporations, and replaced the ties of feudal dominance over the bodies of serfs and subjects with basic freedoms of movement, labour and inheritance, and equality before the law. Increased taxation and other burdens devised by the centralized apparatus of government further impinged on the autonomy of noble estate-owners. Professionalized local administration replaced manorial bailiffs and courts. Noble corporations were pushed aside by elected parliaments, which in many countries boosted their legitimacy by extending the franchise to wider groups of voters. There could be no question of what some historians have argued was a 'persistence of the old regime' all the way up to 1914. The decline of the aristocracy was a standard topic of social commentators all over Europe well before the end of the century. Historically, noble status had derived its meaning from the lord's dominion over his serfs, but over the decades the main functions of the seigneur had been assumed by the state, leaving nobles legally not much different from other subjects.

THE NEW ELITE

Despite its general loss of political power, the aristocracy in late nineteenth-century Europe remained in some areas at least a force to be reckoned with. In England, for example, a country long dominated by capitalist agriculture and almost entirely lacking a class of subsistence farmers or peasants, 363 individuals, all of them with titles, owned almost a quarter of all the land in 1873, with an average of more than 10,000 acres apiece. Magnates such as the Duke of Bedford or the Duke of Devonshire owned vast estates which brought in sufficient income for them to maintain grand country houses teeming with servants, cooks, scullery-maids, butlers, footmen, valets, chambermaids, gardeners, gamekeepers, and many more. Some of them, like Chatsworth House in Derbyshire, were palaces in all but name. In east-central Europe there were even greater landed magnates. On the eve of the First World War, the Schwarzenberg family owned 315,000 acres in southern Bohemia, while in Hungary the Esterházy family's landed estates extended to some 750,000 acres in all. In Silesia the eleven biggest landowners owned 20 per cent of the surface area of the province. Yet while a boom in grain prices that continued through the 1850s and 1860s allowed larger proprietors to make considerable profits, the sharp downturn of the 1870s brought trouble for many of them. In Britain the price of wheat fell by half between 1871 and 1901, and wheat acreage was reduced from 3,500,000 acres to less than 1,500,000. Many tried to adapt by modernizing, but the investment needed was possible only for large farms and estates producing for the market. The British engineer Thomas Aveling (1824–82) devised the first self-propelling steam traction engine in 1859, enabling threshing and other machines to be moved from place to place and operated under steam power. Soon he was doing business all over Europe. In Germany from 1882 to 1907 the number of threshing machines increased by 385 per cent, seed drills by 450 per cent, and mechanical reapers by 1,500 per cent. Imports of agricultural machinery into Italy rose more than twentyfold between 1888 and 1910. Landowners in northern France began to import threshing, reaping and binding machines from America in the 1870s: by 1892 there were 262,000 horse hoes, 234,000 threshing machines and 39,000 mechanical reapers in use in France, and the total weight of imports of agricultural machinery increased more than tenfold between 1890 and 1913. Increasingly, too, Continental countries began to manufacture their own farm machines: the value of the output of agricultural machinery factories in Russia rose more than tenfold between 1890 and 1913, a development paralleled in less dramatic form in other areas of commercially farmed large estates.

These developments left peasant farming largely untouched. Two-thirds of all ploughs used in Russia in 1910 were still wooden, and only 2 per cent of peasant households were using seed drills. The fact that in the late nineteenth century the total number of farms in France stood at 3.5 million indicated that machinery was used only by a tiny minority; most peasant farms carried on doing things by hand. Agricultural credit banks began to enable at least some investment here too, even if agricultural modernization continued to be confined mainly to the larger estates. Improvements were more rapid and far-reaching in Germany, where more than 10 million people worked in agriculture in 1913. While the increase in output that had taken place earlier in the century was largely the consequence of bringing more land under cultivation, from the 1870s it continued despite a fall in the total land area in agricultural use. Output of potatoes nearly doubled from 1875 to 1884 and 1905 to 1914, while that of sugar beet trebled. By 1910, indeed, Germany was producing a third of the world's entire output of potatoes. Much of this produce went into the distillation of spirits, in factories erected on the noble landowners' estates. Some of it was for export. Nearly 200,000 litres of grain and potato spirit were imported into southern Africa through the Portuguese entrepôt of Lourenço Marques in 1894. Almost half a million litres were imported at the peak of the trade, in 1896, to dull the senses of the thousands of African labourers drafted in to work in the goldmines of the Rand, where, diluted with water, tincture of prunes, green tea and creosote, the potent spirit was sold as 'kaffir brandy'.

Smaller farmers by contrast found it easier to turn to animal husbandry. The number of cattle in Germany increased from 16 million in 1873 to 21 million in 1913, and the number of pigs from 12 million in 1892 to 26 million on the eve of the war, more than compensating for a sharp fall in the number of sheep kept. Pigs required much less land, and pork could be used for a variety of purposes, most notably of course the many hundreds of different kinds of sausage consumed by the Germans, who almost entirely lost their taste for mutton and lamb during this period. In Germany too, producer co-operatives and rural banks, both founded by Friedrich Wilhelm Raiffeisen (1818–88), began to help peasant farms modernize, but the process was a very slow one; farming strips were still not consolidated in many areas by 1914, and tiny holdings predominated, with two-thirds of the farms in the Prussian Rhine province occupying only a quarter of the cultivated area on the eve of the war. Raiffeisen had a European impact, with the co-operative agricultural banks founded by his Italian follower Luigi Luzzatti (1841–1927) pioneering a movement that saw more than 700 of them in existence by 1908, almost all in Lombardy. They also made a major impact in Hungary, where the name Raiffeisen can still be seen in streets throughout Budapest today.

In all these areas of agriculture, the advent of chemical fertilizers played a key role in improving productivity. Phosphates, pioneered by the German chemist Justus von Liebig (1803–83) and the British agronomist Sir John Bennet Lawes (1814–1900), began to replace guano as companies such as Fisons, dating back to 1843, started to manufacture the fertilizer on an industrial scale. In Italy the value of imported fertilizer rose from 4 million lire in 1887 to 60 million by 1910, and there was comparable growth elsewhere. This was also a period of countless small, now largely forgotten inventions that improved agricultural output in various ways. Dairy farming was made easier, for example, by the centrifugal cream separator, perfected by the Swedish inventor Gustaf de Laval (1845–1913), which was particularly useful for small farmers who switched to animal husbandry in this period, unable to compete with large grain producers. Only the larger farmers could afford machinery and fertilizer, however. Some 505 of the 511 steam-driven agricultural machines in Austrian Galicia in 1902 were on farms covering more than 120 acres. Even with improvements of this kind, noble estates and market-oriented farms across Europe were increasingly unable to withstand the rising tide of cheap grain imports from America, where the vast Great Plains of the Midwest were brought under cultivation in the second half of the century. Russian grain production also increased rapidly, more than trebling between the 1860s and the 1880s and nearly doubling again by 1910–13. Much of this produce was exported. Wealthier Russian peasants quickly became attuned to the need to price the wheat they grew for export so as not to be undercut by imports from America. An American observer standing at the quayside at Nikolayev, a Ukrainian port on the Black Sea, noted how 'the peasants on arrival at the market with their grain were asking: "What is the price in America according to the latest telegram?" And, what is still more surprising, they knew how to convert cents per bushel into kopecks per pood.' Yet as the population of Russia grew apace, grain was required to feed its insatiable demand for bread, so that the percentage of wheat exported fell from over a third to less than a quarter between 1897 and 1913. Still, Russia, along with Germany, remained a major grain exporter right up to 1914.

European trade had been facilitated over the decades by the dismantling of tariff barriers in a lengthy series of bilateral trade treaties – twenty-four concluded by Italy in the 1860s, for example, eighteen by Germany, fourteen by Austria-Hungary. But the situation changed dramatically with the economic downturn of the 1870s and the precipitous rise in American grain exports to Europe. In Germany, Bismarck, yielding to pressure from *Junker* and other landowning interests, introduced protection in 1879 and increased duties again in 1885 and 1887, by which time the import duty on grain stood at 30 per cent. Nevertheless, on the eve of the First World War, 40 per cent of all wheat consumed in Germany still had to be imported, most of it from Russia. The landed interest also secured tax concessions for its estates, and managed to ensure that tax assessment and collection was largely in the hands of local administrators drawn from the ranks of the noble landowners, the *Landräte*, who fixed them in the interests of their fellow estate owners. Similarly in France the pressure for import tariffs on grain grew until they were introduced in 1885. Under the 1892 Méline tariff they reached very high levels indeed, making wheat prices about 45 per cent higher than they were in free-trade Britain. Russia introduced new grain duties, above all in the Mendeleev tariff of 1891, as did Austria-Hungary with new tariffs in 1878, 1882 and 1887. The Italians reversed their policy of the 1860s and pushed through new import duties in 1878, 1888 and 1894. In all these cases, and even more so with tariffs introduced by countries such as Bulgaria and Romania, there was a strong element of industrial protection, but a significant part of the pressure to bring in tariffs came from large and medium-sized farms and estates producing for the market.

All of these measures had some effect in shoring up the large estates. But they did not shore up the traditional, post-feudal aristocracy. In many parts of Europe failing estates were increasingly purchased by wealthy middle-class entrepreneurs and investors, who by 1877 had bought up one-eighth of all the land owned by individuals in Russia. In Prussia the

Junker aristocracy gained 990,000 acres of land through the whole process of emancipation, together with 260 million marks in money payments, but even this huge transfer of resources did little to counteract its indebtedness, which doubled from 162 million to 325 million marks between 1805 and 1845. In this situation many landowners had no option but to sell. By 1900 only a third of East-Elbian noble estates were still owned by noblemen, including recently ennobled ones. The middle-class purchase of landed estates from impoverished noble families was one of the most widespread social phenomena of the post-feudal period in nineteenth-century Europe. Following disentailment in Spain, for example, a sixth of the property sold in Valladolid was purchased by people from Madrid, all of them commoners. In 1855 a liberal government ordered all land belonging to the state, the Church, charities and municipalities to be sold at auction, for cash that was to be used to fund public works. As a result, around 615,000 properties covering 24 million acres, up to a third of the total land surface of Spain, came onto the market between 1836 and 1895. In some parts of Europe the great landowners managed to put brakes on this process by reintroducing entailment: thus in Hungary, for example, where in 1844 non-nobles had for the first time been legally permitted to purchase landed estates, sixty-four estates were newly entailed between 1853 and 1867, creating nearly three and a half million acres of 'indivisible and inalienable' land. But this only slowed down the overall process of transfer, rather than stopping it altogether.

Some aristocratic landowners were unable to adapt to the new commercialism even with the aid of massive sums paid in compensation for their loss of income from feudal sources such as the tithe. In Spain the Duke of Osuna, the country's top taxpayer in 1850, had already begun to sell off property in 1841 to reduce his debts, but he was forced to take on further loans until he was unable to meet the interest on them except by selling off more land. By 1877 forty-seven sales, 'some of them worth millions', it was said, had reduced the duke's properties still further, until in 1894, following a lengthy series of lawsuits brought by his creditors, his entire remaining property was sequestrated and sold off. According to one investigation, most of the land fell into the hands of 'substantial farmers, many of whom had been tenants of the House [of Osuna], who added ownership to exploitation and came to reinforce the figure of the capitalist farmer'. Nevertheless, despite such spectacular failures, most large aristocratic landowners in Spain and elsewhere managed to weather the transition to a capitalist agrarian economy, enjoying their new liquidity to invest in a broad portfolio including services and industrial enterprises, or selling off estates in a carefully managed way to reduce their indebtedness. But smaller noble landowners did not always fare so well. 'Sandalled nobility' as they were called in Hungary, or 'buckwheat nobility' in Poland, were similar to the *Krautjunker* or 'cabbage-patch Junkers' in Prussia – men who lacked the land necessary to live off after the ending of serfdom and often had to migrate to the towns. In Hungary bankruptcies multiplied and many small estates were sold to large landowners, often acting through Jewish-owned banks. The number of medium-sized gentry estates fell from 30,000 in 1867 to only 10,000 by 1900; in 1890 alone there were foreclosures on nearly 15,000 farms whose owners had mortgaged them up to the hilt.

For those whose income allowed them to do it, by far the best way to survive was to invest in industry. In Russia the redemption payments that aristocratic landowners received for the ending of serfdom provided ready funds with which to do so. By the 1870s, as Friedrich Engels remarked in one of his writings on Germany, the aristocracy had 'left the old and respectable days behind and now swell the lists of directors of all sorts of sound and unsound joint-stock companies'. From the point of view of industrialists, including a titled aristocrat on the board of a company could lend it a touch of class, while the financial rewards were eagerly sought after by those noblemen who did not regard such activities as beneath them. By 1905 the boards of Hungarian financial and industrial companies counted among their number eighty-eight counts and sixty-six barons; in 1902 noblemen made up 30 per cent of the directors of railway companies, and 23 per cent of large steel and banking companies. In Austria in 1874 the boards of railway companies founded since 1866 included thirteen princes, sixty-four counts, twenty-nine barons and forty-two other noblemen. This reflected among other things the huge shift in the sources of wealth that had taken place over the preceding decades. In France the 1848 inheritance records showed that only 5 per cent of the fortunes left at death were in stocks and shares, while 58 per cent were in land or houses; but by 1900 the former figure had climbed to 31 per cent and the latter declined to 45 per cent.

Investing in industry was even easier for a landowner if there were mineral deposits on his estate. Engelbert, Duke of Arenberg and Croy (1875–1949), not untypical in this respect, allowed mines to be sunk on his land in Westphalia in return for rent that brought him an annual income of more than half a million marks by the 1900s. Other aristocratic landowners settled for a percentage of the mining income, a deal that propelled another Westphalian magnate, Alfred, Prince zu Salm-Salm (1846–1923), to one of the top positions in a *Yearbook of German Millionaires* compiled by Rudolf Martin (1867–1939) as a way of demonstrating the prosperity of the German Reich. Most entrepreneurial of all were the great Silesian landowners, six of whom figured on Martin's list of the eleven richest Prussians in 1913. One of them, Prince Christian Kraft zu Hohenlohe-Öhringen, Duke of Ujest (1848–1926), employed more than 5,000 coalminers and was the world's largest producer of zinc. Four-fifths of his wealth was invested in industry by 1910. Another, Prince Guido Henckel von Donnersmarck (1830–1916), diversified his industrial empire into chrome, viscose, paper and cellulose, and invested in industrial enterprises in Austria, France, Hungary, Italy and Russia. Nevertheless, however energetic they were, rich aristocrats like these found it increasingly difficult to keep pace with the rapid development and expansion of industry. By 1909 the Duke of Ujest's businesses were embroiled in a bitter lawsuit with those of Henckel von Donnersmarck and were teetering on the verge of bankruptcy: Kaiser Wilhelm II was forced to intervene, and the duke had to sell off a large chunk of his land. 'Mere dilettantism,' commented the Austrian ambassador on the scandal, 'was no longer sufficient to manage large estates in a capitalist world.' Increasingly such men turned their business interests into limited companies and employed professional managers to run them.

In many cases landed aristocrats who tried to gain from industrial enterprises founded on their lands were outflanked by the entrepreneurs they called in to run them. In the Donbass region, the Welsh ironmaster John Hughes (1814–89), having received a commission from the Russian government, arrived in 1870 with a hundred skilled ironworkers and miners from south Wales. Renting the land from the Lieven family, originally Baltic German nobility but now occupying high positions at Court and in the army, Hughes set up a vast complex with eight blast furnaces, iron-ore mines, collieries and brickworks. As the settlement grew, he built an Anglican church dedicated to St George and (of course) St David, schools, a hospital, tearooms, bath-houses, and many other amenities. In 1882, unable to cope with the assertiveness of the miners in the rapidly growing industrial settlement, and mired in lawsuits over their properties, the Lievens sold up to Hughes and invested in stocks and bonds and Baltic forests instead. Within a decade of Hughes's death, the town, now under the management of four of his sons, was producing three-quarters of all Russia's iron ore. All this was achieved by a man who was unable to write and could only read if the text was in capital letters, while the aristocratic owners of the land were not even capable of understanding what they had done. Hughes's memory was commemorated in the name of the settlement, Yuzovka (Hughesovka), and it was only changed after the Bolshevik

Revolution when most of the Welsh miners went back home; in 1924 it became Stalino, then, later, after Stalin's name fell into disrepute, Donetsk. The example of Yuzovka, like the experiences of the Silesian magnates, pointed to the fact that even where the landed aristocracy tried to keep up with the times, they were often overtaken by thrusting entrepreneurs of far humbler origin. What emerged in fact from the social changes of the nineteenth century, as bourgeois businessmen invested in landed prop-erty and aristocratic estate-owners invested in industry, was a new kind of elite, based above all on wealth, mixing together large landowners, bankers and businessmen, industrialists and investors, some with titles, some without, but all living more or less the same style of life, wearing the same kind of clothes, and indulging in the same kind of amusements. Increasingly hunting parties and country-house weekends were joined by businessmen, non-aristocratic politicians and other commoners who entered 'Society', as the term was in England, on the basis of their wealth. The very wealthy lived a peripatetic lifestyle, moving from one residence to another as the seasons required. In England, for example, they would occupy a house in London in the late spring and early summer. They would move up to the Scottish moors for the opening of the grouse-shooting season on the 'glorious twelfth' of August, and then to Norfolk for the pheasant shooting, or the Midlands for fox hunting and county balls. They returned to London for Christmas, after which they would overwinter in Monte Carlo or Biarritz, indulging in gambling, card-playing, socializing and intrigue.

It was common for the very rich to own a house in every location where they spent more than a few weeks each year, though only their main country residence would be really large. Wealthy central Europeans tended to spend a good deal of their time in spas such as Karlsbad or Baden-Baden, where the casino was almost as important as the thermal baths. Such locations were meeting places for a wide variety of European high nobility and, increasingly, wealthy bourgeois. Baden-Baden was visited at one time or another by Queen Victoria, Kaiser Wilhelm I and the Emperor Napo-leon III, as well as foreign potentates such as the Persian Shah Nasir al-Din (1831–96). It also featured as a setting for some of the episodes in the novel *Anna Karenina* by Leo Nikolayevich Tolstoy (1828–1910) as well as *The Gambler* by Fyodor Mikhailovich Dostoyevsky (1821–81), who went there to play the tables at the casino, though he could not really afford it. Johannes Brahms (1833–97) had a house there, and Ivan Ser-geyevich Turgenev (1818–83) set his 1867 novel *Smoke* in the town. In such venues the high aristocratic and, increasingly, the wealthy elites of many countries had the opportunity to meet, socialize, gamble, and conduct affairs across national and linguistic divides. Their cosmopolitanism was aided by the universality of French as the basic means of communication. The great cities of Europe, above all Paris, provided more venues of this kind; some noblemen lived almost all the time there, like the post-feudal boyars of Romania, who generally preferred to stay in France or Switzerland rather than in their own impoverished country, where 2,000 of them nonetheless owned 38 per cent of the land at the turn of the century. Later on, the film *The Grand Illusion* (1937) by the French director Jean Renoir (1894–1979) was to recapture this cosmopolitan world of the European elite in the encounter between Major von Rauffenstein, governor of a German prisoner-of-war camp during the First World War, and Captain de Boeldieu, one of his French prisoners: both aristocrats, they remembered dining at Maxim's restaurant in Paris, and even recalled flirting with the same woman before the war.

Not content with sharing in the lifestyle of the landed elite in this way, the upper middle classes even moved in on that most aristocratic of pursuits in the nineteenth century, duelling. In the aristocratic world of the eighteenth century, the pursuit of glory was accompanied by the defence of honour. An insult could only be requited through a challenge. Potential duellists were supposed to be, as the Germans put it, *satisfaktionsfähig*, that is, of suitably honourable standing to give or receive a challenge, but as the century wore on, the definition of who was honourable crept steadily down the social scale. Out of the 232 Prussian duellists known to have fought between 1800 and 1869, 44 per cent were noblemen; among the 303 duellists known to have fought between 1870 and 1914, the figure sank to a mere 19 per cent. Doctors fought over diagnoses, lawyers over court cases, politicians over parliamentary exchanges, army and naval officers, whether titled or not (and 20 per cent of the Prussian officer corps and the great majority of the naval officer corps were not titled even in the 1850s), over tactics employed on manoeuvre. By asserting their honourable status, middle-class men were laying claim to what had previously been the exclusive preserve of the titled aristocracy: all across Europe, writers like Marcel Proust (1871–1922), Alexander Pushkin and Mikhail Yuryevich Lermontov (1814–41), politicians like Pyotr Stolypin, Georges Clemenceau (1841–1929) and Ferdinand Lassalle, even the painter Édouard Manet (1832–83), fought duels. The merging of aristocratic and bourgeois mores signified by middle-class duelling took place at many levels across the century. In Britain, duelling was replaced from mid-century by sporting contests, but the process was the same. Long before 1914 it was clear that a new upper class of the wealthy and the influential had been formed.

Some historians have argued that the aristocracy changed over the course of the eighteenth and nineteenth centuries from a social order to a class, but this is not quite correct. Certainly under the legal regime of agrarian feudalism the aristocracy possessed rights and privileges denied to the untitled, reflecting the *ancien régime* conception of a society where every order not only knew its place but was also kept there by law. But before the decline of feudalism, in most parts of Europe the aristocracy was also a class, that is, it too could be defined economically, as the group in society whose wealth derived from the land. Of course, at its lower borders there was little to choose in this respect between the impoverished *Krautjunker* and the prosperous peasant, and here the web of rights, privileges and duties spun by feudalism was at its most potent and its most restrictive. Nevertheless, the aristocracy's decline in the nineteenth century broadly mirrored the decline of land as a source of wealth and the rise of banking, trade and industry until they outstripped it. The titled aristocracy, increasingly uncoupled from landed wealth, became ever more exclusively a status group, retaining its social prestige but losing its economic identity and merging into the upper ranks of the bourgeoisie. Contemporaries recognized this fact: in France, for example, it was common by the late nineteenth century to argue that the country was run by '200 families' of the wealthy elite, most of them non-noble, who arranged everything to suit themselves (though if there was such an oligarchy, it was certainly much larger than this).

In *Der Stechlin*, the last novel of Theodor Fontane (1819–98), the central figure, the conservative noble landowner Dubslav von Stechlin, lives a tranquil life, interrupted only by an election in which he is beaten by a socialist. Stechlin recognizes that he and his kind are no longer capable of keeping up with the modern world. They had, as one of the characters, Pastor Lorenzen, says, to go 'not necessarily with the new: better with the old, as far as we can, and with the new, only as far as we must'. But perhaps the most powerful fictional evocation of the decline of the aristocracy and the rise of a new bourgeoisie comes from a much later novel, *Il Gattopardo* (referring to the serval, a large wildcat that was hunted to extinction in Italy in the nineteenth century, but known in English as *The Leopard*). Its author, Giuseppe Tomasi di Lampedusa (1896–1957), was a minor Sicilian prince whose incompatible marriage to a Baltic German noblewoman, Alexandra Alice Wolff von Stomersee (1894–1982), strangely mirrored that of Hermynia and Viktor von Zur Mühlen. The novel, based on family stories and documents from the time of Lampedusa's great-grandfather, centres on Prince Fabrizio, an impoverished Sicilian aristocrat who lives off his peasants and does not really work, preferring to occupy himself with pursuing his private hobby of astronomy. The prince is jolted out of his routine when he is confronted with the upheaval of the Risorgimento, in which the Kingdom of the Two Sicilies falls and is incorporated into the new united Italy, ruled from Piedmont by bourgeois politicians, bankers and industrialists. As those who have backed the unification become rich and influential, the prince realizes that he and his estates will only survive in this new world if he follows the advice of his nephew Tancredi, who has joined with Garibaldi to signify the nobility's acceptance of unification: 'If we want things to stay as they are, things will have to change.' Although he does not love her, the ambitious Tancredi marries Angelica, the daughter of the rough and unscrupulous businessman and politician Don Calogero, who has rigged the plebiscite in Sicily to produce a majority for unification. As the novel proceeds, the prince and the businessman grow more like one another, the prince becoming more proactive in his business dealings, Don Calogero beginning 'that process of continual refining which in the course of three generations transforms innocent peasants into defenceless gentry'.

THE WORKSHOP OF THE WORLD

Throughout the nineteenth century, the economy of Europe and indeed the entire world was dominated by Britain. By 1850 over 40 per cent of the world's output of traded manufactured goods was produced in the United Kingdom. Britain was 'the workshop of the world', a status celebrated in the Great Exhibition of the Works of Industry of All Nations held in 1851 in a vast, specially constructed glass pavilion – the Crystal Palace – erected in London's Hyde Park. Despite the invitation to exhibitors from across the globe to display their wares in the pavilion, there was no doubt that the primary intention was to advertise Britain's role as the world's industrial leader. The continuing influence of the landed aristocracy was present symbolically in the choice of the Duke of Devonshire's head gardener, Joseph Paxton (1803–65), to design the Crystal Palace, a larger version of an enormous glass conservatory he had built at Chatsworth in Derbyshire. Six million people visited the Great Exhibition, from all social classes, making the average attendance per day more than 40,000. Queen Victoria was given season ticket number one and visited the Crystal Palace more than forty times. 'The tremendous cheering,' she wrote on the opening day, 'the joy expressed in every face, the vastness of the building, with all its decoration and exhibits, the sound of the organ . . . all this was indeed moving.'

Those who attended were overwhelmed by the novelty and diversity of the exhibits. The novelist Charlotte Brontë (1816–55) noted after her visit:

> It is a wonderful place – vast, strange, new and impossible to describe. Its grandeur does not consist in *one* thing, but in the unique assemblage of *all* things. Whatever human industry has created you find there, from the great compartments filled with railway engines and boilers, with mill machinery in full work, with splendid carriages of all kinds, with harness of every description, to the glass-covered and velvet-spread stands loaded with the most gorgeous work of the goldsmith and silversmith, and the carefully guarded caskets full of real diamonds and pearls worth hundreds of thousands of pounds.

Prizes were offered for the most ingenious mechanical inventions and the most innovative industrial products, and were almost all won by the British; other countries took the prizes for foodstuffs, handicrafts and raw materials. The Exhibition was notable for its social harmony, with workers, admitted on specially discounted tickets, marvelling at the products alongside the middle classes. Queen Victoria's husband Prince Albert (1819–61), a moving spirit of the Exhibition, remarked before the opening that it would demonstrate 'peace, love, and ready assistance, not only between individuals but between the nations of the earth'. Only the German industrialist and arms manufacturer Alfred Krupp struck a discordant note, exhibiting a shiny steel cannon: 'The English will have their eyes opened,' he exulted.

Britain's domination of the oceans in the decades following the defeat of Napoleon ensured that British shipping carried the vast bulk of world trade during the period. At mid-century a quarter of all international trade passed through British ports. More than half of Britain's foreign trade was carried in British ships, generating important invisible earnings that were enormously boosted by the virtual world monopoly in shipping insurance exercised by Lloyd's of London. In 1890, Britain still had a greater tonnage of shipping than the rest of the world put together. Even in 1910, 40 per cent of the tonnage of the ships engaged in world trade was British. For most of the nineteenth century these ships were sailing vessels, with the famous tea-clippers such as the *Cutty Sark* dominating the trade in China tea. American sailing ships were more advanced than their British counterparts in the early decades of the century, carried more cotton and required fewer sailors to man them. But the transition to ironclad and steam-powered vessels transferred the advantage back to the British shipping industry, above all when steamships became powerful enough to cross the oceans, as they did in the early 1830s. A crucial breakthrough came with the invention of the screw propeller by the Bohemian engineer Josef Ressel (1793–1857), who patented the device in 1827 and used it to power the ship *Civetta* across Trieste's harbour at 6 knots in 1829 (unfortunately the ship exploded halfway over, and the Austrian police banned any further experiments). The first steam-powered ship to cross the Atlantic Ocean, the SS *Savannah*, which made the journey in 1819, still carried sail, while the first purpose-built transatlantic vessel, the SS *Great Western*, built by the British engineer Isambard Kingdom Brunel (1806–59) and the largest ship in the world at the time, still used a paddle-wheel for propulsion. But by 1845, Brunel had built a screw-propelled ship for the Atlantic crossing, the SS *Great Britain*. It took further technical innovations such as compound and triple-expansion engines, which hugely increased fuel efficiency by using steam several times over, to make regular long-haul journeys possible. Coaling stations allowed steamships to carry more cargo, and the opening of the Suez Canal in 1869 saved nearly 4,000 miles on the China run.

The hegemony of British shipping was ensured by the largest naval force in the world, which from 1889 onwards was required by an Act of Parliament to have at least as many battleships as the next two largest navies in the world combined. British trade was underpinned by the vastly greater degree of mechanization that gave British industry a huge advantage over its competitors, allowing it to produce more goods, faster, in greater quantities, and to a higher standard. The British economy dominated a global division of labour in which Britain produced industrial and manufactured goods, while the rest of the world supplied raw materials. Some 93 per cent of British exports at mid-century consisted of manufactured goods, and around the same proportion of imports comprised primary unprocessed produce. This situation continued well into the second half of the nineteenth century. The period was dominated increasingly by heavy industry and engineering. Textiles, which still made up more than 60 per cent of British exports in 1850, fell to 34 per cent in 1913, whereas metals and engineering increased from 18 to 27 per cent.

Just how much the economy depended on the British command of seaborne trade can be seen in the case of the Welsh slate-quarrying industry, which came to dominate the world in the nineteenth century. There were major seams of this stone, used above all for roofing the millions of houses built in the urban expansion of the era, in other parts of Europe, notably Westphalia and Spanish Galicia, but these regions lacked the ability to ship out blocks and finished slate products in quantity. The great quarries opened in north Wales transferred their products down to the coast on narrow-gauge gravity railways such as the Ffestiniog, the Talyllyn and the Corris, and from there they were shipped away by small bulk carriers, many of which were built onsite in special harbour facilities such as Port Dinorwic. The Penrhyn Quarry at Bethesda, on the slopes of Mount Snowdon, was carved out of the hills on a gargantuan scale, with twenty galleries together producing over 100,000 tons a year, leaving behind enormous grey slag heaps of discarded and broken rock tumbling down the hillside. In the five-year period 1875–80, 1,125,000 tons of slate were taken by ship from Porthmadog to other parts of Britain, the Continent or overseas, and another 692,000 tons from Port Dinorwic. Slate exports remained at an extraordinarily high level throughout the period, above all to Germany: in 1894, 39,500 out of 48,700 tons of slate went from Porthmadog directly to German ports. The 14,000 or so men employed in the Welsh slate-quarrying industry owed their livelihood in the first place to the British ability to monopolize the means of transportation of this heavy yet fragile bulk material across Europe and the world.

British industrial know-how and capital investment did not spread evenly across the European Continent in the age of high industrialization. Although many major industrial regions crossed state boundaries, as with the north-western European coalfield, industrial production had a growing effect on the economic and ultimately the military power of individual nations. Nowhere was this more obvious than in the case of the German Empire. In western Germany, north of the river Ruhr, the coal seams were deep, and the first successful sinkings of pits were achieved only in the 1840s. Coal output in the Ruhr, a mere 2 million tons in 1850, rose to 12 million in 1870, 60 million in 1890, and 114 million in 1913 (nearly three times the entire coal output of France). By 1913 the Ruhr was producing 8 million tons of pig iron a year. Companies grew at a frenetic pace, uniting coal and iron-ore mining with smelting and engineering in a 'vertical combination' that reduced costs and increased efficiency. Beginning with railways they moved out into other areas, above all armaments. Typical of this process was the Alfred Krupp firm in the Ruhr, which had begun its dizzying ascent to industrial prominence by making crankshafts and axles during the first railway boom in the 1840s. Continuing technical innovations after the middle of the century enabled Krupp to produce cast steel rings for use on railway wheels, then rails, as well as steel plates and propellers and shafts for steamships. In 1862, Krupp installed the first Bessemer furnace, named after the English inventor of a process involving the removal of impurities from pig iron by oxidation, Henry Bessemer (1813–98). Krupp followed it in 1869 with an improved version named after another English inventor, Sidney Gilchrist Thomas (1850–85). The profits allowed Krupp to buy up other firms and acquire iron-ore mines.

The firm went on to make more and bigger steel products, until it was employing 12,000 workers on an 86-acre site in Essen by 1874, three times the size it had been a decade earlier. Major heavy-industrial enterprises like Krupp and Thyssen ensured that Germany had become the leading industrial nation on the Continent well before the end of the century. It began to rival Britain. In 1910 the steam tonnage of the German merchant marine was well over 2 million tons, 11 per cent of the world total. Britain's monopoly on merchant shipping was clearly on the wane. The pace of German industrial growth and innovation was frantic. At the opening of the new port facilities in Hamburg in 1888, Otto von Bismarck surveyed the 16,150-square-foot sprawl of the Blohm and Voss shipbuilding yards, with their three huge construction berths, the recently completed purpose-built 'warehouse city', the bustling tugs and barges, the vast steamships towering over the waterfront, and the forests of steam cranes loading and unloading goods on the quayside, and remarked to his entourage: 'Gentlemen, that is a world I no longer understand.'

Compared to Germany's rapid industrial growth, French industrialization was an oft-interrupted process through most of the nineteenth century. British superiority in heavy industry, manufacturing and engineering in the first half of the century meant that the French had to concentrate on consumer goods, notably textiles. The weight of a peasant-dominated agricultural sector retarded French industrial investment, though German and British banks put considerable resources into the French economy. Population growth in France was far slower than in Britain or Germany, leaving little room for growth-led demand and placing a greater weight on exports. In addition, French agriculture was notably inefficient, with wheat yields in 1911–12 averaging half those of Belgium or the Netherlands. A major agricultural crisis hit France in the 1870s, as a microscopic parasite called pébrine devastated the silkworm industry and a tiny aphid, phylloxera, found its way across the Atlantic in fruit shipments and began eating up grapevines across the country. By 1880 nearly half of the vineyards in St Emilion had been lost. As the English humorous magazine *Punch* commented, 'The phylloxera, a true gourmet, finds out the best vineyards and attaches itself to the best wines.' Of course, the disease badly affected vines elsewhere, notably in Germany, but French wine was a major export commodity, whereas German wine mostly stayed at home, to be exported principally in the sickly sweet variety known in England as 'hock'. Overall, the epidemic cost around 37 per cent of the average annual French gross domestic product in the years 1885–1894, an indication of how important winegrowing was to the economy. The industry gradually recovered, thanks to the importation of disease-resistant vines from America, but the rate of replacement was slow. Germany's output of pig iron, the same as that of France in 1870, had doubled to twice the French output twenty years later, reflecting France's 10 per cent compared with Germany's 50 per cent population increase during these years as well as the chance location of large coal and iron-ore fields within the German borders. In France, 53 per cent of the labour force were engaged in agriculture and forestry in 1870, and 37 per cent in 1913. The railway boom continued through much of this period, and France's coal output rose from 17 million tons in 1875 to 41 million by 1913. But these quantities were small in comparison to those produced in Britain and Germany, and French imports of coal always amounted to between a third and a half of total consumption.

If French industry fell behind in relative terms, then on the southern periphery of Europe economies altogether failed to develop a strong industrial sector. In Spain the poverty of agriculture, the lack of easily exploitable mineral resources, the loss of the Americas, and the high tariff barriers erected in 1891 to levy a duty of more than 100 per cent on foreign grain, meant that the economy continued to be dominated by agriculture. Political instability discouraged investment, and the weak home market inhibited capital accumulation. Most Spanish natural produce was exported, including 81 per cent of Basque iron ores over the period 1881–1913. Portugal was in a similar situation, with one estimate putting per capita gross national product in 1913 near the bottom of the European pecking order, only a little higher than that of the Balkan states. Similarly, Austria-Hungary accounted by 1913 for only 6 per cent of Europe's total industrial output, and within the empire agriculture continued to make up around half of the entire national product on the eve of the war, with foodstuffs, textiles and consumer goods dominant. Heavy industry was concentrated in a few areas such as Bohemia and Moravia, Silesia and Styria, pulled along by the railway boom. But even though the Gilchrist-Thomas process enabled low-grade ore to be smelted and used in steel manufacture, costs per ton were a quarter higher than in Lorraine, coke and even ore had to be imported, and in some parts of the empire charcoal continued to be used in preference to coke as late as the 1890s. The textile industries continued to grow in Austria, with an increase in the number of cotton spindles from 1.3 million in 1851 to 2 million in 1885 and nearly 5 million in 1913, but Hungary was left far behind in the race, and overall continuing rural poverty held demand back across the Austro-Hungarian Empire as a whole. Only in a few centres did imaginative entrepreneurship and the import of modern methods lead to a real success story, as in the shoe industry of Bohemia, where Tomáš Bat'a (1876–1932) brought assembly-line technology back from the United States to his home town of Zlín in 1894 and applied it to the family firm, creating one of Europe's most successful mass-production shoemaking businesses in the process. On the northern slopes of the Carpathians, deep-drilling techniques imported by a Canadian oil company led to a vast increase in production from 2,300 tons in 1884 to more than 2 million in 1909, putting Galicia into fourth place among the world's oil-producing regions.

Patchy and regionally localized industrialization also characterized the Russian economy before 1914. Yuzovka, in the Donbass region of Ukraine, was one, still relatively small industrial area; in the 1890s the iron-ore fields of Krivoy Rog came into large-scale operation, with large metallurgical plants being founded at Ekaterinoslav, on the Dnieper, and industry clustered around the great cities of Moscow and St Petersburg. Industrial production in Russia doubled between 1860 and 1880, again to 1891, and again from 1892 to 1900. Yet this was still a slow pace of growth. Sergei Witte, Finance Minister from 1892 to 1903, previously in charge of Russia's railways, saw that state intervention was needed to speed up the process of economic growth. Witte was determined to bring Russia into the modern world. His policies ranged widely, and included for example a drive to improve literacy rates among the peasantry, in an effort to equip them for success in a market economy. Witte's policies represented perhaps the most dynamic and determined example in Europe before 1914 of state intervention as a deliberate tool of economic and industrial growth. Protective tariffs introduced in 1891 encouraged the domestic market, and in 1897 Witte introduced the gold-based rouble in order to provide a stable financial environment for foreign banks to invest in machines and factories for Russian industry. Witte was also successful in encouraging foreign banks to subscribe to government loans, so that by 1914 nearly half the state debt was held abroad. Coal output in the southern provinces of the tsarist empire more than trebled between 1890 and 1900, while pig-iron production in the area grew from 210,000 tons in 1890 to 1,483,000 a decade later. Right up to 1914, however, heavy industry still lagged behind cotton textiles, beet sugar refining and other consumer goods industries. Around 15 per cent of the empire's spindles were concentrated around Łódź, 'the Polish Manchester'.

As a latecomer, Russian industry imported advanced structural models from western and central Europe rather than building on pre-existing proto-industry. Thus firms tended to be large in scale from the outset. The average number of workers per factory in the metallurgical industries of Ukraine in 1890, for example, was 1,500, and in 1900 that number had risen to 4,600. Companies formed syndicates such as Prodameta, especially in mining and metallurgy, to control prices and divide up the market. Vertical integration proceeded apace; by 1913, twelve of the leading southern metallurgical firms owned or rented iron-ore mines, controlling 80 per cent of supplies in Ukraine, and held enough of an interest in coalmines to produce more than 2 million tons a year surplus to their own requirements. Yet the poverty of rural Russia, where the overwhelming majority of the tsar's subjects still lived on the eve of the First World War, held them back. 'To dream of consolidating our metallurgical industry on the basis of horseshoes, axles, wheels, ploughs and roofs for the peasantry,' a government spokesman observed gloomily, ' . . . is not something in which practical men can indulge.' The fact was that heavy industry was dependent on foreign and especially French investment. Ten of the fifteen companies that dug out three-quarters of Russia's coal in 1899 were foreign-owned, and almost every shipyard from Riga to Odessa was in foreign hands.

After 1905 heavy industry in Russia relied not on the wider market but overwhelmingly on government commissions, above all for armaments, but here too there was major foreign involvement. Thus the French arms firms of Schneider-Creusot and St Chamond transferred their expertise to the Putilov Armoury in St Petersburg, the largest industrial enterprise in the capital and another metallurgical plant that had grown up in the railway era of the 1890s. Similarly, the British arms firms of John Brown, Vickers and Armstrong-Whitworth together modernized the Tsaritsyn Arsenal in 1910–14 to make it 'a private factory such as no other nation possesses, excepting England . . . the most recent, the most modern, and most effective which could be provided in any country in the world'. Yet Russian exports in 1914 were still dominated by agricultural produce – half of their value was accounted for by grain – and manufactured goods made up a mere 8 per cent. In 1913, despite its huge size and massive population, the Russian Empire produced only one-tenth of the coal mined in Britain, half the British output of steel, and one-third of the oil brought to the surface in the USA. Witte's attempt to force industrialization ran into the sands of an agricultural depression at the turn of the century. In 1903, under fire variously from agrarian pressure groups, disgruntled conservatives, and intriguers who looked down on him because he was not only a commoner but also had a Jewish wife, Witte was forced to resign his position as Minister of Finance.

THE SECOND INDUSTRIAL REVOLUTION

By the time the railway boom eventually came to an end, the engineering industry on the Continent had largely taken over the production of locomotives, track and rolling stock. The rapid mechanization of the textile industry displaced British exports as British firms failed to switch from the jenny or mule to the new, faster and cheaper technique of ring-spinning. Ironically, British machinery firms such as Platts in Oldham near Manchester exported the new automatic looms to Japan and other countries but failed to find buyers in the home market. British dependence on what by the late nineteenth century had become traditional industries also inhibited the development of new ones, but also slowed modernization more generally. Continental industries had the advantage of coming late to the game and being able to adopt the latest methods, while British industries began to lag behind. Cotton mills constructed in Lancashire after 1896 to take advantage of new markets for cheap cloth in Africa were still being built on the old lines. Industrial production in Britain, which had grown at an average of 3 per cent per annum since the 1820s, slowed down to under 2 per cent after 1880. Productivity began to fall until output per head in British coalmining was only half of that found in the American coal industry by 1914. Heavy investment in the 1860s and 1870s in plant such as the Bessemer converter made manufacturers reluctant to invest again. American innovations such as the typewriter and the sewing machine invaded British markets. Danish, Dutch, French and Swedish patented dairy equipment followed. Hungarian roller mills started to supplant British ones in the milling industry.

The growing difficulty of their situation from the end of the 1870s onwards led British industrialists to control competition and fix prices through trade associations, trusts and cartels. In 1879, for example, the tea shippers agreed to limit the tonnage competing for trade with China so that their ships would all sail with full cargoes. British consumer goods production was now vulnerable to American intervention, particularly in the tobacco, salt and sewing-thread industries, which prompted British manufacturers and retailers to combine in order to fight the competition. The Imperial Tobacco Company united thirteen leading companies that together accounted for over half of all the tobacco sales in Britain at the turn of the century. In 1906, eleven regional soap businesses merged into a 'soap trust' run by Lever Brothers, reducing costs by pooling research and technical expertise and accounting for some 60 per cent of soap production and sales in Britain by 1910. It was in these decades that many famous brands in the food and drink and other light industries, such as Cadbury and Fry in chocolates, or Lever Brothers' 'Lux' and 'Vim' in washing and cleaning products, became established. At the same time, coal output increased from 110 million tons in 1870 to 290 million in 1913. Ironically, Britain became an exporter of a major raw material – coal – at the same time as its dominance of the European economy in manufactured goods began to decline.

In two industries in particular the British fell behind their competitors in the second half of the nineteenth century. Germany took the lead in the chemical industry, where German research dominated to such an extent that British chemists almost invariably went there to get their training. Soda production was revolutionized by the Solway purification process, invented in Belgium in 1861 and used as the basis for mass production by the German-born industrialist Ludwig Mond (1839–1909). The first aniline dye (christened 'mauvine' from its colour) was discovered accidentally by the British chemist William Perkin (1838–1907) while working on quinine, a treatment for malaria, with the German chemist August Hofmann (1818–92). Perkin patented the substance, but aniline dyes only became suitable for mass production when the French chemist Antoine Béchamp (1816–1908) developed a way of reducing them and manufacturing them in quantities suitable for commercial use. The Baden Anilin and Soda Factory (BASF), founded in 1865, developed a similar process, using coal tar, ironically mostly imported from Britain, where industrialists did not know what to do with it. BASF developed further dyes, notably indigo, produced from 1897 onwards. Business boomed, and by 1900 the BASF factory, in the company town of Ludwigshafen, across the Rhine from Mannheim, was devoting 80 per cent of its production to dyestuffs.

The pharmaceutical company Bayer, in Wuppertal, founded in 1863 by two men involved in the dyestuffs business, built on the discoveries of the French chemist Charles Gerhardt (1816–56), becoming a joint-stock company in 1881. He was a student of the great German chemist Justus von Liebig, whose discovery of the value of nitrogen as a plant nutrient effectively founded the chemical fertilizer industry. Liebig had studied and worked in Paris, and in 1865 founded a company to produce and market meat extract according to a process he had discovered with a Belgian colleague: in 1899 the product was labelled 'Oxo'. Liebig also developed a technique for producing concentrated extracts of yeast, marketed in England as Marmite or, in Australia, where it became a national icon, Vegemite. Non-German chemical companies were mostly multinational, such as Nobel Explosives, founded in Ayrshire in 1870 by the Swedish inventor of dynamite Alfred Nobel (1833–96), Brunner Mond, founded in 1873, and United Alkali, formed in 1890 from the merger of forty-eight small firms.

Like the chemical industry, the electrical industry, the other field in which Germany took the lead in the late nineteenth century, also developed through international collaboration. Here too the British failed to innovate. It was the British scientist Michael Faraday (1791–1867) who first built a machine to produce a direct current from rotary motion, but it was the American inventor Thomas Edison (1847–1931) who adapted it for commercial use on a large scale. In 1882, Edison opened the world's first steam-powered electricity generating station, on Holborn Viaduct in London. (The previous year a water-powered generator had provided the world's first public electricity supply, in Godalming, Surrey.) Soon electricity was being used to power trams and underground railways in Europe's great cities, and domestic appliances such as hotplates and blankets, already exhibited at the Vienna World Exhibition in 1883. The German engineer Werner von Siemens (1816–92), who made his fortune with telegraph systems based on needles pointing to letters rather than on Morse Code, operated on an international basis, with his brother Sir William Siemens (1823–83) in Britain and another brother Carl von Siemens (1829–1906) in St Petersburg. Other companies too established subsidiaries in Britain: the electrification of the pioneering District and Metropolitan lines on the London Underground, for example, was undertaken at the turn of the century by the American financier Charles Yerkes (1837–1905), and the trains worked on an alternating current system provided by the Ganz Works in Budapest. It was a sign of the British electrical industry's failure to exploit inventiveness that Sir Joseph Swan's incandescent light bulb was outclassed and outsold by the products of his rival Thomas Edison, forcing a merger of the two companies in Britain in 1883 under the trade name Ediswan.

By this time the German chemical and electrical industries had grown to become European and indeed world leaders, leaving their British counterparts far behind. Part of the reason was their employment of trained scientists – 230 in BASF, for example, or 165 in Hoechst, another major chemical firm – reflecting the greater concentration of state-funded German universities on the sciences. In 1913, German chemical companies were producing 28 per cent of the world's exports in the field, with Britain producing only 16 per cent. In synthetic dyestuffs the British only managed 2 per cent of the world's exports, with Germany making up a massive 90 per cent. Similarly, Siemens, and its great rival, AEG (*Allgemeine Elektrizitäts-Gesellschaft*, or General Electricity Company, which applied Edison's patents to the European market), accounted for 75 per cent of

German electro-technical production. The scale of these organizations by this time was gargantuan: Siemens, for example, employed 75,000 workers in Germany in 1913, and 24,000 outside the country. The ambition of their leading figures was boundless. As the writer, politician and business-man Walther Rathenau (1867–1922) noted at the funeral of his father Emil Rathenau (1838–1915), founder of AEG, when he 'saw this little light bulb alight for the first time, he had a vision of the whole world covered with a network of copper wire. He saw electric current flowing from one country to another, distributing not only light but also power.' Backing up these developments was a steady growth in trusts and cartels, in which bank representatives joined the boards of industrial companies and acted as intermediaries in mergers and acquisitions. In Germany they brokered the union of the Phönix Ironworks with the Westende coalmining concern in the 1890s, an example of 'vertical integration', while after the turn of the century the Darmstädter Bank was instrumental in the creation of the Luxemburg-Lorraine Pig Iron Syndicate. So closely were German banking and industrial enterprises interwoven by this time that some historians have even spoken of 'organized capitalism' in which open-market competition became increasingly controlled by large conglomerates, often with close links to the government. Certainly, by 1907 cartelization covered 90 per cent of the German market in paper, 74 per cent in mining, and 50 per cent in crude steel. By 1900 there were 275 cartels in operation in Germany, in all branches of industry, some 200 of them created between the years 1879 and 1890.

It was not only the German economy that was outpacing the British in the 'second industrial revolution', or at least in parts of it. In Italy the development of an advanced electrical industry in the 1890s delivered a sharp stimulus to modern areas of production, notably motor manufacture. Industrial take-off in the Italian north-west, around Genoa, Milan and Turin, already economically relatively prosperous, had to wait for railways – built with imported materials and equipped at first with foreign machinery – to facilitate the bulk import of coal, still however costing up to eight times what it cost in England at the factory gate. It was not until the 1860s that Italy witnessed a real railway boom, with the new national government seeing the railways as a means of unifying the country; three-quarters of all expenditure on public works between 1861 and 1913 went on the construction of railway lines. The length of railway line in Italy grew from just short of 1,120 miles in 1859 to 11,800 miles by 1913, mostly concentrated in the north. The real breakthrough, however, lay in the technological innovation that enabled the vast potential sources of hydroelectrical power in the Alps to be exploited. The development of electric generators from the 1880s onwards soon led to the creation of large-scale hydroelectrical power plants, pioneered by the Schoelkopf Power Station at Niagara Falls in the USA in 1881. From the mid-1890s onwards there was a massive construction boom in Italy, with hydroelectricity replacing 20 per cent of imported fuels by 1911 and operating at a much lower cost. In 1914 the hydroelectrical capacity of Italy reached a million kilowatts, and though some of this was used for purposes such as providing electric lighting for Milan (one of the first cities in the world to be fully lit by this method), 90 per cent of it was employed in industry, which expanded at dizzying speed in the decade and a half before the outbreak of the First World War.

Following a banking crash in 1893–4, new Italian banks emerged, often funded with foreign capital, and they invested heavily in hydroelectric schemes, especially after the nationalization of the railways in 1905. They extended credit to the most modern industries. Other advanced industrial enterprises were emerging in Italy by this time, such as the Olivetti typewriter company, founded in 1908, but technological innovation also produced rapid growth in more traditional sectors, such as food production, where the Buitoni factory employed thermo-mechanical drying for pasta products. Cotton spinning machines and power looms, combined with high import tariffs introduced in 1887, turned Italy into a major exporter of cotton goods, especially to Turkey and the Balkans. Mechanization stimulated the iron and steel industry – steel production grew from 200,000 tons in 1895 to 933,000 tons in 1913. Altogether the industrial growth rate in Italy has been estimated at around 5 per cent per annum between 1897 and 1913, but electricity was growing by 15 per cent a year, chemicals by 13 per cent, and iron and steel by 11 per cent.

Italy was not the only European country to experience rapid industrial growth based on hydroelectric power. By 1915, Sweden was producing 550,000 kilowatts of energy a year, modernizing its iron and steel production, and building a new industrial economy centred on high-precision engineering products. Capital accumulated through the export of timber to Britain for railway sleepers was invested in the new power source and the new industries, which included technologically advanced sawmills and paper mills. Norway depended more on foreign capital, though it had a very large whaling and fishing fleet, but hydroelectric power resources grew here almost exponentially, doubling from 200,000 kilowatts in 1908 to 400,000 in 1912. In this way Italy, Sweden and Norway all leapfrogged the coal-based stages of industrialization and entered the industrial age on the basis of the most modern power technology. Other countries, such as Austria, despite its Alpine potential, found it difficult to follow suit, not least because of the inhibiting effect of the German economy: thus, for example, while German chemical companies could obtain sulphuric acid as a cheap by-product of the metallurgical industries, Austria, lacking modern industries of this kind, had to import it in the old-fashioned form of Spanish pyrites, at a much higher cost. The predominance of highly specialized artisanal production such as watchmaking made the adoption of hydroelectric power schemes in Switzerland and the French Alps seem unnecessary. German demand for untreated wood for use in its technologically advanced and large-scale paper industry meant that Austria-Hungary remained a source of raw material in this area rather than developing a pulping industry of its own, so that exports of wood from the empire between 1904 and 1914 were eleven times greater than exports of wood pulp and cellulose. Similarly, the headlong industrialization of Germany led to rapid urbanization that created rising demand in areas such as electricity supply, tramways, street lighting, chemically dyed clothing, canned or processed food and the like, which was absent from areas such as Spain, southern Italy, Hungary or the Balkans, where industrialization and urbanization were slower and towns few and far between, and even from France, where economic growth and entrepreneurship were too sluggish to take advantage of the potential of hydroelectric power in the French Alps.

The outbreak of war in 1914 interrupted these developments, but already it was clear that Britain was being overtaken by other European countries, especially in the 'second industrial revolution'. Even in heavy industry, Germany, with its newer and more rational organizational structures and improved plant, was outpacing Britain, producing for example 77 tons of steel per man-year in 1913 as against 48 tons. In this later stage of industrialization, too, the state began to play a greater role, not only with orders for armaments but also with infrastructural measures including improved education and legal reform and in some places direct investment in major railway-building and similar projects. A fierce debate broke out among economists in Britain about the reasons for this. One major reason, it was agreed, lay in the primacy of advanced scientific research in countries like Germany. While the technological innovations that brought about the first industrial revolution had been achieved largely by the ingenuity of mechanics, the second clearly required the knowledge of scientists. British universities began to adopt the focus on centrally directed research that characterized German higher education, with Cambridge creating strong faculties separate from the colleges, whereas Oxford refused to take this step, preferring instead to continue focusing on the education of young men for public service. Others considered dedicated research institutions the answer, and Imperial College London was founded in 1907 on the lines of the Charlottenburg Institute, incorporating the Royal School of Mines and the Royal College of Science. But British industrialists seemed to many to be too keen on ploughing their fortunes into becoming country landowners, rather than reinvesting them in productive technical innovation. The widespread belief in Britain that Germany was forging ahead economically before 1914 fuelled anxieties about the rise of an economic rival that translated all too easily into political and military terms.

The scale of social and economic change that swept across Europe from the middle of the nineteenth century to the outbreak of the First World War was staggering. Statistics tell a dramatic story. In 1850 some 52 per cent of the economically active population of France was employed in agriculture; by 1900 this figure had fallen to 42 per cent. In Italy the fall was from 75 per cent (in 1862) to 60 per cent in 1900. In Germany rapid industrialization pushed down the figure more dramatically, from around 60 per cent to 35 per cent. The head start enjoyed by the British in the process of industrialization and urbanization was demonstrated by the fact that already in 1850 only 22 per cent of the economically active population were engaged in agriculture, and by 1900 this had sunk to a mere 9 per cent. A new social world was emerging, one in which society was dominated by people who no longer inhabited the countryside but lived in the cities and towns of the industrial age.

BUILDING THE NEW JERUSALEM

The nineteenth century was the age of Europe's urbanization. Most obvious were the entirely new settlements that mushroomed where industry took root. In the Ruhr, the population of the new industrial town of Duisburg doubled from around 7,000 in 1831 to over 13,000 in 1850, then shot up to 93,000 by 1900. Living conditions were poor. In late-industrializing Russia, workers in the new industrial and mining settlements were housed in barracks, as in the Bryansk metallurgical factory 235 miles south-west of Moscow, where conditions were 'compared without any exaggeration with the quarters of domestic animals' by an inspector in 1892; they were filthy, poorly ventilated and unhygienic. Staying in Salford, a new industrial suburb of Manchester, in the mid-1840s while working in the management of a sewing-thread mill owned by his father's textile company, the twenty-two-year-old Friedrich Engels found 'dirt and filth' everywhere, especially around the river Irk, where 'several tanneries are situated on the bank of the river and they fill the neighbour-hood with the stench of animal putrefaction'. The houses abutting onto the river were 'blackened by soot, all of them are crumbling with age and all have broken window-panes and window-frames'. There was no pumped or piped water, and 'so few privies that they are either filled up every day or are too far away for those who need to use them'. The middle classes insulated themselves from the spectacle of poverty and exploitation behind their shopfronts and villa walls. After speaking on the street to a middle-class businessman about the 'frightful condition of the working people's quarters', Engels reported: 'The man listened quietly to the end, and said at the corner where we parted: "And yet there is a great deal of money made here; good morning, sir." ' It was not only the new industrial settlements that experienced rapid growth. The population of Glasgow, estimated in 1800 at 77,000, nearly doubled in twenty years to 142,000 and increased almost tenfold by the end of the century, to 762,000. Berlin's population grew from 172,000 in 1800 to 419,000 at mid-century, 1,122,000 by 1880, and more than two million thirty years later, on the eve of the First World War. The population of Copenhagen increased from just over 100,000 in 1800 to more than half a million in 1910. After Buda and Pest, facing each other across the Danube, were formally united in 1873, the population of the Hungarian capital grew from 270,000 to 880,000 by the First World War. Lisbon's population, more or less static for most of the nineteenth century, suddenly shot up from 242,000 in 1880 to 435,000 thirty years later.

The effects of such rapid growth were soon apparent as the social geography of such cities began to change. Like many other European capitals, London swallowed up surrounding villages and turned them into suburban settlements for the better-off portion of the population who wanted to escape the dirt and noise of the city centre, seeking out higher ground in areas such as Hampstead. As working-class housing was cleared to make way for railway termini and commercial buildings, the poor were forced to migrate to newly built terraced houses in the East End. The process of social-geographical differentiation can be observed with par-ticular clarity in the case of Hamburg, whose population, under 200,000 in 1820, rocketed to 623,000 by 1890 and over a million by the eve of the First World War. In the eighteenth century and before, merchants and manufacturers had lived in Hamburg's old city, near the harbour, often above their offices and next door to their warehouses. But as the city grew, they moved out of the city centre to plush and spacious villas dotted around the Alster Lake inland of the old town, or downstream on the banks of the river Elbe, leaving the half-timbered buildings on the waterfront to be divided into tenements as the working classes moved in. Soon these became known as the 'Alley Quarters', insanitary and overcrowded, dilapidated and unhygienic. Similar processes took place in many European cities in the nineteenth century. Deteriorating conditions in the older inner-city areas provided the backdrop to the writings of socially concerned novelists. In his novel *Oliver Twist*, Charles Dickens described the 'rookeries' as they were known, of one particular slum district in London, Jacob's Island, in dramatic terms, with its 'dirt-besmeared walls and decaying foundations, every repulsive lineament of poverty, every loathsome indication of filth, rot, and garbage'. Newly built working-class housing was often almost as bad. In *Colonel Chabert*, an 1832 novella by Honoré de Balzac, the eponymous hero, an impoverished Napoleonic veteran, forced to live in a hastily built speculative development every bit as squalid as a medieval slum. 'Though recently built,' Balzac commented, 'this house seemed ready to fall into ruins.'

Most notorious of all were the slums of Naples, a city of half a million people in the 1880s, where the poorest section had to suffer a density of 208,000 inhabitants per square mile, ten times that of London. Housing blocks were so tall that the American writer Mark Twain, on visiting the city, described it as 'a hundred feet high, like three normal American cities piled on top of one another, blocking out the sunlight from the streets'. With an average of only 86 square feet per person in the lower city (compared to 344 in London), these tenements were regularly compared to anthills or rabbit warrens, blackened with smoke and dirt, plagued by swarms of flies that fed on the rotting organic waste thrown into the streets, 'the most ghastly human habitations on the face of the earth', as the Swedish-born doctor Axel Munthe (1857–1949) described them during a visit in 1884. Not only Naples, but most other European cities lacked fresh water supplies well into the second half of the century and in many cases beyond. Hamburg drew its supplies from the river Elbe upstream; so impure was the unfiltrated water in the pipes that carried it into people's houses that small fish could sometimes be found coming out of the taps; indeed, in 1885 a zoologist published a scientific study entitled *The Fauna of the Hamburg Water-Supply*, identifying several dozen types of small worms, molluscs and other creatures in a cross section taken from a water-supply pipe. In 1863 a survey of 8,242 buildings in St Petersburg, housing 90 per cent of the population, revealed that only 1,795 had running water, and its quality was only marginally better than that of the Neva river from which it was taken (visitors were advised not to drink it, since, as a travel guide noted bluntly, 'with most travellers it produces diarrhoea'). In 1911 the biologist August Thienemann (1882–1960) described the Ruhr river as a 'brown black brew, reeking of prussic acid, containing no trace of oxygen, and absolutely dead'. Only 50 per cent of the river's total volume was from natural sources; the rest was provided by millions of litres of sewage from the 1,500,000 people who lived in its catchment area, along with the human and industrial effluent from 150 mines and 100 factories.

Cleaning the streets of Europe's growing towns and cities posed problems every bit as severe as providing pure water to drink. Horses were present in every European city right up to 1914, pulling carts and wagons, buses and trams. Some 12,000 horses were stabled in the inner city and suburbs of Hamburg as late as 1892. It was estimated that 20,000 tons of horse droppings had to be cleared away from London's streets every year in the 1850s; thirty years later, 100,000 tons of dung were being removed from the streets of Berlin each year. In the 1840s pigs were roaming freely around the streets of Gateshead in north-east England. Smaller towns retained the sounds and smells of the farmyard for much longer. Major cities solved the problem of supplying fresh meat to their inhabitants before the age of refrigeration by driving live animals into the centre to be slaughtered. By the middle of the nineteenth century, it was reported, in the course of a single year 220,000 head of cattle and 1,500,000 sheep would pass through the streets to Smithfield, the meat market located in the centre of London. 'Of all the horrid abominations with which London has been cursed,' wrote one observer, 'there is not one that can come up to that disgusting place, West Smithfield Market, for cruelty, filth, effluvia, pestilence, impiety, horrid language, danger, disgusting and shuddering sights, and every obnoxious item that can be imagined.' Dead animals and the like were simply dumped. In Paris complaints multiplied in the 1830s about the vast waste disposal site on the edge of the city, at Montfaucon, a cesspool to which, it was reported, 'some 230 to 244 square metres of human excreta are carted . . . daily and most of the corpses of 12,000 horses and 25,000 to 30,000 smaller animals are left to rot on the ground'.

But civic pride and bourgeois squeamishness gradually combined to overcome these problems. The middle classes may have moved out of city centres but they still travelled there to work, and increasingly they demanded a healthy and salubrious environment. In 1842 a much-publicized report on the sanitary condition of the working classes in English towns by Edwin Chadwick (1800–90) led to the creation of a Public Health Association and a General Board of Health six years later. Chadwick believed strongly in the Victorian maxim 'cleanliness is next to Godliness'.

'How much of rebellion,' he remarked, 'of moral depravity, and of crime, has its roots in physical disorder and depravity.' In 1868 a magnificent new livestock market was opened in Smithfield, with the animals transported to it through a specially constructed underground railway line. By the 1870s there was general acceptance in Britain that local authorities had to provide pure water and dispose effectively of liquid and other wastes, clean the streets and provide a healthy environment, following a Royal Commission on the Prevention of the Pollution of Rivers, which led to the Rivers Pollution Prevention Act of 1876. A crucial aid in achieving the situation was the flush toilet, first mass-produced by the plumber George Jennings (1810–82), whose curiously named 'Monkey Closets', the first public conveniences, were visited by 827,280 people at the Great Exhibition of 1851. Each of them spent a penny on the visit, for services including shoe-shining and the use of a towel and comb – the origin of a much-used euphemism common up to the late twentieth century. Another plumber, Thomas Crapper (1836–1910), often credited with the invention of the flush toilet, was in fact responsible only for the development of the ballcock. Water closets became standard in Britain by the late nineteenth century, required by law in all new dwellings in Manchester from 1881 onwards, and in many other towns and cities as well.

'A good sewer,' declared the art critic John Ruskin (1819–1900), was a 'far nobler and a far holier thing . . . than the most admired Madonna ever painted.' London's new system of sewers, constructed by the civil engineer Joseph Bazalgette (1819–91) between 1858 (immediately after the 'Great Stink', caused by noxious effluvia from the Thames, had closed down Parliament for several days) and 1865, was a great source of civic pride: the opening of the southern outfall down the Thames was attended by 500 guests, who dined on salmon as the effluvia of the great city rushed through the tunnel beneath them and fell into the river below. 'Sewage farms', introduced in Berlin from 1885 onwards by the city planner James Hobrecht (1825–1902), now purified the noxious liquids before they reached the rivers and oceans of Europe. Pure water supplies became available to an increasing proportion of the population of Europe's great cities in the late nineteenth century: within just over a decade after the last outbreak of typhoid in Budapest in 1888, all of the city's dwellings were connected to the municipal water supply. By 1893, Budapest could also boast some thirty-two public conveniences, mostly concealed artfully between the trees of public squares. Chadwick's vision was realized in almost all of Britain's towns and cities from the late 1850s onwards. In other parts of Europe the process took much longer; as late as 1885, for example, only a third of Italian municipalities possessed underground water mains and just half of them had sewage systems.

Among Chadwick's disciples was a young engineer, William Lindley (1808–1900), who as an adolescent had spent time in the 1820s learning German in Hamburg. Because of his linguistic competence, Lindley was sent by Isambard Kingdom Brunel to survey and construct the first railway lines in northern Germany during the 1830s. After a large part of the city of Hamburg was destroyed by fire in 1842, Lindley was commissioned to help plan its reconstruction. An essential part of the scheme consisted in creating a new sewage and water-supply system. He persuaded Hamburg's ruling Senate to build a new set of reservoirs that would draw water from the Elbe above the city, together with steam-powered pumps to push the water through a network of pipes into people's houses and flats; by 1890 there were over 250 miles of pipes, and nearly every house in the city had at least one tap either inside or in the courtyard. The scheme was linked to the creation of a centralized sewage disposal system, built in the 1840s and opened in 1853; in 1875 a Sewage Law required all the city's inhabitants to have their dwellings connected to it. The introduction of a central water supply also enabled Lindley to persuade the Hamburg Senate to build public bathhouses at key locations across the city. As he remarked in 1851, 'a dirty population degenerates and so commits all the more offences against the laws of the state' – an almost exact reproduction of the political principle of urban improvement he had learned from his teacher Edwin Chadwick.

Lindley's reputation spread to other European cities, which soon began to clamour for his services. In 1863 he began work on a new water-supply system for Frankfurt am Main, and then moved on to Düsseldorf, St Petersburg, Budapest and Moscow. Together with his son William Heerlein Lindley (1853–1917) he designed and built a new water-supply system for Warsaw in the 1870s and 1880s. This last-named project, with its huge water tower, reservoirs, filter beds, pumping stations, many miles of pipes, and numerous earthworks and tunnels, was built with the assistance of another of William Lindley's sons, the young Robert Searles Lindley (1854–1925). William Lindley junior went on to construct water-supply and sewage-disposal systems in Prague, where a museum was subsequently devoted to his projects, and Baku in Azerbaijan, while his plans for Łódź, initially shelved because of their expense, were eventually realized in the 1920s. Everywhere, the Lindleys' schemes resulted in a dramatic decline in death rates from waterborne diseases. Between 1868 and 1883 the death rate from typhoid in Frankfurt am Main fell from 80 to

10 per 100,000 inhabitants, while a local historian of Warsaw calculated just before the outbreak of the First World War that the new water-supply system in the city had saved on average 10,000 lives a year since its construction. Only in Hamburg, where the penny-pinching Hanseatic merchants and house-owners had refused, despite Lindley's advice, to spend money on ensuring that the water supply was passed through sand filtration to kill off harmful bacteria, did these death rates remain undiminished (as we have seen, the pipes were full of all kinds of living creatures). Dam construction to create reservoirs of drinking water for the great cities of Europe began towards the end of the century. Invariably dams were built of stone: the age of concrete came later. In the Elan valley, in north Wales, identified as a suitable site with impenetrable rock below, high average annual rainfall, and an elevation above that of the city – Birmingham – that it was chosen to supply, land was compulsorily purchased, three manor houses, eighteen farms, a school and a church were demolished, and one hundred people were displaced (only landowners received any compensation). Workers moved in to begin construction of the dam in 1893, and the project was completed nine years later. A similar dam was built at Lake Vyrnwy in the 1870s to provide water for Liverpool. All over Europe, schemes such as these were in progress, with the first in Germany being completed near Remscheid in 1891.

More than the provision of hygienic water supplies was needed to bring about urban improvement. The most famous of all nineteenth-century projects of urban renewal was begun by the Prefect of Paris under Napoleon III, Baron Georges-Eugène Haussmann (1809–91), soon after his appointment in 1853. His aim was to rid the city of what one critic called 'the tiny, narrow, putrid and tangled streets' that never let in the sun. As he cleared away the narrow alleys and replaced them with broad boulevards, Haussmann the 'demolition artist' (as he called himself) was also removing the ideal sites for the construction of barricades by revolutionary crowds and opening up the city to the forces of order. His grand schemes reduced the Île de la Cité's population from 15,000 to 5,000, destroying almost all the private dwellings there at one stroke. 'It was the gutting of old Paris,' Haussmann wrote with satisfaction in his *Mémoires* (1890), 'of the neighbourhood of riots, and of barricades, from one end to the other.' With a large part of the working class forced to seek accommodation further out, the way was open for the construction of grand public buildings such as the Opéra (1875), the creation of the major railway termini, the homogenization of the central boulevards by lining them with neo-Classical buildings of the same height and the same façade design, and the provision of new squares and public gardens. Haussmann completely transformed France's capital city during the seventeen years of his Prefecture, wielding dictatorial powers unavailable to any of his predecessors. The work of transformation was crowned by an iconic structure he had not envisaged, the Eiffel Tower, built by Gustave Eiffel (1832–1923) for the Paris Exposition of 1889, and improvement continued, albeit at a slower pace, after Haussmann's death

The rebuilding of Paris turned the waste-disposal facility of Montfaucon into a public park complete with trees and grassy knolls. Remodelling the streetscape of the French capital offered an opportunity to create a new underground system of water supply and waste disposal. 'The underground galleries,' wrote Haussmann, 'organs of the large city, would function like those of the human body, without revealing themselves to the light of day.' So capacious was the main sewer constructed underneath the city that journeys along it in what was described as 'a veritable gondola with carpeted floor and cushioned seats, lit up by large lamps' were offered to adventurous tourists. 'No foreigner of distinction', noted the *Larousse* dictionary proudly in 1870, 'wants to leave the city without making this singular trip', and female tourists were as welcome as male: 'The presence of lovely women,' commented an American tourist, 'can add a charm to the sewer.' The Paris sewers even appealed to the literary-minded, who could thrill to the thought that they were reliving the experiences of the hero of Victor Hugo's *Les Misérables*, Jean Valjean.

Parallel to these developments, increasing efforts were made to improve housing conditions in Europe's towns and cities. In 1862 the London-based American banker George Peabody (1795–1869) launched the Peabody Trust, which opened its first housing block for the poor, in Spitalfields, two years later, containing twenty-two flats, nine shops, water closets on each landing, baths and laundry facilities on the top floor. By 1882 the Trust had constructed 3,500 dwellings in London, housing 14,600 people. Social housing in Copenhagen also evolved from private initiative, in this case physicians alarmed at the slum conditions they considered responsible for a major cholera epidemic in 1853. Some 250 houses were built initially, and let at low rents. Yet in many cities housing construction could not keep pace with population growth. In St Petersburg the number of apartments rose from 88,000 in 1869 to 155,000 in 1900, but the average number of people per apartment also rose over this period, from 7.0 to 7.4, and a third of the city's inhabitants at the turn of the century still lived in apartments that were not equipped with basic services such as running water. In the new industrial town of Duisburg, in the Ruhr, the average number of persons per room rose from 1.3 in 1875 to 1.5 ten years later. In the northern French textile town of Lille one building inspected in 1863 was inhabited by 271 people, with an average of 18.3 square feet of living space each.

While housing often proved resistant to reform, however fast speculative builders might throw up tenement blocks for incoming migrants, municipal services did improve dramatically in a number of respects in the second half of the century. City governments cleared the way in many towns for urban expansion by knocking down medieval city walls, as in Hamburg in 1837, where they were replaced by green parkland, or Vienna in 1857, where the famous *Ringstrasse* with its grandiloquent public buildings took their place. Urban roads were renovated and supplied with new surfaces. Up to mid-century, London's streets were paved not with the legendary gold, but in many cases with wood, which was only replaced by granite along Cheapside in 1846 and Fleet Street in 1851. Pavements took a long time to arrive, and in most towns pedestrians took their lives in their hands if they dared to walk in heavy traffic. In larger cities the streets were increasingly clogged with a chaotic jam of horse-drawn carriages, wagons, handcarts, and hansom cabs and their equivalent on the Continent, the *fiacre* or the *Droschke*. There was little attempt at traffic regulation: an effort to introduce a manually controlled gas-powered traffic light outside the British Houses of Parliament in 1868 was abandoned soon afterwards when it exploded, killing the policeman who operated it. After that, no more traffic lights were erected anywhere in Europe until the 1920s. There was no legal requirement to drive on one side of the road or the other in England until 1835, and in Belgium as late as 1899. Different parts of Italy drove on the left or right according to custom, nor was there a uniform rule in Spain. Traffic in the Austro-Hungarian Empire drove on the left, as also in Portugal and Sweden, whereas those parts of Europe affected by Napoleon I's mania for standardization, including Denmark, the Netherlands, and western Germany, drove on the right, along with Russia, where the rule had been imposed by Catherine the Great. Photographs of busy European cities taken in the early twentieth century suggest that in many cases these rules were in any event simply ignored.

But at least, gradually, the streets began to be lit properly at night. Gas lights were already in use in the late eighteenth century, and they illuminated Westminster Bridge and Pall Mall as early as 1815; after the end of the Napoleonic Wars they became more common, spreading quickly to British provincial towns and cities. It was not until the 1840s that gas lighting became generally accepted in Paris, and even in 1860 London alone consumed twice as much gas as the whole of Germany. The first public gas lamp was lit in St Petersburg in 1819, and by mid-century there were 800 of them lighting up the streets and squares of the Russian capital. It was a Russian military engineer, Pavel Nikolayevich Yablochkov (1847–94), who in 1875 first developed an arc light powered by electricity, the 'Yablochkov candle'. The first town on the Continent of Europe to have public electric lighting was Temesvár, in Hungary, where 731 street lights were installed in 1884. By this time Swan or Edison incandescent bulbs had replaced arc lights, and cities, beginning with London, had started to build central electricity-generating stations. Electricity also increasingly powered municipal tram systems, which were built in many European cities in the second half of the century, following the invention of the grooved and sunken rail by the French engineer Alphonse Loubet (1799–1866). Tramcars were initially pulled by horses everywhere, from St Petersburg, where a network of 71 miles was carrying 85 million passengers a year by the end of the century, to Sarajevo, where the first horse-tram ran in 1883, to be replaced by electric trams twelve years later. The cost of keeping, feeding and grooming horses, and the fact that they could only work for relatively short periods each day, thereby requiring frequent replacements, made electrification attractive – once Werner von Siemens had developed a means of transmitting power to the trams, at first through an electrified rail, which he invented in 1879. Within two years the first electric trams were running in Berlin, and after the American invention of the trolley pole in 1885 was adopted in Europe, pedestrians no longer ran the risk of receiving electric shocks by treading on the rails when they crossed the street.

By this time major cities were attempting to solve the problem of street congestion by building underground railways on the model of the first to be opened, the Metropolitan Railway in London, on which ordinary steam trains ran just below the road surface from 1863 onwards. Electric tram technology enabled these railways to be converted to cleaner power, and the three new lines opened in the 1890s used it from the start. The discovery that it was possible to bore through the soft London clay allowed for much deeper and narrower tunnels – 'the tube' in local parlance. The first carriages were not provided with windows because it was not considered that passengers would need to know where they were when they travelled underground: they were popularly known as 'padded cells'. The world's second-oldest underground railway was a funicular system built in Istanbul by a British company and opened in 1875, and the third, in Glasgow, a cable railway inaugurated in 1896. The Budapest Underground, using overhead wires, also opened in 1896. Paris followed suit with the Métro, whose first line began operating in 1900. In many European cities overground and elevated suburban railways complemented the underground system. In Berlin the *S-Bahn* (*Stadtbahn*, or city railway) brought together some existing and some specially constructed lines to carry people to and from work on steam-hauled trains from 1882 onwards.

Urban improvements such as these were attempts to solve the basic problem of moving thousands or even millions of people around efficiently and cheaply as Europe's cities expanded. But there were less tangible reasons for urban improvement as well. As monarchs and rulers attempted to bolster their legitimacy in the decades after 1815, they launched ambitious building programmes. They included the grand neo-Classical edifices and spaces designed for Munich by Leo von Klenze (1784–1864) on the orders of King Ludwig I of Bavaria; and the constructions of Karl Friedrich Schinkel (1781–1841) in Berlin, such as the *Neue Wache* (1816), the Prussian National Monument for the Liberation Wars (1826) and the *Altes Museum* (1830), which transformed the city from a sleepy provincial town into a grand state capital. The Saxon capital of Dresden received similar treatment from Gottfried Semper (1803–79), as did Karlsruhe, the capital of the Grand Duchy of Baden, from Friedrich Weinbrenner (1766–1826) and his pupils. Broad avenues flanked by grand public buildings projected princely majesty onto the public stage in a way designed to cement loyalty by evoking awe. In London these decades saw the laying down on the orders of the Prince Regent, subsequently King George IV, of Regent Street and Regent's Park, under the guidance of the most celebrated of Georgian architects, John Nash (1752–1835). The 'Haussmannization' of Paris under Napoleon III belonged in the same context.

In the 1870s and 1880s it was the turn of Budapest. A long boulevard, Andrássy Avenue, was constructed between 1872 and 1876, lined with large and imposing new buildings: the Academy of Fine Arts (1871), the Academy of Music (1875) and the Opera House (1884). The new boulevard ended at Heroes' Square, designed by the Galician-born German architect Albert Schickedanz (1846–1915), who placed a new Museum of Fine Arts and Palace of Art on opposite sides of the square. In 1906 a Millennium Memorial Monument, celebrating the conquest of the Carpathian Basin by the Magyars, was placed in the middle. A public park along one side of the boulevard completed the grandiose representation of national culture. Where a new state was created, the erection of public buildings and the establishment of the standard accoutrements of a capital city became matters of urgency. Following the foundation of the autonomous Principality, later (1908) the independent Kingdom, of Bulgaria in 1878, the insignificant town of Sofia, with fewer than 12,000 inhabitants, was chosen as the capital. The new monarch imposed by the Concert of Europe, Alexander von Battenberg (1857–93), nephew of the Russian Tsar, appointed two Viennese architects, Friedrich Grünanger (1856–1929) and Viktor Rumpelmayer (1830–85), to design and oversee the construction of two royal palaces (one in Sofia, the other on the Black Sea coast). Foreign-trained Bulgarian architects put up a building to house the National Assembly, the main railway station (opened in 1888), and a range of government Ministry headquarters. Vitosha Boulevard, later to become the capital's main shopping street, was opened in 1883. Gradually Sofia lost its sleepy provincial character and began to take on the mantle of a national capital city.

By contrast, many small towns across Europe survived virtually unchanged through most of the century, often isolated from new industrial developments by poor communications and a primary orientation towards the markets provided by their rural hinterland. Baedeker's 1883 guidebook for tourists in south-eastern Europe warned that the town of Debrecen presented 'the usual Hungarian characteristics. Pavements are unknown, and in rainy weather the mud in the narrower streets is atrocious.' In 1858 *Murray's Handbook for Travellers in Scandinavia* warned adventurous travellers who made it to the Icelandic capital of Reykjavík that they would find only 'a collection of wooden sheds' there. There were no inns anywhere, no roads, and no creature comforts. Would-be tourists were advised to take a tent with them. The poverty of Iceland was extreme, but where there was little or no economic development, urbanization and urban improvement were slow to take root. On entering the Bulgarian town of Plovdiv in 1868, the Bulgarian patriot Lyuben Stoychev Karavelov (1834–79) saw in it only oriental squalor, the product of continuing Ottoman rule: 'Our horses plunged into the mud up to their knees and lurched from side to side together with us; we held our noses to keep from suffocating from the extraordinary stench. In the streets: dead dogs, chickens, even horses swam in the muddy morasses.' Only after the creation of an autonomous Bulgaria in 1885 did urban improvement begin. And even in Europe's grandest metropolises, there were still areas of urban deprivation at and after the turn of the century. In Birmingham there were more than 40,000 houses without any running water in 1900, and nearly 60,000 without a separate sanitary facility. Even as late as 1895 only 42 per cent of Prussian urban communities with over 2,000 inhabitants were serviced by mains water; the other 58 per cent were dependent on wells, springs, river water or rainwater. By the time the century came to an end, urban improvement had come far, but it also still had a long way to go.

THE TRIUMPH OF THE BOURGEOISIE

The headlong growth of industry brought with it a rapid transformation of urban society, creating what was in many ways essentially a new social class: the bourgeoisie. The name itself – *bourgeois, Bürger, borghese* – meant city-dweller. In the pre-industrial urban social order, the dominant elite of guildsmen would include a handful of educated, literate doctors, lawyers, notaries, apothecaries, clerks and scribes. Many long-established towns were dominated by an hereditary patrician elite that increasingly had to make room for bankers, industrialists and professionals without necessarily being displaced by them. In the Swiss city of Basel the patrician elite, which had formed a closed corporation earlier in the century, still provided more than half the members of the ruling institutions in the 1890s even after a reform carried out in 1875 had introduced a democratic element into the city's political system. Nevertheless, the old patrician elite was in effect merging into a new urban middle class as its legal privileges were gradually eroded. In the Adriatic seaport of Trieste, whose population grew from 45,000 in 1815 to 230,000 a century later, the self-co-opting patriciate lost power as a new constitution was passed in 1838 that made provision for the election of 'people . . . on the basis of intelligence, knowledge, personal services and gifts' as well as for those passing the minimum qualifications of wealth and property. In 1850 a further municipal reform defined citizenship (as distinct from mere domicile) in even broader terms of educational and propertied factors, including possession of a degree, exercise of a profession such as architect, surgeon, apothecary and so on; ship's captains and master artisans were included in the list, as were lawyers and tradesmen.

Economic and social change drove up the numbers and increased the significance of the bourgeoisie across many European countries in the course of the century. In Norway the proportion of bureaucrats, teachers, bankers, financiers, lawyers, doctors and other professionals in the population rose from 6 per cent to 22 per cent between 1815 and 1914. Around the end of the century one calculation numbered around 15,000 merchants and industrialists in Sweden, 4,700 engineers, 7,000 higher civil servants, 7,600 teachers at all levels including the universities, and 3,300 doctors and apothecaries. They formed a distinctive social class that provided the driving force of social and political liberalism along with the wealthiest among the independent farmers in a country that was still predominantly agricultural. In even less developed societies the bourgeoisie, though growing rapidly, remained a relatively weak social and political force, often with a minority composition. In Hungary around 1900, 45 per cent of doctors and 35 per cent of medical students were Jewish, while in Poland, the German-speaking element of the bourgeoisie was particularly strong, and was concentrated in predominantly German-speaking towns such as Danzig, Elbing or Thorn. By contrast, in a city like Vienna, with its bloated bureaucracy administering the affairs of the entire Habsburg monarchy, the bourgeoisie was both numerous and strong.

The social formation of the urban middle class in most European countries occurred first of all through the development of associations – the reading circles, coffee houses, social clubs and cultural organizations of the early nineteenth century. The membership of social clubs in German towns, usually with names like 'Casino' or 'Harmony', varied according to the nature of the society in which they emerged – 40 per cent of the members in the university town of Göttingen were professors and teachers, while 70 per cent in the Bavarian capital of Munich were noblemen, army officers and bureaucrats. In the financial centre of Frankfurt bankers, merchants and industrialists predominated. But everywhere these societies made a conscious effort to include a broad spectrum of members from the world of the educated and the well-off. The 1820s and 1830s saw a wave of new foundations across Germany, including in Augsburg alone the Tivoli (1825), the Concordia (1827), the Resource (1829), the Enlivenment (1829) and the Jollity (1830). Subscriptions were kept high enough to deter applicants from lower down the social scale, while internally the constitutions of these societies worked on a democratic and representative basis. As these organizations proliferated, they divided the emerging middle class into religious, political or professional groups, above all after 1850. But multiple memberships also helped class cohesion: thus in the 1870s, 38 per cent of the members of the music society in Mannheim also belonged to the leading social club in the town, the Harmony, which also included 44 per cent of the art association and 56 per cent of the natural history society among its members. Almost half the members of all these clubs were counted in the highest class of taxpayers in the town. Participating in urban cultural life was a key to professional as well as social success for the middle class. For medical men, lawyers and other professionals, a suitable social manner in dealing with other members of the bourgeoisie was an essential part of the job, and belonging to a club or society could be a means of gaining patients or clients as well as relaxing after work.

These societies differed from the traditional salon in a number of ways. Salons were frequented above all by the nobility, and although members and visitors left their social status at the door, there is little doubt that they had a strongly aristocratic character. Women played a central role in convening and presiding over salons, whereas they were barred from participation in bourgeois social clubs. The sexual intrigues common in salons were scarcely in evidence in the rigorously moral world of the social club. Every club drew up its own elaborate rules and standing orders, but the salon remained an informal meeting place dedicated above all to conversation. Literature and philosophy were the topics of discussion there, whereas the clubs covered a vastly broader area, when taken as a whole; and while the salons avoided oppositional politics, the clubs were not at all reluctant to engage in them. Salons continued to exist through the nineteenth century: in Brussels, presided over by the Marchioness Arconati-Visconti (1800–71); in Milan, founded in 1834 by Clara Maffei (1814–86); in Uppsala, where Malla Silfverstolpe (1782–1861) organized informal discussions of art and literature; and in many other European cities. But salons were increasingly outflanked by the new institutions of the emerging bourgeois social world, and these institutions were emphatically male, bound together by a new code of 'manliness', subscribing to the values of stability, solidity, probity, industriousness and self-control, all qualities that their members did not consider women to possess.

Largely absent from both kinds of institutions were the bankers and industrialists who formed the stratum known as the 'economic' or 'entrepreneurial' bourgeoisie. Their income was directly subject to market forces, contrasting with that of the 'educated' or 'professional' bourgeoisie of lawyers, teachers, doctors, engineers and the like. But both sectors of the bourgeoisie were increasingly bound together not only by social but also familial ties. By 1900 only 34 per cent of the wives of senior civil servants in the Prussian Rhineland were themselves the daughters of officials, while 48 per cent of these women's fathers were in business or industry. The bureaucracy was merging into a wider middle class, with 37 per cent of the fathers of senior civil servants in the Prussian Rhineland being civil servants themselves, 30 per cent in business or industry, 17 per cent landowners, and 6 per cent military men. In the late nineteenth century between a half and a quarter of the business elite in France, Britain and Germany had received a higher education. The snobbery with which the wealthy and the educated treated families that made their money through 'trade' was gradually being overcome.

Urbanization, industrial growth, the expansion of the state, the rise in population, all demanded the services of doctors, lawyers, engineers, teachers and many others. This led to a steady expansion in the professions. The total of people in the 'public service and professional sector' in England and Wales, counted at just over 200,000 in 1851, numbered some

560,000 forty years later. As knowledge became more complex, training and validation became more important. On the Continent, these were supplied through studying at universities and obtaining degrees in the relevant subject. In Italy in 1877, 40 per cent of university students were studying law. Between 1830 and 1860 nearly a third of all students at German universities were enrolled in Law Faculties. No wonder that legislative assemblies in this period were peopled above all by lawyers. Repeated revisions of the written legal codes that defined every respect of the application and administration of the law on the Continent provided a great deal of fodder for legal practices. The number of lawyers in England and Wales grew from the already considerable total of 15,800 in 1851 to 22,000 in 1891, and there was a comparable increase in other European countries too.

Everywhere, of course, the legal profession encompassed a wide range of qualifications and abilities, from the poorly paid and badly educated notaries of small-town provincial France to the wealthy City solicitors and high-earning barristers of London. Not surprisingly, lawyers were constantly campaigning against unqualified hucksters, known in Germany as *Winkeladvokaten*, or street-corner advocates, and in Italy as *faccendieri*, fixers. In the 1880s the Naples hall of justice was said to be like a flea market, with would-be lawyers advertising their services at every corner. Small wonder, then, that the 18,000 or so lawyers practising in Italy in the 1880s were keen to regulate their profession, though efforts to pass such legislation were generally frustrated, or the laws emasculated, by vested interests. The model here was England, where the Law Society, founded in 1825, regulated entry to the profession of solicitor, set examinations, and enforced standards. While solicitors prepared cases, barristers, who appeared to plead cases before the court, gained their qualifications from the Inns of Court, where they also lived and based their practice in 'chambers'. It was not until 1894 that a broader-based body, the Bar Council, was brought into existence to deal with breaches of professional standards, previously handled by the judiciary.

A similar process of professionalization took place in the civil service and higher state administration of most European states, which underwent a massive expansion in the nineteenth century. By 1914 there were some 166,000 senior civil service posts in Italy, with 314 heads of division compared to a mere 103 in 1882. In the early decades of the century civil servants and state administrators were often lazy, corrupt and lacking in qualifications, like the mayor satirized in Gogol's play *The Government Inspector* (1836), who mistakes a casual visitor for an auditor sent from St Petersburg. The idea of political neutrality was also slow to take root. In the early part of the century, the higher civil service in France, including the prefects in the regions, was a political body. The Restoration appointed noblemen, especially if they were former exiles; the July Monarchy replaced them with Bonapartists and new men; the Second Empire immediately brought about a fall in the number of titled bureaucrats. Similarly, political instability in Spain had its effects on the bureaucracy; a character in the 1898 novel *Mendizabal* by Benito Pérez Galdós (1843–1920) tells the hero that during twenty-five years as a bureaucrat he has 'seen fourteen administrations and been dismissed seven times'. His job, like others in the Spanish civil service, basically depended on patronage. It was constantly at risk; in an earlier generation the dramatist Antonio Gil y Zárate (1793–1861) noted cynically that 'a government job is nothing more than a way of having an income without doing anything . . . talent is irrelevant and . . . the whole business is reduced to whether the person who has the job is a friend or not'. In Britain the Northcote-Trevelyan Report of 1854, strongly influenced by the model of the Chinese mandarinate, recommended that civil-service appointments be made on the basis of merit, as tested by open examinations, and that promotion should be on the basis of merit as well. The civil service had to be neutral, serving the government of the day without being dependent on it. In France higher civil servants were given a more targeted training at the Free School of Political Sciences, known familiarly as *Sciences-Po*, an elite college founded in 1872.

In contrast to the modern civil service, the medical profession was a long-established and relatively stable institution. The number of qualified medical practitioners in England and Wales barely grew in the second half of the century, increasing from 19,200 in 1851 to 20,800 forty years later. The status of English doctors at mid-century was not particularly high. They had to enter the houses of the rich and powerful by the tradesmen's entrance; in *The Vicar of Bullhampton* (1870), a novel by Anthony Trollope (1815–82), one of the characters 'would not absolutely say that a physician was not a gentleman, or even a surgeon; but she would never allow to physic the same absolute privileges which, in her eyes, belonged to law and the church. There might also possibly be a doubt about the Civil Service and Civil Engineering . . .' In Britain, as with other professions, medicine was largely self-regulating, under the General Medical Council established in 1858. The number of doctors also increased slowly in France, from just over 11,000 in 1866 to a little more than 13,000 in 1906, before leaping to 20,000 on the eve of the First World War. Their education still left a great deal to be desired. Medical students in Paris protested frequently in the 1900s about the lack of practical training, overcrowding in laboratories, and the dominance of a small elite of wealthy doctors; in 1911, dissatisfied with the standard of the education they were offered, they locked the Dean of the Medical Faculty at the Sorbonne in his laboratory, causing the Faculty to be closed for a month. The German Doctors' Society was set up in 1822, aiming not least to eliminate the competition of unqualified and alternative medical practitioners, whom it damned as *Kurpfuscher*, or quacks, and to cement the status of doctors by providing regulatory norms. The growth of mutual benefit societies, health insurance and medical charities made doctors less dependent on well-heeled patients for their income. The number of medical students in the German Empire increased from just over 1,600 in the mid-1840s to more than 5,000 in 1882, while at the turn of the century there were nearly 18,000 qualified doctors in Prussia and more than 22,000 in Italy.

The rate of expansion was far greater in another, much more modern profession, engineering, whose practitioners grew in number as Europe's towns and cities expanded, roads, railways and canals were built, and factories and offices multiplied. There were 900 engineers in England and Wales in 1850 and 15,000 forty years later. Graduation from engineering courses in Italian universities was a compulsory requirement for practice, and the profession was organized in military-style corps answerable to special government offices. The state remained the major employer after unification, when a campaign of road and railway construction provided new opportunities for engineers. In France the dominance of the army in the engineering profession declined sharply over time, but the state continued to be the major employer, and the influence of the Saint-Simonians and the prestige of the École Polytechnique, founded in 1794, ensured a relatively high status for engineers, making the profession a vehicle of upward social mobility as it expanded towards the end of the century. Technical institutes were set up in Germany, with more than 11,000 students enrolled by 1914; at the turn of the century they made up a fifth of all students in higher education. In every European country, engineers, like other professions, cemented their identity and status by founding professional associations like the Association of German Engineers (1856), the Society of Civil Engineers set up in France in 1848, and the Austrian Engineers' Association established at the same time and extended in 1864 to include architects. The first Italian congress of engineers met in Milan in 1872, and the 1875 conference, held in Florence, called for a national register of engineers, though this was unsuccessful, as was a proposal to found a national association. Internal rivalries and dissensions, particularly over the role of government in the profession, prevented further progress until 1908, when twenty-four different associations came together to form a national federation.

Special obstacles barred the way to the formation of an independent bourgeoisie in Russia. Merchants were prevented from owning serfs or purchasing land until the 1860s. They were subject to heavy taxation and treated as a closed caste. In the 1897 census there were merely 500,000 merchants, the same number as Orthodox priests and monks, and only a third as many as nobles and officials. Their social isolation was deepened by the fact that most of them were Old Believer sectarians, like the Skoptsy whose proposal to recruit Savva Purlevsky had so frightened the runaway serf. Many came themselves from servile backgrounds. If merchants eventually managed to escape from the institutional restrictions imposed by the tsarist regime, technical experts and professionals found it rather more difficult. For most of the nineteenth century they were confined to militarized corps under the aegis of the tsarist authorities. Three-quarters of physicians, for example, were public employees, and most of them were trained in military medical academies. Some 94 per cent of mining engineers and more than three-quarters of transport engineers were graduates and members of military corps. Only in the reform era of the 1860s were these corps replaced by universities and technological institutes. What substituted for a middle class in Russia for most of the century was the 'intelligentsia' or *literati*, a small group of educated men and women, university professors or teachers, doctors and lawyers, many of them noble.

In the 1890s with the rise of the *zemstva* local and regional authorities, and the beginnings of the industrialization pushed forward by Sergei Witte, the numbers of technicians and professionals began to increase significantly and start the process of forming a middle class on western European lines. It was not until this final decade of the century that the professions started to organize themselves, albeit only with limited success: the tsarist authorities permitted the physicians to hold congresses from 1885 onwards, persuaded that they were necessary for the exchange of information and the formulation of policy about epidemics, but they banned the lawyers from holding conferences after the first one took place in 1872, and did not allow engineers to organize any at all. The professions mostly had to make do with journals, alumni associations, scientific meetings and informal contacts instead. The creation of broad, self-regulating professional bodies seemed politically dangerous to the Russian authorities. Establishing ethical codes of conduct, a central element in western European professionalization, remained difficult if not impossible in a situation where the lion's share of jobs and contracts remained in the hands of government officials who were a byword for corruption.

In every European country, the expansion of technical and other kinds of expertise also required an expansion in the numbers of people who taught them. Here too, as in the law, or medicine, there was a wide spectrum of status and income. There was a large gulf between, on the one hand, university professors and senior teachers in selective academic schools such as the French *lycée* or the German *Gymnasium*, many if not most of whom possessed doctorates from prestigious universities, and, on the other, the lowly primary-school teacher in a provincial town or village who often had to take a second job to make ends meet and did not really belong to the established bourgeoisie. As government employees, teachers in academic and higher education were vulnerable to political pressure: university professors like François Guizot and Victor Cousin were dismissed in the 1820s for their liberal views, and the case of the seven Göttingen professors sacked for the same reason in 1837 achieved widespread notoriety. As late as the 1890s the physicist Leo Arons (1860–1919), who lectured at Berlin University, was refused promotion on the orders of the Prussian government in 1892 and dismissed eight years later because he had donated money to the Social Democratic Party. Political controls were even more severe in Russia.

The bourgeoisie, with its manifold gradations of income and status, developed unevenly across Europe, but by the end of the century there could be little doubt that its numbers and influence were increasing as European economies grew. To be bourgeois was to employ a live-in servant, avoiding any hint of engaging in manual labour; in the middle-class London suburb of Hampstead, for example, in 1911, there were 737 servants for every 1,000 inhabitants. To be middle-class was also to boast a degree of education above the mere command of literacy, preferably with a high school, university or professional qualification; to engage in associational, public and charitable life; and to command sufficient income to possess, or more frequently on the Continent, rent, a well-furnished house or apartment in a salubrious suburb. Status was won not by title or descent but by hard work, probity, lifestyle, and the outward manifestation of 'respectability'. Within the family, the wife or mother did not engage in paid work outside the home; at most, in the upper reaches of the middle classes, women undertook charitable work of one kind or another. Yet this did not mean they were mere passive advertisements of a higher social status; in the bourgeois household, the mother had to manage the servants and control the family's expenditure as well as ensuring the home was supplied with food, clothing, and all the accoutrements of domestic exist-ence. The family, indeed, was at the centre of bourgeois life.

Over the decades, political systems everywhere, even in reluctant tsarist Russia, had adjusted to the new world of the middle classes. Yet there was also a sense in some quarters that their heyday was over by 1900. In the first year of the new century the German writer Thomas Mann (1875–1955) published his great novel of upper-middle-class life, *Buddenbrooks*, in which a mercantile family gradually falls apart over the decades as its members abandon their core values and sink into self-indulgence and decadence in a process symbolized in the progressively worsening tooth decay suffered by the men of each generation. This trajectory was paralleled almost uncannily in the real-life history of the Morozov family, whose founder, Savva Vasilyevich Morozov (1770–1862), freed himself from serfdom to create one of the largest industrial enterprises in Russia. His grandson, Savva Timofeyevich (1862–1905), departed from family tradi-tion to study chemistry at Cambridge, sponsor the Moscow Arts Theatre on his return, and become a friend of the radical socialist writer Maxim Gorky (1868–1936). He committed suicide in Cannes when his mother ousted him from the family business after he had tried to introduce a profit-sharing scheme for the workers; some alleged it was murder. The lengthy series of realist novels, *Les Rougon-Macquart* (1871–93), pub-lished by the popular writer Émile Zola (1840–1902), charted the influence of hereditary weakness on a bourgeois family. Moral hypocrisy forms the core of *Professor Unrat* (1905) by Thomas Mann's elder brother Heinrich (1871–1950), which satirizes the double standards of the outwardly respectable German professoriate. The middle classes, in all their variety, were still socially and in many ways also politically dominant at the begin-ning of the century, but increasingly they had to share their power with competitors lower down the social scale.

THE PETTY BOURGEOISIE

For Karl Marx and his followers, the petty bourgeoisie or lower middle class was a transitional social stratum doomed to extinction, torn apart by the owners of the means of production on the one hand and those they exploited, the workers who had nothing to sell but their labour, on the other. Writing at mid-century, Marx categorized the petty bourgeoisie as a disparate collection of subsistence farmers, traditional artisans and small independent retailers. The gigantic social upheavals of the second half of the century did indeed create serious competition for these social groups.

But they also generated new additions to the lower middle class, both transforming it and ensuring its future. Thus the massive expansion of educational systems provided jobs for huge numbers of schoolteachers, who were forced to live on the margins of respectability. In Britain, even after the introduction of the 'certified teacher' system in 1846, their salary averaged £100 a year. This was little more than the average earnings of most clerks, of whom there were said to be around 129,000 in England and Wales in 1871 but 461,000 in 1901. Before the age of the typewriter, theirs was a male profession, augmented by scribes, copyists and similar employees in banking, the law, insurance, and the lower ranks of the civil service. 'Clerks as clerks,' wrote one of them in response to a British inquiry about employment in 1870, 'are at a discount. There are swarms of them glad to engage at £180 a year and less. Clerks as clerks never will be in a better position.'

This was the quintessentially lower-middle-class occupation. Charles Dickens's novels graphically conveyed the often miserable conditions in which they worked. In *The Pickwick Papers* (1836) he described 'the clerks' office of Messrs. Dodson & Fogg' as 'a dark, mouldy, earthy-smelling room, with a high wainscotted partition to screen the clerks from the vulgar gaze, a couple of old wooden chairs, a very loud-ticking clock, an almanac, an umbrella-stand, a row of hat-pegs, and a few shelves, on which were deposited several ticketed bundles of dirty papers, some old deal boxes with paper labels, and sundry decayed stone ink bottles of various shapes and sizes'. Bob Cratchit, the decent but ineffectual clerk to the grasping moneylender Ebenezer Scrooge in *A Christmas Carol* (1843), is continually at the mercy of his employer's unrelenting miserliness. In *David Copperfield* (1850) Uriah Heep, the ambitious and manipulative villain of the story, is a clerk whose ambition is to better himself. Some indeed did: Charles Pooter, the hero or possibly anti-hero of *The Diary of a Nobody* (1892), whose trivial social ambitions and dull suburban lifestyle are gently satirized by the authors George Grossmith (1847–1912) and his brother Weedon Grossmith (1854–1919), gains promotion to the lofty position of senior clerk at one point in the novel, with a £100 salary increase, though he remains irritated by his social connections among the local shopkeepers, whom he now considers well below him on the social scale.

Shopkeepers were one of the success stories of the century, at least in economic terms. As towns expanded, the traditional weekly market, with produce brought in from the countryside, became inadequate to meet the needs of a growing population, even when transport links improved. Thus fixed and specialized retail outlets grew rapidly in number. A study of six towns in the north of England, for example, showed that there was one shop for every 136 inhabitants in 1801 and one for every 57 half a century later. After this, the numbers stabilized as new forms of retailing established themselves. Most important of these was the chain store, with branches all over the country. The stationer W. H. Smith was founded in 1792 and expanded to a nationwide business through opening newsstands on railway stations, the first being in 1848. Further competition came from co-operatives and from mail-order retailing, invented by the Welsh entrepreneur Pryce Pryce-Jones (1834–1920) in 1861 and dependent, of course on the establishment of an effective national postal service. Commentators on local government in Victorian England soon came to speak of a 'shopocracy' in which retailers played an influential role on local councils (from 1832 to 1867 they made up a third of the local electorate).

But the most striking innovation in the field was the department store, where a variety of specialized retailing outlets were gathered together under the same roof, thus reducing overheads. The new department stores extended over several floors and offered a variety of goods including luxuries of many kinds. The earliest, such as Bainbridge's in Newcastle-upon-Tyne, founded in 1838, had twenty-three departments by 1849; the *Bon Marché* in Paris, also founded in 1838, sold goods at fixed rates, another innovation in an era when customers were used to haggling over prices with shopkeepers or market stall-owners. The department store was immortalized in Zola's novel *Au Bonheur des Dames* (1883), which described its many innovations, including mail-order sales, aggressive marketing and heavy discounting, and chronicled its devastating effects on small shopkeepers who were unable to lower their prices to meet the competition. These were successful enterprises: the *Bon Marché* in Brussels increased the number of its departments between 1879 and 1889 from eighteen to thirty-two, adding children's clothing, hats, perfumes, flannel and much else besides. In Germany the department-store chains were founded by Jewish cloth merchants. Among them were Rudolph Karstadt (1856–1944), who began trading in Wismar in 1881; Oskar Tietz (1858–1923), who launched his first store in Gera in 1882 and soon possessed a chain of stores across northern Germany, including one on the Alexanderplatz in Berlin; and his brother Leonhard Tietz (1849–1914), who began trading in Stralsund in 1879. By eliminating the middleman and purchasing direct from the producer, they were able to control prices more effectively than conventional retailers.

This model was quickly followed elsewhere, as in Budapest, where the Simon Holzer Fashion House, opened in 1895, occupied four floors of a large building twelve years later, selling ready-to-wear clothing, another innovation. By the turn of the century purpose-built department stores such as Harrods, constructed on the Brompton Road in West London in the late 1890s following the destruction of an earlier building by fire, had become 'cathedrals of consumerism', where shopping became a leisure activity, middle-class women could wander around without the need to be chaperoned, and specially trained staff, also overwhelmingly female, could acquire secure employment, though at the price of spending up to thirteen hours on their feet every day. By the early twentieth century the Párisi department store in Budapest, on the prestigious Andrássy Avenue, close to the Opera House, was selling goods on six floors of a magnificent building whose vast galleries, adorned with specially commissioned paintings and decorations, offered a huge range of goods at all prices, advertised in plate-glass windows along the frontage. The Samaritaine in Paris, constructed in 1910, had steam heating ducts, a pneumatic tube system for messages, motorized conveyor belts to deliver packages, and electrically powered awnings on the exterior to protect the windows from the sun.

Yet all these new forms of retailing did not really account for more than 15 per cent of turnover in the sector. The small shop, the butcher, baker, grocer, greengrocer, dairy and so on, continued to grow in numbers to meet the ever-increasing demand. In Madrid the Almacenes Madrid-Paris department store employed 416 people, but at the start of the twentieth century the 8,851 merchants engaged in 'general commerce' in the city employed nearly 25,000 workers, or just under three each. The number of shops in Germany grew by 42 per cent between 1905 and 1907 alone, at a time when the country's population increased by only 8 per cent. A witness to an inquiry of 1892 in Britain described a plethora of 'small shops in back streets, or perhaps in a parlour window, or small cellar, [that] sell almost everything, a little hosiery, chips, and bath bricks, and all that kind of thing, and sweets; a little bit of everything that they think they can dispose of'. Many such businesses led a precarious existence; in Bremen at the turn of the century a third of all retail businesses lasted less than six years. Nearly half of all grocery stores in Ghent had been in business for less than five years according to an inquiry undertaken in 1905.

It was a similar story with small workshops manned by single master artisans: in Edinburgh a third of them closed down in a typical five-year period, from 1890 to 1895. To defend their interests and provide a social life, small shopkeepers, clerks and other groups within the petty bourgeoisie increasingly established clubs and societies of one kind and another. The Master Joiners' Circle founded in Lyon in 1867 was set up 'with a view to establishing regular and friendly relations between the master joiners; to tighten among themselves ties of fraternity; and to associate for the progress of their trade'; the Master Patissiers of Brussels set up a society in 1887 'to get together from time to time, to see each other, and to talk over the past', as well as to formulate demands for their trade; the Fulham Tradesmen's Association held convivial dinners but also tried to advance their group economic interests. In Germany the Central Association of German Traders and Businessmen (1899), the German Central Association for Trade and Business (1907) and similar organizations acted to defend the economic interests of their members. Well before the turn of the century these were describing themselves as representatives of the *Mittelstand*, the 'middle order', which they contrasted with the workers on the one hand and the bourgeoisie and aristocracy on the other. Competition from large-scale industry and from socialist consumer co-operatives drove members of these associations to the right of the political spectrum and infused them with a dose of paranoid antisemitism, though this has sometimes been exaggerated by historians.

There was no doubt, however, about the anti-Jewish character of the populist German National Commercial Employees' Association, founded in 1896 on the basis of a local Hamburg group set up three years earlier: it also became virulently anti-feminist as the female secretary began to replace the male clerk, and combined its two obsessions in the charge that feminism was a Jewish plot designed to undermine the German family. None of this had much effect, as women – mostly the educated daughters of the middle class – continued to move into new, modern and technologically driven areas of employment such as post offices, telephone exchanges, department stores and all kinds of businesses where the female-operated typewriter, first commercially produced in 1870 by the Danish inventor Rasmus Malling-Hansen (1835–90), quickly replaced the scribe and the copyist. One of the sharpest delineators of the social boundary with the petty bourgeoisie was the fact that the wives and unmarried daughters of teachers, shopkeepers, pettifogging clerks, independent master artisans and small businessmen had to work, either as unpaid assistants or in paid employment outside the home, while those of the established bourgeoisie did not. In Germany in 1907, indeed, 54 per cent of those recorded in an occupational census as working in commerce were members of the owner's family. If the husband should die, it was common enough for his widow to carry on the business. Such activity was considered socially embarrassing for those petty-bourgeois families who aspired to move up the social scale: in one of the numerous novels by the Greek-born Italian writer Matilde Serao (1856–1927) a female character 'did not look down on the life of a shopkeeper. But she would have liked to have been the lady of the house and not of the shop, a housewife and not a seller of sweets, a mother to her family and not a vendor in a shop.' Yet the dividing line of social aspiration and class consciousness between petty bourgeoisie and proletariat remained clearer and sharper than it did between petty bourgeoisie and the social world above.

'NOTHING TO LOSE BUT THEIR CHAINS'

By the early twentieth century, the proletariat of wage-earning manual labourers and their families had grown to become the largest single social class in many industrialized nations. In France by 1914 there were perhaps 4 million industrial workers in a population of around 42 million. In a fully industrialized economy like Britain, with a population of roughly 45 million in 1868, industrial workers far outnumbered all other social classes put together, over 16 million compared with under 5 million economically active members of the upper and middle classes. In Germany manual labourers and their families made up nearly two-thirds of the population, though this figure included agricultural workers as well. Income inequalities were striking. According to one estimate, of the 10 million people with an independent income in Britain in 1867, some 50,000 (the 'upper class') earned over £1,000 a year, 150,000 (the 'middle class') between £300 and £1,000 a year, 1,854,000 (the 'lower middle class') up to £300 a year, and 7,785,000 below £100 a year, of whom nearly 2,250,000 were agricultural labourers and the rest urban skilled and unskilled workers. The well-to-do literally looked down on their social inferiors. A statistical comparison between cadets at Sandhurst, for example, an officer-training establishment, and students enrolled in the Marine Society charity school, shows that the elite students enjoyed a remarkable height advantage of almost 9 inches by 1840. The poor Marine Society boys, many of them from London, were the shortest group ever recorded in Europe and North America. They were even 2–3 inches shorter than the average height of American slaves at the time. Among male Scottish prisoners, Glasgow natives were nearly an inch shorter than other prisoners. Longitudinal studies show that average height in Britain did not start to increase until the late nineteenth century.

These differences reflected gross disparities in health and nutrition. Life expectancy at birth in the prosperous London suburb of Hampstead around 1900 was fifty, whereas in the deprived working-class London borough of Southwark it was thirty-six – the disparity reflecting above all a huge difference in the rates of infant mortality between the two districts.

By 1900, 96 per cent of babies born in the middle classes in England survived the first year of life, whereas 33 per cent of those born in the poorest London slum districts did not. Average mortality per 1,000 inhabitants in the Parisian *arrondissements* with the wealthiest population was 16 points below the average for the city as a whole in 1817, 27 by mid-century, and 23 by 1891; by contrast, mortality in the poorest districts was 23 to 24 points above the city average throughout the first half of the century, falling back to 6 points by 1891. Death rates were highest in the industrial towns where the working classes were crowded together in cramped and poorly ventilated living quarters: in the early 1890s, for example, 4.5 per thousand population in the industrial areas of the Ruhr and the Lower Rhine died of tuberculosis every year compared to under 2 per thousand in the rural districts of eastern Prussia. In the city of Hamburg around the same time death rates per thousand in the two wealthiest precincts stood at 1.3 from tuberculosis compared to 3.3 in the waterfront slums, while the figures for overall infant mortality were 11.4 and 25.1 respectively. Diseases such as cholera struck the poor much harder than the well off; in Hamburg in 1892 mortality rates among taxpayers earning 800–1,000 marks a year – a manual labourer's income – were 62 per thousand, among those earning 2,000–3,500 marks a year 37 per thousand, and among those earning 50,000 marks or more a year a mere 5 per thousand.

As cities grew, and people crowded into them looking for work, getting fresh food in from the countryside and keeping it from going rotten became ever more difficult. Icehouses, storing blocks of ice imported from glaciers and snowfields in the mountains or the far north, were used only by the very wealthy. The Scottish engineer James Harrison (1816–93), based for most of his life in Australia, patented the first vapour-compression refrigeration machines in the 1850s, using them mainly to cool beer. It was not until 1911, however, that the first domestic refrigerators became available, manufactured by the General Electric Company in the USA. They sold for $1,000 each, twice the price of a motor car. Not surprisingly, the great mass of ordinary people had to do without them. And as if the problem of food deterioration in the summer months was not enough of a burden for the health of the poor, general standards of food hygiene were in any case minimal. In Hamburg, milk, unsterilized until the end of the century, was distributed through the streets in open red-painted pails carried on small carts pulled by dogs, which were said to quench their thirst on hot days 'by lapping the dripping milk-pails'. In cities where breast-feeding was uncommon because young mothers had to return to work almost immediately after giving birth, sour or tubercular milk was a major contributor to infant mortality. The working classes often had to live off food bought as leftovers even for their good meals; on broken eggs, stale bread, bruised fruit, offal, and unsold and unfresh meat and fish. Bread, potatoes, polenta or other starchy foods provided the bulk of their diet. An average working-class family in the mining and iron and steel town of Bochum in the Ruhr in 1875 spent an average of 60 pfennigs a day on bread, 39 pfennigs on butter, fat, grease and lard, 24 pfennigs on potatoes, 15 pfennigs on coffee mixed with chicory, and 15 pfennigs on vegetables. Of these items, bread was by far the cheapest, so that its place in the diet was even more prominent than these expenditure statistics would suggest.

As the consumer became ever more separated from the producer, with supplies increasingly passing through the hands of wholesalers and other middlemen before they reached the shops, the possibilities of adulterating food were seized on with alacrity by traders looking to maintain or increase their profits at a time of growing competition. An official report commissioned by Bismarck in 1878 found that barite, gypsum and chalk were added to flour to increase its weight, while in southern Germany 'egg noodles' were coloured yellow with picric acid and even urine. In 1889, 60 per cent of samples of butter investigated in Hamburg were found to be adulterated with margarine (a French substitute patented in 1869 and based on vegetable oil and beef fat). Some 24 per cent of tests on a range of foodstuffs and drinks carried out in Berlin in 1890 found evidence of adulteration. The substitution of worthless additives diluted the nutritional value of food and could even in some cases be positively dangerous. In 1855 the English doctor Arthur Hill Hassell (1817–94) found alum in flour and bread, gunpowder in tea, water added to milk, and oxide of lead used as a colouring agent in coffee. The Adulteration of Food Act, passed in 1860, had no discernible effect, largely because the trade interest stopped local authorities from appointing official food analysts. Only after a new Act was passed in 1872 did the number of investigations increase, and only following more sophisticated techniques of chemical analysis in the 1880s did comparable legislation in countries such as Germany begin to have an effect. In France the first investigative laboratory was set up in 1878, serving the interests of retailers who wanted to check the quality of foodstuffs they purchased from wholesalers; it was only in 1905, however, that a general law was introduced to criminalize adulteration and the fraudulent advertising of food and drink. The law established among other things the *appellation controlée* designation of the origin of wines that has persisted to the present day. Only in the last two decades of the nineteenth century did nutritional standards begin to rise.

Better diet accompanied urban improvement and the 'hygienic revolution' in many European towns and cities. Yet employment was unstable, reflecting both the economic instability of capitalist enterprise and the attitudes of first-generation industrial workers, many of whom still retained their links with the land. In the mines of Carmaux in southern France, for instance, the company often laid off its workers without pay when demand was low. This occurred on as many as fifty-six days in 1886. On the other hand, absenteeism sometimes had an effect too, especially at harvest time, when workers often went back to their families in the countryside to help gather in the crops. Miners at Carmaux were even awarded a prize if they achieved as much as 23 per cent attendance in a month. All over Europe workers customarily took Mondays off, to add to the weekend – 'Saint Monday' as it was known in England, or 'Blue Monday' in Germany. In the coalfields of Asturias in north-western Spain as many as three-quarters of the miners were accustomed to stay away from work not only during the numerous religious holidays but on the day after too. In many trades, in any case, employment was casual and ad hoc; in ports, workers were hired in gangs separately for each ship coming into or leaving the harbour, and therefore in lean periods, notably winter time, they were left without an income. In the Voortman cotton mill in Ghent, hourly pay replaced daily wages, enabling the owner to increase the working day when demand rose, without facing protests from the workers. By 1858, however, Voortman's employees were working a 75-hour week, an average of nearly 13 hours a day. During times of heightened demand the company increased the length of each cloth to be made by pieceworkers (who were paid per piece of finished cloth produced), whereas during an economic downturn it cut wages, at all times keeping wage calculations a secret from the workers.

In many trades, piece rates, with workers paid according to how much they produced, were common. In coalmines wages were calculated by the amount of coal produced by each particular team of miners. Because the coal was hard in some seams, soft in others, and also varied in quality from one part of a seam to another, the rate of pay for each truck of coal had to be constantly renegotiated to ensure that effort was fairly rewarded. The coal was cut by hand and taken along the galleries by pit ponies pulling trucks on a narrow-gauge railway before being hauled to the surface by a steam-powered winch; it could take as long as an hour for miners to reach the coalface in the deeper pits, and 'winding-time' was a constant source of dispute, especially when mine owners refused to pay for it. Hours everywhere were long and the facilities poor. In Budapest in the 1880s, most factory employees worked a twelve-hour day; yet only 109 out of

5,000 factories surveyed in 1910 had toilet facilities, and a mere 75 had canteens. Accidents were common. Spectacular mine disasters like that of the Courrières mine in northern France in 1906, when a massive dust explosion killed over a thousand workers, including many children, hit the headlines, but the daily toll of injury, death and disease on workers of all kinds exacted an even greater price over the long term. Chronic illnesses like the lung diseases silicosis and pneumoconiosis were barely recognized by the medical profession. The annual report of Britain's Chief Inspector of Factories and Workshops for 1899 listed 22,771 industrial accidents reported to the certifying surgeons, 871 of them fatal; 150 involved the loss of a limb, 2,521 part of a hand; there were 2,706 scalds or burns, and 1,202 fractures. In Russia in 1890 alone 245 people were killed in accidents in metallurgical factories, and there were 3,508 serious injuries; by 1904 these figures had climbed to 556 and 66,680 respectively, affecting 11 per cent of the labour force.

In the textile mills where so many women worked, it was easy for clothing to be caught in a machine. Cases of operatives losing fingers were far from uncommon until safety devices were introduced and improved, the dust-filled atmosphere was damaging to the workers' lungs, and the deafening noise of the power looms frequently led to hearing loss. Few factories had facilities catering for mothers with small children – only seven out of the 5,000 factories in Budapest surveyed in 1910 provided a crèche, for example. New industries posed new hazards, as in the manufacture of self-igniting white-phosphorus matches, invented in 1830 by the Frenchman Charles Sauria (1812–95). Already by mid-century some 250 million matches were being struck every day in the United Kingdom, the majority of them strike-anywhere 'Lucifers'; the safety match, which was far less dangerous in every respect, never became popular in Britain. In the London-based Bryant and May company the fumes from the white phosphorus used to make the combustible match-heads began to have a terrible effect on the workers – almost all of them women and teenage children – whose job it was to prepare the phosphorus solution and dip frames of matchsticks into it. Their gums began to ulcerate, their teeth fell out, and their jawbones began to rot, exuding a vile-smelling pus, sometimes through the nose. This was 'phossy jaw'. The use of white phosphorus was eventually banned by an international convention signed at Berne in 1906 and ratified by the British Parliament two years later.

Women such as the match-girls at Bryant and May were predominantly young and single, as they were in the textile industries and domestic service. In Spain, 4,046 of the 4,542 employees of the Seville tobacco factory were women. Tobacco workers were famous for the combativeness that led to five days of rioting at a Madrid factory in 1830 in protest against a wage cut. Their reputation caught the attention of the French composer Georges Bizet (1838–75), who adapted an 1845 novella by Prosper Mérimée (1803–70) to create in 1875 the most famous of all fictional Spanish women workers, the gypsy girl Carmen. Women were generally believed to be more dexterous and better at delicate work than men, but their employment outside the home was also concentrated in areas that extended their conventional domestic roles to the outside world, in the food and drink industries, in clothing manufacture and cleaning, and in domestic service. During the first phase of industrialization, dominated by the textile industry, the new spinning and weaving machines were operated predominantly by women. In the textile town of Roubaix in northern France during the mid-nineteenth century, 55 per cent of employed women worked in the textile mills. Here, 33 per cent of all women over the age of ten were in employment, and 18 per cent of married women worked, half of them in the mills. But this was exceptional. Married working-class women with children usually had to work at home. New possibilities were opened up by the modern sewing machine, invented in 1829 by the French tailor Barthélemy Thimonnier (1793–1857). It was developed commercially by the American inventor Isaac Singer (1811–75), a man whose volcanic energy found one outlet among many in fathering at least twenty-four children by a number of different women. Singer's machine was patented in 1851 and was soon being mass-produced, spurring the development of a new putting-out system, through which a clothier would order garments from a middleman who would employ up to twenty women in a workshop using Singer sewing machines.

Most legislation on female employment was directed towards factory work, where women's hours were regulated in Russia in 1885, and in Germany at around the same period, with the aim, as one (male) Reichstag deputy declared in 1890, of ensuring 'that the ennobling spirit of family life and the blessings of hearth and home, which seem at present to be seriously under threat, remain assured to the worker and his own'. It was far more difficult to regulate domestic service, which had become one of the largest areas of employment for working-class women by the late nineteenth century, when there were 2.5 million servants in Germany alone. In Spain there were 322,000 female domestic servants in 1887, out of a female labour force of around 1.5 million. From 1851 to 1871 the total of live-in female servants in England and Wales grew twice as fast as the general population, from 750,000 to 1,200,000. Most worked in single-servant households employing a 'maid of all work'. In the garrison and county town of York in the north of England, in 1851, nearly 60 per cent of all employed women were servants. In Hamburg in 1900, 90 per cent of domestic servants were female, the majority coming from the surrounding areas. Some 75 per cent of them worked as the only employee of a middle-class family. The records of a local Hamburg tribunal dealing with disputes between servants and their employers – about 2,000 cases a year by the 1880s – demonstrate frequent complaints on the servants' part about bullying, name-calling, long hours, poor living conditions, minimal or unpaid wages, and above all restrictions on their freedom. And if an employer did not like a new servant's first name, he or she would arbitrarily change it to something different, and the servant simply had to acquiesce.

Industrial conditions of employment began to spread to the countryside too, above all where farmers produced in large quantities to sell on the national or international market. The harshness of agricultural work in the late nineteenth century can be illustrated by the experience of the Pomeranian labourer Franz Rehbein (1867–1909), a self-taught man whose autobiography was published in 1911. Son of a washerwoman and a tailor who died of tuberculosis when Franz was still a child, he had to earn his keep as a farm labourer. After finding work in a sugar refinery he subsequently became a farm servant on an estate before running away to Hamburg and then being called up for military service. On his discharge he went back to agricultural work. Steam-powered threshing machines were by now widely used in Schleswig-Holstein, but only the richest estate-owners could afford their own, so most of them were hired out, with their operators, by independent contractors who moved the machines from farm to farm as required. The quantity of labour needed was considerable – up to thirty men for each machine, carrying out tasks such as stoking and carrying water to the engine, baling the straw, collecting the ears of corn, and so on. A few machine-owners also used a mechanical binder or baler, which reduced the number of men needed, but mostly the work was done by hand. Conditions of work were almost unbearable. The machine made a deafening noise, and the dust it threw up stopped the workers' noses, made their eyes swollen, and got in their throats and lungs, so that they coughed up 'black lumps of black mucus', as Rehbein reported. If it rained, the dust clung to their skins in a thick layer. The labourers were paid an hourly rate that could be as low as 15 pfennigs. Work often began at three in the morning, and carried on until nine or ten in the evening, sometimes even longer. Breaks were allowed only for meals, or to allow the machine to be oiled. 'The man had to go out with the machine,' Rehbein wrote, 'he becomes its slave, becomes himself part of the machine.' The threshing machines were also dangerous: in 1895 Rehbein's arm became caught in one of them and had to be amputated.

The free market in labour and the increasing numbers of landless rural labourers living, like Rehbein, on piece rates in miserable poverty resulted in a growing migration of young men from the countryside to the towns in search of steadier and, by the late nineteenth century, better-paid work – what the Prussians called *Landflucht*, the flight from the land. This meant that male labour had to be replaced by female, as the women stayed behind until their husband or betrothed had made enough money to support them by buying a smallholding. The temptation of leaving the land to work in the factories was obvious from the 1913 statistics of average per capita annual income in urban and rural areas of northern Germany: 480 marks in the 'flat land' region of West Prussia, and 576 in Pomerania, contrasted with 1,254 marks in Berlin and 1,313 in Hamburg. Even taking into account the greater numbers of middle-class incomes in the towns, and allowing for the possibility that rural workers could subsist from a smallholding or cottage garden, this demonstrated that the towns and cities of an advanced industrial economy had finally acquired a higher standard of living for the masses than was possible in the countryside.

There were many social gradations within the urban and rural working class. There was a marked disparity in wages between male and female workers – in the Spanish textile industry, for example, female wages were about half those of men in the 1850s, rising to two-thirds by 1914. But social gradations also affected men and families at different levels. In London skilled artisans looked down on the unskilled; and among the latter, shipworkers looked down on shore workers, and the permanently employed despised the casually hired. English workers felt superior to the Irish, just as in the Ruhr German workers looked down on Italians and Poles. These differences often reflected differences in earnings. In France in the late nineteenth century, glassblowers earned around 10 francs a day, whereas weavers only earned 1 franc 65 centimes. Yet such differences paled beside the gulf that existed between all these manual, waged workers on the one hand, and the far smaller number of the better off and the wealthy in the middle and upper classes on the other. The experience of poverty, oppression, social disadvantage and, in much of Europe for most of the period, lack of basic rights was common to all these workers and helped bind them together into a single social class, much as Marx had predicted. This happened over time with the development of a permanent, hereditary proletariat. When a railway-engine factory was founded in the south German town of Esslingen in 1846, it was initially unable to recruit a permanent workforce. Although there were over a thousand operatives in the factory by 1856, most left after a few months, or migrated elsewhere, or, above all, went home in summer to help with the harvest. The pattern of migration reflected the agricultural cycle rather than the pattern of demand in the industry. During the summer, when the regular workers were away, their jobs were filled by local textile workers. It was not until the agricultural crisis of the late 1870s that this pattern changed and workers began to remain at their posts through the summer, gradually severing their contacts with the farming communities from which they came.

In the slate-quarrying districts of north Wales it was common for quarrymen to live away from the workplace on a hill farm or smallholding, where their wives and families looked after a few cows and sheep, a pig and some chickens during the day or, if the farm was far away and the men forced to live in quarry barracks, during the entire week. One quarry manager complained of his workers in 1892 that 'in the summer, for instance in hay harvest, a good many go away'. Two-thirds of the coalminers of Asturias in north-western Spain were said by the State Mining Directorate in 1911 to be 'farmers who have their homes and their lands, alternating their work in their fields with that in the mines'. In St Petersburg young workers retained their links with their home villages to the extent that a survey of 570 skilled wage earners carried out in 1908 revealed that 42 per cent of married and 67 per cent of single respondents sent part of their money back to relatives in the countryside. Even here, however, as the 1910 census showed, nearly 20 per cent of men in the 'peasant' category in St Petersburg had been born there, and 25 per cent of the women; in 1902, 16 per cent of the male and 21 per cent of mill operatives in the city were second-generation workers. A permanent, hereditary proletariat was in the process of formation here too. This development was already beginning to have major political consequences before the century came to an end.

THE 'DANGEROUS CLASSES'

The urbanization of Europe aroused widespread alarm among conservative contemporaries. The conservative German social theorist Wilhelm Heinrich Riehl felt that big cities broke down traditional structures of family and status, so that people became 'intoxicated, confused and discontented'. Rising crime rates were the inevitable consequence. Indeed, social commentators noted with alarm the creation of an 'irredeemably criminal class', as the London *Times* put it in 1863. In 1852, Karl Marx described the criminal underclass, the *Lumpenproletariat* or 'ragged working class', in drastic terms:

> Alongside decayed roués with dubious means of subsistence and of dubious origin, alongside ruined and adventurous offshoots of the bourgeoisie, were vagabonds, discharged soldiers, discharged jailbirds, escaped galley slaves, swindlers, mountebanks, lazzaroni, pickpockets, tricksters, gamblers, pimps, brothel keepers, porters, literati, organ-grinders, ragpickers, knife grinders, tinkers, beggars – in short, the whole indefinite, disintegrated mass, thrown hither and thither, which the French call *la bohème*.

Marx's picture was echoed by that of the army officers who suppressed the Paris Commune in 1871, blaming the uprising on 'the dangerous classes', 'black with powder, haggard, ragged . . . their sordid females with them'. Scarcely less notorious than the Parisian underworld or the *lazzaroni* of the Neapolitan slums were the impoverished criminal classes of London, the subject of a four-volume survey by the journalist Henry Mayhew (1812–87) in his *London Labour and the London Poor* (1851–61). With his collaborators, Mayhew interviewed a wide variety of offenders, from 'sneaks or common thieves' to 'housebreakers and burglars', and recorded the experiences of the urban underclass including the 'mudlarks' who made a living by stealing coal from barges on the Thames and selling it to the poor. In Charles Dickens's novel *Our Mutual Friend* (1864–5) the main female character, Lizzie Hexam, helps her father in his business of riffling through the pockets of dead bodies of people who have fallen into the river, or thrown themselves in, as they float downstream with the tide.

Many commentators titillated the horrified fascination of their bourgeois readers with the existence of this supposedly separate social class that had its own customs, habits and language. In Dickens's *Oliver Twist*, indeed, there is a whole criminal underworld in London peopled by characters such as the prostitute Nancy, the violent burglar Bill Sykes, and the sinister 'fence' Fagin, who employs a gang of juvenile pickpockets for which Oliver is at one point forced to work. In France, a similar literary exploration of the urban criminal milieu was conducted by Eugène François Vidocq (1775–1857), a convicted thief, forger and jailbird who had become a police spy in prison. In the late Napoleonic period he founded the *Sûreté*, the French detective force, and went on to publish a series of (mostly ghostwritten) books on the underworld, including one on its argot. The German policeman Friedrich Christian Benedikt Avé-Lallemant

(1809–92) wrote four volumes on the criminal classes, the final one being a dictionary of their language, known as *Rotwelsch*. But the concept of an entirely separate substratum of society was largely a literary conceit. Many of the casual poor drifted in and out of crime as their circumstances dictated, earning their living as best they could, constructing for themselves an economy of makeshifts in which legal activities intermingled with illegal ones. The social investigator Charles Booth (1840–1916) acknowledged this reality in his famous street maps of London in the late nineteenth century, colour-coded to indicate degrees of wealth and poverty: blue was reserved for streets occupied by 'vicious, semi-criminal' elements, the lowest of the low.

Yet many workers who in other respects were law-abiding citizens saw nothing wrong in stealing from their employers. In the mines they considered it perfectly legitimate to take coal home for heating since the coal was the product of their own labour; indeed some 3,000 miners went on strike in Upper Silesia in the early 1870s when the mine-owners proposed checks on workers going off shift to make sure they were not taking any coal with them. Similarly, in the docks, goods from incoming cargoes to sell or use later on were routinely appropriated by wharfmen and stevedores. 'If people work all night alone and without supervision,' wrote the *Hamburg Stock Exchange Journal* in 1891, 'is it then any wonder that the one or the other of them gains a few pounds in weight during the night and that this extra weight consists in fact of coffee?' Parts of London's small-scale industry existed almost entirely on stolen or pilfered goods, with furniture workshops using stolen wood and clothing shops stolen fabrics. This did not make their suppliers into full-time thieves. Still, professional criminals certainly did exist. Arthur Harding (1886–1981), who grew up in a slum known as 'the Jago' in the East End of London, recalled in old age how he had begun his criminal career as a pickpocket, before graduating to more ambitious enterprises. In 1908 he was described as the 'king' or 'captain' of the Brick Lane van-draggers – 'a most slippery and dangerous criminal . . . the leader of a numerous band of thieves'. 'I got my first gun about 1904,' he recalled. Harding and his gang were soon operating a racket extorting protection money from illegal gambling dens: 'When we made a raid on a club, we made everyone stand up, and waved our guns about to show that we were serious.' Many other port cities harboured a similar criminal class. In January 1906, across the North Sea in Hamburg, as a massive political demonstration occupied the attention of the entire city police force, the people of the Alley Quarters near the harbour emerged from their houses and threw stones at the street lights, putting them out before smashing the windows of the jewellery shops in the city centre and pulling down the security bars: 'As soon as the window was destroyed,' one eyewitness reported, 'and the iron bars broken off, greedy fingers grabbed at the watches and gold in the display . . .' The visibility of occurrences such as these did much to convince contemporaries that urbanization led inevitably to an increase in crime and disorder.

'Criminal statistics,' noted a Russian journal in 1893, 'attest that crime is greater in cities than in villages.' Life was insecure, city-dwellers were cut adrift from their families and were without the moralizing influence of the Church. There were far more temptations in towns and cities than in the impoverished countryside. Rural crime was thought to be mostly violent and interpersonal in nature; with the growth of towns came a shifting of the balance towards property crimes. Thus in Russia from 1874 to 1913, for instance, 85 per cent of murders occurred in rural areas, 89 per cent of manslaughters, and 85 per cent of assaults. By contrast, only just over half of all cases of theft and dealing in stolen goods occurred in the countryside, though this was still where the overwhelming majority of Russians lived. But these figures were deceptive. Not only did they in many cases fail to incorporate cases dealt with by local courts in rural areas, but most importantly they also ignored the fact that crime in the countryside often represented a clash of values and beliefs between the peasantry and the authorities.

Popular belief made a distinction between property created by human industriousness and property created without a human contribution. The latter included wood, essential for making furniture, huts and houses, and implements of many kinds, as well as fuel for heating and cooking. Former serfs in many areas refused to accept the consequences of the privatization of woodland that accompanied their emancipation. Between 1815 and 1848 convictions for wood theft in Prussia reached astonishing proportions as a result. Throughout the 1830s and 1840s the number of convictions for wood theft in Prussia (not including the Rhine Province) continued to grow, from 120,000 in 1836 to 253,000 ten years later. There were 351,000 convictions in 1856 and 373,000 in 1865. Indeed, wood theft was by a very long way the most common recorded criminal offence in Prussia during this period, with 1,000 successful prosecutions per 100,000 inhabitants of the kingdom in 1836, in contrast to a mere 236 per 100,000 for all other kinds of theft put together, and a mere 23 per 100,000 for grievous bodily harm and assault. Whole communities were involved, leading to armed clashes between the foresters of the landlords, who now sought to use their forests as a source of profit, and the local peasants, who continued to regard them as a common resource. The clash of cultures that lay behind the disputes between peasants and foresters was never fully resolved.

In many ways rural society for most of the century, and in some areas up to the First World War and even beyond, was self-sufficient in the administration of justice. Those who transgressed against the rules of the village were liable to be punished through the communal village practice known in France as *charivari*, in England as 'rough music' or 'skimmington', in Germany as *Haberfeldtreiben*, and in Italy as *scampanate*. The *charivari* in France could take various forms, but most commonly the young men of the village would gather, hold a mock trial, and decapitate or burn an effigy of the offender. In some areas they would smear the offender's face with honey and feathers, put a nightcap on his head, place a distaff in his hand, and drive him through the village as he sat on a donkey facing backwards. More usually, however, especially in England, as described in the novel *The Mayor of Casterbridge* (1886) by Thomas Hardy (1840–1928), they would assemble outside the offender's house in the early hours of the morning, burn the offender in effigy, shout insults and sing specially composed songs, blow horns, ring cowbells, clash pots and pans and make what the Germans called *Katzenmusik* ('caterwauling'), often repeating the process for several nights on end. In Bavaria, if a farmer had seduced his maid, the village youth would take a cart from his stable, dismantle it, and carry the parts onto the roof of his dwelling, reassemble it there, and fill it with dung in the practice known as *Mistwagenstellen*. But theft, defamation, even infanticide courted such punishments as well, and they could also be applied to brewers who watered down their beer, usurers who demanded excessive interest, or farmers who transgressed repeatedly across the boundaries of someone else's property.

Such practices were common not only in England, France and Germany but also in Italy, Austria, Hungary, Holland and Scandinavia. In Russia the *charivari* was directed mainly against thieves; indeed, it was known as *vozhdenie* ('leading the thief'). It involved parading the offender through the village, sometimes wearing a horse's collar, to the accompaniment of a noisy banging of pots and pans, buckets, washtubs and iron oven doors. Most reviled of all were horse thieves; in 1887 villagers in Umansk even broke into the district jail where five horse thieves had been imprisoned, took them out and tortured them as a crowd of onlookers cried 'Beat them, beat them to death!' 'Almost daily,' noted an article in the Russian magazine *The Jurist* in 1905, 'the telegraph brings news about cases of vigilante justice against thieves, robbers, hooligans and other criminal elements . . . One might think that Russia has been brought temporarily to the

American prairie and that lynch-law has been granted citizenship by us.' Tsarist officialdom and educated opinion saw these practices as evidence of the barbarism and backwardness of the peasantry. 'Nothing is sacred,' complained one writer in 1912: 'There is anarchism, atheism, a complete decay of morals.'

In southern Europe vendettas and blood feuds were still common at the end of the century. Here a transgression of social custom, such as the refusal of a marriage, a brawl, the theft of property, disputes over land boundaries or flocks, or merely an insult offered, even in jest, to a leading villager, might be requited by the killing of the culprit by the rival clan or family, inaugurating a blood feud that could continue for decades until it was ended by the payment of blood-money. In the villages of the Mani peninsula in Greece families built high towers for their own protection, emerging to track down members of the rival family against whom they had declared a blood feud. Truces were concluded at harvest time, but as the feud continued whole families could be wiped out. On the small island of Corsica, between 1821 and 1852, no fewer than 4,300 murders were recorded by the French authorities as products of the vendetta. But despite the horrifying statistics, the blood feud was as much a way of regulating and ritualizing violence as a spur to spreading it. In Montenegro the offended family would formally appoint someone to exact revenge, an oath had to be sworn, and if the offender had committed a crime, the victim's family could seek ritual approval from his family to deal with him. Custom dictated who was to kill and be killed (normally the closest male relative of the most recent perpetrator). In Albania there was even a set of rules, the *Kanun Leke*, preserved in oral tradition until it was finally published in excerpts in 1913, that provided the regulations for murder in defence of clan honour. 'Spilled blood,' the code declared, 'must be met with spilled blood.'

The disorder created by such events increasingly brought down the wrath of the state. In England the practice of 'skimmington' was outlawed by the Highways Act of 1882, though in a few places it continued into the twentieth century. In Germany the last examples of *Haberfeldtreiben* took place in 1894; all the participants were arrested by the police. In the Balkans the state was less able to impose itself. Blood feuds increasingly spilled over into intercommunal violence, as Montenegrin families fought Albanian ones, while feuding declined among Serbs as the major families realized it was only helping their Ottoman overlords. In Corsica and southern Italy the state made some limited headway in controlling the violence, and the death rate from vendettas fell. However, in Sicily the blood feud took on a new and dangerous form in the 1860s as the landowners' private armies, disbanded by the new Italian state, were replaced by rival clans – the Mafia – who first worked to enforce the landowners' sanctions against their tenants, then drifted into protection rackets and other forms of criminality, and finally began to fight each other over the spoils. As long as the state was too weak to penetrate mountainous or remote areas like Albania, Catania, Corsica and the Mani, the blood feud and the vendetta continued to flourish.

Social conservatives who viewed the countryside as a haven of peace and tranquillity, morality and orderliness, were thus wide of the mark. Indeed, as Britain underwent a vast expansion of its towns and cities, the statistical record showed a steady decline in the rate of recorded acts of theft and violence until, as the *Criminal Register* noted in 1901, it was clear that there had been 'a great change in manners: the substitution of words without blows for blows with or without words; an approximation in the manners of different classes; a decline in the spirit of lawlessness.' The Bavarian Georg von Mayr (1841–1925) was the first to compile 'moral statistics', correlating food thefts with food prices, and soon states were issuing official criminal statistics in every part of Europe. Annual convictions for crimes against the person in Germany actually fell, from 369 in 1882–5 to 346 in 1914. Berlin, by far the largest city in Germany, experienced overall crime rates only just above the national average. In Wales, a country experiencing rapid industrial growth in the coalfields of the south and the slate-quarrying regions of the north, the rate of criminal indictments fell from one person per 845 in 1851 to one in 2,994 by 1899. Religion, self-discipline, temperance, improvements in living standards, and not least, education, all had an influence. The decline in crime, reported the British Home Secretary Sir William Harcourt (1827–1904) to Prime Minister Gladstone, was 'a bright and encouraging light on our social horizon'. The more urban and industrialized an area became, the more its overall crime rates tended to fall.

Nevertheless, criminals and crimes became the focus of growing public interest as legal reforms such as the Criminal Law Code of 1851 in Prussia, the French-influenced Criminal Law Code of 1863 in Italy, and many similar enactments, established trial by jury in open court, a gift to the newly emerging mass popular press towards the end of the century. Sensational murder trials began to make headlines, whether of the American homeopath Dr Hawley Crippen (1862–1910), found guilty of the murder of his wife and arrested on board a transatlantic liner with his young mistress, or of the former miller and repeat offender August Sternickel (1866–1913), executed in Frankfurt an der Oder in 1913 for strangling a farmer in the course of a robbery after a trial that made press headlines day after day. Readers were mesmerized by stories of fictional detectives, whether Dickens's Inspector Bucket in *Bleak House* (1852–3) or Dostoyevsky's Inspector Porfiry in *Crime and Punishment* (1866). England above all saw the rise of the fictional professional detective who worked independently from the police, notably Sherlock Holmes, the creation of Sir Arthur Conan Doyle (1859–1930); elsewhere, as in Germany, the primacy of the confession over circumstantial evidence in gaining a conviction made it more difficult to write a story based on the reading of clues, and the danger to authors of criticizing the police made it harder to write a story based on a civilian detective whose work constantly showed the police to be incompetent. To suit their largely middle-class readership these writers focused on middle-class crimes and criminals, or brought in exotic villains from foreign parts; the mundane criminality of the urban residuum was seldom thought worthy of their attention, as it had been of social novelists like Dickens or Vidocq. Parts of Europe's great cities remained dangerous for the respectable to visit, but contrary to the alarmist warnings of critics of urbanization, crime rates were steadily falling.

THE GREAT EXODUS

All through the nineteenth century, Europeans in their millions sought to escape from poverty and oppression by leaving the Continent for a new life overseas. Their motives were often mixed. The lure of American freedom, and the chance of acquiring land cheaply and farming it not just for subsistence but for profit, were irresistible to many whose future in Europe seemed bleak and without hope. Political persecution provided another motive, especially for the radicals and revolutionaries of 1848. Some 30,000 'forty-eighters' settled in what became known as the 'over-the-Rhine' neighbourhood of Cincinnati, Ohio, where they led violent protests at the visit of a papal emissary in 1853. Within Europe itself, London was the first port of call for revolutionaries of all stripes, from Karl Marx to Lajos Kossuth. They had been preceded by a wave of political émigrés from Poland following the uprising of 1831, though many of these settled in Paris. Polish nationalists played a part in the conflicts of 1848 in many European countries, fought in the American Civil War, and, more than most émigrés from other countries, refused to sever their links with their homeland. During the 1863 uprising a Polish Central Committee was formed in the United States to aid the insurgents. A characteristic figure was Julian Ursyn Niemcewicz (1758–1841), a revolutionary nationalist in the early 1790s who emigrated to the USA following the defeat of the

1795 Polish uprising. Niemcewicz returned to Poland after the Napoleonic invasion, and in 1817 wrote the first major Polish antisemitic tract, *The Year 3333, or an Incredible Dream*, in which he painted a horrifying portrait of a distant future in which his country was ruled by Jews. Published posthumously in 1858, its espousal of an elaborate conspiracy theory in which 'Judeo-Polonia' was already beginning to replace the social structures of the old Polish Commonwealth had a powerful influence on the emerging Polish nationalist right wing. During the relatively liberal 1820s, Niemcewicz served in a number of official capacities in the administration of Congress Poland, only to be forced into exile again after participating in the insurrection of 1831. Driven to despair by the setbacks he had experienced, he wrote shortly before his death that 'Everyone has a homeland; but the Pole only has a grave.' On his own grave in a suburb of Paris was inscribed the epitaph: 'And there, where tears are banished, he still shed Poland's tear'.

Political exiles continued to find their way to London or the USA, or in some cases Latin America, throughout the century, though never in such numbers again as in 1831 and 1848. But the major reason for leaving was economic. The most spectacular exodus was from Ireland. Between 1848 and 1855 the island's population fell from 8.5 to 6 million, and while much of the decline at the beginning of the period can be ascribed to the famine, the continuing fall, to under 4.5 million by the census of 1921, was almost entirely due to emigration. More than 700,000 had arrived on the British mainland by 1861, over 200,000 went to Canada, and 289,000 left for Australia (many of them to join in the gold rushes of the 1860s). But the bulk of the migrants found their way to the United States – more than three million in all between 1848 and 1921. By 1900 there were more Irish-born men and women living in the USA than in Ireland itself. They were not entirely destitute – between 1846 and 1851 the Irish withdrew over £1,200,000 from banks in gold, much of it to pay for the transatlantic passage – but many were funded by landlords eager to clear their estates, some had government subsidies, and a number were supported by family members already living in America. The average emigrant was a man in his mid-twenties. 'There are very few boys left on our side of the country,' wrote a woman in County Wicklow, south of Dublin, '. . . there will be few men soon, for they are pouring out in shoals to America.' Desperate families grouped together to raise funds. 'All we want is to get out of Ireland,' wrote one group: 'We must be better anywhere than here.'

If Ireland was the most spectacular case of a desperate people driven out of Europe by economic catastrophe, then Germany showed that the morcellization of landholdings, especially in the south-west, where partible inheritance prevailed, and the rapidly deepening crisis of the artisan trades as British industrial competition undercut them, could be almost as powerful. Some 21,500 people emigrated from the German Confederation in the 1820s, 140,000 in the 1830s and nearly 420,000 in the 1840s. The 'hungry forties' played a role here too, and between 1846 and 1857 well over a million people left Germany in the wake of the great agrarian crisis. The USA became more attractive after 1862 with the passage through Congress of the Homeland Act, which allowed settlers to fence off land for farming in the Midwest at little or no cost. News soon reached Europe. Another million people left Germany between 1864 and 1873, before the economic downturn of the 1870s made America less attractive. As the world economy recovered, around 1880, a fresh wave emigrated, with 1,800,000 Germans leaving the country by 1890, this time mostly from the impoverished north-east. As German industry expanded headlong in the 1890s, however, the possibilities of finding work inside the country soaked up most of the remaining emigration potential, so that between 1895 and 1913 a total of little more than half a million left the country. Still, between 1820 and 1914 well over five million Germans went to live in the USA; between 1820 and 1860 they constituted 31 per cent of all immigrants there, the second largest contingent after the Irish, and from 1861 to 1890, with nearly 29 per cent, the largest contingent of all.

A rather similar picture emerged in Scandinavia, where little land could be used for cultivation. More than half of the surface area of Sweden was covered in forest, while mountains and other unusable land covered three-quarters of the land area of Norway. In 1890 the US national census reported 800,000 people who identified themselves as Swedish-American. Some 150,000 Swedes left Europe in the 1860s, nearly 140,000 in the 1870s, 347,000 in the 1880s and over 180,000 in the 1890s. Initially driven to emigrate by famine, later on they were enticed over to America by relatives promising a better life and in many cases sending them funds to purchase their passage. This was a lucrative business for the shipping lines that took them to New York, usually via Hamburg or Bremen and Liverpool or Southampton, and the companies were soon advertising for custom in the major Swedish towns. Letters home describing the idyllic conditions on the Great Plains, where everyone was equal and there was no aristocracy as there was in Sweden, prompted whole communities to leave. Americans welcomed the Swedes as hard-working, law-abiding, orderly, sober and Protestant. As one Congregational minister wrote in 1885, Swedish immigrants 'do not seek the shelter of the American flag merely to introduce and foster among us ... socialism, nihilism, communism ... they are more like Americans than are any other foreign peoples'. Similar positive attitudes, combined with crop failures and a dearth of cultivable land, also encouraged some 800,000 Norwegians to emigrate to America and Canada between 1825 and 1900. Peaking at 188,000 in the 1880s, Norwegian emigration was higher as a proportion of the domestic population in the nineteenth century than that of Britain and Ireland – 971 per 100,000 in the 1880s, for example, compared to 608 per 100,000 at the height of the Irish emigration in the 1860s. Harsh climatic conditions and a major volcanic eruption in 1875 also drove 15,000 Icelanders to leave for North America between 1870 and 1900, out of a total population of 75,000, or around 20 per cent, an extraordinarily high proportion. Some 3 per cent of the entire population of the island emigrated in 1887 alone.

In Denmark, by contrast, where the land is flat and the summers are longer, and arable and pasture made up a majority of the land at the turn of the century – 75 per cent, as opposed to a mere 12 per cent in Sweden and 3 per cent in Norway – relatively few people decided to seek a better life overseas. Here the economy developed on the basis of the mechanization of food processing and a switch from grain to meat and dairy products. Danish butter and Danish bacon became major exports in this period. The Danish example was noted elsewhere: the Anglo-Irish agrarian reformer Horace Plunkett (1854–1932) exclaimed in 1908: 'I have always felt that Ireland as a second Denmark was no bad ideal for our reformers to set before them.' But rural Denmark enjoyed advantages that rural Ireland did not possess: an independent middling farmer community, a high level of education, a network of small rural banks, and lack of deep political or religious divisions. In Denmark farmers pooled their resources in co-operative dairies (from 1882), abattoirs (1887), egg-packing stations (1891), and bacon-producing plants (1887) – a development that did not take place in Ireland. By 1900 there were more bacon-producing co-operatives in Denmark than there were private enterprises. As a result of all this, emigration was very limited.

The pace of emigration from Austria-Hungary was steady, rising from 183,000 in the 1860s to 286,000 in the 1870s, 294,000 in the 1880s and 496,000 in the 1890s. As with other countries, there were also a substantial number of returnees, ranging from a sixth to a half of emigrants; thus in 1904, for example, while 101,000 people left Hungary, some 47,000 came back. From 1900 to 1914 over a million people were recorded as leaving the Habsburg Empire, the overwhelming majority of them bound for the USA, their numbers increased by an agreement signed by the Hungarian government with the Cunard Shipping Company in 1903. A contemporary commentator ascribed this high rate of emigration to 'the deplorable condition of the working classes, the long hours, low wages, and the lack of proper workmen's dwellings', as well as 'the methods of management of the large estates and the dearth of small holdings', though agricultural workers tended first of all to head for Germany, Russia or Romania rather than deciding to move overseas at the outset.

Emigration from Spain was also overwhelmingly economic in character. It was severely restricted until eased by a new law in 1853, but it was not until the 1880s that it became large in scale: 360,000 Spaniards left for the New World between 1882 and 1896. Figures for the decade 1904–15 show another 1.7 million crossing the Atlantic, 500,000 of them bound for Argentina. They came from Galicia, Asturias, Santander and the Canary Islands, all poor agricultural regions unable to feed their growing populations. On a smaller scale, Spanish migrants, most of them temporary, also left for north Africa, especially after the French colonization of Algeria in 1830, and for France, where there were 80,000 Spaniards living in 1900 and 105,000 by 1911. In 1907 recruiting agents even arrived in Málaga offering 'emigration with free passage to the State of Hawaii' for agricultural workers under the age of forty-five, and by 1914 some 7,735 mostly landless labourers had left, though the majority later moved on to California.

Russian emigration, which began on a large scale with Jews fleeing the pogroms that were initiated after the assassination of Tsar Alexander II in 1881, showed a mixture of political and economic motives. Tens of thousands left every year from this point on, with a total of nearly 800,000 from 1881 to 1890, 1.6 million between 1891 and 1900, and again 1.6 million between 1901 and 1910. No fewer than 868,000 people left in the years 1911 to 1914 alone. Crowded into the Pale of Settlement on the western side of the tsarist empire, the Jewish population sank into desperate poverty; a third were said to be living on welfare by the turn of the century. Following their expulsion from Moscow and a major famine in Russia in 1891–2, some 94,000 Russian citizens left for the USA through the ports of Bremen and Hamburg in 1891 alone, and another 70,000 the following year. Between 75 and 85 per cent of these migrants were Jewish, and they were followed after the turn of the century by many Old Believer sectarians fleeing the persecution visited upon them by an increasingly aggressive Orthodox government. One Old Believer sect, the Dukhobortsy, left en masse in 1900, when 7,500 of them made the journey to western Canada, where they aroused controversy by living in communes, rejecting education and practising nudism.

The final wave of European emigration overseas came from southern Italy, which remained mired in agrarian backwardness even after the turn of the century. Commercial agriculture was confined to the north, where there was sufficient capital to support mechanization and the use of chemical fertilizers. State grants for land reclamation, road-building, water supplies and the like became available after the turn of the century, but of the 869,800 acres improved in these various ways by 1915, only 5,680 were in the south. Northern farmers could benefit from the growth of the canning industries and sugar-beet refining. These changes barely affected southern Italy. Income per head in the south was only about half that of the north-west. Trapped in an unremitting cycle of poverty and backwardness, people in southern Italy began emigrating overseas in increasing numbers. At least 150,000 people left the country every year between 1898 and 1914, more than two-thirds of them from the south and a quarter from Sicily, and in some years the figure was much higher. No fewer than 873,000 emigrated in 1913 alone; the percentage of the entire population of Italy leaving the country increased from 0.6 in the 1880s, many of them northern Italians leaving for skilled jobs in other parts of Europe, to 1.8 between 1900 and 1913. With fast steamships guaranteeing a quick passage, around 40 per cent of these emigrants came back between 1897 and 1906, and by 1913 this figure had risen to 66 per cent. Most of them were young, unskilled rural labourers, but a portion of these returned to Argentina or the United States more than once, and overall it has been estimated that around one and a half million Italians emigrated permanently in the first decade of the twentieth century. When Prime Minister Giuseppe Zanardelli (1826–1903) visited Moliterno in the southern region of Basilicata, the first Italian head of government ever to do so, he was shocked to be greeted by the local mayor 'on behalf of the eight thousand people in this commune, three thousand of whom are in America and the other five thousand preparing to follow them'.

Almost no part of Europe was exempt from this massive exodus. Nearly a sixth of the entire population of Greece emigrated between 1890 and 1914, either to America or to Egypt. European states with overseas empires, from Britain and France to Portugal and the Netherlands, also witnessed extensive waves of emigration. The major exception was France, where the low birth rate and the security of land tenure kept people in the home country. Altogether some 60 million people are thought to have left Europe between 1815 and 1914: 34 million for the USA, 4 million for Canada, and maybe a million for Australia and New Zealand. Between 1857 and 1940, 7 million Europeans left for Argentina, and between 1821 and 1945, 5 million for Brazil. Altogether over a quarter of the natural increase in population in western Europe between 1841 and 1915 was absorbed by emigration, with a net population loss of 35 million people.

As a result, the world balance of population was beginning to change. At mid-century the population of the USA was not much larger than that of Britain, the same as that of France, and a little less than the area covered by the future German Empire. By the eve of the First World War the USA was well ahead, with a total population of more than 92 million. Yet Europe's share of world population actually increased over most of this period, from 22 per cent in 1850 to around 25 per cent in 1900 (for comparison, its share by the early twenty-first century was around 10 per cent). Overall the population of Europe increased from 188 million in 1800 to 458 million in 1914, and this increase formed the major driving force behind the massive emigration waves of the century. Within this global figure, there were marked contrasts between different areas and different countries. Russia's population expanded by 300 per cent, partly because of the conquest and incorporation under the tsar's rule of large areas of Central Asia, the Caucasus and Siberia. The population of Great Britain grew by a remarkable 400 per cent, that of Italy and Spain by nearly 100 per cent. France's population, by contrast, grew slowly, by only 50 per cent.

This vast human replenishing of the earth was the social dimension of a process of globalization that reached its peak in the years immediately preceding the outbreak of the First World War, as capital, goods, people and ideas began to flow with increasing rapidity and intensity from continent to continent. More rapid communications boosted trade and reduced the price gaps of commodities between Europe and the USA as well as Europe and Asia by a half or three-quarters in the period 1870–1914. Investment overseas, dominated by Europe during this period, accounted for 32 per cent of the net national wealth of Britain in 1913. Foreign investment reached nearly 20 per cent of domestic savings in France by 1900. Much of this was in other European countries (60 per cent in the French case, 53 per cent in the German) but capital also flowed overseas, with 21 per cent of British foreign investment going to America in the period 1870–1913 and 16 per cent of German foreign investment (the same figure as for German investment in Latin America, only slightly below the British figure). Technology transfer took place on every level and in virtually every industry, with America increasingly the innovator in new industries such as motor manufacture. This was the first age of globalization, one in which Europe remained the dominant force. This fact was reflected in the particular intensity with which European countries developed ties with their formal and informal colonies in Africa, Asia, Australasia and Latin America.

The results could be seen at the most prosaic levels of everyday life by 1914. If the great department stores that sprang up in Europe's cities in the last quarter of the nineteenth century prided themselves on offering for sale goods from all over the world, then small retailers also sold imported commodities, most notably of course tea and coffee, but also tropical fruit, spices, tobacco, rice, cane sugar, and much more besides. In Germany the term 'colonial wares' came to denote such exotic imports, and some retail outlets devoted themselves exclusively to their sale. Overseas trade lent a cosmopolitan character to a substantial portion of the bourgeoisie. Most of the larger trading houses in Liverpool trained apprentices sent to them from merchant firms in other countries, including Latin America as well as Germany and France. In the 1870s there were said to be in Hamburg 'dozens of older gentlemen who knew "every town on the Mississippi" from personal experience and had been "twenty times in London"', but who had never visited Berlin at all. By the end of the century, too, professionals of most kinds were participating in international congresses and associations, exchanging ideas and practices across national boundaries. Political exiles, the printing press, the telegraph and finally the radio aided the transmission of ideas between continents. Socialists, feminists and others came to regard themselves as part of global movements of political emancipation that had their international congresses and conferences too. All these developments were summed up and symbolized in the great World Fairs inspired by the example of London's Great Exhibition of 1851. Just two years later New York held an Exhibition of the Industry of All Nations, complete with its own Crystal Palace, and in 1876 it was Philadelphia's turn to host a World's Fair, followed by Chicago in 1893, with many others held in a variety of European and other American states. If Britain had advertised itself as the workshop of the world in 1851, by 1914 it was clear that it was no longer alone.

Well before the outbreak of the First World War, Europe had undergone a social revolution of major dimensions, but of a very different kind from that imagined by Marx or Bakunin. Alongside the political transformations that had convulsed the Continent between 1848 and 1871, the relations between classes had also been transformed, though over a longer period. The traditional landowning aristocracy had been undermined by the forces of economic change, by political reforms such as the abolition of serfdom, by the advent of elected legislatures, however limited their powers, by the ending of corporate privileges such as those that had sustained the Baltic nobility earlier in the century, and by the increasing wealth and ambition of the business, banking and professional classes. A new, hybrid social elite had emerged, based on bourgeois values of thrift, hard work, sobriety and responsibility. These values had come to dominate society and politics in large parts of Europe, finding their expression in urban renewal, sanitation and hygiene, agricultural improvement, penal reform, and the attempt, not always successful, to impose order on the criminal or semi-criminal underworld. They percolated down in various forms to the petty bourgeoisie and the respectable working class, however much their politics may have differed from those of doctors, lawyers, teachers, or businessmen. This was a very different social world from that which emerged from the upheavals of the French Revolutionary and Napoleonic Wars. It was also one, as we shall now see, that had a major, and not always positive, impact on the natural environment that surrounded it.

5

The Conquest of Nature

TAMING THE WILD

In 1835 the poet Bertalan Szemere (1812–69), a liberal Hungarian nobleman interested in improving the condition of his native land, decided to travel through Europe to discover what people living in other countries were like and find out something of their knowledge of his homeland. Szemere was well-read and had a gift for languages, speaking English, French, German and Italian. He kept a diary of his travels and published it on his return, in 1840. His first encounter with foreign ignorance about Hungary occurred almost as soon as he left. At the Bohemian town of Teplice he was forced to listen to a Czech police sergeant as he pontificated to his family about the backwardness of Hungary:

'Oh, and it is dangerous to travel there in wintertime,' he continued, 'as one comes across wild beasts all over the place. Bears, for example.' 'In our country, bears sleep all through the winter,' I replied, thinking that now I had caught the old fellow. But that was not the case at all. 'Ha-ha-ha-,' he laughed, 'what, the bears? In the winter? I know they do not! They keep jumping through the snow, like young lambs!' 'Bears!' his wife and children exclaimed, and all of a sudden they stared at me tactlessly. I flattered myself that they took pity on me, since I lived in such a horrible country. 'Yes,' the father began again, 'and wolves. Sometimes you have no fewer than twelve chasing the poor soldier who delivers the mail. Surely many of them end up being unfortunate, since the wolves maul the horses, and the next day, only the boots are to be found. Once I was returning from Galicia on a sledge, and they chased me, and the only way to get rid of them was to slice up the kitbag and throw it away slice by slice . . . In the winter, it is excessively cold . . . and it is also tremendously snowy. The mountains, the forests are all white, and in the villages, one cannot see the houses – the poor residents are all stuck inside, as they cannot open their snow-jammed doors.'

Consciously proud of being Hungarian and anxious to rebut this calumny, the traveller ventured hesitantly to remark that the snow in his native land was no deeper than it was in Bohemia, and yet ' "people walk on the roads here in the winter." "Yes," the sergeant replied with great satisfaction, "because here we clear the snow away from the roads once a day." ' Alas, Szemere was obliged to admit to himself ('although I did not say it out loud'), 'we do not do it in our country. But we know that it is not out of laziness, but from our acceptance of Providence. The Lord gives us cold and snow in the winter, which keeps it, and the Lord sends heat in the spring, which melts it.'

Hoping, perhaps, for a less ignorant and more positive view of his native land, Szemere made his way from Bohemia to the north-west, into Prussia. But he encountered the same prejudices there too. 'Hungary,' he was told firmly, 'is a very fertile land and it is abundant in things that grow naturally, but the country is deserted. In its forests wild beasts are present in such large numbers as tame animals are in other lands . . . Its uncultivated deserts are teeming with groups of bandits, its swamps make the air unpleasant and the heat is like in Italy . . . Darkness prevails, the country is inhabited by helots and lords.' The further west he travelled, the less people knew. All that his French interlocutors had to say about Hungary was that there were a lot of bandits there. In Britain he encountered absolute and total ignorance; people knew nothing about the country at all except that it produced a sweet wine called Tokay. Despite the depression these views engendered in him, Szemere tried to make the best of the situation. Thus he gave the Hungarians' close relationship to nature a patriotic interpretation, claiming it gave rise to a strong spirit of freedom. He appreciated London because of its huge parks, where nature could roam freely. He admired the artist John Constable (1776–1837) because of his realistic landscape paintings, where instinct and wildness could be seen, in contrast to the academicism of French painters. Rather than depicting Classical themes, the English painted the nature of their own country. This was what gave them their spirit of freedom, a spirit that Szemere wanted to emulate in Hungary, where politics were corrupted by money and oppressed by the rule of the Habsburgs. Other liberal reformers in Hungary disagreed, seeing in the country's closeness to nature a sign of its backwardness. István Gorove (1819–91), one of the leading figures in liberal politics, observed in 1846 that 'the wild man lives within the thicket of the forests as he wishes, but the one that moves to the city must accustom himself to the ones he lives amongst. That is our situation in Europe.' Like many others, Gorove considered that Hungary had to become more civilized and more European, a view given practical expression by another liberal reformer, István Széchenyi, in his enterprise of smuggling industrial machinery out of England.

Szemere's commitment to natural freedom led him to become involved in the 1848 Revolution as Prime Minister of the liberal nationalist government. After the Hungarian surrender, determined to keep the crown of St Stephen, the orb and sceptre and other royal regalia out of the hands of the victorious Habsburgs, he buried them on 23 August 1849 at Orşova in the Banat region, leaving a runic sign on a nearby tree. (The regalia were dug up in 1853 by the imperial army after the burial spot had been betrayed by one of Szemere's associates.) From Orşova he crossed the border in secret to Turkey and made his way to Paris and then London. In 1851 he was sentenced to death *in absentia* in Hungary by the Habsburg authorities. Szemere bitterly resented the centralizing rule of post-revolutionary Vienna in the 1850s. 'Estates formerly flourishing are now . . . melting away under a crushing weight of taxation.' Yet closeness to nature and an appreciation of the freedoms it bestowed made Hungary, as he told Lord Palmerston, 'the natural channel by which western civilization must flow into those eastern countries'.

Szemere's wife, Leopoldina Jurkovich (1829–65), whom he had married in 1846, joined him in exile with their first child; a second was born in 1850 but died within two months; two more followed, in 1858 and 1859 respectively, and survived. Plagued by financial difficulties for most of his life, Szemere faced ruin in 1856 when an exiled Hungarian fraudster who had gained his confidence in Paris swindled him out of the savings that had been rescued from Hungary by his wife. He tried to earn some money by exporting Hungarian wine, but it had all turned to vinegar by the time it reached Paris. He quarrelled with the other Hungarian exiles, publicly condemning Lajos Kossuth for selfishly aiming to found a quasi-royal dynasty of his own in Hungary. Isolated and impoverished, Szemere began to feel disoriented and despondent, suffered from frequent headaches, and was plagued by nightmares about the swindler who had robbed him of his money. 'I cannot work and read,' he wrote in his diary in 1856. 'There are many plans echoing in my head. Yet I cannot bring myself to carry them through. This is a huge problem.' Szemere's diary entries became progressively briefer and less coherent, and ended altogether in January 1862. He had a severe mental breakdown in 1863, losing all self-control and descending into bouts of unbridled anger, during one of which, towards the end of 1864, he attacked his family physically in the middle of the night. With his wife's help, Szemere successfully petitioned the Habsburg emperor Franz Joseph for an amnesty and he returned to Hungary in January 1865, but was in a mental asylum by April. His outbursts of rage grew more frequent and intense up to his death four years later. After confronting claims that his country was unable to control its nature, he ended his days by being unable to control his own, losing altogether the veneer of civilization and descending into raw emotion.

In doing so, Szemere seemed to confirm European prejudices about the state of nature in which Hungarians were widely thought to exist. The countryside was full of wild men and bandits. In 1883, Baedeker's guide-book warned its German readers that 'the traveller in some of the more remote districts . . . may still be exposed to the risk of a predatory attack'. It was no accident that both Jules Verne (1828–1905) in *The Carpathian Castle* (1893) and Bram Stoker (1847–1912) in *Dracula* (1897) set their novels about the supernatural fusion of the human and the animal in the vicinity of Braşov, a town in Hungarian Transylvania. But nature was a commanding, dominating, all-pervasive presence not merely in Hungary but also in large parts of the rest of Europe in the nineteenth century. Vast amounts of land were wild and uncultivated. In 1815 a survey of land use in Prussia revealed that just over a quarter of the land was set aside for crops and a fifth for pasturage. The rest, some 55 per cent, consisted of mountains, forests and wilderness. Over the century, under the pressure of population growth, this situation gradually changed. The amount of land under arable cultivation in Prussia doubled between 1805 and 1864; it increased in Romania between 1860 and 1905 from 6.1 to 13.6 million acres; and in Spain some 9.9 million acres of land were newly brought under cultivation between 1818 and 1860. But this process had its limits, especially in the early decades of the century. In Bohemia it was reckoned that arable land increased by a fifth between the 1780s and the 1840s, but even by the latter period it still made up less than half the surface area of the province. In the first half of the century, the area under the plough in European Russia increased by more than 50 per cent, but even in the 1860s four-fifths of the land surface of the tsar's European domains were left uncultivated.

The wildernesses of Europe were inhabited by a variety of dangerous animals. Wolves, as Szemere's Czech interlocutor indicated, were the most feared. Normally avoiding human society, they were liable to attack people if driven by hunger or desperation. Official statistics recorded that around two hundred people were eaten by wolves every year in Russia through most of the century; between 1870 and 1887 the total came to nearly 1,500 altogether. In the Hungarian county of Temes wolf packs were reported entering farmyards in the early 1890s to steal sheep. Up to 1900 and beyond, wolf-hunting was a legal duty in Sweden. Wolf packs roamed parts of Spain, Italy, Portugal, France and the Balkans, above all in mountainous regions such as the Pyrenees or the Apennines; their numbers had increased in many areas during the disorders of the French Revolutionary and Napoleonic Wars. One wolf in Poland, it was reported in 1817, was 'accustomed, during the late campaigns, to live upon the dead bodies of soldiers', and so developed a taste for human rather than animal flesh; a forester eventually shot the wolf after it approached to eat his two-year-old child, whom he had fastened to a tree as bait. As order was restored in France after the end of the wars, hunting resumed, with 1,500 wolves killed each year during the 1820s. Wolves were still being hunted in the Morvan, the Vosges, Brittany and other parts of France in the 1890s. By the end of the century, however, wolves had been driven back to small pockets of marginal wilderness in most of western and central Europe, hunted almost to extinction; unlike foxes, they did not learn to adapt to urban life, and it was only in Russia and the far north that they remained widespread.

By this time, more or less continual hunting had eliminated a wide variety of wild animals from many parts of Europe. Bears, native to mountainous districts of the Continent, were hunted to extinction by Alpine farmers, who blamed them for killing their sheep. By the later part of the century bears were present only in the uplands of southern Europe, the Balkans, and above all in Russia and Finland, in both of which countries they were adopted as the national symbol. Bear-hunting was possible only in very remote areas; Count József Potocki (1862–1922), an aristocratic Polish landowner in Volhynia, had to travel to northern Russia to bag the female bear and three cubs whose stuffed forms were adorning his landing when the English naturalist Richard Lydekker (1849–1915) visited him early in the twentieth century. Brown bears were regularly captured, trained and exhibited as 'dancing bears', especially in Russia, and the zoo-owner and animal dealer Carl Hagenbeck (1844–1913) is said to have offered a thousand bears for sale between 1866 and 1886. His nephew Willy Hagenbeck (1884–1965) possessed a troupe of seventy polar bears and taught them to build a pyramid, a feat he achieved through the ruthless employment of whips, truncheons and starvation to make the reward of meat more enticing for the animals if they succeeded.

By this time town-dwellers were exhibiting a growing sympathy for the bear across Europe. The Alps, complained a tongue-in-cheek article in a Swiss satirical magazine in 1889, would lose 'part of their wonderful mysterious charm' if the bears became extinct. 'Why kill the educable and harmless bear, who is greedy, if at all, for a calf or a cow? He should be trained and employed as a tour guide – then all parties would benefit, and our Switzerland would again boast something novel and unique that diverges mightily from the same old bear hunts found elsewhere!' The bourgeois public, indeed, was beginning to grow fond of the bear. As the director of the Berlin zoo, Ludwig Heck (1860–1951), noted, the bear 'serves as a caricature of mankind, as our own distorted reflection', especially when it stood on its hind legs or ate clutching food with its front paws. The public, said Heck, loved bears 'as much as they did monkeys' – an affection not, it seems, reciprocated by the bears, one of which had bitten off the tips of the first two fingers on Heck's left hand earlier in his career. The domestication of the bear reached a new intimacy after the turn of the century, by which time children in well-off households could play with little clockwork dancing bears, or go to sleep cuddling a teddy bear. The soft toy was invented in America in 1902 in response to an incident in which President 'Teddy' Roosevelt (1858–1919) had refused to shoot a bear that had been cornered, clubbed and tied to a tree for him to dispatch. Teddy bears were soon afterwards being manufactured in their thousands by the Steiff Company in Germany, their origins in the wild entirely forgotten.

Keeping wild animals such as bears in or near princely domiciles became increasingly impractical. The English Royal Menagerie, located in the Tower of London, contained 280 animals at the end of the eighteenth century, but the collection shrank thereafter, with the last of the animals being relocated to Regent's Park in 1835 after one of the lions had tried to eat a soldier. By the late nineteenth century, though many noblemen and royal families kept deer parks and stocked them with a variety of animals – Count Potocki for example kept American bison on his estate – royal menageries had become very rare. Perhaps the only modern menagerie was the collection begun by Ferdinand of Sachsen-Coburg-Gotha (1861–1948), who became ruling prince of Bulgaria in 1887 and almost immediately had a large cage built in his palace park to hold a black vulture. This was soon joined in various parts of the grounds by other animals, including, more practically, cows to supply Ferdinand with fresh milk every day. In 1893 the menagerie opened its gates to the public three days a week, and soon it displayed such exotic creatures as a Tibetan yak and a Mississippi alligator. The cowshed was converted into a house for two African lions. The menagerie was on its way to becoming a zoo.

As urbanization continued apace, so more and more people's familiarity with the wild vanished and had to be recreated in public displays. Animal exhibitions could reflect a scientific mission. But they also reminded people of humankind's mastery over nature. In the late 1830s the young Queen Victoria went six times to Drury Lane to see the show of the celebrated American lion tamer Isaac Van Amburgh (1811–65), whose speciality was putting his head into a lion's mouth. Van Amburgh reportedly achieved his mastery over lions with the liberal use of an iron crowbar during training. But even in zoos, where such blatant cruelty was less common, the average lifespan of a large carnivore, confined within a tiny, cramped cage, was only two years at this time. Some zoos had an overtly economic function. The Jardin Zoologique d'Acclimatation in the Bois de Boulogne, for example, was founded in 1860 in order to domesticate, breed and sell useful animals like angora goats, llamas and alpacas. With 5,000 animals on display, it attracted a quarter of a million visitors in the 1860s, but during the siege of Paris by the Prussians in 1870–1 most of the animals were eaten by hungry Parisians.

The first zoo in Poland was opened in 1871 for indisputably commercial purposes. It was set up by a restaurant owner in the back garden of his establishment in Prussian-ruled Poznań in order to attract customers; in 1883 it moved to a 13-acre site; by 1907 it was displaying 900 animals and a quarter of a million people were visiting it each year. The first giraffe arrived in Budapest in 1868, bought from a German menagerie and displayed along with many other animals on a 40-acre site within the city's botanical garden. The zoo, founded two years previously, was a scientific initiative from the beginning, and it was run at various times either by a learned society or by the municipality. Zoos could also boast a nation's global reach. In 1826 the Zoological Society of London was established by Sir Stamford Raffles (1781–1826) and Sir Humphry Davy (1778–1829) and began planning a zoological garden in Regent's Park. Raffles was a senior East India Company official and founder of Singapore. He believed that though 'richer than any other country in the extent and variety of [her] possessions', Britain did not have any forum for displaying the animals that inhabited the large areas of the globe under British rule. In addition Raffles intended London's Zoological Garden to demonstrate the organizational and scientific principles that he believed underpinned British control over the empire. He did not live to see his dream realized. London Zoo opened to members of the Society two years after Raffles died, in 1828, and to the general public in 1847.

Attitudes to animals were changing. During the nineteenth century the urban bourgeoisie moved increasingly to outlaw the cruel sports that were popular in rural areas. In England the spectacle of bear-baiting, in which a bear was tied to a stake and attacked by dogs, was outlawed along with cockfighting in 1835, as a result of lobbying by the Society for the Prevention of Cruelty to Animals, founded in 1824. But the Cruelty to Animals Act of 1835 did not cover wild animals, so badger-baiting continued to the end of the century and beyond. 'This singular creature,' according to the *Field Book* of 1833, 'is able to resist repeated attacks both of men and dogs, from all quarters, till, being overpowered with numbers, and enfeebled by many desperate wounds, it is at last obliged to yield.' Digging badgers out of their setts was another popular pastime. 'A day spent in the woods or on the hillside badger-digging in the company of gamekeepers, woodmen and others of that ilk is a good day,' wrote another country commentator. 'The only method by which any British wild animal can be preserved from extinction in this age of what is termed progress,' opined the Liberal politician Sir Alfred Pease (1857–1939) in the first monograph devoted entirely to badgers, 'is to hunt it.'

As fox hunting grew in popularity with the rural landowning classes in England, foxes became scarce, so that by the middle of the century more than a thousand fox cubs were being imported every year from Holland, Germany and France, to be sold on at Leadenhall Market in London to fox hunters for release into the wild. In some areas the hunt rescued the fox from the hounds once they had run it to ground, and released it later for another hunt; one well-known fox in Devon had been caught thirty-six times by hounds trained not to kill or injure the quarry. Fox hunting – 'the unspeakable in full pursuit of the uneatable', as Oscar Wilde (1854–1900) memorably described it – survived into a less aristocratic age, whereas purely noble pastimes such as falconry more or less died out, because the hunts managed to extend themselves down the social scale to include gentlemen farmers and country squires while falconry did not. On the European Continent the system of serfdom had reserved hunting rights to aristocratic landowners, but after 1815, where Napoleonic Law had taken root, on the left bank of the Rhine, northern Italy or France itself, only the most limited of the hunting privileges swept away by the Revolution were restored, and they were hedged about with numerous restrictions. In areas still under traditional feudal law the strength of popular feeling on the issue was indicated by the fact that 13 per cent of all the petitions handed in to the Prussian legislature in 1848 were demands for the abolition of hunting privileges. It was in that year that hunting rights were given to landowners (including peasant farmers) exclusively on their own land, in a series of measures that were not rescinded even in the post-revolutionary reaction of the 1850s.

In Spain the staging of bullfights as a form of aristocratic pastime had already been democratized in the eighteenth century with the introduction of matadors on foot and the construction of dedicated stadia. By the end of the nineteenth century the bullfight had gained a huge popular following across Spain, becoming the nation's leading spectator sport. Criticisms from British and European animal-lovers had no effect. In any case there was nothing unusual about the Spanish habit of killing animals for sport. Hunting as a mark of status became one of the principal pursuits of Europe's wealthy elite in the late nineteenth century, carefully staged and organized on special estates where animals and birds were reared for the sole purpose of being shot. Edward VII (1841–1910) was such a passionate hunter that already as Prince of Wales he had the clocks on his Norfolk estate of Sandringham kept half an hour early so he could have more daylight hours in which to shoot pheasants and partridges. The birds were held in sanctuaries on the estate, where buckwheat and mustard were planted for them to eat. Released when adult, some 7,000 birds were shot every year. An entry in the carefully recorded 'game book' at Sandringham recorded that 725 partridges were shot on 7 November 1907. Such feats were made easier as breech-loaders replaced muzzle-loaders, and driving game towards the guns replaced walking it up with dogs. At Balmoral, the British royal family's Scottish estate, stags were the game, and eighty to ninety were killed each year. As a contemporary remarked, Edward, as Prince of Wales, shot his first stag on 21 September 1858 when he was sixteen: 'It is not difficult to imagine the elation which the boy must have felt . . . A throne might await him, and an empire's love, but that supreme moment could never be repeated.'

Still, there were also other, more exotic thrills to be had for the prince. On a visit to Ceylon before his accession to the throne, he was taken on an elephant-shooting party. He waited for five hours, with his elephant gun at the ready, on a high stand surrounded by a stockade that had taken 1,500 men two weeks to build, until the wild elephants, stampeded by beaters who had set fire to part of the forest, came charging towards him. Despite the size of the targets, he only managed to wound two of the beasts. The prince set off on foot through the jungle with his retinue until he found a wounded elephant and shot it dead. Clambering on top of the mountainous corpse, he was handed a large knife with which he cut off the tail, the customary trophy on such expeditions. In India he killed a pregnant tigress with four cubs, taking four shots to finish the animal off. Edward VII's hunting exploits were by no means untypical of those of the wealthy men of his day. The Archduke Franz Ferdinand of Austria is said to have killed around 300,000 animals in his lifetime, including deer, bears, tigers, elephants, crocodiles, and many more, with the double-barrelled Mannlicher rifles he had specially made for his own use. He had a well-deserved reputation as a crack shot, and on one wild-boar hunt staged by Kaiser Wilhelm II he shot dead fifty-nine of the sixty boars that were let out of the pen. Shortly before his assassination in 1914, Franz Ferdinand recorded with satisfaction the killing of his three-thousandth stag. There could be no more striking demonstration of man's superiority over nature.

Yet at the same time the upper classes across Europe were beginning to try and recreate wild nature on their own estates, at least as far as their flora went. Landscaping with a carefully designed natural effect had been in vogue ever since the decline of the formal garden began in the eighteenth century. Under the influence of the English horticulturalist Gertrude Jekyll (1843–1932), who created over four hundred gardens in Britain, on the Continent and in the United States, large, densely planted herbaceous borders, wildflower beds and artfully designed alternations of colour and texture replaced the picturesque garden of the early part of the century, with its artificial bridges, follies, ruins and statues. The idea was for a garden to look natural, even untidy, following the precepts of the Irish originator of the 'wild garden', William Robinson (1838–1935), and to create, as it were, a superior, denser, more colourful, more natural version of nature itself. Yet the idea of preserving nature in the wild had not yet taken root. Across the globe, animals, fish and birds were hunted without hesitation whether they were useful or not. The collection and display of the eggs of rare birds became a cherished and highly competitive pastime. The eggs of the great auk were said to fetch a price equivalent to a whole year's wages for a skilled worker. Eggers drove the great auk, a large flightless seabird rather like a northern version of the penguin, to extinction, aided and abetted by collectors who wanted specimens of the adult bird for taxidermy and display. The last great auk in the British Isles was captured by fishermen in July 1844, who kept the unfamiliar bird alive for three days until a storm blew up, upon which they beat it to death, believing it to have summoned up the tempest by witchcraft. At the same time the last European specimen altogether was killed on Eldey, an island off the Icelandic coast, on the commission of a collector, accompanying other creatures such as the Portuguese ibex (1892), the Sardinian lynx (c. 1900) and the Eurasian wild horse (1909) into extinction.

MASTERING THE ELEMENTS

Nature in nineteenth-century Europe posed major challenges in other ways too. Great mountain ranges cut one part of Europe off from another: the Pyrenees, separating France from Spain; the Alps, dividing Italy from France, Switzerland, Germany and Austria; the Scandinavian Mountains, dividing Norway from Sweden; and the Carpathians, stretching for nearly a thousand miles along the borders of Poland and the Ukraine on the one side, and Slovakia, Romania and Hungary on the other. With the highest peaks rising to around 8,000 feet in the Carpathians and the Scandinavian Mountains, 11,000 feet in the Pyrenees, and more than 15,000 feet in the Alps, these were vast extents of wilderness. On the lower slopes nomadic shepherds grazed their flocks in the summer, and villagers huddled in snowbound settlements cut off from the outside for months on end in the winter, keeping warm by living with their animals and consuming pickled or preserved food left over from the summer. At a maximum height of around 7,000 feet, the Apennines, running down the central spine of Italy, and the Balkan Mountains, which shadowed them along the north-eastern coast of the Adriatic, were all below the regional snowline, but they posed scarcely less effective barriers to communication.

Mountain crossings had been in use for many centuries, but it was Napoleon who took the initiative in constructing paved roads across the major Alpine passes to aid the movement of troops and supplies, though, as in other mountain ranges, these were closed for long periods during the winter. Mountains themselves posed another of nature's challenges to human mastery: conquering them became a sport, pioneered by the English High Court judge Sir Alfred Wills (1828–1912), who climbed the Wetterhorn in 1854, leading to the founding of the Alpine Club three years later. In 1865, Edward Whymper (1840–1911) led a party of climbers up the Matterhorn for the first time; they reached the summit in triumph, but at the cost of four men's lives. Local guides such as the Swiss wood-carver Melchior Anderegg (1828–1914) made a living out of conducting parties up major peaks; but the sport remained above all the province of the British upper and middle classes. Less spectacular but far more popular was the new sport of skiing, brought to the Harz Mountains and the Black Forest by young Norwegians studying at universities in Germany. The locals saw them 'as a blend of madman and clown' as they sped down the gentle slopes, but the sport extended to the Alps when resorts like Davos and St Moritz, initially favoured for their dry mountain air, opened in the winter, benefiting from new road and rail connections completed in the 1880s. By the turn of the century ski clubs were coming into existence, with their members teaching local residents to use skis and claiming that the acquisition of this skill 'transformed local life' and 'afforded an enormous extension of liberty to the mountain dwellers'.

Throughout this period much of the uncultivated area of Europe below the Arctic tree line was covered in dense forest. The situation of England, where only 5 per cent of the land was wooded by the late nineteenth

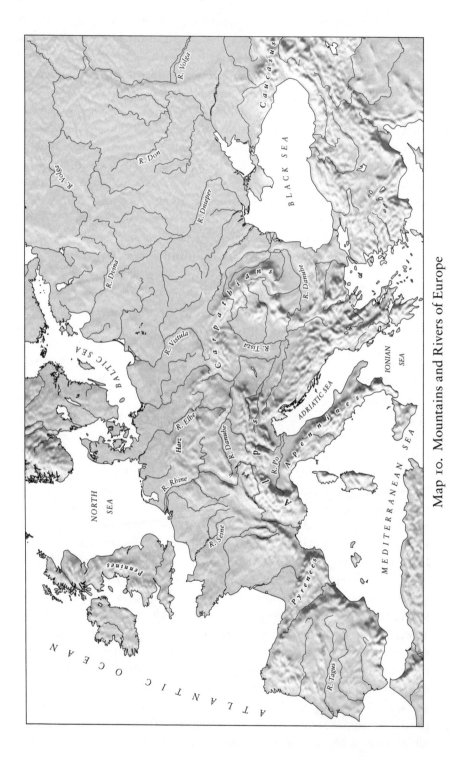

Map 10. Mountains and Rivers of Europe

century, had no real parallel in the rest of Europe. Even in the early twentieth century around two-thirds of Norway and Sweden, a third of Austria, Bohemia and Moravia, Russia and the Balkans, more than a quarter of Germany, just under a quarter of Poland, nearly a fifth of France and Belgium and a sixth of Switzerland was covered in forest. Only where there were major arable areas producing wheat and other farm produce for export was the forest smaller, as in Hungary, with its 11 per cent of woodland, Holland with 7 per cent, or Denmark with a mere 5 per cent covered in trees. Once a traveller passed beyond the inhabited and exploited margins of these vast forests into their inner depths, the civilized and semi-civilized world were left far behind. The folk tales collected by the German nationalists Jacob and Wilhelm Grimm were often set in the woods: Hansel and Gretel, the woodcutter's children, are taken deep into the forest to be abandoned by their wicked stepmother, who does not want to feed them since times are hard; Little Red Riding Hood is trailed by the wolf when she goes through the woods to see her grandmother; the wicked queen tells a servant to take Snow White into the depths of the forest to kill her, only to be frustrated by a hidden community of dwarfs unknown to human society. At the same time, however, the forest could also be a place of freedom, where escaped serfs or wrongdoers fleeing justice might find refuge amid natural resources rich enough to live off. Polish nationalist rebels in 1830 and again later on in the century fled from avenging Cossacks into its depths. The forest was, wrote the conservative critic of the urban-industrial world, Wilhelm Heinrich Riehl, 'the heartland of folk culture' in Germany, 'so that a village without a forest is like a town without any historical buildings, theatre or art galleries'.

The forests, however, were under constant threat. At the forest's edge peasants cut down trees and branches to use for building, firewood, or the making of implements, carts and other artefacts. In Russia it was calculated that on average the wooden huts in which peasants lived had to be completely rebuilt every fifteen years since there was no effective way of preserving the timber from weathering and disintegration. Most towns and cities were also built of wood, and in Minsk alone it was estimated in the middle of the century that more than 600,000 trees had to be felled to build or restore the 8,000 houses and other buildings that fell into disrepair in an average year. Each of the 500 barges that plied Russia's rivers took 500 trees to construct. Logging became a major industry: around 1900 more than 2 million tons of logs were being exported from Russia to Britain, Germany and the Netherlands every year. Warfare could speed up the process still further. Huge areas of timber were cut down along the Bulgarian and Serbian frontiers during the Turkish wars of the

1870s and 1880s, and trees were felled in Spain during the Peninsular and Carlist Wars to remove hiding places from brigands.

Altogether nineteenth-century Europe saw one of the greatest processes of deforestation to have taken place so far. Agronomists began to recognize that the destruction of forests led to soil erosion and even climate change. In 1836 the Russian ethnographer Vadim Vasilevich Passek (1808–42) complained that 'according to the observations of old-timers, the climate of Kharkov province . . . has become more severe, and it is now exposed to more droughts and frosts. It is likely that this change has come about because of the destruction of forests.' With trees gone, water erosion caused by rain or by melting snow began to open up fissures in the steppe. One ravine that appeared near the home of the Aksakov family in the Samara district of south-eastern Russia was one and a half miles long and 140 feet wide. By the 1890s dust storms were said to be 'terrible' in southern Russia, especially in the spring. Within little over half a century, it was estimated in 1890, Italy had lost between 4 and 5 million acres of woodland. Altogether Europe's forests declined by 25 per cent between 1700 and 1850 and by another 5 per cent between 1850 and 1920. Large areas of the Vosges and the Upper Saône valley had been denuded to provide timber for shipyards, while woodlands around Paris, Lyon and other large cities were felled. By the 1830s French travellers were writing of the lower slopes of the Pyrenees and the Alps as 'landscapes of desolation' showing a 'terrible nudity of bare and sterile rocks'. 'In fifty years from this date,' wrote the French economist Adolphe Blanqui (1798–1854) in 1843, 'France will be separated from Savoy by a desert.'

Only towards the end of the century did the increasing use of coal as fuel and iron and steel for buildings and implements begin to slow down the rate of deforestation. In Russia agricultural societies began to plant trees in large quantities, and the government encouraged a policy of reforestation. Between 1871 and 1900 the area planted with new trees in the land belonging to the Don Cossacks increased from just over 59,000 to almost 81,000 acres. But often these policies met with limited success; in 1885 it was reported that fewer than 50 out of the 313 acres of trees planted on appanage (or state-owned) land in Samara and Stavropol provinces were still standing. In other parts of northern Europe, the growing timber industry was a far greater influence on reforestation: the Seafield estates in Scotland were said to have planted more than 50 million trees in the first half of the century, and by 1881 some 30,000 acres had been planted with Scots pine and other commercially exploitable trees such as larch and spruce in Strathspey and the Rothes area. Geologists and agronomists also began to discover that deforestation encouraged landslides and floods. Denuded of the trees whose roots held the soil on their slopes in place, the Apennines began to suffer growing numbers of avalanches. In the province of Cosenza, in Calabria, forestry inspectors reported 156 landslides in 1903 alone, covering 5,000 acres. The river Basento, in the Basilicata region of southern Italy, washed down over 15 million cubic feet of mud from the Apennines into the Gulf of Taranto every year, silting up its estuary. In some areas farming became almost impossible, with the land deteriorating into a barren, rock-strewn wilderness. Where rivers, blocked by increasing quantities of silt, overflowed their banks and created marshland, malarial mosquitoes moved in, rendering the area almost uninhabitable for humans.

Italian governments therefore began to fund land reclamation and improvement schemes on a large scale. The malarial Fucine Lake in central Italy, whose Roman outlet had been blocked many centuries before, was drained between 1862 and 1875 by the Swiss engineer Jean-François Mayor de Montricher (1810–58) on the initiative of Alessandro Torlonia, Prince of Civitella-Cesi (1800–86), son of a successful banker. While the costly scheme was in progress, people were said to remark in Rome: 'Either Torlonia will drain the Fucine Lake, or the Fucine Lake will drain Torlonia.' By 1907 it was claimed that 200,000 acres in the province of Ferrara alone had been won for agricultural exploitation, above all in the Po Estuary, where arms of the river were blocked off one by one, dunes were levelled, and the water was channelled to reduce flooding. But all across Europe floods were a major problem. In one of many such disasters, the Danube overflowed in March 1838 following the melting of the ice upstream, inundating Pest. Great blocks of ice smashed into house fronts, demolishing them entirely. Visiting the city after the floodwaters had receded, the Croatian writer Ion Codru-Drăguşanu (1818–84) noted that 'a great number of houses had toppled over, having been built from such poor materials, unfired brick and pounded earth, since there is not much wood hereabouts, the forests being far off'. In 1879 the river Maros overflowed its banks and completely destroyed the town of Szeged in southern Hungary. Only 265 of the 5,723 houses remained and 165 people died. Emperor Franz Joseph visited the site and promised to rebuild the city, which eventually emerged from the catastrophe with broad boulevards and modern public buildings.

Many of the rivers that now flow peaceably through well-ordered fields and meadows were as yet unchannelled and unnavigable. Over time, however, increasing efforts were made to bring them under control. In 1876 after the Tiber river had silted up repeatedly following futile dredging operations, stone embankments were built on either side to direct its course. The Isère river in south-eastern France was channelled between two dykes each 26 miles long in a project begun following a major flood in 1816 and completed in 1854. A more rapid intervention was undertaken in the case of the Danube, where the course was straightened and the Hausstein rock in midstream dynamited between 1853 and 1866, eliminating the notorious rapids that had impeded traffic for centuries. The shallows at the Iron Gates between Bulgaria and Romania were deepened in the 1830s, then bypassed by a new canal at the end of the century. The grandest of all these engineering projects was executed on the Rhine. Before the nineteenth century the river had spilled outwards from its central gorge across the plains, creating bogs and marshlands inhabited by swarms of mosquitoes that made malaria the main killer disease of the region. Between Basel and Mainz the river was up to two and a half miles wide, and navigation for large craft was difficult if not impossible. In 1812, however, the military engineer Johann Gottfried Tulla (1770–1828) devised a plan to dig a new, deep riverbed along the whole stretch between Mainz and Basel, using dams to hem it in and channel its tributaries into the main stream, cutting off loops and meanders and straightening it out, and creating barriers to stop the water overflowing into the adjacent marshland. Tulla's project shortened the length of the river by 51 miles, and restricted its width to 656 feet. After this, floods happened seldom and the marshes dried out, with a gain of around 24,700 acres of fertile farmland, though this gain was achieved at the price of devastating the marshland flora and fauna. By the time of the project's completion in 1876, Tulla himself was long since dead, carried away by the malaria that was an endemic feature of the riverside in this region.

If the danger of catastrophic inundations was gradually lessened, the same could not be said of another major peril that periodically visited Europe's peripheries: earthquakes. On 21 March 1829 a large earthquake hit Spain, with the worst effects felt in Murcia in the south-east, where it was reported that numerous villages had suffered extensive damage: 'La Mata is a heap of ruins . . . Guardamar is no longer in existence; two windmills only are standing, the village having entirely disappeared.' In 1880 an earthquake hit Zagreb, severely damaging the cathedral and weakening or destroying well over 1,500 buildings. The following year an earthquake devastated the island of Chios, destroying twenty-five out of sixty-four villages and causing 7,866 casualties, adding to the island's reputation for ill-luck garnered already in the Turkish massacre of its inhabitants in 1822. In 1904 a quake devastated the area south of Sofia in Bulgaria, where 'the barracks', as a correspondent reported, 'have been destroyed and the great powder magazine completely wrecked'. On 28 December 1908 an earthquake completely flattened the towns of Messina and Reggio Calabria in southern Italy, with a death toll estimated at between 75,000 and 200,000. It was made worse by a 40-foot tsunami that struck lengthy stretches of the coast. Precautions against earthquakes were non-existent, nor had the construction techniques needed to limit earthquake damage been developed. Equally alarming, volcanic eruptions could not be predicted, and several caused widespread devastation, notably the massive eruption of Askja in the central highlands of Iceland in 1875, which sent a huge ash cloud into the air, poisoning livestock and causing serious damage as far away as Sweden. Vesuvius erupted eight times in the nineteenth century; the 1906 eruption caused so much damage in Naples that the Olympic Games, scheduled to open there in 1908, had to be relocated to London.

A more widespread terror by far was caused by the fires that frequently swept across European towns and cities in an era when most buildings were still made of wood. The greatest of all nineteenth-century fires was one that devastated Hamburg in 1842. It began on 5 May in the early hours of the morning, in a half-timbered building on the waterfront, and quickly spread to nearby warehouses, consuming their stores of shellac resin, rubber and other, similarly combustible materials. Before long, over a thousand men were fighting the fire, using thirty-four fire engines taking their water from the harbour. But dry weather and strong winds fanned the flames, and soon a large part of the city stretching from the harbour to the Inner Alster, the lake that divided the eastern and western quarters of Hamburg, was in flames. The city authorities began blowing up houses in the fire's path, but the wall of flames simply jumped over them. The city hall was levelled with 800 pounds of gunpowder, after the official files had been removed. Churches were reduced to rubble, and the fire only died down when the wind veered from its original southerly direction to blow harmlessly across the harbour. Some 20,000 people had lost their property; 1,100 houses, 102 warehouses, ninety-four bars and hotels, seven churches, two synagogues and numerous official buildings had been burned to the ground. Tsar Nicholas I of Russia sent more than 50,000 marks to aid relief, the largest donation in a total of nearly 7 million marks, while neighbouring towns and cities provided soup kitchens, loaves and provisions for the homeless, who were housed in temporary accommodation. Meanwhile looters ransacked the smouldering ruins, undeterred by the mobilization of the citizens' militia, and could be seen dividing their ill-gotten gains in public on the Goosemarket.

The Great Fire of Hamburg was far from being the only such event of its kind. In one famous conflagration the ancient Palace of Westminster in London, containing the Houses of Parliament, burned to the ground in 1834, causing William IV (1765–1837), who visited the still-smouldering ruins, to be 'amazed at the fury of the flames which could have hurled so much destruction through and over these enormous buildings and, in many instances, terrifically thick old stone walls'. Too many tinder-dry wooden tallies (obsolete medieval tax records or 'nick-sticks') had been stuffed into the furnaces that supplied the heating, and the blaze had got out of control. Prime Minister Lord Melbourne (1779–1848) declared the fire 'one of the greatest instances of stupidity upon record'. It was some time before the ruins were replaced with the magnificent neo-Gothic structure of the Houses of Parliament familiar from the 1860s onwards. On 10–11 May 1861 a fire broke out in the middle of the night at the Adler Hotel in the Swiss town of Glarus. A strong south-west wind, 'or "Föhn" as it is there called, was blowing at the time, and the flames soon spread on all sides with irresistible fury, so that by morning two-thirds of the place lay in ashes, and the church, council-house, post-office, school-buildings, and other public places were destroyed'; 593 buildings were razed to the ground, including the telegraph office and the railway station, 'making reporting of the blaze difficult'.

In May 1862 a series of fires broke out in St Petersburg. One entire precinct, the Soldiers' District, was set alight, with forty buildings going up in flames, leaving only 'heaps of metal and skeletons of houses', while at one point fires were raging simultaneously in five different parts of the city. Arson was widely blamed, attributed variously to 'students', 'radicals' and 'Poles', and a number of left-wing intellectuals were arrested, though no connection was ever proven. In *The Devils* (sometimes known as *The Possessed*), written a few years later in 1871–2, Fyodor Dostoyevsky portrayed an entire suburb ablaze, a sight which guests at a ball, seeing it through the window, immediately blame on disgruntled factory workers, 'those poor devils who can only be stirred by fire'. Alongside such major conflagrations, towns and cities experienced an almost continuous series of more minor blazes. Living in Istanbul with her diplomat father, the young Hermynia Folliot de Crenneville reported 'an extraordinary number of fires in this part of the world. Red flames were continually leaping up into the night sky, the air was filled with the smell of burning, and the silence was shattered again and again by the rattling of fire engines heading to the scene of a fire.' The fire brigade was commanded by an elderly Hungarian count, who liked to ride the fire engines to the conflagrations himself, though the horse-drawn vehicles seldom arrived in time to do much good. Proportionately the most devastating fire of all took place in the Norwegian town of Ålesund, which was completely destroyed by a conflagration on the night of 23 January 1904, rendering 10,000 people homeless, although there was only one fatality.

Fires were far more common in the countryside, especially where cottages and barns were roofed with thatch. In 1857 alone two entire villages were destroyed in France: 114 dwellings burned to the ground in the village of Fresne-sur-Apance in the Haute-Marne, and 100 people were left homeless when all seventeen houses in the hamlet of Fretterans in Bresse were consumed by flames. Fires could of course be started deliberately: an analysis of 114 cases of rural arson in Bavaria between 1879 and 1900 has shown how these surprisingly frequent crimes were motivated by feelings of resentment against mean farmers or brutal employers, older brothers inheriting the property, abusive parents, or revenge for real or imagined slights. One man accused of setting fire to the family mill after it had been inherited by his older brother confessed: 'I committed the arson . . . because I was angry with my brother because he treated me and my mother badly.' The playwright Anton Chekhov (1860–1904) began his sketch of rural life, *Muzhiki*, published in 1897, with a village fire, portraying the male peasants standing around dumbfounded with 'a helpless expression and tears in their eyes', while the women of the village ran around crying hysterically, or wailing 'as if they were at a funeral'. A 'genuine arson epidemic has broken out in many, many villages,' reported an official in Ekaterinoslav Province in Russia in 1902. Discontent was to erupt in a wave of arson attacks on an even greater scale during the revolutionary months of 1905–6.

The frequency of fires, especially in towns and cities, and the losses of life and property they caused, prompted widespread efforts in the nineteenth century to prevent such disasters and deal with them promptly and effectively should preventive measures fail. In 1867 the Paris fire brigade was transformed into a military regiment commanded by a colonel; it numbered forty-eight officers and 1,800 men by 1914. Each *arrondissement* of the city had its own fire station. The arrival of motorized fire engines shortened the response time, but even in 1914 many of the Parisian fire engines were still horse-drawn. It was not until 1875 that firefighting services were standardized on similar lines across the whole of France. Municipalities were slow to introduce building regulations that would lower the risk of fire. In other countries, professional, dedicated fire brigades were even slower to emerge, with Hamburg only creating one in 1869 despite the experience of the Great Fire twenty-seven years before. Most fires were fought by volunteer firemen. By 1914 the city boasted a fire brigade 500-strong, equipped with the latest mechanized steam pumps, extension ladders and chemical engines. It was down to municipalities to implement fire-prevention measures. They included the installation of fire alarms, though these continued to be relatively uncommon – 700 in Berlin and only 149 in Budapest in 1914 – as well as the construction of fire hydrants in the streets – 3,260 in Vienna by 1914 and 3,350 in Rome. Telephones began to connect fire stations with each other – seven stations in Rome had them by 1914. Building regulations were gradually introduced in many cities to reduce the risk of fire. Shops in Rome were required to insulate themselves from tenements on upper storeys by installing fire-resistant floors. Gradually, therefore, the hazard of fire was reduced.

Smoke from ordinary everyday home fires was a more persistent problem. As towns and cities expanded, so more people lit their home fires with cheap coal that sent sulphurous fumes into the atmosphere. Uncontrolled noxious vapours emitted from factory chimneys made matters worse. Travellers on their way to Hamburg were said to know they were nearing their destination when they 'saw from afar the layer of black air that always hangs over the city'. As water condensed around the particles of soot and ash floating in the air, the pollution increased the likelihood of a persistent fog. Between 1877 and 1895 there were on average fifty-nine foggy days a year in Munich, but during the following decade the figure increased to eighty. The clouds of soot and ash hanging over the industrial area of the West Midlands in Britain caused it to be described as 'the Black Country' from the 1840s, a region where, as Samuel Sidney (1813–83), writer of railway guides, put it, 'a perpetual twilight reigns during the day'. 'In some districts,' noted an early pilot flying his airplane over the Ruhr in 1913, 'there spreads so thick a layer of smoke and haze that it was impossible to orient oneself and we had to make emergency landings'. Trees were stripped of their leaves and grass turned black. Edinburgh was so full of smoke that it became known as 'Auld Reekie'.

Most dramatic of all were the great yellow fogs that afflicted London during the winter months, as natural mist was thickened into the consistency of yellow split-pea soup by the sulphurous particles that hung in the air. In 1873 a fog was so dense that animals were asphyxiated at the Smithfield Cattle Show. The fogs increased in frequency and intensity up to the 1880s, when they served as cover for striking dockers when they invaded the prosperous retail district of the West End. Writers made metaphorical use of these 'London particulars', from the elaborate opening paragraphs of Bleak House (1853) by Charles Dickens, where they stand for the obfuscation caused by the Court of Chancery, to the Strange Case of Dr Jekyll and Mr Hyde (1886) by Robert Louis Stevenson (1850–94), where fog is used to denote the mystery surrounding the murderous activities of the eponymous split-personality criminal. As English artists fled to Italy to experience the purity of the air, foreign artists came to London to capture the atmospheric effects of the fog, most notably the Impressionist Claude Monet (1840–1926), who composed over a hundred paintings of fog on the Thames from the window of his room in the Savoy Hotel. Beautiful though they seemed to Monet, the thick yellow fogs in which, as Dickens put it in *The Old Curiosity Shop* (1841), 'every object was obscured at one or two yards' distance', continued to cause deaths from bronchitis and other respiratory afflictions right up to 1914 and beyond. All attempts to control noxious emissions foundered on the twin obstacles of the resistance of industrialists to costly smoke abatement devices and the reluctance of politicians to violate the sanctity of the blazing hearth in the citizen's home.

THE SHRINKAGE OF SPACE

The conquest of nature in the nineteenth century extended not only to the wilderness and its denizens, the elements and their effects on everyday life, but also to the fundamental factors that framed life and experience. Among the major constraints on human action and communication were distance, space, and the slowness and difficulty of travel. For most of the period many villages and rural communities, especially in mountainous areas, remained difficult of access, particularly in the winter months. In France in the 1820s travellers noted that villagers managed to produce almost everything they needed themselves, weaving their clothes from local wool, hemp or flax, baking bread from their own corn, slaughtering a pig, a goat, a lamb or a bullock and smoking or curing the meat for the winter months, and buying the few metal utensils they needed from itinerant peddlers. They also married within the locality. In the first half of the century, for example, 77 per cent of brides and grooms in the village of Hetzenhausen in Bavaria originated from a radius of one mile of the village. Similar figures can be found for numerous villages in France and other parts of Europe. The local and restricted nature of space experienced by most Europeans through most of the nineteenth century was expressed not least in the staggering diversity of the ways people used to measure it. The *ell*, for instance, originally the distance between the elbow and the fingertip of a normal adult male – itself a changing measurement as the average human grew larger – varied in practice from country to country. The French ell was more than twice the length of the Swedish ell, and there was also a Flemish ell, a Scottish ell and a Polish ell. The German ell measured between 15 and 32 inches depending on what part of the country one was in, but even within individual states it could vary in length: in Saxony there were 7.5 ells to the old rod and 16 feet to the slightly longer new street-rod. In both Baden and Bavaria there were, more conveniently, 10 feet to the rod, but the rod differed in length between the two states, so that a Badensian rod was a little longer than a Bavarian rod. The Danish rod was shorter, but was the same as the Prussian rod; however, there were 10 feet to a rod in Denmark and 12 in Prussia. Longer distances tended to be measured in miles, but the mile too varied greatly in length, from 1,000 modern metres in Wiesbaden, demonstrating the influence of the French metric system on this part of western Germany, to 4,630 metres in the Palatinate and 11,100 metres in Westphalia. Surface area was often traditionally measured by the amount of land a man could work in a day, and so it varied according to the nature of the land, the methods used to work it, and the tools employed. In Lorraine a *journal* was 20.44 acres; in the Haute-Marne 25.85 acres; in Sarthe 44 acres; in the Landes 42 acres of poor land but only 35 of good land.

Whatever officialdom might decree in the interests of uniformity, peasants generally ignored. A local French schoolteacher noted in 1861 that nine-tenths of peasants still paid no heed to the official system of weights and measures even though it had been introduced many decades before. Why should they bother with it, unless they regularly engaged in trade? In the remote and impoverished Tarn in the south-west of France, the economist Henri Baudrillart (1821–92) found that nobody knew what a hectare was; people used local measures that varied from one parish to another. Increasingly, however, Europeans measured distance by the metre and its various multiples and subdivisions: this was a product of the French Revolution, when a scientific expedition dispatched from Paris undertook the measurement of the Earth's circumference along a line from pole to pole. (They did not, of course, actually go to the poles but merely measured the distance from Dunkirk to Barcelona and scaled it up.) The line passed, predictably enough, through Paris. One ten-millionth of the circumference became a metre, and though later scientists discovered that the overall measurement had not been entirely accurate, it stuck. This was not least because the growing needs of trade and industry were forcing governments to consider standardization. In 1875 an international metric convention was signed by seventeen countries. However, it was ignored by the British, who, along with the United States and much of the rest of the world, used the imperial system defined by the British Weights and Measures Act of 1824, and stuck to miles, furlongs, chains, yards, feet and inches for length, and roods, perches and acres for surface area. The Russians carried on with their own standardized measurements introduced in the early eighteenth century, based on but not identical with the imperial system. The *fut* was the same length as the English foot and the *diuym* the same as the English inch, but the *verst*, or turn of the plough, was 3,500 feet, much shorter than its English equivalent, the 5,280-foot mile.

The adoption on most of the Continent of the metric system was one of many consequences of the fact that the second half of the nineteenth century was the age of railway-building, when railway companies needed a standard measurement of length. By 1880 there were over 100,000 miles of railway track across Europe. Many countries previously more or less untouched by railways now took them up. In Spain the Railway Law of 1855 provided subsidies to construction companies and allowed them to use public land. They were allowed to import fuel and building materials tariff-free for ten years. This encouraged foreign businesses to get involved, and the French in particular took advantage of this provision. By 1858 nearly 3,000 miles of track had been built in Spain, but the foreign companies who ran the system paid no attention to Spanish economic needs, so that the lines simply radiated out from Madrid or Barcelona instead of following traditional trade routes. Thus there was for a long time no cheap and reliable means of getting coal from the mines of Asturias in the north to the foundries of Vizcaya 200 miles to the east, which were obliged to rely on imports of Welsh coal instead. The railway boom reached Russia in the 1860s, driven by private firms operating under government guarantee. From a mere 750 miles of track in the mid-1850s the system expanded to some 14,000 miles in 1881. Altogether the mileage of railway track increased from 27 in Russia in 1840 to 53,000 by 1900, in Italy over the same period from 20 to 16,000, and in Austria-Hungary from 144 to 36,000. In 1860 there were only 527 miles of railway track in Sweden; by 1900 there were 11,000.

The greatest of all railway-building projects was undoubtedly the Trans-Siberian Railway, extending from Vladivostok on the Pacific coast to Chelyabinsk in the Urals, where it connected with the railway network in European Russia. Begun in 1891 simultaneously at both ends and in the middle, it was largely complete by 1904, and served above all the military and strategic purposes of the Russian government; it enabled troops to be transported quickly across huge distances, it ran through a part of Manchuria leased from the Chinese Empire, which was thus opened up to Russian penetration, and after the Russo-Japanese War of 1905–6 a new line was begun north of the Amur river, entirely within Russian

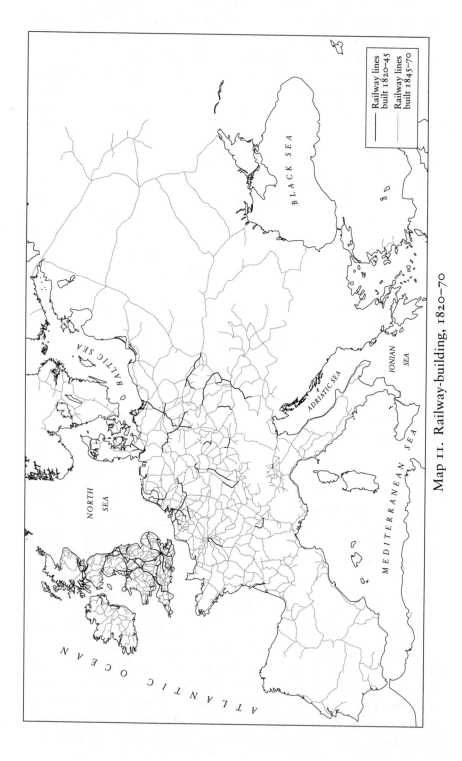

Map 11. Railway-building, 1820–70

territory, in anticipation of another conflict with Japan. Thus passengers could now travel by rail from the Atlantic to the Pacific Ocean, and a luxurious 'international' train was provided, with a grand piano in the saloon and marble tiles in the bathrooms, though its average speed was no more than 20 mph and it could only run on the broad-gauge Russian lines. While most of Europe adopted George Stephenson's standard gauge, there were still problems caused by differing signalling technologies, working practices, safety regulations and insurance provisions. A series of international conferences held in Bern from 1878 to 1886 worked out a number of regulations governing these and other issues, making international travel easier.

Carriages became more comfortable in many respects after 1850, with glass window panes and upholstered seats in the first class, hot-water bottles provided in winter months, and even, eventually, a toilet on the train; however, it discharged its contents, somewhat unhygienically, directly onto the line, a practice that continued into the second half of the twentieth century in most parts of Europe. Restaurant cars and sleeping cars, pioneered by the American George Pullman (1831–97), were introduced in the 1870s, made possible by modifications in carriage design that allowed people to pass from coach to coach. The Belgian banker's son Georges Nagelmackers (1845–1905) founded the Compagnie Internationale des Wagons-Lits, and created a series of international services culminating in the famous Orient Express, launched on 5 June 1883. With its one-way fare of 300 francs – two whole weeks' wages for a manual labourer – its uniformed attendants, and its requirement for passengers to wear evening dress for the seven-course dinner served in the restaurant car, a train like the Orient Express was explicitly designed for the well-to-do. Travelling at 45 mph in France and Germany, 30 mph in Hungary and 20 mph in Romania, it took eighty hours to travel the 1,900 miles from Paris to Istanbul by a sometimes circuitous route; by 1894 a new Romanian section had been added to the line and ten hours cut from the total journey time; and in 1906 the opening of the Simplon Tunnel allowed the train to take a new route through Venice, Zagreb and Belgrade, reducing the journey time still further, to a mere fifty-three hours.

The railway and the steamship shrank global space as well, for it became increasingly possible to travel huge distances in an extraordinarily short time, as depicted in 1873 by Jules Verne in his novel *Around the World in Eighty Days*. Railways, steamships and the telegraph had become essential tools in the creation and maintenance of Europe's overseas empires; they were an important part of the technological underpinnings of British and European domination of the world in the nineteenth century. Without rapid and efficient communications, metropolitan control of vast, far-flung global empires would not have been possible. The combination of railway expansion and the spread of literacy also made the nineteenth century the golden age of letter-writing. The number of letters sent each year in France rose from 64 million in 1830 to 94 million a decade late. In 1839 the inventor and social reformer Rowland Hill (1795–1879) inaugurated standardized letter charges in the United Kingdom. Two years later the invention of the adhesive stamp further boosted the amount of mail sent. The number of letters carried annually by the British Royal Mail rose from 564 million in 1860 to 1.2 billion in 1880 and 2.3 billion in 1900. The circulation of postcards, initially pre-stamped blanks without a picture, grew especially quickly after 'private' illustrated cards were introduced in the 1890s: 75 million were sent in 1870, rising to 927 million by 1914. To cope with this increase, every major town in Britain had four deliveries every day. In Germany each state had its own postal service until the creation of the Reich Postal Service in 1871, directed by Heinrich von Stephan (1831–97). Stephan was also the instigator of the Universal Postal Union in 1874, which immeasurably improved the efficiency of global and indeed European postal communication by abolishing the rule by which international letters and parcels had to carry the postage stamps of every country through which they passed. From this point on, foreign and domestic mail were accorded equal treatment, each country was entitled to retain all the revenues it gained from international postage, and a uniform, flat rate was agreed for all international post.

Not only letters and postcards but also cheap, mass-manufactured goods were increasingly carried to previously remote parts of Europe by the extension of the railway network. Branch lines brought policemen, teachers and other agencies of the state, newspapers, books and magazines, different kinds of food, chemical fertilizers and new types of agricultural implements and machines to towns and villages far from the major urban centres. Among other things this prompted a massive growth in the efficiency and productivity of farming, which enabled its output to keep pace with the growth of population in the towns. Local cottage industries and handicrafts vanished under the impact of industrialized textile production, artificial fibres, mechanized engineering, and iron and steel manufacture. The new network of communications enabled wealthier farmers to export their produce rapidly and cheaply to the towns; it also carried young men away from the villages to new factories and industrial centres far from their home, further disrupting the traditional structures of rural life. Branch lines brought a new, cheap means of travel to millions, but just as this process of democratization was getting under way, it was put into reverse by the arrival of the self-propelled motor vehicle. This was a German invention, the brainchild of Karl Benz (1844–1929), who in a long series of technical experiments patented the battery ignition system, the spark plug, the carburettor, the gearshift, the water radiator and the clutch. In 1886 he presented the world with the first automobile or horseless carriage. After his wife borrowed it without his knowledge and drove it 66 miles to visit some relatives, inventing brake-lining on the way by getting a cobbler to nail leather pads to the brake blocks, Benz added another gear, and built a larger factory, and soon companies in other countries were following his lead. Some of the new 'horseless carriages' were powered by a different type of engine invented by the engineer Rudolf Diesel (1858–1913), who illustrated the international character of these new industries neatly through his birth and upbringing in Paris and his education in Germany. Benz himself had close connections with the French engineering firms of Panhard and Peugeot, which began making cars in their own right, importing most of their machine tools from the United States. The excellence of the French road system meant that touring was possible from the start, and country doctors and small landowners were soon purchasing economy models. The small-scale firms common in French industry were ideally suited to take advantage of this demand, and soon Darracq (1896, the first company to standardize production), Renault (1898), Peugeot (1899) and De Dion-Bouton (which produced the first V8 engine, in 1907) were ensuring that French car output, numbering 45,000 vehicles by 1914, was the largest in Europe, while the pneumatic tyres developed by Michelin (1889) allowed drivers and passengers to travel in relative comfort.

Perhaps the most dynamic motor-manufacturing industry was to be found in Italy, however, where, boosted by government sponsorship and cheap electric power sources, there were no fewer than seventy-one such companies by 1907. These were based above all in Turin, and focused on high-performance vehicles to sell to wealthy foreigners on the lookout for new thrills driving fast cars produced by firms such as Bugatti, founded in 1908 by the eponymous Ettore Bugatti (1881–1947), or Alfa Romeo (1910), originally founded in 1906 as an offshoot of the French car maker Darracq. The Fabbrica Italiana Automobili Torino (FIAT), established in 1899 by a group of former cavalry officers including a liberal sprinkling of aristocrats, entered its cars for races, but its managing director, Giovanni Agnelli (1866–1945), saw relatively early on that there was more money to be made from mass production. He travelled to the United States to learn from the example of Henry Ford (1863–1947), who was already earning huge profits by turning out motor cars in the thousands. When

Agnelli was asked during his visit whether the streamlined manufacturing methods used to make Ford's famously inexpensive Model T, first produced in 1908, could be introduced into Europe, his interlocutor noticed that 'Monsieur Agnelli avoided answering. His eyes lit up briefly but his face, which I was scrutinising, remained impassive. He changed the conversation rapidly.'

The answer was not slow in coming. By 1912, FIAT, now a public company in which Agnelli owned most of the shares, was making a new cheap car, the Model Zero, production of which accelerated from 150 vehicles in 1903 to 4,500 in 1914. Britain could not keep up. In 1890, Frederick Simms (1863–1944), a businessman and engineer who invented the word 'petrol' and the term 'motor car' and founded the Royal Automobile Club, acquired the United Kingdom and British Empire rights for a high-speed petrol engine devised by the German inventor Gottlieb Daimler (1834–1900), although he used it at first to make motor launches. In 1896, Simms opened a factory producing Daimler cars. He also invented and built the first armoured car in 1899. Others followed suit, most notably Herbert Austin (1866–1941), who is generally credited with building the first all-British car. A new company founded in 1906 by Charles Rolls (1877–1910) and Henry Royce (1863–1933) focused on high-powered luxury cars. This was not a stable industry. Of the 200 motor-manufacturing companies that started up in Britain at this time, only half were still in existence in 1914, by which time the largest producer of cars in the United Kingdom was an American company, Ford.

Motor cars were still relatively uncommon before the First World War, but the future was already becoming clear. In France there were 3,000 automobiles in 1900; by the eve of the First World War this number had shot up to over 100,000; double this number of cars were being driven around the roads of Britain by this time. In 1865 an Act of Parliament, aimed at steam traction engines, had limited the speed of 'locomotives' on roads to 4 miles per hour and decreed that they had to be preceded by a man on foot holding a red flag. Under heavy pressure from motorists, this law was repealed in 1896, allowing motor vehicles to travel at speeds of up to 14 miles per hour. A new national speed limit was introduced in 1904, imposing a maximum of 20 miles per hour on all public highways. In France, by contrast, there was no speed limit outside the towns, and the country, as a British motorist noted, was ideal 'for the devotee of speed', a land 'where he can peg down the accelerator pedal and go out all day'. Car ownership before 1914 was overwhelmingly the preserve of the wealthy, like the car-loving *nouveau riche* Mr Toad in the children's story *The Wind in the Willows* (1908) by Kenneth Grahame (1859–1932). The motor car enabled them once more to revert from the public nature of railway travel to the privacy of an individual mode of transportation, exhibiting their prosperity and modernity to an astonished world. Royalty also took to the automobile with enthusiasm: by 1910, Tsar Nicholas II was maintaining a fleet of twenty-two cars in the Imperial Personal Garage, including a staff of chauffeurs to drive him about in a French Delaunay-Belleville for short journeys and a 90-horsepower Mercedes for longer ones. Kaiser Wilhelm II had a horn specially made for his car, blaring out the leitmotif of the thunder-god Donner from Richard Wagner's 1854 music drama *Das Rheingold*.

A more democratic form of locomotion could be found in the humble bicycle, whose forerunner the dandy horse, a wooden-framed two-wheeler pushed along by the rider's feet, was invented in 1817 by the German Karl Drais (1785–1851), a retired forestry official. It was not until the 1860s that a series of inventors, all of whose individual claims remain disputed to this day, began to experiment with pedal propulsion, leading to the creation of the velocipede, known as the boneshaker because of its solid wooden, iron-rimmed wheels. The larger the front wheel, the faster the machine would go, so that in the 1870s the 'ordinary bicycle' had a huge front wheel and a tiny rear one – the 'penny-farthing' as it was later known. The British inventor James Starley (1831–81) got round these problems by devising the differential gear and the chain drive; his nephew John Kemp Starley (1855–1901) used these devices in 1885 to make the new 'Rover' safety bicycle, a far more stable machine than its predecessors. Two years later the Scotsman John Boyd Dunlop (1840–1921) began to market the pneumatic tyre, opening the way for a veritable cycling craze in the following decade. As the price of bicycles fell, sales began to rise. Already in 1911 some 11 per cent of Dutch taxpayers owned a bicycle, and most of them were in the lowest tax bracket, signalling the penetration of the bicycle into the working class. Understandably, cycling was most popular in countries, like the Netherlands, where the land was flat. Cycling clubs began to emerge, like – to take a random example – the Willesden Cycling Club, established in 1884 in a London suburb for largely social purposes, which included a Smoking Concert and an annual pantomime on its programme. Bicycle races began with a 1,200-metre race held on 31 May 1868 in Paris, won by James Moore (1849–1935). Soon there were two international cycling associations, founded respectively by the British in 1892 and the French in 1900. Up to half a million people gathered in French towns in 1903 to watch the first Tour de France pass by – and not only in French towns; the organizers advertised their patriotism by running a stage through Alsace-Lorraine, annexed by the Germans in 1871.

The bicycle was important not least as a vehicle of female emancipation. The Austrian feminist Rosa Mayreder (1858–1938) declared that it had done more to emancipate women than all the efforts of the feminists put together. It allowed them to go out unaccompanied, required them to exchange impractical billowing clothing for the 'rational dress' of divided skirts, and gave them an active, healthy sporting image that bolstered their claims to social equality. Cycling gained popularity among middle-class women: 'It couldn't be helped,' recounted a story in a Berlin magazine in 1901: 'It was too beautiful, too new, too chic, too practical, too healthy. And so one day the mayor's daughter got onto a bicycle, and a few years later even her mother bought herself a little iron horse.' 'If ever I have a daughter,' says Marie, a character in Zola's novel *Paris* (1898), 'I shall put her on a bicycle as soon as she's ten years old, just to teach her how to conduct herself in life.' The lesson was not lost on reactionaries. One elderly aristocratic lady in Vienna, observed the young Hermynia Folliot de Crenneville, 'had her gardener collect flint-stones and lay them on the garden table. Then she sat behind the hedge of her garden and watched for women cyclists. If one of the immodest creatures passed her way, she was showered with a rain of stones, and the old Countess would shout: "Hussy! Hussy!"' When male undergraduates at Cambridge hanged a woman in effigy as a sign of their opposition to the admission of women to the university in 1897, they put the effigy on a bicycle.

As horizontal distances shrank, vertical space also became more easily accessible. Grand department stores began to install escalators once a workable model had been devised. Harrods in London installed a 'moving staircase' in its Brompton Road store in 1898. A single leather belt consisting of 224 linked slats, it carried customers up somewhat unsteadily to the first floor, where shop assistants were waiting with brandy and smelling salts to revive those who had been unnerved by the experience. Eight years later a spiral escalator was installed at the Holloway Road underground station in north London, though it was taken out of service after a few hours and never saw public use. A more modern version of the escalator, with slats that continued moving horizontally at the top and bottom of the incline, was displayed by an American lift firm at the World Exhibition in Paris in 1900, but practical problems prevented it from gaining widespread currency before the First World War. By contrast, the lift had become a common feature of tall buildings by this time. Elevators of a kind had of course been used for many decades in coalmines, powered by a steam winch that lowered and raised the cage conveying miners to and from the underground galleries. The modern elevator owed its existence to Elisha Graves Otis (1811–61), who in 1854 had invented a safety brake that prevented the car from falling if the cable snapped. By the late nineteenth century his hydraulic power system, which used a water-filled counterweight, had been replaced by an electric motor. As buildings became higher in New York and Chicago, the use of the elevator became more common and spread quickly to Europe, where it was adopted first by luxury hotels.

Safety regulations rapidly introduced by police and municipal authorities required lift operators to be trained and qualified, and tested them on their ability to start and stop the elevator exactly at each floor, there being as yet no automated way of achieving this result. A series of unfortunate accidents in which people stumbled through lift doorways and plunged to their death down the shaft led to the introduction of safety doors both in the elevator itself and in every lobby, similarly controlled by a uniformed liftboy. Soon hotels were boasting that guests could reach their upper floors without having to climb the stairs, and Baedeker's tourist guides were pointing to desirable accommodation in establishments like the Grand Hôtel de Rome in Berlin, 'optimally situated, with 120 rooms, elevator, electric lighting and baths'. In 1892, when this description was published, elevators were still something new; twenty years later they had become a generally expected feature of the luxury hotel, and guidebooks no longer pointed them out, referring to them instead only when it came to describing the inexpensive 'simple hotel, without elevator or central heating'. Not only hotels but also office buildings climbed steadily upwards with the advent of the elevator: the Austrian Postal Savings Bank Building in Vienna, designed and built by Otto Wagner (1841–1918), was eight storeys high and opened in 1905; but it was outdone by the Royal Liver Building in Liverpool, designed by Walter Aubrey Thomas (1864–1934) and built of reinforced concrete. It was opened in 1911 and stood eleven storeys or 300 feet tall, the highest building in Europe at the time.

The elevator upended the social hierarchy of tall buildings. Before its arrival, the cheapest rooms were on the upper floors, which the customer had to climb many flights of stairs to reach. After elevators became a common feature of hotels, these rooms were enlarged and became the most expensive, since they enjoyed the best views and were furthest from the bustle and noise of the street. Attics had traditionally been associated with poverty, famously illustrated in the painting *The Poor Poet* (1839) by Carl Spitzweg (1808–85), which showed the eponymous subject huddling in his bed, protected by an umbrella from a leaky roof, declaiming his verses to an empty, book-filled room. The elevator facilitated a social reversal here too, with the birth of the penthouse and the roof garden. In such luxury buildings there was always a separate elevator for the servants at the back, while in some the guests were even trusted to operate the lift by themselves after electric buttons were introduced in 1903, providing automatic stops on each floor (hotels and department stores kept the old system, given the high volume of traffic). In apartment blocks the elevator reduced the sense of community: as it passed by each floor, the passengers were cut off from its inhabitants, where using the stairs had given them the opportunity to get to know their neighbours below.

However many floors an elevator reached, it had in the end to remain earthbound. The quest to conquer the skies had begun in the eighteenth century with the invention of the hot-air balloon and then the gas balloon, which could go further and fly higher and last longer in the air. Hydrogen-filled balloons were used for exhibitions, most famously by Sophie Blanchard (1778–1819). After numerous exploits, including crossing the Alps, she eventually came to grief in the Jardin de Tivoli in Paris when the fireworks she let off from her basket, to the accompaniment of an orchestra, ignited the gas in her balloon and caused it to plummet to the ground with fatal results. The accident set back the cause of ballooning until it was taken up again by Charles Green (1785–1870), who lowered its cost by purchasing pit gas from coal companies and made 526 successful ascents during his long career. In 1836, starting at Vauxhall Gardens in London, he crossed the Channel with an assistant, consuming a large picnic in the basket along the way, reached a height of more than two miles, and eventually came to land north of Frankfurt after a flight lasting eighteen hours. The flight ignited a new ballooning craze, and Green even proposed an Atlantic crossing, though wisely perhaps, he never put this idea into practice.

Victor Hugo, enthused by the possibilities of flight, proclaimed optimistically that balloons, if their direction of flight could be controlled, would 'bring the immediate, absolute, instantaneous, universal and perpetual abolition of all frontiers everywhere . . . Armies will vanish, and with them the horrors of war.' The reality was rather different. Balloons had already been in use since 1858 for aerial photography, and in flights such as that undertaken in 1862 by the English meteorologist James Glaisher (1809–1903) to take air pressure and other measurements in the upper atmosphere (Glaisher reached a height of almost 30,000 feet, nearly freezing to death in the process). But they soon acquired a military function. The opposing armies sent officers up in them to spy on enemy dispositions and carry dispatches during the siege of Paris by Prussian forces in 1870–1. Novels like the best-seller *Five Weeks in a Balloon*

(1863) by Jules Verne proclaimed the superiority of the European fliers over the African tribesmen on the ground below, while European armies began to use observation balloons in the numerous colonial wars of the day. The key to the future, however, as Victor Hugo had suggested, lay with finding a safe and reliable means of directing a balloon and thereby freeing it from the mercy of the winds. After numerous attempts, some of them successful, using steam power or even a gang of men turning a wheel, the arrival of the internal combustion engine and the electric motor finally solved the problem. It was, perhaps inevitably, a military airship, *La France*, which made the first trip that came back to land where it had started off, in 1884.

To manoeuvre successfully, airships had to be bullet-shaped rather than round, and equipped with a rudder for direction and propellers for forward motion. The Paris-based Brazilian Alberto Santos-Dumont (1873–1932), inspired by reading the works of Jules Verne, designed what is thought to have been the first successful dirigible balloon, creating a sensation when he flew it around the Eiffel Tower in 1901. The most celebrated pioneer was, however, Count Ferdinand von Zeppelin (1838–1917), a German military engineer who had served as an observer with the Union Army during the American Civil War. After his retirement, he devoted his time to developing a new kind of airship, consisting of a rigid aluminium framework covered with fabric and containing a multitude of separate gas cells capable of expansion and contraction. With the aid of government subsidies and the income from the creation of a limited company, Zeppelin built a series of large, torpedo-shaped airships, the most successful of which aroused widespread public attention on its first flight in August 1908. Huge crowds gathered to watch it pass overhead. By August 1914 twenty more had been constructed, six of them for the purpose of providing commercial flights for wealthy customers, the rest for military functions. A veritable Zeppelin craze swept the country, with Zeppelin magazines, Zeppelin postcards, Zeppelin ornaments and Zeppelin toys. The Zeppelin became a symbol of German technological prowess and national pride. It would 'drop something on the head' of anyone who 'scolds Germany', one song proclaimed.

By this time, an even more decisive breakthrough had taken place, with the first successful flight by a machine that was heavier than air. The brothers Orville (1871–1948) and Wilbur (1867–1912) Wright piloted the first powered 'Flying Machine' in 1903 on Daytona Beach, North Carolina. The German Otto Lilienthal (1848–96), a pioneer of glider design, had already devised a number of aircraft, including flapping-wing machines, and built towers from which he jumped off in them, but had broken his neck in a fall before he could develop his idea of a powered machine any further. Hearing of the Wright brothers' achievement, however, and quickly dropping his enthusiasm for airships, Alberto Santos-Dumont constructed a biplane on the model of a box-kite and logged the first officially recorded airplane flight in Europe, just outside Paris, on 23 October 1906. Before long, designs had improved sufficiently for Louis Blériot (1872–1936), the inventor of the car headlamp, to fly across the English Channel in his monoplane on 25 July 1909, thereby netting a prize of £1,000 put up by the London *Daily Mail*, his departure watched by a crowd estimated at 10,000 strong. Commercial flights still lay in the future, but even before the outbreak of the First World War, the Schneider Trophy, announced in 1912 by the French financier Jacques Schneider (1879–28), was being offered to the fastest small airplane, spurring technological developments that were to come to fruition in the dogfights above the Western Front during the war.

By this time, dreamers, fantasists and science-fiction writers were already beginning to look beyond the Earth's atmosphere to worlds beyond. The great discoveries of observational astronomy had already been made: the sole new planet found in the nineteenth century, Neptune, was discovered on 23 September 1846 by the German astronomer Johann Galle (1812–1910), as a result of its location through mathematical calculations based on evidence of perturbations in the orbit of the planet Uranus. Telescopes improved in range and precision, particularly after the introduction of silver-coated mirrors in 1857, but they proved a mixed blessing: twenty years later the Italian astronomer Giovanni Schiaparelli (1835–1910), using a 22-inch telescope, observed lines, which he called *canali* (channels), on the surface of Mars during one of its periodic oppositions to the Earth. Mistranslated as 'canals' by over-enthusiastic American readers of his report, the discovery sparked intense speculation about the possibility of intelligent life on the red planet, even though subsequent observations failed to locate the lines and they eventually turned out to be optical illusions. The French author and balloonist Camille Flammarion (1842–1925) had already advanced the idea that the universe was teeming with sentient life, though he derived this belief from his spiritualist convictions, positing the transmigration of souls between the planets. He became an avid proponent of the idea that Mars was home to an alien civilization 'much more intelligent' than its counterpart on Earth. A skilled publicist, he wove an air of mystery about himself, often telling the story of how the manuscript of a chapter on 'wind' in his book *The Atmosphere* (1888) was blown off his desk and out of the window one stormy night, landing with implausible accuracy in the correct order of pages in his printer's office the following day.

Flammarion believed in astronomy as a force for good. If only people 'knew what profound inner pleasure awaits those who gaze at the heavens,' he wrote, 'then France, nay, the whole of Europe, would be covered with telescopes instead of bayonets, thereby promoting universal happiness and peace'. But most writers preferred to take a gloomier view. In the novel *On Two Planets*, published in 1897 by the German mathematics teacher Kurt Lasswitz (1848–1910), a group of Arctic explorers are abducted to Mars by aliens from the red planet; the expedition finds the planet's surface criss-crossed by innumerable canals and the Martians a nautical race who then send a fleet of battleships to England to defeat the Royal Navy, a piece of wishful thinking that demonstrated the navalist ambitions of some Germans even before a German navy had been built. The British writer H. G. Wells (1866–1946) went even further, depicting in his novel *The War of the Worlds*, published in serial form the same year, the invasion of Earth by a fleet of advanced 'fighting machines' on stilts, manned by cephalopodic Martians, who obliterate everything in their path with their heat rays and black smoke until they fall victim to mundane bacterial infections and die. Writers of the new genre of science fiction continued to describe civilizations on Mars or even the Moon, as in Wells's *The First Men in the Moon* (1901), despite warnings from the English naturalist Alfred Russel Wallace (1823–1913) that both bodies were too cold for life to exist on them. Another schoolteacher, the Russian mathematician Konstantin Eduardovich Tsiolkovsky (1857–1935), in his little-read work *The Exploration of Cosmic Space by Means of Reaction Devices* (1903) worked out the mathematical equation that laid down the principles on which a rocket would be able to escape the gravitational pull of the Earth, though it was to be many years before it was put into practice. For the time being, the conquest of space stopped at the limits of the Earth's atmosphere.

THE MAKING OF MODERN TIME

Limitations on communication were imposed not only by the problems inherent in traversing horizontal and vertical space, but also by the complex and – in the early nineteenth century – largely unregulated nature of time and its measurement. In the pre-industrial world, time was calculated in relation to the solar noon, which of course occurred at different times according to where one was located on the Earth's surface, and changed everywhere with the passing seasons. Few people had learned to tell the time from looking at clocks, a skill that was not taught in schools even where they existed, and the hour was only a very rough guide to the passage of time; in most rural areas, church bells only tolled for services such as matins and evensong, providing an even more approximate indication of the time of day. The vast majority of people had little need to reckon time accurately to within the minute; often, indeed, clocks only possessed one hand, and the convention of marking the minutes as well as the hours only gained currency gradually. As increasing numbers of men and women migrated to the cities and worked in factories and mines for wages paid by the hour, so timekeeping became more important for employers and employees alike. In 1890 a machine was invented in America that stamped employees' cards with the time they entered the factory and the time they left. 'Clocking on' and 'clocking off' soon became widespread. To avoid being fined for late arrival, workers needed watches. World production of pocket watches, around 400,000 a year in the early nineteenth century, rose to more than 2.5 million a year by 1875. By the turn of the century, the German historian Karl Lamprecht (1856–1915) was claiming that between them the 52 million inhabitants of Germany owned no fewer than 12 million pocket watches.

In the early nineteenth century, each town or city in Europe kept its own time, setting its watches and clocks without much regard for the hours observed by its neighbours. Early factories still set their clocks by local time, but soon the impulse to standardize time became irresistible, and it was driven above all by the spread of the railways. Even in the mid-1870s, after Germany had been united in a single state, railway timetables within the empire were still forced to base themselves on a bewildering variety of local times that varied from city to city, leaving it up to passengers to convert the time on the local clock to the time on their pocket watch. Railway companies found it necessary to standardize times for their own internal use, and were able to make use of synchronizable electric clocks, invented in 1840 by the Scotsman Alexander Bain (1811–77) and produced in large numbers from the mid-1840s onwards by the German clockmaker Matthias Hipp (1813–93). In Britain the Irish Mail train leaving Euston Station in London every morning carried an Admiralty messenger with a watch giving the correct London time, passing it on to officials on the Irish steam-packet at Holyhead to take to Dublin, and receiving it from them on the way back to return to London. By 1855, however, virtually all public clocks in the United Kingdom were set by Greenwich Mean Time, well before they were forced to do so by law twenty-five years later, largely following the initiative of railway companies that decided it was too complicated to take local times into account. In Britain many station clocks continued to have two minute-hands up to the end of the century and sometimes beyond, one showing Greenwich time and the other the traditional local time. Belgium and the Netherlands did not introduce a standard time until 1892, Austria-Hungary and Italy until 1893. The French railways, recognizing the centrality of Paris to their system, had standardized their timetables according to Paris time, but although an 1891 law made this legally binding for the whole of France, the railways fixed their station clocks five minutes behind this so that passengers would have time to board their train, while time on the tracks remained fixed at the national standard. In Germany it was not the railway companies or other economic pressure groups that proved the most powerful advocates of standard time, but the Prussian Field Marshal Helmuth von Moltke. He had already used railways to good effect in the wars of German unification to move troops rapidly across the land, and saw the continuing chaos of variable time zones as a major obstacle to military efficiency in the future. In the early 1890s he complained that 'we have in Germany five zones, a ruin that has remained standing out of the once-splintered condition of Germany, but which, since we have become an empire, it is proper to abolish'. Accepting the primacy of the Greenwich meridian, and advocating a national standard time based on the 15th meridian, just east of Berlin, Moltke went on to declare that what was needed was 'a unity of time reckoning for the whole of Germany'. It came eventually in 1893.

The need to standardize time had already become urgent with the spread of telegraphing systems across not only Europe but also the world. The first submarine cables were laid across the English Channel in the early 1850s, and already in 1852, Edward Highton (1817–59), a pioneer of the electromagnetic telegraph, commented: 'Time and space are all but annihilated. Years are converted into days, days into seconds, and miles have become mere fractions of an inch.' It was not until 1865 that the *Great Eastern*, then the largest ship in the world, succeeded in laying a cable across the Atlantic Ocean. A frenzy of cable-laying followed, and by 1871 punters in Calcutta could learn the result of the Derby no more than five minutes after the famous horse race was over. The scale of the British Empire and the dominance of British industry ensured that in 1890 nearly two-thirds of the telegraph lines in the world were owned by British companies, which controlled 97,000 miles of cables. But the influence of the system extended far beyond the British Empire. The growth of the new global communication networks meant, as the Hungarian writer Max

Nordau (1849–1923) noted in 1892, that the simplest villager now had a wider geographical horizon than a head of government a century before. If he reads a paper he 'interests himself simultaneously in the issue of a revolution in Chile, a bush-war in East Africa, a massacre in North China, a famine in Russia'. This new system of communication was too valuable, perhaps too potentially dangerous, to be left in private hands, so all over Europe the telegraph system was gradually taken over by the state. The majority of users were private, but news organizations quickly saw the potential uses of the telegraph, and the enterprising Paul Julius von Reuter (1816–99) established the first agency telegraphing news across the world in Aachen in 1851, setting up his British headquarters seven years later. The telegraph arrived in time for the intrepid correspondent of the London *Times*, William Howard Russell, to cable back reports on the inadequacies of the British conduct of the Crimean War to his editor in London, helping to create a political storm through the immediacy of his accounts of the terrible sufferings of the troops, the incompetence of the officers, and the squalid conditions of the field hospitals.

While the telegraph depended for its operation on trained specialists, anyone could use a telephone, following the patenting of the first model and transmission system in 1876 by the Scottish-born engineer Alexander Graham Bell (1847–1922). Early lines were seldom private: when a call was made on a 'party line', bells rang at every station along its length, and anyone could listen in on the conversation. Advice issued on telephone etiquette included the injunction to begin a conversation by shouting 'ahoy!' down the line, and for gentlemen to keep their moustaches out of the mouthpiece. By the eve of the First World War there were more than half a million subscribers to what was now a national telephone service in Britain; in Budapest there were around 27,000, who could also enjoy a telephone news and music transmission service invented by the electrical engineer Tivadar Puskás (1844–93), which had 6,437 subscribers in 1900. Telephones speeded up the distribution of news more generally. As early as 1880 the London *Times* put a direct phone line into the House of Commons in order to be able to report late-night debates for the following morning's edition. More revolutionary again, though still in its infancy before the First World War, was the new system of wireless telegraphy patented by Guglielmo Marconi (1874–1937), an Italian who became a naturalized British citizen. Made operationally viable by the establishment of the British Marconi company in 1897, it was used particularly for seaborne communication.

In order to carry out such operations, people needed among other things to be sure of the time to the hour, minute, even second. As the

1. *Windmill near Norwich* (1816) by John Crome (1768–1821), showing the skies turned yellow by the sulphur emissions from Mount Tambora, which erupted in April 1815 and made 1816 'the year without a summer', causing widespread famine in Europe.

2. The Congress of Vienna: Austrian Emperor Franz I, Friedrich Wilhelm III of Prussia, Tsar Alexander I, the Prince Regent, and Joachim Murat, King of Naples divide up Europe. Napoleon, his son at his side, snips away France on his return from Elba; Talleyrand crouches under the table clutching a medallion of Louis XVIII.

3. *The Massacre at Chios* (1824) by Eugène Delacroix. This large painting depicts atrocities committed by Ottoman troops after lifting the siege of the Turkish garrison of the island by Greek insurgents. Up to 30,000 inhabitants of the island were killed and many more sold into slavery. Greek rebels had previously carried out many massacres of Muslim Turks in the Peloponnese.

4. *The Fighting Temeraire* (1839) by J. M. W. Turner. One of the last of the wooden men-of-war that fought at the Battle of Trafalgar in 1805 is towed by a steam-powered tug to be broken up, symbolizing the dawn of the industrial age and the changing face of British sea power, which remained dominant despite the anxieties evoked in this picture.

5. *The Emancipation of Russian Serfs in 1861* (1907) by Boris Mikhailovich Kustodiev (1878–1927), showing a local official reading out Tsar Alexander I's proclamation ending centuries of servile status for millions of peasants, the single most important act of emancipation carried out anywhere in Europe in the nineteenth century.

6. *The Great Famine* (1850), by George Frederick Watts (1817–1904). Originally entitled 'Irish Eviction', this painting is one of the few depictions of the avoidable human suffering caused by the most disastrous of all nineteenth-century famines, which killed a million Irish men, women and children in the late 1840s and prompted mass emigration from the island in the following decade.

7. Open-cast copper mine at Falun, Sweden, around 1850. The mine, in operation for centuries, produced a large portion of Europe's supplies of copper but was superseded from the mid-nineteenth century onwards as other sources of supply were located in Chile and the United States and mined using more modern methods.

8. Arrival of the first train from St Petersburg to Tsarskoye Selo on 30 October 1837, by Friedrich von Martens (1800–1875). Russia was slow to construct railways, and used a wider gauge for the rails than elsewhere in Europe. This line was used mainly for taking courtiers and aristocrats to and from the Catherine Palace, the tsar's country residence.

9. 'New Harmony' as envisaged by the Utopian socialist Robert Owen, a wealthy British industrialist who purchased the town of Harmony, Indiana, in 1825, intending to build an ideal socialist community. Like other such experiments, almost all of them carried out by European Utopian socialists in the USA, it did not last.

10. Windischgraetz bombards Prague in June 1848. Divisions between Czech and German nationalists in the city hampered the cause of the liberal revolutionary uprising against the Habsburgs, and the Austrian Field-Marshal's attack led to their surrender on 17 June 1848, the beginning of the counter-revolution in Central Europe.

11. The Battle of Sadowa or Königgrätz, 7 July 1866: Prussian troops commanded by Helmuth von Moltke outmanoeuvred the slow-moving Austrians and broke through their centre, driving them from the field, opening the way to German unification without Austria or Bohemia.

12. Napoleon III's army crosses the Mont Cénis pass, using the road built by his uncle Napoleon I, on its way to aid the Piedmontese forces fighting to expel the Austrians from northern Italy. Following the Battle of Solferino on 24 June 1859 the process of Italian unification became unstoppable.

13. The social world of the aristocracy: the City of Vienna Ball, 1904, by Wilhelm Gause (1853–1915). In the centre, Vienna's anti-Semitic mayor Karl Lueger (with chain of office) chats with the Archduke Leopold and other dignitaries, signifying his acceptance in Habsburg high society.

14. A painting from the year 1871 by the Scottish inventor James Nasmyth (1808–90) of the steam hammer he had invented and installed in his foundry in Manchester. It allowed iron to be wrought for machine parts with the minimal exertion of human muscle-power: a classic innovation of the industrial revolution.

15. The metro station beneath the prestigious Andrássy Street in Budapest, pictured in 1896, the year it was opened. It was only the second electrically operated underground railway in the world, after London's, and carried up to 35,000 passengers every day, a proud testimony to urban modernity in the Hungarian capital.

16. *Emigrants* (1894) by Raffaello Gambogi (1874–1943), showing Italians embarking at the port of Livorno for New Zealand, in response to advertisements from an emigration agent. The mass emigration of Italians did not begin until the turn of the century, after which over 150,000 left every year, mostly for Argentina or the USA.

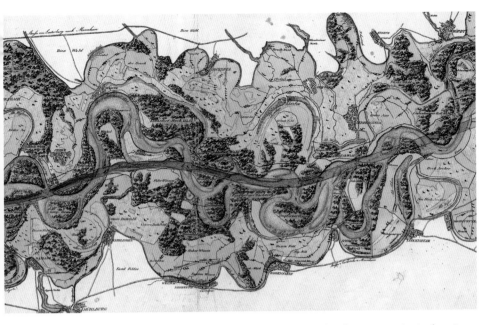

17. Hydrographic map of the Rhine between Neuburg and Sondernheim (1822/25), showing (in red) the new course of the river planned by the engineer Johann Gottfried Tulla. Over several decades the Rhine was straightened out and made more navigable and shortened by 50 miles, one of many such river projects carried out in the nineteenth century.

18. *Bullfight* (1892) by Vicente Garcia de Paredes (1845–1903). It was in the nineteenth century that bullfighting became a truly popular spectator sport in Spain, at a time when fox-hunting in England was so widely practised that fox-cubs had to be imported in their thousands from the Continent to satisfy the demand.

19. Loading the transatlantic cable onto a storage compartment in the *Great Eastern* steamship (1865). From this point onwards, almost instantaneous global communication became possible, leading to the introduction of time-zones and the International Date Line at the Washington Conference in 1884.

20. The conquest of disease: preventive hygienic measures such as disinfection, applied here to reluctant travellers on the Danube entering Serbia in 1911, when cholera was spreading into Europe from the Middle East, did much to reduce the danger of epidemics and lower the European death rate. In this case the disinfectant spray is unlikely to have done much good.

21. The execution of Karl Ludwig Sand in Mannheim on 20 May 1820, for the murder of the pro-Russian playwright and propagandist August von Kotzebue. Capital punishment was carried out in public in many European countries until after the 1848 Revolutions, after which fear of popular disturbances led most states to move them to closed prison yards.

22. Memorial of the liberation of the Bulgarian Church from the Greek Ecumenical Patriarchate after fifteen years of struggle (1872) by the Bulgarian artist Nikolai Pavlovich (1835–94). The creation of an independent Bulgarian Exarchate reflected a much wider European clash between nationalism and universal Christianity in the nineteenth century.

23. Advertisement for an 1886 edition of Victor Hugo's popular novel, first published in 1862, by Jules Cheret (1836–1932). *Les Misérables* was one of many works of fiction that explored the underworld of the poor and dispossessed in the new urban-industrial society of the nineteenth century.

24. *At the Zielony Balonik* ('The Green Baloon') (1908), a popular Cracow literary cabaret, by Kazimierz Sichulski (1879–1942). Opened in 1905, it was forced to close six years later by the Russian police. Like other, similar institutions in Paris, Barcelona and Berlin, it was closely associated with the modernist movement in the arts.

25. Hubertine Auclert and other French women's suffrage activists invade a polling station and overturn the ballot box in May 1908 as a protest against the disenfranchisement of women. Norway and Finland both introduced voting rights for women before 1914, but Frenchwomen had to wait until 1944 until they were granted the vote.

26. Assassination of the Spanish prime minister Antonio Cánovas del Castillo on 8 August 1897, while the politician was relaxing at a thermal spa. The murder, carried out in revenge for the execution of five Spanish anarchists ordered by Cánovas shortly before, was one of many such outrages carried out in Europe in these years.

27. *The Attack* (1899) by Euto Isto (1865–1905), showing the Russian eagle attempting to snatch the law book from the hands of the Finnish Maiden. The painting was widely reproduced and became a symbol of national resistance to the attempted Russification of Finland, which began around this time.

28. The Norwegian legislature, the *Storting*, declares independence from Sweden on 7 June 1905: tinted photograph by Frederik Hilfling-Rasmussen (1869–1941). The separation of Norway from the Swedish crown was achieved without bloodshed thanks largely to the threat of a general strike against military intervention by the Swedish labour movement.

29. Relief of the German garrison of Windhoek, besieged by Herero warriors, shown in a colour lithograph in the French popular magazine *Le Petit Journal* (21 February 1904). The armed forces sent from Berlin to put down the rebellion in Namibia deliberately exterminated the majority of the Herero tribe, one of many colonial atrocities committed by European powers in the age of imperialism.

30. Defeat of Bulgarian forces by the Turks at the Second Battle of Adrianople on 21 July 1913 during the Second Balkan War. Note the trenches, the Ottoman aeroplane, the use of heavy artillery, and the khaki uniforms worn by the Bulgarians – all harbingers of the way in which the First World War was to be fought just over a year later.

31. *The Wolves (Balkan War)* (1913) by Franz Marc. The ravenous Balkan states, turning on each other and blowing away the fading flower that symbolizes humanity, are shown in Cubist style by the young German artist, who was himself killed at the Battle of Verdun on 4 March 1916.

32. The assassination of the Archduke Franz Ferdinand and his wife, Countess Sophie Chotek, on 28 June 1914 in Sarajevo. This newspaper sketch clearly derives from an eyewitness report. Unlike most illustrations of the event, it depicts the protagonists in the right positions and the archduke in the correct headgear. However, the Archduke was shot first, not as shown here. Note the position of the steering wheel: Austria-Hungary drove on the left.

Scottish-born Canadian engineer Sir Sandford Fleming (1827–1915) pointed out, the standardization of time was required by the creation of an international telegraph network which 'subjects the whole surface of the globe to the observation of civilized communities and leaves no interval of time between widely separated places proportionate to their distances apart'. In the global communication network created by the telegraph, 'noon, midnight, sunrise, sunset, are all observed at the same moment' somewhere on Earth, and 'Sunday actually commences in the middle of Saturday and lasts until the middle of Monday'. This created intolerable uncertainties of many kinds, in areas such as insurance, or legislation, by leaving indeterminate the exact point when laws came into force, or insurance policies began to operate. In 1884, yielding to the pressures that came from the globalization of communication, delegates from twenty-five states met in Washington to standardize world time. Sailors had already synchronized time using chronometers set by longitudinal measurements based on the Greenwich Meridian, reflecting British dominance of seaborne mercantile traffic. This was the standard adopted at the Washington conference, which divided the world into twenty-four time zones by longitude, treating the meridian as the zero line, dividing the eastern from the western hemisphere and creating an International Date Line drawn through the least inhabited part of the Pacific.

It was particularly galling for French officialdom to have to admit the primacy of Britain in setting world times. In 1894, indeed, the French anarchist Martial Bourdin (1868–94) gave practical expression to this resentment by detonating a bomb in Greenwich, an incident later used in *The Secret Agent* (1907) by the Polish-British novelist Joseph Conrad (1857–1924). Further objections came from the Church, one of whose representatives, the Abbé Cesare Tondini de Quarenghi (1839–1907), campaigned unsuccessfully in the late 1880s for the meridian to be moved to Jerusalem, the Universal City regarded as the centre of the Earth by medieval mapmakers. A law of 1911 managed to fix French time without reference to Greenwich at all, defining it as 'the mean Paris time slowed nine minutes and twenty-one seconds'. Keen to recapture the initiative from the British, the French government organized an International Conference on Time in 1912, which established a generally accepted system of establishing the time and signalling it around the globe. The Eiffel Tower was already transmitting Paris time by radio signals, receiving calculations of astronomical time from the Paris Observatory. At 10 a.m. on 1 July 1913 it sent the first global time signal, directed at eight different receiving stations dotted around the world. Thus, as one French commentator boasted, Paris, 'supplanted by Greenwich as the origin of the meridians, was proclaimed the initial time centre, the watch of the universe'.

In the universe described by the mathematician and natural philosopher Sir Isaac Newton (1642–1727) time was uniform and absolute and flowed in a single direction. Not coincidentally, this concept provided the underpinning for that most universal of nineteenth-century ideas, the idea of progress. The concept of a uniform time proceeding everywhere in a linear fashion enhanced people's ability to imagine a distant past beyond their own experience, in which things had been different. The French Revolution had already created a sense of the pre-revolutionary past as different, renumbering the years from its outbreak as Year I, Year II, Year III and so on. This practice itself did not survive. But the idea of the past as different became widespread in European culture, in contrast to the eighteenth century, which had depicted the people and societies of the past as largely similar to those of its own age. The past also began to stretch back further in the imagination. Making their calculations on the basis of statements in the Bible, Christian theorists such as Archbishop James Ussher (1581–1656) had dated the creation of the world to 4004 BC, but geological investigations began to tell a different story, and by 1863 the British physicist William Thomson, Baron Kelvin (1824–1907), was calculating the Earth's age as around 100 million years, based on the rate of its cooling. Time began to stretch back far beyond what people had previously imagined; it became larger, as well as more uniform and more organized.

Yet just as time expanded in the past, it also contracted in the present. As the century progressed, people felt increasingly that they were living, as the English essayist William Rathbone Greg (1809–81) put it in 1875, 'without leisure and without pause – a life of *haste*'. 'The most salient characteristic of life in this latter portion of the 19th century,' Greg concluded, 'is its SPEED.' Comparing life in the 1880s with the days of his youth half a century before, the English lawyer and historian Frederic Harrison (1831–1923) recalled that whereas people seldom hurried when he was young, now 'we are whirled about, and hooted around' without cessation. In Britain railway companies on the east and west coast lines competed to see who could reach Scotland from London first. Fast sailing ships raced to be the first to bring the new year's tea from China back to Europe, with the tea-clipper *Cutty Sark* losing a famous race against its rival *Thermopylae* in 1872: both ships left Shanghai on 18 June, and arrived back in London on 19 and 10 October respectively. The opening of the Suez Canal in 1869 gave a key advantage to steamers, since sailing ships still had to go via the Cape of Good Hope. Competition was even fiercer for transatlantic crossings, and the rivalry between shipping lines soon became a symbol for the prowess of the countries where they had their onshore headquarters, with the Germans taking the prize from the British in 1897 but losing it in 1909 to the British liner *Mauretania*, which logged an average speed of more than 26 knots, a record that stood until 1927. The great luxury liners of the German *Imperator* class and the White Star company's *Olympic* class were floating palaces, equipped with amenities of all kinds, launched amid massive publicity, each more grandiose than the last. On 15 April 1912, however, the sinking on its maiden voyage of the newest vessel of the White Star company, the *Titanic*, at the time the world's largest ship, dented this feeling of confidence; 1,500 people were drowned, and the poor safety precautions, the insufficient provision of lifeboats, and the privileging of the upper-class passengers, led to a public outcry, followed by the International Convention for the Safety of Life at Sea, passed two years later.

On land as well as on sea, time was becoming ever more pressing. The Italian artist Giorgio de Chirico (1888–1978), founder of the 'metaphysical school' of painters, executed a series of works between 1912 and 1914 in which clocks dominate an empty landscape, dwarfing the few, tiny human figures with which it is populated. In several of them, a train is depicted; one is even entitled *Gare Montparnasse (The Melancholy of Departure)*. Time, de Chirico seemed to suggest, ruled human intercourse; paintings could only depict a single moment, identified by the clearly visible hour shown on the clock. His paintings showed scenes arrested at a single, immovable point of time. Some painters, notably the early Italian Futurists, or the French artist and *provocateur* Marcel Duchamp (1887–1968), in his 1912 picture *Nude Descending a Staircase*, attempted to incorporate movement in their work through painting an object on a single canvas at several different stages of its progress through time. Motion pictures, first developed in the 1880s, could speed up time, freeze it, jump over minutes, hours, days or even longer periods in their narratives; even more startlingly, as the brothers Louis (1864–1948) and Auguste Lumière (1862–1954) showed in 1895, they could reverse time by the simple device of projecting a film backwards, so that divers appeared to leap out of the water to land on the diving board, broken eggs put themselves back together in their shells, and shards of glass flew up onto a table and reassembled themselves into the unblemished form of a wineglass. Time began to seem malleable, changeable, uncertain, a development represented in science by the theory of relativity, first announced to the scientific world by Albert Einstein (1879–1955) in 1905. The papers in which he developed his theory were highly specialized but their implications were not: time and space were relative to the observer, so that moving clocks might tick more slowly than an observer's stationary clock, and if two observers were in relative motion, the same two events could be simultaneous for one but not for the other. The speed of light was constant and in a vacuum the same for all observers, and it could not be exceeded; mass and energy were equivalent. These conclusions put time and space into a new context far more complex than that of conventional mechanical physics. The implications of these theories were only to become apparent when Einstein completed his general theory of relativity in 1915, but already to a small number of physicists they had revolutionized basic concepts of time and space.

THE END OF THE GREAT PLAGUES

Time for the inhabitants of Europe in the nineteenth century was limited in another sense: their life on Earth was mostly very brief compared with that of later generations. For most of the nineteenth century, Europeans had to live with the constant presence of debilitating and sometimes fatal diseases. In low-lying, swampy areas with a warm climate, malaria was endemic, spread by mosquitoes living in brackish water. The disease was present around the Mediterranean and the Black Sea, and common along the coasts of France and Holland and along the Rhine and Danube before these rivers were channelled and controlled. In 1826 an epidemic along the North Sea coast affected 20,000 people, with considerable loss of life. As late as the end of the century there were two million cases a year in Italy, with 20,000 deaths and innumerable sufferers from recurring, debilitating 'quatrain fever'. The best treatment – quinine – was isolated from the bark of the cinchona, a commonly used therapy in Bolivia and Peru, by two French medical scientists in 1820, and made into a principal constituent of 'Warburg's Tincture', a drug developed in 1834 by Carl Warburg (1805–92), a German doctor based in Guyana. It was not until 1897, however, that Sir Ronald Ross (1857–1932), a British surgeon working in colonial India, established the role of mosquitoes in the transmission of the disease. Meanwhile, quite independently of any medical research, the incidence of malaria had been declining steadily in Europe as marshes were drained and rivers canalized – an accidental if welcome by-product of a policy largely carried out in the interests of trade.

The most universal of the serious and potentially fatal diseases to afflict nineteenth-century Europeans was tuberculosis, an infection that particularly affected the lungs in the form of 'consumption', which 'consumed' the body until the sufferer, coughing blood from the decaying organs, finally expired. In 1815 the physician Thomas Young (1773–1829) estimated that it was 'a disease so frequent as to carry off prematurely about one-fourth part of the inhabitants of Europe'. Some 250 out of 696 autopsies performed in the main Paris hospital in the early nineteenth century reached a diagnosis of tuberculosis as the cause of death. It was an affliction 'where youth grows pale, and spectre-thin, and dies', as John Keats (1795–1821) wrote in 'Ode to a Nightingale' in 1819; he himself was to die of the disease just two years later. In the second half of the nineteenth century almost half of all recorded deaths in England and Wales in the age group of twenty to twenty-four were from consumption. The relatively mild symptoms, the generally slow progress of the disease, the lack of any link to immoral conduct, all made consumption seem almost ennobling. It was widely regarded as intensifying the sufferer's experience of life. The composer Frederyk Chopin, whose health was euphemistically described as 'extremely delicate', continued to write music during his last years, as one of his pupils later remembered, improvising at the piano and 'transporting us to regions none of us had known before and none of us would revisit again', before his death from tuberculosis in 1849.

The moral elevation that many writers and commentators saw as a by-product of consumption belied the fact that it was a disease above all spread by overcrowded homes, unhealthy working conditions and poor nutrition; it was, in other words, a disease not of artists, intellectuals and socialites, but of the poor. The Russian novelist Fyodor Dostoyevsky, with his brutally realistic view of Russian society, saw this clearly enough. There are few more terrifying scenes in literature than the death in *Crime and Punishment* (1866) of the consumptive widow Katerina Ivanova, thrown into poverty by the alcoholism of her irresponsible husband and made destitute by his eventual death. In delirium and desperation, she takes her small children out onto the streets to sing and dance for a few kopecks. Arrested by a policeman, she runs breathlessly away, stumbles and falls dead in the street, blood gushing out of her throat: 'I've seen it before,' says the policeman: 'That's consumption.' Her death is undignified and grotesque, the product of the extreme poverty that has driven Katerina Ivanova not into an exalted state of mind but into indignity and madness.

The disease hit the poorest hardest because the poor lived and worked in overcrowded, damp and unhealthy conditions. The most popular treatment was the provision of fresh air, a dry and pure atmosphere, a healthy diet and rest for body and spirit far away in milder southern climates or high mountainous regions, or at the seaside. Of course, such luxuries were available only to the well off. Sanatoria were in the end used by too few people to have a measurable statistical impact. Yet death rates from tuberculosis fell almost everywhere in the second half of the century. The decline in tuberculosis mortality accounted for around half the overall decline in mortality between 1850 and 1900, though in 1894 it was still claimed that each year it caused as many deaths in Europe as had been caused by the whole of the Crimean War. The most important factor in the decline is likely to have been improved diet. Direct medical intervention, by contrast, had little effect. The German physician Robert Koch (1843–1910), who had discovered the cause and mode of transmission of anthrax in 1870, succeeded in 1882 in demonstrating through the use of differential chemical staining of microscopic samples the presence of the tuberculosis bacillus in all the sufferers he investigated. He managed to cultivate the bacilli in his lab and show their effect by injecting them into healthy animals, producing within a short time the classic symptoms of the disease. Koch repeated these experiments on a large scale until his discovery became indisputable. The disease, he showed was spread by coughing It was a major achievement and made him famous across the world. Yet it was to have no real impact on reducing the incidence of the disease: that had to wait until the era of the BCG vaccine (1921) and the development of antibiotics later in the twentieth century.

The greatest success of medical science had been scored in the fight against smallpox, which in the late eighteenth century had killed as many as 200,000 victims a year in Europe. The practice of preventing the disease by scratching the skin with an infected needle, developed early on in China, was introduced to Europe via the Ottoman Empire in the mid-eighteenth century. Its treatment was revolutionized at the end of the century, in 1798, by an English country doctor, Edward Jenner (1749–1823), who noticed that milkmaids never caught smallpox, and concluded that the reason for their immunity was because they had already caught a related disease, cowpox, which did not pose any threat to humans. Jenner's new preventive treatment, which he called vaccination, after the Latin for 'cow', soon became widely practised. State authorities began to make it compulsory. By the middle of the nineteenth century the Kingdom of Prussia had passed laws refusing to admit young people to school, apprenticeships, employment or the army without a vaccination certificate. Sixty-six vaccinations were recorded in Prussia annually for every 100 births. Other states followed suit. In France, the government had been far less successful; 125,000 French troops in the Franco-Prussian War of 1870–1 caught the disease, of whom some 28,000 died, compared with 8,500 cases and a mere 400 deaths among the Prussians and their allies. After the troops returned home, smallpox spread across Europe, killing a total of half a million people by the mid-1870s. In 1871 the British

government made vaccination compulsory as a result. Due to such measures, smallpox had become rare in Europe long before 1914.

Other diseases actually increased with industrialization. Growing
pollution in cities boosted the death rate from typhoid, a water-borne
disease, from 87 per 100,000 in London in the 1850s to 89 in the following decade. Its victims included Albert, the Prince Consort of Queen
Victoria, in 1861. By the eve of the First World War, the rate had fallen
to less than 9 per 100,000 following the great clean-up of the city in the
late Victorian era. The discovery of the bacterial causative agent by Robert
Koch's assistants in the early 1880s led quickly to the conclusion that it
could be carried by people who did not develop any symptoms, like the
famous 'Typhoid Mary', Mary Mallon (1869–1938), an emigrant to the
United States who in the 1900s caused epidemics wherever she went
despite the fact that she did not appear to suffer from the disease herself.
Public health campaigns duly took account of this fact, soon confirmed
in a number of other diseases too, including notably diphtheria, as well
as scarlet fever, meningitis, polio and typhoid, all of which could be carried in fresh milk as well as in water. Education in personal cleanliness
combined with public health measures such as water purification were the
most effective way of preventing diseases of this kind.

Most striking of all was the gradual disappearance of the great epidemics that had swept over Europe from time to time. For centuries, bubonic
plague, the 'black death', had ravaged Europe, but after the end of the
great epidemic in Bosnia in 1815–18 it was held at bay at the military
frontier established by the Habsburgs in south-eastern Europe and by
quarantine measures imposed in Mediterranean ports. More persistent
was typhus, a disease spread by the human body-louse. It had often been
spread by war, carried by large concentrations of troops living in unhygienic conditions, and by famine. The relative absence of wars and famines
in the nineteenth century was a major reason for its decline. Famines bring
large masses of people from the countryside to the towns in search of food,
and typhus broke out during the potato famine in Ireland in the late 1840s
as well as in central Europe. For radical liberals such as the German
pathologist Rudolf Virchow (1821–1902), typhus was not so much a sign
of ignorance and slovenliness born of a backward state of civilization, as
the result of oppression and the deprivation of basic human rights. Commissioned by the Prussian government to investigate an outbreak of the
disease in Upper Silesia in 1848, Virchow condemned the filth, squalor,
idleness and drunkenness of the people but rejected any idea that these
habits were the product of the fact that the area was largely inhabited by
Poles. The people, he declared, did not bother to take care of themselves

because they had lost their right to participate in cultural and political life. Virchow's report earned him dismissal from his post, but in retrospect it can be regarded as one of the first great classics of social medicine. It is not surprising that its author subsequently became a leading liberal and opponent of Bismarck, who was so angered by his persistent criticisms that in 1865 he challenged Virchow to a duel. As the person challenged, Virchow had the right to choose the weapons to be used, and famously he chose two sausages – one thoroughly cooked, for himself, and one raw, and stuffed with lethal trichinae larvae, for Bismarck. Sensibly on all counts, Bismarck then withdrew his challenge.

The association of typhus with dirt and poor hygiene was well established, and as towns and cities became cleaner, and people developed a more hygienic way of life, the incidence of the disease fell dramatically. Epidemics affected St Petersburg every year throughout the century, with a peak of more than 8,000 cases in 1878, as troops returned from the Russo-Turkish War, and over 300 deaths in 1891 as peasants flocked to the city during a famine. But in normal years morbidity and mortality rates were already falling even in Russia, as a result of improvements in public and personal hygiene. The actual discovery of the cause and mode of transmission of typhus did not in fact happen until 1909, when the French bacteriologist Charles Nicolle (1866–1936), director of the Pasteur Institute in Tunis, noticed that typhus patients only infected others if they had not changed their clothes. He investigated the dirty clothes and established that they carried body lice. He then placed some of these on a healthy chimpanzee, which caught the disease. Nicolle was awarded the Nobel Prize for Medicine for his discovery.

Alongside the decline of typhus and smallpox and the virtual disappearance of the bubonic plague, nineteenth-century Europeans also had to contend with an entirely new threat to their life and health: Asiatic cholera. The disease spread to Europe as a result of the opening up of new trade routes through Afghanistan and Persia following the British conquest of northern India, escaping from its reservoir in Bengal in 1817 and making its way westwards initially with troop movements and then with trade. Cholera spread to Europe because Europe's strategic power was spreading across Asia. Soon christened 'Asiatic cholera', the disease was widely understood as Asia's revenge: a deadly invasion from the supposedly backward and uncivilized East, launched just as Western civilization, in the eyes of many Europeans, was reaching the height of its progress and achievements. Once it had arrived in Europe, cholera quickly battened onto another central aspect of Europe's nineteenth-century expansion and growth. Industrialization ensured the disease spread quickly by road, river and rail, and was transmitted easily from person to person in the overcrowded and insanitary towns and seaports of the new industrial society, passed on either through contaminated water supplies and food-stuffs or through direct human contact. The extremely high death rate, averaging 50 per cent of those affected, was only one of the terrifying aspects of the disease. Almost as important for nineteenth-century bourgeois sensibilities was the fact that its onset and progress were sudden, often running from the first symptoms to death within twenty-four hours – massive vomiting and diarrhoea, the uncontrollable loss of bodily fluids – a shock to Victorian prudery and concealment of bodily functions. Death from cholera was the antithesis of a beautiful death.

Cholera killed millions in Asia and Europe in the 1820s and early 1830s. It returned in 1848–9, spreading again from east to west, and reaching the United States by ship across the Atlantic Ocean. It came back again in the mid-1860s, again crossing the Atlantic, and once more in the 1880s, in a series of epidemics lasting until the early 1890s. The coincidence of these major epidemics with periods of war, upheaval and revolution was noted by contemporaries. Cholera was brought westwards by Russian troops suppressing the Polish national uprising in 1830–1. In 1848–9 it followed the forces of order, including once more Russian troops, as they put down the Europe-wide revolutions of that year. The epidemic of 1854–6, which in similar fashion swept across Europe from Russia, was also the only one that then spread back across the Continent from west to east, carried to Turkey, Bulgaria and the Middle East by British and French troops fighting in the Crimean War. The epidemics of 1866 and 1871 were spread by Bismarck's wars of German unification. In 1892 cholera came westwards to central Europe with a wave of Jewish migrants fleeing antisemitic persecution in Russia and looking for a new home in America via ships sailing from Hamburg.

Here the hot weather and brackish water of the tidal Elbe river provided ideal breeding grounds for the bacillus, which entered the river from the cheap lodging houses and primitive, insanitary barracks where the migrants were housed, and was swept upstream by the tide. It soon reached Hamburg's water-intake point, spread through the unfiltered reservoirs, and was pumped into homes and houses across the city before the medical authorities had taken steps to diagnose the disease in its first victims or take any measures to deal with it or warn people of its presence. Soon victims were being collected in their thousands from infected homes and taken to hospital, in 50 per cent of cases never to return. Altogether some 10,000 people died in the city in the space of little more than six weeks. Hamburg was the only city in western or central Europe to suffer an epidemic on this scale in 1892. The disease hit the poorest most severely, living as they did in overcrowded and unhygienic dwellings, sharing toilet facilities and unable to take precautions such as boiling water before drinking it – as advised by Robert Koch, who had discovered the causative bacillus in 1884 and was sent from Berlin to deal with the epidemic. Surveying the slum quarters by the harbour where the impact of the disease was greatest, and remembering the squalid dwellings he had seen in Egypt and India, Koch turned to his team and said: 'Gentlemen, I forget that I am in Europe.' At the height of Europe's age of imperialism, it was hard to think of a more damning verdict.

In addition to Koch, the French chemist Louis Pasteur (1822–95) had made significant discoveries based on the germ theory of disease, developing vaccines for anthrax and rabies, and inventing the technique of 'pasteurization' to heat milk and kill any germs it might be carrying. But direct medical intervention did little to prevent and still less to cure infectious diseases in the nineteenth century. The sanitary revolution that took place in Europe's cities in the second half of the century, with the provision of clean water and proper sewage disposal, certainly helped stop the spread of cholera, just as it reduced the incidence of typhus and typhoid and similar diseases. After 1892, border controls, the disinfection of railway travellers and other similar measures were remarkably effective in preventing the spread of cholera across Europe. This was the last of the great epidemic infections to be conquered. It returned to the Ottoman Empire in 1910, from which it spread to Naples, returning in 1911. By this time the Neapolitan and national Italian authorities had learned the lesson of the 1884 epidemic, which had caused major public rioting in the city. Instead of coercive policing measures, they formed sanitary squads consisting mainly of working men from the areas in which they operated, instructed them to use courtesy and persuasion and not force, and avoided alarming publicity. The sale of food on the streets was banned, wells and cisterns were sealed, sewers were disinfected, the water supply was monitored, swimming in the harbour was stopped, the streets were swept, and the homes of victims were cleaned and their clothes destroyed. After some initial resistance, there was widespread popular acceptance of these measures, as there had been in Hamburg in 1892.

OUT OF THE SHADOW OF DEATH

Epidemics might hit the headlines, but the real killers were the everyday ones: poor nutrition, lack of hygiene, chronic conditions of one kind and another. At Europe's extremes these could have a devastating effect. In

remote, treeless Danish-administered Iceland, the harshness of the northern climate, just south of the Arctic Circle, was mitigated by the mildness
of the North Atlantic Drift, bringing warmer water up the Atlantic from
the Gulf Stream. But the long dark winters made for a short growing season – only four to five months – and nothing much more could be grown
than grass to feed livestock. Three-quarters of the island was covered in
barren lava fields, glaciers, mountains and deserts, and human habitation
clung to the margins, near the sea. Centuries of over-grazing had eroded
the grasslands and reduced the livestock, which numbered around
300,000 sheep and 25,000 cattle at mid-century. Volcanic eruptions and
epidemics, cold winters and famines had brought the population from its
medieval maximum of around 100,000 down to little more than half that
number by the early nineteenth century. When ice floes appeared in
strength off the coast, the temperature on the coastal plains plummeted
and the grass failed to grow.

In the nineteenth century, Icelanders lived mainly off mutton, beef and
fish; scurvy was common, and standards of cleanliness were so low that
visitors frequently commented on what the intrepid Austrian explorer Ida
Pfeiffer (1797–1858) called in 1852 the 'unparalleled filthiness' of the
turf-roofed, smoke-filled farmhouses. She found the floor of one house
'actually slippery from the incessant expectorations'. Malnutrition had
lowered the average height of Icelandic men (measured by skeletal remains)
from 5 feet 8 inches in the Middle Ages to 5 feet 6 inches by 1800. The
crude death rate stood at just under 30 per 1,000 population up to the
1870s – more than twice that of the city of Hamburg in 1892, the year of
the great cholera epidemic. Much of the mortality was among infants. In
the 1840s infant mortality in Iceland ran at an annual average of 35 per
cent, more than twice that of Norway and Sweden. Life expectancy at
birth in the 1850s was only thirty-two. Birth rates were correspondingly
high, at nearly 40 births per 1,000 population from the 1830s to the 1850s.
Iceland was by no means an extreme case in its demographic misery. In
Spain the death rate remained stubbornly at around 30 per 1,000 until
1900, not least because of the failure to carry out vaccinations against
smallpox in the rural interior of the country, despite their general availabil-
ity since 1798. The situation was made worse by an increase in the number
of children sent to foundling hospitals during the first half of the century,
where 58 per cent of them died before reaching the age of five. Rural
poverty could be deadly. In the 1880s infant mortality rates were regularly
around 20 to 30 per cent per annum in the sharecropping district of Ber-
talia, in the Emilia-Romagna region of Italy.

Yet the nineteenth century experienced a widespread fall in mortality rates, above all among infants, across most of Europe. Deaths per 1,000 population fell in England and Wales from 27 in 1800 to 14 in 1913, in Germany from 26 to 15, in France from 30 to 18; in Italy from 30 in 1850 to 19 in 1913. Even in Russia a fall was registered, from 39 in 1850 to 27 in 1913. In Austria-Hungary the decline was slow, from 28 in 1800 to 20 in 1913, but it occurred all the same. The reduction in infant mortality, the end of the great epidemics, the improvement in hygiene and sanitation, the arrival of effective methods of disease prevention – all this meant that for an average European born in the last two decades of the nineteenth century through the first decade or so of the twentieth century, the chances of surviving into adulthood and middle or even old age improved dramatically. Life expectancy at birth rose in Sweden from around thirty-seven in the early 1800s to forty-three by mid-century and fifty-eight by 1910; in the Netherlands it rose over the same period from thirty-two to fifty-four, with the bulk of the improvement coming after 1880; in England and Wales life expectancy rose steadily, from thirty-six to fifty-three; and France experienced a similar improvement, from thirty-four to fifty. By contrast, life expectancy at birth in Russia was still only just above thirty-two in 1910, with Spain, at thirty-two precisely, not much better.

With death ever present, its central place in nineteenth-century culture was hardly surprising. Funerals were very public affairs, often attended by large crowds, numbering hundreds of thousands in the case of the Duke of Wellington, buried with state honours in 1852 in St Paul's Cathedral. Following the death of Tsar Alexander III of Russia (1845–94) the city of St Petersburg was plunged into mourning, everyone had to wear black clothes, and theatres and concerts were cancelled. The tsar's hastily embalmed body embarked on a two-week tour from Livadiya in the Crimea, where he had died, to the capital, via Moscow and many other towns and cities, to arrive in St Petersburg for interment in the Peter and Paul Fortress, by which time the body was in a visible state of decomposition. Scarcely less impressive were the obsequies for the novelist, poet and political campaigner Victor Hugo in Paris in 1885, when two million people are estimated to have followed his coffin from the Arc de Triomphe to the Panthéon. Some 200,000 people are said to have followed the hearse bearing the body of Wilhelm Liebknecht (1826–1900), co-founder of the German Social Democratic Party, through the streets of Berlin, in a procession accompanied by '1,500 wreaths each with a red ribbon'. Funeral processions indeed became a standard form of socialist demonstrations in Germany's major cities, an occasion for party members and trade unionists to parade in vast numbers with banners held aloft.

The funeral rites of ordinary citizens were scarcely less elaborate. In the urban middle classes it was common to buy mourning teapots, black-edged stationery, black crêpe to cover the brass knocker on the front door, even special mourning umbrellas for a rainy day. A London under-taker's order book dating from 1824 records the following requirements for a particularly elaborate funeral:

> A strong coffin with white padded satin lining and pillow, mattress, sheet and a padded satin-lined lid; a very strong outside oak case, covered with superfine black cloth, best silvered nails, and rich ornaments also silvered; a rich plume of black ostrich feathers, and a man to carry ditto; silk scarves, hatbands and gloves for attendants; gifts of ditto for mourners; feather-pages and wands; mutes on horseback; silk dressings for poles; best black velvet pall and saddlecloths for horses; more ostrich feathers; cloaks; pages with truncheons and staves; hatbands and gloves; crape; attendants; rooms on the road; coachmen; feathermen; and turnpike fees to the family seat in Herefordshire – costing total of £803.11.0.

This was a huge sum at the time. The average funeral costs for a British aristocrat in the 1840s ran at between £800 and £1,500, for a gentleman £200 to £400; the Duke of Wellington's funeral cost all of £11,000, and was widely criticized for its extravagance. Already there were voices call-ing for the reduction of the expense and ceremony. *The Lancet* noted in 1894 that 'the cost of funerals has been very greatly reduced among the upper and upper-middle classes. It is found that the expenditure of £10 to £15 will allow of everything being completed in good taste and reverence, but without any excess.' The commemoration of the dead did not stop there. Social convention required that a widow should wear full mourning black for two years before the transition to half-mourning clothes, usually grey or lavender, for six months. The five years during which Queen Vic-toria formally mourned Prince Albert were exceptional only in length, not in their basic principle.

Memorials were made permanent in the elaborate headstones and monumental sculpture of Victorian graveyards – one reason why the burial of the dead in mass unmarked graves during major epidemics caused so much public disquiet. The advent of photography in mid-century even enabled mourners to pose with the dead laid out in a coffin before they set off for the burial, or with the deceased loved one, eyes opened and dressed as if still alive. King Oscar I of Sweden and Norway (1799–1859) was the first but by no means the last monarch to order his dead body to be photographed in its coffin. Death was ever present in poetry, perhaps most notably the influential and widely read long poem *In Memoriam* by

Alfred, Lord Tennyson (1809–92), commemorating his deceased friend Arthur Hallam (1811–33). Heroic death was especially prized, as in the endlessly copied and reproduced contemporary painting by Arthur Devis (1762–1822) of the death of Admiral Horatio Nelson in 1805 at the Battle of Trafalgar. In all these representations, literary as well as visual, it was striking that the body remained intact; there was no blood, there were no gaping wounds, no *mess*; and the same was true of the Victorian funeral, where the arts of the embalmer were employed to render the deceased as much as possible like he or she had been in life. The often sordid realities of death were concealed, in an attempt to make death respectable.

The Christian emphasis on dying a good death, so evident in the death-bed scenes in Dickens's novels, demanded clarity of mind to the end; a deathbed struggle against the delusions brought on by fever could become a metaphorical struggle for repentance and forgiveness. Religion guaranteed triumph over suffering, however severe it might be. Families, even children, gathered round the deathbed to witness the dying person's transition to the life everlasting. Yet attitudes were changing. Avoiding suffering in the present became the paramount consideration. By the late nineteenth century it had become regarded as a blessing when someone died without knowing that they were dying; a sudden death, or death in one's sleep, were thought of as ideals. In Tolstoy's story 'Three Deaths' (1859) a rich businessman refuses to tell his wife that she is dying (saying, somewhat illogically, 'it would kill her'); eventually a poor relation is called in to give her the bad news, but the woman stops him. 'Don't try to prepare me,' she says. In a later, more famous story by Tolstoy, 'The Death of Ivan Ilyich' (1886), the friends of the eponymous central figure conspire to try and convince him he is not really dying at all. They 'laugh at his fears, as if this horrible and nameless thing that had taken root in him, gnawed at him constantly, and was drawing him inexorably no one knew where, were some sort of amusing joke'. Even his doctor tries constantly to give him hope of recovery: 'We'll fix you up in no time!' he says reassuringly. When Ivan Ilyich collapses, he tells his wife: 'It's nothing . . . I . . .' 'What's the use of telling her,' he says to himself. 'She wouldn't understand.' Death was becoming an unusual occurrence, especially among adults in the prime of life, and the middle and upper classes at least were losing the ability to cope with it.

Such attitudes were wholly alien to the great mass of Europeans who lived in the countryside, where death rates remained high right up to the turn of the century and beyond. A death in the family in Sicily or Greece or the Russian steppe brought in the women of the community, who washed the body, engaged in ritual keening, and supervised the burial preparations. If there was a clock in the house, it was stopped; mirrors were turned to the wall to stop the dead person's soul seeing itself, water vessels were emptied to prevent it from drowning. In Sweden, rural France and other areas the death knell of the local church was rung in a pattern that denoted the age and sex of the deceased person. It was common for the funeral to be held no more than three days after death, with the open coffin filled with jewellery for women, a pipe or a bottle of wine for men, and toys for children; everywhere a small coin was added, to pay St Peter at the gates of Heaven. In Russia sharp stones were sometimes placed in the coffin to remind the deceased of the sins they would carry with them. Only gradually were funerals handed over to commercial undertakers.

Country folk took precautions to make sure that nobody was buried while still alive. In Germany a cemetery in Frankfurt had a room with bells connected to cords tied to the fingers of the deceased. The eyes of corpses were closed to prevent the dead from summoning the living with a glance. In many parts of Europe, and not just in Transylvania, legends of vampires rising from the dead caused widespread anxiety, even terror. Burial in consecrated ground could to some extent avoid this threat, but with the growing population cemeteries began to experience overcrowding. Corpses piled on top of one another could break through to the surface, constituting a serious health hazard. Secularist, socialist and anticlerical movements began to advocate civil rather than religious interment; by 1880 fully a quarter of all burials in Brussels were civil ceremonies. Increasingly graveyards were moved out of city centres, but the long-term solution lay in cremation, anathema to those who believed in the physical resurrection of the body at the Day of Judgement. In 1864 a corpse was experimentally cremated in Dresden by a closed device designed by Siemens, and a similar device was exhibited at the Vienna Exposition of 1873 by two Italian scientists. Impressed by the demonstration, Sir Henry Thompson (1820–1904), a well-known surgeon and sometime physician to the king of the Belgians, founded the British Cremation Society the following year. In 1888 twenty-eight cremations took place at the Society's crematorium in Woking, Surrey. The custom began to spread. The Swedish physician and politician Richard Wawrinsky (1852–1933) campaigned for cremation on hygienic grounds, resulting in the construction of the first crematorium in Sweden in 1887, and others soon followed despite a ban on the practice by the Catholic Church that lasted into the second half of the twentieth century.

The growing practice of cremation was another sign that death was becoming much less of an everyday experience for the middle and upper classes of Europe, as falling mortality rates reduced their familiarity with it. As the Duke of Argyll (1823–1900), a retired politician, was dying, after falling into senile dementia some years before, his daughter Frances Balfour (1858–1931) expressed nothing but horror, and her letters to her brother-in-law Arthur Balfour (1848–1930) included no descriptions of the deathbed scene at all. Death had become something to avoid talking about. Indeed people even began to seek for supposedly scientific evidence that it was only a transition to another life, as Christian certainties began to ebb away. Spiritualism, a movement that spread from America, where it began in the 1840s, reached the height of its popularity towards the end of the century, as séances proliferated, offering a variety of supposed proofs that the soul continued to exist in the afterlife: the dead could speak to the living through the voice of a medium or inspire him or her to commit automatic writing to a blank sheet of paper, they could even manifest themselves physically through movements of chairs and tables. By 1914, in urban society at least, death had become something to deny, an attitude that was to make the mass slaughter of the First World War all the more traumatic.

CONTROLLING THE PRIMAL URGE

The fall in death rates that was one of the most striking aspects of the demographic history of nineteenth-century Europe was followed, at an interval, by a corresponding fall in birth rates: taken together the two trends constituted what historians call the 'demographic transition'. Birth rates fell across Europe, from 31 live births per 1,000 population in Sweden in 1800 to 14 live births in 1913; in England the decline was from 38 to 24 live births, in Germany 40 to 28, in France 33 to 19, in Austria-Hungary 41 to 30. By contrast, in Italy the decline was far slower and less marked, from 37 in 1850 to 32 in 1913. Russia lagged noticeably behind the rest of Europe, with a birth rate of 51 in 1850 falling to 43 in 1913. The movement, however, was in the same downward direction all across Europe. It meant that the average number of children per woman of childbearing age also fell – between 1800 and 1910 in England and Wales from just under six to just under three. From 1870 to 1910 the average fell from 4.6 in the Netherlands to 3.3, and from 5.3 in Germany to 3.5. Across the Continent as a whole the average number of live births per woman of childbearing age fell from 4.7 in 1870 to 3.4 in 1910. Another, more precise statistic, the total number of children born alive to the average woman during her marriage, leaving out illegitimate births in other words, told the same story: this fell from 6.8 in Austria in 1880 to 5.9 in 1910, from

6.8 in England and Wales in 1851 to 4.7 in 1911, and from 7.6 in Germany in 1867 to 5.4 in 1910. To put it in more general terms, a woman in most parts of Europe just after the middle of the nineteenth century could expect to have between six and eight children during the course of her marriage, whereas by around 1910 she could expect to have five or fewer, except in Ireland, Norway, Russia and Sweden, where the figure remained static at around seven.

The difference in scale and chronology between various European states was a cause for concern for those that felt they were lagging behind, notably France, where 'pro-natalism' became a significant political force by the end of the century. The population of France grew from 30 million in 1800 to only 40 million in 1910; that of Britain more than doubled over the same period, from 20 to 45 million; Russia's population growth was even more impressive, from 48 to 142 million, though a large part of this was a consequence of eastward territorial expansion. The Austrian Empire increased in population from 29 to 51 million, and the Italian state from 23 million in 1860 to 35 million in 1910; but it was German population growth, from 41 million in 1860, not much larger than the population of France, to 65 million in 1910, that really worried the French. By the 1890s births per 1,000 inhabitants in Germany were running at a rate of 36, as they had been since mid-century, but in France they had fallen from the already low figure of 27 down to a mere 22 per 1,000. For German governments and nationalist commentators, this signified the youth and vigour of their own nation, and the decline and decadence of the French, until the turn of the century when German population growth levelled off and then began to fall, sparking an intense debate that led to increasingly desperate and completely futile attempts to stop the decline.

How was this remarkable fall in the number of births achieved? This was a world in which there was no contraceptive pill, while mechanical methods of contraception were ineffective and not widely available. The vulcanization of rubber in 1844 enabled the Goodyear tyre company to produce rubber sheaths from the mid-1850s (they were apparently about the thickness of a bicycle inner tube), but they were expensive and still unreliable. Moreover, their marketing and sale were frowned upon by governments anxious that the decline of the birth rate would compromise their military effectiveness. In Germany advertisements for condoms came under a law of 1900 banning the display of objects 'for obscene use'. Moral disapproval was widespread. 'The use of contraceptives of any sort,' declared the gynaecologist Paul Zweifel (1848–1927) in 1900, 'can only serve lust.' Midwives, especially in rural areas, could supply diaphragms and chemical contraceptives, but these too were illicit as well as unreliable.

Other methods of contraception, including withdrawal, promoted by the sex manuals that began to be published from the 1820s onwards, were poorly understood and even less effective, though coitus interruptus was the method most commonly used in France according to a survey of doctors carried out in 1899, and most probably elsewhere too. The same survey reported that condoms were hardly used at all. Abortions as reported by doctors and midwives became increasingly widespread before 1914 despite being outlawed almost everywhere: in Germany there were an estimated 100,000 to 300,000 every year in the period 1905–10, mainly among single women of all social classes, but especially within the petty bourgeoisie.

The only completely safe contraceptive method was abstinence, and since it was women who bore the risk of pregnancy and all the consequent burdens, it was women who began to repress their sexual feelings. The idea that women were incapable of sexual activity, an idea that would have seemed strange in the eighteenth century, became more common, above all among the bourgeoisie. Daughters had to remain chaste until marriage, for here too an unwanted pregnancy could ruin a family's reputation and impose undesirable financial burdens on it. It was to reinforce such behaviour that the notorious phenomenon of Victorian prudery emerged. Its most celebrated exemplar was Thomas Bowdler (1754–1825), editor of *The Family Shakespeare, in Ten Volumes; in which nothing is added to the original text; but those words and expressions are omitted which cannot with propriety be read aloud in a family.* The omissions were indeed striking. Derogatory references to clergymen were expunged, parts of the body were not referred to, the word 'body' itself was generally replaced with the word 'person', and immoral characters such as the prostitute Doll Tearsheet in *Henry IV Part II* disappeared entirely. Bowdler's edition, largely compiled by his sister Henrietta (1750–1830), was first published in 1807 and reached its final form in 1818; it went through fifty editions all the way up to 1896. While the early editions were heavily criticized for what one reviewer called their assumption that families would be too 'squeamish' to read Shakespeare aloud in the original, as early as 1820 a leading periodical, the *Edinburgh Review*, was declaring that 'it is better every way that what cannot be spoken, and ought not to have been written, should now cease to be printed'. Such views became more common later in the century and fuelled the political drive in many countries to ban pornographic literature. The German police compiled lengthy lists of obscene books, while in 1891 the Italian Minister of the Interior, Giovanni Lanza (1810–82), declared that 'all those who are honest and moral know how much obscene images and licentious books harm young people . . . The corruption of mores leads to the decadence of the nation.'

With expurgated and 'popular' editions of literary classics coming into vogue, and censorship laws in place in many countries, middle-class women were generally beleaguered by the forces of prudery. Given the pressures to reduce expenditure on children with the spread of education and the concomitant reduction in children's earning power, it was not surprising that the decline in the birth rate affected them first. But it soon spread to the working classes as legal restrictions on child labour and the extension of primary education turned children from an economic asset into an economic burden lower down the social scale too. Working-class sexuality may to some extent have been less repressed than its middle-class counterpart, but the unbridled lust portrayed in Zola's *Germinal* (1885), where a night-time walk in a coalmining community reveals copulating couples round every corner, owed more to the novelist's overheated imagination than to sober social observation. Not surprisingly, the illegitimate birth rate also began to fall across Europe, beginning in the 1840s, and continued to decline until the end of the century; women in other words were having less sex outside marriage as well as within it.

Giving birth out of wedlock, with its consequence of social stigmatization, was frequently cited as a major reason for women being forced to engage in prostitution, which underwent a considerable expansion in the nineteenth century. In 1899 there were 2,000 registered prostitutes in Madrid and perhaps 7,000 illegals, and the capital contained 150 officially sanctioned brothels, which were subjected to regular health inspections. According to the novelist Pio Baroja (1872–1956), writing in 1911, the women in them were relentlessly bullied by the madams, who kept their earnings, fed them poorly, and reduced them to the condition of a 'sad proletariat of sex'. A quarter of the city's registered prostitutes were former domestic servants, and another quarter, probably textile workers, had been driven into the trade by poverty. The 1869 census in St Petersburg recorded some 2,000 prostitutes in the city, but these were said to constitute only a quarter of the true number. The registered prostitutes lived in the inner city, concentrated in state-licensed brothels. In Berlin a survey of 2,224 registered prostitutes carried out in the 1870s showed that nearly half were the daughters of artisans, 20 per cent of factory workers, and 14 per cent of minor officials and clerks. They were mostly in their late teens or twenties, and came from a variety of jobs, of which domestic service and waitressing were the most prominent, accounting in Munich in 1909–10 for 1,261 and 1,162 respectively out of a total of 4,560 prostitutes. The ranks of the many thousands of clandestine prostitutes swelled when times were bad in trades like dressmaking and textiles, and declined when these recovered; most prostitutes slipped in and out of the game as their need for additional income required.

As Europe's cities grew with the influx of young men looking for jobs, so prostitution grew to satisfy their sexual demands. The best statistical indicator of the extent to which men used the services of prostitutes can be found in death rates from syphilis, which in England and Wales rose very sharply from 1850 up to the end of the 1860s, then levelled off, to decline from the mid-1880s onwards. Since the disease had a generally low mortality rate, this means that the number of people infected must have been many times greater. In 1864, indeed, nearly 30 per cent of all troops in the United Kingdom were said to be infected with sexually transmitted diseases, including syphilis. The annual incidence of new cases of syphilis in St Petersburg was running at around 30,000 by the end of the 1870s, or 45 patients per 1,000 inhabitants. It was not until 1905 that the causative agent of syphilis was discovered, by two German scientists, Fritz Schaudinn (1871–1906) and Erich Hoffmann (1868–1959). Unusually, relatively effective treatment followed very quickly in this case. In Frankfurt the scientist Paul Ehrlich (1854–1915) had for some time been engaged in experiments to develop a way of attacking microbes with arsenic compounds without causing collateral damage to other cells. In 1909, in his 606th experiment with different compounds, he succeeded in developing a chemical treatment for syphilis, which he called Salvarsan, marketed by the drug company Hoechst AG the following year and in an improved version a few years afterwards. Ehrlich dubbed it the 'magic bullet'.

Male clients using prostitutes went unstigmatized: they were merely young men 'sowing their wild oats'. Protecting them from disease appeared to the male authorities to be a priority. French prostitutes had to be registered with the police from 1802 onwards. Official regulation was introduced in most other European countries in the following decades. Medical authority for these measures was provided by the hygienist Alexandre Parent-Duchâtelet (1790–1836), whose hugely influential tract on prostitution in Paris appeared posthumously in 1836. He charted the distribution of prostitutes across Paris, and declared that women of loose morals deserved to be registered, locked up, subjected to regular medical examinations, and sent if ill to a locked hospital ward until they recovered, because 'they make themselves unworthy of . . . freedom by abandoning themselves to their unbridled passions and all the excesses of a dissolute life. Freedom in this case,' he concluded, 'amounts to licentiousness, and licentiousness destroys society.'

Of course, further up the social scale 'courtesans' and the *grandes horizontales* escaped formal control. In high society sexual favours were more likely to be exchanged for benefits such as lodging, clothes, jewellery and the like, to escape the stigma of commercial prostitution. This was also one way for a small number of women, such as Lola Montez, to achieve political power and influence. Women such as the singer-actress Blanche d'Antigny (1840–74), the model for the eponymous heroine of Zola's novel *Nana* (1880), was said to have had lovers at one time or another in Paris, Romania and Russia, where she had an affair with the chief of police in St Petersburg, and also Egypt, where she became the mistress of the Khedive. High aristocrats and monarchs frequently took mistresses or had serial affairs; on his frequent visits to Paris, Edward VII, according to the French police, received a string of aristocratic women from the Russian Embassy in his hotel rooms, no doubt rewarding them amply for their services. Lower down the social scale, novelists portrayed downtrodden and exploited young women like Nancy in Charles Dickens's *Oliver Twist* or Fantine in Victor Hugo's *Les Misérables* as good-hearted victims of the criminal underworld; Nancy is eventually beaten to death by her brutal lover, the burglar Bill Sykes, while Fantine is forced to sell her hair and front teeth to avoid destitution, dies in a fit, and is buried in a pauper's grave.

It was for such women that police regulation was devised. It was justified in Britain in the 1860s by the Paris-trained gynaecologist Dr William Acton (1813–75), who believed that the women who became prostitutes were morally and physically disordered, untypical of the female sex as a whole. Acton stated baldly: 'The majority of women (happily for them) are not very much troubled with sexual feeling of any kind.' Men, on the other hand, were in his view driven by strong sexual urges that required expression. Acton thought that spotting the women who should be arrested and incarcerated was easy enough. 'Who,' he asked:

are those fair creatures, neither chaperones nor chaperoned: those 'somebodies whom nobody knows', who elbow our wives and daughters in the parks and promenades and rendez-vous of fashion? Who are those painted, dressy women flaunting along the streets and boldly accosting the passer-by? Who those miserable creatures, ill-fed, ill-clothed, uncared-for, from whose misery the eye recoils, cowering under dark arches and among bye-lanes?

Acton's answer, and that of the administrators of the Contagious Diseases Acts, passed in 1864, 1866 and 1869 to impose confinement in locked medical wards for women diagnosed with sexually transmitted diseases, was clear: they were all prostitutes. But of course in effect they could simply be women engaging in sex before marriage, or carrying on serial non-marital relationships, or simply just walking around unchaperoned. The view that prostitution helped preserve the institutions of marriage and the family was widespread across Europe. The Italian politician and anthropologist Paolo Mantegazza (1831–1910) declared roundly that 'paid sensual pleasure is one hundred times better than infidelity in the home, than adultery integrated into our moral customs'.

Such views were precisely what angered social reformers like the British feminist Josephine Butler (1828–1906), who, when a National Association for the Repeal of the Contagious Diseases Acts was founded for men only in 1869, quickly set up a Ladies National Association that soon took the lead in the campaign. The state regulation of vice in Butler's view merely encouraged men to indulge in it in the belief they could avoid being infected with a sexually transmitted disease. And the prostitutes themselves were forced into a life of vice that was surely alien to their natural modesty as women. 'The fallen woman who lives off her trade,' declared one social purity pamphlet, 'is a pest to society. Pity her, reform her by all means, but do not feel bound to give her liberty to ply her harmful trade any more than you give liberty to any other corrupters of society.' The series of murders of prostitutes in the poverty-stricken East London district of Whitechapel in 1888 by the mysterious killer known as 'Jack the Ripper', far from arousing sympathy for the victims, acted for most as a confirmation of this negative view. The exposure of the most extreme form of sexual coercion and exploitation, child prostitution, by the journalist William Thomas Stead (1849–1912) in his article series 'The Maiden Tribute of Modern Babylon' (1885), caused a sensation, but led to few concrete results except the raising of the age of consent from thirteen to sixteen.

Butler's movement eventually secured the repeal of the Acts in 1886. But her attempt to carry her campaign to the European Continent, recounted in her *Personal Reminiscences of a Great Crusade* (1896), was an unmitigated failure. Police authorities across Europe, as she recorded indignantly, treated her with indifference or scorn. It was not until the turn of the century that feminists in France, Germany and elsewhere began to gain public support in their campaigns against the registration of prostitutes. In one city after another, police-approved brothels were closed down: their number in Hamburg, for example, after growing from 98 to 191 between 1834 and 1874, fell back to 157 by the 1880s. In Britain the Criminal Law Amendment Act of 1885 gave the police wide-ranging powers to close down brothels. In France a law of 1906 also raised the age of consent and led to the imprisonment of many prostitutes, who had now come under even closer police supervision than before, leading most of them to work illegally. Many sex-workers bitterly resented this 'neo-reglementarism', leading in 1908 to a mass revolt in Rouen, where mutinous registered prostitutes attacked the police who arrested them, biting and kicking them, tearing their clothes to pieces and shouting obscenities. At the Gare St-Lazare in Paris, as they were being transferred to another institution, they escaped from the train, opened their bodices, lifted up their skirts and shouted insults at the police. There could be no more dramatic demonstration of the gulf between these young women, who repeatedly shouted 'we are good-time girls', affirming their identification with their trade, and the morality societies who treated them either as innocent victims of male depravity or evil corrupters of the social order.

The campaign against prostitution in Britain led among other things to an amendment to the 1885 Act, put by the ambitious Liberal politician Henry Labouchère (1831–1912), providing for up to two years' hard labour in prison for acts of gross indecency between men. Labouchère claimed that in doing this he had been prompted by the prevalence in England's cities of male prostitution, but in effect it applied to all forms of homosexual activity between men. The new law was certainly less draconian than the previous English laws against buggery, which had provided the death penalty on conviction (removed in 1861), but it was much more all-encompassing. The Labouchère amendment also reflected a general belief among social purity campaigners that male homosexuality was a product of the same unrestrained male lust they were trying to curb in their campaign against the double standard. In both cases, too, public decency was invoked, along with the need to protect young people, a concern voiced particularly in the trial of the playwright and wit Oscar Wilde in the mid-1890s. This was also the case with public scandals in other countries where homosexual relations between men were outlawed, as in Germany in 1907–8 when the journalist Maximilian Harden (1861–1927) became embroiled in a lengthy series of libel actions after accusing Philip, Prince of Eulenburg (1847–1921), a close friend and companion of the Kaiser, and various other senior figures at court and in the military, of carrying on homosexual relations with one another. The scandal led to a nationwide panic, fanned by the opposition Social Democrats, the disgrace of Eulenburg, prosecuted for perjury, and serious damage to the reputation of the Kaiser. Paradoxically, the criminalization of homosexuality was an important factor in creating a greater sense of sexual identity and a stronger network of subcultures among homosexuals.

That the outlawing of homosexuality in the United Kingdom did not extend to homosexual relations between women was not, as legend would have it, because nobody in the British government dared broach the subject with Queen Victoria, but in reality because of a belief in the absence of the sexual impulse between women that underlay the entire social purity campaign. The same distinction between men and women also underlay the criminalization exclusively of male homosexuality on the Continent, as in the 1871 German Criminal Law Code or successive Russian criminal laws in 1835, 1845 and 1903. Lesbian sexual relationships could be accommodated under the concept of 'romantic friendships'; women who were explicitly conscious of their homosexuality – such as the wealthy Yorkshirewoman Anne Lister (1791–1840), whose mannish appearance, black clothing and openly cultivated sexual relationships with other women aroused considerable disapproval in local society, where she was known as 'Gentleman Jack' – were rarities, but in any case they did not cause major social anxiety. It was male lust that was the object of the reformers. An even worse manifestation of male lust than homosexuality in the eyes of some was masturbation, against which there was a veritable moral panic at this time. As the social purity campaigner the Reverend James Wilson (1836–1931) declared: 'Rome fell; other nations have fallen; and if England falls it will be this sin, and her unbelief in God, that will have been her ruin.'

By this time a counter-movement was in progress, with erotic publications like the *Yellow Book*, with woodcuts by Aubrey Beardsley (1872–98) aided by the subversive wit of Oscar Wilde, challenging key Victorian values. The Italian poet Gabriele D'Annunzio (1863–1938) made a point not only of conducting a very public affair with the actress Eleanora Duse (1858–1924) but also of writing literary works such as *The Child of Pleasure* (1889) that led to his condemnation by the Church as a perverter of public morals. Even greater scandal was caused by the plays of the Munich-based Frank Wedekind (1864–1918), notably *Spring Awakening* (1891) and the two 'Lulu' dramas, *Earth Spirit* (1895) and *Pandora's Box* (1904), which attacked sexual repression and featured subjects such as lesbianism, prostitution and group masturbation. But the emergence of the Decadent movement only signalled the complexity and diversity of late Victorian and Edwardian attitudes to sexuality. The physician Max Nordau denounced the new trends in his 1892 book *Degeneration*, seeing them as symptoms of a wider social and moral decline. And the core idea of the Suffragettes' classic poster demand, 'Votes for Women and Chastity for Men', continued in many ways right up to the introduction of the contraceptive pill in the 1960s. A pamphlet by Christabel Pankhurst (1880–1958), *The Great Scourge and How to End It*, advocating male abstinence as the only way to end the evil of prostitution, was perhaps not so eccentric as many historians have suggested. The play *Ghosts* by the Norwegian dramatist Henrik Ibsen (1828–1906) still caused a public scandal when it was first performed in 1882, because it featured the long-term effects of a sexually transmitted disease on one of the principal characters. The *Daily Telegraph* was one of many publications that condemned what it called 'Ibsen's positively abominable play entitled *Ghosts*'.

The serious study of sexuality had begun in the late 1860s, with a campaign by the Hungarian journalist Károly Kertbeny (1824–82) to stop the German Criminal Code then in preparation outlawing homosexuality, a word he himself invented in 1860. The greater openness with which sexuality was discussed towards the end of the century was reflected in, and perhaps also influenced by, the publication of a range of books and treatises on the subject. The most notable of these was by Baron Richard von Krafft-Ebing (1840–1902), a practising psychiatrist, who explored previously unmentionable forms of sexuality in his textbook *Psychopathia Sexualis* (1886), a treatise for medical and legal professionals written in a deliberately dry academic style, with copious use of Latin, in order to discourage the prurient. The book dealt with homosexuality ('sexual inversion'), paedophilia and bisexuality, and gave currency to the terms 'sadism', derived from the cruel sexual practices of the Marquis de Sade (1740–1814), and 'masochism', after the writings of Leopold von Sacher-Masoch (1836–95), in whose novel *Venus in Furs* (1870) the hero submits himself voluntarily to various forms of sexual humiliation. Krafft-Ebing was a stern moralist who thought all forms of sexual expression were perversions unless they were directed to the end of procreation, but his work, for all the precautions he took, helped bring discussion of sexuality into the open. He did not, however, contradict the prevalent view of female sexuality. If a woman was 'normally developed mentally,' he wrote, 'and well brought up, her sensual desire is small'.

Krafft-Ebing's English counterpart, Havelock Ellis (1859–1939), published his own medical textbook, *Sexual Inversion*, in 1896. Ellis introduced the terms 'narcissism' and 'autoerotism' into the language, and his ideas had an influence on the Austrian neurologist Sigmund Freud (1856–1939), who developed his practice of 'psychoanalysis', based on the use of hypnosis or free association to help patients deal with their nervous disorders by recovering memories of childhood sexual traumas, real or imagined, from their unconscious mind. Through discussion of these ideas at the Wednesday Psychological Society, founded in 1902, Freud began to acquire increasing influence among psychiatrists, leading to the foundation of an International Psychoanalytic Association. Some of his disciples began to develop rather different ideas, notably the Swiss psychologist

Carl Gustav Jung (1875–1961), who invented the terms 'extraversion' and 'introversion' and posited the existence of a 'collective unconscious' shared by all and constituting the essentially religious foundations of the human psyche. But it was Freud who dominated the psychoanalytical mainstream, though it was not until after the First World War that his ideas became really influential. The fact remained that, for all the public discussion of sexuality and for all the histrionic eroticism of a man like D'Annunzio, the continuing fall in the birth rate throughout the period and well beyond made it clear that most people were more concerned to repress their sexual urges than to act on them.

THE MANAGEMENT OF PAIN

Before the nineteenth century, human beings had been condemned to live with almost constant pain, alleviated at best by folk remedies of one kind or another. Major operations had to be conducted without anaesthetic, the patient's senses dulled only by the application of copious quantities of alcohol or opiates. Even small operations, such as tooth-pulling, which had become a frequent necessity after the arrival of large amounts of sugar in the European diet during the eighteenth century, could cause almost unbearable pain. Attempts were made to dull the senses by 'animal magnetism' or 'mesmerism', devised by the Austrian doctor Franz Anton Mesmer (1734–1815) in the 1790s and popularized by French physicians in the 1820s. It became popular in a series of experiments carried out by Dr John Elliotson (1791–1868) at University College Hospital London in 1837 on two domestic servants who suffered from hysteria and epilepsy. Elliotson claimed to have cured them by passing an invisible magnetic fluid from his own body to theirs, thus warming them up and driving the ailment away. Mesmerism, or what we would nowadays call hypnosis, quickly gained currency in a wide variety of social circles until it was discredited by the revelation that Elliotson's subjects had in fact been pretending all along; as a result of this damning discovery, doctors quickly abandoned its use as an anaesthetic in operations, common in the early 1840s, and turned to chemical anaesthesia instead.

The chemical management of pain began in the mouth. Laughing gas (nitrous oxide) was first deployed in America in 1844 as a way of eliminating pain during dental operations, but like two other anaesthetics first used in the 1840s, ether and morphine, it proved unreliable and had unwelcome side effects, including in some cases addiction. The most popular anaesthetic of the era was chloroform, whose effects were discovered by the Scottish surgeon James Young Simpson (1811–70). It became widely accepted after Queen Victoria took it to dull the pain of childbirth in 1853: 'The effect,' she recorded in her journal, 'was soothing, quieting & delightful beyond measure.' However, objections were raised to the use of anaesthetics even during amputations; they scorned nature, some argued. Least of all were they required during natural events such as childbirth. They were dangerous. And they were unnecessary, particularly with men such as soldiers who were inured to pain. The Russian surgeon Nikolai Ivanovich Pirogov (1810–81) was the first to use anaesthetic on a battlefield, applying ether to amputees during the Crimean War (he also invented the plaster cast for broken bones), but many soldiers during the war had to undergo surgery while fully conscious. As Florence Nightingale wrote in November 1854 shortly after her arrival at the military hospital in Scutari:

> I am getting a screen now for Amputations, for when one poor fellow, who is to be amputated tomorrow, sees his comrade today die under the knife it makes an impression – and diminishes his chances. But anyway, among these exhausted frames the mortality of operations is frightful. Now comes the time of haemorrhage and Hospital Gangrene, and every ten minutes an orderly runs, and we have to go and cram lint into the wound till a Surgeon can be sent for, and stop the bleeding as well we can.

Many patients refused to undergo a general anaesthetic for fear they would not wake up afterwards. One clergyman told Simpson that chloroform was 'a decoy of Satan' that would 'harden society and rob God of the deep earnest cries which arise in time of trouble for help'. Suffering was good for the soul; mere mortals should not try to avoid it. Dr John Hall (1795–1866), a long-serving officer who was chief of medical services with the British forces in the Crimea and a stubborn opponent of Florence Nightingale, declared that 'the smart use of the knife is a powerful stimulant and it is much better to hear a man bawl lustily than to see him sink silently into the grave'. Given the dangers of general anaesthesia, surgeons, especially where minor operations were involved, sought a means of dulling pain in small areas of the body as required. The Austrian ophthalmologist Karl Koller (1857–1944) was the first to use a local anaesthetic to stop patients involuntarily reacting when their eyes were touched by a surgical instrument: he employed cocaine successfully, experimenting on himself to begin with, and its use soon spread to dentistry as well. Folk medicine had long been adept at applying pain-reducing natural remedies such as willow bark and spiraea, and their active ingredient, salicylic acid, was isolated in the eighteenth century. In 1859 its structure was determined, and in 1897 the chemical company Bayer produced a synthetically altered version derived from the herb meadowsweet (*spiraea ulmaria*), acetylsalicylic acid, to which it gave the trade name Aspirin. Two years later it was being marketed all over the world as the first effective modern painkiller.

Until the advent of anaesthetics, surgeons prided themselves in sawing off a leg in a matter of minutes, but while this might reduce the suffering of the patient it did not mean the operation was going to be successful, especially since surgeons did not wash their hands or sterilize their equipment and reused old bandages without disinfecting them. The risks of infection in hospitals more generally were first recognized by the Hungarian physician Ignaz Semmelweis (1818–65), who in 1847 observed that around a third of the women who gave birth on the doctors' wards in the Vienna General Hospital, where he worked, died of 'puerperal fever', whereas the death rate on the midwives' wards was only around 10 per cent. Noticing that medical students came to the delivery room straight from dissecting corpses without washing their hands, Semmelweis put a basin of chlorinated water outside the delivery room and instructed all students to use it to disinfect themselves before entering. The death rate fell to a mere 1 per cent.

But Semmelweis could provide no scientific explanation for this dramatic result, and alienated fellow doctors with his obsessive pursuit of his theory. Neither the humoral nor the miasmatic theory of disease supported his ideas. Many doctors, including James Young Simpson, considered that the cause of puerperal fever was more likely to be person-to-person infection. Medical men felt insulted by the suggestion that they might themselves be spreading disease. Semmelweis's contract at the Vienna General Hospital was not renewed, and though appointed to a teaching post in obstetrics he was only allowed to practise on leather mannequins. He resigned in frustration with the authorities just a few days afterwards. Moving to a position in Budapest, he again succeeded in virtually eliminating deaths from childbed fever in the hospital where he worked. The book in which he defended his approach in 1861 was savaged in the medical journals, however, and rival textbooks ascribing puerperal fever to other causes were more widely used. Emotionally exhausted by his futile campaign to get the medical profession to accept his arguments, Semmelweis began to behave increasingly strangely in public. He was eventually confined to a mental hospital, where an attempt to escape led to a beating by the guards, confinement in a straitjacket, and death two weeks after his incarceration from his wounds, which had become infected.

It was not until much later that aseptic methods of surgery and antiseptic precautions taken before operations became widely accepted. The germ theory of disease provided at last a scientific foundation for its practice. Joseph Lister (1827–1912), who had studied Pasteur's work, came to believe that germs could be prevented from infecting the wounds that so often caused surgical patients to die in agony after an operation. He applied a dressing of lint soaked in linseed oil and carbolic acid to an eleven-year-old patient with a compound fracture of the leg caused when he fell under a cart. Lister wrapped the dressing in tinfoil to stop evaporation. The bones reset successfully and were not infected, and the boy walked out of the hospital six weeks after the operation. 'Laudable pus' had previously been regarded as a sign that bad humours were being excreted from a body, but Lister argued that it was a sign of a dangerous infection. Soon Lister's techniques of expelling blood from a surgical wound, washing hands before an operation, bathing a wound in carbolic acid and applying a dressing were being widely applied, especially after he moved from Glasgow to London in 1877 to train young surgeons. At Newcastle Infirmary the death rate from operations of all kinds fell from 60 per cent to 1 per cent after Lister's practices of 'antisepsis' were applied.

The year after Lister moved to London, Robert Koch discovered the germ that caused blood poisoning or septicaemia. This led to further improvements such as the thorough cleaning of surgical wards, the steam sterilization of surgical instruments (1887), and the use of sterilized rubber gloves (1894) and face masks, introduced by the Polish surgeon Johannes von Mikulicz-Radecki (1850–1905). Yet antisepsis was slow to become regular practice in the operating theatre. In the Franco-Prussian War (1870–1), French surgeons amputated some 13,200 limbs, with a mortality rate among patients of 76 per cent. All of the amputations performed on people wounded in the Paris Commune resulted in death. It was not until 1875 that the first manual of antiseptic and aseptic procedures was published in France, by the surgeon Just Lucas-Championnière (1843–1913), who had observed Lister's methods in action. The introduction of these methods not only reduced pain: it also enabled surgeons to embark on more lengthy operations, accessing internal organs of the body that had previously been beyond their reach.

These innovations, together with the use of anaesthetics, brought about major changes in the role and reputation of hospitals. Early nineteenth-century hospitals were places where the poor went to die. Across the Continent they were mainly run by female religious orders in fulfilment of their vows of charity. Even at the beginning of the twentieth century only 3,000 out of a total of 75,000 nurses in Germany were professionally trained; the rest were nuns or deaconesses. In France, by contrast, the anticlerical Third Republic introduced professional training programmes in the 1870s, while in Britain, Florence Nightingale set up a school for nurses on her return from the Crimea. By the eve of the First World War, the professionalization of nursing had extended to the military sphere, as armies recognized the need to reduce infection and death rates among their troops in wartime. Medical science, and above all the triumphs of bacteriology, enormously boosted the reputation of the medical profession by 1900, while the spread of sickness funds and similar schemes began to open up hospital treatment to the masses. Knowledge of disease and its causes was revolutionized, and with it came dramatic changes in therapy. The anatomy schools that flourished in the early decades of the century helped educate the medical profession on the structure and function of the internal organs. It had long been standard medical practice to apply leeches to the sick to restore the balance of humours in the body. François-Joseph-Victor Broussais (1772–1838), a French physician who served in Napoleon's armies successively in Germany, the Netherlands and Spain, found a new reason to use these slug-like bloodsuckers, arguing that by removing blood from a patient they would eliminate the inflammation of the blood that he considered the basic cause of disease. Under his influence French imports of leeches reached the imposing number of 33 million a year by the mid-1830s. It was only with the advent of bacteriology towards the end of the century that the practice of bloodletting declined.

Diagnosis was revolutionized by the invention of the stethoscope in 1819 by the French physician René Laennec (1781–1826). Its employment on his return from Paris by the fictional English doctor Tertius Lydgate, a leading character in Middlemarch (1871–2, but set in the 1830s) by George Eliot (1819–80), was portrayed as raising strong objections from his English medical colleagues back home. Other inventions included the laryngoscope, developed in 1855 by a Paris-based Spanish baritone and voice teacher, Manuel García (1805–1906), and soon adopted by the medical profession. The ophthalmoscope was invented in 1855 by the German physicist Hermann von Helmholtz (1821–94). They all furthered the development of specialist medicine and specialist hospitals, including children's hospitals, established in St Petersburg in 1834 and Vienna in 1837 among other places. Eye hospitals, cancer hospitals, dermatological hospitals, orthopaedic hospitals and similar institutions helped improve the reputation with the public of the hospital as an institution. Yet most diseases remained stubbornly resistant to the discovery and application of successful cures. It was not until the advent of antibiotics after 1945 that common infections became susceptible to medical intervention. The medical profession had begun to master pain, but it would be a long time before the process came anywhere near completion.

MADNESS AND CIVILIZATION

The nineteenth century saw many attempts to understand and ultimately to control human nature through scientific means. The lead here was taken initially by the new science of phrenology, developed early in the century by Franz Gall (1758–1828) and Johann Spurzheim (1776–1832), who lectured in Edinburgh and passed on his method to George Combe (1788–1858). Combe's writings on the subject were crucial to its popularization in England. His book *The Constitution of Man, Considered in Relation to External Objects*, published in 1828, had sold 300,000 copies by 1859, making it by one estimation the fourth-best-selling book in England of the second quarter of the century, after the Bible, *Pilgrim's Progress* and *Robinson Crusoe*. At the height of its popularity, phrenology was popularized by more than two hundred lecturers who toured the United Kingdom spreading its tenets to Mechanics' Institutes, where it was particularly popular as an easily comprehensible, secular, rational and scientific way of determining personality traits. Phrenologists believed that the mind was made up of a variety of different mental, spiritual and moral faculties each located in a different part of the brain – an important insight that lay at the root of the later development of neuropsychology. Each individual possessed these faculties in a different combination and to different degrees. This was reflected in the size of the area each faculty occupied in the brain, so that one could determine someone's personality structure by measuring the area of the skull overlying each particular faculty, or rather, where the phrenologists thought the faculty was located. Combe believed that the individual could work to improve himself and thereby alter the pattern of bumps on his head, and he encouraged thrift, orderliness, punctuality, hard work and cleanliness, so it is not surprising that phrenology was popular in the age of headlong industrialization. Yet its reputation declined sharply after 1850, as the arbitrariness and medical absurdity of its central tenets became steadily more apparent, until it was formally rejected by the British Association for the Advancement of Science, founded in 1831. Phrenology never had much influence elsewhere, especially not in France, where it was associated with left-wing, secularist and materialist currents of thought.

While phrenology rose and fell, institutional care for the mentally ill and handicapped was undergoing a revolution. Enlightenment rationalism prompted a sharpening of the division between the sane and the mad, and led to the creation of separate 'lunatic asylums' for the mentally ill and disturbed, distinct from the prisons where they had previously been randomly incarcerated alongside criminals. Psychiatry emerged as a distinctive sub-discipline within medicine, and reformers campaigned for the removal of restraints from mental patients and the adoption of therapies to attempt to cure or at least alleviate their symptoms. The French psychiatrist Jean-Étienne Dominique Esquirol (1772–1840) was a leading advocate of separate facilities for the insane, declaring that 'the lunatic hospital is an instrument of cure'. He was the main architect of a French law of 1838 that required the establishment of mental hospitals in every French department, run by qualified physicians. He coined the term 'hallucination' and devised the diagnosis of 'monomania' and its varieties including 'kleptomania', 'nymphomania' and 'pyromania'. In the asylum at Charenton south-east of Paris, where the Marquis de Sade was confined until his death in 1814, Esquirol introduced a new method of treatment by 'removing the lunatic from all his habitual pastimes, distancing him from his place of residence, separating him from his family, his friends, his servants, surrounding him with strangers, altering his whole way of life'. When this had been done, the psychiatrist would then introduce new stimuli that would restore the patient to sanity. Even 'idiots' were subjected to training, particularly after the Cornish physician John Langdon Down (1828–96) identified what became known to posterity as 'Down's syndrome'.

A similar degree of optimism was expressed by the chief representative of the physiological school of psychiatry, Wilhelm Griesinger (1817–68), who put forward the widely influential argument that 'every mental disease is rooted in brain disease'. He proposed that mental illnesses could be divided into the chronic and the acute. Sufferers from the former should be put in rural asylums, from the latter in urban ones. If a patient moved from one state to the other, he or she should be moved to a different asylum accordingly. This meant an integrated system of asylums in which the powers of the individual director were considerably reduced, leading not surprisingly to widespread objections to his scheme. Rather than being simply confined, let alone put under permanent restraint, patients should be made to work, to stimulate their minds and to offset the costs of building and maintaining the large new asylums being constructed everywhere. Griesinger succeeded in establishing psychiatry as an academic discipline and was appointed to the first chair in the subject at the University of

Berlin in 1865. Despite their disagreement on the aetiology of madness, both Esquirol and Griesinger represented a new, more optimistic view of mental illness that found its expression in the establishment of purpose-built institutions for the insane in many European countries.

Just as it began to reform the poor laws, so the state also began to take on responsibility for those it was now persuaded were unable to look after themselves. The French law of 1838 proposed by Esquirol was imitated by similar laws in other European countries such as the Netherlands in 1841. These laws established state mental hospitals under medical supervision. In England and Wales the care of the insane by private lunatic asylums ran into growing criticism as the abuses of the 'trade in lunacy' became clearer. Already in 1828 a law established inspections by 'commissioners in lunacy' and a system of licensing and approval. Most of the 21,000 inmates of asylums in 1844 were still in private institutions, but a law passed in 1845 established medically supervised state mental hospitals for the poor in every county, leading to the transformation of private asylums into places where the middle and upper classes sent their mentally ill family members. The new asylums like the Middlesex County Asylum, already constructed at Hanwell in 1831, were situated in rural areas, did away with restraints, and encouraged their inmates to walk in the grounds and undertake useful employment. With 450 inmates, Hanwell was at one time the largest mental hospital in the world. The need to cope with the growing numbers of people committed to such institutions led to the building of ever-larger asylums for the insane: the frontage of Colney Hatch asylum to the north of London, for which Prince Albert laid the foundation stone in 1849, was over a quarter of a mile long.

The first mental hospital in the progressive and highly urbanized Rhineland was founded by the local Prussian administrators at Siegburg in 1825, financed from the local land tax. It was intended for 200 inmates; the chronically mentally ill, the mentally deficient, the senile and epileptics were not to be admitted. Applications for admission could be made by the local authorities or private persons, and were decided upon by the director. Their maintenance was mostly paid for by relatives. By 1842 patients admitted since 1825 numbered 255 people from military or professional families, 528 from an artisanal or business background, 177 tradespeople, 162 farmers, 28 pensioners, and 311 wage-labourers, who were thus in a small minority among the inmates though they comprised a large majority of the population. Despite the hostility of the traditional representative Estates, who resented the cost of the institution, liberals managed to preserve its character as a charitable and progressive institution that its director Carl Wigand Maximilian Jacobi (1775–1858) told the Estates in 1843:

has liberated the insane from the cages and holes, these dungeons, in which they lay, has broken the chains that bound them, has put them in dry and brightly lit living quarters, has provided them with clean beds, protective supervision, gardens and fields, purposeful occupation alternating with manifold varieties of amusement, caring medical treatment and the consolation of religion, as far as their capacities allow, in short, has granted to them everything that is understood in today's normal conception of a well-equipped mental institution.

Yet the foundation of this and similar institutions raised the question of why some people were diagnosed as insane, and others not. The lunatic asylums, indeed, owed their foundation and expansion not so much to medical advances as to changing social mores.

Thus at the Eberbach asylum in the same period, located in the Prussian province of Hessen-Nassau, a high proportion of the inmates were diagnosed as suffering from religious mania, after exhibiting forms of public communion with the supernatural that were tolerated in the village milieu but not in the bourgeois society of the era. Religious mysticism or melancholia, prophecy, possession, even enthusiasm, ran up against the bourgeois belief in self-restraint and moderation and were explained by the emerging psychiatric profession in terms of mental disorder. Treatment in the asylum included not only therapies designed to restore the balance of fluids in the body and brain, such as bloodletting or plunging the patient into cold water from a great height in a kind of medical bungee jump ('we used an eighty-foot high church vault to unfurl them from a swing,' reported one of the doctors at Eberbach), but also mechanical devices aimed at driving out the mental disturbance, for example by fastening the patient in a chair that would then be turned on its axis at high speed. All these therapies could also be used as instruments of discipline. They were directed particularly against the lower-class patients who formed the bulk of the asylum's inhabitants. The middle-class patients living at the Eberbach asylum, by contrast, were invited to attend regular salons, or 'casino evenings' with the senior staff, to sip tea with them and engage them in polite conversation and games of billiards. At Eberbach these sessions were customarily opened by a speech from a patient who thought he was the French *dauphin*. Not just class norms but also gender norms were central to the process of diagnosis and treatment. Notions of appropriate behaviour for men and women were vital components of the emerging public sphere. Violation of these norms, especially by lower-class people, increasingly led to their stigmatization as insane. Women who behaved in public in a bold, aggressive, independent manner were labelled 'nymphomaniac', a diagnosis often confirmed by their use of traditional, often vulgar and sexualized forms of protest at their incarceration once they were inside the asylum. Men who behaved in a dull, passive, weak manner, avoided society, and failed to live up to the new bourgeois cultural ideal of active manhood, were hospitalized, allegedly suffering from 'masturbatory insanity'.

At a Norwegian lunatic asylum constructed in the 1850s the causes of insanity were listed as 'hereditary' (thirty-three cases), 'onanism' (thirty), 'disappointments in love' (twenty-three), 'intemperance and intoxication' (twenty-two), 'domestic sorrows' (twenty-two, almost all of them female), 'vexation' (thirteen), syphilis (eleven) and 'fright or over-exertion' (ten). There were five wings for, respectively, 'quiet patients of the better ranks of life', for paupers, for the 'noisy and turbulent', for the 'violent, excited, and destructive', and for the 'dirty and degraded'. The staff read professional psychiatric journals in all the main European languages, and tried to accustom the patients to something like a normal life, with individual or at most double rooms, a canteen and exercise. A common room was made available for socializing. 'The gentlemen have their billiard-tables, and the ladies their pianos, as we have,' reported the English physician William Lauder Lindsay (1829–80) when he visited the asylum in 1857. The men were given work felling timber, the women sewing. Their insanity, he reported, took the form of melancholia (seventy-one cases), mania (forty-three) or dementia (thirty). Opium was freely administered to calm the patients when it was thought necessary. Overall some sixty-five out of a total of 250 patients were released every year, allegedly either cured or considerably improved.

Most of the new European asylums were built in relatively remote areas, in part at least because townspeople frequently objected to the presence of the insane in their neighbourhood. In September 1892, for example, a residents' association in the Steglitz district of Berlin petitioned the German Reich Chancellor to stop the 'spread of private lunatic asylums in this place . . . Not only will the peace and safety of their neighbours be endangered to the highest degree, but the surrounding area will suffer in reputation and the neighbouring properties will lose considerably in value.' In any case, however, the leading psychiatric doctrines of the later nineteenth and early twentieth centuries emphasized the need for natural surroundings, light, fresh country air and room to exercise for patients. A model institution, the Steinhof mental hospital, located in the Vienna woods and built to designs by the Vienna Secession architect Otto Wagner, was opened in 1907 with forty small pavilions arranged in rows on a hillside, topped by a spectacular art nouveau chapel. By this time the huge institutional blocks of the mid-century years were going out of favour with progressive psychiatrists, and a less regimented form of hospitalization was preferred, though there were seldom funds available for knocking down the earlier giant buildings and constructing something more progressive in their place.

Not even the most advanced institutions could deal with the incurably insane. One well-known example was the composer Robert Schumann (1810–56), who began experiencing alternate moods of exaltation and depression from 1853 onwards, with visions of angels or demons. On 27 February 1854, fearing he would harm his wife, the pianist and composer Clara Schumann (1819–96), he threw himself off a bridge into the river Rhine. Rescued by boatmen, he had himself admitted to a small private asylum at Endenich, in Bonn, where his condition deteriorated rapidly until he died on 29 July 1856. His symptoms may have been caused by a brain tumour, or by tertiary syphilis compounded by mercury poisoning. Another celebrated case was that of the artist Vincent van Gogh (1853–90), who suffered from bouts of depression and mental disturbance. On 23 December 1888, following a quarrel with his friend and fellow artist Paul Gauguin, he sliced off a portion of his left ear with a razor, wrapped it up and left it with a prostitute in a local brothel. Coming to the realization that he needed treatment, he admitted himself to the St-Rémy Asylum of St Paul in Provence, where he stayed in 1889–90. He was given access to the grounds, and supervised carefully so that he did not smoke or drink or try, as he had earlier done, to consume paint and turpentine. 'I feel happier here with my work than I could be outside,' he wrote. 'By staying here a good long time, I shall have learned regular habits and in the long run the result will be more order in my life.' The treatment, which was minimal, consisting mainly of a two-hour bath twice a week, had no effect. He did not stay long, but discharged himself, remaining under medical supervision, and shot himself in the chest with a revolver on 27 July 1890, dying two days later from an untreated infection brought on by the wound.

The failure of the mid-century model of the large mental institutions occurred not least because they were permanently understaffed. The fundamental problem was that the numbers of inmates were increasing with unprecedented rapidity, while the numbers of those released remained small. In the single year of 1901 in Ireland, for example, 3,700 people were admitted to asylums across the island and 1,300 were discharged. Many hundreds of the latter would soon be re-admitted; a report issued in 1904 confessed that 'it is a very common thing to have people removing their insane relatives from the asylum to work for them during the summer months'. These 'cure-rates' had not increased since the 1870s, while the numbers admitted to asylums on the island had rocketed, reaching a level of 490 inmates per 100,000 in 1914 compared to 298 in England and Wales – a result of the generous provision of state-funded facilities for the Irish poor in the post-famine decades. Already in 1838, William Ellis (1780–1839) felt obliged to resign as superintendent of the Hanwell Asylum because of continual demands from the local authorities for the admittance of more patients. By 1844 visiting inspectors reported: 'The two resident Medical Officers have between them nearly 1,000 patients to attend.' The situation had deteriorated still further by the latter decades of the century.

Most of the work in asylums was done by the attendants, recruited, as one report put it in 1837, from 'the unemployed of other professions . . . If they possess physical strength and a tolerable reputation for sobriety, it is enough; and the latter is frequently dispensed with. They enter upon their duties completely ignorant of what insanity is.' Keeping order was all they could do, and they were none too subtle about the way they went about their business. One inmate at Hanwell, who had himself committed in the mid-1860s, reported that the behaviour of the attendants only made his depression worse:

> The manner of feeding the patients, the language used, the filthy allusions, the disgusting and obscene retorts – attendants vieing with patients in exciting the loudest laugh; the attendants' coarse bawl, the obstreperous shove, the stamping on toes; the pitching about the ill, the unruly, and the helpless patients, heedless of the result; the shameful scenes tended *then* to strengthen my preconceived impression that I was accursed of God.

In 1895, Connolly Norman (1853–1908), superintendent of a number of asylums in Ireland, demanded that two attendants who had broken an inmate's rib during a beating should be dismissed by the governors of the institution. They refused to support him and the attendants remained in post. Complaints multiplied in the 1890s and 1900s, with overcrowding leading to growing numbers of violent incidents and governors and staff looking the other way. When Norman interviewed attendants after the death of a patient, he reported that 'they say that they will not give any evidence while living here, as it would not be safe to do so'.

By the turn of the century the population of mental institutions was increasing even faster. In the middle decades of the nineteenth century most mentally ill or handicapped people were still looked after by their own families. Of the 55,043 persons classified in the Prussian census of 1871 as 'mad', 41,262 lived at home, 75 per cent of the total. Yet this balance shifted markedly in the following decades. The general population of Prussia grew by 60 per cent between 1875 and 1910, the urban population by 137 per cent, and the number of inmates in mental institutions by 429 per cent. In 1910 there were 79,000 male and 64,000 female inmates, more than half of them labelled as suffering from 'simple disturbance of the mind'. Similarly, in the Netherlands there was an increase from fifty-two inmates of mental institutions per 100,000 population in 1850 to 144 per 100,000 in 1910, while in Switzerland the number of inmates per 100,000 doubled over the same period. With continuing rapid urbanization it was more difficult for families to keep the mentally disabled and disturbed at home, and more likely that such people came to the attention of the state.

Added to these developments was a transition in psychiatric theory towards a belief that far from being curable, many mental afflictions were hereditary. University professorships in psychiatry were founded in Göttingen in 1866, Heidelberg in 1871, Leipzig and Bonn in 1882. However, they did not train practising doctors in the asylums but engaged in research and theoretical work, particularly on the brain; the asylum doctors were ordinarily qualified physicians who learned their trade on the job. Ultimately it was the academics who created this change in attitude, introducing the idea that mental disability or disturbance was mainly physical in origin. Mental influences were still allowed by Jean-Martin Charcot (1825–93), 'the Napoleon of the neuroses', who established a psychiatric clinic at the Salpêtrière hospital in Paris, and was the first to describe multiple sclerosis and Parkinson's disease (which he named after James Parkinson [1755–1824], author of an influential treatise on the 'shaking palsy' published in 1817). Charcot's major psychiatric work was on hysteria, generally thought to be a symptom of female orgasmic dysfunction. Charcot argued it was as common among men as among women, with psychological rather than physiological causes. Here his influence largely failed to percolate down to the practitioners, who continued to prescribe belts, injections and internal appliances to girls regarded as suffering from the condition. Treatment included female genital mutilation, widely applied to women who, as claimed by one British practitioner, Isaac Baker Brown (1811–73), had become 'restless and excited . . . and indifferent to the social influences of domestic life'. Brown, who had performed many operations of this kind at his London Surgical Hospital since 1859, was expelled by the Obstetrical Society in 1871 for abusing his authority, but claimed, perhaps with some justification, that he was doing nothing unusual and had been punished unjustly.

The most pessimistic views were expressed by Emil Kraepelin (1856–1926), whose handbook of psychiatry was published in 1883 and frequently reissued and extended. It argued that mental disturbances were primarily of hereditary, physical origin. He declared that psychiatry had taken a 'decisive step from a symptomatic to a clinical view of insanity'. Symptoms were merely expressions of a syndrome, a hereditary disorder such as schizophrenia or manic depression that no amount of therapy could correct. Kraepelin extended this concept far beyond what was commonly understood as mental illness, to embrace alcoholism, petty criminality and deviance of all kinds. The police and local authorities leaped upon this as a way of dealing with the refractory poor, adopting with medical advice a redefinition of binge-drinking as 'a form of periodic mania' and consigning alcoholics to mental hospitals, often despite strong resistance from their families. Thus the great asylums became dumping grounds for the deviant. As John Bucknill (1817–97) of the Devon County Asylum noted in an annual report:

> The law providing that madmen, dangerous to themselves and others, shall be secluded in madhouses for absolutely needful care and protection, has been extended in its application to large classes of persons who would never have been considered lunatics when this legislation was entered upon. Since 1845, medical science has discovered whole realms of lunacy, and the nicer touch of a finikin civilization has shrunk away from the contact of imperfect fellow-creatures, and thus the manifold receptacles of lunacy are filled to overflow with a population more nearly resembling that which is still at large.

After a century of trying to cure insanity, little progress seemed to have been made in controlling the uncontrollable; indeed, if anything, the problem had become even worse. Deviance and insanity now seemed two sides of one coin.

DISCIPLINE AND PUNISH

In 1858, in the Hanoverian university town of Göttingen, a convicted murderer was led out from the town gates onto an execution platform, or 'ravenstone' as it was popularly known, where a large crowd had gathered to witness the event. An eyewitness, the anatomist Heinrich Wilhelm Gottfried von Waldeyer-Hartz (1836–1921), described what happened next:

Under his chin they placed a leather sling, by means of which one of the assistants pulled his head back tightly, and held it there . . . The executioner drew the great, broad, sharp, highly polished sword of justice from under his cloak, stepped to the left side of the condemned, drew back his arms, and in a trice severed the head from the rump, cutting through the neck more with a smooth stroke than with a blow. The head remained in the leather sling, and two columns of blood spurted up from the neck-wound, to fall back and rise, and fall again a few more times, ever lower and weaker, with the succeeding heartbeats . . . Close by the scaffold a few sufferers from epileptic fits had posted themselves. They had handed the assistants glass vessels in which the assistants caught the blood as it bubbled over and gave it to the epileptics, who drank it immediately.

It seems astonishing that an event like this should take place as late as 1858, but such public rituals, attended by vast crowds sometimes estimated at 20,000 people or more, and accompanied by ancient folk superstitions, the selling of food and drink, and the singing of ribald songs and ballads, were common in many parts of Europe well into the second half the nineteenth century.

In England public executions by hanging were often accompanied by brawls between members of the offender's family and men sent by the anatomy schools to procure the malefactor's body for dissection. In cases where the corpse was left to rot on the gibbet – the last instance in England was in Leicester in 1832 – people sometimes raided it for body parts to be used in folk medicine. In Prussia public executions were carried out either with a hand-held axe, or, up to 1848, with a heavy cartwheel, which the executioner dropped on the limbs of the malefactor as he was spreadeagled on the scaffold. In the Rhineland the judicial authorities used the guillotine, introduced under the French occupation, but its revolutionary associations caused it to be rejected by conservative administrations in many parts of Germany, including Prussia and Bavaria. In Austria and England capital offenders were put to death by hanging, while in Spain the method, standard across the country from 1820, was the garrotte, a device in which the prisoner was tied to an upright post and strangled as a metal collar was tightened from behind.

Increasingly, bourgeois squeamishness and the growing anxieties of governments began to limit the ritual of public execution and then finally to abolish it altogether. As Charles Dickens complained of a hanging he witnessed in 1840, there was no 'emotion suitable to the occasion . . . No sorrow, no salutary terror, no abhorrence, no seriousness; nothing but ribaldry, debauchery, levity, drunkenness, and flaunting vice in fifty other shapes'. After 1848 authorities everywhere feared large public gatherings, whatever the reason for them. Executions were moved to prison yards in Prussia in 1851, in Saxony in 1855, and in all other German states by 1861. Public executions were brought to an end in Britain in 1868. By contrast, the last public execution in Russia took place as early as 1826, when five of the Decembrists were hanged before a large crowd; as the ropes split, saving the lives of the condemned men, the crowd clamoured for mercy, in a tradition that regarded such occurrences as the expression of God's will; but the implacable Tsar Nicholas I ordered new ropes to be attached to the gallows and the hanging went ahead. In France from 1832 onwards the executions took place outside the gates of the prison where the offender was being held, and from 1870 the elevated scaffold was also abolished, bringing the ceremony to ground level and making it more difficult to witness. But attempts to abolish public executions in France foundered on the opposition of conservatives on the one hand, and abolitionists on the other, the latter believing that to put executions behind prison walls would make them more respectable and so reduce the chances of doing away with them altogether.

Parallel to these developments, a process of reform and a reduction in the incidence of capital punishment also took place. By 1815 the death penalty was restricted almost exclusively to first-degree murder and high treason almost everywhere in Europe except Great Britain. Here, exceptionally, it applied to theft as well as homicide – three-quarters of those hanged in England and Wales in the 1820s had been convicted for property crimes, and only one-fifth for murder. Some 200 offences were punishable by death under what came later to be called the 'Bloody Code', and although 90 per cent of the sentences were commuted, still, from 1816 through 1820 no fewer than 518 hangings took place in England and Wales. There were 364 from 1821 up to the end of 1825, and 308 from 1826 to 1830. This compared to an annual average of only four or five in Prussia, whose population at the time, at 16 million, was about the same as that of England and Wales. The steady fall in executions in Britain brought the rate to somewhere near the European average by the 1840s (around thirty-four a year in France, for example). In the 1820s there was only one execution per 100,000 population in Russia, a ratio that continued roughly for the rest of the century. But during the aftermath of the 1905 Revolution the average rose from around fifteen death sentences a year in the 1880s and 1890s to 627 in 1907 and 1,342 in 1908, almost all of which were actually carried out – a reflection more of political anxiety and the determination of Nicholas II to clamp down on dissent rather than penal policy on the part of the state.

Already in the eighteenth century the Italian jurist Cesare Beccaria (1738–94), who introduced the principle of punishment graded to fit the severity of the crime, had advocated the abolition of the death penalty because capital punishment had manifestly proved useless as a deterrent. In the 1830s and 1840s reformers such as the German jurist Carl Mittermaier (1787–1867) backed this up with statistics showing that the ending of executions, wherever it had occurred, had not led to any demonstrable increase in the murder rate. The rise of psychiatry began to introduce into the courts the principle of diminished responsibility by virtue of insanity. To be sure, monarchs and heads of state were keen to retain the death penalty because it allowed them to exercise a symbolic right of sovereignty through commuting it into a lesser sentence and thus demonstrating their God-given power over life and death. However, increasingly they began to have religiously motivated scruples about signing death warrants. Some, such as the king of the Netherlands after 1855, the king of Italy after 1863, the king of the Belgians after 1865, the king of Saxony after 1866, the king of Norway and Sweden after 1872, and King Wilhelm I of Prussia after 1878, refused to confirm them in case there had been a miscarriage of justice or in anticipation of the death penalty being abolished in the near future.

Liberal critics argued that capital punishment was an outmoded relic of medieval times, unworthy of modern civilization. Punishment should be used not merely to deter people from offending but also to improve and reform them if they had committed a crime. This was the principle that eventually triumphed as legislatures acquired more power after 1848, leading to the legal or de facto abolition of the death penalty in many European countries. When new law codes came into being, they frequently included a clause outlawing capital punishment, as in Belgium in 1866 or the Netherlands in 1870. In some countries, such as Greece, where the guillotine was the normal method, or the firing squad when, as sometimes happened, a guillotine could not be found, capital punishment continued. In Prussia, Bismarck overcame liberal opposition to engineer its retention in the Criminal Code of the North German Confederation in 1866–7. It was taken up again with enthusiasm when Wilhelm II, anxious to advertise his sovereign powers by any means possible, acceded to the Prussian throne in 1888. His habit of signing death warrants quickly produced a sharp decline in the murder rate, as courts and juries became more reluctant to convict than they had been under his more lenient grandfather, Wilhelm I.

Capital punishment was in many ways the last relic of a long-established punishment regime that focused on the body of the malefactor. Corporal punishments were widespread under serfdom, and whipping was a common punishment across Europe into the second half of the nineteenth century. It was abolished in most German states in the 1860s, in the Netherlands in 1870, and in other countries at roughly the same time as capital punishment, but it continued in Britain for long afterwards, and in virtually every country it carried on regardless within prisons. In Germany all new prisoners were given a 'welcome' with a whipping, and received another beating on their release; in southern Europe the *bastinado*, or foot-sole whipping, was a standard disciplinary measure in penal institutions until the middle of the twentieth century and in some countries even later. In Russia corporal punishment only ended with the abolition of serfdom despite a law to the contrary passed in 1845; nose-slitting was only abolished in 1817. By and large, however, corporal punishment as a formal judicial sanction had more or less disappeared by the late nineteenth century, including in the Ottoman Empire, where it was removed from the Penal Code in 1858, though whipping continued to be imposed by the Islamic courts for offences such as adultery.

The decline of old-established forms of punishment posed governments with the problem of finding an alternative. One that offered itself immediately was transporting felons out of the country, which combined the advantages of punishing offenders for their crimes, removing the threat they posed to society, and providing a labour force for the colonies. The Russians were the most wedded to this practice, sending some 865,000 convicts to Siberia in the course of the nineteenth century. Political exile was also used to punish Polish rebels, some 20,000 of whom were sent to Siberia after the revolt of 1830–1 and another 20,000 after the uprising of 1863. Many stayed there for the rest of their lives. The revolutionary Vladimir Ilyich Lenin (1870–1924) met some of the 1863 exiles when he himself was sentenced to Siberia for three years in 1897. Exiles were often dispersed over a wide territory to prevent them from associating with each other, as with the Decembrists, no more than three of whom were kept in any one place. Brutal mistreatment on the march to Siberia, which the exiles had to undertake partly on large sleds, partly on foot, was common. Dostoyevsky, sentenced for revolutionary activities, was flogged twice on the road to Omsk in 1850, and was shackled hand and foot during his four-year imprisonment with hard labour. But political exiles were relatively well treated in comparison to ordinary convicts, who were frequently forced to undertake dangerous and exhausting hard labour in the salt mines of Nertchinsk, near the Chinese border. The system of exile was only brought to an end at the turn of the century.

For much of the eighteenth century the British transported convicts to America, but when this became impossible after 1776 they turned to Australia, where by the 1820s some 3,000 were being transported every year. By the 1840s the number of private settlers had grown, and they began objecting to the continual arrival of convict shipments. Transportation began declining under the weight of public criticism at home and in Australia in the 1850s and came to an end in 1867. Ironically, perhaps, this was just the period in which transportation from France actually began. In 1852, Napoleon III's government established a penal colony on Devil's Island in French Guiana, an unhealthy, brutal, often fatal prison through which 80,000 offenders passed before it was eventually closed down in 1946. French political prisoners were sent not to Devil's Island but to the remote Pacific island of New Caledonia, forming a significant minority among the 20,000 offenders who had been incarcerated there by the time it was abandoned in 1897. In some German states prisoners were given the choice of emigrating voluntarily, as with a group sent to Brazil from Mecklenburg in the early 1820s. Up to mid-century the Kingdom of Hanover routinely offered free passage to America to convicts as an alternative to a costly term of imprisonment, issuing them with false passports concealing their criminal record if they agreed to go.

The only long-term answer to the demand for alternatives to capital and corporal punishment was the prison. Prisons existed in the eighteenth century, but they were mainly used for people awaiting trial. As they began to be used more for punishment, their inadequacies quickly became obvious. Penal reformers demanded purpose-built reformatories and penitentiaries that would establish a prison regime designed to break the will of the offender and remould his or her character to make it useful to society. Rough food, coarse clothing and hard labour were the basis of the new system, first developed at the Walnut Street prison in Philadelphia in 1790 and widely reported and admired in Europe, particularly through a two-volume treatise published by Gustave de Beaumont (1802–66) and Alexis de Tocqueville, *On the Penitentiary System in the United States and its Application in France* (1833). In 1842 the first new model prison on American lines was opened at Pentonville in London. It was quickly imitated across Europe. Prisoners were given numbers, to which they always had to answer; they were kept in single cells, arranged in galleries, and when they went out of the cell had to wear a mask to conceal their identity; the prison chapel – religion, the reading of the Bible, chapel services and religious instruction were central aspects of the reformation of prisoners – was constructed so that no prisoner could see another, but all could see and be seen by the preacher (the perfect example of the panopticon, an idea conceived by the philosopher Jeremy Bentham). Inmates were inured to hard work by the treadmill, a continuously moving device that produced nothing of any use at all; the prisoner had to keep treading, usually for a two-hour spell; anyone who ceased treading would get trapped between the steps and could be seriously injured.

Prison reform swept across Europe in the middle decades of the century. In Britain it was pioneered by the Quaker Elizabeth Fry (1780–1845). In 1817 she was so shocked by the conditions prevailing in Newgate Prison in London that she founded a reform society that led to the creation of the British Ladies' Society for Promoting the Reformation of Female Prisoners, often seen as the first nationwide reform movement in Britain that was led by women. A regular writer on prison reform, Fry became famous enough for Friedrich Wilhelm IV of Prussia to make a detour from a state visit to the United Kingdom in 1842 in order to discuss prison reform with her. A previous visitor, the German Protestant pastor Theodor Fliedner (1800–64), who met Fry in 1823, was inspired to found a society for 'the improvement of prisons in Rhenish Prussia' three years later, and persuaded the authorities to build a new penitentiary on the Walnut Street model, the Klingelpütz in Cologne, in 1835. In Italy the Milanese reformer Carlo Cattaneo championed the Philadelphia system in an influential tract written in 1840. In the new system, he claimed:

> The scaffold with all its barbarous rites is banished; punishment becomes at once sublime and spiritual in the silence that reigns in the solitary cell. The supreme defence adopted against those who threaten to disturb society is no longer mere animal pain, but a pain that affects the whole spirit: a pain that is exquisitely social because it consists in denying the ordinary comforts of social intercourse to those who disturb the peace.

New penitentiaries were built on American lines in Piedmont, while in Tuscany a new single-cell male prison was constructed at Volterra and a women's prison in San Gimignano. In France, where there were more than 100,000 prison inmates at the beginning of the 1840s, new prisons were built on a modified version of the Philadelphia system requiring solitary confinement only during the night-time. This was intended to replace the traditional institution of the *bagnes*, waterside buildings originally housing offenders condemned to the galleys but who were now, like Jean Valjean, the hero of Victor Hugo's *Les Misérables*, sent out in chain gangs to work on road-building. The French prison reformer and critic of the death penalty Charles Lucas (1803–89) urged the separation of offenders by crime, and the reform of character by strict discipline. In 1885 the principle of surveillance and control was extended into the community with the introduction of suspended sentences and parole.

Yet the zeal and optimism of the reformers repeatedly ran up against the budgetary constraints imposed by governments, and the low priority given to the penal system by politicians and administrators. In France even after the reform of 1885 only 10 per cent of inmates were kept in solitary confinement. The number of people sentenced to terms of imprisonment increased with the population; prison-building was never able to keep pace, and overcrowding was the result. Before long inmates in the new jails were kept two or three to a cell, undermining the basic principle of isolation. In Italy almost all prisoners were made to work after a reorganization of the penal system in 1864, but overcrowding was desperate, and in most penitentiaries, convicts were kept chained in pairs until 1901, watched over in large open halls and guarded by warders armed with whips, carbines and clubs. In Russia the number of prisoners rose from 88,000 in 1884 to 116,000 in 1893, and was further increased by the ending of the system of exile to Siberia in 1900. Frequent amnesties marking imperial occasions such as the birth of an heir to the throne had reduced the prison population to 75,000 by January 1905, but in the post-1905 repression the prison population expanded rapidly, with 140,000 offenders in prisons by 1913. There was a corresponding sharp deterioration in prison conditions, with mortality rates among inmates, roughly the same as in the general population until 1906 (11 per 1,000 as against 14), rising to nearly 50 per 1,000 by 1911. Here, prison reform was trumped by political anxiety rather than by budgetary constraints.

Perhaps the most extreme example of the failure of prison reform, despite the best of intentions, was in the Ottoman Empire, where the drive to improve conditions was sparked by a critical memorandum issued in 1851 by the influential British ambassador, Sir Stratford Canning. Prisons administered by the regime, he complained, were makeshift structures crammed with all kinds of offenders in a random assortment of petty criminals and murderers, accused and convicted, men and women, adults and children. By 1871 a model penitentiary had been constructed in Istanbul in response to Canning's critique. New regulations were issued in 1880, separating different categories of prisoner. But these measures were never backed by a formal decree, and were widely disregarded. The model Istanbul penitentiary did not find any imitators. The lack of central control over the Ottoman provinces allowed regional and local officials to disregard the sultan's attempts at reform. As more and more prisoners crowded in, conditions deteriorated. Corruption was rife, overcrowding led to the spread of disease, the lack of guards allowed fights and prison riots to take place, and prisoners had to cook their own food, which was supplied not by the prison authorities but by relatives or by charitable organizations.

Stories of the maltreatment of prisoners abounded: the Armenian-American lawyer Vahan Cardashian (1882–1934) even claimed sensationally that during the reign of Sultan Abdülhamid II, Christian prisoners were beaten and branded to extract information, and if that failed, their 'hair was shaved off, incision made, and vermin placed in the skull'. Only with the coming to power of the Young Turks was a central prison administration established, in 1911, leading to a series of edicts attacking corruption, outlawing the smuggling in by prison warders of intoxicants, imposing sanctions against the misappropriation of food by guards, and curbing other abuses. The new rulers of Turkey also tried to appoint more staff, but even in 1914 the ratio of guards to inmates was 1:16, comparing with a European average of 1:7.

Everywhere in Europe, despite the introduction of the new system of separate detention and disciplining, prisoners were not reformed but kept returning to jail. Already in 1875 a French deputy warned the Chamber of Deputies that 'a floating population exists in France, oscillating between the prison and free society'. In this situation and under the influence of the theory of evolution propounded by Charles Darwin (1809–82), Cesare Lombroso (1835–1909), who served with the Italian Army in 1863 fighting brigands in Calabria, came to the view that criminals were not made but born, representing throwbacks to an earlier stage of human evolution. In 1876 he published *Criminal Man*, which took advantage of the development of photography to argue that born criminals had long arms, simian features and other physical attributes of the ape. Lombroso's idea of atavism, of criminals as evolutionary throwbacks, never received much support, and as time went on he modified his arguments to suggest that hereditary criminality was also the consequence of generations of alcoholism, or sexually transmitted diseases, or malnutrition; but more generally the basic idea that criminality was inherited began to exert a growing influence across Europe in the late nineteenth century.

The consequences of Lombroso's basic argument, popularized by his student Enrico Ferri (1856–1929) in Italy, by Gustav Aschaffenburg (1866–1944) in Germany, by Francis Galton (1822–1911) in Britain, and by Rafael Salillas (1854–1923) in Spain, were momentous. The study of crime and criminality became the province not of law and its practitioners but of medicine and of professional criminology. Increasingly, in the 1890s and beyond, arguments began to be raised in favour of the compulsory sterilization of the 'inferior' who might be found work but should not be allowed to reproduce. Lombroso himself, along with many others who shared at least some of his views, began to argue for capital punishment on new grounds, namely that the extremely degenerate offender, the criminal with inherited violent traits, could neither be rendered safe nor removed from the chain of heredity unless he or she was eliminated altogether. Punishment had come full circle, from the medieval and early modern punishment of the body to the Enlightenment and Victorian punishment of the mind, and back to the turn-of-the-century punishment of the body again.

Ultimately what underlay all these changes was the growing power of the state to enforce the law and hence the increasing number of people arrested and condemned for criminal offences. The nineteenth century began with banditry, theft, smuggling, and crime of many kinds rife all over Europe, in the disorder created by the French Revolutionary and Napoleonic Wars. As European states re-established themselves, creating and maintaining political and social order was a priority. The most important instrument of this was the French-style *gendarmerie*, a mounted semi-military force stationed in rural areas, such as the *Guardia Civil*, established in Spain in 1844, the Corps of Gendarmes created after the Decembrist revolt in Russia in 1825, or the spiked-helmeted *gendarmerie* set up in the Habsburg lands during the post-1848 reaction; this force numbered nearly 19,000 in 1857, including 1,500 mounted police. In some areas the gendarme was meant to be a civilizing influence on the rural population, 'a friend and the authority to whom people frequently look for support', as a document of 1910 from Bukovina noted, an area where the force was regarded by the Habsburg government as spreading Western civilization to the population (among its functions, the document reported, was to help people 'write an address on an envelope').

The rapid growth of towns during the nineteenth century raised a rather different problem of policing, however. The traditional nightwatchmen left a great deal to be desired. In Hamburg the Night Watch was described in 1840 as 'an asylum for a local and foreign pack of ruffians' who were often drunk and seldom active; in the 1850s it was merged into a new police force. The growth of towns indeed required the creation of a new type of uniformed police force, the *sergeants de ville*, with blue coats and bicorne hats, introduced in Paris in 1829 by the Prefect of Police Louis-Marie de Belleyme (1787–1862); or, six months later, the constables of London's Metropolitan Police, with a uniform consisting of a blue tailcoat and a black top hat. 'The essential object of our municipal police,' declared de Belleyme's deputy in 1828, 'is the safety of the inhabitants of Paris. Safety by day and night, free traffic movement, clean streets, the supervision of and precaution against accidents, the maintenance of order in public places, the seeking out of offences and their perpetrators . . .' It took some time before the new forces were accepted by the public; in

London they were regarded by some as an instrument of continental despotism, and were often attacked in the streets. In 1830 the murder of the first London constable to be killed in the line of duty – he had intervened in a fight between two drunks, who then joined forces to beat him to death – was declared by a jury to be 'justifiable homicide' because of the policeman's 'over-exertion in the discharge of his duty'.

In Germany the army was frequently used to maintain order and prevent or combat even petty crime in garrison towns, which contained half the urban population of Prussia in 1840. During the 1848 Revolution, the liberal administration in Berlin created a new uniformed police force on the London model, with top hats to signify the officers' non-military character. From 1848 to 1856 this *Schutzmannschaft* – literally, 'body of protection men' – was commanded by Karl von Hinckeldey (1805–56), who made extensive use of the very broad powers he possessed to improve prisons, introduce social welfare schemes, set up public baths, get the streets cleaned, and much else besides. In Prussia the fire brigade, the prison service, and major parts of the poor-law administration were in the hands of the police, who also supervised markets, registered newcomers to the city, arrested vagabonds, oversaw all public meetings, licensed places of amusement, controlled public brothels, and authorized vets and pharmacists. The police could issue ordinances and impose fines under their own powers, which remained in place up to 1914. Here too, as in France, the police drew their officers and men from the ranks of army veterans, who were given an exclusive claim on them in return for signing on for twelve years in the ranks of the military. They were organized on military lines, and equipped with sabres in place of the wooden truncheons used by their British counterparts. Aspects of the military model of policing thus managed to survive the reforms of the revolutionary year.

A partial and gradual separation of urban police from military institutions such as the *gendarmerie* took place in most European countries in the course of the nineteenth century. This could sometimes lead to rivalry and confusion. In Italy, for example, the urban police had wide-ranging powers similar to those possessed by their German counterparts, but there were overlapping competences between the *carabinieri*, the Italian equivalent of the French *gendarmerie*, and the Public Security Guards, a civil force established in 1860, while the army took a central role in dealing with major problems involving the use of violence, such as brigandage, especially in southern Italy. Towns also appointed Municipal Guards who frequently engaged in demarcation disputes with the Public Security Guards. Despite the existence of all these different forces, their numbers failed to keep pace with the growth of Italian cities. It was only after the turn of the century that the Italian government attempted a reform, but even this failed to remedy the chronic disorder that reigned in southern Italy, compounded by the influence of organizations such as the Mafia and the Camorra as they extended their reach from the country into the city.

The limits of policing were apparent in other parts of Europe too. In Russia in 1900 there were fewer than 50,000 police officers for a population of some 127 million. A new force of constables had been introduced in 1878, and 1903 saw the establishment of another force of 40,000 mounted gendarmes aimed at establishing law and order in the villages. However, they were soon occupied in suppressing the uprisings associated with the revolution of 1905, and did not return to regular policing functions afterwards. The force's strength was pathetically inadequate. In Ryazan province, for instance, there were just fifty-eight captains and 251 constables for a rural population of more than two million in 1913. Judges, policemen and officials were notoriously corrupt and inefficient. In many European countries the police were more successful: in Hungary, for example, they kept order on the main thoroughfares and patrolled the streets, acting as a deterrent to crime, so that recorded petty offences dropped by half in two districts of Budapest between 1908 and 1912 after the local police increased their presence there. But in general the strenuous attempts of nineteenth-century governments and administrators to control or reform the baser criminal instincts of the deviant elements in the population met with only limited success.

The conquest of nature thus ran up against the limits of the possible in many different areas. In taming the wild and mastering the elements, it met with some success, but also produced unwelcome consequences, from the extinction of species to the damage caused by deforestation. Urbanization and the rapidly increasing use of fossil fuels to provide heat, light and power brought atmospheric pollution, with consequences that were to become ever more serious in the twentieth and twenty-first centuries. Despite the rapid expansion of the concept and experience of time and space, most human beings in Europe, as everywhere else, proved unable to move very far from the surface of the Earth, or very fast across it. New experiences and perceptions of time and space led many people to believe they were living in an era of unprecedentedly rapid change. This feeling was bolstered by major advances in medicine. The great epidemics were banished, infections sharply reduced by antisepsis, and human pain brought under some degree of control; even animal pain had become the focus of a movement against cruel sports, which had scored some notable successes by 1914. Human nature proved more intractable, but the decline of birth and death rates was bringing about major changes in attitudes to life. The conquest of nature opened up many possibilities, for women, for travellers, and not least for the military, but it also cut off possibilities from others, above all the deviant, the marginal and the mentally disturbed. It also threw up existential challenges to religion and belief, as science uncovered facts about the Earth and its history that undermined the traditional narratives of the Bible. Along with technological change in the form of photography and, at the end of the century, cinema, radio and audio reproduction, this posed new problems for the expression of human emotion and the representation of the natural world in literature and the arts, as we shall now see.

6

The Age of Emotion

FROM THE PRESENT TO THE PAST

Fredrika Bremer (1801–65), a writer now largely forgotten outside her native Scandinavia, had become by the middle of the nineteenth century one of Europe's most celebrated novelists. She was born near Åbo, Swedish Finland (Turku in Finland today), into what eventually became a family of five girls and two boys. Her father Carl Fredrik Bremer (1770–1830), a wealthy merchant, moved with his family to Stockholm in 1804 when Fredrika was three, and purchased a country house at Årsta ten miles to the south, as well as an apartment in the city centre. She learned the conventional accomplishments of the upper middle-class girl: English, French and German conversation, playing the piano and dancing, sewing, embroidery, drawing and painting, with the help of a French governess and a variety of private teachers. But Fredrika suffered under a handicap in the marriage market: she was not considered as good-looking as her older sister, a fact of which she was only too well aware: 'I wish I were more beautiful,' she would reply to admirers even at the relatively late age of fifty. She took increasing refuge in the world of the imagination. The family would read aloud in the evening, mostly serious history books chosen by their father; the girls preferred the works of Jean-Jacques Rousseau (1712–78). Later the family turned to the historical novels of Sir Walter Scott (1771–1832), with their noble rebels such as Rob Roy or Robin Hood, their romantic entanglements, and their picturesque representations of old Scotland and medieval England.

Fredrika's frustration at the restrictive regime imposed on the girls by her father drove her to depression, until in 1826 she was left at Årsta one winter to look after the two most sickly of her four sisters while their parents were in Stockholm. She began treating the young women with herbs and soon acquired a local reputation as a healer. Unable to meet the growing demands of her philanthropic work, Fredrika turned to writing in order to make some money. Her stories dealt with the bourgeois family world in which she had grown up and continued to live, but she also combined domestic realism with poetic descriptions of the sublime, with picaresque incidents and with sentimental idylls. One of the main characters in her first novel, *The H— Family* (1831), the beautiful blind girl Elizabeth, goes out onto a cliff-top in the middle of a violent thunderstorm, raises her arms and delivers a confession of unrequited love: 'The lightning crossed the whole country with its glowing streaks; the storm raged around; and the thunder, now rolling, now crashing, increased above our heads. The blind girl stood upon the cliff, as though the spirit of the storm, with a wild, terrible countenance.' She sings a song, her voice rising above the tempest: 'Hail to the day of freedom . . . I am free . . . My hour is come.' She tells her guardian: 'You have fettered my body, you have bound my tongue, and now I stand before you, powerful and strong.' Unexpectedly, however, Elizabeth does not throw herself over the precipice but returns, exhausted, to die in her bed. Indeed, elevating, romantic deathbed scenes are so common in Bremer's novels that in one of them she pauses to address her audience with a direct question: 'Will not my friendly readers be astonished that the pen, which ought only to be dedicated to pleasure, passes on from one deathbed to another, just as if everyday life were a continual procession of corpses?'

Full of depictions of Gothic dreams, wild-looking young men, weeping girls, endless pine forests and woodland fountains, Bremer's novel was an instant success, winning a medal from the Swedish Academy. Dissatisfied with her 'chaotic' education she engaged a tutor, Per Böklin (1796–1867), a local headmaster, author of a learned dissertation on Ancient Greek accents, part-time publisher and translator from German. Böklin took her through a course on German philosophy and its relation to Christian faith. Her second full-length story, *The President's Daughters* (1834), drew on Bremer's experiences with her tutor and indeed quoted directly from his letters to her as well as reproducing the reading list he had supplied. It focuses on the four daughters of a wealthy man and their governess, whose liberal views of female education clash with the more conventional vision of her employer. The governess describes with savage irony women as men would like them to be: 'We fill the room, and yet deprive nobody of a place; we neutralize the warring elements of life, which without us would destroy one another . . . We put our houses in order, salt our meat according to the book; gossip moderately about our neighbour, think only as much as necessary.' By the end of the novel, however, after many vicissitudes, the women of the family have won their father round to the idea of allowing them to develop their own individuality and creativity, and the story, unusually for Bremer, ends happily.

The relationship between Bremer and Böklin, a bachelor, developed with such intensity that he eventually asked her to marry him. But she refused him, claiming that she needed to be alone and free from wifely burdens in order to write. To get over the relationship she escaped to Norway, where she stayed with friends and wrote her most popular novel, *The Neighbours: A Story of Everyday Life* (1836), in which an overly strict parent ends by being struck blind, one of many such instances in Bremer's work. By this time her depiction of the tragic situation of women who were prevented from gaining their independence had acquired a grim parallel in her own life. Since she was unmarried, and thus legally still a minor whatever her age, her brother Claes Bremer (1804–39) had full legal control over her increasingly substantial income as an author after their father's death in 1830. This was exactly at the point when she began her successful career as a novelist, and in the course of less than a decade Claes gambled a large portion of her earnings away. It was only when he died a wastrel's death in 1839, following the demise a few years earlier of her only other brother, that Fredrika Bremer was free to manage her own affairs.

In her novels of the 1840s and early 1850s, such as *Midnight Sun: A Pilgrimage* (1849), the theme of religious conversion and Divine revelation entered her work. Continuing her reading, unsystematic though it might have been, she came across the phenomenon of Utopian communities, described in a novel she published in 1848, where two characters return from a visit to the phalanstery at Lowell, Massachusetts, and try to set up an imitation of it in Sweden. The following year Bremer travelled to America and visited Lowell. She met Ralph Waldo Emerson (1803–82), 'a quiet nobly serious figure with a pale complexion, starkly marked features and dark hair', conversed with leading politicians and literary figures, and was too busy being lionized to find time to read 'the thick volumes of Hegelian philosophy' she had brought with her in her continuing quest to educate herself. More significantly, however, Bremer was appalled by her discovery of the evils and brutalities of slavery, a 'heathen institution that is leading to acts so incomprehensible, so inhuman in this country, the Christian and free-minded America, that it is hard for me at times to believe, to grasp that it is reality and not a dream'.

Back in Sweden, she wrote her most impassioned plea for women's emancipation from legal and social slavery so far, in her novel *Hertha* (1856). In a situation that recurs in many of her stories the father of the eponymous Hertha is bad-tempered and overbearing and tells her 'that she possessed no right at all over her own property, over herself, or her future, otherwise than in as far as her father would consider it'. The father mismanages the family estate, but is seriously injured in one of the many fires that occur in Bremer's novels, and for a time allows Hertha to earn money as a schoolmistress. Finally, Hertha marries her sweetheart Yngve over her father's protests ('Will you defy me?' he shouts) – if only, inevitably, at the young man's deathbed, after he has been mortally injured while rescuing passengers from a blazing steamboat. With her income assured by this novel, Bremer embarked on an extensive tour first of Europe, searching for religious inspiration, then of Palestine, returning to Sweden to write a six-volume account of her travels, and finally moving back to Årsta, where she died of pneumonia on New Year's Eve 1865.

Fredrika Bremer's stories brought together two of the main cultural currents of the age. They combined emotionalism, love of nature and Gothic imagery with a setting that was usually family-oriented and domestic. Other writers of the period, often known as Biedermeier (1815–48), in central Europe under the impact of Metternich's repression of open political discourse turned inwards towards the home, or to depoliticized stories about country life. Annette von Droste-Hülshoff (1797–1848), a well-educated aristocratic poet and composer of *Lieder*, was characteristic of these tendencies in writing mainly religious and nature poetry; in Austria the Bohemian-born writer Adalbert Stifter (1805–68) became celebrated for his depictions of nature. For a poet such as William Wordsworth (1770–1850) inspiration and emotion were rooted in the beauties of nature, above all in the mountains and streams of the English Lake District where he lived. Similarly, Biedermeier artists depicted with painstaking accuracy scenes of domestic and country life, telling a simple story in an often pious or sentimental manner. The style spread to Scandinavia, as did the simple, natural style of furniture for which the term Biedermeier is best known. Just as the English Romantic poets eschewed Classical allusion and, for the most part, elaborate metaphor in favour of the directness of ordinary speech, so Biedermeier furniture expressed a reaction against the ornate mahogany chairs, tables and other pieces produced under the French Empire; it appealed to the new middle classes with its clean lines and utilitarian designs, and was brought within their financial range by the usage of European woods such as cherry or oak rather than expensive imported hardwoods. In Sweden it was known as Karl Johan furniture, after Karl XIV Johan (1763–1844), the reigning monarch of the period, who had finished his military career as Marshal Bernadotte, a leading figure in Napoleon's armies.

In music, too, there was a turn towards the domestic. The aristocratic and clerical patronage that had sustained the composers of the eighteenth century was no longer available, at least not on such a scale as before.

Although the music of Ludvig van Beethoven (1770–1827), Carl Maria von Weber (1786–1826), Gioachino Rossini, Hector Berlioz (1803–69) and Ferenc (Franz) Liszt (1811–86) was celebrated in public performance, musical life in some respects retreated into the private sphere, into the family or the salon. The music of Franz Schubert (1797–1828) provides one of the best examples: much of it was written for musical evenings or weekends within the home or a circle of friends. Even so, Metternich's police regarded all gatherings even in private with suspicion, especially if those who took part in them were young. In 1820, Schubert and four of his friends were arrested for subversion; the composer himself was severely reprimanded and one of his friends was imprisoned. His comic opera *The Conspirators* (1823) – one of a number of attempts at making money from public performances, almost all of which came to nothing – was banned by the official censors because of its title. In fact, Schubert managed to hold only one public concert of his own music and focused on chamber works and songs for solo voice and piano, all of which could be performed by competent amateurs within the home. He ushered in the private world of the narrative song-cycle with *Die schöne Müllerin* (1823), *Die Winter-reise* (1828) and *Schwanengesang* (1828), works that are most evocative when performed in a small venue.

Similarly, Robert Schumann wrote only piano music early in his career, combining composition with music journalism in order to make a living. His piano cycles such as *Carnaval* (1834–5) and *Davidsbündlertänze* (*Dances of the League of David*, 1837) celebrated friendship among lovers of the arts, their pieces referring to individuals within Schumann's circle and identified by musical cryptograms. The deceptively simple *Kinderszenen* (*Childhood Scenes*, 1838) are perhaps the best known of all musical depictions of a child's life, with its toys ('Ritter vom Steckenpferd', or 'Knight of the Hobbyhorse'), games ('Hasche-Mann', or 'Blind Man's Buff') and imaginings ('Träumerei', or 'Dreaming', perhaps his most famous composition of all). Only later in his career did he turn to writing *Lieder*, building on Schubert's pioneering production of song-cycles to produce vocal works that told a story, usually of unrequited love. In the final phase of his life, Schumann wrote chamber music along with several powerful orchestral works, notably the Piano Concerto (1845) and Cello Concerto (1850); by this time public concert performances were bringing in a more reliable stream of income.

The rhythmic ambiguities even of these late works by Schumann are combined with an inwardness that takes them a long way from the showy virtuosity favoured by some other composers of the time such as Liszt, whose public performances during the 1840s aroused hysterical audience reactions dubbed 'Lisztomania' by Heinrich Heine: a 'veritable insanity' in which women fought over his handkerchiefs and gloves after a performance and attempted to cut off locks of his hair. Liszt's career pointed to the obverse of Biedermeier domesticity, the cult of the genius. While almost all of the instrumental and chamber works of the eighteenth- and early nineteenth-century composers can be performed by competent amateurs – even the final fugue of the *Hammerklavier* Sonata (1818) by Beethoven, if the retrospectively inserted metronome marks are disregarded – the 1820s also saw the arrival of the virtuoso, whose speciality was performing music that ordinary people found far beyond their capacities. The pioneer in this respect was not so much Liszt as the violinist Niccolò Paganini (1782–1840), whose fingers were so long that he could play three octaves across four strings simultaneously. Such was his virtuosity that he was said to have sold his soul to the Devil in exchange for it, a legend he did little to counter. To show off his talents, Paganini, like Liszt, wrote his own music, most notably the *Caprices* (1802–17), but he also commissioned works from professional composers such as Berlioz, who described him in his memoirs as 'a man with long hair and piercing eyes and a strange, ravaged countenance, a creature haunted by genius'.

Berlioz's own compositions breathed the unmistakable spirit of Romanticism, the new artistic movement that reacted to the rationalism of the Enlightenment by emphasizing the emotions, the exotic and the wild. Their themes encompassed not only a Byronic hero's encounter with brigands and his experiences wandering alone in the mountains (*Harold in Italy*, 1834), but also, in another Byronic piece, *The Corsair* (1844), the world of the Mediterranean pirate; and in the *Symphonie Fantastique* (1830) the drug-induced dreams of an artist, including a 'March to the Scaffold' and 'Witches' Sabbath'. A number of early Romantic works were written under the influence of opium, including, famously, the poem *Kubla Khan* (1816) by Samuel Taylor Coleridge (1772–1834), who became a serious addict, consuming up to four quarts of laudanum (tincture of opium) a week. The drug's impact was recorded in detail by Thomas de Quincey (1785–1859) in his *Confessions of an English Opium Eater* (1821). Opium distorted perceptions of time and space and heightened emotional experience, something that strengthened its appeal to the Romantics. Whereas the Enlightenment had stressed the need to subordinate the emotions to the intellect, Romanticism instead stressed feeling as the fundamental source of truth and authenticity and their expression in art.

The characteristic Romantic figure was a lone individual such as the *Wanderer above a Sea of Fog* (1818) by the German painter Caspar David Friedrich (1774–1840), standing on a mountain top above a sublime landscape after conquering its peaks, and, with his back turned to the viewer, contemplating an unknown and uncertain future, perhaps in the next life. The idea of the tortured genius was central to this ideal of art: art and suffering were intertwined in the Romantic agony in the figure of Beethoven, who was afflicted by increasing deafness from his mid-twenties until he had lost all his hearing by 1814. His deeply personal late string quartets met with general incomprehension – his fellow composer Louis Spohr (1784–1859), whose agreeable music is seldom heard today, described them as 'indecipherable, uncorrected horrors' – but all his symphonies, including the Ninth (1824) with its choral finale, were performed in a concert series in 1825 in Leipzig and again the following year, and he managed to stay financially afloat in his last years with income from commissions, chamber music and piano works, including the great Opus 111 Sonata (1822), with its ethereal, ecstatic second (and final) movement, and the endlessly inventive *Diabelli Variations* (1819–23). Beethoven was a transitional figure, beginning firmly in the Classical tradition and breaking free of it in his late works, whose inspiration followed Romantic principles by eschewing rule-bound forms (for example, in the number and length of different movements) and expressing emotion in seemingly spontaneous and unfettered fashion.

The Romantic hero as emotional being was expressed most dramatically perhaps in the character of Heathcliff, the protagonist of *Wuthering Heights* (1847) by Emily Brontë (1818–48): a 'dark-skinned gypsy', as she described him, who is adopted as a child by a Yorkshire gentleman farmer, is spurned in love by his daughter, and, consumed by rage and despair, spends the rest of his life in pursuit of revenge upon the family. Critics preferred the novels of Emily's more famous sister Charlotte. In her best-known work, *Jane Eyre* (1847), she described the eponymous heroine's growing independence and her rejection of the constricting conditions of governessing and teaching. Romantic themes continually recur in the novel, above all the ghostly and mysterious noises which, it is eventually revealed, are caused by a madwoman kept hidden in the attic of the remote Yorkshire house where Jane is employed by Mr Rochester. The two fall in love, but the madwoman in the attic is revealed as Rochester's wife, whom he had married unwisely in his passionate youth, and so Jane and Rochester are prevented by law from marrying. The novel ends with the madwoman setting fire to the house, which burns down, blinding its owner. Jane, who narrates the story, returns to rescue him, and opens the concluding chapter with the famous words: 'Reader, I married him.'

Jane Eyre contains many tropes familiar from Fredrika Bremer's work – blindness, injury and death caused by fire, women's thirst for emancipation, the law's restriction on women's freedom. Jane herself, like Bremer's heroines, is a committed Christian with a desire for self-improvement. Set in the wild moorlands of Yorkshire, the novels of the Brontë sisters depicted raw nature as something not to be ordered and controlled, but to be admired as sublime. Romantic art aimed at arousing strong emotions, not just happiness and sadness, but particularly in its choice of subjects, awe, terror, even revulsion, as in *Frankenstein* (1818) by Mary Shelley (1797–1851), which depicts a scientist's disastrous creation of an artificial human being made from the parts of various bodies. Romantic painting rejected the Classicizing traditions of the Academies in favour of depictions of wild natural scenes, such as *Horse Frightened by a Storm* (1824) by Eugène Delacroix, in which the animal, rearing on its hind legs, expresses nothing but pure emotion; or in the seascapes and atmospheric studies of J. M. W. Turner, rendered in the free style he developed in his late thirties. In pictures such as *The Slave Ship* (1840) or *Snow Storm: Steam-Boat off a Harbour's Mouth* (1842) the human figures are subordinated to the effects of light, so that they are often barely discernible within the wash of colours: nature is all. To conservative reviewers who disapproved of Turner's departure from strict Classical proportions, the influential critic John Ruskin responded that his painting fulfilled the central obligation of the artist – to be true to nature.

In showing slavers throwing overboard their dead and dying captives as a typhoon loomed, *The Slave Ship* struck a political note that could be found in many works of Romanticism. Byron's influence, evident in so many of them, was political as well as aesthetic: Delacroix painted not only a scene from one of his plays in *The Death of Sardanapalus* (1827) but also *The Massacre at Chios* (1824), and *Liberty Leading the People* (1830), produced on the occasion of the overthrow of Charles X. Similarly, the Russian poet and dramatist Alexander Pushkin was closely engaged with the war of Greek independence and published poems that inspired the Decembrists. Polish nationalism was expressed in the national epic written by the poet and dramatist Adam Mickiewicz, *Pan Tadeusz* (*Sir Thaddeus*, 1834), with its appeal to the memory of the formerly independent Polish-Lithuanian Commonwealth: 'My fatherland! You are like good health; I never knew how precious you were till I lost you!' Polish identity was musically expressed in the martial *Polonaises* and more gentle *Mazurkas* of Fryderyk Chopin. Like many other works of early Romanticism, Chopin's *Preludes* and *Ballades* abandoned Classical forms (in this case, the Sonata) for a more free-flowing, improvisatory structure, embodying the spontaneous expression of emotion (Schubert's *Impromptus* for piano even embodied this principle in their title). The emotions that early

Romanticism expressed were predominantly inward and private rather than public: poets, novelists, *Lieder* composers and painters dealt with love and despair, hope and belief, the wild and the sublime, but on a very personal level of experience.

In pursuit of emotional authenticity, artists and writers reached back beyond the Enlightenment to remoter periods for inspiration. Sir Walter Scott's historical writings inspired Berlioz to write overtures on *Waverley* (1828) and *Rob Roy* (1831). Their Romantic depiction of Scotland lay behind the *Scottish Symphony* (1842) by Felix Mendelssohn-Bartholdy (1809–47), with its imitations of bagpipes and its Scottish dance rhythms; the opera *Lucia di Lammermoor* (1835) by Gaetano Donizetti (1797–1848) was based on a novel by Scott. The French writer Alexandre Dumas declared he had experienced a '*coup de foudre*' on reading *Ivanhoe* (1820) and settled down to write a series of historical romances including *The Three Musketeers* (1844), *The Count of Monte Cristo* (1844–5) and *Robin Hood* (1863). The Hungarian Jósika Miklós (1794–1865) even included direct quotations from Scott in his *Abafi* (1854), set in Transylvania, the first historical novel in the Magyar language. Pushkin called Scott 'the Scottish sorcerer'. Germany's most famous writer, Johann Wolfgang von Goethe (1749–1832), who championed the principles of Classicism while exercising a substantial influence on the Romantics through his most celebrated work, the poetic drama *Faust* (1808, part I, and 1832, part II), said of Scott: 'I discover in him a wholly new art with laws of its own.'

Victor Hugo took Scott's technique of elaborate descriptions of land-scape and pageantry as an inspiration for his massive novel *Notre-Dame de Paris* (1831). Here he provided a fifteenth-century setting for a Gothic love story centring on the disabled and impoverished bell-ringer Quasimodo and the gypsy girl Esmeralda (Scott's *Ivanhoe* also featured a sympathetic portrait of an outcast girl, in his case Rebecca, daughter of a Jewish moneylender). Much later, responding in a similar way to the influence of Scott, Sir Arthur Conan Doyle, the creator of Sherlock Holmes, regarded his medieval novels *The White Company* (1891) and its sequel *Sir Nigel* (1906), along with other historical works, as his real contribution to literature. He even killed off his fictional detective at one point because he was eclipsing what he thought of as his more serious work, only to be compelled to resurrect him in response to popular pressure. A reading of Scott's work prompted the German historian Leopold von Ranke (1795–1886) to declare, famously, that every epoch was equal in the sight of God. The task of the historian, he thought, was to penetrate empathetically to its inner essence, to discover 'how it essentially was' (*wie es eigentlich gewesen*), not to dismiss it as backward or barbarous, as the historians of the eighteenth century had done.

Music also began to look to the past, most obviously in Mendelssohn-Bartholdy's rediscovery of the great works of Johann Sebastian Bach (1685–1750), previously thought of as hopelessly old-fashioned. On 11 March 1829, Mendelssohn staged a public performance of the *St Matthew Passion* (1727) before an audience that included the King of Prussia, the poet Heine and the philosopher Hegel. The work had not seen the light of day since Bach's death, and the performance was a triumph. 'It is as if I heard the roaring of the sea from afar,' commented Goethe, when he heard of the performance's success. The age saw the beginnings of the now almost universal practice of playing old as well as, or even rather than, contemporary music. Yet to make Bach's work palatable to audiences in the age of Romanticism, Mendelssohn cut half the numbers in the *Passion*, changed the orchestration, altered the harmonies, and modified the lines the soloists had to sing. The oratorio *Messiah* (1741) by George Friedrich Handel (1685–1759) was far more popular than any work by Bach, and inspired composers such as Mendelssohn himself to compose their own counterparts. However, in nineteenth-century performances there was little resemblance to the original, as the orchestration was strengthened and solidified and the choral forces grew ever larger: at the 'Great Handel Festival' held at the Crystal Palace in London in 1857 the work was sung by a choir of 200 and an orchestra of 500 players. Gargantuan performances of this kind became the staple of the many amateur choral societies that emerged during this period.

The discovery of the past indeed frequently involved its 'improvement' to suit contemporary tastes. In the 1820s architecture was still dominated by the neo-Classical style expressed in official buildings in many European capitals, from the Royal Museum (1823–30, now the Altes Museum) in Berlin, designed by Karl Friedrich Schinkel, to the Royal Palace in Oslo (1824–48) built by Hans Listow (1787–1851). But in the Romantic era it was challenged and eventually eclipsed by the neo-Gothic style introduced in Britain by Augustus Pugin (1812–52). Pugin began his career by designing sets for an operatic version of Scott's *Kenilworth* in 1829, and in 1833 he published his influential treatise, *Examples of Gothic Architecture*. This led to his commission, with Charles Barry (1795–1860), to build the new Houses of Parliament in Westminster following the destruction of the old ones by fire in 1834. The vast neo-Gothic building took thirty years to complete, and was rivalled in scale and grandeur only by the huge Parliament Building in the same style constructed in Budapest between

1895 and 1904 by the Hungarian architect Imre Steindl (1839–1902). Neo-Gothicism had already triumphed by the 1840s, by which time architects and designers were busy 'improving' buildings of all kinds to make them conform more closely to what they thought of as the spirit of the Middle Ages. Pugin insisted on putting rood-screens into the many churches he restored, despite the lack of contemporary justification for them. Eugène Viollet-le-Duc (1814–79) 'improved' the great Parisian Cathedral of Notre-Dame, adding gargoyles, which had not been part of the original building at all, and replacing some of the medieval statues with modern ones he thought looked more authentic. In 1849, when the French government decreed that the tumbledown walls of the southern French citadel of Carcassonne should be pulled down, an energetic campaign by the mayor resulted in a commission to Viollet-le-Duc to restore them, which he did partly by importing inappropriate northern French components such as slate roofs.

But the improving activities of Pugin and Viollet-le-Duc gave way later in the century to the movement to preserve the national heritage, fostered not only by pressure groups within each country but also by international journals, conferences and societies. Governments were gradually persuaded that leaving old buildings intact rather than adding to them was a better way to connect the present to the past. Growing national cultural pride aided the preservationists in their campaigns. International agreements, notably at The Hague in 1899 and 1907, enjoined the victors in wars to act as the guardians of the conquered nations' cultural possessions, rather than looting them, as had been the custom of war up to and including the time of Napoleon. By the end of the century scholarly editions of Handel's work were starting to appear, and were used as the basis for more authentic public performances than had become customary since Mendelssohn's time. And from 1851 onwards the Bach Society in Germany began its monumental project of publishing all of the great composer's works without editorial emendations, dissolving itself in 1900 when the task was finally completed. The ideas of national heritage and historical authenticity had finally come together.

ROMANTICISM AND RELIGION

By emphasizing the primacy of the emotions in the human spirit, Romanticism opened the way for religion to escape the scorn of Enlightenment rationalists and to come back into the cultural mainstream. The process was assisted by the drastic reduction in the secular power of the Church during the French Revolutionary and Napoleonic Wars. Ordinary Catholic parish clergy, liberated from dependence on aristocratic patrons, now looked above all to Rome for leadership. In northern and central Europe this meant fixing their gaze to the south, across the Alps, and so they were known as 'Ultramontanes'. Their militant Catholicism, strongly encouraged by the Vatican, was fuelled by fear and loathing of the French Revolution and its consequences, and they turned to new forms of religious devotion as sources of emotional mobilization, including the cults of the Immaculate Conception, promulgated by Pope Pius IX in 1854, and the Sacred Heart, celebrating the corporeality of Christ. Mass pilgrimages got under way once more, the most remarkable perhaps taking place in the western German town of Trier, where the lifting of state restrictions on Catholic assemblies by the Prussian King Friedrich Wilhelm IV prompted Bishop Wilhelm Arnoldi (1798–1864) to stage a demonstration against Enlightenment scepticism by inviting the pious to venerate the Holy Robe supposedly worn by Jesus before his crucifixion and displayed in the cathedral. Half a million predominantly poor people streamed past the relics in a disciplined procession, demonstrating the strength and popularity of the new Catholic piety.

Visions and revelations, including those of the French domestic servant Estelle Faguette (1843–1929) and the French teenager Thérèse Martin of Lisieux (1873–97), also gained a strong following. Most popular of all was the cult of the visionary Bernadette Soubirous (1844–79) in the Pyrenean mountain village of Lourdes, who saw the Virgin Mary in a local grotto. 'I am the Immaculate Conception,' the Virgin announced. Sick people began to make their way to the grotto and, later, the chapel she had instructed Bernadette to build on the site, seeking cures. Many of them claimed to have recovered from their illness following their visit. In 1862, after a thorough investigation in which Bernadette, a simple, illiterate and obviously pious girl, stuck to her story, the Church declared the visions genuine. In 1876, 100,000 Catholics, including thirty-five bishops, gathered in the village to crown a new statue of the Virgin. Other, similar apparitions were less widely accepted. When three girls living in the Saarland mining village of Marpingen claimed in July 1876 to have seen a woman in white describing herself as 'the Immaculately Conceived', 20,000 pilgrims appeared at the scene within a week, many of them claiming miraculous cures at the spring which the Virgin, according to the children, had indicated as a source of healing. Part of the reason for the visions' popularity lay in a widespread feeling among German Catholics that the Virgin, having revealed herself to the French, would surely show herself to the Germans as well. The Prussian police intervened, sending a detective to the village under the pseudonym of 'Marlow', who manufactured evidence that was thoroughly discredited when he appeared in the witness box at the trial of a number of villagers for fraud. A company of Prussian infantrymen arrived in the village, fixed bayonets, and dispersed several thousand pilgrims by force. The Church, cowed by the Prussian state's firm reaction to the events, refused to confirm or support the authenticity of the visions. Popular religious emotion was proving a difficult nut for the formal institutions of Church and State to crack. The girls eventually admitted they had made their story up as a prank, but had been too afraid to retract it when the story quickly became so widely accepted.

In Britain, driven on by the Evangelical revival of the early nineteenth century, voluntary associations such as the Society for the Suppression of Vice (1802) sprang up across the country, and in many of them, middle-class women played leading roles. Moral entrepreneurs from William Wilberforce (1759–1833) onwards campaigned and brought prosecutions against what they regarded as immoral art and literature. Bourgeois respectability was triumphing over aristocratic licentiousness and plebeian immorality. Good causes were not to be doubted or made fun of; and what censorship could not suppress, fashion consigned to oblivion. Part of the process of reform that transformed religion in Britain in the late 1820s and 1830s was the partial dismantling of the privileged position of the Anglican Church. Ever since the sixteenth-century Reformation, Catholicism had been regarded as a form of national treachery. Catholics like Protestant dissenters had long been barred not only from the universities of Oxford and Cambridge but also from public office, which was reserved for fully paid-up members of the Church of England. In 1828 and 1829 these restrictions were removed by Act of Parliament, not least in the Catholic case to defuse mounting tension in Ireland. A growing number of Anglican clerics saw these developments as threatening, especially when the government reduced the number of Irish bishops and proposed to secularize some of their revenues, following this with the commutation of church tithes, the legalization of civil marriage and marriages carried out in Dissenting chapels, and the establishment of a permanent Ecclesiastical Commission to reform diocesan administration, all in 1836.

A group of Anglican clerics centred round the University of Oxford and led by John Henry Newman (1801–90), John Keble (1792–1866) and Edward Pusey (1800–82) began publishing a series of tracts in which they accused the reforming Whig government of 'national apostasy' and Parliament of a 'direct disavowal of the sovereignty of God' by interfering with the Church and extending rights to Dissenters. The Tractarians, as they were known, believed that the Church of England's possession of Apostolic continuity demanded the greater use of ritual, vestments and Catholic observances in services: Pusey was banned from preaching for two years and eventually, following his own logic, Newman joined the Roman Catholic Church in 1845, later becoming a cardinal. In 1851 another prominent Anglican, Henry Edward Manning (1808–92), also converted, later becoming Cardinal-Archbishop of Westminster and heading the Catholic hierarchy in England, which was re-established in 1850. This step was taken not least in response to the arrival of large numbers of Irish Catholic immigrants following the famine of the previous few years. It did not, however, prevent the continued identification of Catholicism and Irish nationalism, which by the 1880s had constituted itself in large part as a movement of opposition to the Protestant Ascendancy in Ireland. An even more intense level of identification had developed across the other side of Europe, in Poland, where the oppressive rule of Protestant Prussia and Orthodox Russia placed Roman Catholicism at the centre of the nationalist movement. Even the Church's condemnation of the uprisings of 1831 and 1863 failed to dent this symbiosis, which was cemented by the development of a Marian devotion more powerful in Poland than almost anywhere else in Europe.

At the other end of the Christian spectrum, the Methodist movement, founded in England by John Wesley (1703–91) in 1739, grew strongly in the early nineteenth century, numbering 489,000 members by 1850. There were Evangelical revivals in Wales and Scotland, and sects such as the Baptists and Unitarians won mass adherence in mining and industrial districts across Britain. Among agricultural labourers too, the turn to Nonconformity was unmistakable, as the proliferation of Primitive Methodist chapels across Norfolk testified. However much they differed in points of doctrine, all these sects emphasized a simple form of religion, reliant on the Bible, shorn of ritual, and using open-air sermons to attract support. These were generally followed by the lower classes, often presenting the spectacle of mass hysteria in the revivalist meetings that led to conversion. Here the rationalism of eighteenth-century religion was replaced by an emotionalism similar in degree though diametrically opposed in doctrine to that of the Anglo-Catholic movement. Nonconformity emphasized above all the need for a sober and orderly lifestyle, opening the way to self-improvement for the working classes. From one point of view, all this could be a means of inculcating the habits of hard work, regularity and sobriety that capitalism required of the new industrial workforce, combined with a predestinarian submission to the grim realities of everyday life. From another, however, it was a spur to democratic reform in the political world. Nonconformity encouraged reading and education, and it engendered a sense of self-respect among workers when employer paternalism was being replaced by the ruthless exploitation of industrial capitalism.

These developments were ultimately a reaction to the influence of the Enlightenment, and of French revolutionary anticlericalism. In Prussia, King Friedrich Wilhelm III decreed the merger of the Calvinist and Lutheran Churches in 1817 in order to foster a religious revival. He placed them under a new government department, the Ministry of Spiritual, Educational and Medical Affairs, or *Kultusministerium*. The merger was followed in a series of other German states (for example, in Baden in 1821). The Prussian king introduced a new, standard liturgy, complete with altar cloths, crucifixes, candles, silk cassocks for bishops and other accoutrements of Catholicism. This ran into strong criticism from many pastors, though 5,343 out of 7,782 Protestant congregations were using the liturgy by 1825. The resistance of many pastors was fortified by the fact that the General Prussian Law Code of 1794 had declared freedom of conscience in religion, but nonetheless a lengthy struggle ensued, with Friedrich Wilhelm III eventually being forced to concede defeat in 1834, marking the effective recognition of parochial autonomy and liturgical diversity. After this, it was easier for individual pastors to retain an identity that leaned either one way or the other, towards the Lutheran or the Calvinist tradition. Similar developments occurred elsewhere in northern Europe, with for example a Department of State in the Norwegian administration running the Church from 1818 onwards.

In a reaction to both the Enlightenment and the state sponsorship of quasi-Catholic ritual, a movement based on the idea of 'awakening' spread across Protestant Germany, spearheaded by itinerant preachers such as Hans Nielsen Hauge (1771–1824), a farmer's son who preached strict Sabbatarianism and Puritanism to his flock. At his meetings converts abjured pleasure and frivolity and demonstrated their commitment by destroying instruments of pleasure – 'fiddlers burned their fiddles', as one shocked observer reported. The Moravian Church, which practised Bible reading, private prayer and the confession of sins, and advocated a life of simplicity and piety, won many new adherents in the Baltic littoral, boosting its membership in Courland from 9,800 in 1818 to 26,300 in 1839, and in Estonia from 21,900 in 1818 to 75,000 in 1839. Elsewhere in Europe, Protestantism underwent a similar 'awakening' in the quest to rescue religion from the rationalism of the Enlightenment. In Lutheran Finland the Karelian Revival found expression in prayer meetings and hymn-singing festivals; the Russian administration of the country saw in these a potential source of nationalist unrest and attempted to suppress them, which of course only strengthened the identification of Lutheranism with the cause of Finnish independence. In Hungary the proportion of Protestants, most of them Calvinists, rose to around 22 per cent of the population by mid-century. The fact that liberal revolutionaries like Lajos Kossuth were mostly Protestants led to the promulgation by the government in Vienna in 1859 of a decree placing the Protestant congregations under state control. But pressure from Britain forced its withdrawal the following year, and with the gaining of national autonomy under the Austro-Hungarian Compromise of 1867 the legal rights the Protestants had won in 1848 were fully regained. The Protestant 'awakening' of the early nineteenth century was even more marked in Switzerland, where men like François Gaussen (1790–1863) campaigned for the employment of 'sound doctrine' and the use of the Bible as the infallible guide to faith and practice. Some congregations declared their independence, leading eventually to the disestablishment of the Swiss Reformed Church between 1907 and 1909.

In Russia, the reaction against Enlightenment rationalism was led by Alexander I. The tsar was personally inclined to mysticism after he fell under the influence of the prophetess Juliane von Krüdener (1764–1824), who told him that he would be the instrument of the downfall of Napoleon, the Antichrist. So convinced was Alexander that his crusade against the French Emperor was sanctified by God that he once invited Juliane to an intimate dinner with Metternich at which a fourth place was laid for the absent Christ. Alexander's genuine belief in the Divine inspiration of the Holy Alliance, which he founded under Juliane's influence in 1815, was turned into pragmatic policy by his more down-to-earth successor. Nicholas I regarded the Orthodox Church as an arm of his autocracy and inaugurated a long tradition of subordinating other religions and denominations in the Russian Empire to the state's control. Nicholas was particularly hostile to the so-called Old Believers, schismatics who had faced the disapproval of the tsars ever since they had rejected ecclesiastical reforms introduced two hundred years before. Some groups of Old Believers thought that the world was ruled by the Antichrist, and refused to have priests or pray for the tsar. Many wanted to simplify the act of worship and condemned the use of polyphony in Church services. Most insisted on the sacrality of the ancient Church Slavonic text of the Bible. A few even repudiated marriage and refused to use money. One group rejected icons and prayed to the East through a hole in a wall: they were known as the Dymiki, or hole-worshippers. The Nyetovtsy, as their name implied, said 'no' to churches, priests and sacraments. The Skoptsy practised

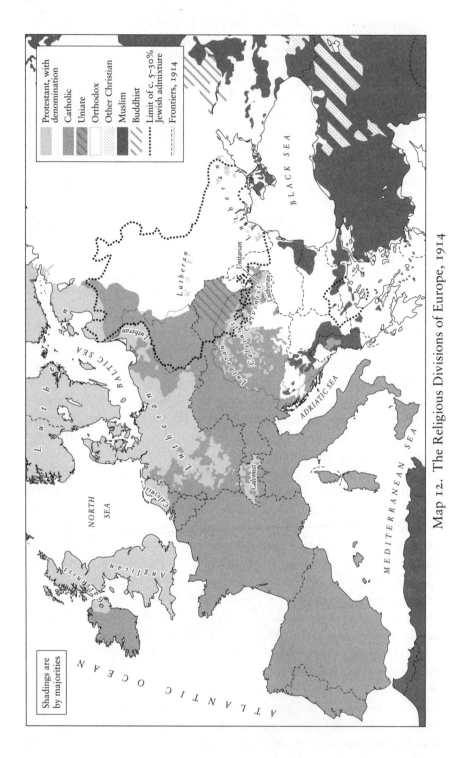

Map 12. The Religious Divisions of Europe, 1914

self-castration as a mark of sanctity. Not surprisingly, the Filippovtsy, who had practised self-immolation as a form of sacrifice to strengthen the faith, had died out in the eighteenth century.

The Old Believers caused a good deal of anxiety for Metropolitan Philaret (Vasily Mikhailovich Drozdov, 1782–1867), who served as head of the Orthodox Church in Moscow from 1821 until his death more than forty years later. Under his influence the Jesuits were banned from the empire in 1820 and the Freemasons two years later. Increasingly aggressive Christian proselytizing led to the baptism of half the 50,000 Jewish youths under the age of eighteen recruited into the army between 1843 and 1855, and the conversion between 1845 and 1847 of 74,000 Courlanders and Estonians to Orthodoxy in the diocese of Riga, established in 1836. However, such conversions were often in name only. The formal reunion of the Uniate Church in Poland and Ukraine with Orthodoxy was announced more than once, without any noticeable effect on the parishioners' adherence to Papal authority. Following Tsar Alexander II's revocation of the requirement for Lutherans in mixed marriages to bring up their children in the Orthodox faith, some 40,000 Estonians and Courlanders brought up in this way reverted to Lutheranism between 1865 and 1874.

The status of the Orthodox Church as an officially sanctioned state institution was severely shaken by the 1905 Revolution in Russia, when Tsar Nicholas II was forced to proclaim freedom of religion. 'Everyone – secular and clerical,' complained the former Procurator of the Holy Synod, Konstantin Petrovich Pobedonostsev (1827–1907), 'has gone out of his mind.' The lapsed hieromonk Iliodor (Sergei Mikhailovich Trufanov, 1880–1952) countered the liberal tendencies among some priests by congratulating the forces of reaction after the 1905 Revolution on their 'great and holy work of emancipating the dear Motherland from atheists, robbers, blasphemers, bomb-throwers, firebrands, lying journalists and slanderers – all of them cursed by God and condemned by men'. He began a popular movement against the government, but in 1911 Tsar Nicholas II summoned him to a meeting and told him to attack the Jews instead; shortly afterwards, Iliodor was promoted to the rank of archimandrite. He remained, however, a disruptive influence. Undermined from within and without, the Orthodox Church in Russia was becoming increasingly fragile as the spiritual arm of a crumbling state.

The Greek Orthodox Church, which strongly backed the independence movement of the 1820s, was declared autocephalous – independent of the Ecumenical Patriarchate of Constantinople – by the Greek Parliament in 1833, but immediately following this, King Otto confiscated church lands and closed down 600 monasteries, implementing in Greece the secularizing legislation that had been put into place in his native Bavaria during the Napoleonic era. However, the Patriarchate of Constantinople carried on being dominated by Greeks, and the Greek Orthodox Church continued to function throughout the Balkans in other areas outside Greece itself. The various branches of the Orthodox Church were keen to collaborate in the face of a resurgent Roman Catholicism. In 1848 a synod of the four main Orthodox Patriarchates formally declared the Roman Catholic Church to be heretical and schismatic. Later on, the new doctrine of Papal Infallibility was condemned as blasphemous, and the dogma of the Immaculate Conception was stigmatized as false. The Church also faced problems within its own ranks, however: in 1901 there were riots in Athens over a new translation of the New Testament into demotic Greek, carried out in London and published in Athens by the daily newspaper *Acropolis*. After it was condemned as blasphemous by the Patriarchate, students took to the streets, trashed the paper's offices, and on 8 November held a mass demonstration outside the Temple of Zeus to demand the excommunication of the translators. The Prime Minister called in the army, who shot eight demonstrators dead and wounded another seventy. In the ensuing furore he was forced to resign, along with the Metropolitan, who had approved the translation. Although most Greeks could not understand it, the sacred Ancient Greek text was given a monopoly of usage in the Constitution of 1911.

In Bulgaria, as in other parts of the Ottoman Empire, Christians formed a separate community on their own, under the suzerainty of the Greek Orthodox Patriarch. With the rise of Bulgarian nationalism, Greek ecclesiastical and especially episcopal appointees were gradually replaced by Bulgarian ones. In 1870 the Ottoman authorities, ever ready to encourage divisions among their Christian subjects, granted permission for the establishment of an autonomour Bulgarian Exarchate, vital to Bulgarian nationalists because the school system was run by the ecclesiastical authorities. The Christian populations of the bishoprics of Skopje and Obrid voted in 1874 to join by 91 per cent and 97 per cent respectively, bringing a substantial part of Macedonia under the control of the Bulgarian Church. In 1872, Atanas Mihaylov Chalakov (1816–88) was elected Exarch; his links with the nationalist movement were made clear by his appointment as President of the Constituent and then the National Assembly in 1879. His declaration in 1872 of the autocephaly of the Exarchate prompted the Patriarchal Synod in Constantinople to defrock him, excommunicate him along with his leading followers, and convict them all of the heresy of ethnophyletism. Nevertheless, the Exarchate flourished, founding or taking over thousands of schools and other educational institutions. Church and state were moving closer together in emerging nations such as Serbia and Bulgaria, leading to the severing of ties with supranational ecclesiastical institutions. A similar process was also taking place further west.

DISSENT, DOUBT AND DISBELIEF

The revival of piety was intimately connected with a deepening crisis in the relations between Church and State, above all in Catholic Europe. In the process of Italian unification, Pope Pius IX faced the incorporation of the Papal States into the Kingdom of Italy – sealed by a plebiscite that delivered 133,000 votes in favour and only 1,500 against. The new Italian legislature passed a law recognizing Pius as a head of state, providing diplomatic immunity for foreign ministers attached to the Vatican, and assigning him a generous annual income. But Pius and his successors rejected this settlement and turned down the subsidy. In the ensuing stand-off, which lasted all the way up to 1929, the Pope issued a futile ban on Catholics taking part in Italian politics, declaring that it was 'inexpedient' for them even to vote. Describing himself as 'the prisoner in the Vatican', he did not leave the city until his death in 1878. He issued protests against the actions of the Italian state with tireless regularity. This was not surprising. In its efforts to establish control over the peninsula, the united Italian state dissolved 38,000 separate ecclesiastical bodies and corporations and sequestrated their assets. Seminarists were made liable to compulsory military service. Civil marriage was made a legal obligation. Scores of bishops and cardinals were arrested. In practice Church schools continued in existence, as did some religious orders, and, on the other hand those Catholics who were qualified continued in their great majority to vote in elections. But the alienation of Catholic institutions from those of the Kingdom of Italy remained deep.

In response to his loss of secular power Pius IX issued a Syllabus of Errors in 1864. The Syllabus proclaimed that it was an error to believe that human reason contradicted Christian faith, or to hold that Protestantism was merely another form of Christianity, or to claim that the Catholic religion should not be the sole religion of the state, to the exclusion of all other forms of worship. Article 80 proclaimed that it was an error to believe that 'the Roman Pontiff can and ought to reconcile himself to, and agree with, progress, liberalism, and civilization as lately introduced'. Civil marriages were to be regarded as null and void, and matrimonial causes should only be dealt with by the Church (Articles 73–4). Education had to be carried out by the Church not the state (Articles 45–7). Pius strengthened his position by summoning a Council, which met in 1870 and issued a Declaration of Papal Infallibility. From this point onwards the Pope could issue decrees and encyclicals with the force of God, brooking no dissent. Liberal Catholics were appalled. Some, like the theologian and historian Alfred Loissy (1843–1922), who tried to apply modern critical methods to the study of the Bible, were sacked from their professorships, to be condemned in 1893 by the Papal Encyclical *Providentissimus Deus*, which reaffirmed the literal truth of the Old and New Testaments. Perhaps the most famous reaction came from the historian and sometime editor of a liberal Catholic periodical, Lord Acton (1834–1902), who declared, referring to the Pope: 'Power tends to corrupt, and absolute power corrupts absolutely.'

A similar clash between Church and State took place during the 1870s in France. While the monarchists dominated the legislature, which was for most of the 1870s, the Third Republic was powerless to act. But as their electoral influence waned, Jules Ferry (1832–93), who controlled French education policy in the late 1870s and early 1880s, pushed through a series of fiercely anticlerical measures. 'My aim,' he said, 'is to establish humanity without God and without King.' He expelled the clerical teaching orders from France and worked hard to laicize the educational system. During Ferry's time as Education Minister or Prime Minister, or under his general influence on government, the Sunday observance laws were repealed (1879), the cemeteries were made non-denominational (1881), and divorce was legalized (1884). Anticlerical politics did not end with Ferry's departure from the scene. In the early 1900s all monastic orders were dissolved (except the Trappists, whom Republicans considered harmless because they never said anything). Some 10,000 religious schools were closed. Finally in 1905 the Church was formally disestablished and separated from the state, which ended its financial support altogether but took over the ownership of most church buildings. The appointment of bishops was made subject to state approval. Pope Leo XIII (1810–1903), elected in 1878, launched a diplomatic campaign to try and bring the conflict to an end, and issued a famous encyclical, *Rerum Novarum*, calling on Catholics to take action to deal with the many social problems thrown up by industrialization and urbanization. He urged the priesthood not to involve itself in politics. In France this led to the so-called *ralliement*, in which Catholics were urged to come to terms with the Third Republic. This dismayed many parish priests, who continued to attack the Republic from the pulpit, while nothing was done on the state's part to repeal the many anticlerical laws in force; rather, if anything, the opposite.

The Church-State struggles of the late nineteenth century were equally fierce in Germany, though they came to an end sooner than in France. Here again a newly created political system sought to cement the loyalty of its Catholic subjects by extending its powers over them just as Pius IX was trying to make them subordinate to the papacy. Bismarck in particular regarded the large Catholic minority in the German Empire as 'enemies of the Reich', since most of them had been citizens of the southern German states that had fought alongside Austria against Prussia in 1866. In addition the substantial Polish minority in the provinces of Posen and Silesia derived a great deal of its nationalist commitment from its passionate allegiance to Catholicism. In 1871, Bismarck began by legislating against clergy who used their pulpits for political purposes, before going on, in 1872, to subject Church schools to government inspection, banning the Jesuits, who seem to have been a particular object of suspicion to almost all European governments at least since the mid-eighteenth century, and breaking off diplomatic relations with the Vatican. In 1873 the so-called May Laws passed over the training of clergy to the state, while clerical appointments were subjected to government confirmation.

Half the seminaries in Prussia were closed in the following five years. In 1875 the Prussian state ended subsidies to the Catholic Church; all religious orders were dissolved, and civil marriage was made compulsory. The flames of conflict were fanned by the German liberals, who cheered Bismarck on in what they came to call the 'struggle of civilizations', or *Kulturkampf*, pitting enlightened progressivism against reactionary obscurantism. The Catholic clergy would not bow to the new laws. They boycotted state training institutions, and refused to submit clerical appointments for government approval. The police moved in and by the mid-1870s some 989 Catholic parishes were without incumbents, 225 priests were in prison, two archbishops and three bishops had been removed from office, and the Bishop of Trier had died shortly after ending a nine-month jail sentence: the furore over the alleged apparitions at Marpingen occurred at the centre of this conflict. German Catholics flocked to the colours of the new Catholic Centre Party, founded in 1871, which forcefully articulated their grievances on the political stage. Here again the election of Pope Leo XIII in 1878 opened the way to a reconciliation, especially since Bismarck was now gunning for a new 'enemy of the Reich' in the form of the Social Democratic Party. In 1880 he introduced a law renouncing the government's right to remove clergy from their posts. In 1882, Prussia reopened diplomatic relations with the Holy See, and the following year the most oppressive features of the *Kulturkampf* legislation were softened. But this did not halt the continued rise of the Catholic Centre Party, which soon provided the largest single group of deputies in the Reichstag.

Italy, France and Germany were not the only states in which there were clashes of this kind. The liberal Ministry in power in Austria during the 1870s made appointments to the priesthood dependent on government approval. It revoked the Concordat concluded with the papacy signed in 1855, secularized marriage and subordinated Church schools to the state. However, Emperor Franz Joseph vetoed proposals to make civil marriage compulsory, and a powerful Catholic political movement emerged in the form of the Christian Social Party, founded in 1891. Similarly, from 1879 to 1884, Belgium was convulsed by a 'school war' in which a liberal attempt to secularize education met with fierce resistance from Catholics, who mobilized in demonstrations and riots; two protesters were killed by police in the town of Kortrijk, and when a Catholic national government was elected in 1884, 200 liberal-dominated municipalities staged massive demonstrations that called forth equally impressive Catholic counter-demonstrations. The king finally was forced to intervene, dismissing the two most radical Ultramontane ministers and forcing the Catholic government to moderate its stance. In the Netherlands, where a substantial Catholic minority inhabited the southernmost provinces, the Pope's appointment of a number of bishops in 1853 led to protests from the Protestant clergy. A law restricting religious processions led to violent clashes with the police in 1872, and in 1878, when columns of pilgrims attacked a police cordon near Roermond in the Limburg province. In Spain the century was peppered with anticlerical legislation, and from 1900 onwards there were numerous clashes and demonstrations as secularists went on the march, following the example of France. They staged banquets on Good Friday, normally a day of fasting, and scheduled an 'anticlerical week' to coincide with Holy Week.

The hostility of new or restructured European states and reforming liberal governments was not the only challenge with which the Churches had to contend. Potentially more serious in the long run was the secularization of the masses. The religious sections of the 1851 national census in Britain revealed that in most large towns fewer than 10 per cent of the inhabitants had attended a place of worship on census Sunday. As one English bishop put it in 1852: 'It is easy to see how the artisan and labourer fresh from the country villages, where, at least, they might find room, and often sought it, in the House of God, should generally lose the habit of worship and devotion, where there was neither place for them to worship nor pastor to lead them in the ways of God.' Similar developments were taking place in Russia. In the diocese of St Petersburg only eighty-five new churches were built between 1876 and 1887. Money for building churches had to be raised locally, a difficult task in working-class districts, not least because so many of their inhabitants were new arrivals or soon moved on to other places of employment. In 1891 a statistical survey of the churches in Germany found that in Hamburg the ratio of pastors to inhabitants was one to 8,000 and in the capital city Berlin it was one to 10,000, a sharp fall from the ratio of one to 3,000 at the beginning of the century. While the overall annual communion rate in Prussia in 1891–5 was forty-three per hundred members of the Church, it stood at only sixteen in Berlin. In Stockholm only 10 per cent of adult males were communicants in 1880, in Paris 15 per cent attended mass around the turn of the century, and in London church attendance stood at 22 per cent around this time. Legislation also made it easier for people to abandon their religious duties: the Dissenter Law passed in Norway in 1845 freed citizens from the legal obligation to belong to a church, an example followed by Denmark in 1849.

The revivalist movement did its best to counteract the effects of secularization in big cities and industrial areas, most notably, in Germany, through the 'Inner Mission', established in 1848 by a leading Evangelical philanthropist, Johann Hinrich Wichern (1808–81), with the aim of using charitable work among the poor to bring a conservative social message to them, based on Lutheran principles. Founded as an imitation of and reaction to the growth of missionary societies that aimed to convert the heathen and the indifferent outside Europe, Wichern's movement spread to other northern European countries, including Denmark, where it was founded in 1861. The Danish movement offered communal activities in rural areas, bringing different social classes together on a religious basis and perhaps preventing the exodus of congregations from the state Church to the kind of radical Protestant sects that were emerging in Sweden at the time. The Catholic Church was not slow to pick up the idea. In Spain socially concerned priests organized Workers' Circles in Valencia, Madrid and other cities from the 1890s onwards, establishing 258 of these institutions with a total of 180,000 members by 1912. In Orthodox Russia itinerant preachers organized themselves in the Society for the Propagation of Religious and Moral Enlightenment in the Spirit of the Orthodox Church. Founded in 1881, the Society held meetings in factories in St Petersburg and won many adherents. A comparable organization, the Alexander Nevsky Temperance Society, had 75,000 members in 1905, a year in which it printed 10,000 copies of a pamphlet on the workers' question. Such efforts easily led to political activism by committed priests. Not surprisingly, they were suppressed by the authorities after Father Georgiy Apollonovich Gapon (1870–1906) had led the demonstration of workers that sparked the 1905 revolution.

For all the anxiety expressed in such movements, the contrast between supposedly devout country folk and secularized, non-believing town-dwellers could easily be overdrawn. Eighty-seven per cent of male and 91 per cent of female believers were recorded as attending confession and communion in urban and rural Russian Orthodox churches in 1900. The parish certainly remained the centre of rural community life in many parts of Europe. But religious observance in the countryside often fell far short of clerical ideals. In France enquiries in the diocese of Orléans revealed that by 1850 only 10.6 per cent of the population took Easter communion; regular attenders at church were even fewer in number. Behaviour in rural churches was frequently rowdy: a French *curé* complained in the 1850s that his flock never listened to his sermons but instead made a deafening noise while he was preaching, spitting, slamming doors, coughing, shuffling and chatting. Urban industrial workers and their families may not have attended church with any regularity, but they still valued religion when it came to marking the great rites of passage in life. In Berlin, 89 per cent of babies born to Protestant parents in 1910 were baptized, and 72 per cent of babies born to Catholic parents. In 'red' Saxony in the years 1896–1900, 90 per cent of couples were married in church and 99 per cent of the dead were given religious funerals. In baptizing their children, Social Democratic workers sometimes signalled their political allegiance by giving them demonstratively socialist names – 'Lassaline', a girl's name after the early German socialist leader Ferdinand Lassalle, was a particularly popular one – but they had them baptized nonetheless.

The process of secularization affected men and women unevenly. In the diocese of Orléans around the middle of the century, 11.6 per cent of women took Easter communion but only 2 per cent of men. Within the area covered from 1830 by the state of Belgium, the ratio of nuns to monks changed from 40:60 in 1780 to 60:40 eighty years later. Most of the women were in teaching, nursing or philanthropic orders. Similarly, in Russia between 1850 and 1912, while the number of monks doubled to just over 21,000, the number of nuns increased from 8,533 to 70,453. Critics of the Church saw this as evidence of the emotionalism of the female sex. The French historian Jules Michelet (1798–1874), an ardently anticlerical Republican, talked of confessors 'seducing' wives or 'flagellating' them with 'spiritual rods', spreading a reactionary influence throughout society by exercising a malign influence over women. Perhaps Michelet was upset by the fact that his mistress, on her deathbed, turned to her confessor rather than to him. But his views were widely shared. Such anticlerical gender stereotyping was a major influence behind the French Republicans' refusal to endorse the enfranchisement of women up to the end of the century and far beyond.

For all the concern of religious people in the nineteenth century about the declining power of the Church, the encroachments of the state, and the growing tendency of ordinary men, and to a lesser extent women, in the industrializing centres of population to cease religious practice except in social rites of passage such as baptisms, marriages and funerals, Europe remained an overwhelmingly religious culture right up to the First World War. Indeed, the nineteenth century was the age above all others when Christians in Europe sought to carry their message to the rest of the world through a vast array of missionary societies. These took advantage of Europe's global hegemony, backed by greatly improved communications, to embark on Christianizing efforts across the continents. Overseas missionary societies, already active in Britain since the late eighteenth century, were founded in Basel in 1815, Denmark in 1821, France in 1822, Berlin in 1824 and Sweden in 1835. They set up schools and colleges, ran newspapers, built churches, and did their best to keep the missionaries of rival Christian denominations at bay. Although the new missionary effort was pioneered by Protestants, the Catholic Church followed suit in 1868 with the 'White Fathers', secular priests who wore a uniform of white cassocks and mantles, and of course the Jesuits had been undertaking missionary activities long before this. Many missionaries met a violent end at the hands of the unconverted, but an armed 'militia of Christ' founded by Cardinal Charles Lavigerie (1825–92) to protect them did not meet with widespread approval: it made the missionary effort look too much like the return of the Crusades.

While missionaries were setting out to evangelize the world, Christianity was coming under intense and growing sceptical scrutiny within Europe itself. The sociologist Max Weber (1864–1920) identified as a central feature of the age what he called the 'disenchantment of the world', a process in which the common view held by rural society that the natural world was a kind of magical creation governed by supernatural power was replaced by goal-oriented, rational systems of belief based on scientific understanding. Initially, this change in belief was confined above all to parts of the urban working class, especially in central Europe, and to the liberal bourgeoisie. Here, however, it fed on the increasingly explicit challenge to religion mounted by modern scientific discoveries and their champions. One of the most profound influences on Fredrika Bremer, evident in particular in her book *Morning Watches* (1842), was exercised by the writings of David Friedrich Strauss (1808–74). His book *The Life of Jesus, Critically Examined*, published in 1835–6, when he was twenty-seven, used modern philological methods of textual criticism to dismiss the miraculous elements in the Gospels as mythical and demonstrated how little hard evidence there actually was for the existence of the historical Jesus. Such ideas horrified Christian apologists. The English translation of his work by George Eliot, which appeared in 1846, was described by the Evangelical social reformer Anthony Ashley-Cooper, 7th Earl of Shaftesbury, as 'the most pestilential book ever vomited out of the jaws of Hell'.

Strauss's work convinced the young classical philologist and philosopher Friedrich Nietzsche (1844–1900) that Christianity had been utterly discredited by historical research. Writing in his customary aphoristic style, Nietzsche declared 'God is dead'; the universal value system propagated by Christianity could no longer possess any validity in a modern world in which there were so many value systems that the individual had in effect to make up his own in an act of will. Those who created a new set of values beyond conventional notions of good and evil were, accordingly, superhuman beings, whose effective use of the will to power Nietzsche contrasted with the mediocrity of the masses and the triviality of popular culture. Much of Nietzsche's work was unread or unpublished in his own lifetime, which ended in silent dementia brought on by the onset of tertiary syphilis; but he had a considerable impact on the Danish writer Georg Brandes (1842–1927), whose 1873 lectures attacking Christianity as a dead ideology were said to have inspired the introduction in Denmark of civil confirmation (though the church rite continued to be used by the vast majority of families).

Philosophical scepticism could sometimes be rivalled in its corrosive effects on faith by Christian despondency, most notably in the work of the Danish philosopher-theologian Søren Kierkegaard (1813–55), who attacked the atheistic determinism of the Young Hegelians by emphasizing the absolute autonomy of the individual conscience. Organized religion, especially if it was state-controlled, infantilized people, he thought, and subverted their faith by compromising with the world. 'The Christian view,' he wrote, ' . . . is one of suffering, of enthusiasm for death, belonging to another world.' By the time of his own death, Kierkegaard's ideas were beginning to have a significant impact on the Danish Church, as his official obituary noted in 1855: 'The fatal fruits which Dr. Kierkegaard showed to arise from the union of Church and State, have strengthened the scruples of many of the believing laity, who now feel that they can remain no longer in the Church.' In the same year the Danish Church freed its members from the obligation only to attend services in their own parish, permitting them to choose any pastor they wished; and two years later it abolished compulsory infant baptism, following the view that religious faith should be a matter of adult choice.

But of all the intellectual challenges to Christianity in the nineteenth century the most serious was the rise of scientific materialism. A good deal of damage was done by the demonstration in the three-volume *Principles of Geology* by Sir Charles Lyell (1797–1875), published in 1830–3, that there was no evidence for Noah's Flood and the world had not been created on the eve of 23 October 4004 BC as claimed many years earlier by the cleric James Ussher (1581–1656), but was far older. Christian writers and thinkers initially reacted to the work of men like Lyell or Strauss by taking refuge in a naturalistic theology that posited the existence of a grand divine plan of nature, putting human beings, the only creatures endowed with a soul, at the centre of God's design. But it became increasingly difficult to uphold this view. An anonymously authored book, *Vestiges of the Natural History of Creation*, published in 1844, actually written by the Scottish publisher and geologist Robert Chambers (1802–71), laid out a description of the natural world that began with the solar system and ended with the emergence of humanity. It asserted that man was simply one kind of animal, 'considered zoologically, and without regard to the distinct character assigned to him by theology'. The naturalist Charles Darwin issued an even more profound challenge to Christian belief. Darwin had collected fossils and observed the variety of species on the Galapagos Islands during his voyage on the *Beagle* from 1831 to 1836. Another naturalist, Alfred Russel Wallace, had independently come to similar conclusions, and in 1859, to forestall him, Darwin published his celebrated book *On the Origin of Species*. It opened with the boldest possible statement, that 'the view, which most naturalists until recently entertained, and which I formerly entertained – that each species has been independently created – is erroneous'. Species had not been made in their final form by God, he declared, but had changed and evolved over time.

Darwin's linkage of evolution to mid-Victorian optimism, along with his manifestly Christian interpretation of the natural order and the preparatory work done by Chambers and Lyell, softened the blow to religion struck by the publication of his book. But in the biologist Thomas Huxley (1825–95) the modest and retiring Darwin acquired an aggressive proponent of his ideas that quickly brought them widespread publicity. In 1860, Huxley debated Darwin's theories with Samuel Wilberforce (1805–73), the Bishop of Oxford, at the British Association for the Advancement of

Science. Wilberforce was a noted public speaker, generally known as 'Soapy Sam' after Disraeli had described his rhetorical style as 'unctuous, oleaginous, saponaceous'. According to Isabella Sidgwick (1825–1908):

> The Bishop rose, and in a light scoffing tone, florid and fluent, he assured us there was nothing in the idea of evolution; rock-pigeons were what rock-pigeons had always been. Then, turning to his antagonist with a smiling insolence, he begged to know, was it through his grandfather or his grandmother that he claimed his descent from a monkey? On this Mr Huxley slowly and deliberately arose. A slight tall figure stern and pale, very quiet and very grave, he stood before us, and spoke those tremendous words – words which no one seems sure of now, nor I think, could remember just after they were spoken, for their meaning took away our breath, though it left us in no doubt as to what it was. He was not ashamed to have a monkey for his ancestor; but he would be ashamed to be connected with a man who used great gifts to obscure the truth. No one doubted his meaning and the effect was tremendous. One lady fainted and had to be carried out: I, for one, jumped out of my seat.

The debate made Darwin and his theories famous. Whether he liked it or not, evolutionism was pitched against creationism, facts against faith.

CHRISTIANITY AND BEYOND

Like Darwin himself, the vast majority of scientists and scholars believed that their discoveries were compatible in one way or another with Christianity, though some writers, like Brandes, and many rank-and-file socialists, believed that the authority of the Bible had been fatally undermined by the discoveries of science. At the other extreme of the scale of belief, magical and superstitious practices still ran in parallel to Christianity across the rural world, many of them deriving ultimately from the pre-Christian era. In the Outer Hebrides one observer reported in 1899 a continuing belief in the existence 'of all forms of evil influence'. In Germany the practice of obtaining the blood of executed criminals for magical healing was only one of a vast number of superstitious habits designed to ward off or cure disease. Country folk prescribed ingesting herbs picked at a particular time, singing incantations or anointing an injury with a magical potion made, as in Portugal, of the ground remains of a dead lizard steeped in the victim's urine. Gifts could be laid beneath a juniper or hawthorn or some other tree by a sufferer from fever. In Pomerania on the Baltic coast peasants reacted to the arrival of cholera by digging up the corpse of the first victim and ritually decapitating it. For scrofula the people of the Bourbonnais in central France sought the aid of the eldest of seven sons to touch the victim before sunrise on the night of St John, in ceremonies that attracted crowds hundreds strong. Sacred places, fountains, groves, wells, fairy rings, all had their various powers. Cases of witchcraft still came to light from time to time: in 1863 a bricklayer in the Ardennes was convicted of commissioning the murder of a supposed sorcerer for casting an evil spell on his kilns; in 1887 a young couple in Sologne in north-central France were condemned to death and executed for murdering the wife's mother on the advice of a sorcerer. Books of spells were on sale at country fairs, particularly popular versions of the works of the medieval alchemist Albertus Magnus (c. 1200–80), the *Grand Albert* and the *Petit Albert*; if a man experienced an unusual run of good luck, people would say 'He has the *Petit Albert* in his pocket!'

Country clergymen often continued to engage in magical practices despite the disapproval of the hierarchy. Church bells in French villages customarily rang the tocsin to dispel storms despite repeated ecclesiastical decrees against the practice. People placed phials of holy water obtained from the church to protect their crops and buildings, or put them on top of their chimneys. From here it was only a small step to go to sites of Christian pilgrimage such as Lourdes in search of cures, or to place votive tablets or handwritten prayers in churches to pray for success in examinations. The Church lent its blessing to the belief in miracles, but the line between the miraculous and the magical was a fine one. Fortune-tellers remained popular at fairs and festivals; it was a particular speciality of gypsy women, who also earned money by selling charms to ward off illness. However, the spread of secular education and the disapproval of the law increasingly undermined the belief systems that underpinned such actions. Parents might continue with the old superstitions, but children learned very different ideas at school. Law courts grew more sceptical in cases involving accusations of magical practices, the use of love-potions, and allegations of witchcraft. Magistrates in Norwich in 1843 dismissed a case in which a woman accused her sister of paralyzing her husband with a potion made of dragon's blood mixed with water in an oyster shell and enriched by the man's nail-parings. In 1894 an English traveller in France observed bottles of holy water placed on chimneys as protection against lightning, but already the Church and the state were pressing for the installation of lightning conductors. Magical practices underwent an even more marked decline in urban society, where in any case the need to regulate relations with the natural world was much less imperative than it was in the countryside.

Even more uneasy than the relationship between Christianity on the one hand and superstition on the other was the relationship between the majority religion and minorities who followed other faiths. Islam was the established religion of the Ottoman Empire, though the numerous Christians who lived in its European territories enjoyed extensive toleration. Islamic scholars differed over how far to adapt to the growing challenge of European science and culture. On the whole, while trying to introduce modern secular institutions to the empire, Sultan Abdülhamid II did his best to keep to a traditional interpretation of the Islamic faith, banning the importation of copies of the Qur'an printed outside the Ottoman territories, attempting to convert Shia schismatics, and insisting on the validity of his claim to the caliphate. There were substantial Muslim communities in the empire's Balkan territories. In Bosnia around two-thirds of the population followed the Sunni branch of Islam. Some 120,000 Muslims were recorded as living in western Thrace in 1912, some of them descended from Greek converts, some from Turks, some from Bulgarian Muslims. Almost 60 per cent of Albanians were Muslims, most of them Sunnis, though a minority were followers of the Bektashi sect, an order of Sufi dervishes regarded as heretics by mainstream Sunni Muslims. Albanian Muslims like the notorious Tepenedeli Ali Pasha in the early 1820s played a significant part in the administration of the Ottoman Empire, and were noted traders and entrepreneurs. In the Russian Empire the conquest of the Caucasus led to the mass southward migration of hundreds of thousands of Muslims, leading to an increasing emphasis on the Islamic character of the Ottoman state. Partly as a consequence of this, towards the end of the century tensions rose between Christians and Muslims in the Balkans, finding violent expression during the Balkan Wars of 1912–14.

In contrast to previous centuries, Islam in the nineteenth century was not regarded by Christians as a threat to Christian Europe. The same was not always true, however, of Europe's various Jewish communities. At the end of the nineteenth century there were about nine million adherents of the Jewish faith in Europe, the largest number by far of non-Christians in the Continent. Some 5.2 million lived under the rule of the tsar, or just under 5 per cent of the Russian population. They were required to live within the Pale of Settlement, whose boundaries roughly coincided with those of the old Polish-Lithuanian Commonwealth and included parts of modern-day Lithuania, Poland, Ukraine, Belarus, Moldova and western Russia. Created in 1791, the Pale amended its boundaries several times, and certain categories of Jews were sometimes permitted to live outside it, though in 1891 thousands of Jews were expelled from Moscow and St

Petersburg and forced to return to it. There were legally prescribed limits on the numbers of Jewish students in universities (10 per cent within the Pale, 3 per cent in Moscow, St Petersburg and Kiev). Living mostly in poverty in settlements known as *shtetls*, the Jews of the Pale mainly spoke Yiddish and developed a variety of strict religious practices reinforced by identifying forms of dress. Persecution and discrimination by the Orthodox Christian population, encouraged by the state, were common, and there were major pogroms launched by Christian mobs following the assassination of Tsar Alexander II in 1881, in which over forty Jews were killed and more than 200 Jewish women raped. There were further anti-Jewish riots between 1903 and 1906, in which some 2,000 Jews died in more than 200 towns, above all in Ukraine. Encouraged by the authorities and often led by Christian priests, these violent outbreaks destroyed whole villages and did incalculable damage to Jewish property. Not surprisingly, in the late nineteenth century and the early twentieth, more than two million Jews left the Russian Empire for a new life in England or, above all, America. Often they were assisted by Jewish philanthropists, such as Baron Maurice de Hirsch (1831–96), a German-Jewish banker who lived in Paris and spent a fortune made in railway speculation on founding a charity, the largest in the world at the time, to help thousands of Russian Jews emigrate to Argentina, where they rode across the pampas as 'Jewish gauchos'.

There were also two million Jews in the Austro-Hungarian Empire in 1900, or 4.6 per cent of the total population. They included more than 800,000 living in Galicia, part of the former Poland; they shared most of the cultural characteristics of the Jewish inhabitants of the Pale. Growing numbers of them left Galicia and took up residence in Budapest in the late nineteenth century, until they formed almost a quarter of the city's population. In Romania there were a further 250,000 Jews according to contemporary estimates; in the Bukovina they made up 13 per cent of the population by 1914. The Jewish community in Germany grew in the same period from half a million to more than 600,000, particularly with an influx of emigrants from Russia. Around 1900 there were perhaps a quarter of a million Jews in Great Britain, 100,000 in the Netherlands, 86,000 in France, 35,000 in Italy and much smaller numbers in other countries. Everywhere Jews were the object of heavy discrimination in the early years of the nineteenth century. The restrictions that Napoleon had swept away were in many cases reimposed after his defeat in 1815, as in Frankfurt, although here as in almost every other European city the requirement to live in the old ghetto was not renewed. The exception was Rome, where Jews were still forced to live within a walled ghetto established in 1555; opened by the 1848 revolutionaries, it was closed again by Pius IX when he was restored to power, though in 1850 he abolished the poll tax levied on its inhabitants. The last remaining ghetto in Europe, it ceased to operate when Rome was incorporated into the Kingdom of Italy in 1870; its walls were torn down eighteen years later. The Pale of Settlement in the tsarist empire was a similar attempt to restrict the movement of Jews, though on a much larger scale.

Even where they were free to live where they wished, Jews were still denied basic civil rights in many European states at the time of the Restoration. The French Revolution had swept away discrimination in 1791, and Napoleon had brought equality to Jews in the lands he had conquered, even though in some of them it was later rescinded. Belgium and Greece accorded Jews full equality from the outset. But emancipation came more slowly to other European states: Württemberg in 1828, the Netherlands in 1834, Sweden and Norway in 1835, Hanover in 1842, Denmark and Hamburg in 1849. Often a major political upheaval such as the 1848 Revolution was required; the Jews of Austria-Hungary were emancipated in 1867 and the North German Confederation and then the German Empire included full rights for Jews in its constitution. By contrast, Jews had to wait until 1878 to become full citizens in Bulgaria and Serbia, 1910 in Spain and 1911 in Portugal. It was not until near the Revolution of 1917 that they gained civil emancipation in Russia, and they only obtained equal civil rights in Romania in 1923. In Great Britain the struggle for equality lasted for decades. The Catholic Emancipation Act of 1829 did not include Jews; proposals to extend its provisions to them were defeated by the conservative House of Lords, led by the Duke of Wellington, until the Religious Opinions Relief Act was passed in 1846. Jews were still debarred from Parliament, however, by the requirement to swear a Christian oath, until the Jews' Relief Act (1858) allowed them to drop the words 'on the true faith of a Christian' when sworn in as an MP.

By this time Jewish communities in Europe and indeed in the United States were beginning to split between Orthodox and Reform Judaism, between those congregations who wanted to retain traditional beliefs and practices and those who sought to modernize the faith. The first reform synagogue was established in Britain in 1841 and was immediately excommunicated by the German chief rabbi, whose remit still extended to the British Isles. In 1858 a United Synagogue was formed, but the division continued to hamper the campaign for full emancipation. Nevertheless, religious equality was a major achievement, brought about not least by continuing pressure from new and already established voluntary associations representing the Jewish community, and paralleling the emancipation of Christian minorities across Europe. One consequence was the conversion of increasing numbers of Jews to Christianity. Some 11,000 German Jews converted in the first seventy years of the nineteenth century, and then the rate increased dramatically, with 11,500 converting in the remaining three decades. Intermarriage with Christians reached a total of 18 per cent of marriages involving Jews in Berlin in 1900, and nearly a third in Düsseldorf by 1914. In Hamburg there were seventy-three intermarriages for every hundred purely Jewish marriages on the eve of the First World War. In Hungary, by contrast, though most Jews were highly acculturated, there were only 5,000 religious conversions to Christianity between 1895 and 1907 in a population of 830,000 Jews. The Jewish religious communities in central and western Europe attempted to counter this process of gradual dissolution by founding their own cultural organizations, newspapers, clubs and youth groups, but this did little to stem the tide of conversion in most countries.

Thanks to centuries of legal prohibitions on landowning and their long-established exclusion from the feudal system, Jews, traditionally exempted from the Christian prohibition of usury, were overwhelmingly concentrated in banking, finance and the professions, or, among the poorer sections of the population, the garment industry (brought to the East End of London by Russian Jewish emigrants in the 1890s). In Budapest, according to the census of 1910, Jews made up 85 per cent of self-employed people in the banking and financial services sector, and 42 per cent of their employees; 54 per cent of self-employed traders and 62 per cent of their employees; and 13 per cent of industrialists and 22 per cent of their employees. Some 45 per cent of the lawyers and 49 per cent of the doctors in Hungary were Jewish. There were less dramatic, but still disproportionately high figures in Berlin, Frankfurt and Vienna. The wealthiest Jewish bankers attained international fame, notably the Rothschilds, originally court bankers in Frankfurt, whose members were influential enough to be ennobled in a number of countries, including Austria in 1818 and England in 1847. There were many other prominent Jewish banking concerns, though none matched the Rothschilds for sheer wealth and influence. Gerson von Bleichröder (1822–93), only the second Prussian Jew to be ennobled, became Bismarck's personal banker and enabled him to finance the wars of German unification in 1864 and 1866 without having to go to the German Confederation for approval.

Most Jewish bankers were actively engaged in philanthropy, but none outdid the Italian-born Sir Moses Montefiore (1784–1885). Six feet three inches tall, and very long-lived, Montefiore built the Jewish almshouses of Mishkenot Sha'ananim overlooking the walls of Jerusalem, a city he visited several times. He intervened with the Ottoman sultan on behalf of Jews in trouble, and visited Romania in 1867 to help the beleaguered Jewish community there. Montefiore's charitable work for the small Jewish community in Palestine laid some of the first foundations of Zionism, but the real movement to end the diaspora was begun by the German-speaking Hungarian Theodor Herzl (1860–1904), whose book *The Jewish State* (1896) urged the return of all Jews to Palestine. A skilled lobbyist, he timed his first trip to Jerusalem to coincide with a much-publicized visit by Kaiser Wilhelm II of Germany, whom he met personally to put forward his views. Herzl's World Zionist Organization held a number of conferences to promote the cause, but after his death the character of the movement changed, gravitating away from Orthodoxy and towards the socialist left. It remained a marginal force until the First World War.

The Christian Churches had been hostile to the Jewish religion for centuries, and provided a tradition from which a new and more virulent form of prejudice emerged, based on the supposedly scientific doctrines of racial difference. The change was signalled in the spread of a new term, 'antisemitism', first coined by the Austrian Moravian, later Prussian Jewish Orientalist Moritz Steinschneider (1816–1907). It was the German journalist Wilhelm Marr (1819–1904) who popularized the concept in his book *The Way to Victory of Jewdom over Germandom* (1879). Although he renounced these beliefs at the end of his life, Marr reflected a wider current in right-wing German politics, already begun by the Prussian court preacher Adolf Stöcker (1835–1909), who demanded legal restrictions on the number of practising Jews in the professions as well as reductions of their supposed influence in the world of business. Stöcker's main concern in founding the Christian Social Party in Germany in 1878 was, however, to wean the workers away from socialism, and in this he met with only very limited success. As the leader of the Social Democrats, August Bebel (1840–1913), remarked, antisemitism was 'the socialism of fools'. The few activists in the party who blamed the Jews and not the capitalists for the sufferings of the workers were marginal figures, while socialists of Jewish origin such as Paul Singer (1844–1911) were popular not least because the rank-and-file members of the party saw parallels between the discrimination practised by state and society against Jews and against workers. Antisemitic politics found some resonance among Protestant peasants trying to understand why they were in economic difficulties, particularly in the 1870s, but they did not gain wide support. Theodor Fritsch (1852–1933) did much to propagate the ideas and policies at the centre of the antisemitic movement, and the circle that gathered in Bayreuth around the widow of Richard Wagner,

Cosima (1837–1930), gave them a certain respectability in intellectual circles – notably her son-in-law, the Englishman Houston Stewart Chamberlain (1855–1927), and his book *The Foundations of the Nineteenth Century* (1899). But beyond small groups of extreme nationalists, antisemitism only had a limited, though discernible effect on German politics before 1914.

In Austria, antisemitism was instrumentalized for political purposes by Karl Lueger (1844–1910). As well as being a successful Mayor of Vienna, Lueger was also an unscrupulous political agitator who curried favour with the Viennese lower middle class and the rural peasantry by publicly blaming the Jews for their economic problems. It was Lueger, for example, who coined the term '*Judapest*' to refer to the Hungarian capital, where there was a high proportion of Jews among the professional classes (the word *Pest* also means 'plague' in German). Lueger's antisemitic rhetoric did much to make such ideas respectable in Vienna. How sincere his views were is debatable; when a follower upbraided him in a Vienna café for sitting at a table with some Jews, Lueger famously replied: 'I decide who's a Jew.' None of this seemed to put voters off: in 1902 he increased his majority on the council. Lueger was outdone as an antisemite by another Austrian, Georg Ritter von Schönerer (1842–1921), son of a railway magnate. In the early 1880s, Schönerer formed a German nationalist association to campaign for the incorporation of Austria into the German Empire, along with Bohemia. Later he renamed his party 'Pan-German', and said in the national Parliament that he 'longed for the day when a German army would march into Austria and destroy it'. It was Schönerer who invented the greeting *Heil!* in imitation of the supposed Germanic heroes of medieval times. His acolytes also used the title *Führer* when addressing him. In 1888 with some followers he trashed the offices of a newspaper that had prematurely reported the death of the German Emperor. As a result of these antics Franz Joseph stripped him of his noble title (which had in any case only been granted in 1880). In 1898, undeterred, Schönerer led the movement *Los von Rom* ('Free from Rome') to convert Austrians to Lutheranism, which annoyed the Church and the emperor still further. Never more than a fringe politician, Schönerer lost his seat in the Reichsrat in 1907. The antisemitism of both Schönerer and Lueger was to bear fruit in the later ideology of Adolf Hitler (1889–1945), who lived in Vienna as a young man during these years.

Politicians such as these built on antisemitic theories that propounded the idea that the Jewish spirit, indelibly stamped on the Jewish racial character, was imbued with an unalterable purpose – to undermine social institutions such as the family, subvert the economy, and shatter the patriotic foundations of the nation in the interests of a 'cosmopolitan' spirit. Pogroms in Russia were based on a conspiracy theory that blamed Jews for the political misfortunes of the tsar. It was in Russia that the most influential of all antisemitic tracts, the *Protocols of the Learned Elders of Zion*, which purported to be the record of secret plans for world domination by a small group of Jews in Paris, was put together in 1897 from sources including, bizarrely, a French political satire dating from 1864 and a German popular novel translated into Russian in 1872. Its actual contents were rather anodyne; but in its antisemitic packaging it was to have a widespread impact after the First World War. Antisemitism entered European culture well before 1914 and can be seen in a whole range of literary stereotypes, most notably perhaps the figure of Svengali, the greasy, unkempt, dirty and underhand criminal who exercises a hypnotic fascination over the naive young heroine of the novel *Trilby* (1894) by George du Maurier (1834–96). In *Oliver Twist* by Charles Dickens the villainous Fagin, who is explicitly portrayed as Jewish, controls and exploits a gang of young pickpockets, boys taken off the streets, only to meet his death at the end of the hangman's rope.

There were, however, many who attacked antisemitic stereotypes, myths and conspiracy theories: Dickens himself was so mortified by accusations of antisemitism that he created the character of the noble Jew Riah in his last completed novel, *Our Mutual Friend* (1864–5), in an unsuccessful attempt to balance out the far more vivid figure of Fagin, while *Daniel Deronda* (1876) by George Eliot portrayed Jewish culture in a sympathetic light. The outburst of antisemitic hatred in France during the Dreyfus affair, as we shall see in Chapter 7, ran into massive and very vocal opposition, and not just on the left. As long as antisemitic prejudice existed in the continued exclusion of Jews from institutions such as the Prussian Army officer corps, or many clubs and societies in Great Britain, or, more obviously and comprehensively, from the entire Russian political and social establishment, Jewish emancipation remained incomplete, and the emergence of racial antisemitism struck a warning note; but from the vantage point of 1900, the achievement of civil equality by Jews in most parts of Europe was a triumph of social emancipation.

CLIMBING THE TOWER OF BABEL

The spread of political ideologies such as antisemitism reflected in part the rise of nationalism in a more exclusive and aggressive form than it had taken in the early decades of the century. This development depended in the first place on the establishment of national identities based on written language. At the time of the Restoration, levels of literacy, measured by the ability to sign a marriage register or an army recruitment form with one's name rather than with a cross, were patchy at best. Around 90 per cent of men in Prussia could read and write, and over 80 per cent in Scotland, and a small majority of adult males in France and England. Elsewhere, the written word found few able to understand it; between 60 and 80 per cent of grown men in Austria, Russia, Italy, Spain and Ireland were still illiterate at mid-century. Even the gentry in the Hungarian province of Vas were unable to raise their literacy rates above 40 per cent by the early nineteenth century. And the ability of women to read and write was far lower, reflecting the almost complete absence of schooling for them in most parts of Europe: two-thirds of women in France and Belgium were still illiterate in the 1840s, more than half in England, and more than nine in every ten in Italy and Spain. Country-dwellers were far less likely to be able to read and write than townsfolk. While 99 per cent of adults in Berlin could already read in the 1860s, the comparable figure for the rural backwater of West Prussia was only 67 per cent. Within Italy illiteracy was almost universal in the south, much less common in the north. Three-quarters of adult Serbs and Croats, Romanians and Ruthenes were unable to read and write even at the end of the nineteenth century, as opposed to only 1 per cent of the Austrian population of the Alpine province of the Vorarlberg. Artisans and craftsmen, professionals and the middle classes, and the inhabitants of towns and cities, were far more likely to be able to read and write than were rural labourers or the urban underclass. In Russia only 7 per cent of rank-and-file army recruits in the 1860s were able to read and write, and even by 1890 the figure was still under a third.

Lacking a basis in a written national language, identity was firmly rooted not in nationality but in locality. 'Every valley,' commented an economist writing about the Pyrenees in 1837, 'is still a little world that differs from the neighbouring world as Mercury does from Uranus. Every village is a clan, a sort of state with its own patriotism.' When a state inspector of education visited a village school in the mountainous department of the Lozère in south-east France in 1864, he asked the pupils what country they lived in. None of them could answer him. 'Are you English or Russian?' he asked. They did not know. The lack of any popular national consciousness was even more pronounced in countries like Germany or Italy that had yet to achieve political unity. To be sure, language and pronunciation helped advertise social class, so that Sam Weller, in Charles Dickens's The *Pickwick Papers* (1836), is instantly identifiable as a lower-class London Cockney by his pronunciation of *v* as *w*; but they were far more important in most countries as an indicator of region. One knew that someone came from Marseille as soon as they opened their mouth, because they pronounced *r* in a guttural way instead of rolling it, as most Frenchmen did in the nineteenth century. Words often varied from one part of a country to another: in German, for example, if you wanted to buy a potato you would ask for a *Kartoffel* in north-central Germany, an *Erdapfel* in the south, a *Grumbeer* in the west, a *Schucke* in the north-east, or a *Knulle* in parts of Saxony and Brandenburg. In Danish, people put the definite article before a noun if they lived west of a line running vertically down the middle of Jutland, after it if they lived to the east. A majority of Italians spoke local dialects, some so distinctive that they were barely comprehensible outside the region where they were spoken. Travelling in the French provinces, Flora Tristan complained that 'nobody speaks French', not even in towns like Nîmes or St Étienne. In such places, 'one could believe one was in a savage land in the depths of America'.

Entirely different languages existed side by side as the principal medium of communication in many parts of Europe. Minority languages were present in particular regions everywhere – Welsh, for example, or Scottish Gaelic, or Basque in north-west Spain, or Sami among the nomadic Lapps of northern Scandinavia. In Brittany it was reported in 1873 that the people 'do not speak French, and do not want to speak French'. Some dialects were extremely localized. 'Change village, change language', went one proverb in the French province of the Limousin. The smallest of the Slavic linguistic communities, the Lusatian Sorbs, continued to defy the influence of the surrounding majority of Germans well into the twentieth century. In Calabria, in southern Italy, people still spoke a version of Ancient Greek, probably deriving from the years of Byzantine occupation. Especially in central and eastern Europe, centuries of trade and settlement had created a multilayered linguistic palimpsest, so that different languages were often spoken in the same town. Growing up in the small trading town of Rustschuk, on the lower Danube, the writer Elias Canetti (1905–94) remembered hearing 'seven or eight languages' spoken as he walked around the streets: 'There were Greeks, Albanians, Armenians, Gypsies,' he wrote, there were Turks, who lived in their own quarter, while Romanians frequently came to the town from the northern side of the river, and Russian traders came and went from the Black Sea region. Canetti himself belonged to the local Jewish community, who spoke Ladino, an antique dialect of Spanish; the Sephardic Jews, expelled in 1492, had carried it to many parts of Europe and were still speaking it centuries later. They looked down on the Ashkenazi community, who spoke Yiddish, the common, largely Germanic tongue spoken by Jews all over eastern Europe.

Rustschuk was far from unique. German and Jewish traders and settlers turned many towns along the southern coast of the Baltic and across large parts of eastern Europe into mainly German-speaking communities, while rural migration created a large and populous area of German-speakers in Transylvania. In many towns and cities, people spoke more than one language, switching from the one to the other as required: up to the middle of the century, for example, the inhabitants of Prague mostly spoke both Czech and German and regarded themselves as Bohemian; their identity was communal and regional but not national. The lack of any firm national identity for most Europeans was underlined by the absence of passport requirements for travellers crossing state borders: in some countries formal requirements existed, but with the coming of the railways they fell into disuse and were abolished – in Norway in 1850, France and Sweden in 1860, and Portugal in 1863. In Greece a passport requirement was introduced in 1835 but was more or less never put into effect, like so many other government regulations. Only Bulgaria, Romania, Russia and Turkey continued to require identity documents and visas from incoming travellers. Cross-border travel was made easier by the fact that French remained the common European language of the upper and middle classes. Latin could be used to get by when talking to priests in a foreign land where one did not speak the local language.

What changed this fragmented situation was not only the spread of communications but also the expansion of elementary education, especially in the second half of the century. Many states attempted during this period to make primary schooling compulsory. In Britain a law passed in 1880 required all children up to the age of ten – extended to twelve in 1899 – to attend school; from 1910 elementary education was made entirely free, and Her Majesty's Inspectors of Schools, first appointed in 1840, extended their remit of ensuring adequate standards to the whole country. The new industrial working class was held by the political elite to be badly in need of education – 'we must educate our masters,' said the English journalist and politician Robert Lowe (1811–92) after introducing an educational reform measure in 1862: otherwise workers would not be able to understand instructions for operating machinery, let alone grasp the issues involved in the parliamentary political system after the extension of the franchise. Indeed, the 1867 Reform Act was followed shortly by an act establishing School Boards across England and Wales to fund local elementary schools, in a move that significantly reduced the role of the established Anglican Church. By 1883 there were already 3,692 board schools, and the Church schools, of which there were still some 14,000 at the turn of the century, were running into serious financial and other difficulties. A new Education Act passed in 1902 unified the administration of all state-run schools in Britain under Local Education Authorities, allowing the creation of over a thousand new state secondary schools by 1914.

A belief that education and literacy would make the masses less savage also inspired liberal-conservative politicians in France. Guizot passed a law in 1833 requiring every village to have a primary school, declaring: 'Ignorance renders the masses turbulent and ferocious . . . We have tried to create in every commune a moral force which the government can use at need.' 'France,' declared Zola, 'will be what the primary teacher makes it', and there was a widespread belief that the nation's defeat in 1870 was the result of superior standards of primary education in Germany. A further impetus for the extension of elementary education in France came from anticlerical politicians such as Jules Ferry, whose reforms passed between 1879 and 1881 extended compulsory, free and secular education to all children aged from three to thirteen. In place of Catholic indoctrination the new schools were required to teach moral precepts based on secular principles, inculcated through an appeal to the emotions: 'The teacher,' as Ferry declared, 'is not required to fill the child's memory, but to teach his heart, to make him feel, by an immediate experience, the majesty of the moral law.' The encouragement of patriotism was a principal aim of the secular school system: apart from the 'three Rs' – reading, writing and 'rithmetic – teaching focused on the history and geography of France, to the exclusion of other parts of Europe and the world.

Liberal governments were particularly keen to foster primary education, literacy and numeracy. In Spain the liberal Constitution of 1812, already proclaimed the need for every village to possess a primary school, an ambition furthered by a series of education laws passed in 1821, 1836 and 1845. The Moyano Law, promulgated in 1857, made education compulsory up to the age of nine, and free for those unable to pay. Though state funding was minimal, the creation for the first time of a national Ministry of Education in 1900 did result in some increase, and provision gradually improved thereafter. As in other European countries, a principal aim of the liberals was to reduce the influence of the Church over education, and to create a national sense of identity by enforcing unity through the exclusive use of the national language – in this case Castilian. Yet underfunding meant that state schools were unable to implement these policies; schools not subject to them because they were run by the religious orders still outnumbered state schools in Madrid by 411 to 135 in 1908, for example, a situation that could also be observed in Catalonia. Minority languages and regional *patois* could be more easily combated in France, where they predominated in rural areas, than in Spain, where they were concentrated in advanced industrial centres in Barcelona and the Basque country.

In Russia too, primary education was dominated by Church schools until the end of the century. What changed the situation was the activism of the local authorities, the *zemstva*, which devoted time, energy and, crucially, funds to establishing schools for the peasantry. By the time of the First World War there were 34,000 primary schools under the Holy Synod, but 81,000 under the Ministry of Education and the local authorities. However, they were subject to a range of crippling restrictions. Primary schools mostly consisted of one class and taught religion, Russian, arithmetic, writing and singing, though in the larger schools, mostly in towns, there was room for geography and history too. Schools were often inadequately housed: the writer Alexander Sergeyevich Neverov (1886–1923) remembered his village school in the 1890s as 'a low dark building with long desks, a filthy ceiling, partitioned off from a room used by the church caretaker'. Things were little better in the towns and cities: one school in St Petersburg at the same time consisted of two rooms in a three-room family flat, with little more than a blackboard and some desks and chairs. Nevertheless, Russian schools had a discernible effect in raising basic standards of literacy and numeracy.

Deficiencies in popular education were also being made good by the movement to improve standards of knowledge and learning in the adult population. Particularly important here were the 'folk high schools', pioneered by Nikolaj Frederik Severin Grundtvig (1783–1872), a Danish pastor and liberal nationalist. Originally inspired by the Protestant awakening, Grundtvig, a prolific author who published more than 1,500 hymns and innumerable books and pamphlets over the course of a very long life, believed that the common people needed to be trained in practical skills as well as being inculcated with a strong national consciousness and the inspiration to develop their own creativity. His ideas struck a chord in Danish society after the country's defeat in the Schleswig-Holstein War of 1864, and three years later some twenty-one folk high schools had come into being. Different manifestations of the movement spread to Norway and Sweden, and found imitators in many other countries, especially Germany. In Britain the doctor and philanthropist George Birkbeck (1776–1841) founded Mechanics's Institutes in Glasgow and London in the 1820s. By mid-century there were no fewer than 700 such institutions in Britain, aiming to provide a broad education for adults, with a special focus on engineering and science. Mostly they taught through putting on lecture courses and providing libraries from which 'mechanics', or in other words members of the working classes (in many instances including

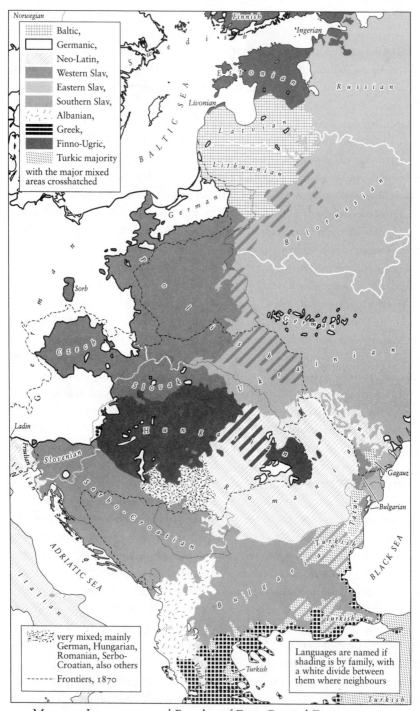

Map 13. Languages and Peoples of East-Central Europe, 1914

women), could borrow improving literature. By all these various means elementary education had a cumulative effect on literacy and the standardization of languages across Europe.

Nationalists tried to develop a standard written and spoken language in order to justify their claim to a national identity and national statehood. Usually they chose some particular dialect. West Bulgarian dialect was used as the basis for the literary language in Bulgaria; in Italy it was the Tuscan dialect, commonly employed in princely courts but in 1860 still only used for everyday communication by 2.5 per cent of the population. Its influence was spread among the educated classes by the 1827 historical novel *The Betrothed* by Alessandro Manzoni (1785–1873). Its anti-Spanish thrust was taken by some nationalists to apply to the Austrian rulers of northern Italy as well (Metternich reciprocated the hostility, referring to Italy as merely a 'geographical expression'). Manzoni later extended his influence by playing a key role on the commission that established Tuscan as the official language of a unified Italy. Sometimes the choice of dialect was made for deliberately political reasons; thus the Croatian writer Ljudevit Gaj (1809–72) changed from the Kajkavian Croatian dialect to the Slovak in 1838 because the latter was also spoken by many Serbs, thus underpinning his campaign for South Slav unity and eventually creating the language known for many decades as Serbo-Croat (written in Roman lettering in Croatia, Cyrillic in Serbia). On occasion, indeed, a nationalist could actually construct a language, as with the Norwegian poet and playwright Henrik Wergeland (1808–45), who developed *Nynorsk* as an alternative to the existing written tongue, which he considered had been corrupted by the influence of Danish (it never found favour with more than a small minority of the population). Linguistic unity was also furthered by the attempts of nationalists to construct an ancient heritage for the national culture. In Finland this task was undertaken by the nationalist poet Elias Lönnrot (1802–84), a regional health officer who collected folk tales and songs in villages and rural communities and shaped them into a national epic, the *Kalevala* (1835, enlarged 1849), choosing the variants that fitted best into an overall structure and adding a few linking passages of his own (amounting, it is now thought, only to around 3 per cent of the total). As Finnish slowly established itself as a literate language (most literate Finns spoke Swedish at the time), the epic became a central focus for the development of national identity and the struggle for autonomous statehood within the Russian Empire.

Not just language, but also history, real and imagined, provided a basis for national identity. In Ireland the nationalist movement began by attempting to recover the autonomous institutions, including the Irish

Parliament, abolished in the Act of Union of 1800. The cultural memory of the Polish-Lithuanian Commonwealth, a powerful state in early modern Europe until its dismemberment by Prussia, Austria and Russia in the eighteenth century, played a key role in Poland. A historical grounding for a national culture could not always be easy to create. For the supporters of Greek independence it seemed natural to call the civilization of Ancient Greece in evidence for the claim to statehood in the nineteenth century. The humanist scholar Adamantios Coraïs (1748–1833), who was educated at the University of Montpellier in south-eastern France, corresponded with Thomas Jefferson, and lived in Paris throughout the Revolution of 1789–94, attempted to revive this connection not only by publishing new editions of the Ancient Greek classics but also by propagating a new version of Demotic Greek, called *Katharevousa*. He aimed to purge the common spoken language of its foreign and particularly its Byzantine accretions and bring it as close as was practicable to the ancient form of the language. But the great mass of ordinary Greeks could not fully understand it and it never became common currency. In any case, language was not always the basis for statehood. In Switzerland speakers of German, Italian, French and Romansch had coexisted in a single confederal state since the era of the Reformation, and the disputes with which the state was riven in the nineteenth century were sparked by issues other than linguistic ones. In the eastern part of Upper Silesia, the so-called *Wasserpolacken*, 'Water Poles' whose Polish speech had been 'watered down' by German influences, resisted being co-opted into the Polish national cause. Similarly, the linguistically hybrid state of Belgium, divided between Flemings and Walloons, persisted in adhering to the statehood acquired in 1830 and did not break asunder, though its unity sometimes seemed precarious.

In the first half of the century nationalists everywhere tended to regard all European nations as moving towards a common state of advanced civilization, though from different starting points and at varying speeds. Germany appeared in British literature in the early nineteenth century as a Gothic land full of wild and untamed nature; its people could be brave and good-natured but also rough and unpredictable. Sarah Austin (1793–1867), who admired German intellectual life and translated German literature into English, thought in 1854 that in the German countryside 'we find a state of civilization which we have been accustomed to regard as past for ever . . . The more we go back to the recollections of what we heard in our childhood from our fathers, the nearer do we approach to the manners of Germany.' Henry Mayhew, author of *London Labour and the London Poor* (1851), a classic investigation of poverty and destitution in the 1840s, found Germany extremely backward. 'Travelling southward from England,' he wrote, 'is like going backward in time . . . In Germany we find the people, at the very least, a century behind us in all the refinements of civilization and the social and domestic improvements of progress.' Closer acquaintance with other countries did little to overcome prejudice. Following the demise of the aristocratic 'Grand Tour' in the chaos and violence of the French Revolutionary and Napoleonic Wars, the new English middle class began to travel to the Continent on commercial tours. Pre-eminent in this business was the company founded by Thomas Cook (1808–92), a Baptist minister who began by organizing trips for temperance campaigners, obtaining discounted tickets from railway companies in return for guaranteed bulk purchases.

By the 1860s, Cook's tours were taking English clients to a variety of continental destinations, and what they saw merely confirmed their feelings of superiority. Their disdain for continentals was widely reciprocated. In 1890 the Romanian writer Nicolae Iorga (1871–1940) complained bitterly about the British in Venice:

> You meet them everywhere, at the hotel, on the narrow streets, on the black gondolas, at the foot of statues, on the platforms atop the towers: correct, with clipped moustaches, Baedeker in hand, holding by the arm (always by the arm) their beloved other half, a doll with glass eyes, rosy cheeks and horse's teeth. Cold and measured, muttering unintelligible explanations in their jumpy language, occasionally in French.

Many French men and women, like Flora Tristan, were not sure whether they wanted a British-style future when it brought with it the misery and oppression of industrialism. 'London may become Rome,' remarked the French writer Théophile Gautier (1811–72) in 1853, 'but it will certainly never be Athens: that destiny is reserved for Paris.' Arguments about the direction to take raged with particular intensity in Russia, where 'Slavophiles' like Konstantin Sergeyevich Aksakov (1817–60) saw the future as based on Russian peasant values and Orthodox traditions, whereas 'Westernizers' like Alexander Herzen, who spent some years in exile in England, wanted to import western European cultural norms. To writers like the Marquis de Custine (1790–1857), Russia, which he visited in 1839, seemed more than half Asiatic. Russia's aristocracy in his view had 'just enough of the gloss of European civilization to be spoiled as savages but not enough to become cultivated men'.

What united all these disparate views was the concept of progress, whether it was welcomed or resisted. English travellers on the Continent complained repeatedly about the filth and dirt of the towns, yet they expected them in due course to undergo the hygienic revolution already experienced in Britain. But in the later decades of the nineteenth century, cultural stereotypes began to give way to racial ones, and the notion of the road to a future along which all nations were travelling was increasingly replaced by the idea of peoples imbued with innate and therefore unalterable characteristics. After the Polish uprising of 1863–4, for example, voices were raised in Russia proclaiming the need to suppress Polish nationality rather than leading it along the path of freedom and progress. The newspaper editor Mikhail Nikiforovich Katkov (1818–87) declared that Poles and Russians were both Slavs, and that Polish identity had to be merged into the greater Russian culture. The Poles were a 'tribe' who with others in 'the Great Russian world, constitute its living parts and feel their oneness with it, in the union of state and supreme power in the person of the Tsar'. Russian reactions to the first stirrings of Ukrainian national identity were even more negative: the Minister of the Interior Pyotr Alexandrovich Valuev (1815–90) warned the tsar in 1876 that 'permitting the creation of a special literature for the common people in the Ukrainian dialect would signify collaborating in the alienation of Ukraine from the rest of Russia'. Other states began to adopt a policy of assimilating national minorities too, most notably Prussia, which introduced under Bismarck and his successors a policy of restricting the use of Polish in the eastern provinces and encouraging German-speaking immigrants to settle there.

Smaller nations and their cultures were widely thought by the apostles of nationalism in larger countries as unlikely to achieve statehood. Not only the English, for example, but also many among the educated classes in Wales, assumed that the Welsh language would 'die fairly, peacefully and reputably', as a Welsh clergyman told a parliamentary inquiry into education in the Principality in 1847: 'Attached to it as we are, few would wish to postpone its euthanasy.' In the event, however, the language survived.

The spread of education, the increasing intensity of cross-border communications, the greater ease with which people could migrate from one country to another, the rise of tourism, and the growing trend for books to be translated from one language into others, did not, as some hoped, lead to greater international understanding. In his book *Unua Libro* (1887) the Polish writer and opthalmologist Ludwik Lazard Zamenhof (1859–1917), author of the first Yiddish grammar (1879), made the most notable attempt to overcome linguistic barriers by inventing 'Esperanto', the 'language of hope'. It attracted enough support for a World Congress of Esperantists to be held in Paris in 1905. But the language never entered the cultural mainstream anywhere.

THE PASSION FOR KNOWLEDGE

While the inculcation of a national language became a principal purpose of primary education, secondary education focused for most of the century on the teaching of the Ancient Greek and Roman classics. In the curriculum laid down for the *Gymnasium*, or academic secondary school, by the Prussian state in 1837, for example, almost a third of the lessons were devoted to Latin, and not much less to Greek. In 1856, in the course of the post-revolutionary turn to conservative values, religious teaching was introduced to the curriculum for the first time. None of this satisfied Kaiser Wilhelm II, who was concerned that an emphasis on authors such as Cicero (106–43 BC), with their doctrines of republican freedom, was nurturing a generation of educated men critical of the monarchical institutions of Imperial Germany. Stressing the need for physical training and character-building, he declared in 1890: 'We must take what is German as the basis of the *Gymnasium*; we want to educate young Germans and not young Greeks and Romans.' A new Prussian national curriculum put into effect in 1892 reduced the hours devoted to Latin by 20 per cent and Ancient Greek by 10 per cent. Similar changes in the parallel system of the less academically oriented *Realschulen* were even more dramatic. In both kinds of school, new requirements were brought in for German literature and history, with an emphasis on the need for teachers to be 'filled with the patriotic spirit'.

With the growth of the middle classes in Germany came an increase in the numbers of students attending academic secondary schools – from just short of 50,000 in Prussia in 1850, for instance, to 108,000 in 1911. There were complaints about overcrowding, only partially met by an increase in the number of academic secondary schools from 261 to 372 between 1875 and 1911. In Russia there were 191 academic high schools by the end of the century, augmented by 115 technical schools. Their social exclusivity was underlined by a notorious decree issued under the reactionary Tsar Alexander III requiring academic secondary schools to be 'freed from the attendance of children of drivers, footmen, cooks, laundrymen, small traders and other persons similarly situated, whose children, with the exception perhaps of exceptionally gifted ones, should not be encouraged to abandon the social environment to which they belong'. Here too the Classics declined as the foundation of secondary education, as the curriculum made room for more practical subjects after the turn of the century. In the academic French secondary school, the *lycée*, where pupils were prepared for the *baccalauréat*, or university qualifying examinations, teaching of the Classics fell sharply and there was a growing focus on modern subjects, especially French language, literature and history, and the sciences. This was a popular measure. Many former students remembered the Classical education to which they had been subjected with retrospective revulsion. 'Merchants of Greek!' exclaimed Victor Hugo in 1856, 'Merchants of Latin! Hacks! Bulldogs! Philistines! Magisters! I hate you, pedagogues!' The secondary-school system expanded, with 30,000 students in 1850, 53,000 in 1881, and 62,000 in 1910. Some 51 per cent of secondary pupils attended state institutions in 1899, as compared to 43 per cent Church schools and 6 per cent lay private schools, but the proportion of boys between the ages of eleven and seventeen who attended any kind of secondary school at all remained consistently below 3 per cent.

Conditions in the French *lycées* were far from ideal. Most were located in former church buildings, hospitals, barracks or convents. One inspector asked in 1877 on visiting one: 'Is this a school, a farm, or an inn, this vast ramshackle hut with rotting shutters and a bare courtyard?' But at least corporal punishment had been abolished in an edict passed in 1769 and reinforced by a Napoleonic decree forty years later. This was emphatically not the case in the leading secondary schools on the other side of the English Channel, where the sons of the elite were educated in fee-paying 'public schools'. In the early decades of the century flogging, carried out before the assembled pupils with a birch on the naked back, was universal and meted out for the tiniest of derelictions, such as making mistakes in the parsing of Latin or Greek. Mr Creakle, the headmaster portrayed in Charles Dickens's novel *David Copperfield* (1850), 'laid about him, right and left, every day of his life, charging in among the boys like a trooper, and slashing away, unmercifully'. Acts of rebellion were just as routine as schoolmasterly violence. One Etonian paid for an artist to paint a portrait of the headmaster on his own back, expecting as all boys did to be flogged: the head was said to have used two birches to obliterate it, breaking the first one in the ferocity of his onslaught. At Winchester in 1818 the boys occupied the towers and sealed up the warden's doors. Eventually twenty-seven were expelled, but the headmaster was forced to resign. At Eton pupils used sledgehammers to break up the headmaster's desk of office, which was raised on a podium and enclosed in a panelled stall. Seven were expelled. Cheaper boarding schools, satirized mercilessly by Charles Dickens in *Nicholas Nickleby* (1839) in the shape of 'Dotheboys Hall', presided over by the ignorant and brutal headmaster Wackford Squeers, could sometimes be used as dumping-grounds for the unwanted, often illegitimate children of the wealthy elite. It was only gradually that this situation began to be reformed.

The main influence here was Thomas Arnold (1795–1842), appointed headmaster of Rugby School in 1828. Arnold described his mission as the cure of souls first: the inculcation of moral principles came second, and the education of minds a distant third. He would rather the boys thought that the Sun revolved around the Earth, he once declared, than that they should neglect the fundamental principles of a moral life: 'Surely the one thing needful for a Christian and an Englishman to study is Christian and moral and political philosophy.' Arnold brought order to school life, enforced by a system in which discipline, including corporal punishment, was applied by senior boys appointed prefects or monitors and kept closely under his control. His reforms were widely copied in other British secondary schools, and became more generally known through the popular novel *Tom Brown's Schooldays* (1857), written by Thomas Hughes (1822–96), a former pupil, who recounted how the bullying, sadism, sexual exploitation, gambling, drinking and whoring common among the senior pupils before Dr Arnold's appointment, and encapsulated in Harry Flashman, the villain of the story, were overcome by the headmaster's firm imposition of the basic principles of Christian conduct.

The purpose of secondary schools everywhere was above all to prepare students for university entrance. Overall numbers of students in higher education were small. There were just over 7,000 university students in Spain in the 1850s, a number that had increased to 12,000 by 1868 and continued to grow slowly into the twentieth century. Spread across ten universities, this was not very impressive. As elsewhere in Europe, the primary function of universities was to train young men for the professions, law and medicine in particular. Students were overwhelmingly the children of prosperous middle-class parents who could afford to pay the steep fee required for the *licenciatura*, the degree certificate that gave them the right to practise. Spanish universities were often of considerable antiquity (the oldest, the University of Salamanca, was founded in 1218, though it was outdone in Italy by the University of Bologna, Europe's oldest, dating back to 1088). The situation was very different in France, where all twenty-two universities had been abolished by the Revolution in 1789 as bastions of privilege, corruption and idleness, and replaced by specialized faculties and colleges that offered training to lawyers, doctors and teachers. Some of these became in due course serious centres of learning and research, such as the École Normale Supérieure, founded in 1795 and re-founded in 1826, where the medical scientist Louis Pasteur pushed through a series of major reforms. (These were not always popular: when he threatened to expel any students caught smoking, seventy-three out of the eighty students in the *grande école* promptly resigned.) There were in general very few students at these institutions – the Faculty of Letters at Caen had only twenty under the Restoration, for example, while the Faculty of Letters at Clermont-Ferrand had only seven in 1876. Rather than being supported by the state, these institutions were funded by examination fees, which meant that they were often in a parlous state of repair.

France's defeat in the war of 1870–1 was ascribed by some to the fact that Germany possessed advanced universities where all the disciplines could be studied independently and in a connected way rather than, as in France, a series of isolated, single-subject, professional training institutions. The amalgamation of the faculties and colleges into proper universities thus became one of the many causes taken up by French Republicans. It took until 1896, however, until the faculties in the provinces were formed into universities along German lines. Still, many subjects, including even French philology, were so much more advanced in Germany that to gain an adequate grasp of them students had to be able to read German. The *grandes écoles* were far more important, especially in the fields of engineering, mining and commerce; the political elite was trained in particular by Sciences Po, Paris, which opened in 1872, while the humanities were catered for by the École Pratique des Hautes Études, founded in 1868. Some of these institutions were highly specialized: the École Nationale des Chartes, founded in 1821, gained a European reputation for training in reading medieval texts, for example, while the École Polytechnique, established in 1794 and run by the Ministry of Defence, focused on military engineering and construction; Napoleon had turned it into a military academy in 1804.

As the move to create universities in France in the late nineteenth century suggested, the strongest and most developed system of higher education in Europe was to be found in Germany. It followed the ideas of Wilhelm von Humboldt, whose work in the Prussian Ministry of the Interior focused on the integration of teaching and research, the freedom of teachers to teach and students to learn what they wanted to, and the adoption of Classical ideals and the unifying intellectual principles of rationalist philosophy. 'To inquire and to create,' he declared: 'these are the grand centres around which all human pursuits revolve.' The University of Berlin, founded under Humboldt's inspiration in 1810, explicitly embodied an alternative ideal to that of the French *grandes écoles*, whose prescriptive curricula and drive to uniformity and discipline he considered damaging to the spirit of innovation and renewal that German intellectual life so badly needed after the humiliations of the Napoleonic Wars. Humboldt intended that universities should research and teach subjects for their own intrinsic intellectual value, rather than specifically preparing students for careers. But this did not happen in the first half of the century. Between 1830 and 1860, for example, 30 per cent of students enrolled at German universities studied theology, to go into the ministry, 30 per cent law, to go into the civil service or the legal profession, 15 per cent medicine, 15 per cent humanistic subjects, to go into teaching, and 5 per cent the natural sciences.

The state kept a firm grip: one third of all full professors of law in German universities appointed between 1817 and 1840 were imposed on faculties by the government Ministry responsible for them without the faculties themselves agreeing or in many instances being consulted. Freedom of teaching was thus in practice restricted by the intervention of the state. Universities were still small, but between 1871 and 1914 the number of students at the twenty-two German universities, including Strasbourg, acquired from France in the Franco-Prussian War in 1871, and Frankfurt, founded in 1914, grew from 13,000 to 61,000. Berlin University's student numbers increased from 2,200 to 8,000, making it the largest in Germany, but Munich could count more than 6,600 students by the eve of the First World War, and Leipzig over 5,300. New technical universities were founded, accounting for a further 11,500 students by 1914. The proportion of students whose fathers had degrees had already fallen during the period 1850–70 from around half to just over a third; in Leipzig it had declined to under 30 per cent by 1909. The students who were sons of industrialists, merchants and financiers were growing in number.

The German model of higher education was widely imitated. In Greece, for example, King Otto founded the Othonian University on German lines in 1837 (it was renamed the National University when he was ousted in 1862), equipped with a range of faculties; the sciences were also taught, though they were hived off into a separate institution, the Kapodistrian University, in 1911. The Royal Frederick University in Oslo was explicitly established in 1811 on the model of the newly founded University of Berlin. Older universities followed suit, including the University of Copenhagen, founded in 1479, destroyed when Admiral Nelson bombarded the city in 1801, rebuilt in the 1830s, and restructured with German-style faculties in the following decade. The founding of a university was a requirement of any self-respecting state: Bulgaria created a three-faculty higher education institute in 1888 that became a university in 1904. State control here remained close, however: King Ferdinand closed it down for six months and dismissed all the professors after he was booed by students at the opening of the National Theatre in 1907. The fate of the Jagiellonian University earlier in the century was even more dramatic: founded in 1364 in Cracow, it was a centre of Polish intellectual life until the Austrians formally annexed Cracow in 1846, when they removed the furnishings from the Auditorium Maximum in order to turn it into a grain store; the university was only rescued when the Emperor Franz Joseph intervened to save it. Polish universities and especially their students continued to be regarded with suspicion in Congress Poland, where the Russian authorities closed the University of Warsaw, founded in 1816, following the 1863 uprising, and replaced it with a higher education institution that aimed to provide education for the military occupation forces and taught only in Russian.

Tight state controls were similarly exercised over universities in Russia itself, where students formed part of the intelligentsia and were the subject of considerable suspicion on the part of the government. The tsarist authorities were caught in a dilemma, however, since if the controls were too tight and teaching was too circumscribed, young Russians would go abroad to learn, above all to German universities, described already by Alexander I as places 'where young people acquire notions that are most opposed to religion and morality'. Later on in the century, they gravitated towards Zurich and other liberal Swiss universities. As part of Alexander II's reforms a University Statute was passed in 1863 ceding the power of self-government to universities, including professorial appointments, and allowing the freedom of teaching and learning that were the ideals of the Humboldtian system. Following student riots at the universities of St Petersburg and Kazan in the autumn of 1882 over demands for improved representation, a new University Statute was passed in 1884 requiring rectors, deans and professors to be appointed by the government. This did not quell student unrest, which broke out again in 1887 following an incident when a student slapped a government inspector of universities in the face at a concert. But it was not until 1905 that university autonomy was restored, following a student strike lasting several months.

In Britain, as in Russia, the primacy of Classical learning was gradually reduced, with Latin and Ancient Greek outflanked by other, modern subjects, although the latter was still required as a condition for entry in all subjects up to 1920 and the former even longer. The links of the ancient universities of Oxford and Cambridge with the established Church were weakened, and new universities, starting with London University (now University College London), founded in 1826, were decidedly secular. In the provinces other colleges initially focused on degree examinations set by London, before amalgamating into new universities themselves, as with, for example, Owens College, founded in 1851, and merged into the Victoria University of Manchester in 1880. Indeed, the expansion of higher education went everywhere together with the professionalization of science and scholarship. German universities, well organized and well funded, took the lead in scientific research. The prizes endowed by Alfred Nobel, the Swedish inventor of dynamite and owner of the Bofors arms company, were awarded to a number of scientists from Germany before 1914. In 1901, for example, the first Nobel Prize for Physics went to Wilhelm Röntgen (1845–1923), who had discovered electromagnetic radiation, or X-rays, in 1895, while nearly half the Nobel Prizes for Chemistry in the same period were awarded to Germans. Although science was still overwhelmingly the province of men, some women did break through science's glass ceiling, most notably the Polish-born French physicist Marie Curie (1867–1934), whose research led her to coin the term 'radioactivity'. With her husband Pierre Curie (1859–1906), in 1898 she discovered two new elements, which they named 'radium' and 'polonium' (she was a passionate Polish nationalist). On her husband's death in a road accident, she was appointed to his chair at the University of Paris, the first woman to become a professor there. She was awarded two Nobel Prizes, one for physics, the other for chemistry, the only woman to achieve this distinction. The status of women scientists, however, was indicated by the fact that when she and her husband were invited to present their research in London, the Royal Institution only allowed Pierre to address the audience; Marie was required to remain silent.

Marie Curie had emigrated to France in 1891 to carry out her research, but Russian and Polish universities, despite political repression, were far from backward in this respect. Kazan Imperial University in Russia, founded in 1804, built a chemical laboratory and astronomical observatory in 1830 and established medical, chemical, mathematical and geological schools. Its Professor of Mathematics, Nicholas Ivanovich Lobachevsky (1792–1856), was one of the founders of modern, non-Euclidean geometry, which indeed is sometimes known as Lobachevskian geometry; its Professor of Chemistry, Alexander Mikhaylovich Butlerov (1828–86), discovered the naturally occurring organic compound formaldehyde in 1859, putting generations of embalmers in his debt; and another chemist, the Baltic German Karl Klaus (1796–1864), discovered the element ruthenium in 1844. Similarly, in Austrian-ruled Galicia in the 1870s, mindful of the rising tide of Polish nationalism, the authorities allowed the Jagiellonian University in Cracow more autonomy and provided funds for new buildings and equipment, especially in the sciences. These enabled the physicist Zygmunt Wróblewski (1845–88), who had studied in Germany, to pioneer the liquefaction of oxygen and nitrogen with his colleague Karol Olszewski (1846–1915) before dying of burns sustained while carrying out experiments. However, elsewhere university-based scientific research took longer to get under way.

The term 'scientist' was only coined in English in 1833, by William Whewell (1794–1866), while the Cambridge Natural Sciences Tripos was founded as late as 1851. Laboratories earlier in the century existed only in establishments like the Royal Institution. The Irish mathematical physicist William Thomson, later ennobled as Lord Kelvin, had to set up his laboratory at Glasgow University in mid-century in a disused wine cellar and the adjoining coal cellar where, as one of his students later complained:

> there was no special apparatus for students' use in the laboratory . . . no special hours for students to attend, no assistants to advise or explain, no marks given for laboratory work, no workshop, and even no fee to be paid . . . students experimented . . . in spite of the atmosphere of coal dust, which settled on everything, produced by a boy coming periodically to shovel up coal for the fires.

Only in 1874 did Cambridge establish a purpose-built physics laboratory, named after the chancellor of the university, William Cavendish, 7th Duke of Devonshire (1808–91), who helped fund it. As time went on, standard procedures were developed in teaching and research – dissection in biology, for example – replacing the old system whereby students had set up whatever experiments they fancied, often with disastrous results. Technical assistants were appointed and standardized equipment manufactured, taking advantage of the opportunities offered by industrial production. Microscopes and telescopes became more sophisticated, chemical dyes made it easier to observe microbes and bacilli, and by the end of the century scientific research and education had become fully professional. By this time, British research in physics had reached an advanced stage: James Clerk Maxwell (1831–79), Joseph Thomson (1856–1940), and the New Zealander Ernest Rutherford (1871–1937) were responsible respectively for the theory of electromagnetism (1861), the discovery of the electron (1897), and the concept of the radioactive half-life (1899). Overall, the number of university teaching posts in science and technology in Britain, excluding medicine, rose from sixty in 1850 to 400 half a century later.

By the turn of the century there was widespread optimism about the future of science, a concept that had been expanded to cover all forms of organized knowledge. Positivism, the doctrine developed by Auguste Comte in the 1840s, and made available in English in his major work *A General View of Positivism*, (1865), held that scientific observation was the only legitimate basis for action. A priori beliefs had to be jettisoned; only what could be seen and verified was true. If the scientific method was applied to every discipline, then all the facts would be known about everything. History, for example, should, in the view of Lord Acton, Regius Professor of Modern History at Cambridge University from 1895 to 1902, satisfy 'the scientific demand for completeness and certainty'. It was widely thought that history had been established as a science by Leopold von Ranke, and history professors everywhere emphasized the application of standard methods of source criticism in order to establish the authenticity of the documents on which historians now began to base their work. Ranke found imitators in universities all over Europe, who dismissed earlier historians, including even the extremely popular author and Whig politician Thomas Babington Macaulay (1800–59), as mere amateurs, historically inaccurate and politically biased. Macaulay's work was too emotional: a dispassionate approach was what was needed, and Ranke was thought to supply it.

Yet this was an illusion: the rhetoric of objectivity based on source criticism and original research was itself little more than a cloak for commitment. In putting forward the proposition that the historian's task lay primarily in identifying the leading currents in every age, Ranke opened the way for the next generation of German historians to identify the rise of Prussia and the unification of Germany as the leading currents of the nineteenth century. Any opposition to German unification was vilified as a struggle against historical inevitability, and the Bismarckian solution to the question of German unity was inserted into the narrative as the only one possible or, indeed, desirable. The chief exponent of this view, Heinrich von Treitschke (1834–96), author of a multi-volume history of Germany in the nineteenth century (which, however, had only reached the year 1847 by the time of his death), was an unabashed German nationalist, not to mention a virulent antisemite. His influence was exercised well into the twentieth century through his many pupils, who included Otto Hintze (1861–1940), Friedrich Meinecke (1862–1954) and the Pan-German politician Heinrich Class (1868–1953). Perhaps, therefore, Rankean history was not so unemotional after all; its exponents claimed to be scientifically objective but their work served a clear political purpose.

THE GENDERING OF EMOTION

In 1848 the entry on 'specific characteristics of the sexes' in a popular German encyclopedia explained that as well as physical differences, men and women could also be distinguished by mental and spiritual features:

'The female is a more feeling creature . . . The man . . . is a more thinking creature . . . Everything that mainly lays a claim on the emotions affects the woman more.' Similar statements can be found in many other encyclopedias of the age. Emotion in the nineteenth century was a gendered phenomenon. 'Intelligence and thought' were the sphere of men, another lexicon declared in 1904: women by contrast were 'removed from the common bustle of life', because they were creatures of imagination, sensibility and love. The encyclopedias of the previous age remained silent on the issue, or treated it only very briefly. By 1887, when the German sociologist Ferdinand Tönnies (1855–1936) wrote his famous tract *Community and Society*, the difference between the sexes had been elevated by some into a universal principle. Tönnies himself regarded the organic community of pre-industrial times as held together by feminine emotion, whereas the industrial society that was (to his regret) replacing it was dominated by masculine reason. Women were being alienated from their true nature: a factory girl who, inevitably, fell under the influence of 'society' in this sense, according to Tönnies, 'becomes enlightened, cold, knowing. Nothing is more alien to her original character, nothing more harmful.'

In the age of Romanticism it was common for men to weep openly at the slightest prompting. Charles Dickens cried over the death scenes in his novels as he wrote them, while the reaction of some of his readers was even more extreme. When the Irish nationalist leader Daniel O'Connell, for example, reading *The Old Curiosity Shop* (1841) on a train journey, came to the passage that described the death of the pure young heroine Little Nell, he found it unbearable: his eyes 'filled with tears', and, sobbing, he shouted 'He should not have killed her!' and threw the book out of the carriage window. Like many others, Lord Byron wept copious tears while watching tragic scenes in the theatre; he described succumbing during a performance in Italy to a kind of 'choking shudder'. The judge James Shaw Willes (1814–72), when pronouncing the death sentence on a woman found guilty of murder, 'bent forward and wept for some few seconds', even though he knew that extenuating circumstances made it overwhelmingly likely that the sentence would be commuted. On this occasion, according to the contemporary report, not only the judge but also 'the jury were in tears', along with 'the greater part of the public'.

Yet increasingly in the second half of the century tears became a sign not of Romantic sensibility but of female frailty. In his book *The Expression of the Emotions in Man and Animals* (1872), Charles Darwin put forward the view that crying was a sign of weakness. 'Englishmen,' he wrote, 'rarely cry, except under the pressure of the acutest grief; whereas in some parts of the Continent the men shed tears much more readily and freely.' But similar views could be found on the Continent too. A man who 'weeps copiously without adequate occasion,' declared the Hungarian writer Max Nordau in 1892, was clearly 'degenerate', suffering from a hereditary taint of emotional weakness. In the second half of the nineteenth century, 'manliness' became a key term of approval in public discourse, at least among men. The growth of a public sphere and in particular the gradual emergence and extension of parliamentary systems was predicated on the assumption that only men possessed the rationality and sense of responsibility to engage in political and legislative activity. The female-dominated *salons* of the late eighteenth and early nineteenth century were replaced by men's clubs, many of which, as in the Frankfurt Parliament of 1848, or in the Carlton Club (1832) and the Reform Club (1836) in London, performed a vital political function. The emphasis on the manly culminated in the cult of the hero as championed by Thomas Carlyle in *On Heroes, Hero-Worship, and the Heroic in History* (1841), in which he wrote 'History is nothing but the biography of the Great Man' – the titanic superhuman who swept all his enemies aside and dominated history with his power and aggression. In a very different version the idea of the great man reappeared in the philosophy of Friedrich Nietzsche. One consequence of this concept was drawn by the Austrian writer Otto Weininger (1880–1903) in his huge tract *Sex and Character*, published posthumously in 1903 after his suicide at the age of twenty-three. Weininger thought that only masculine women such as lesbians could be truly emancipated; the rest were passive, unproductive and uncreative. Weininger was also profoundly antisemitic: he declared that Jews were feminine by nature, and so incapable of fulfilling men's true destiny of becoming geniuses. Since he himself was Jewish, his suicide, carried out in the house in Vienna where Beethoven, the greatest of all geniuses, had died, could be regarded as a logical final step in his life: perhaps the most extreme of all examples of Jewish self-hatred.

Manliness for Victorian Englishmen and their continental counterparts was expressed physically in the form of beards and moustaches. The fashion began around the middle of the century. By the 1870s half of the men whose pictures appeared in the *Illustrated London News* were wearing a full beard. Some justified their decision to become more hirsute on medical grounds, as the miasmatic theory of disease, dominant in mid-century, prompted the idea that the beard could be a filter against dangerous and unhealthy vapours (Bismarck called his moustache 'my respirator'). More importantly, a beard made it easier for a man to present an impassive face to the world, avoiding the expressions of emotion that were felt to be the characteristic of the female sex. On the European Continent full beards were less common among the educated classes than they were in Britain. In Greece, for example, moustaches were ubiquitous among men of all classes, but a beard was mostly only chosen by politicians like Eleftherios Venizelos (1864–1936) who wanted to make a good impression on the international stage, and even here he kept it well groomed and relatively short, like that of Tsar Nicholas II of Russia (1868–1918) or his near-identical cousin King George V of Britain (1865–1936). International fashion may have prompted Tsar Alexander III of Russia to wear a full beard, but in general the association of a full beard with the *muzhik*, the peasant, deterred upper- and middle-class Russian men from sporting it – though this was precisely why the novelist Leo Tolstoy wore a particularly large and unkempt specimen.

In Germany moustaches were more common, but could also be very luxuriant. Friedrich Nietzsche took particular trouble, as his contemporary the Swiss philologist Jacob Mähly (1828–1902) remarked, with the cultivation of 'his huge moustache, which protected him from any charge of having feminine characteristics about him'. German men were particularly notable for the variety of exotic growths on their faces, from Kaiser Wilhelm I's bristling mutton-chop side-whiskers to the long forked beard sported by Admiral Alfred von Tirpitz (1849–1930) and the famous moustache worn by Kaiser Wilhelm II (1859–1941), with its carefully tended upturned ends. Before the 1840s beards had been a sign of cultural or political unconventionality, the property of artists and Chartists. Following the collapse of the Chartist movement and the defeat of the European revolutions in 1848, beards became respectable, their allure increased though not caused by the heroic reputation of the soldiers who returned unshaven from the Crimean War in 1856. This trend had little to do with shaving technology, or its absence; in fact it defied it as more and more men spurned the advantages that came in 1847 with the invention of the safety razor by William Henson (1812–88). Henson himself seems to have made little use of his own invention and sported a fine set of whiskers. The chronology of the British beard was followed roughly by men – many of them artists – on the Continent; almost all the French Impressionists, for example, sported beards. The Russian composer Mikhail Ivanovich Glinka (1804–57) was clean-shaven in the 1840s but had acquired a neatly trimmed full beard by 1856, and was followed by his fellow composer Pyotr Ilyich Tchaikovsky (1840–93). Johannes Brahms stopped shaving in the 1860s. An accepted alternative was provided by the kind of mutton-chop whiskers worn by the Norwegian playwright Henrik Ibsen from the mid-1860s onwards. But Ibsen abandoned his whiskers when they were no longer fashionable, and by the eve of the First World War the mutton-chops which the Austro-Hungarian Emperor Franz Joseph continued to wear had become a sign of his survival from a world that had long since passed into history.

Masculinity was also signified in the nineteenth century by the top hat, which had replaced the tricorne by the 1820s, after which time it became virtually ubiquitous among the middle classes. Once Prince Albert started wearing one, in 1850, the triumph of the top hat in Britain was assured, and it was soon imitated on the Continent. As silk replaced beaver skin in their manufacture, top hats grew ever higher, extending in America into the 'stove-pipe'. It was not surprising that collapsible top hats began to go on sale, particularly useful when attending the opera or theatre. Unlike the full-length beard, the top hat persisted until the First World War and beyond. Combined with a dark frock coat and, from the 1830s, trousers instead of knee breeches, it was a symbol of bourgeois respectability, advertising the wearer's status and power. Its main function was not to protect the head but to be doffed when greeting others: social gradations were observed by the order in which hats were doffed. Not wearing a hat was an obvious sign of insanity or distance from civilization. A Berlin newspaper reported in 1893 that 'a hatless man' had been spotted wandering about the streets and bothering passers-by; clearly he was mentally disturbed. In Charles Dickens's novel *Our Mutual Friend* (1865) Gaffer Hexam, who makes a living by fishing dead bodies out of the Thames and emptying their pockets into his purse, is described as 'half savage' because he has 'no covering on his matted head'.

In earlier times, including the eighteenth century, aristocratic men had worn clothing that distinguished them as members of the titled nobility, but the triumph of the top hat and frock coat reflected the blurring and then the disappearance of the social boundary that separated the nobility from the upper echelons of the bourgeoisie. While masculinity was advertised through generally dull grey or black clothing, women's dress was more colourful, with the waist coming down from the high 'Empire line' and then from the 1850s the crinoline, a skirt billowing outwards supported by a series of hoops, completely concealing the body's natural shape beneath. With the growth of feminist ideas, however, the impracticality of such styles gave way to the more close-fitting 'princess line', while the more advanced feminists began wearing divided skirts, known as 'bloomers' after their American inventor, the temperance and women's rights advocate Amelia Bloomer (1818–94), who had adopted them in imitation of Turkish pantaloons in the 1850s. Women's fashions began to change more rapidly as paper patterns and sewing machines became more

widely available, and the fashion industry began to emerge, with its advertising campaigns for new styles for every season. The 'bustle', attached to
the back of a skirt to keep its hem from dragging, was for instance only
current for a few years in the 1880s. Common throughout the century,
however, were corsets, usually made of whalebone, to bring in the waist,
and, as with men, hats, though for women these were often of very modest
dimensions, at least until the first decade and a half of the twentieth century, when extravagant wide-brimmed hats became fashionable, often
sporting an array of ostrich feathers, imported from the colonies and dyed
in a variety of different colours. Fashions such as these were only available to the well off, though with the spread of the department store it
became easier for women of the lower middle class to acquire stylish
dresses as well.

The rise of the beard from mid-century onwards can perhaps be best
understood as a reaction to the emergence in many European countries
of a new feminist movement, which began to bring women into the public
sphere as campaigners for the recognition of equal rights in many areas
of life. In the early decades of the nineteenth century, the characterization
of men as rational and women as emotional was expressed in the law's
placing of women in the same category as children, their rights exercised
by their husband, or by their father if they were unmarried. Women were
barred from most professions in most European countries as the professionalization of medicine and the law raised further the barriers against
them, while their lack of legal rights prevented them from being active in
business, banking and finance. More fundamental, perhaps, was discrimination against women in education. Most professions required a university
degree, but women were not admitted to universities across the greater
part of Europe until the latter decades of the century. In the *Code
Napoléon*, which governed civil law not only in France, Belgium, Spain,
Portugal and Poland, but also in significant parts of western Germany,
and had a strong influence over the Romanian Code of 1864, women were
not legal persons but were treated as minors until they were married, after
which they were represented legally by their husband. They could not sign
contracts, and they required the permission of their father or husband if
they wanted to engage in paid employment, change residence, or conduct
a lawsuit. The law required the wife to obey her husband. He was entitled
to use force to compel her to reside at a place of his own choosing. If she
committed adultery, she could be imprisoned for up to two years; adultery
by men, in contrast, was not a crime at all. If a husband discovered his
wife committing adultery and killed her, he could not be prosecuted for
murder, while a wife had no legal protection if she committed an act of

violence against her husband. The *Code Napoléon* had originally allowed divorce, but this right was deleted in France in 1816, after the Restoration.

In Russian law the Code of 1836 required that a wife was obliged in law to go with her husband wherever he went, unless he was sent to Siberia. She was not a legal person and needed her father's permission, or her husband's, to work, study, travel or trade. Divorce was theoretically possible on grounds of adultery, five years' unexplained absence, or deprivation of civil rights, but in practice it was hard to obtain. Thus in Tolstoy's novel *Anna Karenina* (1877) the eponymous heroine, married to a government official she does not love, has an affair with Vronsky, a younger man, and bears his child. But despite her husband's eventual consent, she is unable to divorce him because the law only allows the innocent party to sue for divorce and requires either a confession from the guilty party or evidence of infidelity, both of which would ruin her reputation. Despairing of ever resolving the situation, Anna commits suicide by throwing herself under a train. In Germany the Civil Law Code of 1900, which replaced all previous provisions and was valid throughout the German Empire, removed the few rights that women had possessed under the laws of the Prussian Enlightenment, by giving all a woman's property to her husband on marriage, and making divorce considerably more difficult by introducing the principle of guilt.

Yet despite the persistence of many of these inequalities, one of the most striking features of the nineteenth century was the gradual improvement of women's rights. In Sweden this was pioneered by none other than Fredrika Bremer, whose work bore political consequences in 1858, following what was called 'the *Hertha* debate'. From this point onwards unmarried women in Sweden enjoyed full legal equality. In 1862, Bremer declared publicly in favour of women's suffrage, and indeed in the same year municipal voting rights were extended to women of legal majority. Organized feminism in many countries had its origins in female philanthropy, and Bremer too engaged in educational and charitable work for the poor. Such activities brought women into the public sphere, and confronted them with many of the problems caused for poorer women by their lack of rights. One way of improving the situation of at least some women was by entering the professions. A campaign led by Sophia Jex-Blake (1840–1912) resulted in the admission of women to the entrance examination for Edinburgh University in 1869 (152 candidates sat for the exam, with four women passing among the top seven candidates). However, the medical students, egged on by some of the more conservative professors, blocked their way into the examination room at Surgeons' Hall on 18 November 1870, pelting them with garbage and mud. Despite the fact that the rioters were fined by the university, the Court of Session, the supreme legal body in Scotland, ruled in 1873 that the women should not have been admitted and had no right to sit examinations. The women qualified abroad instead, and returned later on to take up practice. Scottish universities admitted women on equal terms from 1892.

The Englishwoman Elizabeth Garrett Anderson (1836–1917) gained a licence to practise medicine through a loophole in the statutes of the Society of Apothecaries, a loophole the Society closed immediately afterwards. She opened a private practice and dispensary in London, having obtained a medical degree from the Sorbonne in Paris, although with some difficulty, in 1870. Three years later she was admitted through another loophole to the British Medical Association, which also changed its rules immediately afterwards to stop any other women from joining. The first woman to practise medicine in Britain was not, however, either Anderson or Jex-Blake, but Dr James Barry (c. 1792–1865). Born in Ireland and brought up as Margaret Ann Bulkley, a girl, she secretly took on a masculine identity after puberty as James Barry in order to be able to enter medical school at Edinburgh University (a plan hatched by family members). Barry obtained a medical degree in 1812, lived as a man thereafter and became a successful military surgeon, travelling to postings in South Africa, Mauritius, St Helena, Canada and the Caribbean accompanied by a black manservant and a dog called Psyche. Barry's true sex was only discovered after her death, causing considerable embarrassment to the medical authorities.

The preferred universities for women on the Continent were mostly Swiss. Zurich opened its university to women in 1847, twelve years after its foundation. Similarly, the University of Bern, established in 1834, admitted women to study for degrees in the 1870s; around half the 2,000 students were from other countries, and here too Russian and German women found the opportunities denied to them in their own universities. Just across the border, the universities of the liberal South German state of Baden admitted women in 1902, and by 1908 all German universities allowed women to study. Women were briefly admitted to Russian universities in the liberal heyday of 1860–1, but they were all expelled in 1862 and henceforth Russian women studied abroad. However, the tsarist government disapproved of this too, since it considered foreign study to be a source of political radicalism, and so it recalled all female students studying at foreign universities to Russia. A solution was eventually found in the form of special women's study courses held in St Petersburg. Nearly though not quite of university level, they were supported by the spread of women's secondary education in the 1870s, but in the reaction of the 1880s all of them were closed down apart from one, which was closely supervised by the secret police. A fresh wave of women departed to study abroad as a consequence. Alarmed at this development, which can hardly have been surprising in the circumstances, the government of Tsar Nicholas II re-established the women's study courses in the 1890s. By 1904 between five and six thousand students were attending the women's study courses, compared to a mere 150 twenty years previously. After 1905 women were finally allowed to take state university examinations. The situation was similar in many other countries. The first state-funded girls' grammar school in Germany, for example, was opened in 1893. In France a regular system of girls' secondary education was only established in 1880, but this still did not prepare girls to take the *baccalauréat*. The first women's college, Girton, was set up in Cambridge in 1869, but its students were not allowed to take their degrees until the mid-twentieth century even if they passed their examinations. Progress was slow but it was under way.

Women's rights in the private sphere improved as well. In 1857 the Matrimonial Causes Act allowed divorce for the first time in England without the passage of a special private Act of Parliament; it also included provisions for legal separation. A new divorce court was set up in London, and such was the scale of business that it dealt with a thousand cases during its first six years of existence. However, it still treated men and women differently, allowing men to petition for divorce on the sole ground of adultery, and requiring them to name the co-respondent, while women had to prove cruelty, bigamy or other offences in addition and were not required to name the co-respondent. In 1870 a further improvement in women's rights took place in Britain when Parliament passed a Married Women's Property Act, which provided that any income a wife earned through her own work remained hers, a measure extended in 1882 to the property she brought into the marriage. In 1884 divorce was finally legalized in France, and in Germany women were legally recognized as independent persons by a law passed in 1875. By the turn of the century women's rights over their property and their children had improved in many jurisdictions, and women had made their presence felt in the public sphere as editors of magazines and writers of newspaper columns, fatally undermining the claim that they were too emotional to take part in public life.

The feminist organizations that pressed almost everywhere for legal and educational improvements in the status of women mostly emerged in the liberal atmosphere of the 1860s and 1870s. Organized feminism in Sweden began with the Association for Married Women's Property Rights in 1873, which actively campaigned on economic issues. The Danish

Women's Association, founded in 1871 in the wake of a reorientation of liberal politics, was pulled to the left in 1883 as the ending of state-regulated prostitution became a central issue; similarly, in Norway, a series of speeches denouncing the double standard of morality by the nationalist writer Bjørnstjerne Bjørnson (1832–1910) in 1887 led to the creation of a White Ribbon Society in 1892 and campaigns for social purity, temperance and women's suffrage. Early feminism in France was closely associated with Republicanism. The two leading figures were Léon Richer (1824–1911) and Maria Deraismes (1828–94), both Freemasons. In 1875 their organization, the Society for the Improvement of Women's Lot, was banned by the pro-monarchist government; at the time the organization had a mere 150 members and its meetings featured an average attendance of ten or twelve. In 1882–3, Richer launched a new female emancipation society, the French League for Women's Rights, but it was dominated by men, who made up around half its membership, and in 1883 it was outflanked by a more radical organization, the Women's Suffrage Society, led by Hubertine Auclert (1848–1914). Both remained limited in numbers and influence. German feminism was dominated by middle-class Protestant women, one of whom, the social novelist Louise Otto-Peters (1819–95), who had already been an active feminist during the 1848 Revolution, took advantage of the revival of liberal politics to found the General German Women's Association in 1865. For thirty years its politics were ultra-cautious. It was unable to raise the demand for the vote because women were barred by law from engaging in political activities at all in most parts of Germany, including Prussia. It petitioned the Reichstag to write married women's property rights into the Civil Code promulgated in 1900, though without success.

Until the late nineteenth century feminism was everywhere an almost exclusively middle-class movement. It had little to say to the great mass of the peasantry who constituted the majority of Europe's population throughout the period. In some respects the situation of women in rural society worsened during the nineteenth century. As young men left for the towns in the age of heavy industrialization, lured by the prospect of higher wages, so the women they left behind had to shoulder an increasing burden of work while still running the household, raising the children and doing the domestic chores. As a local doctor in the Zeitz district of northern Germany wrote in 1912, there had been a 'change in the division of labour', which 'places heavy demands on the women's physical resources'. This was only partly balanced out by the greater freedom women had to marry as serfdom was abolished and better communications made it easier for them to travel away from the village and so obtain a wider choice of potential spouse. Divorce, however, was still beyond the reach of most of them. In England the high cost of divorce even after it became easier to obtain meant that popular justice continued to assert itself in the practice of wife-sales, described disapprovingly at the opening of Thomas Hardy's *The Mayor of Casterbridge* (1886), as the hay-trusser Michael Henchard, drunk on furmity laced with rum, parades his wife Susan at market and auctions her off to the highest bidder. In practice, the purchaser was usually pre-arranged. In 1833 the sale of a woman for two shillings and sixpence was reported at market in the Essex town of Epping. Brought before the magistrates, the husband claimed that he had not lived with her for some time, 'and that she had lived in open adultery with the man Bradley, by whom she had been purchased'. The authorities stamped this practice out by the First World War; but it indicated a widespread lack of sentimentality about marital relations in rural society that shocked the urban middle classes. The focus of the feminist movement on property, educational improvement and marital rights did not really apply to the great mass of working-class women either, whose lives were taken up by hard work, childbearing and the struggle to survive.

Nevertheless, what the feminists achieved paved the way for the extension of meaningful rights to all women. Even if only a handful of women entered professional life before 1914, the fact that they were able to practise as doctors or study at university in itself established a vital precedent for the future. The feminists won the argument not so much on the basis of equal rights for all individuals as on the principle that women would exercise a beneficent influence on society because they were more moral, more sympathetic, more feeling than men. Women proved their worth, many of them declared, by their engagement with charitable and philanthropic activities, through which they showed not only that they could apply their motherly instincts to society as a whole but also that they could organize and channel these instincts in a responsible manner, to the benefit of all. So women had to appear to be strong as they entered the public sphere and the industrial and administrative world, and began to present themselves in less emotional terms. 'The woman who indulges in the luxury of a "good cry"', declared the *Daily Mirror* in 1911, 'no longer exists.' The article was headlined: 'Women Who Never Cry: Business Girl's Grit Replaces Victorian Tears and Hysterics'. However much feminists might stress women's closeness to nature and the world of feeling, the end result of their efforts was to ensure that middle- and upper-class women also developed, like men, what the Americans called 'the stiff upper lip'.

THE PURSUIT OF HAPPINESS

People in Europe, as in other parts of the world, have generally sought happiness, among other things, through cultured activities. This search has not always been conducted separately from the world of work. In pre-industrial society, men and women sang to set the rhythm of their work during sowing and reaping, spinning or weaving, relieving the boredom and repetition of their tasks as well as setting a pace for themselves in performing them. 'When the ploughman sings', went one saying in France, 'the plough goes well.' In the Pyrenees women were hired to follow the reapers to sing out the rhythm of their scything. Musical instruments such as fiddles, bagpipes and drums were brought out for special occasions such as weddings or dances; people played them and sang songs handed down to them from their parents, bought ballads from pedlars, or listened to itinerant minstrels singing for their supper on the village green or square. German *Bänkelsänger* – 'bench-singers' – would travel around with a satchel full of songsheets or illustrated pamphlets telling rhymed stories of miraculous events, strange happenings, grisly murders and tragic love affairs; these were known as *Moritaten* because they frequently ended with a strong moral message. Often, especially in areas that experienced hardship and oppression, folk songs lamented the poor country people's lot, articulating complaints about hunger, hard work, taxes, conscription and other miseries of daily life: 'They lead us like oxen', as one Romanian folk song had it, 'they shear us like sheep.' Ribald songs accompanied village weddings, just as folk songs were adapted for political purposes during upheavals such as the 1848 Revolutions.

Folk songs seldom survived the transition to the urban-industrial environment. 'The beautiful old folk-song,' wrote an anonymous American observer of Russian popular culture in 1893, ' . . . disappears at the sound of the steam whistle.' Slow epics and ballads were being replaced by shorter and livelier songs, communal rituals by songs focusing on individual experience, traditional melodies by new ones imported from the towns. With the spread of the railways and the consequent improvement of communications, young people in the French countryside began to demand popular melodies from Paris sung in French rather than local tunes sung in local *patois*, while both the village priest and the village schoolteacher distributed printed songbooks with edifying patriotic and moral ditties in them, and encouraged the formation of *orphéons*, or choral societies, to bring village music under their control. In 1864 a school inspector in the department of the Aude in the south reported with satisfaction that 'the lewd songs that wounded even the least modest ears have been replaced by the religious and patriotic choirs of numerous choral societies due to schools and the initiative of teachers'. Itinerant balladeers could not compete, and their trade died out. Traditional country dances, with men and women facing each other in lines or in a round, had provided opportunities for courtship regulated by the community, but by the 1870s the young had come to prefer dancing in pairs to the strains of a waltz, a polka or a quadrille – 'the dances of city people', as one observer called them in Lorraine in the 1880s. 'The old dances,' it was reported in Lauragais in the south-west in 1891, 'are disappearing progressively, and most already survive only as memories.' Dancing became separated from the ritual year, and became a form of organized leisure and popular entertainment.

Rural popular culture also attracted the growing hostility of the state. Officials tried to curb fairs and processions because they considered them a threat to public order. Rough and often bloody village games were suppressed in the interests of health and safety, while shooting and throwing competitions with live animals as the targets were banned in the cause of animal welfare. In Russia officials and middle-class moralists deplored the drunkenness and violence they observed in popular fairs and ceremonies. During patronal festivals, one temperance campaigner complained in 1908, the peasants 'drink themselves into a complete frenzy, bite off one another's fingers, often thrash each other to death . . . The same is true on religious holidays . . . Vodka flows like rivers and there is widespread immorality and disorder.' The organized mass fistfights common on such occasions often ended in serious injury or even death. Already by the late 1890s almost fifty Russian cities and towns had outlawed or curtailed holiday markets, deterring the peasants who came to town to take part in them. In England, as elsewhere, the enclosure of common land took away many of the venues traditionally used for country recreations. By 1840, as William Howitt (1792–1879), writer and husband of Fredrika Bremer's translator Mary Howitt, noted, 'a mighty revolution has taken place in the sports and pastimes of the common people . . . In my own recollection, the appearance of morris-dancers, guisers, plough-bullocks, and Christmas carolers, has become more and more rare.'

The consequences, as the economist and circuit judge Joseph Kay (1821–78) observed, were particularly unfortunate as the lower classes flocked into the new industrial towns. 'In England,' he noted in 1850, 'it may be said that the poor have now no relaxation but the alehouse or the gin palace.' Alcohol was the lubricant of industrialization. Pubs and bars proliferated in the new urban world. In the industrial French department of the Nord there was already one bar for every forty-six inhabitants in

1890, catering for the thirst of the predominantly urban working-class population. By 1910 the French were drinking nearly 5 billion litres of wine every year, though very often it was watered down by both the growers and the barkeepers, so that it was not always very potent. The authorities everywhere tried to curb the taste for alcoholic beverages, but with little success: to circumvent the licensing laws in Prussia, for example, cheap and informal *Schnapskasinos* opened up, often in rooms rented privately by groups of workers. By 1893 there were more than 100 of these in the mining districts of the Ruhr, with over 16,000 members. As the name implied, they served not only bottled beer but also hard liquor. While Germans drank Schnaps, the French preferred absinthe, a green-coloured spirit based on the medicinal plant wormwood: they were consuming 36 million litres a year by 1910. A spectacular murder committed by an absinthe addict led to a ban on the drink being written into the Swiss Constitution after a referendum in 1908, followed by similar bans in the Netherlands in 1909 and France itself in 1914.

In Russia the government was reluctant to attempt to reduce alcohol consumption even before it established a monopoly over the distilling of vodka in the 1890s, when the alcohol revenues of the Russian state began to increase almost exponentially, from 250 million roubles a year to nearly a billion by the eve of the First World War. Taxes on vodka supplied nearly a third of government revenues for much of the century. Dostoyevsky's *Crime and Punishment* (1866) – originally intended to be called *The Drunkards* – is full of scenes of inebriation in the bars and taverns of St Petersburg, opening with a drunken monologue by the hopeless alcoholic Marmeladov, who sells his daughter into prostitution to subsidise his addiction. Similar reports could be heard from social commentators all over Europe. In *The Condition of the Working Class in England* (1844), Friedrich Engels described how on being paid on a Saturday afternoon, 'the whole working class pours from its own poor quarters into the main thoroughfares, [where] intemperance may be seen in all its brutality'. Early on in the industrial era, indeed before it even began, temperance organizations emerged across Europe, often inspired by religious movements, to combat drinking both through moral exhortation and through pressure for legislation and tax increases. Such organizations were particularly powerful in Scandinavia: in Sweden the government established a monopoly on the sale of liquor, which could only be obtained in carefully regulated outlets, while in Norway, where there were similar arrangements, the average annual consumption per head of *akvavit* fell from 32 pints in 1833 to 12 pints by 1851. Pure water and soft drinks became more widely available to quench the worker's thirst, so that between

1899 and 1913 a 25 per cent reduction in alcohol consumption was registered across Germany. In Britain consumption of beer began to fall from the 1880s onwards, from 40 gallons per person per year in the 1870s to under 30 gallons on the eve of the First World War. For the British bourgeoisie, tea-drinking was already a central part of domestic life by 1800, but with urban growth tea trickled down into the lower middle and respectable working classes as well, with average annual per capita consumption rocketing from 1.6 pounds in the 1840s to 4.4 pounds in the 1870s and 5.7 pounds in the 1890s.

Clubs and societies offered further alternatives to drinking. In the northern industrial town of Lille under the French Second Empire, for example, there were sixty-three drinking clubs, but also thirty-seven clubs for card-playing, twenty-three for bowls, thirteen for skittles, ten for archery and eighteen for crossbow-shooting. Miners commonly kept pigeons or greyhounds for racing, symbolizing perhaps the freedom and speed of movement they were unable to achieve for themselves in the cramped conditions of the coalface. Football clubs were founded in many areas and helped cement the solidarity of new urban communities. Initially in England the Football Association, founded in 1863 in an attempt to enforce the 'Cambridge rules' – drawn up in 1848 by representatives of the public schools at Trinity College, Cambridge – was dominated by elite educational establishments. But in 1883 the working-class team of Blackburn Olympic inaugurated a new era when it defeated the Old Etonians in the Football Association Cup Final. The game rapidly spread to the Continent, usually taken there by the British. As early as 1863 *The Scotsman* newspaper reported that 'a number of English gentlemen living in Paris have lately organized a football club . . . The football contests take place in the Bois de Boulogne, by permission of the authorities, and surprise the French amazingly.' The Dresden English Football Club was set up by British workers in 1874 and was soon followed by others. A. C. Milan was founded by the English lacemaker Herbert Klipin (1870–1917) in 1899, under the name of the Milan Cricket and Foot-Ball Club (the cricket did not last very long). The first football match in Poland was played between Lwów and Cracow in 1894. It was won by Lwów with the first recorded goal in Polish history, scored by Włodzimierz Chomicki (1878–1953) in the sixth minute, after which the referee ended the game: an understanding of the rules was slow in coming. Football was already on the way to becoming an international sporting phenomenon by 1914, with an increasingly dominant working-class following; indeed, many teams were set up in industrial towns, like the Ruhr club of Schalke 04, the number signifying its date of foundation; its players were popularly known as 'the miners'.

As literacy rates improved, entertainment of a different kind was provided by the rise of the popular press. In Russia the gradual relaxation of censorship from the time of Alexander II onwards encouraged the rise of the 'penny press', single-sheet newspapers sold on the street rather than by subscription. The best-selling of these 'boulevard newspapers' was the *Moscow Sheet*, whose editor Nicholas Pastukhov (1831–1911), a former innkeeper described by one of his own journalists as an 'illiterate editor who in the midst of illiterate readers . . . knew how to speak their language'. A rival penny paper in St Petersburg was dismissed in 1870 as 'a sort of junkyard of all sorts of rumours, gossip, and news'. The young writer Anton Chekhov was told by his editor that 'we'll grab the readers with stupidities and then instruct them with learned articles'. In practice, the latter continued to be in short supply. In France local newspapers began to be produced from the 1870s onwards, though they were read mainly by the middle classes at first; in 1896, however, the police described one such paper, *L'Avenir du Cantal*, as 'much read by the peasant'. Its sales had climbed to 2,300 three times a week, more than the entire press of the south-central department of Cantal two decades before. 'The taste for newspapers', it was noted in the Breton commune of Guipel in 1903, 'is creating serious competition for legends and traditional stories. It is expelling them from thought and conversation.'

Cheap newspapers in France were no more immune from sensationalism than they were in Russia. Murders, scandals, sensations of many kinds filled the pages of *Le Petit Journal*, founded in 1863. The proprietor, Moïse Polydore Millaud (1813–71), told the first editor that he must be 'bold enough to appear stupid . . . Find out what the average man is thinking. Then let yourself be guided by this.' The paper achieved sales of more than half a million by 1880. Such papers were not only sold on street corners but also in railway kiosks, whose number in France exceeded a thousand by the turn of the century. The circulation of the daily press in Paris mushroomed from one million in 1870 to five million in 1910, aided by the passage of a liberal new press law in 1881 and by the importation of rapid rotary printing presses manufactured by the Hoe Company in America. Newspaper circulation in Britain leapt as a result of the abolition of stamp duty in 1855, but long after this even the relatively popular papers like the *Daily News*, with a circulation of 150,000, or the *Daily Telegraph*, which reached 190,000 by the 1870s, were staid in appearance and respectable in content.

It was not until the 1896 that a truly popular press arrived, with the creation of the *Daily Mail*. By 1902 the paper was enjoying a circulation of over a million copies, the largest in the entire world. With its sensational headlines and stunts, such as the offer in 1906 of a prize of £1,000 for the first airplane flight across the English Channel, it quickly exerted an unrivalled popular appeal. If the press was becoming more sensational, it was in a new way, therefore, linked to the reporting of real-life events rather than stories of miracles and wonders. This was particularly the case in Germany, where generally high literacy rates and the effective ending of pre-censorship after the 1848 Revolution created a thriving newspaper industry. By 1862 there were thirty-two newspapers appearing in Berlin alone, six of them twice a day. In 1866 some 60,000 copies of the *Cologne Newspaper* were being printed daily. Illustrated weeklies like *Die Gartenlaube* with 400,000 subscribers by 1875 and satirical journals such as *Kladderadatch* and *Simplicissimus* were even more popular than the newspapers. The number of newspapers in Germany increased from around 1,500 in 1850 to 4,221 in 1914. However, sensationalism did not become a significant feature of German newspapers until the 1920s, when the highly respectable and well-organized Social Democratic subculture that provided newspapers and magazines for the industrial working class began to be sidelined by the rise of the commercial press.

Besides newspapers and magazines, the emerging working classes of the industrial age also read books with increasing enthusiasm, helped by the spread of public libraries. Reprints of popular novels could be bought for two shillings by the 1850s, while the publisher Richard Bentley (1794–1871) was producing one-shilling books in his 'Railway Library' at the same time. Such improving popular literature did not plunge into a cultural vacuum; it was largely aimed at replacing what serious-minded reformers regarded as the vulgar and corrupting influence of sensational 'penny dreadfuls'. In Germany the equivalent of the latter was the *colportage* novel, sold door-to-door or on the streets as a cheap serial publication. *The Executioner of Berlin*, published in 130 weekly instalments in the early 1890s, was typical of the genre, and included executions, murders, kidnappings, duels, exhumations, drownings, accidents, arson and espionage, all within the first few chapters. Publishers also produced cheap editions of the classics as a kind of moral counterweight; popular biographies of heroic figures such as Garibaldi had a broad appeal; and improving literature was churned out by organizations such as the Society for the Dissemination of Useful Books, founded in Russia in 1861; but there is little doubt which genre sold the best. Concern about the quality of working-class reading led in Britain to the Public Libraries Act of 1850, which established the principle of free libraries funded by local authorities. Yet the idea was slow to spread across the Continent, with the Frenchman Eugène Morel (1869–1934) only pioneering the idea in 1910. More common were reading clubs and societies, and small libraries founded by trade unions in the social centres they built.

Cheap fiction was also used as the basis for melodramas, which reached the height of their popularity during the Victorian era. Typical was *The String of Pearls* (1846–7), which featured as its villain Sweeney Todd, 'the demon barber of Fleet Street', who murdered his customers to make fillings for meat pies. Apart from the villain, customarily hissed loudly by the audience on his every appearance onstage, there was also usually a rather dim and unsuspecting young hero and an equally innocent damsel in distress, along with an aged parent and a servant. Melodrama merged seamlessly into the music hall, which emerged as a form of popular entertainment in the 1850s. The first to be opened was the Canterbury Hall in Lambeth, in 1852; by 1878 there were seventy-eight large music halls in the capital city. Songs and dances, with comic and acrobatic or juggling acts, were introduced by a compère while the audience ate and drank their way through the evening, which often ended in riotous disorder. English music halls were described by one commentator in 1868 as 'gleaming temples of dissipation' where audiences were 'debased by low songs and vulgar exhibitions'. The messages purveyed in music-hall songs were hardly revolutionary – as one song had it, 'It's a *little* bit of what yer fancies does yer good' – but moral reformers strongly disapproved of the ribaldry of performers such as Marie Lloyd (1870–1922), whose performances were deemed unacceptably risqué by middle-class critics.

In France simple *cafés chantants* such as the *Cabaret des Assassins* in Montmartre, founded in the 1850s and under its later name the *Lapin Agile* the haunt of artists and writers, were eventually trumped by more elaborate venues with stand-up comics, bands, dance routines and lavishly costumed performers. The most famous of these was the *Folies Bergère*, founded in 1869. The *Moulin Rouge*, which opened for business in 1889, was the birthplace of the cancan, a dance performed by a high-kicking line of chorus girls, and the haunt of the painter Henri de Toulouse-Lautrec (1864–1901), who designed its advertising posters. Here too there were risqué performances by *artistes* such as Mistinguett (Jeanne Bourgeois, 1875–1956), who catered for a mixed audience of all kinds avid for entertainment. *Le Chat Noir* (also known briefly as the *Cabaret Artistique*), opened in 1881 in Montmartre – the composer Erik Satie (1866–1925) earned his living playing the piano there – but it closed in 1897 following the death of its founder and host, Rodolphe Salis (1851–97). The working-class equivalent of the music hall in Germany, the *Tingeltangel*, so called after the noise customers made when they jangled the cutlery against their glasses while singing the refrain of a song, was born in Berlin in the 1870s, and soon spread across northern and western Germany. By 1879 the *Tingeltangel* was being attacked in the Reichstag. It was to be judged immoral 'partly', as one speaker declared, 'owing to the frivolous or suggestive content of what is performed, and partly because of the suggestive nature of the performances themselves'.

Outside France the fashion for literary and artistic cafés spread until they found imitators like the *Zielony Balonik* (Green Balloon) in Cracow, established in 1905 explicitly for writers and painters; it was forced to close in 1912 under the weight of censorship and police interference. In Germany the *Überbrettl* cabaret, founded in Berlin in 1901, employed the Austrian composer Arnold Schoenberg (1874–1951) as its director of music. *Els Quatre Gats* in Barcelona, which opened in 1897 as a beer hall, tavern and hostel, was explicitly modelled on the Parisian original and specialized in traditional Catalan puppet shows. But despite – or possibly because of – its habit of displaying modernist paintings to try and sell them to the public, it closed after a few years, in 1903. The *Café Central* in Vienna, which opened for business in 1876, proved more durable: in 1913 alone customers included Sigmund Freud, the later Yugoslav Communist Josip Broz Tito (1892–1980), Adolf Hitler and Vladimir Ilyich Lenin. On the eve of the First World War the Austrian socialist leader Victor Adler (1852–1918) warned the Foreign Minister, Count Leopold Berchtold (1863–1942), that a European war would cause a revolution in Russia. 'And who will lead this revolution?' Berchtold asked sarcastically: 'Perhaps Mr Bronstein sitting over there at the *Café Central*?' Lev Davidovich Bronstein (1879–1940) was indeed a revolutionary, though in his political activities he went under the name of Leon Trotsky.

In Munich the great beer cellars of the 1880s, such as the *Bürgerbräukeller* (1885) or the *Löwenbräukeller* (1888), with their large halls and outside gardens, provided entertainment as well as food and drink for thousands, with a resident band playing background music and on Saturday evenings a series of singers, comedians and variety acts taking the stage. In Russia such institutions were less closely linked to the consumption of alcohol because factory owners and temperance organizations set up their own theatres and put on performances of short dramas, operettas, farces and vaudeville shows, and acts by clowns, magicians, comedians and other popular entertainers. In 1899 alone the Guardianships of Popular Temperance organized 1,332 theatre performances and 1,356 outdoor entertainments: by 1904 these numbers had increased to 5,139 and 4,238 respectively. Around 40 per cent of their offerings consisted of serious drama, and they were reported to have driven the popular theatrical entertainments put on at the Shrovetide Fair – celebrated in the ballet

Petrushka (1911) by Igor Fyodorovich Stravinsky (1882–1971) – and other folk festivals out of existence. In 1908 it was claimed that 'the Guardianship has managed to fight the uncultivated masses' aspiration for spectacles of a baser sort and arouse in them a love for classical art'. Nevertheless, melodrama remained the most popular form of theatre in Russia; one manager complained in 1902 that 'no innovations, even in the guise of artistic ensemble, interested the public, who were captivated only by melodramatic acting in heartrending plays'.

An alternative to the theatre or the beer cellar, the bar or the café, was offered to the working class across Europe by the dance hall, often little more than a pub room cleared of its furniture. This was a world away from the formal waltzes at middle- and upper-class balls danced to the strains of music by Viennese composers such as Johann Strauss (1825–99) on the one hand, or the elaborate communal dancing that could be seen in villages and rural communities across Europe on the other. In the dance hall the steps were simple, the music basic, and the dancers couples. The German theologian and social investigator Paul Göhre (1864–1928), who lived as a worker for three months to observe the life of the proletariat, thoroughly disapproved of the goings-on at the Sunday-night dance halls in an industrial suburb of Chemnitz in 1895: 'In these halls, in the nights from Sunday to Monday, our young labouring people are losing today not only their hard-earned wages but their strength, their ideals, their chastity.' Authorities everywhere began to impose restrictions on these and similar institutions in the name of public order and morality. By the early 1900s a licence was required to open a music hall in Britain, and on the eve of the First World War alcohol was finally banned on music-hall premises. Similar measures were taken in Germany: in Düsseldorf the police moved the closing time for public dances forward to 10 p.m., a step followed in many other German industrial towns.

Before 1914 music for dances had to be played by live bands. The phonograph, invented by Thomas Edison in 1877, using wax cylinders for recording, was little more than a novelty. However, by recording the voices of Gladstone, Kaiser Wilhelm II, Tennyson and others for publicity purposes, the phonograph left a record of what they sounded like that can still be heard today. The German-born American Emile Berliner (1851–1929) improved the technology by inventing a flat disc in 1887 that could be played on what he called a 'gramophone'. But the rotation speed was difficult to control, the record only provided two minutes of music, and full orchestras had to be replaced by bands numbering only a dozen musicians or so, because the recording equipment could only pick up sounds emitted close to it. It also took a long time to invent a method of copying discs, so that musicians had to record the same piece fifty times if they wanted to sell fifty records. All this made gramophones and records very expensive. Nevertheless, the great Italian tenor Enrico Caruso (1873–1921), whose resonant voice was ideally suited to the new medium, caused a sensation with his first recordings. By 1914 he was earning £20,000 a year from sales of his records. Tchaikovsky called the gramophone 'the most surprising, the most beautiful, and the most interesting among all inventions that have turned up in the nineteenth century'. He made sure that his own voice was recorded for posterity by Edison as well.

At the end of the century all these activities began to be put into the shade by the rise of the entertainment medium that was soon to dominate the leisure time of the masses: the cinema. Already in 1839 the Frenchman Louis Daguerre (1787–1851) had produced the first photograph – known as the daguerreotype – and technical improvements by the 1850s enabled the British photographer Roger Fenton (1819–69) to take dramatic pictures of the Crimean War. Early photographs needed a long exposure to achieve results. Sitters had to remain still for as much as half an hour if they wanted an unblurred portrait. Often they were assisted by neck-braces, armbands and waist restrainers to stop them from moving. The photographer had to place the camera on a tripod and cover his head in black cloth to keep out unwanted light. Only towards the end of the century did gelatin plates open up the possibility of capturing a body in motion, while cheap, hand-held Kodak box cameras, first manufactured in America in 1888, brought photography within the compass of ordinary people. At the same time experimentation with multiple lenses and perforated celluloid reels led to the invention of motion pictures, the first of which was shown by the brothers Auguste and Louis Lumière in 1895. When one film showed a train coming towards the screen, members of the cinema audience panicked, threw themselves back into their seats, or jumped up and ran to the back of the auditorium. By 1897 the first studios had been built, and a rotating camera had been devised for panning shots. Far cheaper to put on than live entertainment acts, movies spread with extraordinary rapidity across Europe. Already in 1895 the Wintergarten Theatre in Berlin was showing an early one-take film. New techniques were developed that allowed for multi-shot and then multi-reel films, companies were set up to create and sell them, and dedicated cinemas began to appear, pioneered by the Nickelodeon in Pittsburgh in 1905.

The rapidity of the spread of the cinematograph – the term invented by the Lumières – can be illustrated by the example of Spain, where the first one-shot film was shown as early as 1896. Movies became hugely popular in the working-class districts of the larger towns, where initially they formed part of variety shows in basic premises like sheds and basements, known as *baracas*. By 1910 there were more than 100 venues in Barcelona alone, with grand purpose-built cinemas along the Ramblas providing 1,000 seats or more, segregated by ticket price so that the middle classes were not inconvenienced by the rowdiness of the working-class patrons. In such venues a pianist was often hired to provide dramatic musical accompaniment to the silent events being shown on screen; there might even be hand-tinted colour versions, though normally films were in black and white. A census carried out in 1914 counted more than 900 cinemas in Spain, including mobile shows that went from village to village. The government, worried about immorality, set up a pre-censorship system in 1912. The same happened in other countries: in Britain, for example, the Cinematograph Act of 1909 was followed in 1912 by the creation of the British Board of Film Censors. Surprisingly, perhaps, the most active country in movie production was Denmark, where the Nordisk company churned out sixty-seven films the year after its foundation in 1906. By 1914, however, imported American films were taking the largest share of movie showings in every European country. The European cinema industry had been born, but the global dominance of Hollywood, where movie companies were beginning to move from the East Coast by this time, was already on the horizon.

REALISM AND NATIONALISM

The realism of photography and moving pictures had a profound effect on the development of art. By mid-century the age of Romanticism was drawing to a close with the growing turn to Realism in the work of painters such as Gustave Courbet (1819–77), who eschewed mythical and religious themes of the past for the concerns of contemporary life. His landscapes abandoned the dramatic exaggeration and compositional artifice employed by the Romantics in favour of a naturalistic approach that suggested he had just come upon a scene and decided on the spot to paint it. In *The Stone-Breakers* (1849) Courbet depicted two peasants breaking rocks by the side of a road, while in *A Burial at Ornans* (1849) he showed the funeral of his great-uncle, depicting not richly clad models but the actual people who attended the event, participating in an orderly manner rather than indulging in the emotional gestures that would have been expected in a Romantic representation of the same subject. 'The burial at Ornans,' Courbet remarked, 'was in reality the burial of Romanticism.' Later he complained that 'the title of Realist was thrust upon me just as

the title of Romantic was imposed upon the men of 1830'. But his paintings undoubtedly inaugurated a new cultural style. Courbet was a political
radical and a committed participant in the Paris Commune of 1871, and
he painted scenes of poverty that were intended as social criticism rather
than presentations of the picturesque. In *The Gleaners* (1857) Jean-François
Millet (1814–75) showed poor peasant women bending over to pick up
small ears of corn left on the fields after the harvest, while *The Potato
Eaters* (1885) by Vincent van Gogh depicted a group of rough peasants
sitting round a table eating their potatoes by the light of a little lamp. Van
Gogh wanted, he said, to indicate by their appearance the fact that
they had 'tilled the earth themselves with these hands they are putting in
the dish'.

Realist in a very different way were the English painters of the
Pre-Raphaelite Brotherhood, founded in 1848. From one point of view the
paintings of Dante Gabriel Rossetti (1828–82), William Holman Hunt
(1827–1910), John Everett Millais (1829–96) and their colleagues reflected
the concern of Romanticism, with their focus on the Middle Ages and
religious subjects and their break with Classical models and techniques
in the search for authenticity of expression. But they also followed the
new Realism in using ordinary people, including working-class girls and
prostitutes, as models. Millais' painting *Christ in the House of His Parents*, exhibited in 1850, was widely condemned: instead of employing
transcendental religious imagery, it was set amid the dirt and mess of a
carpenter's workshop and showed the Holy Family as ordinary, poor
people. Even more controversial was the sculptor Auguste Rodin (1840–
1917), whose sculptures were a far cry from the smooth Classicism of the
Academies. Instead of following the Grecian tradition they made a direct
appeal to the emotions through their dramatic and often unconventional
poses and the roughness of their textures. In 1864 the Paris Salon rejected
The Man with the Broken Nose, a bust of a Paris street-porter, because
of what the judges considered its unfinished state. A life-size male nude,
The Age of Bronze (1877), admitted to the Salon after a very close vote in
the selection board, puzzled critics because it did not have an historical
or mythological theme but was 'just', Rodin said, 'a simple piece of sculpture without reference to subject'. By this time, however, he was beginning
to win commissions. Rodin never completed the commission he was given
to sculpt a vast doorway surround entitled *The Gates of Hell*, after Dante.
But some of the figures he created as part of it subsequently became
famous, notably *The Thinker* of which the first of many bronze castings
was made in 1904, and *The Kiss*, an 1889 marble sculpture. Despite the
controversy elicited by his work, Rodin achieved not only popular fame

by the turn of the century but acceptance by the government, bypassing the Academies in the process.

Realism spread rapidly to other countries, reaching Russia for example in the shape of 'the Wanderers', fourteen young artists who abandoned the Imperial Academy of Arts in 1863 to form their own co-operative, painting scenes such as the celebrated *Barge Haulers on the Volga* (1873) by Ilya Yefimovich Repin (1844–1930). Similarly, the Realist novel was often, though not invariably, set in the present rather than in the Romantic past. It allowed readers to inhabit a world parallel to their own, where moral and social dramas were played out in ways that were recognizably similar to their own lives, but more eventful and exciting, and which sometimes prompted the desire to subscribe to the reforming ideas of the author. The chronology of literary Realism did not match that of its counterpart in the visual arts precisely: already in the 1830s, Balzac was turning away from writing historical fiction in the manner of Walter Scott, as in early novels such as *Les Chouans* (1829) and fantasy-fables like *La Peau de chagrin* (1831), to writing in a Realist manner his series *La Condition humaine*. Of course some artists continued to paint Biblical, Classical and historical scenes regardless of the Realist trend. But there is no doubt that artworks and novels addressing contemporary life and attempting to portray it in a manner that was true to life predominated after the middle years of the century.

It was above all industrialization that called forth the Realist novel as a means of portraying the collectivity of society, with its teeming mass of characters and its depiction of the shifting relations between them. The master here was Charles Dickens, many of whose works sought to lay bare in literary form the evils of the age and to advocate by showing their dramatic consequences the urgent need to tackle them: *Oliver Twist* (1837–9) addressed the state of crime and disorder in London, *Bleak House* (1853) the expense and injustice of the antiquated English system of civil law, *Hard Times* (1854) the cruelties inflicted by the utilitarian philosophy of the new industrialists. The 'social novel' carried a strong charge of social criticism: *Alton Locke* (1849) by Charles Kingsley (1819–75) reflected its author's Chartist sympathies in its depiction of the exploitation of agricultural labourers and workers in the garment industry, while *Mary Barton* (1848) by Elizabeth Gaskell (1810–65) showed what its author called the 'misery and hateful passions caused by the love of pursuing wealth as well as the egoism, thoughtlessness and insensitivity of manufacturers'. *Les Misérables* (1862) addressed the three great problems of the age, identified by Victor Hugo as 'the degradation of man by poverty, the ruin of women by starvation, and the dwarfing of childhood by physical and spiritual night'. In *L'Assommoir* (1877), Émile Zola painted a drastic picture of poor housing conditions in a Parisian slum, while his *Germinal* (1885) brought together the political and social features of life in a coal-mining community over several decades in a dramatic narrative of a strike followed by an uprising. More drastic still was the account of impoverished Russians living in a shelter for the homeless in *The Lower Depths* (1902) by Maxim Gorky.

Realist novels could flourish in many European countries not least because of the emergence of a new market for books, as the middle classes grew in numbers and wealth, and merchants, industrialists, lawyers, bankers, employers and landowners were joined in the ranks of the affluent by doctors, teachers, civil servants, scientists, and white-collar workers of various kinds, numbering more than 300,000 in the 1851 census in the United Kingdom for example, the first time they were counted, and more than double that number thirty years later. Books became cheaper and more plentiful as steam-driven presses replaced hand-operated ones in the printing industry, and as mechanical production reduced the cost of paper while hugely increasing the supply. Novels, including those of Dickens and Dostoyevsky, were commonly printed in instalments and read in serial form. Alongside the 'penny dreadful' and the *colportage* serial a new type of bourgeois novel emerged, catering for an educated readership. Altogether, if 580 books were published in the United Kingdom every year between 1800 and 1825, more than 2,500 appeared annually in mid-century, and more than 6,000 by the end of the century. In 1855 some 1,020 book titles were published in Russia, and by 1894 this figure had increased tenfold, to 10,691, a figure equal to the output of new titles in Britain and the United States combined.

In all of this, despite the growing taste for non-fiction, ranging from encyclopedias and handbooks to triple-decker biographies, the proportion of works of fiction published in Britain increased from 16 per cent in the 1830s to nearly 25 per cent half a century later. Novel-reading, once the province of upper-class women, became a general habit among the middle classes of both sexes. Perhaps by necessity, in order to gain a following, Realist artists and writers focused on the comfortably off as well as on the poor and the exploited. Portraits continued to be a significant source of income for painters, while in literature the bourgeoisie featured centrally in the family sagas of the age. *Fathers and Sons* (1862) by Ivan Turgenev dissected the fraught relationship between a conservative older generation and young nihilistic intellectuals; Zola's *Les Rougon-Macquart* (1871–93), a cycle of twenty novels, attempted, as the author said, 'to portray, at the outset of a century of liberty and truth, a family that cannot restrain itself in its rush to possess all the good things that progress is making available and is derailed by its own momentum, the fatal convulsions that accompany the birth of a new world'.

In *Middlemarch: A Study of Provincial Life* (1871–2), George Eliot tackled the impact of change brought by the railways, medicine and other harbingers of modernity on a deeply conservative small-town society; *Madame Bovary* (1856), written by Gustave Flaubert after his friends had persuaded him to abandon early efforts at historical fantasy, described in realistic detail the daily life and love affairs of the bored wife of a weak provincial doctor; both Theodor Fontane in *Effi Briest* (1894) and Tolstoy in *Anna Karenina* (1877) dealt with adultery, real or imagined, and the constrained lives of married women in the upper reaches of society; and in the six-novel sequence *The Barsetshire Chronicles* (1855–67), Anthony Trollope traced the fortunes of the leading inhabitants of an imaginary provincial town, while *The Pallisers* (1865–80) focused on the engagement of a much grander family with parliamentary politics. As the American writer Henry James (1843–1916) remarked, in a somewhat backhanded compliment, Trollope's 'inestimable merit was a complete appreciation of the usual'. However quotidian their concerns, Realist novels and paintings shared one thing in common with the cultural products of Romanticism: their appeal to the emotions, achieved not least by plumbing the depths of character and arousing sympathy and identification in the reader or the viewer.

Literary Realism was a broad European movement. In Portugal it was represented by José Maria de Eça de Queirós (1845–1900), who was influenced by the Realist novels of England, where he worked during the 1870s as Portuguese consul in Newcastle-upon-Tyne. He did not like England much ('Everything about this society is disagreeable to me,' he wrote on a visit to Bristol, 'from its limited way of thinking to its indecent manner of cooking vegetables'). So he set his stories in Portugal, most famously *The Sin of Father Amaro* (1875), whose depiction of a young priest's affair with the daughter of his landlady caused considerable scandal when it was first published. In Scandinavia the Realist movement found its most powerful expression on the stage. The Swedish playwright August Strindberg (1849–1912) followed the precepts of Zola's essay 'Naturalism in the Theatre' (1881) in his plays *The Father* (1887) and *Miss Julie* (1888), which eschewed elaborate dramatic structures in favour of the exploration of character. Meanwhile his Norwegian counterpart Henrik Ibsen, writing in Danish, used carefully constructed plots to expose the sordid and oppressive realities behind the respectable facade of bourgeois life in plays such as *A Doll's House* (1879) and *The Master Builder*

(1892). Ibsen was a strong influence on the Irish playwright George Bernard Shaw (1856–1950), who conveyed a strongly social-critical message in plays such as *Widowers' Houses* (1892), an attack on slum landlords, *Mrs. Warren's Profession* (1893), an exposure of sexual hypocrisy, and *Pygmalion* (1912), a comedy of manners centred on the cultural gulf between the classes. *The Weavers* (1892) by Gerhart Hauptmann (1862–1946) dramatized the plight of poor and oppressed Silesian workers in the 1840s. Before the advent of Realism contemporary drama had tended to be both superficial and artificial, as for example in the farces of Georges Feydeau (1862–1921), with their convoluted plots and unlikely coincidences; afterwards, though comedies and farces continued to be produced, contemporary theatre acquired a serious cultural cachet.

Realism even entered the highly artificial world of opera, which, after the unification of Italy, came under the influence of *verismo* in Italian literature. This was spearheaded by Luigi Capuana (1839–1915), who had begun as a Romantic poet but began writing in the 1870s what he called 'the poetry of the real'. With his contemporaries such as Giovanni Verga (1840–1922) he turned from history to the present, and from Romanticized subjects like the *carbonari* to the actual lives of the people. In 1890, Verga's play *Cavalleria Rusticana (Rustic Chivalry)* was turned into a one-act opera by the Tuscan composer Pietro Mascagni (1863–1945). It told the story of the love affairs of a group of Sicilian peasants, a whole world away from the normal historical or fantastical subjects of Italian opera. *Cavalleria Rusticana* was often performed in the same bill as another one-act opera set in a village, *I Pagliacci (The Clowns)* by Ruggero Leoncavallo (1857–1919), first performed in 1892. In tune with the changing fashion, the ageing Giuseppe Verdi (1813–1901) turned from Romantic subjects such as *La Traviata* (1853), based on Dumas' *Lady of the Camellias*, to Shakespeare for his final works, *Otello* (1887) and *Falstaff* (1893). Neither of these operas used typical Realist subject matter, but both abandoned the traditional operatic alternation of recitative and aria for a flowing, through-composed musical style in which the sung parts follow conversational rhythms.

Verdi's successor was generally agreed to be the Tuscan Giacomo Puccini (1858–1924), who began as a Romantic composer, with operas such as *La Bohème* (1896), based on the 1851 book by Henri Murger, but then gravitated towards *verismo* with *Tosca* (1900), a work his publisher described as 'the opera I need, with no overblown proportions, no elaborate spectacle, nor will it call for the usual excessive amount of music'. *Madam Butterfly* (1904) and *The Girl of the Golden West* (1910) were more obviously indebted to Realism, being set in the present or very recent past, whereas the action of *Tosca* took place during the Napoleonic Wars. Perhaps the most extreme example of Realism in opera was provided by the Moravian composer Leoš Janáček (1854–1928), whose *Jenůfa* (1904), a story of infanticide and redemption set in an impoverished Moravian village, was one of the first operas to be written in prose and sung to conversational speech rhythms. Realist operas often caused a scandal when they were first performed. The everyday setting and working-class characters of *Carmen* (1875) by the French composer Georges Bizet, for example, shocked the audience, who received the work in stony silence. 'All these bourgeois,' Bizet complained, 'have not understood a wretched word of the work I have written for them.' *Carmen* ran to half-empty houses, and after a brief revival in 1876 it was not performed in Paris again until 1883. It did rather better in Vienna in October 1875, but its success reflected not least the fact that the spoken dialogue was partly replaced with recitatives, while a ballet using other music by the composer was now interpolated into the second act. Bizet himself did not live to see this dubious triumph; he had died of a sudden heart attack in June the same year, at the age of thirty-six.

In many countries the turn to Realism coincided, not fortuitously, with the rise of literary and cultural nationalism. One of the century's greatest examples of literary nationalism, the novel *The Doll* (1890) by Bolesław Prus (pseudonym of Alexander Glowacki [1847–1912], a journalist by profession), set in a precisely delineated Warsaw, depicted the failure of Polish aspirations in 1848 and 1863, with the protagonists caught in a social order dominated by snobbish aristocrats and unwilling to engage in revolutionary action to free the country from foreign rule. Russian writers turned especially to the defeat of Napoleon in 1812, above all in Tolstoy's *War and Peace* (1869), though this vast book – a work that the author himself said is 'not a novel, even less is it a poem, and still less a historical chronicle' – is of course about far more than the celebration of Russian resilience in the face of invasion, and its depiction of the Battle of Borodino is anything but heroic. French painters until the end of the century and beyond engaged in repeated representations of the Napoleonic Wars, just as Italian painters gloried in the triumphs of the Risorgimento. Zola's novel *The Débacle* (1892) is an indictment of the incompetence of the French military leadership and the ruthlessness of the Prussian army during the Battle of Sedan (1870). In Realist art the Russian painters who called themselves 'the Wanderers' developed a genre of landscape painting designed to display the beauties of the Russian countryside as well as the hardships endured by those who lived and worked in it. In a similar way the series of tone poems entitled *Má vlast (My Homeland)*, written by the

Bohemian composer Bedřich Smetana (1824–84) between 1874 and 1879, contained musical representations of the Czech countryside, along with the nation's heroes and legends. The German painter Anton von Werner (1843–1915) specialized in precisely observed patriotic depictions of events during the unification of Germany (such was his fame, indeed, that he was even engaged for the thankless task of trying to teach Kaiser Wilhelm II to paint).

By the middle decades of the century, opera in Italy had become a genuinely popular art form, its tunes played by village bands across the country, and patriotic songs, or songs that could be interpreted as patriotic, gaining the status of modern folk melodies. Not least for this reason it took on a significant role in the development of Italian nationalist culture. Even though the arts had been heavily censored earlier in the century, it had still been possible to get a nationalist message across, as for example in the opera *The Italian Girl in Algiers* (1813) by the immensely popular Gioachino Rossini, where Italian slaves are urged to 'think of your fatherland, and boldly do your duty: Behold throughout Italy, examples of daring and valour are reborn once more.' *Norma* (1831) by Vincenzo Bellini (1801–35) featured an uprising by Gauls against the occupying Romans, while Verdi's *Nabucco* (1841) was full of not so subtly coded references to the Austrian occupation of northern Italy, notably in the famous 'Chorus of the Hebrew Slaves'. A performance in Parma of *The Horatii and the Curiatii* (1846), a now-forgotten opera by Saverio Mercadante (1795–1870), with its depiction of Italian resistance to a German invader in the Middle Ages, even caused a riot: when the words 'let us swear to triumph for the fatherland or to die in the attempt' were sung, the audience burst out onto the streets and forced the Duke of Parma to flee. Richard Wagner made the triumph of 'German art' the central theme of his music drama *The Mastersingers of Nuremberg* (1868), incorporating in it a prophecy from the Middle Ages that 'Evil deeds threaten us; once the German people and the German empire fragment under false foreign domination'. 'I am the most German being,' he had declared three years earlier in one of his frequent outbursts of cultural megalomania: 'I am the German spirit.'

Nationalism permeated the work of Russian composers throughout the century. Modest Petrovich Mussorgsky (1839–81) wanted his music to be 'an independent Russian product, free from German profundity and routine . . . grown on our country's soil and nurtured on Russian bread'. In his songs and in the early versions of his opera *Boris Godunov* (1873) he sought to reproduce Russian speech rhythms and intonation. *The Year 1812* by Tchaikovsky, first performed in 1880, with its bombastic concluding rendition of the national anthem to the accompaniment of cannon-fire, celebrated the Russian victory over Napoleon. The unfinished opera *Prince Igor* by Alexander Borodin (1833–87) provided a justification for Russian imperial conquests in Central Asia. Later in the century nationalism was expressed in the use of folk melodies, as for example in Smetana's opera *The Bartered Bride* (1866), which used Czech dance forms such as the Furiant in its typically Realist setting of a peasant village community. Following Smetana's example, Antonín Dvořák (1841–1904) also incorporated folk tunes into his work and turned them into concert pieces for his *Slavonic Dances* (1878–86). The Finnish composer Jean Sibelius (1865–1957) pressed his music into the service of the Finnish struggle for national identity and independence from Russia with compositions such as the *Karelia Suite* (1893) and above all *Finlandia* (1899–1900). In England, Edward Elgar (1857–1934) prefaced his first set of *Pomp and Circumstance* marches (1901–07) with the words 'I hear the Nation march/Beneath her ensign as an eagle's wing'. The concert pianist and composer Isaac Albéniz (1860–1909) used flamenco dance rhythms and Spanish folk music for virtuoso piano works such as *España* (1890) and *Iberia* (1905–9); many of his compositions were successfully transcribed for that most Spanish of musical instruments, the guitar. Edvard Grieg (1843–1907) was even granted a pension by the Norwegian government in recognition of his music's role in the formation of Norwegian national identity. However, he came to dislike what was perhaps his most famous composition, 'In the Hall of the Mountain King', part of his incidental music for Ibsen's 1867 play *Peer Gynt*, 'because it absolutely reeks of cow-pats [and] exaggerated Norwegian nationalism'.

RITES OF SPRING

With the decline of Romanticism, the standard forms of classical music staged a revival, though they had never entirely gone away. Demand from amateurs ensured that piano and chamber music found a ready market, and with growing middle-class prosperity and urban pride came the construction of purpose-built concert halls such as the Music Hall in Aberdeen (1859), the Gewandhaus in Leipzig (1884), the Concertgebouw in Amsterdam (1888), the Stadsgehoorzaal in Leiden (1891) and the Victoria Hall in Geneva (1894). The cult of the virtuoso led composers to collaborate with performers to produce concerti for them to perform. The relationship between Brahms and the Hungarian violinist Joseph Joachim (1831–1907) was a particularly famous example, though Brahms often ignored his technical advice, so much so that one critic described the Concerto for Violin (1878) as not so much for the violin as against it. After a period of eclipse following the death of Beethoven in 1827, the symphony moved once more to the centre of the orchestral repertoire. Robert Schumann did not begin to compose symphonies, concerti and chamber music until relatively late in life, while Brahms found the precedent of Beethoven so daunting that he took over two decades to write his First Symphony, which paid direct homage to his great predecessor's Ninth Symphony in the main theme of the last movement. So dominant did the symphony become as the central expression of musical genius that several composers later in the period, such as Anton Bruckner (1824–96), Gustav Mahler (1860–1911) and Jean Sibelius, wrote few other large-scale compositions. As a mark of its importance, the symphony increased both in length, with Bruckner's Eighth (1892) and Mahler's Third (1896) each lasting around an hour and a half, and in scale, with vast orchestral forces and sometimes a chorus as well. So many performers were involved in Mahler's Eighth Symphony (1910) that it was popularly known as the 'Symphony of a Thousand'. 'A symphony must be like the world,' Mahler told Jean Sibelius in a famous exchange: 'It must contain everything.' The Finnish composer, whose symphonies were much shorter and more tightly organized than those of his Austrian counterpart, preferred to stress the symphony's need for 'profound logic and inner connection'.

Such works stood, sometimes self-consciously, as in the case of Brahms, in a tradition going all the way back to Beethoven. With string quartets, concerti, piano sonatas and trios, the choral *A German Requiem* and other works in classical genres, traditional musical forms were at the heart of Brahms's output, like that of Mendelssohn-Bartholdy. They were, however, written off as conservative by the proponents of the 'new German school'. Here, new musical forms such as the symphonic poem, invented by Liszt, or the music drama, created by Wagner, were regarded as the music of the future: free-flowing, narrative, representational. For Wagner music drama was a 'total work of art', whose performance was a kind of sacred rite, literally so in *Parsifal*, his final work, performed in 1882 at the innovatory theatre he had built in Bayreuth for his operas in 1874–6. For critics like Eduard Hanslick (1825–1904), music could awaken emotion in the listener but it could not represent it in itself. Wagner for his part condemned Hanslick and his supporters as a 'musical temperance society' afraid of emotional expression, and sneered at Hanslick's 'gracefully concealed Jewish origin'. Yet the 'war of the Romantics' concealed the fact that the two sides had much in common. Brahms declared privately 'I am the best of Wagnerians', and his music was often regarded as highly unconventional: an early performance of his First Piano Concerto in 1859 was hissed by the audience, who found its vast first movement and delayed piano entry too strange to stomach. Both sides represented different variants of late Romanticism. Wagner was thought to have pushed forward the boundaries of harmony into new realms of chromaticism, especially with *Tristan and Isolde* (1857–9), but as Schoenberg later pointed out, Brahms's own handling of tonality was just as innovatory.

The search for a 'new music' by the Wagnerians expressed a growing dissatisfaction with conventional cultural forms that could be found in many branches of the arts in the later decades of the nineteenth century. In painting the camera was beginning to subvert Realism and representation and forced artists to rethink the nature of their business. Sharing many of the basic features of Realism, above all its focus on the ordinary and the everyday, a group of Parisian artists led by Claude Monet, Pierre-Auguste Renoir (1841–1919), Alfred Sisley (1839–99) and Camille Pissarro (1830–1903), and influenced by Édouard Manet, broke free of the conventions of the Academy to paint not so much static, finished representations of reality as works recording its often fleeting impressions on the observer. They reacted to the rejection of their work by the Academy's annual Salon by forming a *Salon des Refusés* (Exhibition of Rejects) in 1863. Eventually known as the Impressionists, a term invented by a critic of Monet's *Impression, Sunrise* (1872), they used free brushstrokes and paintings created *en plein air* rather than in the studio to record the effects of light in bold colours. Monet even painted the same subject – haystacks, for example, or Waterloo Bridge, or Rouen Cathedral – scores of times in succession to show the impression it made on the viewer in different kinds of sunlight, mist, fog, or shade, at different times of the day or the year. The use of vivid and constantly changing colour offered the Impressionists a conscious alternative to photography, at a time when colour film had been invented only on an experimental scale without entering general circulation. Met initially with public ridicule, the Impressionists had gained widespread acceptance by the end of the nineteenth century.

Impressionism found its way into music through the compositions of Claude Debussy (1862–1918), though he himself denied that his works were what 'imbeciles call "impressionism" a term employed with the utmost inaccuracy'. Eschewing traditional musical form, he composed piano and orchestral pieces that used unconventional harmonies and subtle timbres to evoke the moods and emotions aroused by subjects such as mists, gardens in the rain, reflections on the water, a submerged cathedral, the hills of Anacapri or, in his most extended orchestral work, *La Mer*

(1903–5), the play of the waves and their dialogue with the wind. His compatriot Maurice Ravel (1875–1937), who also rejected the categorization of his works as Impressionist, produced more abstract music, but several of his pieces, such as the piano suite *Miroirs* (1905), with its evocations of a boat on the waves or church bells in a valley, could fairly be described as belonging to the genre. A major influence on Debussy in particular was the French Symbolist movement in literature, which represented a significant move away from Realism and towards spirituality and the imagination. It was futile, argued a 'Symbolist Manifesto' published in 1886 by the Greek-born poet Jean Moréas (1856–1910), to attempt to represent reality in a direct way: what was required was, as in the work of the Impressionists, to depict 'not the thing, but the effect it produces'. The three poets named in the manifesto, Charles Baudelaire (1821–67), Paul Verlaine (1844–96) and Stéphane Mallarmé (1842–98), used the sounds of words as much as their meaning to convey the impression of their subject. Debussy and Ravel were inspired by the Symbolist poets to write a number of compositions, notably Debussy's symphonic poem for orchestra *Prélude à l'après-midi d'un faune* (1894) and Ravel's *Trois Poèmes de Stéphane Mallarmé* (1914) for soprano and chamber ensemble.

Symbolist painters such as the German Franz von Stuck (1863–1928), whose painting *Sin* (1893) showed a female nude emerging seductively from the shadows, the Norwegian Edvard Munch (1863–1944), best known for *The Scream* (1893), and the Austrian Gustav Klimt (1862–1918), whose *Judith and the Head of Holofernes* (1901) surrounded an erotically charged female semi-nude with Byzantine-style gold, retained a figurative core to their work while placing it in a determinedly non-figurative context. The emphasis on surface decoration in Klimt's paintings paralleled the emergence of *Art Nouveau* or *Jugendstil* in the decorative arts in the 1890s, with its curves and parabolas and cursive scripts. The new style was evident, for example, in the architectural decoration of the Norwegian town of Ålesund, rebuilt in three years after its complete destruction by fire in 1904, and in many buildings of the newly constructed Hungarian city of Pest. In Russia writers such as Alexander Alexandrovich Blok (1880–1921) and Andrei Bely (pen-name of Boris Nikolaevich Bugaev, 1880–1934) incorporated sound-pictures and experimental rhythms into their poetry. The Symbolists were rebelling against not only the notion of realistic representation but also the conscription of the arts into the service of nationalism, arguing instead that the arts were entirely autonomous from social or political life. The French writer Joris-Karl Huysmans (1848–1907) dealt in his novel *Against Nature* (1884) what Zola called a 'terrible blow' to Realism: the action, or rather inaction, of the novel takes place in a hallucinatory world in which the imagined becomes more real than the real. In Oscar Wilde's novella *The Picture of Dorian Gray* (1890) the ravages of the protagonist's dissolute life are visited upon his portrait, while his own physical appearance remains untouched by age or the consequences of sin. Art, argued Wilde and the other proponents of Aestheticism in the 1890s, should be pursued for art's sake, and for no other purpose.

These developments opened the way to the separation of art from representation and the severing of its ties with centuries-old conventions. The English painter and art critic Roger Fry (1866–1934) coined the term 'Post-Impressionism' in 1910 for an exhibition in London of the work of Paul Gauguin, Vincent van Gogh and others, who departed from the subtleties of Impressionism by employing vivid and increasingly arbitrary colours in their paintings. Gauguin's pictures of life among South Sea islanders, such as *Spirit of the Dead Watching* (1892), used colour not as a representation of the subject but as an interpretation of the subject's emotions, as did the whorled clouds in van Gogh's *Starry Night* (1889). Another of the featured artists, Paul Cézanne (1839–1906), used geometric forms that underpinned figurative representations of landscapes, departing further from the representational conventions of Impressionism. A further step was taken in the paintings of Henri Matisse (1869–1954), where the pigments bore no relation at all to the natural colours of the subject: in his *Woman with a Hat* (1905), for example, brushstrokes of green cover the nose and forehead of the sitter. *Charing Cross Bridge* (1906) by André Derain (1880–1954) was coloured in strident greens, blues, reds and yellows. A critic compared the work of Matisse and Derain to that of wild animals – *Fauves* – and so they became known as the Fauvists. Their work had parallels in Germany, where in Dresden in 1905 Ernst Ludwig Kirchner (1880–1938) and others formed the group known as *Die Brücke* (The Bridge), whose works sought to express the inner creative urge of the artist: hence the name 'Expressionist'. More radical still was *Der Blaue Reiter* (The Blue Rider), a group formed in Munich in 1911 after a painting by Franz Marc (1880–1916) of a blue horse against a background of red, yellow, purple and blue hills.

'We have ceased to ask: "What does this picture represent?" and ask instead: "What does it make us feel?"' wrote the art critic Clive Bell (1881–1964) in 1912 on the occasion of a second Post-Impressionist exhibition in London, in words that equally applied to other trends in the visual art of the time. Another of the Blue Rider's members, the Russian émigré Wassily Wassilyevich Kandinsky (1866–1944), set not only colour but also form adrift from its moorings in figurative representation and created the first abstract paintings, with titles such as *Squares with Concentric Circles* (1913). In Paris the 'Cubists' Georges Braque (1882–1963) and Pablo Picasso (1881–1973) dissolved the surface of pictures into a complex set of geometric patterns representing a view of the subject from a variety of different angles, replacing the bright colours of the Fauvists with a uniform pale wash of colour, usually grey or brown. The subject of the painting could still be discerned but was broken up like a kaleidoscope, as in Braque's *Violin and Candlestick* (1910). But by 1912 the Cubists were using collage to eliminate the perception of depth and perspective altogether, as in Picasso's *Glass and Bottle of Suze* (1912), where pieces of newspaper are stuck onto the surface of the painting seemingly disconnected from its ostensible subject. These developments quickly exerted a general European influence, leading to paintings with titles such as *Amorpha: Fugue in Two Colours* (1912) by the Czech artist František Kupka (1871–1957), or *Abstract Speed and Sound* (1913–14) by the Italian Futurist Giacomo Balla (1871–1958). Futurism was yet another of the numerous groups and movements that emerged in the last decade and a half before the outbreak of the First World War. Created by the poet Filippo Tommaso Marinetti (1876–1944), it attempted to capture noise and movement as well as other aspects of what his 1909 *Futurist Manifesto* described enthusiastically as a future dominated by machines, by conflict, and by aggression. 'We will glorify war,' he wrote, 'the world's only hygiene – militarism, patriotism, the destructive gesture of freedom-bringers, beautiful ideas worth dying for, and scorn for woman.'

The Futurists' worship of the machine stood in sharp contrast to the revival of disappearing folk traditions that formed part of the effort to create a national culture. Hans Aall (1869–1946), founder of the Norwegian Folk Museum, declared that the purpose of his collection was to remind his fellow countrymen 'that first and foremost we are a people . . . we are Norwegian'. Organizations like the English Folk Song Society sprang up at the end of the century, and musicians such as Ralph Vaughan Williams (1872–1958) began recording on wax cylinders some of the now usually rather old men and women who sang the traditional songs of the countryside. All of this sounded perfectly innocuous. It conjured up images of sandal-wearing, homespun-clad, middle-class intellectuals searching for an alternative lifestyle that would get away from industrially produced goods and an urban way of life and recapture the natural, simple skills and styles of traditional folk art. The Arts and Crafts movement begun in the 1880s by William Morris (1834–96), under the influence of John Ruskin, tried to do just that. So did the *Werkbund*, the German group whose leading figure, the architect Hermann Muthesius (1861–1927), published in 1904 a three-volume survey of the English house written in the spirit of the Arts and Crafts movement. Similar associations were founded in Austria and Switzerland in 1912 and 1913 respectively. Their critique of industrial capitalism lent their work a distinctly left-wing tone.

But there was a more disruptive side to the recovery of 'primitive' folk culture. As the European empires cemented their hold on their African and Asian colonies, African artworks like Benin bronzes were imported into Europe and exerted a strong fascination on artists seeking a way forward from Realism. After Picasso first saw African art in a Paris exhibition in 1907, he began to experiment with incorporating its forms into his own work, above all in his painting *Les Demoiselles d'Avignon* (1907), which portrayed a group of prostitutes, two of them wearing African masks, in a two-dimensional representation that marked an important stage on his road to Cubism. The term 'primitivism' was soon used to describe such work – and not only in the visual arts. In music, composers such as Béla Bartók (1881–1945), who, like Vaughan Williams, travelled the countryside recording folk songs, discovered that the rhythms and harmonies of folk music were often very different from those of the European classics. Previous appropriations by classical composers had smoothed them over, adjusting their rhythms and domesticating their harmonies. Instead, Bartók left them raw and unvarnished when he began incorporating them into his own work.

Other composers also started pushing up against the boundaries of tonality, already extended by Wagner, and eventually burst through them altogether. It was a personal experience that prompted Arnold Schoenberg to begin composing music without any definable key – his wife's affair with the painter Richard Gerstl (1883–1908), who committed suicide when she returned to her husband. In the Second String Quartet (1908) and the song cycle *The Book of the Hanging Gardens* (1908–9), Schoenberg cut the music adrift from traditional tonality. With his atonal 'melodrama' *Pierrot Lunaire* (1912) he tried to compensate for the loss of harmony by deploying a series of elaborate formal devices in the accompaniment provided by a small chamber ensemble to the poems half-spoken, half-sung by the soprano performer. 'Away with stylized and protracted emotion,' he wrote: his music, he said, was 'not built, but expressed'. Schoenberg was followed on his journey into atonality by two of his pupils, Alban Berg (1885–1935) and the meticulous Anton Webern (1883–1945). But other composers too, while retaining tonality in their work, reacted against the lush harmonies and hyper-romanticism of music such as the enormously popular *Der Rosenkavalier* (1911). In this opera Richard

Strauss (1864–1949) turned from his earlier flirtation with dissonance in his operas *Salomé* (1905) and *Elektra* (1909) to a more conventional late-Romantic style. Sibelius wrote his grim, spare and dissonant Fourth Symphony (1913) explicitly 'as a protest against present-day music,' he wrote, referring to Strauss rather than to Schoenberg, adding that unlike late Romanticism, 'It has absolutely nothing of the circus about it.'

Modernist music frequently encountered protests, sometimes very vocal, in the opera house and the concert hall. On 31 March 1913 there was a riot during a performance of works by Schoenberg, Berg and Webern in Vienna; fights broke out, the police were called, and the concert ended prematurely. At a subsequent court trial brought over a punch thrown by the concert's organizer at a protester, one witness, the operetta composer Oscar Straus (1870–1954), commented acidly that the noise of the punch had been the most harmonious sound in the entire evening. But this event was eclipsed by the scandal caused by the first performance of the ballet by Igor Stravinsky, *The Rite of Spring*, on 29 May 1913, in the Théâtre des Champs-Élysées in Paris. Stravinsky had already written two very successful ballets on Russian folk themes for the enterprising impresario Sergei Pavlovich Diaghilev (1872–1929) and his Ballets Russes. The first of these, *The Firebird* (1910), had established him as an exciting new presence on the Parisian musical scene; the second, *Petrushka* (1910–11), proved even more popular, though it included episodes of bitonality – music played in two keys at the same time – and ended, despite Diaghilev's objections, on a note outside the main key. As soon as *The Rite of Spring* began, however, a faction of the packed audience broke out into derisive laughter; a rival faction began loudly to object, and soon the dancers onstage could not hear the music from the orchestra in the pit, into which, as the conductor Pierre Monteux (1875–1964) later remembered, 'everything available was tossed' by the rioters. The powerful, irregular, repeated rhythms and the dissonant phrases and chords issuing from the orchestra pit, combined with the heavy stamping of the dancers as they enacted a pagan rite that ended with a young girl dancing herself to death, drove the audience into a frenzy. One onlooker recalled that the man sitting behind him 'began to beat rhythmically on top of my head with his fists', though he himself was so excited that he failed to notice for a time. A countess got up from her seat, her tiara awry, and shouted, 'I'm sixty years old and this is the first time anyone had dared to make fun of me!' Insults were exchanged and at least one challenge to a duel was issued. Amid loud whistling and shouting, the lights were turned up and forty of the offenders were escorted from the theatre, while the performances carried on doggedly to the end amid the uproar.

Press reaction the next day was uniformly negative. The music and the dancing had been 'barbaric', and the Ballets Russes should go back to Russia. Stravinsky later remarked that music was merely an abstract arrangement of notes, incapable of expressing anything but itself: but the powerful, uncontrollable emotions aroused by *The Rite of Spring* belied this verdict. The primitivism of the music, its framing in a pagan rather than a Christian context, and its use of multiple conflicting rhythms and tonalities, all broke through the smooth surface of European culture to disturb and upset. A challenge had been issued to the mellifluous late Romanticism of composers like Camille Saint-Saëns (1835–1921), Gabriel Fauré (1845–1924), or the much younger Sergei Vasilievich Rachmaninov (1873–1943). When in 1914 the English composer Gustav von Holst (1874–1934; he dropped the 'von' during the war) wrote *Mars, the Bringer of War*, its loud, repeated chords, harsh dissonances and pounding rhythms seemed to presage the end of the peaceful, complacent, cultural world of the prewar era. But that world had already been shaken to its foundations by modernist artists, writers and composers. Critics referred to the *Rite*'s 'barbarity', upset not only by the music but also by the choreography's departure from the classical balletic traditions of costume, dance and design. Just over a year after the riot in the Théâtre des Champs-Élysées, real barbarity was to spread across Europe with the outbreak of a world war.

7

The Challenge of Democracy

THE FINAL FRONTIER

One of the best-known news photographs of early twentieth-century Britain is a picture of a small, elegantly dressed woman, her feet well off the ground, being carried upright away from the gates of Buckingham Palace on 21 May 1914 by a large, burly policeman in a cap, her mouth open perhaps in protest, perhaps in pain. The woman was Emmeline Pankhurst (1858–1928), and she had been attempting to present to King George V a petition in favour of women's right to vote. Always respectable in appearance – 'beauty and appropriateness in her dress and household appointments,' one of her daughters commented, 'seemed to her at all times an indispensable setting to public work' – she had already had many brushes with the police as a result of the vigorous and often illegal campaign she had been waging for female suffrage. On this occasion she was hauled off – and not for the first time – to the women's jail at Holloway. Pankhurst always claimed that she was predestined to be a revolutionary because she had been born on Bastille Day, although her birthday was actually a day later, on 15 July 1858; she counted Carlyle's history of the French Revolution among her favourite books (it 'remained all my life a source of inspiration', she once said). There was certainly a political tradition running in her family; her grandfather had been present at the Peterloo massacre in 1819, and her grandmother had been active in the Anti-Corn Law League (1838–46). Emmeline's father, a comfortably off Manchester merchant, had been involved in the campaign to end slavery in the United States and had read his daughter the anti-slavery book *Uncle Tom's Cabin* (1852) by Harriet Beecher Stowe (1811–96) when she was a child. As in so many fields of nineteenth-century politics, the language of emancipation from slavery played a part in the campaign for the emancipation of other groups in society, in this instance women.

Both of Emmeline's parents supported women's suffrage. Her mother subscribed to the *Women's Suffrage Journal*, edited by Lydia Becker (1827–90), another Manchester woman, who in 1867 founded the National Society for Women's Suffrage; Becker also campaigned for the inclusion of women on school boards, and in 1870 stood successfully for election to the Manchester School Board. In 1874, Emmeline attended a meeting organized by Becker, and later wrote: 'I left the meeting a conscious and confirmed suffragist.' In 1878 she met a barrister known for his support for female suffrage, Richard Pankhurst (1834–98), twenty-four years her senior. Emmeline suggested they live together in a free union, but he objected that this would lead to social ostracism, at least for her, so they married in 1879, moving to London in 1886; she had five children with him over the course of their marriage. In 1889 the couple moved house to Russell Square, in Bloomsbury, which became a centre for suffrage campaigners, including a leading American, Harriet Stanton Blatch (1856–1940). Emmeline and Richard founded the Women's Franchise League in 1889 to work for women's right to vote in local elections. Before long, however, it fell apart, largely over the issues of trade unionism and Irish Home Rule. In 1903, frustrated by the lack of progress in the campaign for women's suffrage, Emmeline, her daughter Christabel (1880–1958) and four others founded the Women's Social and Political Union. It began recruiting supporters, particularly in Lancashire, it published a newsletter, it organized petitions and it held rallies. In May 1905, after a Bill for women's suffrage had been filibustered within the House of Commons, Emmeline and her supporters staged a noisy protest outside.

The publicity that the demonstration won them seemed to her to mark the arrival as a political force of the Women's Social and Political Union, whose members were dubbed 'suffragettes' by the *Daily Mail*. Their tactics grew bolder. In February 1908, Emmeline was arrested while trying to enter the Houses of Parliament to deliver a protest to Prime Minister Asquith. Charged with obstruction, she was sentenced to six weeks in prison. So welcome was the publicity this generated that in June 1909 she struck a police officer twice in the face to make sure she was arrested again. Her campaigns won massive public attention, with between a quarter and half a million people attending an open-air meeting organized in London's Hyde Park by the Women's Social and Political Union on 21 June 1908. The lack of reaction to the meeting shown by Asquith's government prompted the suffragettes to raise the level of radical action. Two of them threw stones at the windows of the Prime Minister's official residence at 10 Downing Street (there were no security barriers to prevent access). At the same time others smashed shop windows in the West End. When they were arrested and imprisoned in the women's jail at Holloway, fourteen women, including Emmeline Pankhurst, went on hunger strike in protest against the conditions under which they were held. The prison authorities responded by force-feeding suffragette prisoners through a painful procedure in which steel clamps were held in their mouths to keep them open, and tubes were inserted down their throat. Emmeline successfully resisted by threatening the officers with a heavy earthenware jug. 'Holloway,' she wrote, 'became a place of horror and torment. Sickening scenes of violence took place almost every hour of the day, as the doctors went from cell to cell performing their hideous office.'

In 1913 the government enacted the Prisoners (Temporary Discharge for Ill-Health) Act, dubbed by the suffragettes the Cat and Mouse Act. Under this statute prisoners, including Pankhurst, would be released from prison if they were suffering from ill health because they had gone on hunger strike, only to be re-arrested when they got better in order to serve the rest of their sentence. Meanwhile the police had become extremely rough in dealing with suffragette demonstrations, and Emmeline recruited a squad of female bodyguards trained in ju-jitsu and armed with clubs. Her supporters radicalized their attacks on property, unsuccessfully attempting to set fire to the Theatre Royal in Dublin, where the Prime Minister was due to speak. They threw an axe at Asquith's carriage and set fire to postboxes. They burned down a pavilion in Regent's Park, an orchid house at Kew Gardens, and some empty railway carriages at King's Norton station. The Canadian suffragette Mary Richardson (1882/3–1961), who had also blown up a railway station and broken in windows at the Home Office, slashed the *Rokeby Venus*, a painting by Diego Velázquez (1599–1660) in the National Gallery in March 1914, declaring: 'I have tried to destroy the picture of the most beautiful woman in mythological history as a protest against the Government for destroying Mrs Pankhurst, who is the most beautiful character in modern history.' Other suffragettes used acid to burn the slogan 'Votes for Women' on golf courses used by MPs, and assaulted individual politicians. Emily Wilding Davison (1872–1913), who had previously committed acts of arson and attacked a man in the mistaken belief that he was the Chancellor of the Exchequer, stepped out in front of the king's horse at the Epsom Derby on 4 June 1913, probably with the intention of attaching a slogan to it, and was run down. She died of her injuries a few days later, the first suffragette martyr.

This campaign of 'outrages' created severe strains within the suffragette movement. Emmeline Pankhurst tried to quell them by cancelling the annual meeting of the Women's Social and Political Union, denying members the right to object, and concentrating all decision-making processes in a small coterie she gathered round her, which included her daughter Christabel. Democracy was beside the point, she said: the suffragettes were 'an army in the field'. Several prominent members had already left in 1907 to form the Women's Freedom League, whose supporters soon outnumbered Pankhurst's: it confined itself to passive civil disobedience. Others were summarily expelled, including Emmeline's other daughters Sylvia and Adele, who had in her view become too close to the socialist movement. Perhaps, some have claimed, the suffragettes' willingness to use violence and their contempt for democracy foreshadowed the tactics of fascism, but it has to be remembered that their violence was overwhelmingly directed against physical symbols of male society (such as golf courses); unlike the fascists, they made no serious attempt to kill or maim individual people. They undoubtedly gave the cause of women's suffrage publicity it would not otherwise have had, but some contemporaries argued that their violence and extremism backed the government into a corner and made it more difficult for it to support votes for women.

Those contemporaries included many moderate supporters of female enfranchisement, a cause that by the late nineteenth century had a long if chequered history. In 1869 one of the most influential of all feminist tracts, *The Subjection of Women*, was published by the liberal philosopher John Stuart Mill (1806–73). In the early 1830s he had become a close friend of the intellectual Harriet Taylor (1807–58), who was separated from her husband; in 1851, two years after the latter died, the couple married. Her influence was evident in Mill's tract, which defined female emancipation as 'the removal of women's disabilities – their recognition as the equals of men in all that belongs to citizenship, the opening to them of all honourable employments and of the training and education which qualifies for those employments', together with the ending of 'the excessive authority which the law gave to husbands over wives'. Mill did not consider that women were necessarily equal to men in every sphere of life, but he thought it wrong that they should be prevented from finding out if they were; if they were inferior in any area, then free competition would prove it and legal barriers were not needed. The legal and social exclusion of women from many areas of public, political, economic and cultural life, he argued, was depriving society of the use of half its members, to its great detriment. Equality was in Mill's view, however, to be granted only to middle-class women and not the women of the proletariat. 'Where the support of the family depends, not on property, but on earnings,' he wrote, 'the common arrangement by which the man earns the income and the wife superintends the domestic expenditure, seems to me in general the most suitable division of labour between the two classes.'

Mill's tract was quickly translated into Danish, French, German and Swedish; by 1870 it was being debated by Russian feminists. In 1866–7, as the Second Reform Bill was being debated, Mill, now an MP, spoke in the House of Commons in favour of the enfranchisement of women, the first time this demand had been raised in Parliament. The Society for Promoting the Employment of Women, founded in 1859, supported him, leading in 1867 to Lydia Becker's formation of the National Society for Women's Suffrage. But this new body won no backing from Gladstone and the leading Liberals, and its fortunes declined. It was not until the 1880s that it began to revive in the wake of Josephine Butler's campaign for the repeal of the Contagious Diseases Acts, which, it was thought by many, would have succeeded more swiftly had women been in possession of the vote. In 1897 the disparate factions of the moderate women's suffrage movement were reunited in the National Union of Women's Suffrage Societies, led by Millicent Garrett Fawcett (1847–1929), sister of the campaigner for women's right to a medical qualification Elizabeth Garrett Anderson. The Union campaigned in meetings, pamphlets and magazines for the enfranchisement of women, and in 1907 staged a demonstration march through the centre of London. But whereas the House of Commons was now in favour of votes for women, particularly when legislative proposals were debated in 1886 and 1897, the House of Lords was not. Support for the Union grew with the publicity generated by the suffragettes; its membership far outweighed that of the Women's Social and Political Union – in 1913 it numbered 50,000 compared to the suffragettes' 2,000. But, like that of the suffragettes, the Union's campaign still showed no sign of success at the outbreak of the First World War.

Liberal feminism in France faced problems quite different from those encountered in England. While Republican politicians did a great deal to improve the education of women, believing it would wean them away from the Church, they were consistently opposed to giving women the vote, since they thought this would undermine the Republic by strengthening the forces of monarchism. Clerical conservatives for their part were horrified at the idea of giving women any rights as individuals, though ironically women's allegiance to the Church was founded not least on the fact that it provided one of the few spaces outside the home and the family where they could be active without having to run the gauntlet of male hostility. Nevertheless, a female suffrage movement emerged in 1876 and by 1883 it boasted a full range of feminist aims, including equality in the law, education, the professions and pay, as well as the vote. Its leading figure, Hubertine Auclert, was organizing street demonstrations for women's votes as early as 1885, and held a 'shadow election' to coincide with the general election of that year: fifteen women stood and gained a great deal of publicity, though they did not gain admission to the legislature.

In 1904, Auclert led feminist demonstrations in Paris on the centenary of the *Code Napoléon*, publicly tearing up a copy of the famous document. Her associates managed to gain access to a balcony at the official banquet held to celebrate the anniversary and released onto the astonished diners a quantity of huge balloons on which were written the words 'The Code crushes women: it dishonours the Republic'. In 1907, Auclert led another march through the capital, and the following year she invaded the Chamber of Deputies with twenty followers and threw leaflets at the politicians. Her most famous act of protest occurred the same year when she went with a companion into a polling booth in Paris during municipal elections and overturned the ballot boxes in protest against the disfranchisement of women. This gained her huge publicity but little support. The Female Suffrage Society had 10,000 members in 1913 but most of them were members of affiliated organizations such as temperance societies and women's trade unions. Even the biggest feminist demonstration, held early in July 1914, only attracted 6,000 people, a far cry from the hundreds of thousands who attended suffragette rallies in London. In the end, the forces ranged against the feminists in France were too great for them to overcome, and they had to wait until the end of the Second World War in Europe before women were granted the vote.

The largest women's suffrage movement outside Britain was in Germany, where feminists did not have to contend with the hostility of their most obvious political allies as they did in France. However, these allies – the Progressives – were in no way as numerous or as dominant as the Liberals in Britain or the Republicans in France. At an international feminist congress held in Chicago during the World's Fair in 1893, German feminists agreed to create a new umbrella organization, the Federation of German Women's Associations; it was established the following year. By 1914 its membership had risen to a quarter of a million. Within this organization and on its fringes a self-proclaimed radical wing emerged, led by the actress Marie Stritt (1855–1928) whose father was a lawyer and Reichstag deputy. The radicals campaigned against the state regulation of prostitution, bringing lawsuits against the police, organizing public meetings, and causing the topic to be debated seriously in the Reichstag for the first time. Police reaction was hostile and the campaign got nowhere. In 1902 the lawyer Anita Augspurg (1857–1943) and her companion Lida Gustava Heymann (1868–1943) founded a German Union for Women's Suffrage, based in Hamburg, where, exceptionally, it was legal for women to attend political meetings. The feminist Helene Stöcker (1869–1943), an admirer of Nietzsche's doctrines of personal liberation from the constraints of convention, advocated legal equality for unmarried mothers and illegitimate children, the free distribution of contraceptives, the legalizing of abortion and other measures which shocked bourgeois moral convention. This was too much for the moderate wing of the feminist movement, which took advantage of the legalization of women's participation in political activities in 1908 to pack the Federation with right-wing Protestant organizations and reject the proposal to legalize abortion. Stritt resigned in protest, to be replaced by a much more conservative figure, the historical novelist and journalist Gertrud Bäumer (1873–1954).

Between 1908 and 1914 the radical wing of the movement fell apart in a welter of mutual recrimination. Stöcker's 'New Morality' movement became caught up in the contradictions of its own ideology, as internal quarrels broke out over whether to focus on welfare measures like women's clinics or on political campaigning for women's rights. The leading women in the dispute accused each other of sleeping with various of the men on the executive committee in order to win their votes, leading to no fewer than seven lurid and highly publicized defamation suits, hardly an impressive advertisement for the consistency or durability of the 'New Morality'. The female suffrage organization split into three rival groups over the issue of whether women should ask for the same electoral rights as men, which would have meant acceptance of the disfranchisement of millions of working-class women through the restrictive property franchise in Prussia, or whether women should demand universal adult suffrage, which would have meant aligning themselves with the socialists in demanding the vote for all adult men as well as women in Prussia. The feminists also attracted growing hostility from radical nationalists on the right, who accused them of undermining the family. In response, they moved away from demanding women's economic and professional independence to emphasize their domestic roles as well. The growing numbers of female social workers in the movement brought in Social Darwinists who saw women's primary role as bearing and bringing up healthy children, while the attacks on feminist pacifists like Augspurg, Heymann and Stöcker from nationalists both within the movement and outside it drove them even further to the margins of politics. Thus German feminism, despite its outward appearance of strength, had become ideologically confused, weak and divided by the eve of the First World War.

If women's political activities in Germany were limited by law until 1908, then in Russia they were almost non-existent. During the 1905 Revolution, Russian feminists, outraged that the October Manifesto, in which Tsar Nicholas II promised wide-ranging reforms, contained no mention of female emancipation, set up the All-Russian Union of Equal Rights for Women. With 12,000 members by 1907, the Union campaigned for female suffrage and legal equality for women. Close to the moderate liberal Cadet (Constitutional Democrat) Party, it also belonged to the Union of Unions, an organization of middle-class professional groups that emerged during the Revolution. 'The struggle for women's rights,' declared the Union, 'is inseparably connected with the struggle for the political liberation of Russia.' It drafted appeals to politicians and deputies in the Duma, the Russian Parliament, as well as securing the endorsement of famous literary and cultural figures. The feminists mass-mailed petition forms, printed them in magazines, and passed them out on the street to be signed before being submitted to the Duma. One contained more than 26,000 signatures. The Union sent delegates to the 1906 Congress of the International Woman Suffrage Alliance (founded by American and British suffragists in 1902) in Copenhagen. In 1908 it organized an All-Russian Congress of Women, which was attended by over 1,000 delegates and debated a wide range of issues. It was presided over by Anna Pavlovna Filosofova (1837–1912), the grand old lady of Russian social feminism.

But the Congress was repeatedly disrupted by the socialist women who attended. They interrupted the speeches of the 'bourgeois' feminists, stamped their feet, and pulled faces. Political rights, they shouted, were irrelevant to working-class women forced to live in grinding poverty. The organizers shouted from the podium 'we don't want to listen to you', and the socialist women staged a walkout. On the right, conservative Duma deputies suggested that the feminists needed a mental examination; one even called them 'whores', bringing Filosofova to tears. The Union collapsed in the face of growing police harassment in 1908. Feminists responded by forming a new League for Women's Equality, which was smaller and better organized than the Union, and focused again on petitioning the Duma for the vote. In 1912 it won the support of forty deputies, and in the following year the leading liberal, Pavel Nikolayevich Milyukov (1859–1943), who had taught at a girls' academy early in his career, brought a universal male and female suffrage proposal forward. However, when he came to the provision enfranchising women, laughter broke out on the right, and the measure was defeated by 206 votes to 106. This marked the end of the campaign for women's enfranchisement. The feminist movement lost support, declining to a membership of a few thousand, mostly professional women and especially doctors. It had fallen victim to the continual rolling back of democratic and parliamentary institutions and organizations in Russia in the last few years before the outbreak of the First World War.

In most parts of Europe the feminists, bolstered by their creation of global organizations such as the International Council of Women (1888), the International Woman's Suffrage Alliance and many others, had at least succeeded by 1914 in putting votes for women on the agenda. The most important factor in determining the fate of the campaign for votes for women was nationalism. Nationalist associations had gained an authoritarian, masculinist, aggressive, sometimes antisemitic cast in Germany by 1914, and out of their milieu there even emerged the German League for the Prevention of Women's Emancipation (1912), complete with accusations, entirely erroneous, that the feminist movement in Germany was dominated by Jewish women. In Hungary, however, it was, since the small urban middle class was heavily Jewish in composition; here too nationalism, dominated by the rural gentry, was socially conservative, and most political parties opposed the very vigorous campaign of the Feminists' Association, founded in 1904 by Vilma Glücklich (1872–1927), the first woman to be admitted to a Hungarian university, and Rosika Schwimmer (1877–1948), a pacifist and close associate of the German radical feminists Anita Augspurg and Lida Gustava Heymann. In 1913 Glücklich and Schwimmer co-hosted the seventh congress of the International Woman Suffrage Alliance, in Budapest. Their campaign in Hungary included a mass demonstration in 1912 attended by 10,000 people, the distribution of placards and leaflets, the sending of telegrams to deputies, and the raising of questions about female suffrage to candidates at election hustings. It made little progress in winning support from Hungarian nationalists, who were suspicious of its Jewish leadership and opposed to its pacifist orientation in international politics.

Yet nationalism could also work in favour of women's rights. Feminists focused in many countries on education, arguing that women had to be taught the values and aspirations of the nation in order to transmit them to their children. In Bohemia this argument galvanized the feminist movement, whose petitions for the vote gathered more than four times as many signatures as their counterparts in Austria. Their arguments won the support of the leaders of the Czech nationalist movement, who were convinced of the need for Czech women to teach their children Czech rather than German. The women's suffrage campaign emerged from a nationalist campaign in 1905–6 for universal male suffrage. The Women's Suffrage Committee formed during this campaign by Františka Plamínková (1875–1942) argued that the issue of votes for women was above politics; in 1909 it demonstrated its nationalist commitment by demanding (unsuccessfully) that Czech become the fourth official language of the International Woman Suffrage Alliance, alongside English, French and German. The women's cause was strongly supported by the leader of Czech nationalism within the Habsburg Empire, Tomáš Garrigue Masaryk (1850–1937). Masaryk had married an American woman, Charlotte Garrigue (1850–1923), whom he had met on a visit to Leipzig: it was not least under her influence that he became a convinced and active supporter of women's rights. All Czech political parties accepted the principle of female suffrage, and put up women candidates for election to the Bohemian Diet, though with one exception for seats which they had no hope of winning (the one female candidate who was elected was in any case vetoed by the Habsburg-appointed governor).

The most successful examples of a symbiosis between nationalism and feminism occurred in Scandinavia. In Norway, which had been ruled by Sweden since 1814, the advocates of complete separation from Sweden, organized in the Radical Liberal Party, supported votes for women. The party had already secured a majority in the autonomous national legislature, the *Storting*, by 1893, though not the two-thirds needed for a change in the Constitution. The following year a petition for female enfranchisement garnered 12,000 signatures, and in 1895 a National Women's Suffrage Association was founded by Gina Krog (1847–1916), a teacher and journalist who had met Millicent Garrett Fawcett in London in 1880. Krog's association campaigned vigorously for the vote, gaining the municipal suffrage for women in 1901. While the Russian Revolution of 1905 distracted the Great Powers, a quarrel between the Swedish and Norwegian governments over the latter's right to appoint its own consular service led to negotiations in which Norway secured complete independence. An available Danish prince was found to serve as King Haakon VII (1872–1957). The new Constitution included a limited right to vote for propertied women in 1907, and led to the introduction of full and equal universal suffrage by a government of left-liberals in 1913.

Links between feminism and nationalism such as these had an even more dramatic effect in the case of Finland, which although part of the Russian Empire still possessed its own political institutions, including the traditional representative Estates. As nationalism grew, based on a campaign to secure equality for the Finnish language with the Swedish, a feminist movement emerged, centred on a reading group formed to discuss John Stuart Mill's *The Subjection of Women*. Linguistic equality was won in 1884, with feminists pointing out the crucial role of women in 'the education of children in their native tongue'. Women already gained the vote at a municipal level in 1872 and twenty years later Lucina Hagman (1853–1946), a schoolteacher whose pupils included the composer Jean Sibelius, founded a Union of Women's Societies to campaign for full political equality. Repression and a Russification campaign by the tsarist authorities brought all Finnish nationalists together. In 1905, when the tsar conceded civil liberties across the Russian Empire, a national legislature replaced the Estates; it introduced universal adult suffrage for men and women in 1906. The tsar clawed back his powers of veto after the crisis had passed, and by 1910 the Russian government was firmly in control again. Still, with women now sitting in the Finnish legislature, equal rights provisions were incorporated into the Finnish Constitution in 1909, though it would not be until 1917 that they came fully into effect.

By 1914 feminist movements in Europe had come to focus overwhelmingly on the right to vote in elections. To feminists, their demand seemed part of an unstoppable international tide of opinion that in the end would sweep them to victory. In some cases they pushed society a little way towards establishing equal rights over property and entry to the professions, though the actual numbers of female professionals were still small on the eve of the First World War. The struggle for the vote, often sparked by wider debates about representation, the extension of male voting rights, or national sovereignty, scored some successes at a local or municipal level in many countries, including Denmark, where the women's suffrage movement numbered more than 23,000 members by 1910. In 1912 a female suffrage Bill passed the Liberal-dominated Lower House of the Danish Parliament by a majority of 100 to 14, though it failed in the Upper House. Swedish suffragists won the right for women to stand in local elections in 1909 and secured a majority in the Lower House of the legislature for full women's suffrage in 1912, though as in Denmark the measure did not pass in the Upper House. Female suffrage was democracy's final frontier, but although feminists had made some advances as democracy's challenge to existing political systems mounted, there still seemed a long way to go by the time war came.

What united all the various national feminist movements, as well as the international associations to which they belonged, was the fact that they were overwhelmingly bourgeois in their composition and liberal in their politics. Even the English suffragettes fought shy of demanding the vote for women of all classes and merely campaigned for equal suffrage. Property laws everywhere still favoured men, so that if middle-class feminists sought equal voting rights for women, they were in effect only seeking them for a very small minority of propertied women. Moreover, the initial demand formulated by John Stuart Mill for equal rights as a recognition of women's simple equality with men as human beings had increasingly given way to a belief that women should be granted equality because they were different. On the radical left of the movement this meant that women's suffrage would bring international peace, an end to sexual exploitation, the abolition of regulated and possibly also unregulated prostitution, and other sweeping changes in social morality. Mainstream feminists thought women's suffrage would strengthen the ties that bound a nation together, as well as allowing female values their full weight in society. These beliefs found their expression in the creation in a number of European countries of the modern welfare state, where the long tradition of female philanthropy, rooted in religious faith, metamorphosed into the rise of modern, female-dominated welfare professions such as social work.

THE RISE OF THE WELFARE STATE

The emergence of women into the public sphere was paralleled by a major reorientation of the state in late nineteenth- and early twentieth-century Europe. This was above all a response to the increasingly powerful articulation of working-class interests, a fundamental aspect of the challenge of democracy in this period. Labour unrest reached unprecedented heights in the last decade and a half before the outbreak of the First World War, fuelled by a renewal of economic growth that reflected not least the increasing demand from governments for arms and ammunition. Some 400,000 workers downed tools in France in 1906, demanding the introduction of the eight-hour day. There were waves of strikes in the Ruhr in 1905 and 1912 as miners demanded improvements in their conditions of work and pay. The number of workers taking industrial action in Spain leapt from 35,000 in 1910 to more than 84,000 in 1913. The first national railway workers' stoppage in Britain took place in 1911 and the first national miners' strike in 1912. Alongside the great collective industrial actions were myriad small-scale, often short-lived strikes in particular factories and mines that addressed perceived injustices of a more localized character. Mounting labour unrest created a growing challenge to the tsarist regime in Russia, culminating in a general strike in St Petersburg in July 1914. Such actions increasingly bore a noticeable political element, as in the general strike and mass demonstration held on 'Red Thursday', 10 October 1907, in Budapest to call for universal male suffrage, or on 'Red Wednesday' in Hamburg on 17 January 1906, when demonstrators tried unsuccessfully to prevent the curtailment of workers' voting rights.

    The increasing scale and frequency of strikes accompanied the growth across Europe of the trade union movement. In many countries this went back to the post-revolutionary decades in the middle of the century. In

1855 the Scottish miner Alexander Macdonald (1821–81) noted that during a strike in Lanarkshire 'our divided condition served well the masters, if they were, in any instances, wishing to resist a just demand'. He urged the creation of a union so that 'our own anarchy should be overthrown'. This led to the formation in 1863 of the Miners' National Association. A national Trades Union Congress was then created in 1868. Its basis was much more secure than that of previous attempts in the first half of the century, because it was essentially a federation of individual craft unions with a strong local base – so-called 'new model unions' like the Amalgamated Society of Carpenters and Joiners, founded in 1860 by Robert Applegarth (1834–1924). The British trade unions became a permanent part of the industrial scene in defiance of all the attempts of employers to stop them. The number of trade union members increased from just over one and a half million in the 1890s to two and a half million in the 1900s and more than four million by 1914.

Unionism in other countries was considerably less successful. In Spain the Socialist Asturian Miners' Union rose in 1910 from the ashes of smaller local unions that had been destroyed by the employers over the previous few years. It formed part of the socialist trade union federation, the General Union of Workers (Unión General de Trabajadores), which had grown in membership from 3,355 at its foundation in 1888 to 40,000 in 1910 and nearly 120,000 in 1914 as individual trade unions signed up. It had to contend with a serious rival, the National Confederation of Labour (Confederación Nacional del Trabajo). Founded in 1910 on the principle of anarcho-syndicalism, the doctrine of overthrowing the capitalist state through a universal general strike, this rival organization won support particularly from railway and electrical workers. Membership covered only a small proportion of workers as a whole. The same was true of Germany. Although more than two million German workers belonged to unions by 1914, these unions were still relatively weak, and the number of collectivebargaining agreements in force was minimal – a sharp contrast to the situation in Sweden, where the national organizations of the employers and the unions formally recognized each other in 1906. Most German employers insisted strongly on their right to take decisions about pay and conditions without consulting their employees. Even in 1910 or 1911, when the German mineworkers were at their strongest, only 40 per cent of miners in the Ruhr were members of any trade union. The movement was divided by the formation of Catholic and liberal trade unions to rival the dominant socialist ones, and, as also in France, strike-breakers countered the trade union movement by forming 'yellow' unions of their own, paid by the employers.

The weakness and fragmentation of the unions in France, and the repeated failure of strike movements to gain their limited and practical ends, prompted a small revolutionary minority to embrace the radical principle of anarcho-syndicalism. The General Confederation of Labour (Conféderation Générale du Travail), founded in 1895, opposed affiliation with any political party. Its leading figure, the journalist Émile Pouget (1860–1931), advocated sabotage as a means of industrial struggle and saw the general strike as a political weapon with which to bring down the state. But its strikes failed, largely because funds were low. Most of its members were reformists, drawn in particular by one of its constituent organizations, the Bourses du Travail (labour exchanges), which offered practical assistance to workers of all kinds in finding jobs and in so doing helped break down barriers of occupational particularism. There were seventy-four of these in France by 1901, but although their guiding spirit, the radical journalist Fernand Pelloutier (1867–1901), thought of them as a revolutionary state within the state, they depended, paradoxically, on government subsidies for their financial viability. Strikes had become legal in 1864 and unions twenty years later, but, as in Britain, the law made unions liable to damages if they prompted workers to break their contract, used threats, or engaged in 'fraudulent manoeuvres'. French trade unions often dissolved themselves and regrouped under a new name to evade these restrictions, but this imposed tight limits on their freedom of action.

Despite such weaknesses, the rise of the trade unions across Europe, along with the repeated occurrence of strikes, was a major force in driving governments to introduce social legislation to try and reduce worker discontent. Sometimes this had a clear political motive. Conscious of the threat to public safety posed by the long hours worked by railway engine drivers – in the 1860s a driver threatened with dismissal for failing to stop at three stations revealed he had been driving for thirty-eight consecutive hours and had fallen asleep in the cab – French governments repeatedly pressed the railway companies to impose limits, and were finally successful in 1891, when the companies agreed to a twelve-hour maximum working day. Public concern could also inform the introduction of improvements. The British Coal Mines Regulation Acts of 1860 and 1872 introduced numerous safety precautions enforced by an inspectorate. In 1880 legislation was finally passed in the United Kingdom making employers liable for industrial accidents, reflecting the pressure of the new trade unions and the public sympathy that often greeted reports of deaths and injuries. Other laws required proper sanitation in workplaces, and regulated conditions in all kinds of trades. However, a comprehensive programme of social welfare still had to be introduced. Especially if they became too old to work, or fell ill, workers faced an uncertain and often extremely impoverished future.

The major change in this respect was initiated by none other than Bismarck, who introduced a range of state welfare measures in the 1880s. The state, declared the Iron Chancellor, had to 'meet the justified wishes of the working classes . . . through legislation and administration'. Linked to aristocratic paternalism in Bismarck's own mind, this 'state socialism', as he himself called it, soon outgrew its political roots. In 1883 he introduced health insurance through sickness funds, to which workers themselves had to contribute two-thirds but were rewarded by the right to stand for election to the managing committees, which they came to dominate after the turn of the century. By 1885 sickness insurance schemes in Germany covered 4.3 million workers. An accident insurance scheme followed in 1884 and a pension scheme for the old and infirm in 1889, all of them backed to a considerable extent by the state. The limitations of these schemes were clear. The old-age pension, for example, covered only men over the age of seventy, and even at the end of the century a mere 27 per cent of male workers lived beyond this age. Still, a few months after Bismarck's departure from office in 1890, the scope of these schemes was extended, night work by women and adolescents was banned, and legislation was passed restricting hours of work. By the eve of the First World War more than 15 million Germans were covered by sickness insurance, 28 million were insured against accidents, and a million were receiving pensions. None of these measures stopped people from voting for the socialists, but they may well have played a part in preventing the working classes from supporting the socialist left wing.

Bismarck's initiatives in Germany were followed in other European countries. In Hungary a factory inspectorate was established in 1884 and compulsory health insurance, inaugurated in 1900, covered over a million workers by 1911. In 1907 the government introduced compulsory accident insurance, providing free medical care for up to ten weeks and paid sick leave for the victims of industrial accidents. A limited old-age pension fund was set up in Italy in 1898 with state backing, while in Sweden state grants for health insurance were inaugurated in 1891 and a universal public-pensions insurance scheme, the first fully comprehensive system in Europe, was introduced in 1913. In France workers' pensions were introduced in 1910 ('the greatest and finest reform of the Third Republic', as its *rapporteur* said in the Chamber of Deputies), and although only a third of those eligible actually made a contribution, it was a start. A law of 1905 provided for old-age pensions and sickness benefits, and by 1914 over half a million people were receiving at least some support from the scheme every year, while a law of 1898 established accident compensation supported by the state, removing the previous requirement for the victims to prove negligence on the part of the employer. In Britain the modern welfare state was established by the Liberal governments of the immediate pre-war years, driven partly by a genuine social conscience and partly by a wish, similar to that of Bismarck, to prevent the working classes from drifting away to socialism. These measures included old-age pensions (1908), labour exchanges (1909), the imposition of improved standards for house-building and town planning (1909), and National Insurance to provide for sickness benefits and unemployment pay (1911). All this began to undermine the Poor Law of 1834, although it was not actually repealed until well into the twentieth century.

These measures represented the extension of welfare schemes from the upper reaches of the working class targeted by Bismarck much further down the social scale. Hitherto poverty in its deepest and most radical form had been the object of religious philanthropy, which was gradually being replaced by private and municipal initiative. In Britain it was driven forward in particular by middle-class women such as Octavia Hill (1838–1912), who pioneered the 'model dwelling' movement for improved working-class housing, and founded the Charity Organization Society in 1869. This introduced into England the Elberfeld System of poor relief, pioneered in 1852 as a response to the 1848 Revolution in the industrial conurbation where Friedrich Engels grew up. The System established a network of overseers whose task it was to visit the poor, recommend a suitable level of support, check on the probity of their domestic circumstances, and find them a job as soon as possible, which they were obliged to accept on pain of forfeiting their benefits. It took the problem of poverty out of the hands of the Church and turned relief into an instrument of secular social control. The changing roles of secular and ecclesiastical charity over the decades can be observed with particular clarity in the case of the Netherlands, where a new law passed in 1854 made the Churches the primary relief agency; municipalities were only to step in as a last resort. More and more however, the state had to take on the burden of support – covering 40 per cent of the costs of poor relief in 1855, and 57 per cent in 1913. The medical profession increasingly urged a more dynamic approach to health care, because as the Dutch social commentator Jeronimo de Bosch Kemper (1808–76) wrote in 1851: 'Improve the health of the people and you will have removed a major, a very great cause of poverty.' The debate continued until in 1901 the Netherlands finally introduced a Public Health Act, a Housing Act and an Industrial Injuries

Act, taking away the primary task of combating poverty from the Churches to which it had been entrusted in the previous century. In many respects, however, such secular institutions were not so different from the traditional charitable institutions of the Christian Churches such as the Society of St Vincent de Paul, founded in Paris in 1833, which specialized in home visits to the poor that would not have seemed unfamiliar to the overseers of the Elberfeld System.

The rise of the welfare state was in essence a response to the growing popularity of left-wing politics, especially among the working class. Conservatives and liberals in the late nineteenth and early twentieth centuries could see no greater threat to their political position than that posed by socialism, whose central tenets were diametrically opposed to the priority given by mainstream political parties to the idea of the nation. Under the influence of Marx and Engels and their disciples, socialists came to believe that workers in industrialized or industrializing countries were so exploited and oppressed that they owed no allegiance to the capitalists who ruled them nor to the nation state they controlled. Still less did they have an interest in fighting wars, which would only use them as cannon fodder while industrialists grew fat on war profits. The declared aim of the socialist movement was to overthrow the central institutions of 'bourgeois' society, including private property, business corporations, the police, the army, the Church, and even the family. They were to be replaced by a state in which property would be owned collectively, children brought up communally, religion abolished, and businesses run by the workers. In practice, however, the politics of socialism turned out to be more complex, and less frightening, than these terrifying visions suggested. The socialists' bark was often worse than their bite, and the grand intentions stated in party programmes were in many cases belied by the pragmatism of socialist politicians in practice. Part of the reason for these developments was indeed the rise of the welfare state, which gave the workers a growing stake in the society that socialist theory said should be destroyed. To that extent, the political intentions of its architects could be said to have been fulfilled.

THE SECOND INTERNATIONAL AND ITS RIVALS

The Working Men's International, founded in 1864, had collapsed at the beginning of the 1870s and was formally dissolved in 1876, destroyed by internal dissension between the followers of Marx and Bakunin, and by the massive police repression that followed the Paris Commune of 1871. By 1889, however, the time was ripe for another attempt at uniting Europe's workers in a single movement, and a successor organization, generally known as the Second International, was founded in Paris. It stayed in being until 1914, holding regular congresses at which resolutions were taken and policy guidelines formed that were intended to be binding on all the different national sections. The dominant power in the International was the German socialist movement, which dated from the Prussian constitutional struggle of the 1860s, when Ferdinand Lassalle had founded the General German Workers' Association. Lassalle's policies and those of his successors included producer co-operatives controlled by the state, parliamentary sovereignty and universal male suffrage. In 1868–9 a second socialist party emerged, the German Social Democratic Party, under the leadership of Wilhelm Liebknecht, a schoolteacher, journalist and veteran of 1848, and the young turner and carpenter August Bebel, son of a Prussian non-commissioned officer. Both were strongly influenced by the ideas of Marx and Engels. In 1875 the two groups united at a conference held in Gotha, forming the Socialist Workers' Party of Germany. But in his *Critique of the Gotha Programme* (1875), Marx suggested that the ideas of the new party owed more to Lassalle than to himself. It was radical-democratic rather than socialist, and it made no mention of the laws of economic development, the class basis of the state, or the need for revolution. Bebel himself followed the principles of Eugen Dühring (1833–1921), who was not only not a socialist but actually an antisemite. The polemic written by Engels in 1877 in an attempt to counter his influence over the party, the *Anti-Dühring* (full title: *Mr Dühring's Revolution of Science*), was successful in winning Bebel and many others in the movement over to the basic principles of Marxism.

From 1878 to 1890 the Socialist Workers' Party of Germany was illegal. The years underground increased enormously the gulf between German socialists and German liberals and strengthened the party in its hostility to the Bismarckian state. The revolutionary ideology of Marxism and its promise of ultimate victory guaranteed by the laws of history proved irresistibly attractive in these circumstances. In 1887 at a Congress in St Gallen, Switzerland, the last representatives of the Lassalleans were defeated. In 1891, at a conference in Erfurt, the party, now legal again, renamed itself the Social Democratic Party of Germany (*Sozialdemokratische Partei Deutschlands*, or SPD) and passed a new programme, strongly Marxist in character. Marx having died in 1883, it was now Engels who dominated the party's ideology. He implanted in it a belief in economic determinism. Continued industrialization would bring the capitalist system to ruins on its own contradictions, as the working class increased in strength and numbers and experienced ever-increasing levels of exploitation. All the institutions of the capitalist state, from the Church to the army, the schools and the judicial system, were mere tools of indoctrination and would be swept away when the proletarian revolution came, to be replaced by a socialist, egalitarian, classless society.

Engels added to this set of beliefs, derived from Marx, a second element in the SPD's ideology which subtly altered its significance: Darwinian evolutionism, adopting it instead of the dialectical view of historical development, which was associated with the 'Prussian philosopher-royal' Hegel. Well before Engels's death in 1895, Karl Kautsky (1854–1938), a professional journalist, had emerged as the SPD's chief ideologue. Since it was a scientifically proven fact that the course of social evolution would bring the working class to power, all it had to do in Kautsky's view was to remain in existence and the revolution would come of its own accord. Thus from 1890 onwards the SPD tried to avoid the danger of being banned again, and laid ever greater stress on its peaceful and law-abiding character. The party focused obsessively on building up its own organization for the revolution. It rejected any co-operation with 'bourgeois' parties such as the Liberals, in order to keep itself socially and ideologically pure until the revolution came. The party also claimed that since the bourgeoisie had failed in its historic mission of creating a liberal society in Germany, the mantle of liberal reformism had fallen on the shoulders of the proletariat. This meant not only a commitment to working to mitigate the worst excesses of the system, but also a reliance on the parliamentary road to revolution. It was through gaining a majority in the Reichstag, the party believed, that it would grasp the reins of power. Confirmation of this thesis was seen in the steady increase in the SPD vote and membership from 1890 onwards, until in 1912 it became the largest party in the national legislature, with 110 seats. By the eve of the First World War, the SPD, with over a million members, was the largest political party not only in Germany but in the entire world.

Yet the SPD was increasingly beset by a sense of political paralysis. Attempts were made to find a way forward both on the right and on the left. On the right were the revisionists, led by Eduard Bernstein (1850–1932), son of a Jewish train driver in Berlin. Bernstein had been active in the socialist movement since 1872 and was one of the authors of the Erfurt Programme, but he had imbibed the principles of reformism during a period of exile in England. In a series of articles published at the turn of the century, he suggested that Marx's predictions of the growing immiseration of the proletariat had been falsified by events. The working class was actually becoming more prosperous, revolution was not going to happen, and it was time for the party to convert to liberal reformism. Bernstein's criticisms unleashed a furious debate within the party. Its rank and file saw these disputes as divisive, and backed the leadership as it silenced the discussion. The revisionists were a small, isolated group of intellectuals with no power base in the party and their ideas made little headway in the end. Much more numerous, and far more influential, were the growing numbers of pragmatists in the party, people to whom ideology, considered so important by Bernstein and his followers, was irrelevant. Men such as Ignaz Auer (1846–1907), a saddler who was the key figure in building up the party machine in the 1890s, believed in simply getting on with the job of recruitment and representing the interests of the working class. The Bavarian socialist leader Georg von Vollmar (1850–1922), a former army officer, was prepared to co-operate with left-liberals or with the state if it would help bring about necessary reforms. Thus in southern Germany the parliamentary representatives of the SPD voted for state budgets and worked closely behind the scenes with the liberals. More generally, members of the party took an active role in the elective parts of community services and health insurance administration. The trade unions focused on immediate, practical benefits for their members, and exerted a growing influence over the party. Its transformation into a mass organization required the appointment of a permanent, paid staff, which increased the number and the influence of the pragmatists by placing in positions of power people whose concern was with the day-to-day running of the party rather than with the wider issues of socialist theory, political principle and long-term strategy.

In Germany the police did not require specific legislation to harass and molest the political activities of a party regarded as hostile to the very existence of the state. The police exploited to the full their right to attend and 'maintain order' at public meetings, and used even the most trivial excuse to dissolve Social Democratic assemblies, while extending a wide tolerance to those held by parties of the right. By 1914 the great majority of SPD newspaper and magazine editors had spent months if not years in jail for offences ranging from defaming the police to lèse-majesté. Social Democratic party members or supporters were excluded from all forms of government service. There were no SPD army officers, judges, or civil servants. When the physicist Leo Arons (1860–1919), inventor of the mercury vapour lamp, became an active member of the SPD, Kaiser Wilhelm II declared: 'I will not tolerate socialists . . . as the teachers of our youth at the Royal universities'. A law was passed in 1898 specifically in order to sack Arons from the University of Berlin, where he taught. More generally, heavy industrialists like Krupp monitored the activities of their workers, employing a private police force to do so, and fired any who were found to be socialists.

Such discrimination aided the emergence of a left wing of the SPD that considered the reformist programme unworkable and urged direct action to bring about a revolution. The leading figure here was the journalist and writer Rosa Luxemburg (1871–1919), who in 1889 had fled Congress Poland for Switzerland in order to escape arrest by the Russian authorities. She studied at Zurich University, gaining her doctorate in 1897 with a dissertation on the economic history of modern Poland, then moved to Germany, where she married, thereby obtaining German citizenship. (The marriage was purely pragmatic and the couple never lived together, divorcing five years later.) Luxemburg's closely argued theoretical tracts, culminating in *The Accumulation of Capital* (1913), sought to identify the economic forces driving imperialism. But it was for her opposition to war that she became best known. Luxemburg argued that war could and should be stopped by a mass strike of proletarians in all potentially participating countries. She successfully introduced a motion into the Second International's Congress at Stuttgart in 1907 calling for a European general strike if war threatened. 'Social democracy,' she said, 'is simply the embodiment of the modern proletariat's class struggle, a struggle which is driven by a consciousness of its own historic consequences. The masses are in reality their own leaders, dialectically creating their own development process.' But while these beliefs made her a more democratic figure than, say, Lenin, her reliance on the masses to produce a revolution without leadership was doomed to failure. Her fellow radical Karl Liebknecht (1871–1919), son of the early socialist leader Wilhelm Liebknecht, a lawyer and Reichstag deputy, put forward similar arguments against the recruitment of workers as cannon-fodder in imperialist wars in his *Militarism and Anti-Militarism* (1907). But Luxemburg, Liebknecht and their handful of followers remained isolated figures on the fringes of the party until the outbreak of war.

Closely allied to the German Social Democratic Party was its Austrian counterpart, founded early in 1889. The Austrian socialists stood out from the Germans through their greater concern with theory (even the major theorist of the SPD, Kautsky, was an Austrian). Given their situation in the multinational monarchy, they were particularly concerned with nationalism, a subject hitherto rather neglected in the Marxist tradition. In *The Nationality Question and Social Democracy* (1907), Otto Bauer (1881–1938) conceded that nation states added a great deal to the sum of human culture through their differences, but he still subscribed to the Second

International's policy of preventing war by staging a general European strike. This was ultimately to prove futile. However, there was one successful socialist campaign to prevent war, namely in Sweden, where Hjalmar Branting (1860–1925), an astronomer-turned-journalist and founder of the Social Democratic Party in 1889, led a movement after the turn of the century to stop reservists being called up for a military campaign against the secession of Norway. Branting called a general strike under the slogan 'Hands off Norway, King!' Alarmed at the prospect of being unable to recruit an effective military force to mobilize against the Norwegians, the Swedish government caved in, and the two countries divorced peacefully. This was probably the only entirely successful example of a political general strike in Europe before the war.

The socialist movement in Britain was far less ideological than its counterparts on the Continent. The new model trade unions that emerged after the collapse of Chartism were closely linked to the Liberal Party. Only in the 1880s did socialist radicalism re-emerge. The first of the new socialist bodies was the Social Democratic Federation, led by Henry Hyndman (1842–1921), son of a wealthy businessman, graduate of Trinity College, Cambridge, and among other things a first-class cricketer. Appalled by the bloodshed of the Austro-Italian War of 1866, a sight he witnessed as a journalist, Hyndman was converted to Marxism when he read *Das Kapital* on an Atlantic crossing in 1880. His associates included William Morris, Karl Marx's daughter Eleanor (1855–98), and two skilled workers, the trade unionists Tom Mann (1856–1941) and John Burns (1858–1943). Once he had read Marx, Hyndman expected capitalist society to collapse of its own accord by the end of the 1880s at the latest. In 1890, undaunted, he revised the date to 1900, also to pass without incident in due course. His programme included the abolition of the monarchy and the army, and, paradoxically, the prevention of women's emancipation, which he regarded as a deviation from the purposes of socialism. Hyndman's dictatorial manner alienated all his main associates, and they had resigned by the end of the 1880s, at which time the Social Democratic Federation only had around 3,000 members. It was never more than a sect, but it was the only movement in Britain to keep Marx's ideas under discussion, even if it did not subscribe to them all. A more intellectual group, the Fabian Society, founded in 1884, named after the Roman general who had defeated Hannibal by delaying tactics rather than open confrontation, had around 2,000 members but made up for its tiny size by producing the influential *Fabian Tracts* (1884–1901). Their publications included contributions by prominent figures such as the playwright George Bernard Shaw, editor of

Fabian Essays (1889), and the social reformers Beatrice Webb (1858–1943) and her husband Sidney Webb (1859–1947). The major political representative of the working classes in Britain was the Labour Party, whose origins lay in the trade unions. These had acquired some 750,000 members by 1888, mostly organized in the Trades Union Congress. In 1886–7 the Congress set up an electoral committee to press for stronger working-class representation in Parliament. In Scotland and the north of England the trade unions broke with the Liberals and put up independent working-class candidates in elections to Parliament. In 1892 one such candidate, the Scot Keir Hardie (1856–1915), was elected for the impoverished London constituency of West Ham South. Hardie was of illegitimate birth, a former coalminer and miners' trade union leader. He was not a Marxist. 'More inspiration for the work,' he said, 'has been drawn from the teachings of Jesus than from any other source.' In 1893, Hardie founded the Independent Labour Party, based in Bradford, with representatives from Hyndman's Social Democratic Federation and the Fabians. It aimed to achieve the 'collective ownership of the means of production, distribution and exchange'. Initially dependent on local electoral pacts with the Liberals, the party won twenty-nine seats in the House of Commons in 1906, alongside twenty-six miners' union representatives elected on the Liberal Party ticket. In 1910 more than forty Labour candidates were successful, though Labour was not to displace the Liberals as the main party of the left until after the war.

French socialism was similarly weak and divided. The most important faction, and the one that bore the closest resemblance to the German model, was led by Jules Guesde (1845–1922), a veteran of the Commune who spent most of the 1870s in exile in Italy and was converted to Marxism in 1876. Guesde, a journalist and former clerk, was a frightening figure for the bourgeoisie: tall and thin, with shoulder-length hair, a large black beard, a pale countenance and metal-framed spectacles, he was ideologically rigid and intransigent. In collaboration with Marx, whose son-in-law Paul Lafargue (1842–1911) was a personal friend, Guesde formed the French Workers' Party in 1880. Marx, however, wrote to both men in 1883, shortly before his death that year, accusing them of 'revolutionary phrase-mongering'. When they assured him they were Marxists, he is said to have responded: 'What's certain then is that I myself am not a Marxist.' Guesde had a power base among the textile workers of northern France, where he used local social life to win adherents. In east-central France his party emerged from a secret society popular among the miners, *La Marianne*, while in the south of France he relied on the radical post-Jacobin lower middle class. With this rather disparate social base, the French Workers' Party had gained 16,000 members by 1898 and won thirteen seats in the Chamber of Deputies – the largest of the socialist factions in France but tiny by German standards. Unlike the German Social Democrats, the Guesdists never succeeded in winning over the trade unions, a crucial condition for success.

From 1881–2 the Guesdists had to face a rival group, the so-called Possibilists, led by Paul Brousse (1844–1912), a medical man. As with so many political parties, the Possibilists were originally given their name by their opponents, in this case Guesde himself, as a term of derision for supposedly selling out to the bourgeoisie. Brousse's response to this criticism was that he accepted the name and that Guesde was an Impossibilist. Brousse thought socialism would eventually be brought about by economic change; revolution was not necessary. In the meantime he focused on municipal issues and winning power at a local level. In 1889 the Possibilists won nine seats on the municipal council of Paris and two seats in the Chamber of Deputies. As his medical practice became more lucrative, so Brousse became more centrist, arguing that revolution in the end was not going to happen. His pessimism caused the typographer Jean Allemane (1843–1935), a former Communard and exponent of the general strike as a political weapon, to break away in 1890 to form another faction, the Socialist Workers' Revolutionary Party. Dominated by workers, it won five seats in the Chamber in 1892, but the deputies were so closely tied to the local constituency parties, who treated them as delegates who had to refer back for guidance on every issue, that they found life in the legislature impossible and broke away from the party themselves in 1896.

By this point a new figure was emerging who would unite and eventually dominate French socialism: Jean Jaurès (1859–1914). Jaurès called himself a 'cultured peasant'. He wore bourgeois clothes including a black frock coat, but dressed so untidily, with his trousers too short, and his pockets stuffed with books and papers, that he did not really seem to belong to any social class. His untidiness betrayed the fact that he was a professor of philosophy by profession. A brilliant speaker with a sixth sense for the mood of a crowd, he left the Radical Party to become an independent socialist when he realized the Radicals were not serious about social reform. He was joined by Alexandre Millerand (1859–1943), a lawyer who had made his name defending strikers in court actions brought against them by the state. Millerand tried to bring together the various socialist deputies including the Guesdists and Possibilists on the basis of a minimum programme that included the nationalization of monopolies, the municipalization of public services and the independence of small proprietors. In 1899, however, he accepted the offer of the post of Minister of Commerce and Industry in a Cabinet led by Pierre Waldeck-Rousseau (1846–1904), which included General Gaston Galliffet (1830–1909), notorious for his part in the repression of the Paris Commune. As a result the socialists disowned Millerand as an opportunist, and indeed he ended up after the First World War as a rather conservative President of the Republic.

Jaurès succeeded where Millerand failed. He benefited from the break-up of the Possibilists and the growth in the number of independent socialist deputies. In 1900 he formed a party of his own, concluding electoral alliances at a local level with the Radicals to boost the numbers of his deputies in the Chamber. He repaid the debt by backing the anticlerical legislation introduced by the Radicals in the early 1900s. Following the German line of non-co-operation with bourgeois parties, Guesde persuaded the 1904 Amsterdam Congress of the Second International to issue a condemnation of Jaurès. Cleverly accepting this, Jaurès ended his co-operation with the Radicals and brought about the unification of all the socialist factions in 1905 as the French Section of the Workers' International. The 1908 programme of the party, rather like that of the German Social Democrats, offered something to everyone. Drawn up by Jaurès, it offered ultimate revolution to the Guesdists, use of the general strike when opportunity arose to the remaining Allemanists, and immediate electoral campaigning, municipal reform and the support of trade unions to those of a Possibilist cast of mind. On this basis the French Socialists doubled their membership to more than 90,000 by 1914. However, this was still less than one tenth of the membership of the SPD. The French movement remained prone to factionalism, with dissidents led by the fervent anti-militarist Gustave Hervé (1871–1944) on the left and the patriotic Alexandre Varenne (1870–1947) on the right. The party never forged close links with the unions, and despite some electoral successes never really succeeded in mobilizing a significant section of the peasantry. Nevertheless, by 1914 it was a force to be reckoned with, commanding 102 out of 601 seats in the Chamber of Deputies, almost double the number it had won in 1906.

French socialism also had to contend with a powerful rival on the left, namely the anarchists. While both wanted, in theory at least, the destruction of the existing order and the creation of a classless society, the socialists blamed inequality and oppression on the class rule of the bourgeoisie, whereas the anarchists blamed the very existence of the state itself. The socialists were prepared to wait for the revolution, whereas the anarchists wanted it immediately; the socialists were willing to a degree to work through the parliamentary system, whereas the anarchists repudiated parliamentary democracy and wanted direct revolutionary action, or 'propaganda by the deed'. Following Bakunin's defeat in the First International by Marx and his followers, the anarchists focused on destabilizing the state through acts of individual violence and terrorism. Their newspapers ran lotteries in which pistols and daggers were offered as prizes. Individual anarchists perpetrated outrages on bourgeois society through robberies, murders and explosions, in a campaign that culminated in 1894 with the assassination of the President of the French Republic, Marie-François Sadi Carnot (1837–94), stabbed to death in Lyon by the young Italian anarchist Sante Geronimo Caserio (1873–94) as he left a public banquet in an open carriage. Caserio declared his crime was committed to avenge the execution of another anarchist, Émile Henry (1872–94), who had detonated a bomb at the Café Terminus in the Gare Saint-Lazare in Paris, killing one person and injuring twenty; when reproached with killing innocent victims, Henry had replied: 'There are no innocents.'

Henry in his turn had let off the bomb as an act of revenge for the execution of Auguste Vaillant (1861–94), who had thrown a bomb into the Chamber of Deputies in 1893 (a home-made device, it was not very effective, and did not kill anyone, though it caused several injuries). Vaillant's last words before he was guillotined were 'Death to the bourgeoisie! Long live Anarchy!' These men entered the long list of anarchist martyrs and heroes, of whom the most famous was probably François Ravachol (1859–92). He tried to blow up apartment blocks where judges lived, and was convicted of murdering an ancient hermit near Saint-Étienne and stealing his savings, as well as killing a rag merchant and two elderly women. As the sentence was read out, he shouted 'Long live Anarchy!' The motivation for these seemingly random attacks was lucidly explained by Émile Henry at his trial: 'I wanted to show the bourgeoisie that their pleasures would no longer be complete, that their insolent triumphs would be disturbed, that their golden calf would tremble violently on its pedestal, until the final shock would cast it down in mud and blood.'

Such incidents lay behind the popular image of the anarchist, bearded and unkempt, beret on head and bomb in hand. It was also from this period that the most celebrated literary portraits of anarchists emerge – in novels such as *Germinal* (1885) by Émile Zola, *The Princess Casamassima* (1886) by Henry James, and *The Secret Agent* (1907, set in London in 1886) by Joseph Conrad. In fact, there were relatively few of these anarchist terrorists, and their main effect was to terrify bourgeois society and produce drastic police repression, most notably in the so-called *lois scélérates* ('villainous laws') of December 1893 (passed two days after Auguste

Vaillant launched his bomb), which allowed the French authorities to close down most of the anarchist press. Anarchism had an even greater impact in Italy and Spain, where the influence of Bakunin proved decisive. During a three-year stay in Italy, from 1864 to 1867, the Russian revolutionary had won the admiration of the younger generation of radicals. 'The advent of the social revolution,' Bakunin wrote optimistically, 'is in no country nearer than in Italy . . . The mass of Italian peasants already constitutes an immense and all-powerful army for the social revolution.' In 1874 he took part in an anarchist uprising in Bologna that ended even before it had begun, with the betrayal of the revolutionaries' plans to the police; after considering suicide, Bakunin disguised himself as a priest and escaped to Switzerland. Two years later, his disciple Errico Malatesta (1853–1932) and a Russian revolutionary, Sergei Mikhailovich Kravchinsky (1851–95), later known as 'Stepniak', went into the Campanian hills near Benevento in 1877, declared the king deposed, and began burning town archives. However, the army arrived and despite the support of the local peasants the anarchists were arrested, though they were acquitted by a sympathetic jury at their trial in 1878.

Malatesta survived into the Fascist era, sometimes in prison, sometimes in exile in London, working as an electrician. In this capacity he helped supply equipment used to rob a jeweller's premises in Houndsditch. When the police caught the burglars red-handed, there was an exchange of fire in which three policemen were shot. The robbers barricaded themselves in a house on Sidney Street, where a siege, attended by the Home Secretary Winston Churchill (1874–1965), ended in their deaths. Individual Italian anarchists were among the most active proponents of 'propaganda by the deed' in the 1890s and 1900s – men such as Gaetano Bresci (1869–1901), who assassinated King Umberto I of Italy, Michele Angiolillo (1871–97), who murdered the Spanish Prime Minister Antonio Cánovas del Castillo in revenge for the execution of five Spanish anarchists, and Luigi Lucheni (1873–1910), who stabbed the Empress Elisabeth of Austria-Hungary to death in 1898 with a four-inch industrial needle. In his diary Lucheni had written before the assassination: 'How I would like to kill someone; but it must be someone important so it gets in the papers.'

It was in Spain that Bakunin's influence was greatest. In the 1870s his Italian disciple Giuseppe Fanelli (1827–77) made contact with a small group of followers of Charles Fourier and Pierre-Joseph Proudhon, and succeeded in getting them to form a branch of the International dedicated wholly to Bakunin's ideas. Fanelli did not know any Spanish and spoke in French, but one of his listeners recalled how his voice 'could take on all the inflections suitable to what he was expressing, passing rapidly from

accents of rage and threats against exploiters and tyrants to those of suffering, pity and consolation'. They managed to find a following among
workers by encouraging political strikes in Barcelona, and their ideas had
a huge influence on the dispossessed rural labourers and small peasants
of the south. By the 1890s the anarchists were organizing mass demonstrations in many parts of Spain, leading to the 'tragic week' in Barcelona,
from 25 July to 2 August 1909, in which thousands demonstrated against
a call-up of troops for service in Africa. Over a hundred were killed by
troops brought in by the government, and 1,700 people were indicted for
armed rebellion, of whom five were sentenced to death and fifty-nine to
life imprisonment. These events resulted in the creation of the CNT, the
anarcho-syndicalist trade union, in 1910.

By contrast, anarchism was unable to take root in Germany, largely
thanks to the strength of the organized industrial working class. Its most
notable moment was in September 1883, when a small band of anarchists
put a huge bomb in a drain underneath the path along which Kaiser Wilhelm I, Bismarck and the German princes were due to pass to the unveiling
of the statue of 'Germania' on a hill overlooking the Rhine above
Rüdesheim. The carnage would have been considerable had they succeeded, but being short of money they could not afford to buy waterproof
fuses. It rained the night before the event, so the bomb did not go off. A
few weeks later they blew up the main police station in Frankfurt, and
when they were arrested they confessed to the earlier attempt at the monument. Three were beheaded, two imprisoned and two acquitted. In the
dock one of them shouted as he was sentenced: 'If I had ten heads left, I
would gladly lay them on the block for the same cause!' German anarchism's most lasting influence in fact was not in its home country but in
the United States. The bookbinder Johann Most (1846–1906), expelled
from the SPD in 1880, emigrated to America in 1882, changing his first
name to John. He played an active role in the emerging anarchist movement there, in which Italian emigrants were particularly prominent. In
1885, Most published his *Science of Revolutionary Warfare* (subtitled *A
Little Handbook of Instruction in the Use and Preparation of Nitrogly-
cerine, Dynamite, Gun-Cotton, Fulminating Mercury, Bombs, Fuses,
Poisons, etc., etc.*). For the rest of his life he was in and out of prison, on
one occasion condemned for supposedly having inspired the assassination
of President William McKinley (1843–1901).

One of the most celebrated of Most's followers in America was the Russian émigrée Emma Goldman, 'Red Emma' (1869–1940). In theory at least,
the anarchist and socialist leaders were supporters of female equality,
inspired by classics such as Engels's *The Origin of the Family, Private*

Property and the State (1884). The most widely read of such texts was *Woman and Socialism* (1879) by the German socialist leader August Bebel. It painted a drastic portrait of the social and economic exploitation of working-class women, especially those who were forced into prostitution, and held out the utopian promise of complete female equality in a post-revolutionary world in which the conventional restrictions of marriage and family life would no longer exist. Partly due to its influence, the most important socialist women's organization in Europe was the German one. The movement was brought together in 1896 from a number of small and disparate local groups into a functioning unit by Clara Zetkin (1857–1933), who was the dominant figure until the First World War. Born Clara Eissner in a small peasant village in Saxony, the daughter of a German schoolmaster and his highly educated French wife, she became active in the socialist movement in the late 1870s and met the Russian revolutionary Ossip Zetkin (1848–89), who became her mentor and partner. The couple did not marry, but she followed him into exile, first in Zurich then in Paris, and bore him two sons. Living in considerable poverty, they both contracted tuberculosis, from which Ossip died in 1889. Clara recovered and later married an artist, Georg Zundel (1875–1948), eighteen years her junior: she was no respecter of bourgeois convention in either of her two relationships.

It was in Paris that Clara Zetkin became passionately committed to a socialist conception of feminism after reading Bebel's tract and making the acquaintance of Engels. On returning to Germany after Ossip's death, she took over an ailing socialist feminist magazine and renamed it *Die Gleichheit* (*Equality*). The magazine, which had achieved a circulation of 125,000 by 1914, argued consistently that the proletarian women's struggle was an essential part of the general working-class struggle for the revolutionary transformation of society. Zetkin condemned the idea of a separate feminist movement as 'bourgeois' and polemicized ceaselessly against its leaders. Aided by Luise Zietz (1865–1922), a tobacco worker married to a Hamburg docker, Zetkin built up a team of 'agitators' who devoted themselves to the systematic recruitment of working-class women. At first, hampered by the legal ban on women's participation in politics in most parts of Germany, they met with little success. But after 1905, as these laws relaxed, and especially from 1908, when they were repealed, the movement grew rapidly, reaching 175,000 members by 1914. The members were overwhelmingly the wives of active male Social Democrats and trade unionists who had come to realize that womenfolk hostile or indifferent to their politics would hamper their commitment, especially in time of strikes or lockouts, and would endanger the socialist future by not bringing up their children to support the cause. The principle of women's emancipation, including full enfranchisement, was therefore written into the SPD's party programme.

However, the women in the movement were not expected to show any independent initiative. The biennial women's conferences held from 1900 to 1908 aroused particular hostility from the men of the SPD, who ensured that only one further conference was held before the war, in 1911. Still more controversial within the movement was the International Women's Day, founded on Zetkin's initiative by a resolution of the Women's Socialist International Congress in Copenhagen in 1910, following the lead of the American socialist women. On 19 March 1911 women in Austria, Denmark, Germany, Switzerland and the United States demonstrated for votes for women. The demonstrations, with processions of respectably clad socialist women silently snaking through the streets holding aloft banners demanding the vote, were held again in 1912, 1913 and 1914. Repeated attempts by the male leadership of the SPD to prevent them came to nothing, though the party did wind up its Women's Bureau in 1912. By this time Zetkin had long since gravitated to the extreme left along with Rosa Luxemburg (who kept determinedly clear of women's issues, regarding them as a distraction from her revolutionary activities), and she was replaced as head of the women's movement in 1908. The SPD leadership's commitment to enfranchising women was never more than token, as became clear in 1910, when the prospect of extending the vote to all adult males in Prussia became a possibility and was embraced by the party without any reference to votes for women.

Impressive in its size and its discipline, the German socialist women's movement had no rival anywhere else in Europe. In France a number of radical feminists, the most important of whom was Louise Saumoneau (1875–1950), a seamstress from a working-class family of cabinet-makers, founded a 'Feminist Socialist Group'. Saumoneau took Zetkin's line that a focus on women's issues was irrelevant to the overriding cause of revolution, and ran into open hostility from the mainstream socialists; in 1914 the combined socialists, with 90,000 members, numbered fewer than 1,000 women among them. The influence of the misogynist writings of Proudhon and the family-based economy of the artisan household was still strong in France. And the trade unions never approved of women's work, which they saw as undermining men's wages. There were small but significant women's socialist movements in Austria, Denmark and the Netherlands, and a number of women active in the Labour Party in Britain, but in the area of women's rights the Germans were even more absolutely dominant in the international movement than they were in the Second International as a whole.

Despite their disunity, organized socialist movements were perhaps the most powerful of all the pressures for the democratization of European politics in the quarter-century leading up to the outbreak of the First World War. With millions of followers, overwhelmingly from the industrial working class, the great socialist organizations of the day were publicly committed to achieving full equality for the masses in politics, ministerial responsibility, the abolition of monarchies and titled aristocracies, the overthrow of state religion, the breaking-up of the great landed estates, and the ending of exploitation through the destruction of capitalism and the establishment of public ownership in all areas of the economy. These beliefs were inculcated, especially in Germany and Austria, through a vast and elaborate network of exclusively socialist institutions, newspapers, magazines, clubs and associations, trade unions, educational societies and much more, so that members could live their entire lives in a world informed by socialist values. Socialism transformed the lives of millions of ordinary workers in this way, but it also constituted a growing threat to social stability and order in the minds of the elites who dominated the political establishment of the day. Repeatedly, conservative and, in the end too, liberal governments tried to defuse working-class discontent by passing welfare reforms that gave the working class a stake in society and removed from its life the insecurity and poverty that generated resentment and disillusion with the dominant institutions of the state. By 1900 in almost every European country the age of the masses had begun, as political parties and groupings of every hue vied for their allegiance and competed for their support.

THE AGE OF THE MASSES

If democracy in its modern form is based above all on universal adult suffrage and the responsibility of government to parliament and the electorate, then the tide of history in Europe in the second half of the nineteenth century seemed to be flowing inexorably towards it. The roll-back of revolution in 1848 did not mean the defeat of liberalism; on the contrary, alongside liberal reforms such as freedom of the press, equality before the law, public trial by jury, and so on, a number of countries saw the triumph of constitutionalism and the establishment of parliamentary supremacy. Legislative assemblies emerged at mid-century either as a result of the revolution or as part of an attempt to ward it off, replacing traditional Estates in almost all countries. Sweden was late in replacing Estates with an elected Parliament, in 1865, but more typical was Prussia, where a

Parliament was instituted in the course of the 1848 Revolution. In one country after another the right to vote was extended to new classes of the population.

A number of countries already had universal male suffrage well before the end of the century. Greece was founded on the principle of votes for all adult men from its beginnings in 1829 (though it excluded the unemployed until 1877). In France universal male suffrage was introduced in 1848 and remained in place thereafter, while the German Empire brought it in for national elections on its foundation in 1871. Austria enfranchised all adult males in 1907 and Italy in 1912 following earlier, more limited extensions in 1882 and 1887. In Spain the Constitution of 1869 accorded voting rights to all adult men. In some countries the extension of the franchise was clearly under way but incomplete by 1914: Sweden, where the electorate had already been modestly increased in the 1840s, enfranchised around 20 per cent of adult males in elections for the Upper House of Parliament in 1865, and 40 per cent for the Lower House, with a major though not quite total extension in 1909. In Norway universal adult male suffrage was introduced in 1898 in the course of a sharp rise in nationalist sentiment, as liberal politicians strove to gain the maximum legitimacy for their policy of freeing the country from Swedish rule. In Denmark only one in seven adult males could vote for the Lower House when it was established in 1849, a late fruit of the mid-century revolutions, but voting rights were extended in stages until complete adult male suffrage was achieved in 1915.

In some countries the extension of the franchise to the whole of the adult male population went at a slower pace. In Britain the 1867 Reform Act had already increased the electorate from 1,365,000 to 2,446,000, or about a third of all adult males. The right to vote was still based on a property qualification but on a much lower one than in 1832, so that the urban middle classes but also a limited number of skilled working men now had the vote. Fifty-two small boroughs were disfranchised and the seats redistributed. This was followed by the introduction of the secret ballot in 1872, which reduced the power of the landlords and brought bribery and intimidation of the electorate to an end. In 1884 the provisions of the 1867 Act were extended to the countryside, in a measure followed a year later by a redistribution of 142 constituencies, thirty-nine of them added to London, and others to industrial cities in the north. Nearly two out of every three adult males now had the vote. In Romania the franchise of 1866 was extended in 1884 to most elements of the middle class but left the mass of the peasantry unrepresented, a factor in provoking the violent peasant uprising that swept the country in 1907.

The most influential of all European constitutions in the nineteenth century, the Belgian Constitution of 1831, gained its fame through the incorporation of basic liberal principles such as freedom of religion, the right to education and so on. However, to begin with, it imposed high property qualifications. The number of men who possessed the right to vote, only about 45,000, was doubled to 90,000 in the course of the 1848 Revolution. Only 4.4 per cent of the male population (of all ages) had the vote in 1892; a new constitution, voted through in 1893 amid widespread strikes and noisy street demonstrations in favour of universal male suffrage, gave every man over twenty-four one vote, those over thirty-four with a family and a rateable home two votes, and those with professional qualifications or property three votes. This increased the number of electors tenfold, though most of the votes were cast by the plural electors. In the Netherlands the States General were swept away and indirect elections were replaced by direct ones. The roll-back of Revolution led in 1850 to an actual reduction in the size of the electorate, which numbered around 80,000 out of a population of three million, while in Belgium an electorate of the same size represented a population of four and a third million. By the end of the century, the pressure for democratization from the increasingly powerful socialist movement in the Netherlands, with a growing number of strikes fuelled by the economic downturn of the previous years, had forced the extension of the franchise in 1887 to all men over the age of twenty-three who fulfilled relatively modest tax and residence requirements. The measure meant that the number of voters increased from 14 per cent of the total adult population in 1890 to 31 per cent in 1910.

In some parts of Europe the forces of democratization were obstructed by monarchical or military authoritarianism, but political instability could also benefit the democratic principle. A military coup in Serbia in 1903 actually reduced the power of the monarch and increased the influence of the electorate. On 4 October 1910 in Portugal a group of junior army officers calling themselves the *carbonari* arrested their superiors, armed the people of Lisbon, and declared a republic. The king was forced to abandon a game of bridge in mid-play and make his way to a lonely beach from where he embarked for England and exile. Repeated political upheavals in Spain were succeeded during the last half-century before 1914 by a relatively stable constitutional monarchy in which the alternation of conservative and liberal governments acquired the name *turnismo*. Everywhere the balance between state authority and legislative assemblies depended not least on the character of the individual monarch and the strengths and weaknesses of the political class and the nation's political culture. The principle of ministerial and government responsibility to the elected legislature was established in Norway in 1884, in Denmark in 1901 and in Sweden in 1917. There were many different reasons for these domestic reforms, but it was significant that the introduction of legislative assemblies and the extension of the right to vote owed a great deal to fear of revolution at different points and in different countries, from Britain in 1832 to Austria in 1907. In France and Germany, as well as in Britain in 1867, voting rights were extended by conservative politicians to groups of the population they wrongly thought would outflank the liberals by voting to preserve the existing order. At other times, as in many countries in 1848, Denmark in 1865 or Russia in 1905, these reforms were brought about by a defeat of the ruling system in revolution or war. Moderate liberals believed that only those who had a stake in the country, whether through owning property and paying taxes, or those who were able to contribute to its political culture, for example by being able to read and write, should have the right to vote. But gradually they were forced to extend this right through the pressure for change exerted by the growing power of socialist and democratic movements.

By the turn of the century modern politics were beginning to reach the rural masses. Certainly, traditional riots and uprisings continued, above all where the peasants were denied the right to participate in the national political culture, as in Russia in 1905 and Romania two years later. Yet the peasantry in many parts of Europe was beginning to mobilize politically. In southern Italy and Sicily old-fashioned peasant revolts were now intermingled with adherence to the modern politics of the socialists or the revolutionary ideology of anarchism. In Germany peasants began to organize in the 1890s by setting up farming co-operatives, a thousand of which were newly established every year up to 1914. In Bavaria the Peasant Leagues mobilized a rural population dissatisfied with its neglect by local notables and the middle class, under the slogan 'no aristocrats, no priests, no doctors and no professors, only peasants for the representation of the peasants'. In central Germany the antisemitic parties of Otto Böckel (1859–1923) and Hermann Ahlwardt (1846–1914) exploited peasant discontent for their own purposes, adopting the black, red and gold colours of the 1848 Revolution and declaring themselves 'against Junkers and Jews'. In France middle-class observers began to report that peasants were becoming 'less obliging than they used to be'. Improved communications made it easier for them to get to the polls, which were always held in towns. In 1907, as the ravages of phylloxera were still causing widespread economic hardship, the winegrower and café owner Marcelin Albert (1851–1921) began holding public meetings that attracted hundreds of thousands of people, or so it was said: as a result, peasants stopped paying taxes, local officials resigned, and crowds besieged departmental prefectures in the south. The troops sent to restore order mutinied (and were subsequently sent to man a remote fort in Tunisia). The Prime Minister, Georges Clemenceau, eventually summoned Albert, found that he was frightened by having created a movement that was now out of control, and persuaded him to abandon the campaign. What survived was the Radical Party, buoyed up by the voting power of the peasantry, who obtained significant tax concessions through its agency.

Much more difficult to control was the peasant movement in Ireland. After the potato famine of the late 1840s and the ensuing mass emigration, social antagonisms between a mainly Protestant, Anglo-Irish class of landowners and the mass of the cottagers and landless labourers deepened dramatically; this was in the light of an increase in the number of larger estates (more than 20 per cent in the case of all estates over 15 acres) and a decline in the number of smallholdings (38 per cent of those between 5 and 15 acres, and 52 per cent of those between 1 and 5 acres). As literacy rates grew (rising from 33 per cent in 1850 to 84 per cent in 1900) and a Catholic middle class emerged, a mass movement known as the Land War broke out at the end of the 1870s, convulsing rural society with more than 11,000 'outrages', mostly threatening letters, between 1879 and 1882, and the same number of families evicted from their tenancies. Landlords were attacked, and a few were shot (one commentator claimed that 'the English shot pheasants and poachers, and the Irish shot landlords and agents'). In the 1880s 'agrarian crimes' were running at twenty-five times the level of 1878, including shootings, beatings, the maiming of animals, the disruption of fox hunting and the dispatching of threatening letters. The discontent of the small farmers in Ireland was fuelled by resentment at their deprivation of legal rights, hostility to the dominance of the 'Protestant Anglo-Irish Ascendancy', and an emerging, largely middle-class nationalism.

The increase in literacy, the spread of education, the standardization of national languages, the extension of communications through railways, newspapers, magazines, mass-produced pamphlets and flysheets – all this drew the urban and rural masses into the wider political discourse and intensified a national sense of identity. In countries where universal adult suffrage obtained or significant elements of the masses were enfranchised, men increasingly began to exercise their right to vote. Percentage polls at elections grew steadily until in a country like Germany they reached over 85 per cent by the early 1900s. With more and more citizens participating in political life, modern political parties began to form, organizing themselves to take part in elections and win representation in national legislatures. Increasingly, however, these parties included the representation of national minorities, which soon began to challenge the political systems of Europe's multinational states.

THE CRISIS OF LIBERALISM

In most European states national minorities were either marginal or more or less quiescent from the 1870s to the end of the nineteenth century. Polish nationalism, the cause of major upheavals throughout the century, had finally been curbed by the brutal suppression of the 1863 uprising. Nationalist political parties began to form, but tsarist autocracy and the repression exercised in their respective parts of the former Polish state by Austria and Prussia ensured their activities were kept within strict limits. In France, Italy, Portugal, the Netherlands and Scandinavia national minorities were marginal to the political process. Catalan nationalism in Spain was only just beginning to stir. However, there were two states in particular where the extension of the franchise and the 'nationalization of the masses' gave rise to serious political conflicts. These were the United Kingdom of Great Britain and Ireland, and the Dual Monarchy of Austria-Hungary. In both countries the intransigence of significant national minorities battened onto the decay of liberal hegemony that was the most obvious consequence of the extension of the franchise and began to threaten the very existence of the state by the outbreak of the First World War.

The extension of the right to vote in Britain in 1867 and 1884 spelled the end for the Whigs, the aristocratic liberals who had dominated the British political scene from the beginning of the 1830s to the middle of the 1860s. In 1883 the leading Whig in the House of Commons, Lord Hartington (1833–1908), son of the Duke of Devonshire, said that the purpose of the Whigs was to 'direct and guide, and moderate' the popular will, and to form 'a connecting link between the advanced party and those classes which, possessing property, power and influence, are naturally averse to change'. What he called the 'advanced party', or Radicals, numbered around eighty in the Commons and wanted further democratic and social reforms. The old Whig Party metamorphosed in the decades after mid-century into the Liberal Party, increasingly dominated by the middle classes. The party as a whole was held together by Gladstone, who delayed the advent of mass politics until the 1880s, after which he played a major role in bringing it about.

The pre-eminent practitioner of fiscal conservatism, working for the restriction of government spending, Gladstone regarded all his policies as designed to preserve social and political order. He believed strongly in rule by the elite, packed his Ministries with Whig peers, and deeply disapproved of the Radicals. Yet on the other hand he believed that it was better to move with the masses than against them. He saw his role as bridging the gap between the landed interest and the broader political elite on the one hand, and the new industrial middle and working classes on the other. With his passionate commitment to every cause he embraced, Gladstone dominated the House of Commons. He had competition only from his great rival Disraeli, who employed humour and sarcasm in an attempt to deflate 'that unprincipled maniac Gladstone' as he called him in private, a man who in his view possessed an 'extraordinary mixture of envy, vindictiveness, hypocrisy and superstition'. Gladstone for his part regarded Disraeli as an unprincipled opportunist: 'The Tory party,' he remarked, 'had principles by which it would and did stand for bad and for good. All this Dizzy destroyed.' The oratorical duels between the two men were printed in the newspapers and transformed their rivalry in the Commons into a national spectator sport. This was politics as performance, cementing a sense of the House of Commons as the great forum for national political debate.

Yet Gladstone was more important in his ability to rouse crowds outside Parliament. His deep, resonant and penetrating voice enabled him to address an audience of ten or twelve thousand in the open air, assisted by 'relayers', men with acute hearing and booming voices, who repeated his words to the outer fringes of the crowd. His great series of outdoor speeches in 1879–80, known as the 'Midlothian campaign', in which he brought many thousands to a state of frenzy with his rhetorical attacks on Disraeli's government, marked the creation of the modern electoral campaign, in which he addressed his programme not to his constituency but to the country. The speeches, lasting up to five hours each, were often likened to sermons. Even in a pious age, Gladstone's religiosity stood out. His High Anglicanism infused all his political statements with a moral conviction that made him the national hero of Calvinists, Methodists and other religious nonconformists. In 1868 he declared: 'The Almighty seems to sustain me for some purpose of His own, deeply unworthy as I know myself to be. Glory be to his name.' It was bad enough, Disraeli complained, that Gladstone often had a political trump card up his sleeve: what was completely unbearable was the fact that he always claimed God had put it there. Gladstone's reputation for taking a long time to make up his mind on important issues – the origin of the legend that he chewed each piece of food thirty-two times before swallowing it – was belied by his impulsiveness on many occasions.

Gladstone presided over the creation of the Liberal Party as a modern political movement with a coherent programme and a permanent organization. The National Liberal Federation was founded in 1877 by the leading Birmingham Liberal, Joseph Chamberlain (1836–1914), an industrialist who began as a manufacturer of screws and later became mayor of his home city. The Federation was organized in constituency branches, it had a registered membership, it engaged in fund-raising activities, it founded local social clubs, and it ran co-ordinated campaigns at election time. Its Conservative counterpart, the National Union of Conservative Associations, was set up in 1867 and run from a Conservative Central Office from 1870, though it had decayed by 1880 and had to be subsequently revived. These changes, and the extension of the electorate, increased the number of contested constituency elections, so that whereas 194 constituencies returned an MP unopposed in 1865, only thirty-nine did so twenty years later. Contrary to Disraeli's expectation, it was Gladstone who rallied the new electorate in 1868 to form his first Ministry, which lasted until 1874 and was the first great reforming government since the Whig administrations of the 1830s. Its aim was to introduce liberal principles of free competition into every area of politics and society, and the list and scope of its reforms were breathtaking.

From 1870 all candidates for the Civil Service, except the Diplomatic Corps, were required to take an open competitive examination; nomination and patronage were no more. This opened up the Civil Service to the middle classes. The War Minister Lord Cardwell (1813–86) reorganized the army in response to the Prussian victories of 1864–71, bringing back many troop units from India and creating a home-based expeditionary force. The purchase of commissions was abolished; henceforth appointment as an officer was on merit. Flogging as a disciplinary measure was also outlawed. The Education Act of 1870 created 'Board Schools' funded by local government, effectively rivalling the Church-run voluntary schools and making elementary education universal. A Public Health Act (1872) set up local Health Boards and medical officers of health; a Local Government Board Act (1871) centralized government agencies dealing with local authorities; another measure the same year removed religious tests for holders of teaching posts in the universities of Oxford and Cambridge; a Trade Union (Protection of Funds) Act was passed in 1869; and in 1870 the Married Women's Property Act (strengthened in 1882) gave wives legal power over the property they brought into a marriage. After this outburst of legislative energy it was hardly surprising that in 1873 Disraeli compared the government ministers on the front bench of the House of Commons to 'a range of exhausted volcanoes'; for by this time a number of other measures were running into difficulties. Gladstone called a general election in 1874 but his only clear policy was the abolition of income tax, and he was heavily defeated.

The winner of the election was Disraeli, who served as Prime Minister until 1880. 'I have climbed to the top of the greasy pole,' he boasted. Born into an upper-middle-class Jewish family, Disraeli had been baptized a Christian, and with his goatee beard, his dandified clothing, his profession as a writer of novels (which he continued to publish during his tenure of office), and his often frivolous wit, he hardly seemed cut out to lead a party of stolid gentry and landowners. Part of his secret was that he had a firm belief in the virtues of the aristocracy, strong-minded, independent, and not to be overawed by the mob; indeed, he believed that Jews themselves were natural aristocrats. The architect of the 1867 extension of the franchise, he was the founder of 'Tory Democracy', turning the Conservatives into a modern political party in terms not only of organization but also of ideology. On the death of Lord Palmerston in 1865, Disraeli was quick to appropriate his mantle of patriotism for the Conservatives. His party's fortunes were buoyed up by the growth of the London suburbs, which voted solidly Tory in the elections of 1874. Seventy years of age when he came to office, Disraeli passed a new Public Health Act (1875), the Artisans' Dwelling Act (1875), an Act requiring ships to mark on their sides the minimum freeboard level known as the Plimsoll Line (1876), and other measures. But his domestic record did not compare with that of his predecessor. Overwhelmingly concerned with foreign and imperial policy, Disraeli saw his mission as engineering social calm through a 'return to normality', bringing about minor reforms but not attempting anything major. In 1876 he moved to the House of Lords as Earl of Beaconsfield. His great debating duels with Gladstone had already come to an end. The former Liberal Prime Minister had retired after his defeat in 1874, but, spurred by personal outrage at Turkish atrocities in Bulgaria, Gladstone returned to politics with his Midlothian campaign. Its momentum swept Gladstone back into the leadership of the Liberals and into power in the general election of 1880.

The Midlothian campaign had unleashed forces of popular politics that Gladstone found difficult to control. He was now widely known as the G. O. M. or 'Grand Old Man' – his enemies called him 'God's One Mistake' – or 'The People's William'. With popular support outside Parliament for major reforms, he put through the Corrupt and Illegal Practices Act of 1883, which limited the amount of money that could be spent on election campaigns by candidates and cracked down on corruption during election time. The 1884 Reform Act brought about a significant extension of the franchise to precisely those parts of society that had lent Gladstone's campaign their support. But, declaring that the Liberals were 'ripe for a new departure in constructive Radicalism', Chamberlain also pressed for improvements in housing, inheritance tax on landed estates (eventually introduced in 1894), free elementary education, a progressive income tax and other measures bound to annoy the Whigs. With his elegant dress, orchid buttonhole and monocle, Chamberlain was hardly the image of a wild radical. But as President of the Board of Trade, his rhetoric began to drive offended Whig aristocrats into the Conservative Party.

Chamberlain's radicalism was combined with a strong belief in Empire and in the United Kingdom, and it was this that brought him into conflict with Gladstone, above all over the Irish Question. This was the crucial point at which democracy came into conflict with liberalism. Resentment at English rule and the ascendancy of Protestant landowners, many of them absentees living in England, was rife among the Catholic Irish peasantry. Gladstone had attempted to deal with religious issues in 1869 by disestablishing and disendowing the Anglican Church in Ireland. In 1870 his Irish Land Act had granted more security to tenants, but proved difficult to enforce. The introduction of the secret ballot in 1872 freed Irish electors from the pressure previously put on them by Anglo-Irish landlords and brought fifty-nine Irish MPs to the Westminster Parliament, all of them committed to Home Rule for Ireland. Disraeli neglected the Irish Question except for a Coercion Act (1875), which gave the government powers to stamp out unrest. The Act was a failure, and by 1880 anti-landlord and anti-English violence was spreading across the countryside. Gladstone became obsessed with the Irish problem. 'My mission,' he said in 1880, 'is to pacify Ireland.'

Gladstone passed a second Land Act in 1881, giving tenants more rights, but this was opposed as inadequate by Charles Stewart Parnell (1846–91), a wealthy Anglo-Irish Protestant landlord who had entered Parliament in 1875 and became leader of the Irish Home Rule League in 1880. Founded in 1873, the League was renamed the Irish Parliamentary Party in 1882 and gave Parnell a platform from which to exercise his remarkable oratorical talents. Half-American himself, Parnell toured the United States in the winter of 1879–80 drumming up funds and support from the Irish diaspora. He told his American listeners:

When we have undermined English misgovernment we have paved the way for Ireland to take her place amongst the nations of the earth. And let us not forget that that is the ultimate goal at which all we Irishmen aim. None of us whether we be in America or in Ireland . . . will be satisfied until we have destroyed the last link which keeps Ireland bound to England.

Parnell cultivated the radical nationalist Fenian movement, and was imprisoned under the Coercion Act. In 1882 he was released after agreeing to the Land Act if rent arrears were written off, in the so-called Kilmainham Treaty. The negotiations were conducted by Captain William O'Shea (1840–1905), whose wife Kitty O'Shea (1846–1921) was Parnell's long-term mistress and about to bear his child. For the moment the liaison remained secret, though the captain did try to fight a duel with Parnell in 1881. More immediately, however, the Kilmainham Treaty was undermined by the murder on 6 May 1882 of the Chief Secretary for Ireland, Lord Frederick Cavendish (1836–82), and his top civil servant, Thomas Henry Burke (1829–82), in Dublin's Phoenix Park by members of an Irish nationalist secret society, the Irish National Invincibles. Parnell was arrested and imprisoned in Kilmainham Jail in 1882 for having allegedly supported the murders; he publicly condemned them and was released. Although an inquiry reported that the incriminating documents were forgeries, further progress had become impossible for the time being.

The 1884 Reform Act increased the number of Irish Home Rulers in Parliament to eighty-six in the election of the following year. They were led by Parnell, who had allied with the Conservatives to bring down the Gladstone government. In the new House of Commons the Irish MPs held the balance of power. Gladstone was by this point converted to the idea of Home Rule as the only way out, but the Protestant Whig magnates, appalled by the idea of Anglo-Irish landowners being expropriated by a prospective Irish Parliament dominated by Catholic peasant farmers, refused to join the Cabinet. They were supported by the Radicals, led by Chamberlain, who regarded Home Rule as a blow to Britain's imperial mission. Gladstone's Home Rule Bill was defeated in 1886, and in the ensuing general election his Liberal supporters lost heavily. A coalition of seventy-nine Liberal Unionists led by Chamberlain and 316 Conservatives now led from the House of Lords by Robert Gascoyne-Cecil, Marquess of Salisbury, came into office. With three brief intervals – Gladstone's Third Ministry, in 1886, and Fourth Ministry, from 1892–4, which again foundered on the issue of Home Rule, and another short-lived Liberal government in 1894–5 under the brilliant but indolent Lord Rosebery (1847–1929) – the Conservatives under Salisbury were continuously in power for some two decades, from 1885 to 1905. The Irish question had brought Liberal hegemony to an end.

Gladstone supported Home Rule partly because he realized that Parnell would settle for nothing else. He was not prepared to let the Liberal leadership pass to Chamberlain, whom he saw as a dangerous opportunist in the Disraelian mould, and he feared that the Irish Question would dominate British politics until it was solved. But Home Rule also became a moral crusade, giving Gladstone the will to carry on in politics well into his eighties. He did not succeed. The wreck of the Home Rule cause was completed by the downfall of Parnell, ruined by the public scandal occasioned by Captain O'Shea, who finally sued his wife Kitty for divorce in 1889, naming Parnell as co-respondent. Nonconformist Protestants among the Liberals were outraged by the details revealed at the trial in 1890, Gladstone warned that they would lose the next election if Parnell stayed on, and the Irish leader's followers split over the issue. Fighting for his political life, Parnell fell ill and died in October 1891 of pneumonia in the arms of Kitty, whom he had married just over three months before.

Salisbury became the dominant figure in British politics for the last fifteen years or so of the nineteenth century. An aristocratic landowner and active journalist, he concealed a neurotic, pessimistic character behind an effective mask as a calm and imperious statesman. He served as Prime Minister in 1885–6, 1886–92 and 1895–1902, sustained in the House of Commons by the solid phalanx of Liberal Unionists led by Chamberlain and in the House of Lords by the Whig peers, who by now had mostly defected to the Conservatives. During his first two Ministries, Salisbury was also Foreign Secretary, and this, and the fact that he was in the House of Lords, allowed individual ministers a great deal of initiative in domestic policy. Overall, however, despite a reorganization of local government and some improvements in conditions of work, Salisbury's years in office were quiet ones, reflecting his deeply conservative belief that 'whatever happens will be for the worse, and therefore it is in our interest that as little should happen as possible'. In this sense, perhaps, he held back the rising tide of democracy in Britain. Yet despite these beliefs, Salisbury, an effective public speaker, accepted the new popular politics introduced by Gladstone. In the meantime the gradual departure of Gladstone from the scene allowed the Liberals to reorient their politics with the Newcastle Programme of 1891, which accepted state intervention to bring about social reform and alleviate working-class poverty. This was a new kind of liberalism, one that was abandoning the Gladstonian belief in the minimal state and moving towards a compromise with the ideology of state-sponsored social welfare instead. Not coincidentally, it had the added benefit of bringing the trade unions round behind the Liberals, and a series of electoral pacts at a local level ensured that growing numbers of Unionists and Conservatives met with defeat at the polls.

Salisbury's final years in office were dominated by the imperial issue of the Second Boer War (1899–1902), which provoked an orgy of patriotic enthusiasm in the populace, including many people in the working class, while the Liberals were deeply divided over the issue. When Salisbury, his health failing, resigned office in July 1902, he was succeeded as Prime Minster by Arthur Balfour, who was his nephew (the succession reputedly gave rise to the phrase 'Bob's your uncle' for a done deal). Although he had run the government's business in the House of Commons under Salisbury, Balfour was wholly unable to cope with a new crisis sparked by Chamberlain. Seriously alarmed by the rise of German economic power, the former Mayor of Birmingham launched an energetic campaign for the introduction of import tariffs to reduce the effects of goods 'made in Germany' on the British economy. This breached the principle of free trade that had been held sacrosanct since the abolition of the Corn Laws more than half a century before. The introduction of import duties was to be linked with 'Imperial Preference', which would keep food prices low with minimal duties on imports from the empire. The campaign alienated the Whig aristocrats among the Conservatives, and they broke away from the government in 1903 to form the Unionist Free Fooders. It also aroused the united opposition of the Liberals and the trade unions, who thought that even low import tariffs on foodstuffs from the empire would raise the cost of living for the working classes.

The split in the Conservative Party forced Balfour's resignation in December 1905 and the appointment of a Liberal government under Sir Henry Campbell-Bannerman, which won the general election of 1906 on the issue of free trade. Balfour himself lost his parliamentary seat – to a young war correspondent, Winston Churchill. However, Campbell-Bannerman suffered a series of heart attacks in November 1907 and shortly before his death in April 1908 was replaced by his Chancellor, Herbert Henry Asquith. Asquith was to remain in power for a further eight years. With 377 Liberals, fifty-three representatives of the newly founded Labour Party and eighty-three Irish Nationalists, Asquith had a strong majority over the Conservatives, who were divided between seventy-nine Tariff Reform 'Whole Hoggers', forty-nine Balfourites and thirty-one 'Free Fooders'. A brilliant lawyer and effective debater, the new Prime Minister managed his Cabinet rather than ruling it, and took a relaxed attitude both to political life and to his personal affairs. Married to the socialite Margot Tennant (1864–1945), Asquith carried on a lengthy affair between 1910 and 1915 with a young aristocratic woman, Venetia Stanley (1887–1948), to whom he was soon writing up to three letters a day, some of them penned during Cabinet meetings. He was also notoriously fond of the bottle.

The advent to power of the Liberals was one of a number of events that symbolized the coming of a new era, beginning with the death of Queen Victoria in January 1901. Her successor, Edward VII, was fifty-nine when he came to the throne. He had spent most of his life drinking, gambling – the source of a number of scandals that scarred his public reputation – hunting, and pursuing affairs with a wide variety of women, from Russian princesses to Parisian prostitutes. (He earned a wholly undeserved reputation as a major international diplomat largely because of his frequent visits to Paris, which were very far from being political in nature.) When he died in 1910 he was succeeded by his son George V, who had become heir to the throne on the death of his elder brother in 1892. George had spent most of his life in the Royal Navy (acquiring a tattoo on his arm in the process), and divided his time on dry land between stamp-collecting and hunting. Unlike Queen Victoria, neither Edward VII nor George V played any notable part in politics, which, together with the decline of the Conservatives, allowed the democratizing tendencies of the Liberal Party full rein – or almost, since the Conservatives still possessed a crushing majority among the hereditary peers of the House of Lords.

Asquith's light touch on government allowed two major Liberal politicians to make their mark in the Cabinet. The first was Sir Edward Grey (1862–1933), Foreign Secretary from 1905 to 1916. A stolid figure who had graduated from Oxford with third class honours and had been university champion in 'real tennis', Grey was connected to one of the great Whig landowning families and possessed enough confidence to make foreign policy on his own. By contrast, the other leading figure in Asquith's Cabinet, David Lloyd George, had made his way as a lawyer and then a politician through his charismatic abilities as a public speaker. Radical in temperament, and even more so in his rhetoric, he was committed to using the resources of the state to improve the lot of the poor. Under his influence the Liberals moved quickly to fulfil the promises of the Newcastle Programme and satisfy their trade union supporters. In 1909, Lloyd George as Chancellor of the Exchequer introduced what he called the 'People's Budget', which included a progressive income tax to hit the rich, and a tax on land. In an unprecedented move the Conservative majority in the House of Lords rejected the Budget as an attack on property. The government declared a general election, which it won in January 1910 with Liberals and Labour combined beating the Conservatives in the highest ever poll (87 per cent of the electorate). This was a mandate not only for the People's Budget but also for the removal of the Lords' power of veto over legislation. Asquith introduced a Parliament Bill to achieve this aim. By threatening immediate resignation, the Prime Minister forced the new king, George V, to agree to create 500 Liberal peers should the Lords reject the Bill, which they did. Asquith called a second general election, which took place in December 1910 with the same result as before. Under the threat of the 500 new peers, and against the resistance of almost a hundred 'last ditchers' among the hereditary peers, the Bill passed the House of Lords by seventeen votes and received the royal assent. From now on the Upper Chamber only had delaying powers over legislation approved by the House of Commons, and was no longer able to block it. This was a major step forward for democracy.

From 1910 onwards, in the midst of this constitutional crisis, Asquith's government depended for its majority on the support of the eighty-three MPs of the Irish Party, which demanded Home Rule as a reward once the Lords' powers had been curbed. This moved the Irish Question back to the centre of politics once more, and soon it was threatening to derail the entire political process. In 1912 the government put forward a Bill to give Ireland its own Parliament with powers over everything except foreign policy, defence and some financial and police matters. But it now faced the determined opposition of the Unionists, who had gained control over the Conservative Party after Balfour had been removed as leader in 1911 because he had backed the reform of the Lords. His successor, the Canadian-born businessman and tariff reformer Andrew Bonar Law (1858–1923), was a strong opponent of Home Rule and supporter of the Ulster Protestants, who objected vehemently to being ruled by the Catholic majority in the rest of Ireland. As the Irish Party insisted on Home Rule including the whole of Ireland, the Protestants raised an armed force of 160,000 Ulster Volunteers commanded by a retired British general. British army officers, sympathetic to Unionism, refused to act, and the Unionists, led by the barrister Sir Edward Carson (1854–1935), who had made his name as the counsel for the prosecution in the trial of Oscar Wilde, prepared for civil war.

The crisis imperilled the entire stability of the British state. It was only postponed by the advent of hostilities against Germany in August 1914. The war came on the heels of massive labour unrest, including the first national railwaymen's strike in 1911, a dock strike in the same year, and a miners' strike in south Wales in which troops opened fire on strikers at Tonypandy. The government seemed unable to control events. Suffragette outrages increased the general sense of chaos. The Liberals responded with a minimum wage for coalminers and a system of sickness and unemployment benefits in 1912, but these measures did not satisfy most workers. Trade union membership grew by 60 per cent between 1910 and 1914, and with it the influence of the Labour Party. Asquith's attempt to pacify the forces of democracy with an extension of the franchise in 1912 foundered on the issue of women's suffrage. The Gladstonian alliance of the middle and working classes was coming to an end as the suburban bourgeoisie began drifting away to the Conservatives in step with the decline of the landed interest's domination of the party. Democracy in Britain had made significant advances, but the onward march of political progress was clearly running into difficulties by 1914. What a later historian described as 'the strange death of liberal England' had already begun. By far the most serious threat to the integrity of the United Kingdom was the Irish imbroglio. It was eventually to end in an armed uprising, followed by civil war and the creation of an independent Irish state in the 1920s, with only the six counties of Ulster left within the United Kingdom.

NATIONALISM AND DEMOCRACY

The second major power to witness the subversive effects of the extension of voting rights on liberal parliamentarism through its empowerment of national minorities was the Austro-Hungarian Empire, created through the Compromise of 1867. The enfranchisement of the masses in response to pressure from the socialists, accomplished in 1907 in one half of the monarchy but not in the other, exacerbated nationalist passions, and ended by reducing the influence of elected legislatures rather than increasing them. Throughout the period, the politics of the Dual Monarchy were dominated by the long-lived Emperor Franz Joseph, who had been put on the throne in 1848 and remained on it for nearly seventy years, until his death in 1916. Simply by staying in office for so long, he provided an element of stability and continuity to the empire. Brought up under the guidance of Prince Metternich, who in turn had been a leading figure in the struggle against the French during the Napoleonic Wars, Franz Joseph increasingly seemed like a survival from another era. He believed in the Divine Right of Kingship, interpreting this to imply a punctilious observation of his duties and a strict observance of ceremonial and tradition. Dull, pedestrian and unimaginative, he was nevertheless not without intelligence. He spoke English, French, German, Hungarian, Italian and Spanish, with some knowledge of Czech and Serbo-Croat. Age and experience made him cautious about change, but where it was unavoidable he was flexible enough to concede it. His private life was marred by a series of tragedies, including the execution in Mexico of his brother Maximilian (1832–67), the suicide of his son and heir Crown Prince Rudolf (1858–89), the assassination of his beautiful and headstrong wife the Empress Elisabeth in 1898 by the Italian anarchist Luigi Lucheni, and finally the murder of his nephew the Archduke Franz Ferdinand in 1914.

The leading and most powerful state in Europe up to the mid-1850s, Austria began a long and uneven process of decline after its defeat by Italy and France in the War of Italian Unification in 1859. Geopolitical logic dictated that rather than seeking revenge like the French, the Dual Monarchy had to ally itself, however reluctantly, with the new German Empire from 1871 onwards. It had to face rising nationalism on its border in the Balkans, backed by an expansionist Russia seeking to profit from the decline of the Ottoman Empire. Over time the balance of power between the Dual Monarchy and the German Empire shifted in favour of the latter, especially as German investments in east-central and south-eastern Europe increased. The Dualist system of government meant that there were two separate states, Austria and Hungary, divided roughly along the line of the river Leithe, and known therefore as Cisleithania and Transleithania. Each contained substantial national minorities – in particular, Czechs, Slovaks, Poles, Slovenes, Italians and Ukrainians in the Austrian half of the empire, and Romanians, Serbs and Croats in the Hungarian half. The story of Austro-Hungarian politics up to 1914 is in many ways the story of a rearguard action of the multinational empire against the rising forces of linguistic and ethnic nationalism, intertwined with growing demands for democratic participation from the emerging working classes.

As in Britain, parliamentary institutions underwent a gradual process of modernization. The *Reichsrat*, or imperial legislature, established in 1861 and confined to the Austrian half of the empire from 1867 onwards, was an antiquated institution clearly in need of reform. It was elected indirectly, by the Diets of the Crown lands, and the Diets in turn were elected by four *curiae* representing respectively landowners, towns, chambers of commerce and rural communities. In 1873 the number of deputies was increased from 203 to 353, elected directly by the *curiae*. The change, rather like the 1832 Reform Act in Britain, gave stronger representation to the towns. The landowners elected 85 deputies, the towns 118, the chambers of commerce 21, and the rural communities 128. Only 6 per cent of the population of the empire could vote in these elections. In 1883, as the *Reichsrat* moved into its grand new building on Vienna's Ringstrasse, the tax qualification for entry into the *curiae* was lowered, and in

1896 a fifth *curia* was added, with universal suffrage for all men over the age of twenty-four. It elected seventy-two deputies, shifting the balance of power away from the nobility.

In essence, these changes did not alter the fact that the emperor retained the right to appoint and dismiss ministers, nor did they affect the powers of the hereditary Upper Chamber of the legislature, but they did mark a gradual extension of the franchise in the spirit of cautious liberalism. Here the dominant figure was Prince Adolf von Auersperg (1821–85), whose Ministry was in power for most of the 1870s, despite Franz Joseph's dislike of his liberal outlook, expressed above all in the prince's fiercely anticlerical policies. Auersperg not only broadened the franchise in 1873 but also conceded a greater measure of self-government to the Poles in Galicia, extended trial by jury to cover most serious offences, and passed a number of other liberal reforms. But in 1873 the financial crash of 'Black Friday', in which 700 million gulden were wiped off the Vienna stock market and thousands of firms and individuals were bankrupted, including forty-eight banks and two railway companies, undermined public confidence in the liberals, especially since a number of them had been heavily involved in the dubious financial speculations that had led to the crash. In 1879, Auersperg's failure to take advantage of a major international crisis between Russia and the Ottoman Empire led to his downfall, as both Franz Joseph on the one hand and many liberal deputies on the other finally deserted him.

The ensuing elections gave a narrow victory to the Right, ushering into office Count Eduard Taaffe (1833–95), descendant of an Irish peer who had entered the service of the Habsburgs in the seventeenth century (this also made him an Irish peer, though Irish peers did not sit in the British House of Lords). A childhood companion of Franz Joseph, Taaffe had begun as a moderate liberal and had served as Prime Minister in the late 1860s. By the time he came to office again he had become more conservative. His great achievement was to persuade the Czech deputies, who had been boycotting the *Reichsrat*, to come back, in return for a series of significant concessions on the use of the Czech language in Bohemia and on the representation of Czechs in the Bohemian Diet. Taaffe's reaction to the rising tide of nationalism was expressed in his famous statement that his aim was 'to keep all the nationalities of the Monarchy in a condition of even and well-modulated discontent'. Rather than signifying a deliberate policy of 'divide and rule', this embodied a recognition that discontent was inevitable; all Taaffe could do was to try and keep it under control. It was Taaffe who pushed through the extension of the franchise in 1883, a measure that further undermined the liberals and opened the door for new political parties, including not only the Socialists but also the Christian Social Party, which acquired a popular and energetic leader in the shape of Karl Lueger. A lawyer from a humble background, Lueger had made a reputation for himself by representing the 'little people' in court cases in Vienna. His combination of social reform, antisemitic rhetoric and defence of Catholic interests gained him huge popularity, and in 1890 his party won fourteen seats, including seven in Vienna, at the same time as the liberals lost a quarter of theirs. In 1895 the Christian Social Party won a majority on the Vienna Town Council, but Franz Joseph, who disliked the party's radicalism, refused to accept the appointments; two years later, however, he relented when Lueger won twenty-seven seats in the *Reichsrat*. Before long, Lueger won further support through his implementation of urban improvement, using his position as Mayor of Vienna to give the city modern health, water and transport services, parks, hospitals and schools, and going some way to fulfilling his ambition of turning it into a 'beautiful garden city'.

By the time of Lueger's death from diabetes in 1910, a further, decisive extension of the Austrian franchise had taken place, in 1907, steered through against fierce opposition from the Upper Chamber. The *curiae* were finally abolished, and universal male suffrage was introduced in all the Crown lands, in response to massive and repeated demonstrations by the socialists, which made Franz Joseph fear that the revolution that had so shaken the position of Nicholas II in Russia would be repeated in Austria-Hungary. This reform brought new nationalist splinter groups into the *Reichsrat*, such as Tomáš Masaryk's Czech Realists, founded in 1900 and opposed to the liberal Young Czechs, the conservative Old Czechs, and the Czech Social Democrats (founded in 1878) – a pattern of ideological fragmentation repeated in other national minorities as well. In 1907 the 516 deputies in the *Reichsrat* were divided into some thirty political parties, ranging from eighty-seven Social Democrats and ninety-seven Christian Socials to eighteen Slovene Clericals, seventeen Polish Populists, three Old Ruthenes and two Czech Realists. The debating chamber became an arena where rival national groups did little more than shout each other down in their different languages. The Czech deputies filibustered and disrupted proceedings because they were held in German, so the German deputies in the Bohemian Diet did the same in return. On the occasion of the sixtieth anniversary of Franz Joseph's accession, in 1908, Czech nationalists even signalled their frustration by tearing down Habsburg flags across Bohemia. The chaos and impotence of the *Reichsrat* moved political power upwards into the court and the ministerial clique around Franz Joseph. The emperor's relations with his designated successor, the Archduke Franz

Ferdinand, were not good, not least because Franz Joseph had forced his nephew to make his marriage with Sophie Chotek (1868–1914) a morganatic one, barring their children from succeeding to the throne: she was after all a mere countess, and so of a rank insufficient to become a Habsburg empress. The archduke's ability to bring about a reform of the Dual Monarchy that might mollify the Czechs was therefore limited. More important still was the fact that the concentration of power around the emperor gave the military far greater influence than before.

While military and foreign policy remained the prerogative of the monarch, the political system of the Hungarian half of the Dual Monarchy possessed enough autonomy to oblige Franz Joseph to consult the government when major steps in these areas were taken. Hungary had been extensively reconstructed with the fall of the centralizing absolutist system in Vienna after the 1867 Compromise. It modernized its Constitution, granted civil and legal equality to the Jews (1868), introduced universal elementary education (1868) and separated justice from administration (1869). Hungary settled down in 1875 to a lengthy period of rule by the Liberal Party, formed by the fusion of the two leading nationalist organizations of the 1860s. The Liberals, representing the moderate wing of Hungarian nationalism, were kept in power, as in many other parts of Europe, by a restricted franchise that limited voting rights to about 10 per cent of the population, mainly landowners and professionals but not the poorer classes. Hungarian Liberals stubbornly resisted all attempts to extend the right to vote because they feared this would give more opportunities to Romanians, Croats and others to voice their grievances. The Prime Minister from 1875 to 1890, the landowner Kálmán Tisza (1830–1902), reformed the taxation system, making the state solvent but winning few friends in the process. He found it increasingly difficult to hold the ring between the radical nationalists on the left, who wanted more autonomy for Hungary than the Compromise allowed, and the army and bureaucracy in Vienna, who thought the Compromise had gone too far and wanted to claw back some powers for themselves. The nationalists' allergic reaction to a ceremony in Budapest in 1886 when the Austrian army commander in the Hungarian capital laid a wreath on the tomb of an Austrian general who had fought against the Hungarian revolutionaries in 1848 was only one of many clashes. Tisza eventually tired of trying to deal with such ostensibly rather trivial controversies, and resigned in 1890, though his party continued in office.

Hungarian liberalism was sustained mainly by the Magyar nationalist landowning gentry, who resisted calls for social reform from representatives of the peasantry. The relative backwardness of industry retarded the

growth of a large-scale socialist movement, and labour unions were outlawed after a wave of strikes in the 1890s. Railway workers who went on
strike in 1904 were drafted into the army, and demonstrations were commonly put down with violence by the police (thirty-three demonstrators
were killed at one such event in Bihar). Magyar was made the official
language for all levels of the judicial and administrative systems, and for
all public announcements, even in areas where it was not spoken at all.
Place names were all Magyarized and the language was mandated as the
medium of instruction in virtually all secondary schools. Thus governmental, educational, administrative, judicial and professional systems
were all confined to those who could speak, read and write Magyar. The
1910 census recorded a population consisting of 54 per cent Magyars,
16 per cent Romanians, 11 per cent Slovaks, 10 per cent Germans, and
smaller proportions of other national groups such as Serbs and Croats,
but the figures were manipulated to show a majority of Magyar speakers,
and the real figure was probably below 50 per cent. Magyarization aroused
growing protests from Serb, Croat, Slovak and Romanian nationalists
from the middle of the 1890s onwards, spelling the end of the era of
Liberal domination. Deputies began to defect from the Liberal Party,
which was led by Tisza's son István (1861–1918), and many of them joined
nationalist groups. In 1905 Tisza attempted to revise the rules of the Lower
House to get round the obstructive tactics of the opposition, but when the
Speaker was seen waving a handkerchief to signal that the government
deputies should vote in favour, this 'election by handkerchief' outraged
those who thought he should be neutral. Many more Liberals subsequently
left to join the Independence Party, led by Ferenc Kossuth (1841–1914),
son of the nationalist leader of 1848 and part of a new 'Nationalist
Coalition'.

Alarmed by the breakdown of parliamentary order, Franz Joseph
appointed Géza Fejérváry (1833–1914), captain of the Hungarian
Life-Guards and a career soldier, as Prime Minister and threatened to
double the number of voters in Hungary by decree. In a gesture of compromise he offered the government to the Nationalist Coalition, which
won a substantial victory at the ensuing elections. A new Prime Minister,
the lawyer Sándor Wekerle (1848–1921), was appointed, but the Coalition
fell apart in 1909, and the Liberals returned to government the following
year. By this time the political climate had deteriorated sharply. The rival
nationalist parties cancelled each other out with their opposing demands
for linguistic recognition, defeating measures of educational reform in
the process. Opposition deputies filibustered and made proceedings impossible. When the Magyar Speaker of the Parliament pushed through a

reform of the standing orders that actually made proceedings workable, an enraged opposition deputy fired three revolver shots at him before turning the gun on himself (all four shots missed their target). The government countered by prosecuting nationalist leaders, but here too, as in Vienna, it now effectively ruled by decree. This meant that the decision-making process in government, though it had to be tempered in military and foreign policy by the need to consult with Vienna, became increasingly removed from popular and democratic influences. Far more than in the British troubles with Ireland, therefore, the nationalization of the masses in Austria-Hungary was deeply damaging to parliamentarism and the integrity of the state.

THE ILLUSION OF INSTABILITY

Two European political systems in the late nineteenth and early twentieth century were characterized by the appearance of chronic instability, with weak political parties and coalition governments rising and falling in quick succession: these were the Italian and the French. In both cases governments succeeded one another with bewildering rapidity. In both cases, too, the political system underwent a period of crisis towards the end of the century, when for a while popular dissatisfaction with the apparent ineffectiveness of government threatened to bring a dictator into power. In France shifting political alliances and alignments produced forty-nine successive governments from February 1871 to the beginning of September 1914, with an average duration of under a year each. In Italy a similar system produced thirty-two different governments from 1861 to 1914, with an average duration each that was slightly longer but not significantly so. By contrast, Great Britain experienced only fourteen governments between the 1867 Reform Act and the outbreak of World War I. Austria, with twenty-four governments from 1867 to 1914, and Hungary, with seventeen over the same period, were somewhere in between these two extremes, but still markedly more stable than either Italy or France.

What were the reasons for the chronic political instability of the two Latin nations? To begin with Italy, it was clear that governments suffered from an extreme lack of cohesion. There was no doctrine of collective responsibility and individual ministers felt no qualms about resigning over policies they disagreed with, often bringing down the entire government with them. Disagreements within governments were far more important in bringing about a change of leadership than elections were. This was because, for most of the period, governments always won elections. The

Italian legislature was based on a very narrow franchise deriving from the Piedmontese Constitution of 1848. Only half a million people out of a total Italian population of 22 million possessed the vote, and in the early years of the new state only around 300,000 of these actually bothered to turn up at the polls. Electoral corruption was rife. Banknotes were torn in two at election time and given to electors half before and half after voting; electoral lists contained fictitious names, sometimes gathered from tombstones in the local cemetery; and it was reported on one occasion that forty cows were registered for an election in Predappio. Intimidation was as common as bribery, exercised in Sicily through the Mafia.

The political system was initially run by men from the north, who generally used the south as a source of political patronage and power, working through the great landowners who also dominated the administration and provided numerous delegates for the legislature. From Cavour's premature death in 1861 up to 1876 the coalition of moderate liberals and conservatives he had assembled dominated the political scene. There was a succession of short-lived Ministries. Cavour's successor, the Tuscan Baron Bettino Ricasoli (1809–80), a man of unusual probity known as the 'Iron Baron', offended the king by boasting that his ancestry was longer than that of the House of Savoy, and was dismissed in 1862. His efforts to reconcile the Italian Kingdom with the Vatican were sincere, but they foundered on the rocks of obduracy on both sides; Ricasoli is mainly remembered today not for his political role but for having created the modern recipe for Chianti wine. The next Prime Minister, Urbano Rattazzi (1808–73), who served in 1862, was followed by Luigi Farini (1812–66), who was forced to resign in 1863 after he had threatened the king with a knife in order to get him to declare war on Russia. Marco Minghetti (1818–86), who served over the next two years, was known for his quick temper; he actually fought a duel with Rattazzi in 1863 after they had exchanged intemperate words in Parliament. Ricasoli, Rattazzi and Minghetti all returned to office later on, as the succession of short-lived governments continued. The time and energy of successive governments in the 1860s were largely taken up first by the question of Rome, finally resolved by the conquest of the city and its declaration as the capital of Italy in 1870, and then by a series of battles with the Church. By 1876 the absence of social reforms had become obvious, and the liberal Left, led by the journalist Agostino Depretis (1813–87), came to power.

Prime Minister almost continuously from 1876 until his death in 1887, Depretis was the first really able politician to emerge in Italy since Cavour. His policy, he declared, was 'more democracy'. But his methods were often dubious. He persuaded the Italian legislature to vote funds to build

1,250 miles of roads, and then distributed them to localities in return for the votes of the deputies who represented them. He used the royal influence to pack the Senate. Nevertheless Depretis did achieve some major reforms, including a large-scale programme of railway-building and the establishment of universal, free and compulsory elementary education – important in a society where more than three-quarters of the population were unable to read or write. And most important of all, in 1882 he finally enacted his promise of 'more democracy', steering through an extension of the franchise to increase the electorate from half a million to two million by lowering the property qualification for voting and the age limit for voters from twenty-five to twenty-one. The requirement that voters had to be literate, however, disfranchised almost everyone in the Italian south while at the same time bringing literate artisans in the north and other members of the lower middle class into the electorate.

The newly enfranchised sections of the population formed a significant part of the power base of the Sicilian Francesco Crispi, a former associate of Depretis. Crispi took over as Prime Minister on the latter's death and served from 1887 to 1891 and again from 1893 to 1896. He was descended from an Albanian family, which some thought explained his volatile character. His nationalist credentials were impeccable. A fervent Mazzinian nationalist forced into exile in early adulthood, he had sailed with Garibaldi's Thousand during the Risorgimento. Crispi was endowed with so much energy that although he was sixty-eight when he came to office in 1887, he still ran three major departmental Ministries as well as being Prime Minister. As a man of the liberal Left, he reformed the prisons, legalized the right to strike, introduced a modern code of civil law, and pushed through many other policies, almost all of them using the royal power of decree. His critics began to call him a dictator, and certainly his actions set a precedent for Mussolini in the twentieth century. One thing Crispi did not do was to curb the corruption so rife in the Italian political system. A report in 1891 on banking scandals – Crispi tried to suppress it but it was leaked to the press – revealed that the banks had been printing money in excess of the legal limit (the Banco Romana secretly used a printing press in England for the purpose). The notes were used in order to bribe politicians and officials. The banks also allowed politicians to run up huge debts in return for favours, especially the award to bankers of titles of nobility. The report named names and spared none of the details. One deputy who owed the Credito Mobiliare half a million lire died of a heart attack; a former bank director was murdered on a train; another bank director disappeared and was arrested attempting to take poison when he was discovered disguised as a priest. The scandal caused the fall of Crispi's first government in 1891, but he was recalled in 1893 as the man to deal with a peasant uprising in Sicily, which he did in a predictably ruthless and uncompromising fashion. At this point Crispi pushed through a series of strict legal controls on the banks, which among other things enabled them to play a greater role in financing industry, helping to boost the economy in the years running up to the outbreak of the First World War.

In 1896, Crispi was forced to resign in the wake of the catastrophic defeat of an Italian army in Ethiopia that did much to discredit Italian liberalism. Two years later a major economic crisis, caused not least by a rise in the price of bread during the Spanish-American War, led to riots in cities across Italy. General Luigi Pelloux (1839–1934), a veteran of the Battle of Custoza, had resigned office as Minister of War in order to tackle the riots, after achieving a major reform of the army, and was now appointed Prime Minister as well as Minister of the Interior by the king. Four other government Ministries were placed under active soldiers. Using the royal power of decree, Pelloux banned political meetings, outlawed strikes by state employees, imposed the penalties of banishment and preventive arrest for political offences, and introduced strict press censorship. He announced he would rule by decree alone and brought a Bill before the parliament, giving his decrees the force of law without having to confirm them by a parliamentary vote. When the liberal Left tried to 'talk out' the Bill with an interminable filibuster, there were violent altercations on the floor. Pelloux dissolved the parliament and arrested a number of the deputies. The Court of Appeal ruled his actions unconstitutional, and when he tried to cut short a debate on the issue before a reconvened parliament, the deputies of the Left withdrew from the Chamber in protest. Pelloux called elections in 1900 on a law-and-order platform coupled with a promise to acquire a colony in China as compensation for Italy's failure in Africa. He lost and was forced to retire. The political system was saved. But the episode showed how vulnerable parliamentarism was to authoritarian intervention at a time of national crisis; in the 1920s it fell victim to the far more ruthless Fascist leader Benito Mussolini (1883–1945), who simply ignored the liberal deputies when they withdrew from the Chamber in protest at his role in the murder of one of their number.

The years leading up to the First World War were dominated politically by Giovanni Giolitti (1842–1928), another left-liberal but one without the experience of participation in the Risorgimento. A career civil servant, Giolitti saw that the rapid growth of industrial society in northern Italy made further social reforms necessary to ameliorate the conditions of the working classes. Giolitti never interfered in strikes, and tried not to alienate the Socialists or do anything to prompt social unrest of the sort that had led to the ascendancy of General Pelloux. Following an election victory in 1906, he proposed to increase death duties as well as raise income tax, but was defeated: the issue aroused such passions that one conservative opposition member threw an inkpot at him in the middle of the debate. Normally, however, Giolitti was a past master at putting together coalitions from disparate groups of ministers and deputies, switching the composition of his majority just at the moment when it looked like falling apart. This tactic quickly became known as *trasform-ismo*, the art of converting a failing coalition into a winning one, and it kept him in power for most of the period from the turn of the century to the outbreak of the war. It was backed up by a systematic collection of files on every deputy, listing personal weaknesses and points of pressure. However, Giolitti's careful appeasement of the Socialists did not prevent them from gaining more support – in 1909 the far Left won more than 100 seats, half of them going to the Socialists – nor did it stop them following the line of the Second International in 1913 as they withdrew from collaboration with 'bourgeois' parties.

Giolitti's most important reform was a major extension of the franchise, undertaken to mollify the demands of the Socialists. In 1912 this led to an increase in the electorate from 3 million to 8.5 million voters, the overwhelming majority of the adult male population. The Socialists predictably won seventy-eight seats in the elections of the following year, when fifty-two of their most radical deputies were pledged to the subversion of Parliament as a bourgeois institution. Only half the expanded electorate cast their votes, but clearly, as in other parts of Europe, the more the percentage poll increased, the more the liberals lost seats to the extremes. The Vatican's rescinding of its ban on Catholics participating in politics in 1913 also led to the rapid emergence of conservative Catholic political organizations, which began to assail the liberals from the Right. The political system was clearly becoming progressively less manageable. Giolitti tried to rally popular opinion by engaging in foreign and colonial conquests from 1911 onwards, ultimately with disastrous consequences, and not merely for Italy. There was no doubt that with the progressive extension of the franchise, the country was becoming more democratic, and the dominance of Parliament had survived the Pelloux episode. However, the headlong rush towards an industrial society in the north of the country was creating social tensions that a political system designed for a small elite of middle-class liberals was poorly designed to master.

Up to this point, despite the rapid succession of governments throughout its history, the Italian political system had preserved an underlying stability due to the presence of individual ministers in successive administrations. It had managed to develop effective policies above all when one minister rose above the herd to exercise a dominant influence for a number of years, as with Depretis, Crispi, and finally Giolitti. A similar contrast characterized the Third French Republic, established on the ruins of the Second Empire in 1871, although unlike Italy, it was based on universal male suffrage, introduced by Napoleon III. Republican politicians had removed the authoritarian centralism of the Second Empire and instead given political power to the Chamber of Deputies, whose dominance thus matched that of its counterpart in Italy. Unusually among European states at this time, France possessed both a democratic franchise (for men, at least) and a government responsible to the legislature and thus, ultimately, to the electorate. Yet these achievements repeatedly came under threat. Ironically, it was the Legitimists, the party of France's traditional monarchy, ousted in the Revolution of 1830, who won the first national elections under the Republic on 8 February 1871, taking 400 seats out of 645. The monarchist majority in the new Chamber elected Marshal Patrice de MacMahon, a well-known Legitimist, as President of the Republic in 1873. Such was his reputation as a hero of the Franco-Prussian War that only one vote was cast against him. Initially MacMahon stuck scrupulously to the neutrality of his office, overseeing the promulgation of a new Constitution in 1875. However, two years later, he dismissed a Republican government, leading to accusations that he was preparing a coup d'état; the ensuing elections returned the Left with a majority of 120, upon which he resigned. The Legitimist majority had proved short-lived; many voters had opposed the Republicans in the 1871 elections since their platform included the continuation of the war against Germany; six years later this issue had vanished from the political scene.

Quite apart from the fragility of the Legitimists' support, the official claimant to the throne, Henri, Comte de Chambord (1820–83), was entirely lacking in political skills. He was very lazy (he never learned to tie his shoelaces). He was as obese as his predecessor Louis XVIII and extraordinarily hairy (as one of his courtiers put it, 'his pilose system was very developed'). Worst of all as far as the Legitimist cause was concerned, he was childless. Chambord belonged to the most extreme faction among the Legitimists, who wanted to turn the clock back to pre-revolutionary times. As a child in Austria, he had been taught no history after 1788. He rejected the tricolor as the French flag and insisted on flying the old white lilies instead. The mainstream Legitimists, local notables and aristocrats, wanted power for the localities rather than power wielded by the centralizing absolutism that Chambord desired. He undermined his cause by banning any of his followers from taking office at local or national level under the Republic, since this would imply they recognized it. At one point in the 1870s, Chambord had done a deal with the Orléanists, supporters of the July Monarchy and its heirs, but when he died in 1883 his diehard followers refused to respect the central provision in the agreement and recognize Philippe of Orléans, Count of Paris (1838–94), as the legitimate heir to the throne. In any case, Philippe was hardly a promising candidate. Grandson of King Louis-Philippe, the count lived in Surrey and had few supporters, since most had long since become either Republicans or Bonapartists. The latter gained seventy-five seats in the elections of 1876 and were a political force to be reckoned with. However, Napoleon the Prince Imperial (1856–79), son and heir of Napoleon III, who also lived in Britain, was killed in his twenties by Zulus while fighting in the British Army, leaving no effective claimant to the legacy of Bonapartism either. Philippe of Orléans did at least have a son and successor, also called Philippe (1869–1926), who became a well-known explorer, but that was the end of the Orléanist line too. A law of 1886 banned royal claimants from entering France, to complete the rout.

The leading personalities in French politics during the 1870s were therefore moderate Republicans. Following the death in 1877 of Adolphe Thiers, founder and first President of the Third Republic, the leadership of the Republicans was taken up by Léon Gambetta (1838–82). Gambetta, who had lost his right eye in an accident and always insisted on being painted or photographed from the left, was a charismatic speaker who championed the cause of what he called the *nouvelles couches sociales*, civil servants, artisans, shopkeepers, in general the lower middle class, which he brought into alliance with the professionals, businessmen, middling landowners and others who provided the backbone of Republicanism. It was this social compact that formed the basis for the Republic's longevity and stability. The dominant politician of the late 1870s and early 1880s, Jules Ferry, a lawyer and journalist, built on Gambetta's achievements. A clever and talented manipulator, Ferry deployed anticlerical and nationalist policies that won him a great deal of support, but also aroused considerable opposition. Cold and aloof, he survived two assassination attempts – one critic remarked that this was not surprising, since he had no heart that an assassin could fire at. In 1885 his government fell after military reverses in Indochina, triggering a serious crisis in the Republic's affairs. An economic downturn plunged swathes of the peasantry into debt; import duties were raised in 1887 so urban workers, 250,000 of whom were out of work, suffered; and the President's son-in-law was discovered to have been selling the *Légion d'honneur* and other decorations. Ferry's focus on colonial and anticlerical policies had meant that his ministries passed few social reforms, and in the 1885 elections new groups of disgruntled petty bourgeois were mobilized against the Republic. The Conservative Union, led by the Count of Paris, won 177 seats against the Republicans' 129 in the first round, though the Republicans buried their differences in the second and won 383 seats to the Conservatives' 200. However, the Republicans were split between so-called Opportunists, followers of Gambetta and his political heirs, and Radicals.

A revision of the Constitution seemed necessary, and the Chamber of Deputies turned to the Minister of War, General Georges Boulanger (1837–91), 'General Revanche' as he was known, the French counterpart to the Italian would-be dictator General Pelloux. Boulanger quickly became a symbol of national unity in the midst of the squabbling parliamentarians. When Jules Grévy (1807–91) was forced to resign as President in 1887 over the honours scandal, many thought Boulanger should have taken over, though in the event the post was taken by Sadi Carnot, known for his integrity as Finance Minister, later to be assassinated by an anarchist, in 1894. Boulanger now mounted a vigorous campaign, funded by many who thought he could rescue France's honour and become the new Napoleon. He was elected deputy for Paris in January 1889, heavily defeating the Republican candidate. He urged the dissolution of the Chamber and the election of a Constituent Assembly. But his bluff was called by the Minister of the Interior Jean Constans (1833–1913). A bankrupt manufacturer of lavatory cisterns who became Governor-General of Indochina and then a skilled if corrupt electoral manager, Constans was in many ways typical of the politicians of the Third Republic. He threatened Boulanger with arrest but allowed him time to escape; Boulanger lost his nerve and fled to Belgium, where he eventually committed suicide on the grave of his mistress. Constans was rewarded by being appointed ambassador to the Ottoman Empire. Boulangism continued as a minor political force, but the Republic was saved.

With the collapse of Boulangism, the Radicals rejoined the Republican mainstream, forging an alliance with the Opportunists in a new centrist movement that went by the name of Solidarism, leaving the Socialists behind to form the core of the Left. Since Boulangism had emerged not least because of frustration at the lack of social reform in the first two decades of the Third Republic, the Republican majority elected in 1889 passed laws improving the status of friendly societies and abolishing the *livret*, the workbook employees had up to then been required to carry with them. In 1893 the poor were given access to free medical care 'in the name of the great principle of solidarity', and in 1905 public assistance was extended to the old, infirm and incurable. An arbitration service for labour disputes was inaugurated in 1892, and in the same year limits were set on working hours for women and children. Laws compensating victims of workplace injuries were introduced between 1898 and 1903 and a pension scheme for workers came into being in 1910. The eight-hour day for miners and a ten-hour maximum for many other workers were introduced after the turn of the century. The welfare state finally seemed to have arrived in France. However, the effects of these laws were limited: in 1914 there were still nearly nine million people living in communes without the institutions (the *bureaux d'assistance*) needed to administer the state pension, insurance and medical-care programmes, and local authorities starved them of cash where they did exist (five-sixths of the sum the Chamber of Deputies voted in 1897 for medical care was never spent). The laws on hours of work were full of loopholes and hard to enforce. And towards the end of the 1890s the Republic was plunged into a fresh political crisis even more serious than that caused by General Boulanger.

At the end of 1894 the French Secret Service (officially entitled the 'Statistical Section') obtained a letter in which a French officer informed the German military attaché in Paris that he was sending him some secret military documents. The writer implied that this was not the first time he had passed military secrets to the Germans. The finger of suspicion pointed immediately to a captain of artillery attached to the General Staff, Alfred Dreyfus (1859–1935), whose writing was thought to resemble that of the letter's author. His reply to the accusation that he was the author was an immediate and unequivocal denial. Dreyfus was an Alsatian whose family had chosen French nationality in 1872 rather than take German citizenship. He was well off and had no financial motive for committing treason. But he was also, unusually for a staff officer, Jewish. To prove its efficiency, the Secret Service needed a quick solution to the crime. A secret dossier was compiled, which neither Dreyfus nor his lawyer was allowed to see. On this basis the captain was stripped of his rank on 5 January 1895 in a public ceremony of degradation and shipped off to life imprisonment on the penal colony at Devil's Island in French Guiana.

His family refused to accept his guilt and continued to lobby the press, who the following year discovered that some of the documents in the dossier had been forged by the Secret Service. In 1897 it emerged that the original letter had in fact been written by Ferdinand Esterhazy (1847–1923), a dissolute and deeply indebted officer who had every reason to sell secrets to the Germans. However, Esterhazy had friends in high places. He was portrayed by the right-wing press as the victim of a Jewish plot, and was acquitted by a military tribunal which reaffirmed Dreyfus's guilt.

Outraged by this outcome, the novelist Émile Zola published a lengthy open letter to the President, arguing Dreyfus had been framed. Entitled *J'accuse*, it became an instant best-seller, with 300,000 copies bought within a few weeks. Zola was successfully sued for libel, but the Ministry of War was forced to admit there were forgeries in the dossier, and that the man responsible was Hubert-Joseph Henry (1846–98), a colonel in the Secret Service. Arrested and imprisoned, Henry committed suicide in despair. In 1899, Dreyfus was finally granted an appeal. Brought back from Devil's Island, he was found guilty by a military court once more. However, he was granted a presidential pardon in September 1899, confirmed by the Senate the following year, and in 1906 a civilian court of appeal reversed the verdict of 1895 and declared him innocent.

Throughout the Dreyfus Affair a literary war was waged in the press, in magazines, pamphlets and posters, between Dreyfusards and Anti-Dreyfusards; huge public meetings were held all over France on both sides, revealing deep and irreconcilable passions. Mass anti-Dreyfusard demonstrations in Marseille were followed by violent attacks on Jewish shops. Republicans were shocked to discover that the French Army was still deeply monarchist and remained a law unto itself. As a symbol of French nationalism and the will for *revanche* against the Germans, however, the army was vehemently defended by politicians and writers on the Right. The clergy saw in the Dreyfusards a conspiracy of Jews and Freemasons, showing that the *ralliement* had paid no more than lip service to the Republic. Thus the Dreyfusard campaign became yet another anticlerical cause, leading to the government's dissolution of more than two hundred congregations of religious orders and to the further secularization of education. The Radicals split once more from the moderate Republicans, and with the Socialists gained increased representation in the Assembly in 1902, leading to the appointment of Émile Combes (1835–1921) as Prime Minister. The son of a peasant who engaged in tailoring and ran a wine shop, Combes represented the new social classes identified by Gambetta. Frugal to the point of austerity, he economized on paper by writing 3,600 words to the page, and as a teetotaler, drank reddened water at public banquets instead of wine to avoid attracting unfavourable attention to himself. His Ministry quickened the pace of social reform begun under his predecessors. The Dreyfus Affair removed any last remnants of antisemitism from the socialist movement, while it anchored antisemitism firmly in the politicians and journalists of the Right. Hatred of the Jews was pumped out regularly in the daily paper *La Libre Parole*, edited by Édouard Drumont (1844–1917), which sold 100,000 copies a day and combined religious and racial antisemitism with conspiracy theories of various kinds. Meanwhile the Combes Ministry lasted until 1905, when it was brought down by the withdrawal of support from the Socialists under pressure from the Second International.

In 1906, in the midst of a series of measures of anticlerical and social reform, elections brought a striking victory to the Radicals, who won 42 per cent of the seats in the Chamber of Deputies. They were now led by Georges Clemenceau ('The Tiger'), a combative and aggressive politician who made many enemies. He fought numerous duels, he divorced his wife and had her imprisoned for adultery, and as a newspaper editor he had been the first to publish *J'accuse*. He was a celebrated orator, but instead of delivering the reforms he had promised, Clemenceau spent much of his time trying to suppress labour unrest, using troops to break strikes and alienating the Socialists in the process. His fall in 1909 left the Radicals divided, resulting in a series of short-lived governments. Indeed, the chronic instability of French governments under the Third Republic as a whole was striking. There were many reasons for this. The Chamber of Deputies was divided into numerous small factions rather than mass political parties, and was dominated by local politicians whose main concern was to win advantages for the constituencies they represented. There was little effective co-ordination of government policy since the office of Prime Minister did not formally exist, so the leader of a government had to occupy a Ministry such as Foreign Affairs, leaving little time for implementing a coherent overall line for the government as a whole. The imperfections of the democratic system were obvious, with no secret ballot, no limits on electoral spending, free wine for voters, bribery and corruption. Alliances and alignments among the locally driven deputies shifted with bewildering rapidity. At least to the uninformed, democracy in France did not seem to work very well.

Nevertheless, there was a high degree of continuity behind the appearance of chronic instability. It was striking, indeed, that for all its divisions and fissures, French democracy under the Third Republic weathered the storms of monarchism in the 1870s, Boulangism in the 1880s and the Dreyfus Affair in the 1890s, to achieve a remarkable degree of stability by the eve of the First World War. Among the many reasons for this was the power of the bureaucracy, especially the prefects in the provinces, and the large cohort of civil servants in the Ministries in Paris. Often legislation was couched only in general terms, leaving the bureaucrats to work out the details. The electorate was also remarkably unchanging in its political allegiances, with some regions in the west voting for conservative candidates ever since the Revolution, others, in the south and centre, supporting the Jacobins in the early 1790s and the Socialists a century later.

The slow pace of economic growth and the persistence of a large mass of independent peasants meant that rapid and violent social change did not disrupt the political system as it did in other states. More than half the French in 1914 lived in towns with fewer than 2,000 inhabitants. There was not enough large-scale industry to sustain a mass Socialist Party. And following the defeat of the Commune in 1871, Paris and its inhabitants no longer posed the revolutionary threat they had done ever since 1789: the Third Republic, unlike the Second or the First, was a Republic of provincials. The Chamber of Deputies changed very little over time: at any one moment between 1870 and 1940, a quarter of the members had served for twenty years and 3 per cent for a remarkable thirty-three years. Given its massive political power, it is not surprising that the Chamber met in almost permanent session; and the composition of its influential commissions changed only infrequently. The Chamber could not be dissolved, and so was able to assert its power during the five-year periods between elections without fear of the government. The Third Republic, in other words, was ruled by an oligarchy of professional politicians, most with strong roots in their constituencies.

Although Ministries changed every few months, the same ministers very often stayed on from one to the next. During the whole period of the Third Republic up to the Second World War, 217 out of a total of 561 ministers served once, 103 twice, 71 three times, 48 four times, and 122 more than four times; thus anyone not wholly incompetent in government could expect to serve in office repeatedly. Leading figures did emerge to dominate French politics for several years at a time. The anticlerical Aristide Briand (1862–1932) served three times as Prime Minister from 1909 to 1913, while Charles de Freycinet (1828–1923), an engineer who had become organizational chief of the railway system and was head of the mobilization service in 1870–1, served as War Minister seven times and Prime Minister four times. This long service enabled Freycinet to push through a series of major reforms of the army that were only possible because he occupied the War Ministry repeatedly. Jules Ferry was Minister of Education in five out of eight governments between 1879 and 1885 and Prime Minister twice, which helped him implement major reforms to the French school system. Reforms were therefore frequently achievable, from the anticlerical legislation of Ferry and then Combes, to the social welfare measures of the 1890s and 1900s. Lasting some seventy years in the end, the Third Republic was to prove the longest lived of all French political systems since the Revolution. Like Italy, it only seemed to be chronically unstable.

'FULL STEAM AHEAD!'

While France's combination of parliamentary rule and universal male suffrage marked it out from other political systems until the extension of the franchise in Italy, Austria and other countries shortly before the First World War, the Italian polity displayed significant similarities with that of Imperial Germany. Like Germany, Italy had been created largely by one dominant member state, in this case Piedmont, Italy's Prussia. The institutions of Piedmont were extended to the whole of Italy, however, while Germany retained its federal system of governance and administration. Parliament was far more influential in Italy. The monarch's position in both cases was strong, including as it did the power to nominate and dismiss ministers and to reject their advice, the right to dissolve the national legislature, control over foreign policy and the army, and the independent issuing of decrees. But there were also important differences. It was generally accepted that an Italian government had to possess a majority in the legislature, and a vote of no confidence usually led to the government's resignation or the calling of fresh elections, as it did not in Germany. Unlike in Great Britain or Prussia, the Upper Chamber of the legislature possessed only limited powers. The constitutional rights of the monarch were to prove fatal for democracy in Italy after the First World War, as in Germany, where they were largely transferred to the President after the fall of Wilhelm II. But for the moment, in Italy, they were seldom exercised.

This was not least because the Italian monarchs themselves were less than ambitious or dynamic personalities. Vittorio Emanuele II was a simple military man whose main pursuits, like those of so many European princes in this period, were women and hunting. He publicly maintained at least one mistress, and had numerous illegitimate children (it was observed that the common phrase used for a king, 'the father of his people', was in his case only too true). His successor Umberto I, the fourth Piedmontese monarch of that name, nevertheless took the number 'I' to denote his loyalty to the whole Kingdom of Italy; a passionate fox hunter, he had a military background and was known for his conservative political opinions, which on occasion, though not very often, he expressed publicly and through his choice of ministers. After Umberto's assassination in 1900, his successor Vittorio Emanuele III (1869–1947), a private and withdrawn man who disliked politics, devoted himself mainly to amassing a collection of over 100,000 coins, which he painstakingly catalogued in his *Corpus Nummorum Italicorum*, begun in 1910 and eventually stretching to twenty volumes, the last of which was published in 1943. The only piece of advice his father gave him was: 'Remember: to be a king, all you need to know is how to sign your name, read a newspaper, and mount a horse.' Only five feet tall, Vittorio Emanuele III was mortally offended when on a state visit to Italy, Kaiser Wilhelm II, in one of his numerous ill-conceived practical jokes, brought with him a squad of giant Prussian grenadiers for him to inspect.

The episode was characteristic of the ineptitude of German foreign policy from the 1890s onwards. Yet for its first twenty years, the newly minted German Empire had been cautiously and successfully steered by the architect of German unity, Otto von Bismarck. Here was another political system, like that of France, where the national legislature was elected by universal male suffrage. Following the example of Napoleon III, Bismarck had gambled on the loyalty of the masses. 'In a country with monarchical traditions and loyal sentiments,' he declared with his usual candour, as he defended the introduction of universal male suffrage for the German national legislature in 1871, 'the general suffrage, by eliminating the influences of the liberal bourgeois classes, will also lead to monarchical elections.' But they did not. Throughout the 1870s the Reichstag was dominated by the National Liberals, conditional supporters of the Bismarckian Empire but also convinced proponents of liberal reforms. This was mainly because the great mass of the peasantry did not bother to vote. In the mid-1870s the National Liberals commanded an absolute majority in the legislature, with 204 out of 397 seats. The result was a stream of liberal legislation, ranging from the Reich Criminal Code to the standardization of weights and measures, the creation of a national currency and a national bank. In conformity with the National Liberals' commitment to free enterprise, the remaining restrictions on freedom of trade were swept away.

In Imperial Germany there was no ministerial responsibility or party rule, indeed in a formal sense no national government, merely civil servants heading up a range of Reich institutions as State Secretaries. In practice, however, the Kaiser, the Reich Chancellor and the State Secretaries depended to a considerable extent on the national legislature to be effective. Elections were therefore increasingly fought along party-political lines, and as time went on, organized campaigning became more important. Political parties were quickly formed, ranging from the pro-Bismarck National Liberals and anti-Bismarck Progressives, founded in 1866, to the parties representing national minorities such as Poles and Danes in 1870–1. The SPD was established in 1875, the German Conservative Party in 1876. In the short term, the main beneficiary of universal male suffrage was the Catholic Centre Party, founded at the beginning of the 1870s, and imitated successfully in Italy only after the introduction of universal male suffrage there in 1912. Uniting all social classes of the urban and rural south and west, the party soon established itself as a major force, its popularity boosted by resentment against Bismarck's assault on the Church in the *Kulturkampf*.

The Catholic Centre Party was led by the Hanoverian lawyer Ludwig Windthorst (1812–91), whose background made him an Anglophile (indeed, he had made his reputation by disputing Prussia's right to annex the Kingdom of Hanover in 1866). Windthorst's appetite for work, along with his rhetorical skills, made him indispensable in the debating chamber. With an undersized body and an oversized head, and with such poor eyesight that he had to have the newspapers read to him, he was a gift to caricaturists. Yet he was, noted one of his contemporaries, 'a parliamentary miracle. He alone was equal to Bismarck.' He was particularly adept at the witty put-down. During one debate, Bismarck, who loathed Windthorst, accused him of using the Catholic issue to try and detach Hanover from the Reich, an act of treason. Windthorst responded by remarking that in the past two days 'such an excess of personal attacks has been directed against me, and indeed with such violence, that I am in fact beginning to believe that I possess a significance of which, until now, I had never dreamed [Laughter]'. His letters were steamed open by the Prussian police, but he did not give up (he started using ciphers), and in due course he steered the Centre Party out of the Bismarckian storm and into calmer political waters.

The Centre Party was hampered by the fact that in the early years of the new state, voting, restricted to men over twenty-five, was often neither fair nor secret. Voters had to bring their own ballot papers to the polls, and increasingly these were supplied by the parties that claimed their allegiance, including of course the Conservatives, dominated by landowning interests in rural areas. The ballot papers could be inspected and sanctions imposed by landlords and factory owners on employees who voted the wrong way. In industrial areas magnates or their agents often led the workers to the polls in a procession. It was only in 1903, after a long campaign, that the state was converted to the idea of supplying opaque envelopes for voters to put their ballot papers into, and only in 1913 that standardized ballot boxes were introduced (before, it was reported, they variously included cigar boxes, drawers, suitcases, hatboxes, cooking pots, earthenware bowls, beer mugs, plates and washbasins). Yet if intimidation was widespread, bribery and corruption were not, and the legalistic political culture of Germany ensured that Reichstag elections were on the whole fairer than their counterparts in many other areas of Europe even before the reform of 1903.

This was important not least because the powers of the Reichstag gradually increased over time, due in part to the creation of a growing number of central institutions over which it could claim oversight: these included the Reich Audit Office (1871), the Reich Statistical Office (1872), the Reich Railway Office (1873), the National Debt Administration (1874), the Reich Health Office (1876), the Reich Post Office (1876), the Reich Patent Office (1877), the Reich Justice Office (1877), the Reich Supreme Court (1877), and the Reich Colonial Office (1884). All of these sucked power away from the federated states and directed it towards Berlin. The increasing flow of national legislation through the Reichstag also tilted the balance of power in the Constitution away from the Federal Council, which represented the twenty-five states that made up the empire, and towards the elected legislature. Correspondingly the State Secretaries who headed the various central institutions of the Reich, including the Foreign Office, the most important of them, gradually evolved into the equivalent of ministers in a national government. As in France, therefore, a strong bureaucracy underpinned what all too often looked like a weak and fractious legislative system.

By the late 1870s, Bismarck's ability to manage the Reichstag successfully enough to get legislation through it was running into trouble. The *Kulturkampf* was not working, the economy was going through a lengthy crisis after the crash of 1873, and revenues from customs duties and indirect taxation were unable to pay for the mushrooming administration of the Reich. Germany was becoming dependent on foreign grain imports as the industrial population grew. Landowners and industrialists were clamouring for the introduction of protective import tariffs, anathema to the free-trade National Liberals. Half of Germany's blast furnaces were lying idle in the mid-1870s, and yet the liberals in the Reichstag still defeated a motion to levy duties on imported pig iron. Bismarck tried to square the circle by inviting the National Liberal leader, Rudolf von Bennigsen (1824–1902), to join the government, but the plan failed because Bennigsen wanted a guarantee that his party would occupy other Reich posts and introduce in effect ministerial responsibility and party government to the Constitution. Neither Bismarck nor Kaiser Wilhelm I was willing to take this step.

In 1878 two attempts to assassinate the Kaiser played into Bismarck's hands. On 11 May a young plumber, Max Hödel (1857–78), fired two shots with a revolver at Wilhelm I as he was driving in his carriage along Berlin's main thoroughfare, Unter den Linden. They missed, and Hödel was apprehended by an angry crowd. On 2 June, however, a disgruntled economist, Karl Nobiling (1848–78), using a double-barrelled shotgun, fired at the elderly monarch from an upstairs window overlooking the same street. Wilhelm I's life was only saved by the fact that he was in military uniform and wearing a spiked iron helmet. Nevertheless, he sustained serious injuries and had to retire from public life for a while in order to recuperate. Nobiling shot himself in the head with a revolver as a crowd tried to arrest him, but Hödel was tried and beheaded amid a massive propaganda barrage organized by Bismarck, who blamed the Social Democrats for the assassination attempt (they had in fact expelled Hödel when he had turned to anarchism). Bismarck used these events as a pretext for banning the SPD, whose members he portrayed, in succession to the Catholics, as 'enemies of the Reich'. As Bismarck intended, this presented the National Liberals with a dilemma: should they uphold civil liberties at the risk of being labelled sympathizers of an assassin, or should they agree to the ban at the risk of sacrificing their liberal principles? A similar dilemma faced them when Bismarck now introduced a range of protective tariffs, which were passed by the Reichstag the following year. Both measures, civil liberty and free trade, split the Liberals apart.

This was a major turn to the right in the governance of the empire. Liberally inclined senior administrators were dismissed and replaced by conservatives. At the same time more of the electorate were now exercising their right to vote, so that the percentage poll in Reichstag elections rose from 50 per cent in 1871 to over 80 per cent in 1912. As more peasants and more workers voted, there was a sharp rise in the Social Democratic and Catholic Centre Party votes, while the National Liberals, who depended on the crumbling hegemony of local notables in urban constituencies, underwent a steady decline. In 1871 they won 125 seats as opposed to seventy-six for the anti-Bismarck liberals, the Progressives, ninety-four for the Conservatives and two for the Social Democrats. By 1912 the National Liberals had fallen back to forty-five seats, with the Progressives gaining forty-two, the Conservatives fifty-seven, the Catholic Centre ninety-one and the Social Democrats 110. Here was evidence of a long and steady decline of liberalism of all varieties, balanced by a comparable rise in the forces of socialism on the left and Catholic politics on the right.

Despite its criticisms of German colonial policy, the Catholic Centre, anxious to demonstrate its loyalty to the empire after having suffered during the *Kulturkampf*, had in effect become the major prop of the government in the Reichstag. Yet Bismarck's gamble on universal male suffrage had failed spectacularly, in consequence of his failure to grasp the scale or importance of the industrialization process at work in Germany. As Arthur von Posadowsky-Wehner (1845–1932), State Secretary in the Reich Treasury, complained in 1896:

Germany is becoming more and more an industrial state. Thereby that part of the population is strengthened upon which the crown cannot depend – the population of the great towns and industrial districts – whereas the agricultural population provided the real support of the monarchy. If things go on as at present, then the monarchy will either pass over to a republican system or, as in England, become a sort of sham monarchy.

That this prediction did not come true was partly a result of the continued ostracism of the Social Democrats by the political elite, partly a consequence of the limited competence that continued to restrict the effect of the legislature all the way up to 1914. In addition, wide-ranging powers remained with the twenty-five federated states, which included tiny and insignificant ones like Schwarzburg-Rudolstadt, small but important ones like the city-state of Hamburg, and large and influential ones such as Baden, Bavaria, Saxony and Württemberg.

All these German states were dwarfed by the Kingdom of Prussia, which contained the majority of the empire's population and occupied the bulk of its territory. It was even more dominant in Germany than Piedmont was in Italy, offering a strong contrast to France, where the Third Republic was built on the rejection of Parisian hegemony and reflected the power of the provinces. Crucially, the King of Prussia was always German Emperor. Prussia held seventeen out of the fifty-eight seats on the Federal Council and could always pressure enough of the other states into voting with it to obtain an outright majority. The Prussian Prime Minister was almost always Reich Chancellor (Bismarck held both posts and that of Foreign Secretary as well). Each federated state had its own sovereign, legislature and administration, and each controlled education, health, police, and the levying of most taxes, though the growth of central government slowly reduced their autonomy. Few of these states were democratic, and in many of them the right to vote was linked to property ownership. In Prussia the electorate was divided into three equal classes reflecting the top, middle and bottom third of taxpayers: thus the two richest classes could always outvote the third, poorest class even though the latter heavily outnumbered them in terms of voters. More crucially still, the Prussian Army, which controlled the armies of the other states, above all in time of war, was to a large extent independent of the legislature. In a faint echo of their more radical position in the 1860s, the National Liberals in the Reichstag had attempted in the 1870s to force an annual budget on the army, while the latter did not want any budgetary controls at all. Bismarck managed to patch up a compromise whereby the army estimates were voted through every seven years. This minimized the degree of parliamentary control, though it still led in 1887 to a major clash as the Liberals tried to vote through a three-year period for the army budget. 'The German army,' declared Bismarck, 'is an institution that cannot be dependent on transient Reichstag majorities . . . This attempt to turn the imperial army into a parliamentary army . . . will not succeed.'

Angered by the National Liberals' assault on the independence of the Army, Bismarck dissolved the Reichstag in 1887 and fought an election campaign on the basis of a cynical and alarmist vision of a France that was so hell-bent on *revanche* that he could see 'war in sight'. Bismarck won, and was able to rely for the first time on a Reichstag majority, consisting of the Conservatives and the National Liberals. The *Kartell*, as the new majority was called, did not last long. Despite the introduction of his pioneering social welfare policies in the 1880s, Bismarck realized by 1890 that he had failed to destroy the SPD just as he had failed to curb the Catholic Centre Party. As the twelve-year sunset clause of the Anti-Socialist Law threatened to come into operation, therefore, Bismarck began to prepare for the Law's renewal. But his dominant position had depended not just on his mastery of the Reichstag but also on the trust of the Kaiser ('It's hard being Kaiser under Bismarck,' Wilhelm I had once remarked). In 1888, the old Kaiser died at the age of ninety, and was succeeded by his son, who took the throne using the Prussian royal number of Friedrich III (1831–88). Married to Queen Victoria's daughter, Victoria, Princess Royal (1840–1901), and enjoying the reputation of being a liberal, the new Kaiser did not get on with Bismarck. But he was weak and indecisive. The 'Iron Chancellor' had no problem in browbeating Friedrich III when he wanted to. Although he was a convinced opponent of the death penalty, Friedrich signed Hödel's death warrant as acting monarch in 1878 when Bismarck told him he would be betraying the Reich and the monarchy if he let the would-be assassin live. In any case, however, Friedrich's reign only lasted ninety-nine days before he died of throat cancer, despite the attentions of the best English surgeons.

He was succeeded by his son Wilhelm II, a very different character: restless, bombastic and unstable. The new Kaiser had been born with a withered left arm, which his parents tried to stimulate into growing by plunging it into the warm entrails of newly slaughtered animals, a therapy that can hardly have helped him gain the psychological balance he so obviously needed. Incapable of systematic work, Wilhelm travelled so much that he was popularly known as the *Reisekaiser*, the 'travelling emperor'. In August 1894 one newspaper calculated that he had spent 199 out of the previous 365 days on the move. There was, contemporaries observed, something about him that was 'not quite normal'. On cruises he made elderly generals perform gymnastics and on one occasion ran around them as they did so, cutting through their braces so their trousers fell down. On another occasion he got one rather fat courtier to make howling noises dressed up as a poodle; on a third occasion he forced the head of the Military Cabinet, Count Dietrich von Hülsen-Haeseler (1853–1908), to dress up as a ballerina and perform before the court; the unfortunate general had a heart attack in the middle of a pirouette and died on the spot. Wilhelm II was equally tactless with foreign potentates; when King Ferdinand of Bulgaria (1861–1948) was on a state visit to Berlin, Wilhelm slapped him vigorously on the bottom, in public, then pretended nothing had happened; while at a dinner in 1904, he told King Leopold II of the Belgians (1835–1909) that he should help him invade France. Leopold was said to have been so upset by this bizarre request that when he got up to leave he put his helmet on back to front.

Wilhelm II surrounded himself with a court 'camarilla' that was credited by critics with more power than it probably possessed. But its fawning sycophancy certainly encouraged him in the illusion that he ruled alone, and by Divine Right. 'I am the sole master of German policy,' he declared once, 'and my country must follow wherever I go!' In 1908, Colonel Edward Montagu-Stuart-Wortley (1857–1934) leaked a private conversation he had had with the Kaiser, during the latter's state visit to England, to the British newspaper *The Daily Telegraph*. The report offended almost everyone, from the Japanese, who the Kaiser said were intended as the target of Germany's construction of a high-seas battle fleet, to the French and the Russians, who he claimed had tried to persuade Germany to intervene against the British in the Boer War. 'You English are mad, mad, mad as March hares,' he told his interlocutor at one point. His dilettantism was illustrated by the fact that the most influential figure in the Foreign Ministry, Friedrich von Holstein (1837–1909), spent much of his time trying to neutralize the Kaiser's interventions, but met him only once during his sixteen-year tenure of office; according to legend, the subject of their conversation on this occasion was Pomeranian duck-shooting.

A man of Wilhelm II's qualities was not going to let Bismarck run things, and a series of minor squabbles between the two, augmented by the new Kaiser's reluctance to renew the Anti-Socialist Law, ended in Bismarck's employment of his customary tactic of threatening to resign. To everyone's surprise Wilhelm II accepted. Bismarck left office in 1890 to the accompaniment of a celebrated cartoon by Sir John Tenniel (1820–1914), illustrator of *Alice in Wonderland*, called 'Dropping the Pilot', which has Bismarck disembarking from the German ship of state as the Kaiser looks down insouciantly from the deck. Wilhelm's response was to announce that his policy was 'Full steam ahead!' But in his place Wilhelm appointed a general, Leo von Caprivi (1831–99), a well-meaning man with no experience of politics. To everyone's surprise, Caprivi began to pursue liberal policies, lowering tariffs and making conciliatory gestures to the opposition parties. However, Caprivi proved unable to manage the Reichstag, and the military Bill he got through was not to the Kaiser's satisfaction. By allowing too much freedom to his ministers, the general opened himself up to intrigues and plots, aided and abetted by the 'camarilla'. He resigned, tired of office, in 1894. His successor, the Bavarian Prince Chlodwig zu Hohenlohe-Schillingsfürst (1819–1901), was older than Bismarck had been at the time of his resignation. He stood by as one by one the independent ministers resigned and were replaced by the Kaiser's cronies. The Chancellor did not care. 'I may be weak,' he said, 'but at least I am not a scoundrel.' In 1900 he resigned at the age of eighty.

Hohenlohe's replacement was Bernhard von Bülow (1849–1929), an intimate of the Kaiser and State Secretary in the Foreign Office since 1897. 'Bernhard – superb fellow!' wrote the Kaiser: 'What a joy to deal with someone who is devoted to one body and soul!' This was another of his illusions. Bülow flattered and cajoled the Kaiser, and tried to gather a workable coalition together in the Reichstag, which passed laws providing for the construction of a High Seas fleet in 1898 and 1900, strongly advocated by the Kaiser, and a tariff reform in 1902, bitterly opposed by the agrarian interest, who did not think it went far enough. But convinced that his job was being made impossible by the Kaiser's tactless interventions, Bülow embarked on a covert campaign to limit his influence. Bülow engineered an election in 1907 over the Catholic Centre Party's criticism of German colonial policy. This resulted in a Reichstag majority, the so-called Bülow Bloc, which included the left-liberals, thanks to concessions to their policies, and pushed the Centre Party into opposition. By leaking a series of homosexual scandals at Court to the press, Bülow brought about the disgrace of the 'camarilla'. He made no attempt to stop the embarrassing *Daily Telegraph* interview from being published in full, though the newspaper had submitted it to him for approval in advance, and used the furore caused by its publication to get the Kaiser to promise not to interfere in government any more.

It was, however, not the Kaiser, but splits within the Bloc over the reform of the financial system of the empire that brought down Bülow. Before resigning in 1909 the Chancellor still managed to force Wilhelm to appoint not one of the discredited 'camarilla' but his own nominee as his successor. This was Theobald von Bethmann Hollweg (1856–1921), a career bureaucrat who had been Prussian Minister of the Interior then

State Secretary for the same department in the Reich administration. Inexperienced in politics, Bethmann found it difficult to manage the Reichstag. At the same time, the collapse of the Bülow Bloc opened the way to the emergence of new radical pressure groups on the right, as the Navy League, originally founded to support government policy, broke free from government control and began to criticize the Reich leadership for its supposed lack of enthusiasm for a big battle fleet. Other organizations such as the Colonial Union, the Society for the Eastern Marches and the Pan-German League formed a 'nationalist opposition' to demand imperial expansion and tough, even military action against the Social Democrats. Especially following the SPD's victory in the 1912 Reichstag election, all the signs were that a polarization of politics was in progress. It would culminate in a descent into political violence at the end of the war.

THE POLITICS OF EXTREMES

Despite Kaiser Wilhelm II's repeated insistence that he alone was in charge of the destinies of Imperial Germany, it was clear there was a vibrant political culture in Germany, with lively debates in the political press, mass membership of the parties, and a high turnout at election time. The authoritarian instincts of the state increasingly ran counter to the forces of democratic political participation. Universal male suffrage had given rise to a system of party politics that was forcing the central government to rely on parliamentary majorities to get many of its policies through. However, like the Dual Monarchy of Austria-Hungary, where the paralysis of the legislative system caused by the intransigence of national minorities was putting more and more power into the hands of the monarch and his chief advisers, the German Empire possessed a legislative and political system that had only a limited effect on decision-making at the top. In 1913 the Reichstag actually passed a motion of no confidence in Bethmann Hollweg's administration over the Zabern Affair, where military units occupying the town of Zabern (Saverne) in Alsace had been arresting, imprisoning and maltreating local people without intervention from the Reich government, which ruled the province directly and refused to condemn the soldiers' behaviour. Bethmann's administration continued as if nothing had happened. Parliamentary responsibility clearly still had some way to go before it finally took root in Germany. The crisis of August 1914 was to demonstrate that Germany's civil and military leadership made policy largely without reference to the legislature and the political parties.

The authoritarianism of the central European empires paled into insignificance in comparison to that of Tsarist Russia. The reforms undertaken by Tsar Alexander II following defeat in the Crimean War in 1856 had not altered the basic fact that the country was ruled by an autocracy unaccountable to no one but itself. There was no national legislature before the turn of the century and there were no political parties. The possibilities of public political discussion were limited. Correspondingly, the tactics used by oppositional groups in Russia were far more extreme than elsewhere in Europe. In the absence of a large middle class and lacking any tradition of liberal politics, the challenge of democracy was mounted by a new and in many ways unique social group that emerged in the 1870s in the wake of Tsar Alexander's relaxation of censorship and reform of education. This was the intelligentsia, a term originally coined by the Polish philosopher and nationalist activist Karol Libelt (1807–75) to denote the men and women who actively campaigned for Polish national identity on the basis of language, culture and education. The term meant both more and less than its equivalent in the world of the Baltic Germans, the *literati*: it did not include the whole of the educated middle class (the German *Bildungsbürgertum*), but on the other hand it did have a specific connotation of civic activism, particularly – in the light of official restrictions on freedom of speech – in literature, which thus took on a highly political character. Initially drawn from the nobility, the members of the Russian intelligentsia were gradually joined by people of less well-defined social origins, the *raznochintsy* (people of miscellaneous social rank), largely because of the expansion of the professional classes, the universities and the secondary-school system. In 1833, 79 per cent of secondary school pupils were sons of nobles and bureaucrats, but by 1885 this proportion had fallen to 49 per cent. The proportion of commoners among these pupils had risen over the same period from 19 per cent to 44 per cent. By 1894, too, there were 25,000 students at Russian universities. Long before this students began to organize themselves and produce newsletters with titles such as *The Living Voice* and *The Unmasker*. The students formed the audience for the new intelligentsia and eventually supplied it with new recruits: they were, as one commentator remarked, 'the barometer of public opinion'.

As the students began to demand the dismissal of ineffectual professors, forcing two in Moscow to resign in 1858, a reaction set in. One group of professors complained that 'the student is no longer a pupil but is becoming a master'. Admissions were curtailed and the police came back into the universities to supervise conduct. Exemptions from tax were removed, drastically reducing the numbers of the poor 'academic proletariat'.

Meetings could only be held with permission from the university authorities. This clampdown radicalized many students. A number were arrested and expelled. Similar events occurred in the provinces. More generally, as news-sheets and magazines began to appear in greater numbers, the failure of Alexander II to push forward with more reforms, above all his refusal to introduce an elected national legislature, propelled students and members of the intelligentsia sharply to the left. In the ferment of political discussion that broke out, the criticism of revolutionary ideology as 'nihilism' in Turgenev's novel *Fathers and Sons* (1862) called forth a response by Nikolai Gavrilovich Chernyshevsky (1828–89), editor of a radical periodical, *The Contemporary*, in the form of another novel, *What Is to Be Done?* (1863), which advocated a society based on producer co-operatives along the lines sketched out by the Utopian socialists. His book became a seminal text for the Russian radicals. The idea of using the peasant commune as a basis for a new society, bypassing the evils of capitalism and industrialism, was based on the writings of a radical of the older generation, Alexander Herzen, whose periodical *The Bell* was smuggled into Russia from his exile in London. But Herzen was too moderate for many of the younger intelligentsia, such as Pyotr Lavrovich Lavrov (1823–1900), who believed that peasant society could become the vehicle of a violent revolution once the peasants had imbibed the principles of socialism. Lavrov too had been arrested for anti-government writings and was in exile, in Switzerland, where he quarrelled with conspiratorial revolutionaries such as Mikhail Bakunin.

The situation became worse in 1866, when a young nobleman, Dmitry Vladimirovich Karakozov (1840–66), who had been expelled from university in both Kazan and Moscow, made an attempt on the tsar's life. Karakozov had been chosen by lot from 'Hell', the inner circle of a small conspiratorial society of Utopian socialists at Moscow University. Racked by remorse for his family's exploitation of the peasantry, he was personally enthusiastic about his mission. 'I have decided to destroy the evil Tsar,' he wrote in a proclamation that was never published because it was lost in the post, 'and to die for my beloved people.' On 4 April 1866, the date predicted for the revolution in *What Is to Be Done?*, he rushed towards the tsar as he was leaving the Summer Garden in St Petersburg, but as he took aim with his pistol his arm was jostled and he missed; the guards arrested him as he tried to take a second shot, and found a phial of strychnine in his jacket. 'What do you want?' the tsar asked him. 'Nothing, nothing,' he replied. Despite begging forgiveness and converting to Orthodoxy, Karakozov was executed by hanging on 3 September 1866; ten of his accomplices were sentenced to hard labour. A further clampdown at

St Petersburg University followed, and all societies of any kind were banned (a consequence of the fact that many revolutionary cells were disguised with harmless names: the one to which Karakozov belonged was registered as a society aiming to establish sewing co-operatives). From now on, the radicals organized themselves in secret.

Inspired by these events, the student Sergei Gennadiyevich Nechayev (1847–82) began to plot the tsar's death. An admirer of Chernyshevsky, he was said to sleep on a wooden board and live on black bread in imitation of the ascetic hero of *What Is to Be Done?* Fleeing the police, he went into exile in Zurich, where he met Bakunin, gaining his confidence by pretending to be part of a revolutionary committee whose members had escaped the Peter and Paul Fortress in St Petersburg, though in fact this was not true. The two men then sat down to compose the celebrated *Catechism of a Revolutionary* (1869). According to this document, the revolutionary had to devote himself full-time to the violent overthrow of the social order:

> The revolutionary is a lost man; he has no interests of his own, no cause of his own, no feelings, no habits, no belongings, he does not even have a name. Every thing in him is absorbed by a single, exclusive intent, a single thought, a single passion – the revolution. In the very depths of his being, not just in words but in deed, he has broken every tie with the civil order, with the educated world and all laws, conventions and generally accepted conditions, and with the ethics of this world. He will be an implacable enemy of this world, and if he continues to live in it, that will only be so as to destroy it the more effectively.

Nechayev returned secretly to Russia a few months later, disillusioned with Bakunin (who, he said, was always 'idly running off at the mouth and on paper'), and organized another secret society, the 'People's Reprisal'. When one of its members disagreed with his views and left the society, Nechayev and several of his comrades strangled and shot him and put his body through a hole in the ice covering a lake. But the body was discovered and the details of the incident came to light after the arrest of some of the perpetrators, prompting Dostoyevsky to pen a scathing portrait of the revolutionaries in his novel *The Devils* (1872). Fleeing once more to Swizterland, Nechayev took up again with Bakunin, and began publishing a small magazine, but his behaviour, which included stealing letters from Bakunin and others with a view to using them for blackmail, and threatening to murder a publisher if he did not release Bakunin from a contract, horrified his acquaintances. He was arrested and extradited to Russia, where he died in prison in 1882. This vision of the dedicated revolutionary was to exert a powerful fascination on later generations.

But this cult of violence at first had only limited influence. More important was the discussion and reading circle led by the student Nikolai
Vasilyevich Tchaikovsky (1851–1926) that produced pamphlets advocating
the creation of a peasant-based socialist society. Their ideas led to a movement 'to go to the people', in which students, who quickly became known
as *Narodniki*, or Populists, donned peasant costumes, learned trades, and
went to live with the peasants with the aim of converting them to the need
for revolution. The movement spread, and soon young revolutionaries
were holding meetings in the countryside, working alongside peasants
and gaining their trust. They soon discovered that the peasants could
not be weaned away from their veneration for the tsar. The Populists
distributed revolutionary pamphlets and books but discovered the peasants were unable to read them. Many Populists were denounced by local
priests or village elders. By the end of 1874 the movement was over. The
Minister of Justice reported that 770 people had been arrested, including
158 women. Fifty-three Narodniki had escaped but 265 were imprisoned
on remand.

The sheer extent of the movement was deeply worrying to the tsarist
authorities, who ordered a mass trial of 193 individuals in 1877. Lasting
for several months, the trial was conducted in public, and the defendants,
who also included participants in student demonstrations, heckled the
judges, delivered lengthy political speeches, and impressed the jury to the
extent that 153 of them were acquitted. Forty of them were sentenced all
the same, and the rest had been in prison for many months awaiting trial.
This trial further radicalized the remaining revolutionaries, who formed
a new organization, 'Land and Liberty', the first proper political movement with a title and a programme, rather than a loose network grouped
around a single individual. It sent out its members to the provinces in the
spirit of the movement 'to go to the people', and had considerable influence
among students. It advocated the 'disorganization of the state' by selective
assassinations. In the middle of the trial of the 193, the Governor of St
Petersburg, Fyodor Fyodorovich Trepov (1809–89), was shot by the young
secretary Vera Zasulich (1849–1919), a close associate of Nechayev. Zasulich belonged to a small Bakuninist group in Kiev and, like many others,
was outraged by Trepov's flogging of a political prisoner who had refused
to doff his cap in his presence. Her shot only wounded Trepov, and in her
subsequent trial so much evidence emerged of his brutality that the jury
acquitted her of all charges. Fearing re-arrest, she fled to Switzerland. The
government responded by transferring political trials to military courts.

The revolutionary movement was now pulled in different directions by
the followers of Bakunin and Lavrov. One wing, styling itself 'Black

Partition', and led by Georgi Valentinovich Plekhanov (1856–1918) and Pavel Borisovich Axelrod (1850–1928), eschewed violence; the leaders left for Switzerland in 1880 and continued their political activities in exile, joining Zasulich in the formation of a new Marxist movement. The other wing, 'The People's Will', focused on realizing the anarchist vision of the collapse of the state by killing the tsar. They got one of their members into Alexander II's palace and supplied him with dynamite, which he used to set an explosive device timed to go off under the dining room of the Winter Palace when the tsar was present. Eleven people were killed but the tsar's arrival had been delayed and so he escaped. A second attempt was made, involving digging a tunnel under a railway line and planting a bomb which the People's Will would detonate when the tsar's train passed over it. Through a double agent in the Third Section, they had obtained detailed plans of the tsar's movements, and knew he would be in the first of the two trains, but the order of the trains was changed at the last moment, and the bomb only destroyed the wagons carrying the tsar's baggage. To try and defuse the movement, Alexander II ordered a degree of liberalization to include the first steps towards a system of representative institutions, but on 13 March 1881, as he was riding in a closed carriage to a regular military engagement, two members of the People's Will threw bombs at him in quick succession. The first missed but the second found its target. 'I was deafened by the new explosion,' the police chief, who was accompanying him, later reported:

> burned, wounded and thrown to the ground. Suddenly, amid the smoke and snowy fog, I heard His Majesty's weak voice cry, 'Help!' Gathering what strength I had, I jumped up and rushed to the emperor. His Majesty was half-lying, half-sitting, leaning on his right arm. Thinking he was merely wounded heavily, I tried to lift him but the tsar's legs were shattered, and the blood poured out of them. Twenty people, with wounds of varying degree, lay on the sidewalk and on the street. Some managed to stand, others to crawl, still others tried to get out from beneath bodies that had fallen on them.

Alexander II was taken back to the palace and died shortly afterwards from his injuries.

The new tsar, Alexander III, a burly man over six feet tall, was a gruff and uncompromising conservative who had already made clear his disapproval of many of his father's reforms. Deeply religious, he was under the influence of his former tutor Konstantin Petrovich Pobedonostsev, Procurator of the Holy Synod of the Orthodox Church, on whose advice he cancelled the decree authorizing the creation of representative assemblies, appointed 'land captains' to oversee local administration, and drastically increased political repression. The police now had the power, without consulting anyone, to search, arrest, interrogate, imprison and exile people who were found guilty of any kind of political activity or even just suspected of engaging in it; to prevent 'untrustworthy' citizens from gaining employment; and to supervise all cultural activities. They had the right to declare martial law or a state of emergency. Secret agents were despatched to Switzerland to begin surveillance of political refugees and infiltrate revolutionary organizations. Under Sergei Vasilyevich Zubatov (1864–1917) a new anti-terrorist police department in the Interior Ministry, the *Okhrana*, founded in 1881, even created trade unions to try and divert revolutionary impulses into peaceful channels, and secretly sponsored student societies. The assassination of Alexander II also prompted an outburst of antisemitism in Russia, since the regime imagined a Jewish conspiracy behind the deed (in fact, the People's Will included very few Jews among its members, and none who adhered to the Jewish religion). Jews were confined to the towns, while quotas were introduced in the universities and professions. In 1891 the Jews were expelled from Moscow into the former Pale of Settlement, whose rules had been relaxed by Alexander II. Russian was enforced as the official language of the courts, the university and the schools in Poland, though the Finns continued to enjoy a substantial degree of autonomy. The result was a nascent revival of Polish nationalism, though it remained subdued by the extremely repressive conditions under which it had to exist.

Alexander III's repression lasted for the rest of his reign. The intensity of police activity ensured that further assassination plots came to nothing, and the People's Will fell apart. However, the tsar died unexpectedly in 1894 at the age of forty-nine, of kidney failure, probably as a result of the physical trauma he suffered when the imperial train derailed in 1888 (he was with his family in the dining car, and reportedly held up the collapsing roof with his bare hands as his children escaped from the wreckage). His eldest son and successor, Nicholas II, was at first an unknown quantity. 'What is going to happen to me and all of Russia?' he asked his brother-in-law on hearing of his father's death: 'I am not prepared to be a tsar. I never wanted to become one.' Conscientious but unimaginative, he was a man of limited abilities who was too shy and polite to deal effectively with his subordinates. However, his support for the principle of autocracy was unwavering: 'I want everyone to know,' he declared, 'that I will devote all my strength to maintain, for the good of the whole nation, the principle of absolute autocracy as firmly and as strongly as did my late lamented father.' Yet Nicholas II interpreted this to mean he had to micromanage everything, from petitions from peasants for a change of name to summoning an official for interview. Nothing was too trivial for his attention. He resented his ministers because their functions derogated from his own, and he even refused to appoint a private secretary, preferring to deal with his own correspondence. He was unable to tell the difference between the important and the trivial, and so he was incapable of delegating the latter in order to concentrate on the former. 'He sticks to his insignificant, petty point of view,' Pobedonostsev complained. The tsar increasingly bypassed his ministers and surrounded himself with aristocratic sycophants, but he also spent months away on tours or on hunting expeditions, yachting trips and family holidays, during which time the business of government ground to a halt. It was widely regarded as a bad omen when on the day following his formal coronation, a crowd of up to half a million people attending celebrations on a large military training ground outside Moscow, where free food and beer were supplied, stampeded as the rumour spread that there would not be enough for everyone: people were pushed into military ditches and suffocated or were trampled to death; altogether some 1,400 were killed and 600 injured. Blithely ignoring this unfortunate event, Nicholas continued the celebrations, attending balls, concerts and other festivities as if nothing had happened. Even in the carefully controlled media of Russia at the time, there was widespread criticism of his indifference.

The revolutionary movement soon revived, especially when former members of 'Land and Liberty' returned from exile in Siberia. In 1894 they formed a new organization, 'The People's Right', which joined another, the 'Union of Socialist Revolutionaries', founded in 1896, to create the Socialist Revolutionary Party in 1902. Influenced by the ideas of Herzen and Lavrov, this new party campaigned on the Populist platform of peasant rights as the basis for the creation of a new society, and Russian peasants began to undergo the same process of politicization that was taking place in other parts of the European countryside at the same time. In contrast to peasant political organizations in France or Italy, Germany or Spain, however, the Socialist Revolutionaries also continued the Russian terrorist tradition. They established a secret Combat Organization, which over the next two years assassinated two Ministers of the Interior, a Grand Duke, and many other government officials. The revelation that its deputy head was a police agent persuaded the party that agents provocateurs might be at work, and it abandoned the tactic of 'individual terror' in 1909. By the turn of the century the challenge of democracy was being articulated by more moderate political movements as well. In the 1860s Alexander II had introduced a new network of local government

institutions, the *zemstva*, which included district assemblies elected by
nobility, townsmen and peasant communes, and these district assemblies
in turn elected provincial assemblies, of which there were thirty-four by
1870. Their powers were extremely limited. However, the *zemstva* employed
growing numbers of administrators, doctors, teachers, agronomists, engineers, statisticians and experts of various kinds, who provided a basis of
support for liberal political ideas. There were an estimated 47,000 professionals working in them by 1900. By the 1890s the *zemstva* were also
holding a growing number of conferences that raised the demand for the
liberalization of the political system. Here was a grass-roots movement of
moderate democratic reform that was potentially a far more serious challenge to the autocracy than the small, if dangerous, terrorist milieu.

On the fringes of politics, Plekhanov and other exiled Marxists rejected
the idea of the peasant commune as an agent of revolution, and began to
argue instead that revolution would be brought about by the industrial
working class, which was growing apace as a result of Witte's economic
reforms in the 1890s and 1900s. The year 1898 saw the creation of the
Russian Social Democratic Labour Party to pursue this aim, but amid
incessant quarrels about tactics it split in 1903 into two bitterly opposed
factions, the Bolsheviks (majority) and the Mensheviks (minority), over
Lenin's book *What Is to Be Done?* A tract, not a novel, it was influenced
not so much by Chernyshevsky, who originated the title in his own much
earlier work (1863), as by Nechayev. Adapting the central principle of the
Revolutionary Catechism to Marxist ideology, Lenin argued that a revolution could only be brought about by a dedicated core of professional
revolutionaries under a strong leader (himself). Plekhanov and the Mensheviks, in contrast, argued for a flexible approach focusing on a legal
political and economic struggle, roughly approximating to the model of
the German Social Democrats. The Bolsheviks in turn rejected the idea
of policy formation by votes, pitting against it the doctrine of 'democratic
centralism' as a way of legitimizing their autocratic system of administration.
Doctrinaire and inflexible, Lenin would brook no opposition. He insisted
that the industrial workers should accept the leadership of the party, which
would mobilize them to extract concessions from the middle classes when
they eventually came to power and established a parliamentary government. The Bolsheviks remained for the moment on the fringes even of
revolutionary politics. They were more than willing to use illegal and
violent tactics, as in the 1907 Tbilisi bank robbery, when the young Georgian
Josef Djugashvili (1878–1953), later known as Stalin, organized the hijack-
ing of a coachload of cash on the main square of the Georgian city. There
were many police spies in their midst, including Roman Vatslavovich

Malinovsky (1876–1918), who rose to become a member of the party's Central Committee and the *Okhrana's* highest-paid agent. By 1914 Malinovsky was the only leading member of the party not in prison or in exile, a fact that in itself aroused suspicions which proved to be entirely justified.

After mid-century, the tsarist regime always failed the test of a major war, whether in the Crimea in 1854–6 or, terminally, in the First World War in 1917. A major war arrived shortly after the turn of the century, as Russia, expanding eastwards, clashed with the growing Asian power of Japan in Korea and Manchuria, which a Russian army 177,000 strong had occupied in 1900. Foreshadowing the bombing of the American naval base at Pearl Harbor in 1941, Japanese forces launched a surprise attack on the Russian fleet at Port Arthur, the only ice-free Russian port in the Pacific, in February 1904. After a lengthy siege, Russia surrendered Port Arthur in January 1905. In February, the Russians lost a major battle at Mukden, where their losses totalled 90,000. In May the Russian Baltic fleet reached the scene of the conflict after many months, having been denied use of the Suez Canal by the British, who were allied to the Japanese and had been annoyed by Russian ships firing on their fishing vessels in the North Sea in the mistaken belief that they were Japanese gunboats. The Japanese annihilated the Russian fleet, sinking eight battleships with no major losses of their own, and their ground forces occupied Sakhalin Island. Strikingly, an Asian state with a constitutional political system had defeated a European state without one.

The war was extremely unpopular at home, and the legitimacy of the tsar's rule was badly damaged by the defeat. While a peace settlement was arranged, brokered in London by the United States, the *zemstva*, taking advantage of the army's absence in the Far East, met to demand a constitution. Nicholas II agreed, his hand forced by a massive peasant uprising that now spread to the army, where mutinies broke out as it returned defeated from the front. A deputation of workers on their way to present a petition to Nicholas at the Winter Palace early in 1905 was fired on by troops, even though it was led by an Orthodox priest, Father Georgy Apollonovich Gapon, and carried religious banners and portraits of the tsar, in a massacre that became known as 'Bloody Sunday'. Gapon escaped but when it was revealed that he had been in contact with the *Okhrana* and received financial support from the Japanese military, he was kidnapped and hanged by members of the Socialist Revolutionary Party's Combat Unit. Workers had already downed tools in the capital and now there was a general strike. It was followed in May 1905 by the formation of a general Union of Unions, and in June by a mutiny in the harbour at Odessa by the crew of the battleship *Potemkin*. A strike by railway workers stopped any further troop movements. In St Petersburg a council, or Soviet, of workers' deputies was set up, led by Leon Trotsky, who had developed the theory of 'permanent revolution', meaning that a bourgeois revolution could be pushed straight on into a proletarian or socialist revolution under the right circumstances. Proclaiming that the tsar was 'at war with the entire people', the Soviet declared a general strike and began demanding full democratization.

Under these various pressures, Nicholas II granted the so-called 'October Manifesto', conceding the election of a Parliament, or Duma, and establishing a Council of Ministers on western European lines. The government tried to pacify the peasants by cancelling the last redemption payments, allowing them to consolidate their holdings and reducing the powers of the commune. The architect of these reforms, Pyotr Arkadyevich Stolypin, Prime Minister and Minister of Internal Affairs from 1906 to 1911, believed he could create a class of small landowners who would be loyal to the state. Although he had been dismissed earlier in the year Stolypin was still thought of as a danger by the Socialist Revolutionaries. One of them, Dmitry Grigoriyevich Bogrov (1887–1911), shot him during the interval at a performance of an opera by Nikolai Andreyevich Rimsky-Korsakov (1844–1908) in Kiev in September 1911, in front of Tsar Nicholas and two of his daughters. Stolypin died a few days later. Bogrov was arrested on the spot, condemned by a military court and hanged ten days later. As so often in these cases in late Imperial Russia, the background was murky in the extreme: Bogrov was unmasked as a police informer and there were accusations that extreme right-wing elements in the police had commissioned the assassination in order to provoke greater repression. An investigation was launched but it was halted on the personal orders of the tsar. The truth was never properly established.

Meanwhile the First Duma had been elected on 27 April 1906, though it did not have the power to appoint or dismiss ministers, which was retained by the tsar. Political parties emerged, however, with the Constitutional Democrats or Cadets, mostly *zemstvo* liberals, winning 179 seats, the Socialist Revolutionaries ninety-four, reflecting their growing popularity among the peasantry, the Social Democrats eighteen, the Right thirty-two, and nationalists of various hues the rest. When the Cadets demanded the right to appoint ministers, the tsar dissolved the Duma, declaring most of the deputies ineligible for re-election. The Second Duma, which convened on 27 February 1907, contained more conservatives and fewer Cadets, and was dissolved when the Social Democrats dared to criticize the army. A Third Duma was elected on a restrictive and indirect franchise, in which one elector was chosen by every 230 landowners, while it took 60,000 peasants to choose an elector, and 125,000 workers. Meeting on 14 November 1907, it contained 154 Octobrists, or supporters of the October Manifesto, 127 conservatives, fifty-four Cadets and thirty-three left-wingers; the Fourth Duma, which met on 15 November 1912 and was elected on the same basis as the Third Duma, was more conservative still (though five years later, its deputies were to play a key part in the February Revolution). Not one of Nicholas II's concessions was made sincerely, and on the urging of his reactionary entourage he sanctioned the dismissal of more than 7,000 government employees, mostly in the *zemstva*, and the creation of armed militias known as Black Hundreds, who attacked and sometimes killed liberal deputies, broke up oppositional meetings, and instigated antisemitic pogroms. The tsar himself pointed the accusing finger: 'Nine-tenths of the trouble-makers are Jews,' he said: 'The people's whole anger has turned against them.'

Despite the roll-back of the democratic movement and representative institutions, the arrests, and the suppression of the Soviet, full autocracy was not restored after 1905. The remaining censorship system was shattered, political parties had emerged and continued to function, and universities expanded and became more autonomous, though restrictions on radical students were reimposed in 1910. The system of local assemblies was extended, a limited measure of health insurance was introduced for workers, local justices of the peace were restored, and the corporal punishment of peasants was curtailed though not abolished entirely. Elementary education and literacy spread fast, though in 1913 the peasants were still spending less on printed matter than on oil for icons. Nevertheless the country was still ruled by a small and increasingly irresponsible clique around the tsar. From November 1905, Nicholas and his entourage fell progressively under the influence of the illiterate peasant faith healer Grigori Yefimovich Rasputin (1869–1916), who was said to have healing powers over the tsar's sickly haemophiliac son and heir. Rasputin used his influence in favour of the antisemitic Black Hundreds, and was instrumental in the dismissal of Stolypin as Prime Minister. Scandals and rumours surrounded the monk, including tales of sexual orgies and a liaison with the Empress Alexandra (1872–1918). These had already begun to undermine the tsar's reputation by 1912.

As the court freewheeled into irrationality, the galloping pace of industrialization and the lack of legitimate outlets for union protests and representation led to a growing number of illegal strikes. Between January and July 1912 some 1,450,000 industrial workers went on strike, with 1,030,000 of them putting political items on their lists of demands. The rickety and unstable nature of Nicholas II's rule was becoming steadily more apparent. Politics were polarized: the tsar's repression of the legitimate opposition in the Dumas had hollowed out the moderate centre. The creation of democracy seemed increasingly unlikely, its potential squeezed between a violent right and a terrorist left. As in other European states, some in the government saw in the fostering of nationalist enthusiasms a possible way out of the situation. Shortly before the outbreak of the war with Japan, and only a few months before his own assassination, Vyecheslav Konstantinovich von Plehve (1846–1904), Minister of the Interior, remarked: 'In order to hold back the revolution, we need a small, victorious war.' The war with Japan that broke out a few weeks after he uttered these words was neither small nor victorious. The war that was to come in 1914 was, however, different in scale altogether; it was to sweep away the tsarist regime altogether and usher in nearly three-quarters of a century of brutal Communist dictatorship.

'THE AMERICANIZATION OF THE WORLD'

Halted, or at least temporarily stemmed, in Russia, the tide of democracy still seemed unstoppable in most of the rest of Europe. Yet it was carrying along with it the seeds of its own destruction. The extension of the franchise brought the increasingly literate and educated masses into politics. While the working classes gave their support to socialist movements that at least outwardly seemed to aim at the destruction of capitalism and the overthrow of established institutions, the peasantry were beginning to move away from traditional forms of protest and gravitate towards populist Catholic parties or rural pressure groups of various kinds. Outflanked by these mass movements, middle-class liberalism was in decline by 1914 in many European polities. Above all, perhaps, the nationalization of the masses introduced a new vehemence into political discourse, expressed in episodes such as the rise to power, however temporary, of figures like Pelloux and Boulanger, both of whom built their popular appeal on the promise of national glory. In Germany mass nationalist movements like the Navy League began to push governments towards a more assertive foreign policy. In Belgium the introduction of universal male suffrage in 1893, which enfranchised the monoglot rural masses in Flanders, sparked the emergence of an increasingly vociferous movement for the use of Flemish as well as French in official documents, with demonstrations numbering tens of thousands of shouting protesters. In a similar way, the issue of Irish Home Rule in Britain broke up the existing pattern of politics from the mid-1880s just as the franchise had been extended to new sectors of the population, while in the Habsburg Monarchy it paralyzed the two major legislative assemblies, respectively in Austria and Hungary, altogether. Those who believed in the inevitability of democratic progress had to contend as well with the rise of far-right, ultra-nationalist and anti-democratic movements such as the Pan-Germans or the Black Hundreds – themselves a reaction to the spread of parliamentary and democratic politics. In 1914 these movements were still relatively small, despite being encouraged or at least tolerated by their respective national governments. Nationalism was no longer, as it had been up to 1848, an unambiguously liberal force. In Ukraine the People's Party, rival of the liberal nationalists, proclaimed: 'Muscovites, Jews, Poles, Hungarians and Romanians are enemies of our people.' The Pan-Germans urged the banning of the Social Democrats, the disenfranchisement of Jews, and the establishment of a dictatorship headed by the Kaiser. The influence of such ideas already pointed to the violent roll-back of democracy across Europe after the First World War.

The rival liberal and progressive ideals of the early-to-mid-nineteenth century – the French ideal of a Jacobin-style revolution or the British ideal of a series of gradual reforms – had already began to fade before the turn of the century. The future no longer seemed to hold a universal promise of either kind, particularly as nationalist ideologies began to look inwards to an imagined *Volk* or race and its historical genealogy rather than to universal principles of justice and popular sovereignty. As the European nations and their political cultures began to seal themselves off from one another in these ways, America started to emerge as the image of the future. The mass emigration of Europeans to the United States forged multiple links between the two continents, blurred the previous image of America as exclusively 'Anglo-Saxon', and broadened the conception of America as a land of opportunity for all. Once slavery had been abolished in the Civil War of the 1860s, the major obstacle to a positive image was removed, aided by the rapid rise of American industry and technology, symbolized above all in its massive display at the 1893 Chicago World's Fair. The economic interdependence of America and Europe was becoming obvious to all: 'The French soldier carries canned meats, prepared in Chicago, in his knapsack,' wrote the French social scientist Paul de Rousiers (1857–1934) in 1892. American initiative and example was wielding a growing influence over European political culture by the turn of the century, particularly in the issues of female emancipation and women's suffrage. The historian Gustave Lanson (1857–1934), taking a break from his duties at the Sorbonne to teach as a visiting professor in an American university in 1910, was much taken by 'the American girl type' he encountered among his female students – typically 'a slim, athletic young girl with regular features, a pure profile, blond or brown hair, clear blue eyes, a laughing, frank and firm gaze, free, rich, and joyful expansion of life'. Readers of the novels of Henry James such as *The Portrait of a Lady* (1881) would have known what he meant.

America could still of course appear as a land of rough-hewn pioneers, as in the touring Wild West Show staged by William Cody (1846–1917, known as 'Buffalo Bill'), whose European tours, from 1887 onwards, were hugely popular and attended by every class of society from Queen Victoria and Kaiser Wilhelm II down through the social scale. By contrast, many conservatives were fearful of the impact of American technology on Europe. The novelist Wilhelm von Polenz (1861–1903), who wrote cosy stories about rural German life, reported after a visit to the United States: 'The Americanization of culture means trivialization, mechanization, stupification.' His book, entitled *The Land of the Future* (1904), was mainly devoted to condemning the influence of Jewish immigrants on America and warning Germans of what he saw as the dangers of the growing influence of 'international Jews'. The term 'Americanization' was invented by the English journalist William Thomas Stead in his book *The Americanization of the World* (1901), in which his main aim was to advocate a renewal of the British Constitution through some form of union with the United States, to achieve the global dominance of the Anglo-Saxon race. (His quest to fulfill this aim led him to sail to America in April 1912 on the *Titanic*; he did not survive the journey.) There was growing anxiety about American economic competition, and after the Spanish-American War in 1898 emerging apprehension about America's imperial ambitions.

American economic methods such as 'Taylorism', making the most efficient use of working time, were much admired, and American inventiveness, from the sewing machine to the aeroplane, was quickly applied. Above all, liberals and socialists came to appreciate the virtues of American democracy. In Germany critical attitudes and derogatory references to the 'abstract freedom' and 'rigid' system of American government common in the Romantic era gave way to admiration towards the end of the century, above all on the part of those who saw Britain as a declining power that had not yet achieved full democratic status. Left-liberals admired the minimal state and widespread freedoms guaranteed Americans by the Constitution, and applauded what they saw as the effectiveness of its federal system, an example for Germany to emulate. Wilhelm

Liebknecht rebuked a fellow Social Democrat who had attacked American 'conservatism' by reminding him in 1887 that 'All democratic peoples are conservative. The American constitution has truly earned the right to be "conserved" – in spite of everything. Despotically ruled peoples are never conservative, because they are never content.' In their continuing, painfully slow struggle for democracy, Many Europeans thought America represented the future for which they were striving: prosperous, peaceful, technologically advanced, the free country of a sovereign people.

Those who opposed democracy and espoused a narrow, militant and aggrandizing nationalism, those who feared and disliked the fast-paced world of urban modernity that cities like Chicago and New York seemed to incorporate, and those who condemned American society as the negation of the ideals of racial purity, took a different, more critical view. Whether liberal or conservative, right or left wing, however, almost everyone assumed that the future belonged to Europeans and their diasporas in America, Australasia and other parts of the world. Whatever the future might hold politically, it was generally believed that it would be imperial, and imperial issues played a role of growing importance in the domestic politics of European states. As politicians such as Crispi, Bülow, Ferry and Disraeli discovered, playing the imperial card was a sure route to domestic popularity. In France the dream of revenge for the defeat of 1871 acquired new power through the expansion of empire. In Germany the political elite increasingly wanted a 'place in the sun', an overseas empire fit for a major European state in the twentieth century. In Britain, Joseph Chamberlain and the liberal imperialists put the defence of the empire at the heart of their ambition. Thwarted in East Asia, Russia turned again to its drive towards the Mediterranean. Holding onto the remnants of an overseas empire became a crucial objective in domestic politics in Spain, where, after the First World War, this aim would eventually turn in on democracy and destroy it. Independent nation states, above all in the Balkans, sought to expand their territory, taking advantage of the obvious decay of the Ottoman Empire. In Austria-Hungary the preservation of the empire's integrity seemed to demand the curbing of Balkan instability. Everywhere, national pride, bolstered by the rise of mass politics, exercised a growing influence over policy.

Among the few who doubted the imperial vision of the future was the English writer Rudyard Kipling (1865–1936), in his poem 'Recessional' (1897), written under the overwhelming effect of the review of the Royal Navy, the largest fleet ever assembled, on Queen Victoria's Diamond Jubilee in 1897. The poem ran directly counter to the mood of the time, but acquired a prophetic dimension in retrospect:

Far-called our navies melt away;
On dune and headland sinks the fire:
Lo, all our pomp of yesterday
Is one with Nineveh and Tyre!

Kipling reminded his readers of the transience of all empires, including even the British Empire, on which the sun reportedly never set. Yet, overall, people were optimistic about the future, insofar as they thought about it at all. On 1 January 1901, the very first day of the twentieth century, the *New York World*, guest-edited by Alfred Harmsworth (1865–1922), proprietor and editor of the *Daily Mail*, published a series of people's responses to the newspaper's question, sent to them a few weeks before: 'What, in your opinion, is the chief danger, social or political, that confronts the coming century?' Correspondents identified a variety of threats, from individualism to alcoholism. Clergymen went for Godlessness and 'mammon worship', while Arthur Conan Doyle and other writers somewhat ungratefully pointed to 'the irresponsible press'. Armaments, imperialism and war featured strongly among the responses. But, ignoring all the pessimism, Harmsworth declared: '*The World* is optimistic enough to believe that the twentieth century . . . will meet and overcome all perils and prove to be the best that this steadily improving planet has ever seen.'

8

The Wages of Empire

In 1815 the circus strongman Giovanni Battista Belzoni (1778–1823) arrived in Malta, after having toured Spain, Portugal and Italy, ready to engage in another series of feats of physical prowess, lifting heavy weights, bending steel bars, and breaking iron chains. His speciality was carrying twelve smaller men on a steel frame mounted on his shoulders. Born in Padua, the son of a barber, and initially intended for a monastic life, Belzoni had fled Italy on the invasion of his native city by Napoleonic troops in 1798, and had made his living in the Netherlands as a barber before moving to England in 1803. Here he had married Sarah Bane (1783–1870), a native of Bristol. Six feet seven inches tall and powerfully built, Belzoni had begun to eke out a living on the streets of London performing feats of strength before being recruited by a well-known circus at Astley's Amphitheatre, a popular entertainment venue in the city. Belzoni claimed, with what accuracy is not certain, to have studied hydraulics before leaving Italy, and was fascinated by technology. His shows were often accompanied by magic-lantern displays using back-projection to cast Gothic images of skeletons and ghosts onto a screen. In Malta, encountering an agent of the Egyptian Khedive Muhammad Ali, he offered to show the khedive a machine he had invented to raise the water level of the Nile to assist crop irrigation. They travelled to Egypt for this purpose, but when Belzoni tested the machine it proved unable to move the predicted amount of water, then spun out of control, and the khedive declared it a failure. Facing destitution, Belzoni and his wife went to see the British consul Henry Salt (1780–1827), who as well as being a proficient painter was also a collector of Egyptian antiquities. The two men hit it off, and Salt appointed Belzoni as his agent.

Soon the Italian was in Thebes, the ancient settlement in Luxor. He had been commissioned by Salt to organize the removal of a huge bust of

Rameses II (thirteenth century BCE), subsequently known as the Younger Memnon, weighing seven tons, and its shipment to England. Dressed in Arab clothing, but conspicuous by his great height and his huge beard, Belzoni travelled up the Nile with his wife. ('Mrs. Belzoni,' he later wrote, 'had by this time accustomed herself to travel, and was equally indifferent with myself about accommodations'.) Presenting the local Ottoman official with an order from the khedive, a bag of coffee and some gunpowder, Belzoni recruited 130 labourers who took more than two weeks to move the bust on rollers down to the river, sometimes sinking into the sand. He got into a fight with a local official when his labourers temporarily disappeared, and overcame many other obstacles before the bust was put on board ship. Upstream he found many other antiquities that 'might also easily be removed'. Reaching the great temple ruins of Abu Simbel, he returned laden with more treasures, and transported everything, including the colossal bust of Rameses, downriver to Alexandria and thence by ship to London and the British Museum. Subsequently Belzoni conducted excavations at Karnak, and was the first European to penetrate the second pyramid at Giza. Sarah Belzoni accompanied him on all his travels, lodging with local women and reassuring them about the couple's presence. 'As it was my lot to ascend the Nile,' she wrote, 'I contrived to see the various modes of living among these half wild people', and indeed she later published a book about them.

Salt was pleased with Belzoni's acquisitions, telling his patron the Irish peer Lord Mountnorris (1770–1844) that he was sending 'a cargo of such things as I believe you have not before seen'. His attempts to ship over a mummy were unsuccessful because superstitious ships' captains refused to carry it on board. A stuffed crocodile that Salt intended to transport to England was eaten by vultures. Nevertheless Belzoni was now launched on his new career as explorer and Egyptologist. His way with Egyptian antiquities was none too gentle. He found it hard to squeeze his considerable bulk into the narrow entrance passages of tombs, even on all fours, and once got stuck in a pyramid, needing to be pulled out by his assistants. In the Gournou tunnels, near Luxor, Belzoni wrote, he was choked by the dust and nauseated by the smell:

After the exertion of entering into such a place, through a passage of fifty, a hundred, three hundred or perhaps six hundred yards, nearly overcome, I sought a resting place, found one, and contrived to sit; but when my weight bore on the body of an Egyptian, it crushed like a band-box. I naturally had recourse to my hands to sustain my weight, but they found no better support; so that I sunk altogether among the broken mummies, with a crash

of bones, rags, and wooden cases, which raised such a dust as kept me
motionless for a quarter of an hour, waiting till it subsided again. I could
not remove from the place, however, without increasing it, and every step
I took I crushed a mummy in some part or other.

Belzoni was blissfully unconcerned by the damage he was causing to the
mummies, for, as he explained: 'The purposes of my researches was to
rob the Egyptians of their papyri; of which I found a few hidden in their
breasts, under their arms, in the space above the knees, or on the legs, and
covered by the numerous folds of cloth that envelop the mummy.' He
carved his name into one stone figure to prevent anyone else from removing it. At the same time he executed numerous coloured drawings and
plans of the sites and their contents, including detailed renderings of the
wall panels in the tombs of the Valley of the Kings, which Belzoni was the
first European to enter. On further expeditions he removed many further
objects, including a large obelisk that now stands to the south of Kingston
Lacy, a Dorset country house owned at the time by Sir William Bankes
(1786–1855), who accompanied Belzoni on one of his expeditions up the
Nile and boasted the largest collection of Ancient Egyptian artefacts in
private possession.

In all these activities Belzoni had to contend with obstruction from
local officials and competition from rivals. While removing the Pilae obelisk, he was confronted by a fellow collector, Bernardino Drovetti
(1776–1852), whose way with antiquities was if possible even rougher than
his own (when he found a collection of twenty vases, for example, he
deliberately smashed half of them to boost the price of the rest). Appointed
French Consul-General to Egypt by Napoleon I, Drovetti stayed on to
collect artefacts for French museums, and when he found the obelisk on
Belzoni's boat at Luxor he claimed that it belonged to him. Gathering
his men, he attacked Belzoni, who was mounted on a donkey. A shot was
fired, whereupon Belzoni leapt out of his saddle and felled one of his
assailants, 'seizing his ankles and using him as a club upon the foemen's
heads'. The local Arabs hastily made peace between the Europeans, upon
whom they did after all depend for their livelihood. The Belzonis returned
to England via Padua in 1819, where Giovanni wrote up an account of his
explorations. In 1821–2 he travelled widely on the Continent with an
exhibition of his acquisitions, feeling unappreciated in England ('I scoff
at my foes,' he wrote in a poetic moment, 'and the Intrigoni/If my friends
remember their true Belzoni'). The exhibition was not a financial success.
Borrowing a large amount of money, Belzoni travelled to west Africa and
joined an expedition to discover whether the river Niger was connected

to the river Nile, intending further to locate the legendary desert city of Timbuktu. But he succumbed to a fatal bout of dysentery in Benin. 'I die at last a beggar,' he wrote bitterly from Gwato, not far from the coast, in a letter urging his friends to 'console my dear Sarah' and care for her when he was gone. He died there on 3 December 1823. Sarah lived on in penury, failing to make an adequate income from either her husband's books and drawings or from her own, first in Belgium and then in Jersey, where she died in 1870 at the age of eighty-seven.

Belzoni's activities in Egypt were part of a pattern of European looting and plunder of other parts of the world that continued through the nineteenth century. It had begun already in 1792 with the French invasion of the Rhineland and expanded onto a huge scale with Napoleon I's removal of vast quantities of paintings and ancient sculptures from Italy in 1797, for transportation to Paris, which he considered to be the true heir of Rome. He took with him 167 'learned men' when he invaded Egypt the following year, and similar quantities of cultural objects were seized on their advice. But after Napoleon's defeat by the Prussian General von Blücher at the Battle of the Nations in October 1813, things changed. On reaching Paris in March 1814, Blücher took back by force the art that had been looted from Prussia by the French Emperor. The Duke of Wellington, resisting pleas from the Prince Regent to purchase some of the finer pieces for the royal collection, decided to arrange for the rest of the looted artworks to be returned to the 'countries from which,' he wrote, 'contrary to the practice of civilized warfare, they had been torn during the disastrous period of the French revolution and the tyranny of Napoleon'. In the event, only about 55 per cent of the looted objects were returned; the rest had already been dispatched to provincial French museums, beyond the ken of the occupying Allied armies. Wellington's disapproval of military plunder found an increasing number of supporters as the nineteenth century progressed. The duke himself thought that plunder both distracted the troops from the military operations at hand and also alienated the local population, who, as his experience in Spain had shown, it was important to keep on one's side.

No such reservations applied to European relations with non-European societies. The British had no problem in acquiring much of Napoleon's Egyptian booty, including the Rosetta Stone, key to the decipherment of hieroglyphics, after Napoleon was defeated by Nelson at the Battle of the Nile in 1798. Particularly rich pickings were to be had from the decaying Ottoman Empire, where it was easy enough to bribe officials at every level to allow for the purchase at a knock-down price of Classical Greek artefacts such as the Elgin Marbles. They were removed from the

Parthenon in Athens by the agents of Thomas Bruce, Earl of Elgin (1766–1841), between 1801 and 1812, purchased by the British government in 1816, and subsequently passed into the hands of the British Museum. Later in the century some two hundred bronze sculptures were seized from Benin in west Africa by a British military expedition and also taken to the British Museum. The Germans removed ocean-going outrigger canoes from Pacific islands for display in the national ethnographic museum in Berlin; the German businessman and amateur archaeologist Heinrich Schliemann (1822–90), obsessed with the quest to find the site of ancient Troy, discovered a cache of gold objects on one site in 1873, smuggled it out of Turkey and gave the jewellery to his wife to wear.

Such acquisitions reflected Europe's worldwide hegemony in the nineteenth century. They were made possible by industrial growth, military supremacy, and above all by improved communications, as travel by rail, steamship, river, canal and road made it easier to span the continents and arrive with little difficulty at the starting point for penetration into distant lands. The rapidly growing prestige of science and scientific knowledge fuelled the idea of exploration. Belzoni and his fellow Egyptologists increased European understanding of Ancient Egypt even as they collected and sometimes damaged or destroyed its cultural products, particularly when the French linguist and historian Jean-François Champollion (1790–1832) deciphered hieroglyphic script, using bilingual inscriptions on Belzoni's obelisk. The thirst for scientific knowledge drove the Swedish explorer Sven Hedin to locate the sources of the Brahmaputra and Indus rivers in the Himalayas and uncover parts of the Great Wall of China. In October 1844 the Prussian natural scientist and explorer Ludwig Leichhardt (1813–48?) undertook a 3,000-mile journey across north-eastern Australia collecting specimens, emerging at Port Essington on the northern coast in December 1845 after he and his party had been given up for dead. He declared: 'I have worked for the sake of science, and for nothing else.' In 1848 he mysteriously disappeared with another expedition, probably in the Great Sandy Desert, in an attempt to cross the continent from east to west.

By this time the search for the source of the Nile was fast becoming a public obsession in England, with the Royal Geographical Society funding a celebrated expedition by Sir Richard Burton (1821–90) and John Hanning Speke (1827–64) in 1856. Burton was as much adventurer as explorer, an irascible man of strong passions. Said to command twenty-nine different languages, he became famous for travelling in disguise to Mecca and publishing an unexpurgated translation of the *Arabian Nights* (1886–98) as well as English editions of the erotic classics *The Perfumed Garden* (1886) and the *Kama Sutra* (1883). His books scandalized Victorian opinion by including details of the sexual practices of the peoples he encountered (he even included measurements of the size of the men's sexual organs). With Speke he travelled up the Nile in 1857–8, and was the first to reveal to Europeans the existence of Lake Tanganyika, collecting a livid scar on the way after surviving an attack by a band of Somali warriors in which a spear had penetrated both cheeks. Scarcely less famous were the self-funded Samuel Baker (1821–93) and his wife Florence (1841–1916). Here too was an adventure story tailor-made to inflame the Victorian imagination, for Baker had spotted the young woman, blonde and blue-eyed, while visiting the slave market in Vidin, in the Bulgarian part of the Ottoman Empire; outbid by the local pasha, Baker bribed her keepers and ran away with her, marrying her in Bucharest. After living for a time in Ceylon, he spent the 1860s in African exploration, accompanied everywhere by Florence; in 1869 he was made a major-general in the Egyptian Army and led a force of 1,700 freed convicts on an expedition to suppress the slave trade in the equatorial regions of the upper Nile – his successor in the post was Colonel Charles George Gordon (later Gordon of Khartoum; 1833–85). Baker was knighted for his services to exploration, but Queen Victoria refused to receive him at Court because, as she observed rather severely, he had been 'intimate with his wife before marriage'.

Exploration offered particular opportunities to the women who possessed the courage and the resources to undertake it. The Swiss explorer Isabelle Eberhardt (1877–1904) was the illegitimate daughter of a wealthy Baltic German aristocratic woman and the Armenian tutor she employed for her older children. Isabelle mastered eight languages; dressed as a man, she converted to Islam and explored the Sahara before being unexpectedly drowned in a flash flood. The Austrian Ida Pfeiffer (1797–1858), daughter of a wealthy Viennese merchant, and married to an elderly widower, began her travels after her husband's death in 1838, travelled to Iceland and northern Scandinavia and then through South America and the Pacific, living for a time among the Dyaks of Borneo and the Bataks of Sumatra. The Englishwoman Isabella Bird (1831–1904) became one of the most celebrated explorers of her day, particularly when she began to take a camera with her; her travels, at first financed by her father and then through an inheritance, included America, Australia, China, Hawaii, India, Iran, Japan, Korea, Malaya, New Zealand, the Ottoman Empire and the Persian Gulf. Her fame drew audiences of up to two thousand at her lectures. After one presentation in the Scottish town of Tobermory, on Persia, the audience was said to have been 'delirious with enthusiasm and delight and the vote of thanks was a wild highland uproar of stamping, clapping, hurraring and waving of hats and handkerchiefs'. Bird's achievements were recognized by her election as the first female Fellow of the Royal Geographical Society, in 1892.

Global exploration was often carried out by people who themselves had a global background. One such was the French-American Paul du Chaillu (1835?–1903), who claimed to be the first European to have seen a live gorilla. He brought a number of skeletons and preserved gorilla corpses back to France to exhibit. Chaillu was also the first European to observe pygmies, as recounted in his book *The Country of the Dwarfs* (1872). His account of his discoveries became influential in the development of racial classifications of humanity in the late nineteenth century. Born on the island of Réunion, or possibly in Paris or New Orleans, Chaillu was educated by missionaries in Gabon, where his father was a French trader. He kept chimpanzees as pets, and published the African legends he heard featuring gorillas abducting women. His tales were the main inspiration for *Tarzan of the Apes* (1912) by the American pulp-fiction author Edgar Rice Burroughs (1875–1950). Equally cosmopolitan was Henry Morton Stanley (1841–1904) a Welshman born John Rowlands and brought up in a workhouse. In 1859 he sailed to New Orleans, jumped ship, and found a job with a rich trader called Henry Stanley, who eventually adopted him. Henry Morton Stanley fought on both sides in the American Civil War, then became a journalist, which led to his engagement by the legendary editor of the *New York Herald*, James Gordon Bennett Jr. (1841–1918), to find the missing British missionary David Livingstone (1813–73). 'Dr. Livingstone, I presume?' – Stanley's reputed greeting to the missionary when he finally caught up with him in 1871 in a remote part of Africa near Lake Tanganyika – entered legend as a classic example of cool understatement.

In 1874 the *Herald* commissioned Stanley to trace the course of the river Congo from its source to the sea; starting out with a company of 356, he eventually arrived at the mouth of the river with only 114 left, none of them European. Disease took its toll but so too did Stanley's brutal discipline, which included frequent floggings of his bearers. Even Richard Burton complained. 'Stanley shoots negroes as if they were monkeys,' he said. 'The savage,' Stanley remarked for his part, 'only respects force, power, boldness, and decision.' Not surprisingly he is said to have been the model for the figure of Kurtz in Joseph Conrad's 1899 novella *Heart of Darkness*. Stanley's knowledge of the Congo led to a commission from King Leopold II of the Belgians, who thought that possession of the Congo basin would yield prestige for his country and profits for his own private exploration company. The explorer opened up lakes, mountains and large tracts of territory to European knowledge, but also laid the foundations for Leopold's exploitation of the region. These explorations worried the French, who sent another explorer, Pierre de Brazza (1852–1905), to open up parts of the Congo basin to their own influence and limit that of the Belgians.

It was Stanley's discovery of Livingstone that really made him famous. The older man was already well known and widely admired for his combination of medical and missionary work. Yet he was an ineffective organizer. He quarrelled with his assistants, many of whom resigned or were dismissed, he failed to find a navigable route along the Zambezi, and he did not succeed in discovering the source of the Nile. At the same time Livingstone founded a number of mission schools and wasted few opportunities for religious conversions; many years later some of these schools gave an education to young men who subsequently became leaders of African nationalist movements. The reports Livingstone sent back to England continually stressed the need to combat the slave trade, which still existed in the areas he went through. Yet ironically, as his expeditions steadily got smaller, he came increasingly to depend on the help of Arab slave-traders. In his last expedition he was often ill, and after Livingstone's death in 1873 his bearers carried his decomposing body for a thousand miles to the coast for return to Britain. This combination of courage and piety, science and faith, and determination in the face of adversity, made his life – and his death – an inspiration for Victorians. Helped by Stanley's journalism, Livingstone became a legend. His activities laid the foundation for later British territorial expansion.

Livingstone's unconscious role in stimulating the rise of empire in Africa, in common with that of other explorers, was due not least to the fact that at every point the Europeans' discovery of parts of the globe previously unknown to them was closely bound up with national prestige and ambition. Explorers publicized their exploits in their home countries as examples of fortitude and daring in a way calculated to bring a glow of national pride to those who read about them. This was the case even where there were no apparent economic or strategic interests involved, most obviously perhaps in the attempt to reach what was then the economically worthless North Pole. The Norwegian Fridtjof Nansen (1861–1930), the first man to cross the interior of Greenland (in 1888), reached 86°13.6′N in 1896 after drifting his ship the *Fram* northwards for many months in the pack ice and then continuing on a dog-sled. In 1897 an expedition sponsored by the Belgian Geographical Society sparked a race for the South Pole, in which German, British, French and Japanese expeditions competed. The first to reach the Pole, on 14 December 1911, was the Norwegian Roald Amundsen (1872–1928), formerly first mate on the Belgian expedition. Amundsen had learned from the Inuit during a crossing of the North-West Passage some years earlier that animal skins were lighter and more waterproof than woollen parkas, and that sled-dogs were the best means of travelling in snow. As the sleds became lighter with the progressive consumption of supplies, Amundsen killed those dogs that were no longer required and used them to feed the others. Eleven of the fifty-two dogs that set out survived. A poorly organized British expedition led by Captain Robert Falcon Scott (1868–1912) arrived shortly afterwards on foot, on 17 January 1912. The party of five had tried to use ponies, but these had proved unable to withstand the harsh climate, and the men disdained the use of dogs as ungentlemanly. Wearing unsuitable parkas and suffering from frostbite and scurvy, Scott and his companions perished on the return journey. 'Had we lived,' he wrote on 29 March in a journal he left in the tent where he died, 'I should have had a tale to tell of the hardihood, endurance, and courage of my companions which would have stirred the heart of every Englishman.'

To a degree the exploration of other parts of the world was seen as a common European enterprise carried out in the name of science and civilization – the British Royal Geographical Society, for example, awarded its gold medal to Leichhardt, Nansen, Amundsen and Hedin among others – but at the same time men like Livingstone and Scott became national heroes, the race to the source of the Nile or the South Pole a matter of national prestige. In the longer run, exploration became one of the key sources of empire, as it brought distant parts of the world closer to Europe and underlined for Europeans the destiny of these regions to be 'discovered' and, eventually, subjugated to Europe's will. If they were inhabited by human society, that society was invariably regarded as inferior, backward, ripe for subordination or even, as in Australia, effectively non-existent. The attitudes of the Russian explorer Nicholas Mikhailovich Przhevalsky (1839–88) were typical in this respect. Exploring Central Asia and northern Tibet 'with a carbine in one hand a whip in the other', he described for the first time the breed of wild horse later named after him. He also called the Chinese 'the dregs of the human race' and claimed that 'a thousand of our soldiers would be enough to subdue all Asia from Lake Baykal to the Himalayas'. Explorers were thus, whether intentionally or not, the harbingers of imperialism, above all in the second half of the century.

THE REVIVAL OF EMPIRE

The global colonial conflicts of the late eighteenth and early nineteenth centuries, above all between the British and the French, had by the time of the Congress of Vienna been resolved. From this point on and up to almost the very end of the century, British command of the oceans was absolute. By the mid-1870s the Royal Navy consisted of more than 500 ships, with roughly half of these being in active commission at any one time. Sixty-one of these were modern ironclads rather than the old-fashioned wooden vessels. The Royal Navy was far larger and more powerful than its nearest rivals, the French and American navies, and indeed from the 1870s it was official British policy to ensure that its own strength should be greater than that of any other two navies combined. With such massive naval predominance the British were the only power in a position to acquire and maintain a really large-scale empire. More than 80 per cent of the world's goods were carried in British ships. The British dominated trade with independent Latin America, so there was no obvious reason why they should seek to convert economic power there, or indeed in any other part of the world, into the annexation of territory. They relied on free trade instead. For much of the century there was no specific or explicit ideology of what came to be called 'imperialism', asserting the superiority of European civilization over others, or justifying the acquisition of colonies as a matter of policy. In the eighteenth century the transportation of slaves from Africa to the plantations of North and South America and the Caribbean had been a fundamental part of the trading relations of Europe with the Americas. By the 1820s, however, the importance of this trade was beginning to diminish and the mercantilist policies that underpinned it had been torn to shreds by the American Revolution.

Yet despite all this, European overseas empires underwent a marked revival in the years after the end of the Napoleonic Wars. The impulses for the new expansion came not from conditions within Europe itself but largely from developing situations in other parts of the world. Local events were often decisive, as in the example of the French annexation of Algeria in 1830. Algeria was formally part of the Ottoman Empire, but the autonomous governor of the province, the Dey Hussein (1765–1838) of Algiers, was in financial trouble because his main sources of wealth – slavery, kidnapping and piracy – were declining. In 1816 the British forced the Dey to surrender Christian slaves and return all the money he had received for ransoming Christian prisoners. Putting up taxes to meet these demands led to popular resistance. In 1827 the Dey asked the French to repay money he had lent them during the Napoleonic Wars. The French consul refused to do this. The Dey summoned him to his court, called him a 'wicked, faithless, idol-worshipping rascal' and struck him with a fly whisk. The French press bayed for revenge for this insult. In 1830, after some hesitation, Charles X of France, anxious to win popularity and stave off the prospect of a liberal revolt, decided to invade. The French Army, thirsting to relive the glories of the Napoleonic era, pulled out the emperor's old invasion plans from a bottom drawer. Eighty-four French ships conveyed 37,000 troops across the Mediterranean and set up a well-defended base camp. Some 35,000 Ottoman troops arrived on 19 June 1830, but the French possessed better guns and routed them. On 5 July the Dey surrendered on the condition that people's religion was respected, and the French occupied Algiers. Napoleon had triumphed again – this time from beyond the grave.

The French, needless to say, did not keep their promises, and soon began turning mosques into churches, sparking resistance from the deeply Muslim country, led by the Sufi orders who had already rebelled against the taxation demands of the Ottomans. A young holy man, Abd el-Kader al-Dzejairi (1808–83), who claimed descent from the prophet Mohammed, emerged as a leader, proclaimed a jihad, and inflicted repeated reverses on the French. By 1836 the French were facing defeat, so King Louis-Philippe sent in Marshal Thomas-Robert Bugeaud (1784–1849). The marshal pushed the rebels back, razing their villages to the ground (thus introducing the Arab word *razzia*, scorched earth, to many European languages), and beheading any Muslims taken prisoner. Victory finally came in 1847, when Abd el-Kader gave up and decamped to Damascus. The French at least began to learn the lesson from these events, and started to use Islamic institutions to support their rule. A motley crew of settlers now began to arrive from Europe: French aristocrats, who wanted to recreate a pre-1789 society in Algeria; Cistercian monks, who built a monastery and farm; ex-soldiers granted land in Algeria at the end of their service; socialist disciples of Saint-Simon, who intended to create utopian communities; later on, revolutionaries deported from France after the 1848 June uprising; Italians, Spaniards, Maltese and many others.

By the time of the Second Empire the settlers had lost most of their initial ideals and agitated for the downgrading of the rights of the original inhabitants of the colony. On 24 October 1870 the new republican government in Paris passed a law giving Jews and settlers in Algeria French citizenship. Arabs and Berbers continued to be excluded from full rights. A local Muslim leader, Mohamed el-Mokhrani (1815–71), declared a jihad against the French, outraged that Jews had been placed above Muslims and convinced that the German defeat of the French was a sign of divine justice. In 1868, French rule had been a major factor in a famine in which perhaps a third of a million Algerians died; French propaganda made great play with the famine relief operation mounted by the Church in Algeria, but this too was a bitter cause of resentment. Some 150,000 Muslims rose in support of Mokhrani and began besieging the towns where the French and other settlers had retreated for safety. Within a short time the revolt was defeated. Together with the 1868 famine, the conflict had led to the death of around a million people, a third of the population. The French revenge was harsh. The leaders of the uprising were killed or sent to the Pacific island of New Caledonia. Up to 1,200,000 acres of Arab land were confiscated. Pilgrimages to Mecca were severely restricted in order to cut off Algeria from the rest of the Muslim world. Arabic was even classified as a foreign language. Muslim social and educational institutions thought to encourage resistance to French rule were destroyed. Within a few years the northern part of the country had been turned into three French departments, satisfying settler demands, while the southern part remained under army control.

Algeria was something of an exception to the general nature of European colonialism before 1880. More traditional patterns obtained in the rest of Africa, where three different interests intersected. The first of these was trading. As the slave trade declined then came to an end, European trading bases began to deal in vegetable oils instead of slaves, processing African-grown groundnuts and palms. But this only created an intensified demand for slaves within Africa itself, so that the slave trade in sub-Saharan Africa continued well into the second half of the nineteenth century. By around 1880 trading bases, mainly British and French, were dotted all over the west African coast, and rivalry between them was becoming a source of conflict. Their respective governments tried to make them financially useful by charging customs duties, which in turn meant annexing new entry points to the African Continent in order to stop smuggling. In 1850 the British government acquired the remaining Danish forts on the coast, in 1861 Lagos and in 1872 the Dutch base of Elmina. The French acquired new trading posts on the coast of Senegal. The possibility of these trading bases getting into trouble with African rulers and requiring military protection increased as their numbers and influence grew. For the time being, however, trading interests were paramount and the likelihood of formal colonization seemed remote.

Britain's relative lack of interest in formal colonial acquisitions was illustrated by events in south Africa. London veered between annexing areas settled by the Boers, who were after all British subjects, and allowing them autonomy; the Transvaal was recognized as a free state in 1852, annexed in 1877, and given autonomy again in 1881. This indecision was to have major repercussions at the end of the century. In India, too, expansion was largely unplanned by Britain, but occurred in particular on the initiative of the Governor-General, Lord Dalhousie (1812–60), appointed in 1848. Dalhousie thought Indian-controlled states were inefficient and that income for the East India Company – the powerful British trading organization that in the previous decades had come to rule over large areas of the subcontinent with its own private armies and administrators, in order to provide a stable and secure basis for its operations – would be increased if he annexed them. Disorder in the Punjab following the death of its ruler Ranjit Singh (1780–1839) drew the British in. It was annexed after fighting in 1849, alongside neighbouring Sind, captured in 1843 by a veteran of the Napoleonic Wars, General Sir Charles Napier (1782–1853). Napier in fact far exceeded his orders, which were merely to quell a rebellion. (His famous punning one-word dispatch, *peccavi*, 'I have sinned', was not actually his at all; it was a joke sent to the satirical magazine *Punch* by the translator Catherine Winkworth, which the magazine printed as if it came from Napier.) Both the Punjab and Sind controlled access to the emirate of Afghanistan, but the British had failed to subjugate this state with a military expedition in 1842 – all but one of the 16,000 men were annihilated by tribesmen.

This rapid expansion of British India in the 1840s and especially the mid-1850s, when many parts of northern India were taken under British rule, along with lower Burma, where Dalhousie acted in 1852 to protect British trading interests, illustrated the fact that at least in this area of the globe Britain continued to push forward with the extension of imperial rule. It also created massive tensions and resentments. The arrival of missionaries sparked fears of forced conversion to Christianity. British control was precarious. In mid-century the subcontinent had a population of around 200 million. This was not going to be a colony of settlement for the British; it was not going to be converted to Christianity; it was not going to be culturally assimilated into European ways of living. It did, however, yield massive revenues used to sustain a very large private army belonging to the East India Company and recruited from the Indian population – so-called sepoys – 200,000 in 1857, under Indian officers, alongside 16,000 European troops in separate regiments, under British officers. Territorial expansion meant that Indian troops were now expected to serve further away from their homeland without additional pay, even in such remote areas as Burma and China, and many of them objected to being removed from their own region. Military expansion necessitated an unpopular increase of taxation on the population. Resentments boiled over when a new model of rifle was introduced, with pre-greased paper cartridges that had to be bitten open to release the powder; the tallow used to grease them was made from either beef fat, offending Hindus, or pork fat, offending Muslims. Sepoys refused to use the rifles, and attempts to discipline them led to open rebellion. Soon the subcontinent was in a state of war. Some key Indian states, whose rulers hated their loss of power and objected to British interference with Hindu custom, joined the uprising. Others remained loyal. In some areas the revolt took on a distinctly nationalistic character, though the diverse motives of the rebels, and the fact that many areas stayed calm, make it difficult to describe this as a concerted war of independence.

The British were driven back into their forts, where they were besieged. There were numerous massacres of British troops, most notoriously in 1857 at Kanpur, which inflamed public opinion back home and fuelled a wave of revenge as British forces regained the initiative. They began punishing the rebels, shooting and hanging them in huge numbers, or using the traditional Mughal punishment of firing them from the mouths of cannon. Blamed for the uprising, the military and administrative role of the British East India Company was removed in 1858 and replaced by direct government control. This was the beginning of the 'British Raj'. The number of British troops in India was virtually doubled and sepoy recruitment was confined to more loyal areas in the north, with the army funded by a new and more acceptable taxation system based on Mughal models. British government control was soon extended over the Malayan peninsula, where local states were forced to accept British informal suzerainty in 1873, in an attempt to protect trade with China against piracy – also a major factor in prompting the Dutch to extend their control over Indonesia in the 1850s. Like much else in this period, such expansion was largely piecemeal and unplanned. The same can be said of the activities of the French in Indochina, where Napoleon III sent troops at the end of the 1850s after French missionaries had been persecuted and killed; local French officials argued that further expansion was necessary to protect missions and trading interests, clashes took place with local and regional powers, and by the 1890s France was in full occupation of the entire peninsula, after capturing the key fort of Hung Hóa in 1884.

In almost all of these examples it was local European officials, merchants and missionaries who put pressure on metropolitan governments, and not the other way round. Strongest of all was the pressure coming from European settlers, not only in south Africa but also in Australasia. As the free European population of Australia grew, traders, whalers and sealers began to move eastwards into the Pacific. By the 1830s they were trading guns and liquor with the Maoris in New Zealand, leading to frequent violent clashes and growing disorder, above all in the inter-tribal 'musket wars' that went on for several decades. When Edward Gibbon Wakefield (1796–1892), who had carried out the systematic colonization of southern Australia, set sail with a large number of emigrants for New

Zealand, the British government declared sovereignty in 1840 so as to provide some kind of protection for them. The Treaty of Waitangi, signed the same year, was supposed to guarantee Maori land rights, but settlers ignored it, and a series of wars and small-scale violent conflicts began, lasting till the early 1870s. The British and the settlers were unable to defeat the Maoris. European settlers outnumbered them by the 1860s, and a kind of uneasy stalemate was the end result, in which Maoris had been pushed out to the edge of European settlement but defended their interests there with some success. From New Zealand, European traders fanned out further into the Pacific, looking for coconut oil and guano. They began to kidnap islanders for forced labour on sugar plantations in Australia – so-called 'blackbirding'; the British navy tried to stop this trade, but with only limited success. Traders, whalers and missionaries began to arrive on the Pacific islands, and to protect their interests the British annexed Fiji in 1874, though Hawaii and Tonga managed to resist being taken over by European powers. In North and South America a similar process of European expansion took place, though without the accompaniment of formal colonial acquisition, as millions of migrants pushed into the interior, displacing and drastically reducing in numbers the indigenous inhabitants of the areas they settled.

Increasingly, therefore, European governments felt obliged to intervene when trading interests came under threat. China provided a classic example. The Chinese Empire restricted entry to European goods, while exporting large quantities to the West themselves, above all tea. To redress the balance, the East India Company smuggled Indian-produced opium into China. In 1838, not for the first time, the Chinese Empire intervened to stop the trade. British ships were boarded in international waters and their cargoes of opium seized and destroyed, while British merchants were blockaded in their factories and starved of food till they agreed to hand over their supplies. In retaliation, the British sent a military force from India in what became known as the First Opium War. It seized Canton, and in 1842 the British acquired Hong Kong and opened four other ports for trade; the United States and France soon got their treaty ports too. The Chinese Empire was unhappy with the treaty ports and conflict broke out again, leading to an Anglo-French force of 18,000 marching on Beijing in 1860 during the Second Opium War. Members of a delegation sent to negotiate with the Chinese were arrested and tortured to death. In retaliation the Europeans destroyed the old imperial Summer Palace and forced the Chinese to open ten new treaty ports, pay a large indemnity, and agree to the opium trade so long as they could regulate it. By 1900, domestic opium production in China was bringing the trade to an end.

Expansion into Asia provided an outlet for tsarist ambitions after the Crimean War. As settlers and traders moved eastwards, local or regional officials began acting on their own initiative to conclude treaties with local states or neighbouring powers. By the 1870s the Russians were moving into what is now Turkmenistan. A key role was played by the fact that Russian settlers on the central Asian steppe were threatened by the unstable but powerful Muslim states of Khiva, Bokhara and Kokand, and so government forces gradually subdued these areas, turning the first two of these states into protectorates and incorporating the third into a new province. The Russian Empire moved gradually eastwards, conquering Tashkent in 1865 and Samarkand in 1868. By the end of the 1870s the tsar controlled all of Central Asia, much to the alarm of the British government, which perceived this as a direct threat to its power over India: the jockeying for position in the region became known in London as 'the Great Game'. Of more direct interest to St Petersburg, however, was the securing of access to the Pacific. The province of Amur was seized from the Chinese and in 1858 China accepted this as a *fait accompli*. Sakhalin Island was occupied, bringing Russia up against Japan. Eastward expansion even brought Russians across the Bering Straits into North America. In the eighteenth century, Russian fur traders had hunted and traded in Alaska in increasing numbers. By the early 1800s the Russian-American company had taken control of most of this trade. By the middle of the century, however, otters, beavers and other fur-bearing animals in the region had been hunted to near-extinction, competition from the Hudson's Bay Company was proving increasingly intrusive, and the costs of communication across thousands of miles to European Russia were proving prohibitive. There were never more than seven or eight hundred Russians in Alaska, almost all of them in the two main coastal towns. In 1867, recognizing the intractability of these problems, the Russian government sold the province to the United States for two cents an acre. History might have turned out very differently had it not done so.

THE AGE OF IMPERIALISM

The 1870s ushered in the age of imperialism – a word that first entered the English language around this time and was soon, as noted by the English economist John A. Hobson (1858–1940), 'on everybody's lips . . . used to denote the most powerful movement in the current politics of the western world'. Imperialism was propagated by governments keen to gain popular support for the principle of maintaining, usually at some cost, their

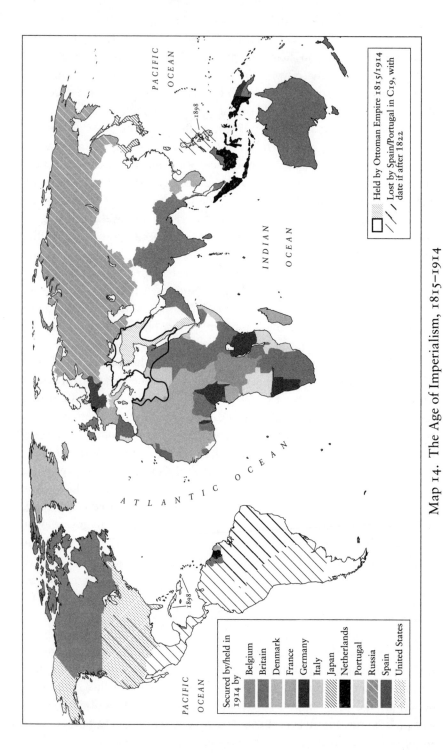

Map 14. The Age of Imperialism, 1815–1914

overseas possessions. The cult of empire began in Britain in 1877 with the proclamation of Queen Victoria as Empress of India. Within a few years British royal ceremonies, including Victoria's golden jubilee were featuring maharajas and colonial troops. Huge publicity was given to the 'durbar' held in India to proclaim Queen Victoria Empress of India. The celebration of empire was relatively slow to take on, but gradually it took hold, above all in the new popular press, and by the 1890s imperial propaganda could be found everywhere, on railway bookstalls, in political meetings, in novels, magazines and history books. The elevation of the monarchy from a national to an imperial status provided an opportunity for the British to celebrate, as a contemporary put it, 'the recognition, by a free democracy, of a hereditary crown, as a symbol of the world-wide dominion of their race'. Already by about 1880, however, nationalist and patriotic politicians in many European countries were beginning to dream of the conquest of other parts of the world.

International expositions, a tradition inaugurated by Britain's Great Exhibition at the Crystal Palace in 1851, began to include 'colonial pavilions' – eighteen of them at the Paris exposition of 1889, clustering around the Eiffel Tower, which was built for the occasion. Colonial museums opened in most European countries to display looted artefacts. Zoos began to include 'native villages' among their exhibits. In Belgium in the 1880s and 1890s exhibitions were held including a typical Congolese village, where imported Africans were told to do what they normally did at home, which was mostly not much, since at home they would not have been sitting in a village but out hunting or in the fields. A pool was provided and stocked with fish, and spectators threw coins in for the Congolese to dive for. Sometimes they threw in bottles of gin and brandy too, to make them drunk. Stages were set up for the men to re-enact battles with spears and shields. The Congolese had to go around half-naked in a display of 'authenticity', and in cold weather many of them became ill. There was no interest in getting the villagers to make or display artworks or put on musical events. The assumption of European superiority over 'savages' was even more powerful or influential than in the colonies themselves. It underpinned the dramatic expansion of European empires that took place during these decades.

Between 1878 and 1914, Europe added more than 8,600,000 square miles to the territory it controlled. Taken together, the colonial possessions of Europe and the United States included 57 per cent of the world's population on the eve of the First World War. A variety of different, rival explanations were offered for this dramatic and precipitate imperial expansion. Writers like Hobson, Lenin and Rosa Luxemburg sought to ascribe economic causes to the expansion of Europe. They argued variously that colonies were needed, as they had not been previously, to provide raw materials for European industry, or markets for its products, or new areas in which to invest its surplus capital in an era when monopolies and cartels were ossifying European capitalist economies and reducing profit margins. Social Democrats in Germany suggested that the acquisition of colonies was used by conservative governments as a way of diverting rising working-class discontent – expressed in the growth of mass socialist parties demanding revolution and the overthrow of capitalism – into nationalist and colonialist enthusiasm. All of these developments were in this view products of the transition to maturity of industrial capitalism in Europe. But while industry did indeed expand rapidly in the 1870s and 1880s, capitalism in Europe did not reach the stage of monopolies and cartels until the 1890s or perhaps even later. There is no convincing evidence that profit margins were declining in the 1880s; on the contrary, European economies were recovering from the sharp downturn of the early-to-mid-1870s precisely at the time when imperialism reached its apogee. The extension of the vote did not lead to the rise of popular pressure groups eager for imperial acquisitions until after the turn of the century, when most new territories had already been acquired. Domestic political considerations were still important, but in the 1880s European powers still thought they could defeat socialism through repression; in Bismarck's Germany the socialist movement was banned from 1878 to 1890, and in the early Third Republic, during the 1870s and 1880s, politics were still conducted in the aftermath of the ferocious and bloody repression of the Paris Commune in 1871. Key players in the imperial game such as Italy only had a very limited electorate, and before the 1890s the extension of the franchise in Germany was not accompanied by the rise of mass politics.

The age of imperialism was accompanied by a change in the international atmosphere in the late 1870s, when the German government ended the era of free trade by introducing import duties into Germany to protect domestic grain producers. International rivalries intensified, as the slow but steady expansion of European possessions overseas began to create collisions between rival European powers, for example in west Africa between the British, the French and the Belgians. The growing penetration of indigenous economies by European traders and merchants increasingly produced crises to which European powers now felt they had to respond by annexing territory. Politicians saw a chance for glory in the growth of empire: Disraeli orchestrated the proclamation of Queen Victoria as Empress of India in 1877, while the French Republican Prime Minister, Jules Ferry, regarded overseas acquisitions as a means of diverting his countrymen from their obsession with the loss of Alsace-Lorraine. France, he declared, had to 'carry everywhere its language, its customs, its flag, its genius'. In Italy, Francesco Crispi promoted the idea of an Italian Empire in the Mediterranean. Yet European powers were initially reluctant to embark on a costly policy of annexation. Bismarck, for example, was adamant that Germany did not need formal colonies for their own sake. They would, he declared, mean unnecessary trouble and expense. 'I am no man for colonies,' he once said. But Bismarck did think that the declaration of interests in particular potential colonies could be a useful bargaining point in the European power-game. As he said to an explorer in 1888: 'Your map of Africa is really quite nice. But my map of Africa lies in Europe. Here is Russia, and here . . . is France, and we're in the middle – that's my map of Africa.'

Yet by this time it was already too late to stop the forward rush of imperial annexations. The chain of events that undermined Bismarck's position had begun back in 1857, when the British and French consuls, joined later by the Italians, had gained the power of supervising the bankrupt administration of the Ottoman ruler, or Bey, of Tunis. Control had then passed in 1869 to an international financial commission, on which the French increasingly gained the leading role. The Bey's government was unable to collect even a small proportion of the taxes imposed on the population, while European powers made the situation worse by forcing down Tunisia's import tariffs until they were no more than 3 per cent, undermining the economy by allowing a mass influx of cheap European goods. In 1881, when the Italians, annoyed by the growing French hegemony, announced their intention of annexing Tunisia wholesale, the French sent a military expedition into the country. This led to a Muslim rebellion, which in turn prompted the declaration of a French protectorate after the Bey Muhammad III (1813–82) was forced to abdicate in favour of his brother Ali III (1817–1902). The decay of Ottoman power in north Africa opened up further sources of conflict between European powers. With relatively few resources, the desert province of Libya remained under Ottoman control throughout the century. But Egypt, far richer in resources, especially cotton, was a different matter. Since the early nineteenth century it had been effectively autonomous, a condition formalized in 1867 by an agreement between the Ottoman Sultan and Muhammad Ali's grandson Isma'il (1830–95), by which time the government had long been fully committed to economic modernization, importing European specialists to help it in the project. In 1854, as part of this programme, the Egyptian authorities had commissioned the former French consul Ferdinand de Lesseps (1805–94) to set up a company to build a canal across the Suez isthmus. Employing over one and a half million workers, the construction project lasted fifteen years. The canal opened in 1869, though it was not fully completed until 1871. Crucially, it made very little money to start with, while Isma'il had invested so much in it that he was effectively bankrupt by 1878. The inevitable Debt Commission, dominated by the French and British, was set up to sort things out, and when Isma'il caused problems it persuaded the Ottoman government to depose him and replace him with his eldest son Tewfik Pasha (1852–92).

This in turn, in what by now had become a familiar pattern, sparked a widespread revolt, led by a senior officer in the Egyptian Army, Colonel Ahmed Orabi (1841–1911, known in England as Arabi Pasha). The revolt was put down at the Battle of Tel el-Kebir in 1882 by a purely British force, since the French Chamber of Deputies had refused to grant credits for an expedition. The British were effectively drawn in to occupying Egypt on their own, and stayed not least in order to guard it against a jihad launched by the sheikh Muhammad Ahmad (1844–85), who took the title of 'Mahdi' or Redeemer, in neighbouring Sudan. This was the uprising that led in 1885 to the famous incident of the death of General Gordon, whom Isma'il Pasha had appointed Governor of the Sudan, at the Sudanese capital Khartoum. The British expeditionary force sent to rescue Gordon came too late; after his death it withdrew, and Sudan was left alone for the time being. Egypt did not become a British colony, but remained under the control of the Debt Commission. This now became the site of Anglo-French rivalry, encouraged by the Germans, who also sat on the commission.

Anglo-French clashes over these issues were exploited in 1884 by Bismarck, who backed the French to try and draw them away from thoughts of taking revenge over Germany for the loss of Alsace-Lorraine in 1871. At the same time, he also wanted to show to the British the desirability of being nice to the Germans by annoying or threatening them in colonial matters (this is what he meant by his map of Africa being located in Europe). There were elections to the Reichstag coming up, and Bismarck needed the support of the powerful National Liberal Party, closely allied to mercantile interests in Hamburg and elsewhere. So he began declaring German protectorates in key areas: Angra Pequena in south-west Africa, where the German flag was raised in May 1884; Togoland and Cameroon (Kamerun) in July 1884; New Guinea (Kaiser-Wilhelmsland) in December 1884; and German East Africa, including present-day Tanzania (without Zanzibar), in February 1885. He also signed a treaty with the King of Samoa giving Germany preferential rights over other European powers – the king thought it prudent to sign for his part when he glimpsed a German warship at anchor off the island. Typically, the moving forces on the ground were German explorers – Gustav Nachtigal (1834–85) in west Africa, Carl Peters (1856–1918) in east Africa – and traders and planters, particularly in New Guinea. But they were all there was: they were not followed by any significant involvement on the ground by the German state.

Bismarck's actions created something like a panic as European states rushed to annex their own territories before somebody else got there first. To underline his friendship with France and his new colonial policy, Bismarck agreed with the French government to call a conference in Berlin, which met from November 1884 to February 1885. It focused almost exclusively on the Congo, where it recognized the claim of Leopold II of the Belgians to annex it as his personal property, as well as ratifying the French claim to the northern bank of the Congo river. Apart from this, however, the conference achieved nothing. Its declaration that a claim to a colony required 'effective occupation' was a dead letter, since such a claim really applied only to coastal areas, and the conference's insistence on free trade along major rivers like the Congo and the Niger was more or less ignored. But by laying down ground rules for annexation, the conference effectively declared that the 'Scramble for Africa' – a British term coined in 1884 – had begun, so it stimulated further annexations. In 1885 the British declared their protectorate over the Nigerian coast and authorized the Royal Niger Company, founded in 1879, to go inland, conclude treaties with local rulers, and exercise British rule, rather like the East India Company of former times. France's rivalry with Britain, stimulated by the quarrels over Egypt, led its local administrators in west Africa to push forward with the idea of an empire stretching from Algeria to the Congo River, and in 1889–90 treaties were signed with the British defining the boundaries of the two empires. All of this was effectively on paper only, since the hinterland was actually controlled by a series of large and powerful Islamic states.

The Germans by contrast were stuck with Togo and Cameroon, and with south-west Africa, since neither Bismarck nor German merchant firms had much interest in going any further. In East Africa, however, Carl Peters, who had founded a Society for German Colonization and concluded treaties in its name with a variety of local rulers in 1884, black-mailed Bismarck into granting a charter for his new East Africa Company by threatening to sell his acquisitions to King Leopold of the Belgians. Needing the support of the National Liberals, who backed Peters, the Chancellor gave in, and soon Peters, returning to Africa in 1885, annexed even more territory until he was expelled from Uganda by the British. Peters got into even more trouble when the activities of his company led in 1889 to a revolt by Arab planters, which the German government – supported by the British – reluctantly sent troops to suppress. This led to the declaration in 1891 of German East Africa as a full colony under German state control, while in 1890 Zanzibar was handed over to the British in exchange for the small but strategically significant British-owned North Sea island of Heligoland, off the German coast. Meanwhile, stories of Peters' scandalous behaviour had begun to reach Berlin. In 1892 it became known that he had had one of his African mistresses hanged when he discovered she was having an affair with his manservant; Peters hanged him too, and both their home villages were razed to the ground. This led to a local revolt, which German troops were brought in to suppress. Peters was recalled and in 1897 dishonourably discharged from government service with the loss of his pension rights; he escaped criminal prosecution only by fleeing to London.

The exchange of Zanzibar for Heligoland reflected a major British concern that the new route to India via the Suez Canal should be properly protected by a string of British possessions and coaling stations along the east African coast. In 1886 and 1890 the exchange was underpinned by British recognition of German East Africa in exchange for German recognition of British control over Uganda and in effect the rest of east Africa north of Mozambique (in Portuguese hands since the early sixteenth century). But the British too had to deal with an awkward imperial adventurer, in the shape of Cecil Rhodes (1853–1902). Sent from England to south Africa as a child to improve his health, Rhodes became a businessman who by the end of the 1880s had bought up all the diamond mines there and acquired an effective monopoly on the world's diamond supplies. He began pushing northwards from south Africa, obtaining mining concessions from local potentates. But his ambitions were not just economic. Rhodes believed in the superiority of what he called the Anglo-Saxon race – among whom he included the Germans – over all others, and he wanted Anglo-Saxon rule over east and central Africa to stretch from Cairo to the Cape. These colonies were, however, to have a large measure of self-government. Rhodes wanted them to escape what he saw as excessive interference from London. These views helped him become Prime Minister of the Cape Colony in 1890, gaining the support of Boer settlers by passing legislation to force Africans off their land. The British government was happy enough to allow his British South Africa Company to occupy and control major areas of central Africa, where missionaries were getting into difficulties, and by 1894 protectorates had been declared over much of the region.

The other European power with an interest in Africa was Italy. Backed by Germany, the Italians acquired territory in the horn of Africa to provide them with ports where Italian ships could refuel before or after negotiating the Suez Canal. There were also scattered Spanish and Portuguese possessions deriving mostly from trading or coaling stations. Large areas of the Sahara and equatorial west and central Africa were claimed by France. Eastern and southern Africa belonged mostly to the British and the Germans. Only Abyssinia and the free state of Liberia, founded by returning freed slaves from the United States, remained independent. Minor adjustments remained: between the French and British in northern Nigeria and in particular on the Upper Nile at Fashoda in 1898, where a military clash between the two powers threatened until the French, feeling very much the inferior power, prudently withdrew in the face of a larger British force. In northern Africa, Italy and France settled claims in Tripoli (Libya) and Morocco in 1900. To all intents and purposes the 'Scramble for Africa' was over by the middle of the 1890s.

It was paralleled by a similar rush for influence and control in Asia and the Pacific, also sparked by Bismarck, who claimed New Guinea, the Bismarck Archipelago, New Pomerania, the northern Solomon Islands, the Marshall Islands and Nauru. In 1885–6 the British and French recognized these claims, allotting north-eastern New Guinea to Germany in return for German acceptance of British rule over south-eastern New Guinea and the southern Pacific, and French suzerainty in parts of the eastern Pacific. European commercial penetration of Indochina brought in French troops to combat nascent nationalist uprisings in 1885–6, uniting Annam, Tongking, Laos and Cambodia and the existing colony of Cochin-China in a single French possession ruled by a governor-general. This sparked the British occupation of Upper Burma in 1885, with the independent kingdom of Siam (Thailand) being retained as a buffer zone between the British and the French colonies. Similarly, the French and British were rivals in the island of Madagascar, where growing clashes produced a stand-off only resolved in 1890 by British recognition of a French protectorate.

There were some parts of the world that never came under direct European rule at any time in history, including Abyssinia, Anatolia, Arabia, Japan, Korea, Mongolia, Morocco, Siam and Tibet. The largest and most significant of them was China. The Chinese Empire was rich, populous, and promising in terms of economic exploitation and investment. From 1850 to 1864 it had been convulsed by the Taiping Rebellion, which caused the deaths of up to 20 million people, the largest armed conflict anywhere in the world in the nineteenth century. The Chinese Empire had recovered, but not before losing control over Manchuria to the Russians in 1860. From 1875, China was ruled by the Empress Dowager Cixi (1835–1908), through her nephew the Guangxu Emperor (1871–1908), whom she had placed under house arrest when he began supporting the reform of the empire along Western lines. As this suggests, she was deeply conservative; contrasting strongly with her Japanese equivalent, Emperor Meiji (1852–1912), who was 'restored' by reformers between 1866 and 1870. After the reformist victory, Japanese emissaries were sent forth across the world to learn and import Western industrial, educational and political ways, while European experts were summoned to the islands to help the task of modernization. In an astonishingly short period of time Japan was well on the way to becoming a major economic and above all military power, not only capable of defending itself against foreign incursions but also increasingly keen to join in the imperial scramble for territory itself. The first opportunity presented itself in Korea, described by a German military adviser to the Japanese government as a 'dagger pointing at the heart of Japan'. Nominally independent, Korea had for a long time been under Chinese control, and when disturbances broke out in 1894 the Chinese sent an army to put them down; this was considered an affront as well as a threat by Japan, which then sent an invasion force that quickly defeated the inferior, poorly equipped and badly organized Chinese forces. The Koreans and Chinese were forced to recognize the transfer of Korea to the Japanese sphere of influence, leading eventually to its annexation in 1910.

These events made European powers view China as ripe for exploitation. What they wanted above all was free access to Chinese markets, and the best way to do this in their view was by taking out ninety-nine-year leases on 'treaty ports' – ports opened to foreign trade and residence due to pressure from the Great Powers. After 1895 there was a massive expansion of this system until the number of treaty ports reached more than eighty. In addition to ports held by the British, there were ports leased to the French, the Russians, the Germans and the Italians. Concessions were taken out by the Japanese, the United States, Portugal, Belgium and even Leopold II's Congo Free State. The rapid penetration of China by European powers inevitably led to a violent reaction. A nationalist movement quickly emerged, known as the Society of Righteous and Harmonious Fists, or Boxers for short, dedicated to reversing the unequal treaties, curbing the activities of missionaries and opium traders, and reducing the activities of the Europeans or even eliminating them altogether. After initial hesitation the Dowager Empress threw the weight of her regime behind them, and they laid siege to the Legation Quarter of Beijing. More than two thousand Chinese Christians were put to death across China in 1900, and a number of European missionaries, merchants and officials were killed. The eight foreign nations involved in the conflict sent a heavily armed force of 20,000 to Beijing to recapture the city. The victorious troops of all armies looted and pillaged on a massive scale, and there were said to have been mass rapes of Chinese women in the occupied city. Boxers or men thought to be Boxers were summarily executed, especially if they fell into the hands of the Japanese. The Germans arrived too late to take part in the fighting, but did their share of the looting all the same. As they embarked at Bremerhaven for the long journey, Kaiser Wilhelm II told them:

> No quarter will be given! Prisoners will not be taken! . . . Just as a thousand years ago the Huns under their King Attila made a name for themselves, one that even today makes them seem mighty in history and legend, may the name German be affirmed by you in such a way in China that no Chinese will ever again dare to look askance at a German.

The speech, especially the comparison with the Hun, was to come back to haunt him in the First World War.

The Allies imposed on the Chinese government financial reparations that would have taken until the end of the 1920s to repay. But the long-predicted carve-up of China never happened. The European powers had received a severe shock from the uprising. If this was the reaction provoked by the existence of mere treaty ports, what might happen if they tried to take over the whole country? Any further territorial advances seemed ill advised in the circumstances. In addition, two of the powers involved, Russia and Japan, were serious rivals for territorial gains in Manchuria, where more than a quarter of foreign investments were held, and a peaceful agreement between the two of them over partition was out of the question: indeed the two states went to war over the issue in 1904. Ultimately, the Chinese government had held together, and it was more profitable to continue lending it money at high interest rates than to invest large sums in trying to defeat it and take over its business. The imperial tax collection service seemed a cheaper and more acceptable vehicle for assembling the debt repayments than a European tax collection service such as had been run by the old British East India Company. So the United States proposed an open-door policy, which everyone apart from the Russians accepted, and in the meantime the powers concluded a series of bilateral treaties promising not to acquire any further territory in China. In 1902 the Anglo-Japanese Alliance, which committed Britain to remaining neutral if Japan was attacked by another power or to joining with the Japanese if two other powers were involved, was widely celebrated in the United Kingdom and presented to the electorate as a classic example of the wisdom of Conservative foreign policy. For the Chinese the humiliation of all this was too much to bear; in 1911 the Qing dynasty was overthrown in a revolution and on 1 January 1912 a Chinese Republic was declared.

China was in the end, therefore, something of a stand-off between European powers and a potential object of colonization. In some other parts of the world, European powers were even forced to retreat. Unrest in Cuba, the rise of a nationalist movement, and reports of atrocities committed by the Spanish trying to retain control over their country's most valuable overseas possession, brought the United States into a war with Spain in 1898 that resulted not only in Cuba being ceded – if only temporarily – to the Americans but also to a US takeover of Puerto Rico, and, in the Pacific, the Philippines and Guam. This marked the end of the Spanish Empire in the Pacific at least: and indeed Spain now actually sold the Caroline, Mariana and Palau to Germany, though Germany had initially wanted to acquire the Philippines. This shakeup was completed by the division of Samoa by Germany and America in return for British disengagement and acquisition of Tonga, some small German islands in the Solomons, and disputed areas in west Africa: all that was left of the once huge Spanish Empire was Spanish Morocco, west Africa and Guinea, the Spanish Sahara and the Canary Islands. The virtual demise of the Spanish Empire administered a tremendous shock to the Spanish political system, despite economic gains in the form of the repatriation of investments from Cuba; the consequences were to work themselves through in the following decades up to the 1930s.

Undoubtedly the greatest humiliation suffered by a European state in the quest for empire, however, was experienced by the Italians in Ethiopia. Italy had already taken control of parts of the horn of Africa and in the 1890s sought to extend its influence over Ethiopia. Here the warlord Menelik II (1844–1913), after conquering the provinces of Tigre and Amhara, had declared himself negus, or emperor, in 1889 and concluded a treaty of friendship with the Italians. Unfortunately the treaty said different things in Italian and Amharic. While the Italians' version gave them control of Eritrea and rights of protectorate over Ethiopia, the Amharic version merely said that Menelik could use Italian diplomats as a proxy in his foreign policy if he wanted to. After this discrepancy came to light, disputes over the treaty intensified until Menelik formally repudiated it in 1893. He began stockpiling modern European weaponry, some of it bought from the Italians themselves, and sent a delegation to St Petersburg, resulting in the attachment of Russian military advisers to the Ethiopian Army. In 1894 the Italians duly began military action, which escalated until on 1 March 1896 a major battle was fought at Adowa in the mountainous area of Tigre.

In this encounter 15,000 Italian troops, many of them raw conscripts, equipped with outdated guns and footwear that broke up on the rough rocky terrain, advanced in three columns that became separated because the Italians did not possess proper maps. They were met by nearly 100,000 Ethiopian troops, raised under the country's feudal system, supplied with modern rifles, and aided by forty-two Russian field guns specially adapted for mountainous terrain. One of the Italian columns retreated in the wrong direction and became trapped in a ravine, where the Ethiopian cavalry slaughtered them in their thousands, egged on by cries of 'reap, reap!' from their commander. At a crucial moment Menelik brought in 25,000 fresh reserves and surrounded the other two columns, forcing them to retreat with heavy losses. Altogether 7,000 Italian troops and *askaris* – Eritrean auxiliaries – were killed. Some 3,000 soldiers in the Italian expedition were taken prisoner by the Ethiopians, and the rest abandoned the field of battle, along with 11,000 rifles, all their artillery, and most of their supplies. The Italian prisoners were treated well, but 800 of the Eritrean *askaris* were condemned as traitors by the Ethiopians, who chopped off their right hands and left feet. The Italians were forced to recognize Ethiopian independence; Menelik was satisfied, and preferred cautiously not to follow up his victory or provoke retaliation by advancing into Eritrea. In Italy people ripped up railway lines in case the government drafted reinforcements. Outraged patriots pelted Prime Minister Crispi's house with rocks until he was forced to resign.

Yet overall the imbalance of forces between European and non-European powers outside the Americas was starkly illustrated in 1898 by the Battle of Omdurman, where an Anglo-Egyptian army led by Major-General Sir Herbert Kitchener (1850–1916) defeated a Sudanese Mahdist force, in what was little more than a massacre: 23,000 Sudanese were killed or wounded, whereas the dead and injured on the British side numbered no more than 430. As the Anglo-French writer Hilaire Belloc (1870–1953) put it: 'Whatever happens, we have got/The Maxim gun, and they have not.' If a non-European state wanted to defeat a European invasion it had to follow the example of Ethiopia or Japan and acquire European weaponry and military hardware itself. Modern weaponry was in turn the product of the great leap forward of European prosperity and industry, science and technology in comparison to other parts of the world. Yet far from being inevitable after 1500, as some historians have claimed, this global imbalance did not really take hold until the third quarter of the nineteenth century. It was the product not just of technological superiority but also of European peace. Things might have been very different had the European nations carried on fighting each other and exporting their conflicts to other parts of the globe, as they had done before 1815. Peace, underpinned by British naval hegemony, allowed the spread of communications networks, telegraph cables, sea lanes and trade routes, and intercontinental railways, leading to further economic development and a dense network of rapid imperial communications. Global trade expanded almost exponentially under these conditions, in a way that would have been impossible had the major industrializing states been fighting one another. Mass European migration to the Americas and other parts of the world helped build a globalized economy of which Europe and the United States were the main beneficiaries. In this sense, Europe's borders had become porous as never before. European states were also politically better organized and more effective in mobilizing their resources. Colonization had its limits, but overall Europe gained a dominance over the rest of the world in the second half of the nineteenth century that it enjoyed neither before nor subsequently.

EXPLOITATION AND RESISTANCE

In 1884–5 the Berlin Conference that set off the scramble for colonies in Africa and other parts of the world laid down the basic principle that in order to establish the formal right of rule over a colony, a European power had to establish 'effective occupation'. The primary of trading interests meant that only coastal areas were occupied to begin with, though explores soon began to penetrate inland. The hinterland of continental Africa was a different matter. Here European states drew straight lines across the map with a cavalier disregard for geographical features, delimiting the territories they claimed from one another but leaving them still to be brought under real control. In many ways the story of colonization in the 1890s and 1900s is the story of how European empires tried to convert paper colonies into real ones. In some colonies, in the age of high imperialism, European settlers began arriving in ever increasing numbers and, with or without the approval of the colonial state, seizing land from indigenous peoples for cattle farming or rubber or palm oil plantations. The clashes such actions sparked were among the most violent in the history of European imperialism, and they almost invariably drew in more or less reluctant European powers to back up settler aggression with state military action. Nowhere were these clashes more dramatic than in German

South-West Africa (Namibia). Initially a protectorate run by a limited company in the classic hands-off manner favoured by Bismarck, the colony was taken over by the state as early as 1888, when the company failed. Much of the land was desert or semi-arid and was inhabited by nomadic cattle herders of the Herero and Nama tribes. During the 1890s, German settlers moved in and began setting up cattle ranches, fencing off the land from the nomads, whose livelihood was also being undermined by an outbreak of a fatal cattle disease, *Rinderpest*, at the end of the 1890s. The nomads retaliated with attacks on German farmers, causing around 150 settler deaths in 1904. Kaiser Wilhelm II took this as a provocation, even a personal insult. Germany was not going to be humiliated as Italy had been in Ethiopia in 1896. Some 14,000 German troops were dispatched from Berlin under General Lothar von Trotha (1848–1920), a hard-line Prussian army officer with previous colonial experience. 'I know,' he said, 'that African tribes yield only to violence. To exercise this violence with crass terrorism and even with gruesomeness was and is my policy.' Herero men were shot, while the women and children were driven into the desert and left to starve. Popular commemorative books were printed celebrating the triumph of German arms in the conflict. Not all Germans agreed with this policy. Social Democratic papers condemned 'the way our national honour is preserved in Africa'. Supporters of the government urged the electorate to 'vote for the honour of the Fatherland against its destroyers!'

The civilian governor of the colony, Theodor Leutwein (1849–1921), elbowed aside by the military because of his policy of compromise with the Herero, declared the policy of extermination a 'grave mistake'. His view – that the Herero should be recruited as labourers instead of being exterminated – won sufficient adherents to bring about the arrest of the remainder of the tribe – mostly women and children – along with the members of the Nama tribe, and their incarceration in 'concentration camps' (the first official German use of this term). Here, however, their fate was no better. At the worst of the camps, on the rocky terrain of Shark Island, off the Namibian coast, the prisoners were used as forced labourers, fed on minimal rations, exposed to bitter winds without adequate clothing, and beaten with leather whips if they failed to work hard enough. Every day bodies were taken to the beach and left for the tide to wash out into the shark-infested waters. The camps also became sites of scientific investigation, as the anthropologist Eugen Fischer (1874–1967), later to become a leading 'racial hygienist' under the Third Reich, descended on the town of Rehoboth to study its mixed-race inhabitants (whom he called, unflatteringly, the 'Reheboth Bastards'). In 1905 'racial mixing' was banned by the colony's German authorities, and in 1909 interracial marriage and cohabitation were made punishable by the loss of civil rights. These measures introduced the term *Rassenschande*, 'racial defilement', into German legal terminology; it was to resurface thirty years later, in the Third Reich's Nuremberg Laws outlawing intermarriage between Jews and 'Aryans'. A superior legal status was ascribed to the German settlers and other white Europeans and Boers in the colony, allowing Herero men to be conscripted for forced labour and compelling them to wear identification tags (another measure later applied by the Nazis to the Jews, though it also had a longer pedigree in Europe). The Herero population, estimated at 85,000 before the war, was reduced to 15,000 by the end, while up to 10,000 out of a total of 20,000 Nama were exterminated. Of some 17,000 Africans incarcerated in the concentration camps, only half survived.

Violence was a constant feature of German rule in many different colonies. In German East Africa, continual military clashes forced the imperial government in Berlin to take over the colony's administration in 1891; but armed conflict continued, with no fewer than sixty-one major 'penal expeditions' launched by the German military in the following six years. In 1905 conflicts over land seizures, taxation rises and forced-labour requirements led to the Maji-Maji uprising, in which some 80,000 Africans were killed. The devastation was immense, with more than 200,000 Africans perishing from the famine caused by the destruction of rebel fields and villages by the Germans. Violence was not just confined to major conflicts such as these. It was a fixed part of everyday life in the German colonies. The officially recorded number of formally ordered public beatings of Africans, certainly an underestimate, rose in Cameroon from 315 in 1900 to 4,800 in 1913. Such acts reflected not least the continuing fragility of German control, with only a small number of colonists attempting to assert themselves over a numerous indigenous population. Colonies like Cameroon were colonies of occupation, where the climate and the terrain were only suitable for low levels of emigration and settlement. They contrasted with colonies of settlement, where large numbers of Europeans emigrated to establish themselves in a climate and under conditions favourable to a European style of life, such as German South-West Africa, which attracted relatively large numbers of settler ranchers.

The relative strength, degree of organization and military preparedness of indigenous societies also played a role in determining the levels of violence and the outcome of conflicts with settlers. Loosely organized nomadic herdsmen like the Herero were in the end far easier to defeat than elaborately structured political systems such as those of the Islamic states that stretched across northern Cameroon and over into British colonies

like Nigeria. In German East Africa, 415 colonial officers and administrators were supposedly controlling nearly 10 million Africans and Arab
traders, but they were not able to extend their remit into the interior. There
were just thirty German military stations across the colony, and they
depended for their effectiveness on the co-operation of local African leaders. The colonizers could of course choose whom to co-opt; during his
twenty-year term of office in Togo, one regional official dismissed all
544 chiefs in his district and replaced them with others, as well as importing black graduates of the Tuskegee Institute founded in Alabama by the
African-American Booker T. Washington (1856–1915), so that 'negroes'
could teach 'negroes' to grow cotton, although in reality the two groups
had little in common. In the end, however, there was no alternative to
relying on the local power-holders. In northern Cameroon the Islamic
Fulbe aristocracy, brought under German control by a series of military
expeditions, actually used German military forces to extend their own
area of influence, so that an effective co-rule between the two was the
result. Given their small numbers in comparison to those of the Africans,
the Germans could only hope to establish islands of power in colonies like
Togo, Cameroon and German East Africa.

How did this compare with the experience of other colonial powers?
The largest of the European empires, the British, was run on decentralized
lines. Westminster law was supreme, but there was no attempt to impose
a uniform system of rule from London. The insistence on free trade across
the empire made central control even less necessary. Power therefore
devolved onto the colonial state on the ground. Major parts of the empire
had been in British possession long before the 'Scramble for Africa'. These
included first of all colonies of settlement, notably Canada, Australia and
New Zealand, and the Cape Colony on the southernmost tip of Africa.
While there was European settlement on some scale in some non-British
colonies, notably Algeria and German South-West Africa, these British
colonies were unique in being mainly intended as goals for emigration.
Many emigrants went of course to the United States, but in Australia,
New Zealand and Canada private settlement companies encouraged emigration from the British Isles and smoothed the way for migrants by
colonizing land and selling it cheaply to them. The main proponent of this
idea was Edward Gibbon Wakefield, who founded a number of colonizing
companies, notably in New Zealand. With his followers he persuaded the
British government that these colonies could support themselves economically and were creating a new British society abroad. In the late 1830s
armed uprisings in Canada, largely caused by the resentments of a French
minority that considered itself disfranchised, prompted a report by Lord

Durham (1792–1840) that laid the ground rules for colonial administration. Its recommendation of colonial self-government, with colonial parliaments and ministries, became the basis for British imperial administration of colonies with a majority of European and especially British settlers. This disqualified colonies where settlers were in a minority, like the West Indies and India, but by the late nineteenth century self-administration had been extended not only to Canada and Australia, but also to New Zealand and the Cape Colony, where the British government did not want to bear the cost of wars against indigenous peoples. Voting rights were confined to the white minority.

To what extent was violence employed in the establishment of the settler colonies? To a large degree in Canada, as previously in the Americas, the settlers' work was done for them by disease. When Scottish settlers led by Lord Selkirk (1771–1820) arrived at Assiniboia in Manitoba in 1816, they were confronted by local 'Indians' who feared the inroads the settlers might make into their fur trading. They killed the governor and twenty-two Europeans in the so-called Battle of Seven Oaks. Selkirk returned in 1817 with a group of fully armed ex-soldiers as settlers, who succeeded in re-establishing the colony. Their success was due not just to their preparedness but also to their introduction, no doubt involuntary, of smallpox. A German traveller in the area in the 1830s recorded it as 'covered with unburied corpses'; the local 'Indians', 9,000 strong, were 'nearly exterminated', he noted: 'They, as well as the Crows and the Blackfeet, endeavoured to flee in all directions, but the diseased everywhere pursued them.' As in the German colonies, so too in British settler colonies, there was constant low-level, small-scale but often deadly violence, meted out, however, more often by settlers than by colonial troops. As the colonists fenced off land in Australia, claiming the country as a vacant possession, nomadic Aborigines began to retaliate for the loss of their traditional areas of hunting and gathering. Aboriginal attacks on sheep stations in the Bathurst area and the Hunter Valley, west of Sydney, in 1824 led the Governor of New South Wales, General Sir Thomas Brisbane (1773–1860), to impose martial law, allowing ranchers to shoot Aborigines on sight. A missionary, Lancelot Threlkeld (1788–1859), reported that 'a large number were driven into a swamp, and mounted police rode round and round and shot them off indiscriminately until they were all . . . destroyed, men, women and children!' The squad collected forty-five skulls from the corpses, macerated them, and sent them back to England as trophies.

One of the relatively few occasions on which concerted government action was taken against Aborigines was in Tasmania. Initially, the governor attempted to show the Aborigines that they would receive equal justice to the settlers. But clashes erupted and continued until 1830, when Governor George Arthur (1784–1854) gathered 3,000 Europeans, including 1,000 soldiers and 700 convicts on parole, paid for by the British Treasury, to form a 'Black Line' across the country to drive the Aborigines onto the Tasman peninsula south-east of Hobart. By this time the original population of 7,000 in 1800 had been reduced to a few hundred through sporadic private violence and above all disease. This remainder, Governor Arthur claimed, would 'murder every white inhabitant, if they could do so with safety to themselves'. The British Colonial Secretary, General Sir George Murray (1772–1846), refused to send out troops to help in the enterprise, commenting that 'the extinction of the native race' would leave 'an indelible stain on the character of the British government'. Except for one small group of five who were caught napping and shot, however, the Black Line failed to find any Aborigines; they had all slipped through it under cover of the dense bush. In 1834 the remaining 200, when told they would be given their lands back and reunited with their families, surrendered. The promises were lies; they were transported instead to Flinders Island, 34 miles north of Tasmania, where most of them perished, leaving only a sad remnant behind.

The killings of Aborigines were part of the disorderly early history of modern Australia. Frequently they were carried out by freed convicts. The state was keen to impose order, and indeed after a massacre of thirty Aborigines by a gang of former convicts at Myall Creek in central New South Wales in 1838, seven of the perpetrators were convicted and hanged, though 'they all stated that they thought it extremely hard that white men should be put to death for killing blacks'. The massacre prompted the government of the state to reject the idea that it should 'abandon all control over these distant regions – and leave the occupiers of them unrestrained in their lawless aggressions upon each other and upon the Aborigines'. It created a Border Police Force, whose aim, however, was not least to protect ranchers against attacks by Aborigines. Small-scale, often individual killings continued, but government control was more or less established by mid-century. The main damage to the indigenous population was done, as elsewhere, by disease. From an estimated half to three-quarters of a million in 1788, the Aboriginal population of Australia had declined to 72,000 by 1921.

Where the British confronted not nomadic hunter-gatherers in a sparsely populated country but settled farmers on rich agricultural land, the situation was more complex. When Xhosa land to the east of the Cape Colony was impounded by the governor to distribute to former slaves, a Xhosa army invaded on 21 December 1834 and claimed it back, killing British and Boer settlers alike. The governor, Lieutenant-General Sir Benjamin D'Urban (1777–1849), declared that the Xhosa had to be 'exterminated', an emotive word that earned him considerable criticism in Britain. The Xhosa chief was shot and his ears were removed by soldiers as trophies. But Xhosa resistance was fierce and after several months a compromise was reached, brokered by a new Whig government in London under Lord Melbourne (1779–1848) that was appalled by D'Urban's actions and terrified of the massive cost of continuous warfare in the Cape. The British withdrew and left the Xhosa with their land. This did not go down well, especially with the Dutch-descended Boer farmers, who bitterly resented the abolition of slavery by the British government in 1834 and were outraged by the minimal scale of the compensation paid to them. Some 5,000 Boer farmers expressed their lack of confidence in the British Empire by migrating northwards between 1835 and 1837 in the 'Great Trek'. Violent clashes with the Zulus and Ndebele ensued, with 135 trekkers reportedly massacring a force of 9,000 Ndebele warriors in 1837. In February 1838, Zulus killed Dutch settlers who had moved onto their land; in December the Boers retaliated by slaughtering 3,000 Zulu warriors at the Battle of Blood River. In 1843 the British annexed the Republic of Natalia, founded by the Boers who had migrated northwards in the Great Trek. Clashes between the British and Boers on the one hand, and the Zulus on the other, continued for several decades. At the Battle of Isandlwana in January 1879 a British force was heavily defeated by Zulu warriors, and though at the same time an outpost at Rorke's Drift held off another Zulu force, the British army had to retreat, suffering further losses. A second, stronger invasion force finally defeated the Zulus in July and established British control, leading to the decision by the British to annex Zululand in 1887.

This did not bring the three-sided conflict to an end. In 1881, shortly after the outbreak of what became known as the First Anglo-Boer War, a Boer force had defeated the British at the Battle of Majuba Hill and re-established the Republic of the Transvaal, founded as a result of the Great Trek and annexed by the British in 1876. The situation was transformed, however, by the discovery of rich gold deposits in the Transvaal in 1884, leading to a massive gold rush two years later. By the 1890s the huge wealth of the mines was proving an irresistible temptation to the British, and when the Boers rejected a demand for voting rights to be extended to the non-Boer white inhabitants of the Transvaal in 1899, the British invaded, beginning the so-called Second Anglo-Boer War. An early Boer counter-offensive against Natal and the Cape was defeated by a British army under Lord Roberts (1832–1914), which relieved besieged towns, notably Mafeking, and in 1900 occupied the main Boer centres including the capital of the Transvaal, Pretoria. For another two years the Boers continued the war in a series of guerrilla campaigns, leading the new British commander Lord Kitchener systematically to destroy Boer farms and set up forty-five concentration camps for Boers, mainly women and children. Some 25,000 Boer soldiers were deported overseas as prisoners of war. Both sides used large numbers of black soldiers, and the British established sixty-four concentration camps for black families as well. About 28,000 Boers, mainly children, died of disease, exposure and malnutrition in the tented camps, a death rate of around one in four. Of the 107,000 black Africans held in the camps, at least 14,000 perished. Conditions in these concentration camps were not part of a deliberate policy of genocide, as their counterparts were to be in German South-West Africa a short while afterwards, but they were murderous enough nonetheless. When, in 1909–10, the Union of South Africa was created as a self-governing Dominion, neither black Africans nor immigrant Indian workers had equal rights with the whites.

The other major territories acquired by the British Empire in the 'Scramble for Africa' were very different. They did not have any formal self-government, legislative assemblies or voting rights. They were not colonies of settlement; by and large there were few white settlers in them, except in British East Africa. Palm-oil, hardwood, ivory, cocoa, ground-nut and cotton production began to make the new west African colonies economically important, whereas east African colonies from Egypt southwards were mainly of significance in protecting the route to India through the Suez Canal. Apart from a small number of states like Zanzibar, Brunei, Tonga, Malaya or most importantly Egypt, they did not retain indigenous rulers but were directly controlled from the Colonial Office. Land seizures by colonists were of limited importance given their small numbers in areas sometimes called 'the white man's grave'. Economic motives remained paramount in the establishment of empire. As the British Prime Minister Lord Salisbury said in 1897 in a speech on British colonization in tropical Africa: 'The objects we have in our view are strictly business objects.' Like Bismarck, Salisbury wanted colonization to be carried out by chartered companies rather than by the state. It was, for example, the Royal Niger Company that led the way in colonizing what later became known as Nigeria, signing 237 separate treaties with local rulers between December 1884 and October 1886 alone. The chiefs made over their land and legal authority to the Company in return for being allowed to mine and farm and maintain their own laws. The Company for its part declared that it had no 'desire to interfere more than is absolutely necessary with the internal arrangements of the Chiefs of Central Africa'.

Such arrangements proved no more permanent in the British than they had been in the German case. Joseph Chamberlain, the Liberal Unionist who became Colonial Secretary in 1895, was a far more thoroughgoing imperialist than his Prime Minister, Lord Salisbury. He was not satisfied with the loose, treaty-based arrangements by which the new African parts of the empire were ruled. British interests had to be asserted more powerfully. In west Africa the Ashanti fought a long series of wars against the encroachments of the British that only ended in the mid-1890s with the British occupation of the Ashanti capital. There was resistance elsewhere too. At the beginning of 1897 an expedition of 250 African soldiers sent by the Acting Consul-General of the Niger Coast Protectorate made its way towards the west African kingdom of Benin. The expedition had purported to be peaceful, but the King of Benin had got wind from a trader that its true aim was to depose him and take over his territory. His forces surprised the column and massacred almost everyone in it; only two survived. A punitive expedition later in the year sacked Benin and looted numerous bronze and other artefacts. The powerful slave-owning Muslim emirs of northern Nigeria also needed bringing to heel, in Chamberlain's view, and in 1900 a West African Frontier Force was created that waged a series of military campaigns against them until the emirs gave in to British demands. The previous year a Royal Navy force bombarded and machine-gunned the port at Zanzibar, killing or wounding 500 people, to express British disapproval of the fact that the sultan's nephew had declared himself ruler on his uncle's death without first seeking the permission of the British consul. Violence therefore lay at the heart of the British as well as the German Empire in Africa.

'THE WHITE MAN'S BURDEN'

In 1889 a world anti-slavery conference gave King Leopold of the Belgians permission to levy import duties in the Belgian Congo, in order to pay for the elaborate infrastructure of roads, railways, steamboats and military posts that he claimed was needed to bring slavery and the slave trade to an end in his private possession. Seduced by the promise of acquiring the territory on his death, and by the prospect of profits from economic enterprises there, the Belgian Parliament advanced him a huge loan with which to begin the work. Leopold saw in the Congo the opportunity for quick returns and big profits. He tried producing cotton, importing American planters to start up cultivation, but conditions were unsuitable so he moved on to ivory. His agents sallied forth into the territory, shooting elephants and buying up or seizing ivory from traders. A Belgian senator travelling through the Congo in 1896 reported constantly encountering files of African porters:

> black, miserable, with only a horribly filthy loin-cloth for clothing, frizzy and bare head supporting the load – box, bale, ivory tusk . . . most of them sickly, drooping under a burden increased by tiredness and insufficient food . . . They come and go like this by the thousands . . . requisitioned by the State armed with its powerful militia, handed over by chiefs whose slaves they are and who make off with their wages.

Discipline on local populations was enforced by beatings with a hippopotamus-hide whip, the *chicotte*. One Belgian magistrate in Leopold-ville came across thirty small children being mercilessly flogged because some of them had laughed on seeing a white man. To enforce control, Leopold used a private army, the *Force Publique*, which by the turn of the century numbered 19,000 men and consumed half his entire budget for the colony. The pattern of conquest was similar to that observable elsewhere, with local and regional African chiefs and rulers resisting the encroachments of Leopold's men. In Katanga, a clash with members of the Sanga people led to their chief taking refuge in a large cave, outside which the *Force Publique* then lit fires, asphyxiating 178 men inside. By the end of the 1890s, Leopold's forces had conquered the remaining centres of resistance.

It was not the conquest of the Congo that marked out the Belgian colony from others, however, but the way it was then run. A worldwide boom in rubber, stimulated by the spread of the pneumatic tyre, insulations for electrical, telephone and telegraph wires, and much more besides, prompted Leopold to devote frantic efforts to harvest the wild rubber that grew in profusion in the Congo before cultivated rubber trees in Latin America and Asia could reach maturity and undercut the prices he got for the wild variety. Profits for Leopold's Anglo-Belgian India Rubber Company and other concessionaries reached more than 700 per cent and Congo rubber earnings increased nearly a hundredfold between 1890 and 1904 alone. Workers were sent ever deeper into the forest to cut the rubber vines that grew up into the canopy, collecting the sap but destroying the plants. The work was difficult and dangerous and Belgian officers forced the men to undertake it by taking their families hostage until the required amount of rubber was delivered. The men then carried the solidified sap to collecting depots under the close supervision of the *Force Publique*. If the quantity was too small, the hostages were shot and the women raped before being killed.

If a village resisted, Leopold's men, African troops under white command, shot everyone in it, and then to prove to their officers that their bullets had not been wasted on hunting for food, they severed the right hands of the victims, smoking them to preserve them on the way back to the depot. One traveller, reaching a village in an area where resistance was strong, noted eighty-one hands being smoked on a slow fire. 'See!' he was told: 'Here is our evidence. I always have to cut off the right hands of those we kill in order to show the state how many we have killed.' If the number of hands was insufficient to match the number of spent cartridges, soldiers simply cut off the hands of the living. Trade carried diseases such as smallpox and sleeping sickness to areas from which they had previously been absent. The birth rate plummeted as women refused to have children and men were taken away to work in the rubber forest or on the 241-mile railway that Leopold had built to transport his booty. By 1924 the Belgian authorities were so concerned about a shortage of labour in the Congo that they ordered a census. When compared with late nineteenth-century estimates, it found that the population had fallen by 50 per cent, from 20 millon to 10 million.

These atrocities soon reached the notice of critics of colonialism in Europe and the United States, fed with information by the young Edmund Dene Morel (1873–1924), a clerk in a shipping company trading with the Congo, who had forged contacts with missionaries in the area who were horrified by Leopold's cruelties. More detail was added by Roger Casement (1864–1916), a British consular official in the Congo. Their cause was taken up by the writers Mark Twain (1835–1910) and Sir Arthur Conan Doyle. King Leopold was forced to hand over control of the Congo to the Belgian government not long before his death in 1909. The state administrators began to replace wild-rubber collecting with the planting of rubber trees. However, the campaign against the atrocities in the Congo did not touch the French Congo, where similar outrages took place. A study of one French trading post showed that the fluctuations in rubber production correlated statistically with the number of bullets used by company police between 1904 and 1907, and one estimate puts the population loss in the French Congolese rainforest area at 50 per cent as well. Inequality was built into the French colonies, where the rights of citizens were denied to the majority of the colonized, with rare exceptions. Apart from Algeria, where European settlement was on a large scale in the north, this meant that the colonies were run in an authoritarian fashion by local administrators. Earlier in the century the French had still believed in the 'civilizing mission', or in other words spreading the benefits of the French Revolution, liberty, equality and fraternity, across the globe, but despite the continuing power of this ideology, the experience of colonization forced a partial retreat from this lofty principle. When indigenous kingdoms like Dahomey, whose female soldiers and customs of mass human sacrifice fascinated and horrified Europeans, were taken over, it was thought that their inhabitants could not be turned into French men and women; it would simply cost too much in money and lives. As a book by the French doctor and explorer Jules Harmand (1845–1921), *Domination and Colonization*, concluded in 1910, it was necessary to 'better the lot of the aborigine in all ways, but only in directions that are profitable to him – by letting him evolve in his own way . . . by *indirect rule*, with a conservation . . . of the institutions of the subject people . . .'.

The principle of indirect rule derived above all from the long history of British control over India. India was different from all other colonies in the British Empire; in fact there was no other colony like it in any European empire. It was very large, with a population of around 200 million in the 1860s, and it had previously been ruled by another great power, the Mughal Empire, which in some respects provided a ready-made infrastructure of rule and to which the British claimed to be the successor. India was not suitable for emigration and settlement. Christian missions did not achieve very much in a land dominated by great religions such as Islam and Hinduism. The assimilation of Indians into British culture was an impossible ideal. After the 1857 rebellion (the 'Indian Mutiny') the subcontinent was ruled autocratically by an appointed governor-general whose power was limited only by a small council of civil servants. Over time this was expanded, and in 1909 it was enlarged to include elected members, but the council had no power to introduce laws or stop whatever the governor-general was doing. Until the First World War, therefore, India was a kind of *ancien régime* autocracy.

British rule in India rested on two key institutions. First of these was the civil service, a central, elite organization operating across the entire country, and staffed by British men, with only 5 per cent of the posts occupied by Indians as late as 1915. The Indian Civil Service was well paid and after the corruption scandals of the late eighteenth century it had become reasonably honest and conscientious. It collected the taxes already levied by the Mughals, above all the land tax, which under the Mughals had been administered by officials known as zamindars, often indistinguishable from high aristocrats. It administered justice under a codified system begun in 1861 that mixed British and Hindu principles and customs, and it provided political advisers to the 600 or so mostly small princely states that survived the uprising of 1857 (not least because the move to assimilate them into British rule was thought to have been one of its causes). The princely states collected their own taxes and ran their own affairs, but under the advice of British officials who encouraged reform. Over time the growing habit of educating the younger generation of princes at British schools and universities, as well as the intensification of communications through better transport, telegraph and so on, and the increasing employment of British or British-trained civil servants to administer them, the princely states developed an amalgam of Indian traditions and European modernity that struck many as an ideal example of what could be achieved by indirect rule. Not just in the princely states, however, but also in the areas under direct rule, British control depended effectively on the passive co-operation of Indians, both elites and masses. This was achieved above all by the retention of Indian customs, institutions and basic structures of administration, along with an attempt to provide good and honest government. Thus the full panoply of modern Victorian administration was applied to India, with the founding of educational institutions such as the University of Madras (1857), and the adoption of the principle put forward in Thomas Babington Macaulay's 1835 report on Indian education that schools and colleges teaching in English should be used to create a new Indian administrative elite to act as an intermediary between British and Indian society. Police forces were created from the 1860s and unified in 1905. Free trade was used to destroy autonomous industries such as textiles in the early part of the century, but India's incorporation into a rapidly globalizing world economy stimulated new industries and an increasing rate of urbanization, helped by the construction of roads, railways and canals. The shock of the 1857 rebellion had stimulated the British to be both cautious and conservative in their handling of Indian society and traditions, and to engage in a sustained policy of improvement and development to convince Indians of the benefits of British rule.

Yet underpinning all this was the application, or threat, of force, in the form of the second great institution of British rule in India, namely the Indian Army. The British regular army numbered around 250,000 men and had to defend and garrison colonies all over the world. The Indian Army was almost as large, and it could quickly be expanded by calling up reserves. It was paid for by taxes levied in India and indeed consumed around a third of all Indian tax revenues. In the key area of the 1857 rebellion, Bengal, the proportion of European to Indian troops was fixed at one to one; in Madras and Bombay one to two. Altogether there were

73,000 British and 154,000 Indian troops in the charge of British senior officers in 1885. British regiments served in India in rotation, with 'sepoy' regiments remaining separate. Recruits were taken from so-called 'martial' areas like the North-West Frontier, Nepal, or the Punjab, which had largely stayed loyal in 1857, as well as from the poorest and most illiterate social groups, who were seen as less likely to get ideas of rebellion and revolt. The Indian Army was an asset not only in ruling the subcontinent but also in establishing British supremacy more generally, among other things in providing backing for the British acquisition of colonies in east Africa.

In major respects, however, British rule in India brought disaster for the population. The intensive land taxes levied by the Raj, and collected with considerably greater efficiency than their equivalents had been under the Mughals, caused changes in land use and turned bad harvests into famines, with two million people dying of starvation in northern India in 1860–1, six million across India in the 1870s, and another five million with a monsoon failure in 1896–7, when the situation was made worse by an outbreak of plague. Communications were still not good enough for effective relief operations to be mounted, and as late as 1921 only 3 per cent of Indians had any formal education, making disease prevention difficult; reading and writing were the prerogative of only a small elite. These catastrophes were not new – the Bengal famine of 1770 is estimated to have killed nearly 10 million people, and famines were also recorded in pre-colonial times – but there is little doubt that they increased in frequency and intensity under British rule, nor did the authorities of the Raj undertake adequate measures to deal with them and mitigate their effects. India also became the major global reservoir of indentured labour, a kind of quasi-slavery where workers were paid but had neither freedom nor any significant rights. Some 60,000 South Asians were sent to Fiji to work between 1879 and 1920, 25,000 to Mauritius, and 30,000 to build Kenya's railways in the 1890s, more than a third of them suffering death or serious injury during the construction. The total number of South Asians, almost all of them Indian, working across the British Empire by 1900 totalled more than a million. Sometimes they were sent across vast distances to replace the slave labour that had now become illegal: nearly 75,000 Indians arrived in Trinidad between 1874 and 1915 in this way. The spread of Indian labour across the British Empire indicated its global nature, but it also caused disruption to Indian communities on the subcontinent, and led to racial tensions in some colonies, notably Fiji.

Despite these problems and the failure of the British administration to deal with them adequately, in India and increasingly after 1918 in other parts of the British Empire reform was seen as the best means of bringing stability and order to colonial societies. Conquest was followed in the end by Victorian 'improvement'. A case in point was the Kingdom of Upper Burma. Fear of growing French power in Indochina prompted British concern when the death of the Burmese king, Mindon Min (1808–78), sparked a struggle for the succession in the course of which the majority of his 110 children were strangled then trampled by elephants (it was taboo to spill royal blood). The victor, King Thibaw Min (1859–1916), was not disposed to yield to the British. Indeed it was not so much disapproval of this violence as concern that the new king had begun to open negotiations with the French, who agreed to build a railway and set up a bank, which led the British Conservative government of Lord Salisbury to send in 10,000 troops in 1885. The Burmese forces were defeated and the territory was annexed in 1886 at the end of what became known as the Third Anglo-Burmese War. This was denounced by Liberal MPs as 'an act of high-handed violence . . . an act of flagrant folly', through which the Burmese political system had been destroyed, leaving chaos behind. Guerrilla resistance proliferated, led by some of the remaining royal princes, and soon the British had 40,000 troops in the country, engaging in a 'pacification' campaign that involved the execution of alleged 'dacoits', or rebels, and the burning of their villages.

By 1890 peace had descended on Burma. It would last up to the 1940s. The 'Burman', remarked one British civil servant in the governor's office, was 'a happy-go-lucky sort of chap, the Irishman of the East'. He needed keeping in order. As another commentator declared: 'If riches and personal comfort, protection of property, just laws, incorruptible judges and rulers, are blessings as a set-off against Utopian dreams of freedom, then Jack Burman has a happy future.' What this meant in practice was the wholesale conversion of the countryside to commercial rice production, with vast tracts of forest being felled and British firms bringing in thousands of indentured labourers from India to do the work. This in turn meant roads, railways, seaports, urban and commercial development. Burma became a vitally important source of rice for large parts of the British Empire, notably eastern Africa and above all India, where it supplied 15 per cent of the rice consumed. Meanwhile the habit of British soldiers and administrators of taking Burmese women as their wives or more usually concubines, much complained of in the 1890s, led to the emergence of a new Anglo-Burmese elite that came to dominate the administration of the country in the interwar years, in a comparable development to the creation of the social stratum of 'Anglo-Indians' who fulfilled a similar role on the subcontinent in the same period.

Imperialism thus continued an ideology of improvement, summed up in 1899 in a famous poem by Rudyard Kipling urging colonizers to:

> Take up the White Man's burden –
> Send forth the best ye breed –
> Go bind your sons to exile
> To serve your captives' need.

To administer the colonies, educated clerks and administrators were required, and given the numbers that were necessary, this meant educating a select number of the colonized. This in turn, whether it involved local education or education in Britain or other European countries, began to create new indigenous elites that imbibed European notions of nationalism, democracy and liberal values. In some colonies, including Burma, a sense of national identity pre-dated colonization. In others national identity required the language of European liberalism to find its articulation, and the model of European political parties in the age of mass democracy in the late nineteenth century to find institutional expression.

As these developments took hold on the subcontinent, 1885 saw the formation of the Indian National Congress, based at first on the ideas of the Theosophical movement, a quasi-religious organization dedicated to world brotherhood, and involving English people as well as Indians. The aim of the Indian National Congress at first was to exert pressure for educated Indians to take a greater part in government and administration, but soon it gained widespread support among Indian elites and began to exert pressure on the government. In 1892 the Raj conceded the Indian Councils Act, allowing corporations to nominate educated Indians to legislative councils, and in 1909 it permitted them to stand for election. The British had been able to take advantage of the break-up of the Mughal Empire and the ensuing disunity to take over one Indian state after another, or play them off against each other. But by uniting India themselves and binding it together with a unitary system of administration and communications, the British had created the potential for a new united nationalist movement. The Raj had on the other hand fastened onto traditional Indian institutions from the land tax to the maharajas and princely states, and to the new educated elite these were beginning to seem like an obstacle to progress. It was indeed possible to take an altogether different view of the 'white man's burden', one in which the imperialist was imposing a burden on the colonized, not the other way round.

THE 'EASTERN QUESTION'

In the second half of the nineteenth century the major European powers still managed to settle colonial questions by peaceful negotiation. But once the process of colonization reached its limits, as it did shortly after the turn of the century, almost the only way a European power could acquire fresh territory was by seizing it from another European power. One area within Europe that dangled low-hanging fruit before the eyes of greedy imperialist politicians was the Ottoman Empire, which at the turn of the century still governed a huge swathe of south-eastern Europe. The empire was catastrophically incompetent at managing its economy. It was not until 1845 that the first bank was opened in Constantinople; the first banknotes were not numbered and they were thus extremely easy to forge. There was no state budget until the 1840s; the Ministry of Finance was only set up in 1839. Although things had improved a little by the mid-1850s, the finances of the empire were utterly unable to cope with the huge costs of the Crimean War. So Ottoman administrators arranged a large loan from the British and French, and soon they became accustomed to asking for more in order to cover the expenses of running the empire. With a return of 10 per cent, private banks in western Europe were only too happy to lend. At the same time the Ottoman government tried to raise money by imposing internal trade tariffs and levying an export tax of 12 per cent. International agreements negotiated to facilitate the loans prevented the empire from levying more than 5 per cent on imports, so it was flooded with European industrial goods.

All of this provided rich pickings for crooked Ottoman administrators. 'Corruption,' a British observer smugly though far from inaccurately noted, 'is the rule from the highest to the lowest . . . The first thought of modern Turkish statesmen is to amass money. They know their tenure of office is insecure and they seize the opportunity.' By the early 1870s the state finances were in a condition of acute crisis; by 1875 interest payments on the state debt were eating up 44 per cent of total government revenues. To be sure, the creation of a state bank, budgets and a Finance Ministry had been part of the *Tanzimat*, the wide-ranging series of reforms that went on through the 1850s and 1860s. They included the guarantee of basic civil rights, the reform of the army, the introduction of civil and criminal law codes, the establishment of Western-style universities, the construction of railways, the opening of a stock exchange, and much more. Central to these was the introduction of equal rights for all religious groups, and the creation of an Ottoman national identity, bolstered by the invention of a national flag and a national anthem.

But these reforms were undermined by a massive influx of more than a million Muslim refugees, who were fleeing first from the chaos of the Crimean War and then from the Russians as they invaded the Caucasus. Many of these refugees found their way into Christian areas in the Balkans, where religious tensions grew rapidly. In many cases the Ottoman regime forcibly evicted Christians from their homes to make room for them. Then in 1873 a major financial and economic collapse across Europe, following the boom of the early 1870s, brought disaster. The loans stopped coming. A drought in 1872 had led to massive harvest failures across the empire. Locust swarms denuded Cyprus of crops. A harsh winter resulted in widespread starvation. Dead bodies were seen on the streets of Constantinople and packs of wolves were observed attacking people in the suburbs. Flooding caused by the spring thaw made matters worse. By early 1874, an estimated 90 per cent of the livestock in Anatolia and the southern Balkans had been slaughtered for food. The local and regional administration was completely unable to cope. The transport infrastructure was inadequate to ferry supplies to stricken areas. And crucially, the Ottoman government, rather than cutting expenditure, urged tax-collecting agencies – mostly tax farmers, independent entrepreneurs who had bought the right to collect taxes – on to ever greater efforts in an attempt to meet the state's overwhelming tax obligations. As the peasants fled to the towns or took to the hills to escape their depredations, the collectors and the gendarmes who accompanied them looted the villages and took away contributions in kind. Resistance quickly spread, above all within Christian areas in the Balkans.

The Russians were quick to take advantage of the rapidly developing situation. Having completed their conquest of the Caucasus, they exploited Prussia's defeat of Austria in 1866 and France in 1870–1 to repudiate the neutrality of the Black Sea laid down in the settlement concluded after the Crimean War in 1856. The British objected but had no support from the other powers, and a conference in London in January 1871 allowed the Russians to send warships into the Black Sea once more. One of the constants of Russian foreign policy through the century had been the drive to secure an ice-free port in the Mediterranean. This drive had been in abeyance in the years after their defeat of 1856. Now it was under way again. Russia's chances of achieving this aim grew as the Ottoman Empire declined. And a new factor now entered the mix: Pan-Slavism, which emerged in Russia in the 1870s with the opening up of public debate following the reforms of Alexander II. It spread to the Balkans, as Orthodox Christian intellectuals and students began to argue that the smaller Slav nationalities belonged to a large family of nations headed by Russia. Such

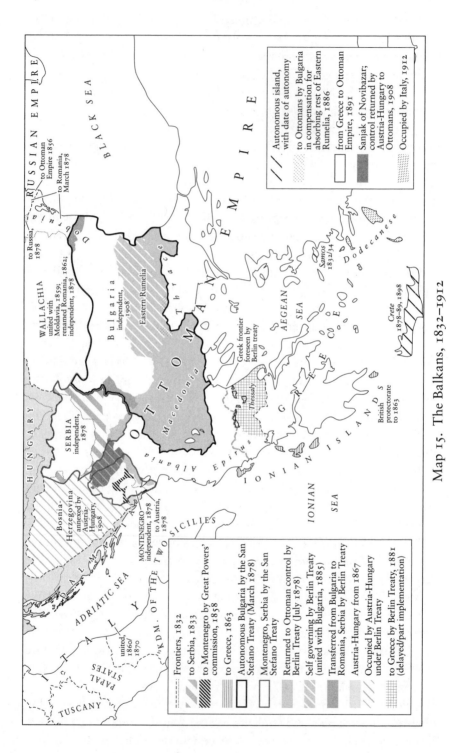

Map 15. The Balkans, 1832–1912

RUSSIAN EMPIRE

BLACK SEA

to Ottoman
Empire 1856

to Romania,
March 1878

to Russia,
1878

WALLACHIA
united with
Moldavia, 1859;
renamed Romania, 1862;
independent, 1878

HUNGARY

Bosnia-
Herzegovina
annexed by
Austria-
Hungary,
1908

to Austria,
1878

MONTENEGRO
independent, 1878

SERBIA
independent,
1878

Bulgaria
independent,
1908

Eastern Rumelia

Thrace

Macedonia

Albania

Epirus

Thessaly

Greek frontier
foreseen by
Berlin treaty

OTTOMAN EMPIRE

AEGEAN
SEA

Samos
1832/34

Dodecanese

Crete
1878–89, 1898

GREECE

IONIAN ISLANDS

British
protectorate
to 1863

IONIAN
SEA

ADRIATIC SEA

ITALY

united,
1860/
1870

PAPAL
STATES

TUSCANY

KDM. OF THE TWO SICILIES

Autonomous island,
with date of autonomy

to Ottomans by Bulgaria
in compensation for
absorbing rest of Eastern
Rumelia, 1886

from Greece to Ottoman
Empire, 1891

Sanjak of Novibazar;
control returned by
Austria-Hungary to
Ottomans, 1908

Occupied by Italy, 1912

Frontiers, 1832

to Serbia, 1833

to Montenegro by Great Powers'
commission, 1858

to Greece, 1863

Autonomous Bulgaria by the San
Stefano Treaty (March 1878)

Montenegro, Serbia by the San
Stefano Treaty

Returned to Ottoman control by
Berlin Treaty (July 1878)

Self governing by Berlin Treaty
(united with Bulgaria, 1885)

Transferred from Bulgaria to
Romania, Serbia by Berlin Treaty

Austria-Hungary from 1867

Occupied by Austria-Hungary
under Berlin Treaty

to Greece by Berlin Treaty, 1881
(delayed/part implementation)

ideas were increasingly influential in areas still nominally under Ottoman rule but strongly sympathetic to the Christian rebels who were rising up against Ottoman tax demands in the Balkans. Serbian radicals infiltrated Bosnia to support a peasant uprising there, while in Bulgaria in April–May 1876 a poorly prepared revolt led by nationalist revolutionaries was put down by the Ottoman Army within a few weeks.

The consequences of the short-lived Bulgarian revolt, however, were momentous. After the insurgents had massacred a number of Muslim civilians, the irregulars who accompanied the Ottoman forces, the *bashi-bazouks*, engaged in the wholesale slaughter of Bulgarians as they suppressed the rebellion. Arriving in the town of Batak some weeks after the *bashi-bazouks* had retaken it, the American correspondent of the *London Daily News*, Januarius MacGahan (1844–78), reported: 'We . . . all suddenly drew rein with an exclamation of horror, for right before us, almost beneath our horses' feet, was a sight that made us shudder. It was a heap of skulls, intermingled with bones from all parts of the human body, skeletons, nearly entire, rotting, clothing, human hair, and putrid flesh lying there in one foul heap.' He estimated that 8,000 people had been killed by the irregulars altogether, though others put the number at nearer 30,000. The Bulgarians' plight aroused widespread public sympathy in western Europe. Governments, like that of Disraeli in England, were reluctant to intervene, since any further weakening of the Ottoman Empire would open the way to advances by the Russians. However, popular sentiment, led in England by Gladstone, who made his political comeback on the strength of a huge public campaign against what he called the 'Bulgarian horrors', demanded action. 'Let the Turks,' he thundered, 'now carry away their abuses, in the only possible manner, namely, by carrying off themselves. Their Zaptiehs and their Mudirs, their Bimbashis and Yuzbashis, their Kaimakams and their Pashas, one and all, bag and baggage, shall, I hope, clear out from the province that they have desolated and profaned.'

Nationalist sentiment was also boiling up in Serbia. Austria, Russia and Germany tried to intervene in Bulgaria in May 1876 with a general plan of reform for the Ottoman provinces in the Balkans, but they were rebuffed by the sultan. Following this, the Serbs declared war on the Ottoman Empire on 30 June. Tsar Alexander II had to yield to Pan-Slav pressure to allow volunteers to go and fight with the Serbs. On 11 November, indeed, he praised 'our volunteers, many of whom have paid with their blood for the cause of Slavdom'. But the Serbs did not do well. They had failed to train their forces, and they only had 460 officers, augmented by 700 Russian volunteer officers, to command a rabble of 125,000 peasants. They were poorly armed, with weapons that were either obsolete or homemade, and relied on numbers rather than equipment. Recent Ottoman Army reforms, by contrast, had created an effective force, armed with Martini-Henry and Snider-Enfield rifles and Krupp field artillery. Led by a Russian general, 68,000 Serbs attacked the Ottoman fortress of Niš and were soundly defeated in August 1876, with 5,000 dead and 9,500 wounded. At this point the Russians stepped in and threatened war on the Ottomans unless peace was concluded on the basis of the *status quo ante*, which it was on 17 February 1877.

These events had major repercussions in Constantinople. Sultan Abdül-aziz (1830–76) was deposed in a military coup led by the so-called Young Ottomans, most of whom had been educated in western European universities, on 30 May 1876, and murdered a few days later. His successor and nephew, Murad V (1840–1904), was not a strong character; on hearing the news of his uncle's death, he fainted, and on coming round is said to have vomited continuously for a day and a half. The Young Ottomans had wanted Murad to grant a constitution, but he failed to do anything, so they deposed him on grounds of insanity on 31 August 1876 in favour of his brother Abdülhamid II (1842–1918). Realizing the need to keep in with the Young Ottomans, Abdülhamid granted a constitution almost immediately. Together with the defeat of the Serbian Army, this made him for the moment extremely popular. He thus felt strong enough to reject another attempt at international mediation in the so-called London Protocol, agreed by all the major powers on 31 March 1877, which contained a demand for further reforms in the Balkan provinces. The inevitable result was that on 24 April, yielding finally to Pan-Slav pressure, Alexander II of Russia declared war on the Ottomans, having previously secured the support of the Austrians by promising them Bosnia, and the Romanians by promising to defend their territorial integrity if they allowed Russian armies safe passage.

During the spring of 1877, Russian forces moved southwards and crossed the Danube. In July they arrived at the well-defended Bulgarian town of Plevna, which had been reinforced by a large Ottoman army under Osman Nuri Pasha (1832–1900). As the Russians failed twice to take the city, the tsar agreed to accept Romanian support, but a third major assault failed as well, with the loss of 18,000 Russian and Romanian lives. In desperation the tsar brought in the Baltic German military engineer General Totleben who had organized the defence of Sevastopol in the Crimean War. Increasing the Russian and Romanian armies' strength to 100,000, Totleben successfully cut off Plevna, captured outlying positions, and repulsed an enemy attempt to break out. On 9 December 1877, Osman

Pasha surrendered, taking 2,000 officers and 44,000 men with him into Russian captivity. Elsewhere, in the Caucasus, fierce fighting in a series of battles ended with the capture of the town of Kars by the Russians on 17 November, leading to a headlong Turkish retreat in which 17,000 of the fleeing troops were taken prisoner. It was in the Balkans, however, that the decisive actions took place. A force of 71,000 Russian troops took the Bulgarian city of Sofia on 3 January 1878 and then defeated a Turkish army at the Battle of Plovdiv two weeks later. Another Russian force of 50,000 led by the dashing General Mikhail Dmitrievich Skobelev (1843–82) destroyed a Turkish army in a three-day battle between 5 and 9 January 1878, at the Shipka Pass, forcing the surrender of 22,000 Turkish troops. This was the last straw for the Ottomans. Shortly after the Russians entered Adrianople, opening the way to Constantinople itself, an armistice was signed on 31 January 1878.

The Russians lost no time in signing a formal treaty, at the town of San Stefano, where negotiations were completed on 3 March. The treaty created an independent and large Bulgaria, which included the whole of Macedonia except Salonika, and, crucially, gave it access to the Aegean via western Thrace, cutting off the Ottomans' overland access to their possessions in the Balkans. This was clearly going to be a Russian client state. The treaty thoroughly alarmed the British, who had already sent a fleet to the Sea of Marmara on 13 February 1878. It also ignored the Austrians by leaving Bosnia and Herzegovina in Ottoman hands. Together with Russian gains in the Caucasus, it looked as if the Ottoman Empire was going to be broken up, and the main beneficiary would be the tsar. And indeed, things looked very black for the Ottoman Empire in the 1870s. Unable to finance its military operations in view of the massive public debt with which it was burdened, amounting by this time to more than half the state's revenue every year, the Ottoman government had declared bankruptcy in 1875. In 1881 an international agreement created the Ottoman Public Debt Administration, which soon had a staff of more than 5,000 officials. It was run by the empire's creditors, effectively on behalf of the British and French banks to which most of the money was owed, and it had the right to collect taxes and customs dues and finance profitable ventures such as railway construction. This humiliating situation continued until after the First World War.

With the outbreak of war in 1877, Sultan Abdülhamid II saw no need to continue with the Constitution he had granted on his accession, and suspended it indefinitely. Mindful of the fate of his two immediate predecessors, the sultan locked himself away in his palace and kept the Ottoman battle fleet inside the Golden Horn, because he thought that the navy

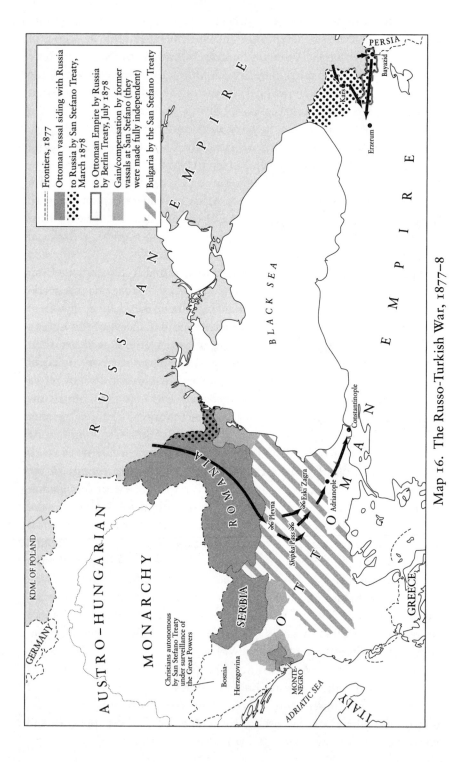

Map 16. The Russo-Turkish War, 1877–8

Legend:
Frontiers, 1877
Ottoman vassal siding with Russia
to Russia by San Stefano Treaty, March 1878
to Ottoman Empire by Russia by Berlin Treaty, July 1878
Gain/compensation by former vassals at San Stefano (they were made fully independent)
Bulgaria by the San Stefano Treaty

PERSIA
Bayazid
Erzerum

RUSSIAN EMPIRE

OTTOMAN EMPIRE

BLACK SEA

GERMANY
KDM. OF POLAND
AUSTRO–HUNGARIAN MONARCHY

Christians autonomous by San Stefano Treaty under surveillance of the Great Powers
Bosnia-Herzegovina
SERBIA
MONTE-NEGRO
ADRIATIC SEA
ITALY

ROMANIA

Plevna
Shipka Pass
Eski Zagra
Adrianople
Constantinople

GREECE

officers were liberals who would conspire against him if they were allowed out of his sight. This made it difficult for the empire to do anything to stop the further loss of territory in the longer run, most notably Egypt and the Sudan. In 1897, Ottoman forces defeated a Greek invasion of Crete, but the Great Powers intervened and gave the island to Greece anyway. In the immediate aftermath of the Treaty of San Stefano, however, with the British and Austrians in the lead, the Concert of Europe was revived, and the Russians were forced to agree to an international Congress, to be held in Berlin in June 1878. After frantic behind-the-scenes negotiations, the Russians managed to get most of what they wanted. Although Bulgaria was cut down to size at the Congress of Berlin, depriving it of access to the Aegean, and the province of Eastern Rumelia was returned to the Ottoman Empire, Russia annexed Bessarabia, in the north-east corner of Romania, which received some territorial compensation in northern Dobrudja. In the Caucasus, Russia occupied Batum and Kars. The Congress recognized Serbian independence along with that of Romania and Montenegro, and all three states gained territory from the Ottoman Empire in addition. Bosnia, Herzegovina and Novi Bazar were left nominally under Ottoman rule by the Congress but were from now on to be administered by Austria.

In effect the Treaty of Berlin created two spheres of influence in the Balkans: the Austrian in the west, including Serbia – much to the annoyance of the Serbs – and the Russian in the east. Russian public opinion was outraged, since the comparison it made was not with the situation before the war of 1877–8 but with the situation created by the Treaty of San Stefano. Pan-Slavism grew in vehemence as a result, and its obvious hostility to Germany, the host of the conference, led Bismarck to conclude an alliance with Austria the following year, expanding it with the inclusion of Italy in 1882 into the Triple Alliance. In 1881 he renewed, this time secretly, the League of the Three Emperors, between Austria, Russia and Germany, that had been publicly announced in 1872 and came into effect the following year. In the long run this attempt to square the diplomatic circle was bound to fall apart because of growing Austro-Russian antagonism in the Balkans. But for the moment it papered over the cracks more or less successfully. As a by-product of the negotiations, the British occupied Cyprus, another Ottoman possession, in exchange for agreeing to defend Turkish territories in Asia against further Russian aggression. For the rest of the century, indeed, the British were in a continual state of anxiety about Russian ambitions in Afghanistan, in Persia and Turkey, and on the north-west frontier of India, the focus of the intrigues and conspiracies that constituted the 'Great Game'.

The effect of dividing the Balkans into Austrian and Russian spheres of influence was to prove disastrous in the long run. It tied the unstable Balkan states and territories to the interests and prestige of two Great Powers, and at the same time fomented resentments and ambitions among these states that would eventually create major conflicts. None of them was satisfied with the territorial settlement it received. All of them resented the Congress of Berlin's insistence in 1878 that they insert into their Constitutions the guarantee of freedom of religion – mainly for Muslims in Serbia and Montenegro, and for Jews in Romania. Montenegro was given access to the sea but told it was not allowed to have armed vessels and that all its merchant ships had to fly the Habsburg flag, a provision that was hardly going to be accepted by the Montenegrins in the longer term. As the British consul in Constantinople remarked following the Treaty of Berlin: 'Those who think themselves strong enough to support their aspirations by arms will be ready to rebel against the authority under which they believe they have been placed in violation of justice and of the principle of "nationality". Those who cannot recur to force will have recourse to intrigue and conspiracy. Both processes have already begun.'

Conflicts began almost immediately with an ethnic Albanian rebellion against Montenegro, and a Macedonian uprising against the Ottomans. Muslims in Bosnia, as in Albania, rebelled against the Christian rule imposed by the Treaty of Berlin. There was a peasant revolt in Serbia. In 1885 a mass uprising backed by Alexander of Battenberg (1857–93), a minor German royal who had been appointed Prince of Bulgaria by popular acclaim, brought Eastern Rumelia back under Bulgarian control despite a Serbian invasion, which was easily defeated by the regular Bulgarian Army. However, the Russians ousted him in favour of Ferdinand of Sachsen-Coburg-Gotha, who was appointed regent the following year. European opinion was taken aback. Ferdinand was thought to be more pliant than his predecessor. 'He is totally unfit,' declared Queen Victoria, referring discreetly to rumours that Ferdinand was homosexual, ' . . . delicate, eccentric and effeminate . . . Should be stopped at once.' In fact, he proved a survivor, lasting until the end of the First World War and gaining the sobriquet 'Foxy Ferdinand' for his skill at political intrigue. The Russians did not get what they wanted from him. His appointment delivered the country into the hands of the ruthless Stefan Stambolov (1854–95). The son of an innkeeper, Stambolov was a leading figure in the 1875–6 uprisings, an architect of the coup that brought Ferdinand to the throne, and regent until the new prince's formal election. Stambolov tried to deal with continuing Russian interference, and the chronic economic problems that plagued the country, by establishing what in effect became a police state, arresting and imprisoning his opponents, muzzling the press, and billeting troops in villages that refused to pay their taxes.

When the Minister of Finance was assassinated in 1891, Stambolov, convinced that Russian agents were responsible, threw more than 300 leading Russophiles into prison. His authoritarian stance as Prime Minister after 1887 brought repeated clashes with Ferdinand. In the mid-1890s the conflict came to a head. In 1893, Macedonians based in Salonika formed a secretive terrorist group eventually called the Internal Macedonian Revolutionary Organization, or IMRO, dedicated to using violence to free Macedonia from Ottoman rule. It was soon dominated by Bulgarians, many of whom had fled Macedonia in the face of Ottoman oppression and taken up residence in Sofia. Stambolov's foreign policy was based on the attempt to counter Russian influence by a rapprochement with the Ottomans (who were still nominally suzerains over Bulgaria). This aroused the violent hatred of the Macedonian refugees, and his position became increasingly precarious. In 1894, King Ferdinand judged the time right to dismiss him. Stambolov did not long survive his fall from power. On 15 July 1895 an assassin fired a gun at him as he was riding in his carriage through the streets of Sofia. Stambolov leapt from the carriage and returned fire with the revolver he always carried with him, but three more assassins jumped on him, threw him to the ground, and, knowing he always wore a bullet-proof vest, stabbed him repeatedly in the head. He tried to protect himself with his hands, but the assassins severed these at the wrists with their knives in the frenzy of their assault. Fatally wounded, Stambolov was taken home by his bodyguards after they had chased the assassins away. 'Bulgaria's people will forgive me everything', he is said to have remarked on his deathbed, 'but they will not forgive that it was I who brought Ferdinand here.' It was rumoured that the assassination had been orchestrated by the king himself, but it was more likely that the IMRO was responsible for the attack. Macedonian jeers at Stambolov's public funeral a few days later were only stopped when his widow held up two jars containing his pickled hands. His grave was destroyed by a bomb less than a year later.

While this grisly pantomime was in progress, Romania enjoyed a period of relative calm after the ousting in 1866 of Prince Alexandru Cuza (1820–73), who had made the mistake of trying to reform the complex and oppressive agrarian structures of the two Principalities of Modavia and Wallachia, united to form Romania in 1859. The leading figure in the coup, Ion Brătianu (1821–91), a large landowner and, like the others in his group, a veteran of 1848, quickly found the inevitable German princeling to occupy the throne, in this case Prince Karl of Hohenzollern-Sigmaringen

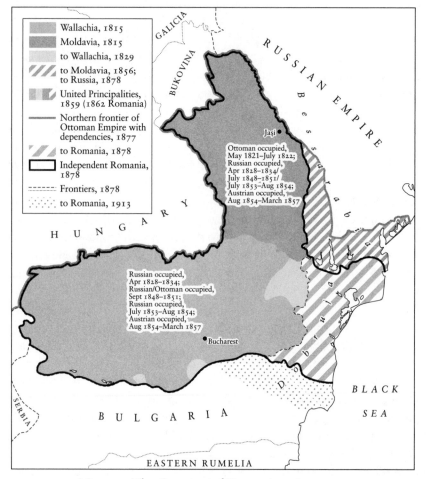

Map 17. The Creation of Romania, 1815–1913

(1839–1914), known as Carol I in Romania. The prince quickly adapted to his new political environment, taking advantage of the Russo-Turkish War of 1878 to declare his country independent of the Ottomans, and raising it to the level of a kingdom in 1881. The extensive powers of the monarchy, combined with the very restricted franchise of the Constitution of 1866 (modelled on the Belgian Constitution of 1831), provided a measure of political stability, based on government coalitions between varying shades of liberal and conservatives. This was coupled with a policy of cultivating good relations with the Great Powers. Trade treaties were signed with both Austria-Hungary and Russia, and Romania remained neutral during the Bulgarian uprising of 1875. Disillusioned with their rough treatment by the Russians in the Treaty of San Stefano, the Romanians initially turned to Germany and Austria-Hungary, building an alliance that lasted in formal terms at least until the First World War. But a Hungarian crackdown on Romanian nationalists in Transylvania created growing tensions, and the Austrians' backing for Bulgaria in resisting Romanian claims on Dobrudja drove the Romanian government, now led by Brătianu's son Ionel (1864–1927), to align itself with France and Russia instead, driven not least by fear of a massive arms build-up across the border with Bulgaria. Torn between the two camps into which Europe was dividing itself, Romania was eventually to opt for neutrality when the First World War broke out.

RACISM AND NATIONALISM

The increasing depth of nationalist passions in the Balkans reflected not only a sense that the days of the Ottomans were numbered, but also the rapid spread of racist concepts of identity, deriving from the expansion of Europe's overseas empires. For much of the nineteenth century, dominant European notions of racial and cultural superiority over the rest of the world were mostly relative rather than absolute, and they had a strong moral and religious content. British geography textbooks pointed out that the Egypt of the pharaohs had been 'full of ancient learning when Britain was inhabited by savages'. However, Britain had eventually emerged from the Dark Ages, and there was hope therefore that Africa would one day cease to be the Dark Continent. Backwardness in other cultures was a product not of lack of intelligence but of lack of progress and religion. As the British *Juvenile Missionary Magazine* told its 'young friends' in 1866: 'you see that man, through all his varieties, has a common parentage' and thus any human being of any race could 'acquire the knowledge of reading and writing almost as speedily as Europeans'. Underlying these views was the strong commitment to human equality embodied in the anti-slavery movement of the early decades of the nine-teenth century.

Victorian Christianity held that all human beings were capable of salva-tion, and indeed offered the prospect of the ultimate conversion of the whole of humankind. The major British missionary societies were all founded in the 1790s to work among settlers, but their role in the anti-slavery campaign encouraged them to extend their efforts into indig-enous societies. Throughout the century missionaries were the main vehicle of the spread of European-style education and – as in Livingstone's case – medical care in Africa, Asia, Australasia and Oceania. Justifications for imperialism were not only religious but also political and historical. The history of England had been one of the steady growth of freedom, in the dominant view of the day, and even towards the end of the Victorian era, intervention in other parts of the globe was justified in terms of libera-tion and progress. Time and again, British school textbooks informed children that Britain had been forced to intervene against oppression: 'The Kingdom of Oude, which was under the rule of its own princes', one schoolbook declared in 1883, 'was so badly governed that it was found necessary, in 1856, to add it to our possessions.' Everywhere, then, the 'white man's burden' was imposed on Europeans by the universality of liberal principles and the impossibility of ignoring them if they were flouted, wherever in the world that might be.

The 1850s and 1860s administered a series of shocks to Britain's con-fidence in its international superiority and civilizing mission. The shortcomings of the British military administration in the Crimean War, the 'Indian Mutiny', the failure of British forces to defeat the Maori in the New Zealand land wars, and the stalemate of the second Ashanti War in west Africa, were bad enough, but they all paled into insignificance in comparison to the upheavals generated by Bismarck's wars of German unification, culminating in the foundation of the German Empire in 1871. In the light of this fundamental change in the balance of power, Britain needed in Disraeli's view to assert herself more vigorously on the world stage. Already in 1872, pursuing his mission of rallying the working classes, many of whom had been enfranchised on his initiative in the Reform Act of 1867, to the Conservative cause, Disraeli declared that they were 'proud of belonging to an Imperial country, and are resolved to maintain, if they can, their empire'. Once he became Prime Minister for the second time, in 1874, Disraeli did all he could to bolster the British Empire at home and abroad. In 1875 he secured for Britain a controlling interest in the French-built Suez Canal, vital for communications with India. By the time his premiership came to an end in 1880, he had mobilized British forces in Afghanistan and south Africa, and played a leading role in the 1878 Congress of Berlin. Above all, as we have seen, Disraeli persuaded Queen Victoria to assume the title 'Empress of India', bringing the concept of empire to the centre of British national identity.

Empire, the African colonizer and entrepreneur Cecil Rhodes thought, would bring concrete economic benefits to Britain that would improve the lot of the masses. But it was also an instrument of patriotic propaganda. As the *Daily Express* proclaimed in 1900: 'Our policy is patriotic; our faith is the British Empire.' By this time, jingoistic enthusiasm for the Boer War was rife in London, and the empire was being celebrated in popular stories by authors like George Alfred Henty (1832–1902), magazines like the *Boys' Own Paper*, and even in early films, one of which portrayed to an enthralled public the bombardment of Mafeking, though it was actually shot on a Home Counties golf course. 'To inculcate patriotism in my books,' Henty claimed, 'has been one of my main objects.' Along with all this went cheap, mass-produced prints and reproductions of imperial scenes. British schools began to celebrate 'Empire Day', marked by a parade through the centre of London, as indeed in almost all other towns and cities across the United Kingdom, while organizations like the Boy Scouts (1908) were formed to raise a new generation for military service in the colonies. By the eve of the First World War, the empire was a central part of British national identity in a way that it had not been in the middle of the nineteenth century.

The new attitude to empire contained a strong element of racism and the denigration of other cultures and civilizations. British schoolbooks now dismissed oriental culture as ornamental rather than useful, and told their readers, of monuments like the Taj Mahal, that 'it might be supposed that they had originally been erected to commemorate the virtues of some great benefactor of our species, instead of being the whim of some prince who dawdled away his years in indolence or pleasure'. Different races were no longer depicted as equal in the sight of God, sharing a common humanity, if at an earlier stage of historical development than that of the Victorian Englishman. Instead, textbooks now emphasized racial difference and the alleged racial inferiority of subject peoples: 'The Australian natives are an ugly, unprepossessing people, with degrading and filthy habits', as one geography textbook put it: 'Like beasts of prey . . . the Malays are always on the watch, to assuage their thirst of blood and plunder'; 'The tribes [of Nigeria] . . . are extremely savage, practising horrible forms of religion, accompanied by human sacrifices.' In such circumstances, it now seemed to be agreed, rule by the British was morally justifiable as well as politically necessary.

The British, indeed, were, in the view of the imperialists of the 1880s and 1890s, destined not only to rule inferior races but also to lead the entire world into the future. As Joseph Chamberlain declared in 1895: 'I believe in this race, the greatest governing race the world has ever seen; in this Anglo-Saxon race, so proud, tenacious, self-confident and determined, this race which neither climate nor change can degenerate, which will infallibly be the predominant force of future history and universal civilization.' Belief in racial hierarchies based on descent had become more widespread once it had become possible to lend it scientific legitimacy. This was not least a product of the growing influence of Darwinism in the second half of the century. In the hands of the biologist and anthropologist Herbert Spencer (1820–1903), who coined the phrase 'the survival of the fittest', Darwinism became a harsh creed of competition, and phrases such as 'the struggle for existence' and 'the strongest prevail' soon became part of what has been termed 'social Darwinism', the application of Darwin's ideas, or a version of them, to human society.

Social Darwinism's influence spread across Europe in the late nineteenth century. It had a progressive version, which laid on the state the duty to improve the race by better housing, hygiene and nutrition. The German zoologist Ernst Haeckel (1834–1919) popularized Darwin's ideas in his best-selling book *The Riddle of the Universe* (1901), though he gave them a twist by arguing that human characteristics could be acquired by adaptation to the environment as well as being inherited. He divided humanity into ten, or, including their subdivisions, thirty-two races, of which the 'Caucasian' was in his view the most advanced. Africans he considered close to the apes, and he concluded that no 'woolly-haired' person had ever contributed anything to human civilization. Haeckel believed that criminals were racially degenerate and should be executed to prevent them passing on their criminal characteristics to the next generation: 'rendering incorrigible offenders harmless' would have 'a directly beneficial effect as a selection process'. The same would be desirable for the mentally ill and handicapped. Children's diseases, he thought, should be left untreated so that the weak could be weeded out from the chain of heredity by natural causes, leaving only the strong to propagate the race. Haeckel also believed, however, that war was eugenically counter-productive since it eliminated the best and bravest young men of every generation, so his self-styled Monist League (1906) campaigned vigorously in the cause of pacifism, leading the German military authorities to keep it under close surveillance during the First World War.

In the world view of Darwin's cousin Francis Galton (1822–1911), who was already beginning to apply Darwinian principles to human society in the 1860s, genius was the product of heredity, and by breeding the clever with the clever it would be possible to improve the intelligence of human-kind. The prime example of course was his own family and its various connections, in which brilliance and scientific ability occurred in succes-sive generations with notable regularity. Galton, wavering between designating himself as scientifically able or generally brilliant, opted in the end for the latter. Of course, like other eugenicists, he did not pause to consider whether wealth, education and circumstances played a role as well. Conversely, Galton thought that inferior peoples were threatening the future of the race by producing too many sub-standard children. What he termed 'eugenics', the idea of degeneracy or reverse evolution, began to be discussed in educated circles. The *reductio ad absurdum* of this view could be found in H. G. Wells's 1895 novel *The Time Machine*, where the time traveller discovers in the distant future that the working classes have degenerated into the 'Morlocks', a race of subterranean savages, while the middle and upper classes, the 'Eloi', have lost almost all their sense of self-preservation and competitiveness. On the other hand, a Social Darwinist like Cesare Lombroso (1835–1909) could argue that the lower classes were closer to the apes, and so inherited savage, criminal instincts that were absent in the law-abiding sectors of the population.

Social Darwinism became even more pessimistic in the hands of Gal-ton's disciple and biographer Karl Pearson (1857–1936). The remedy for eugenicists such as Pearson was to encourage the breeding of superior humans, and discourage the increase of inferiors. While this might be possible within British society, the same principles were much less encour-aging when applied to the world as a whole. Here Pearson was influenced by the French racial theorist Arthur de Gobineau (1816–82), whose ideas were first developed in his *Essay on the Inequality of the Human Races* (1853–5). Gobineau, a pro-German whose enthusiasm for the aristocracy was so great that he awarded himself the title of 'Count' to stake his own claim to noble status, argued that interbreeding could only dilute the characteristics of superior races, rather than improve those of inferior ones. Gobineau did not win many adherents in France for his claim that the French aristocracy was mostly German or, as he put it – borrowing from earlier theorists such as Friedrich Schlegel (1772–1829) and Ernest Renan (1823–92) – 'Aryan' in origin, until after France's defeat by Ger-many in the war of 1870–1, which soon sparked a debate about the extent to which the victory of the Germans had proved them to be racially supe-rior. Not surprisingly, Gobineau's ideas were most popular of all in

Germany itself, where a Gobineau Society was founded in 1894. Taken to fresh extremes by the composer Richard Wagner's son-in-law, the Germanophile Englishman Houston Stewart Chamberlain (1855–1927), in his 1899 book *The Foundations of the Nineteenth Century*, these ideas became the vehicle for a racialized antisemitism, in which the Jew was portrayed as the eternal enemy of the pure-bred Aryan, and Jesus Christ was portrayed as an Aryan and not a Jew.

Scientific racism arranged racial types on an evolutionary scale and implied that mixing them together would pull what were now increasingly known as the 'higher races' down to the level of the 'lower' ones. Contemplating the British Empire and its history, Pearson declared:

> History shows me one way, and one way only, in which a high state of civilization has been produced, namely, the struggle of race with race, and the survival of the physically and mentally fitter race. If you want to know whether the lower races of man can evolve a higher type, I fear the only course is to leave them to fight it out among themselves, and even then the struggle for existence between individual and individual, between tribe and tribe, may not be supported by that physical selection due to a particular climate on which probably so much of the Aryan's success depended.

In this pessimistic view, education and improvement were futile when applied to inferior races. Conquest, assimilation or even extermination were the only possible ways forward. The nations with 'the greatest physical, mental, moral, material and political power' would win in the struggle for survival, or supremacy, and they would be justified in doing so, declared the German general Friedrich von Bernhardi (1849–1930): 'Without war, inferior or decaying races would easily choke the growth of healthy budding elements, and a universal decadence would follow.' 'Eternal and absolute enmity is fundamentally inherent in relations between peoples,' wrote a close adviser to the German Chancellor Bethmann Hollweg, the journalist and Foreign Office press agent Kurt Riezler (1882–1955).

In the early and mid-nineteenth century there was a widespread view, and not only in Britain, that the progress of human society was linear in nature, with Britain in the lead in terms of industrialization and democratization, and other European nations following. But while liberals regarded the nation state as a universal phenomenon, and nationalism in the first half of the nineteenth century was linked closely to the implementation of liberal values such as the freedom of the press, trial by jury, and the sovereignty of elected assemblies, things began to change in the decades leading up to the First World War. Where British commentators, for example, had once condescendingly regarded Germans as hopelessly impractical, backward, and mired in Gothic medievalism, they started well before the end of the nineteenth century to express admiration for German industrial and scientific progress, and give vent to anxieties about being overtaken by German economic growth. For their part, German nationalists started to think of the French as racially degenerate, not least because of the slow pace of French population growth. The German sense of superiority was rudely challenged in 1912 when an official report revealed that the German birth rate had started to decline as well. German newspapers and politicians pointed in anxiety to the continued growth of Russia, where the population was booming, with potentially major effects for the future strength of the armed forces. Austro-Hungarian politicians and generals looked with alarm on the spread of Slav nationalism across the border with Serbia into parts of the empire itself. French opinion treated Germany as an enlarged version of Prussia, rigid, militaristic, unimaginative and threatening. Increasingly such anxieties were expressed in racial terms, with 'Slavs' pitted against 'Teutons', 'Anglo-Saxons' against 'Latins', in the inevitable struggle for survival and supremacy.

Such views did not go unchallenged. In colonial administration, race could often take second place to the need to reward the native elites whose collaboration was essential to the maintenance of imperial control. British royal honours, knighthoods and orders were doled out liberally to maharajas and sultans across the colonies. Critics of empire like Hobson, Lenin and Luxemburg emerged to excoriate the economic exploitation they thought underpinned the colonial enterprise. Colonial atrocities, particularly in German South-West Africa, aroused criticism from Catholic politicians, and Social Democratic parties across Europe agreed that the next war would be fought in the interests of capitalism, resolving to prevent it by staging a Europe-wide general strike should war seem imminent. The Austrian pacifist Bertha von Suttner (1843–1914) published her best-selling novel *Lay Down Your Arms!* in 1889 and lobbied ceaselessly for peace. She persuaded the Swedish manufacturer of dynamite, Alfred Nobel, to endow a Peace Prize, which she herself duly won in 1905. In 1899 and 1907 two peace conferences held at The Hague on the instigation of the Russians laid down an important series of ground rules for limiting the damage caused by war. They banned the killing of prisoners and civilians, and declared that an occupying force was the guardian of the cultural heritage of the areas it conquered, and should not loot or destroy cultural artefacts. But an attempt to establish a binding system of arbitration for international disputes failed because of the opposition of the Germans. Some thought that war would not happen anyway. The

British pacifist Norman Angell (1872–1967), in his book *The Great Illusion* (first published in 1909 as *Europe's Optical Illusion*), argued that Europe's economies had become so closely integrated that war was futile and counter-productive. It was an illusion to imagine therefore that any country would gain by attacking another. Even so, he observed, the gathering arms race was making such a war more likely. Already, in the Balkans, indeed, armed conflict was becoming increasingly violent and uncontrollable, the expression of ethnic and religious hatreds that were beyond the power of any larger nation to contain.

THE BALKAN WARS

The initial crucible of Balkan violence was to be found in the disputed territory of Macedonia, home to a complex mixture of Serbs, Bulgarians, Greeks, Albanians, Jews and Vlachs. It had been ceded to Bulgaria by the Treaty of San Stefano but restored to the Ottoman Empire by the Congress of Berlin in 1878. The area was also riven by religious rivalry between Orthodox Christians and Muslims. The Greeks, Serbs and Bulgarians all demanded the cession of the region from the Ottomans. Bulgarians were the most radical. IMRO agents within Ottoman Macedonia attacked and killed Ottoman officials and confiscated their funds as a matter of routine. Their violence degenerated into simple criminality as they increasingly relied on extortion and intimidation to raise money to buy arms. In 1897 the Ottoman authorities seized huge quantities of weapons and ammunition from an IMRO cache. This only increased the radicalism of the revolutionaries, and in 1903 they took over twenty-eight villages near the Bulgarian border, killing more than 500 Turkish troops. As the Turkish Army poured in reinforcements, terrorist murders and bomb attacks spread, until they merged into a general uprising, which was eventually put down by regular Turkish troops and *bashi-bazouks*. They burned 119 villages to the ground, razed 8,400 houses and drove 50,000 refugees into the mountains. This effectively crushed the revolutionary movement. But it seriously alienated international opinion. The Austrians and Russians, acting in a rare moment of unity, sent in an international police force, which was reluctantly accepted by the sultan.

Behind the scenes Abdülhamid II turned in desperation to Germany for help. Soon German officers were training Ottoman troops, and German engineers were building a new railway to Baghdad, financed by German banks. All of this, however, undermined the sultan's authority within the empire, as foreign intervention, repression, and his refusal to reintroduce the 1876 Constitution led to the emergence of conspiracies to try and oust him. Shortly after his accession, Abdülhamid had abandoned the policy of trying to create an Ottoman national identity. Perhaps reacting to the loss of a very large proportion of the empire's Christian population in the Balkans, and the migration of hundreds of thousands of Muslims from the Caucasus and from the new Balkan states to Anatolia, he had substituted the policy with a new ideology of pan-Islamism. From now on the sultan's religious status as the Caliph was emphasized in Ottoman propaganda as the basis for the allegiance of his people. Increasingly, Abdülhamid put his empire's troubles down to an international conspiracy of the Christian world, and in particular to the Christian Armenian minority in Anatolia, mostly well-off traders and merchants, whom the Treaty of Berlin had obliged him to protect. In 1892–3, Muslim crowds, egged on by officials who claimed the Armenians were trying to destroy Islam, began massacring the area's Armenian population. When Armenian nationalist groups retaliated, they were crushed by the Ottoman Army, after which local and regional officials encouraged further violence against them, aided by Kurdish irregulars sent in by the sultan.

The worst atrocity occurred with the burning alive of more than 3,000 Armenians in the cathedral of Urfa in December 1895. A protest demonstration of Armenians in Constantinople was suppressed and was followed by widespread killings of Armenians in the capital. Foreign intervention, again urged by Gladstone, never became a reality. The massacres continued until 1897, by which time between 100,000 and 300,000 Armenians had been killed. Another 30,000 died in the town of Adana in 1909 when a reactionary movement to suppress calls for the return of the 1876 Constitution degenerated into a series of pogroms. Already by the end of the 1890s the Armenian massacres had lost Abdülhamid any sympathy he still enjoyed in the international community. Domestically, too, his days were numbered. Suspicious of the younger officers, many of whom had visited western Europe and imbibed western ideas, the sultan starved the army of funds. Corruption meant that often officers did not get paid. In 1907–8 conspirators organized in a self-styled clandestine Committee for Union and Progress assassinated many of the police agents who had infiltrated the army, then moved into action. Garrison after garrison now openly declared its support for the Committee. Abdülhamid, afraid for his life, hurriedly agreed to reintroduce the 1876 Constitution. But it was too late. This was the Young Turk Revolution. Remarkably, in declaring its support for freedom and democracy, it had the support of minority nationalist groups, including even IMRO. But the Young Turks had little idea of how to put their ideas into action beyond getting rid of Abdülhamid, which they did by deposing him the following year and putting one of his many relatives on the throne as Mehmed V (1844–1918).

Meanwhile, in the period since the Serbo-Bulgarian War of 1885, all the Balkan powers had been arming themselves to the teeth, buying up the latest weaponry from Europe's leading arms manufacturers with loans supplied by the British, French and German governments, who were keen to boost exports. Urged on by Macedonian officers in its army, Bulgaria bought arms so lavishly that by the mid-1890s a third of the state budget was being spent on the army and in 1902, unable to pay the interest due on all the loans, the country had to declare state bankruptcy. It was not alone in its national insolvency. The Serbs also devoted massive resources to building up their army, resulting in a state bankruptcy in 1893, when the government declared itself unable to pay the interest on loans it had taken out. The debts were consolidated, the currency issue was reduced, and an autonomous financial control authority was put in place. In Greece things were even worse. By 1893 state indebtedness amounted to ten times the national income and here too the government declared national insolvency. Nothing was done to resolve the situation, however, until 1897, when Greece launched a war against Turkey over disputes between Christians and Muslims on the island of Crete after furious crowds in Athens had accused King George I (1845–1913) of betraying the national cause by trying to come to a peaceful settlement over the issue. The war was fought on a number of fronts, but in the decisive action, at Domokos, in Thessaly, where around 45,000 troops were assembled on each side, the Ottoman forces drove the Greeks into retreat. The 'Black 97' or the 'Unfortunate War' led to a series of minor territorial losses and obliged Greece to pay massive financial reparations to the Ottomans. Realizing that Greece was unable to pay, an International Financial Control Commission now stepped in to ensure payment of the reparations to the Ottoman government by cutting back on the issue of currency to stabilize the drachma, and also by collecting indirect taxes on behalf of the Greek government.

The problem for all these countries was that they were inhabited mainly by subsistence farmers and so had low export volumes, while the tax-collecting administration was largely ineffective. None of these financial difficulties, however, proved an obstacle in the end to military expansion, fuelled by growing nationalist passions. In Greece young army officers, fired up by the example of the Young Turks, overthrew the government in a coup d'état in August 1909, eventually handing over power to a skilled nationalist politician, Eleftherios Venizelos, who immediately reformed the state finances but combined this with a programme of renewed rearmament. In Serbia the change came earlier, and in a more violent way. When King Alexander Obrenovíc (1876–1903) attempted to purge the Serbian Army in 1903 in order to reduce its power and save money, a group of young officers led by Dragutin Dimitrijević (1876–1917), known as Colonel Apis, decided to get rid of him. They had the implicit support of many leading figures who objected strongly to the king's rapprochement with Austria-Hungary, fearing it would turn Serbia into a Habsburg client state. Alexander was already unpopular because he ruled in an authoritarian manner, closed newspapers, disregarded election results, and alienated senior politicians. These last included the influential Minister of the Interior, Djordje Genčić (1861–1938). Like many ministers and officials, Genčić objected to the king's marriage to Draga Mašin (1864–1903), whose reputation in society was so bad that the entire Cabinet resigned when the couple became engaged. 'Sire,' Genčić told the king, 'You cannot marry her. She has been everybody's mistress – mine included.' The king's response – a slap in the face – was enough to drive Genčić into the arms of Apis's conspiracy.

After careful preparation, twenty-eight Serbian officers led by Apis burst into the royal palace late in the evening of 28 May 1903. In the ensuing exchange of fire Apis was shot three times; he survived, but carried the bullets in his body for the rest of his life. His fellow conspirators rushed up the stairs, then found a concealed entrance to the small dressing room where the king and queen were hiding. After swearing that they would remain loyal to their oath to the monarch as officers, the insurgents shot King Alexander and Queen Draga as they emerged into their bedroom, and hacked their corpses to pieces before throwing them out of the window. One of the conspirators cut off a piece of the queen's skin and carried it about with him subsequently as a trophy. Elsewhere in Belgrade other members of the conspiracy shot dead members of the Cabinet including the Prime Minister. Installing a leading member of the rival Karadjordjević family as King Peter (1844–1921), the army now had free rein to order whatever weaponry it wanted. It built up a huge state debt to the French, from whom it purchased its military hardware. The apparatus of Alexander's authoritarian state was dismantled, and a degree of popular sovereignty restored.

This gave power to a profoundly nationalist electorate, to the benefit of the liberal politician Nikola Pašić (1845–1926), whose popular Radical Party had been a principal victim of Alexander's clampdown. The main international loser in this revolution was Austria-Hungary. From now on, Serbia remained profoundly hostile to the Habsburg state and aimed to undermine its hold on Bosnia-Herzegovina. In 1908 the advent of the Young Turk regime was taken in Serbia and the rest of the region as a further sign of Ottoman weakness and a signal for action. Austria-Hungary, worried about Serb irredentism, and taking advantage of the chaos in Constantinople, annexed Bosnia-Herzegovina, nominally an Ottoman province but under Habsburg control since the Congress of Berlin thirty years before. At the same time, and certainly not coincidentally, Ferdinand of Bulgaria declared his country an independent sovereign nation free from Ottoman control, and appointed himself king. The Russians had to agree to the amendment of the Treaty of Berlin in recognition of these events, but were left determined not to tolerate a repeat of the situation. They encouraged the creation of a series of mutual alliances in the Balkans and supported a campaign of subversion within the annexed provinces, which were inhabited by a mix of Serbs, Croats and Muslims. The disorder spread to Montenegro, which had achieved independence at the Treaty of Berlin in 1878 following a series of armed clashes, most notably a Montenegrin victory at the Battle of Grahovac in 1858. Following the Treaty of Berlin, Prince Nikola I (1841–1921) had consolidated independence with skill, marrying off two daughters to Russian archdukes and signalling his alliance with Russia by the purely symbolic gesture of declaring war on Japan in 1904. Nikola took advantage of Ottoman weakness to declare himself king of his impoverished country in 1910. Parallel to this action, the neighbouring Albanians, subjected to military conscription, denied the use of their language and deprived of any kind of education system by the Young Turks, even though they too were Muslims, rose up in a confused but violent rebellion in the same year.

What actually lit the Balkan tinderbox, however, was a series of events that began in north Africa. When, in 1911, the Sultan of Morocco appealed for French military assistance in putting down a rebellion, the German Kaiser sent a gunboat to Agadir in order to force a climb-down. But the British intervened on the French side and forced Germany to accept a French protectorate over Morocco in return for a transfer of territory from the French Congo to the German colony of Cameroon. It was at this point that the Italian government saw its chance to revive its ambition of an empire in north Africa and invaded Libya, declaring war on the territory's nominal sovereign power, the Ottoman Empire. The war was notable for the first example of aerial reconnaissance and aerial bombardment, by the Italians, who also for the first time in history deployed armoured cars on the ground. Initial setbacks prompted the Italian Army to send reinforcements until their forces numbered 150,000. The Ottomans recruited Arab auxiliaries but, unable to reinforce their army except by sea, failed to muster more than around 30,000 men. Gradually superior Italian numbers and weaponry drove the Turks back. Meanwhile an Italian fleet annihilated the Ottoman navy off Beirut, and the Italians occupied the Dodecanese islands in the Aegean Sea.

The Ottoman government, already in serious difficulties at home, sued for peace, and the Treaty of Ouchy, signed in October 1912, gave Italy control over Libya in return for the islands' return. However, this part of the agreement was not honoured by the Italians and in fact was not implemented until the end of the Second World War. The final dismemberment of the Ottoman Empire now seemed to be under way. Already in August 1912, 20,000 poorly organized but well-armed Albanian tribesmen had occupied the Macedonian town of Skopje, forcing the Ottomans to concede autonomy to its surrounding province, where there were large numbers of Albanian speakers. Together with the Italian victories, this convinced Bulgaria, Greece, Montenegro and Serbia that the moment had come to attack. In October 1912 the region rapidly descended into chaos as the Bulgarians invaded Thrace, the Bulgarians, Greeks and Serbs Macedonia, the Montenegrins and Serbs northern Albania and Kosovo, and the Greeks southern Albania. A war on so many fronts proved impossible for the already demoralized and disorganized Ottoman forces to cope with. Within days the Serbs defeated a Turkish army at Kumanovo and entered Skopje. An eyewitness in the town of Kumanovo reported how the 'Turk divisions ran amok through the town in chaotic retreat . . . maimed, blood-soaked and barefoot . . . Serbian shrapnel began falling on the station, and the railway personnel scattered as if being shot at like sparrows.' Serb forces moved through the area, largely populated by Albanian Muslims, setting light to villages and massacring their inhabitants. A Serbian socialist in the army reported how the people of Skopje woke up 'every morning to the sight . . . in the very centre of the town . . . of heaps of Albanian corpses with severed heads . . . [It was] clear that these headless men had not been killed in battle.'

The lead in the massacres was taken by Colonel Apis, founder of 'National Defence', a nationalist organization set up in 1908 following the annexation of Bosnia-Herzegovina. When the Austrians forced the Serbian government to ban the organization, Apis set up another, secret terrorist organization, 'Unification or Death', also known as the 'Black Hand'. Its aim was to create a Greater Serbia, including Bosnia, Croatia and Macedonia. Before long it was controlling the Serb-occupied areas of Macedonia. Following the defeat of a Greek army at Monastir between 16 and 19 November 1912, the Serb forces, 110,000 strong, attacked 90,000 Turkish troops in a three-day battle that left 12,000 Serbs and 17,000 Turkish soldiers dead. The general in charge of the Ottoman troops finally surrendered, leading 45,000 of his troops into captivity while another 30,000 fled to the nearby hills. Meanwhile a Greek force raced

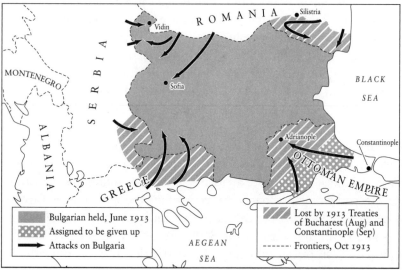

Map 18. The First Balkan War, July 1912–May 1913
Map 19. The Second Balkan War, June–October 1913

to Salonika, occupying the city just before the Bulgarians arrived. Relations between the two small states soon deteriorated sharply as a result. Elsewhere, however, the Bulgarians had more luck, taking possession on 24 October of the key fortress of Lozengrad in Thrace and driving the Ottoman forces out of the region in disorder. While the retreating Turks massacred civilians on their way out, the incoming Bulgarians burned down every mosque they found on their way in. At the fortress of Çatalca the Bulgarians unleashed a massive bombardment from 900 field guns. The noise could be heard in Constantinople more than 20 miles away. The Turks dug in, casualties began to mount, and the two armies fought each other to a standstill. The conflict was largely over by the end of 1912, but Bulgarian-Turkish hostilities resumed in February 1913 at Adrianople, sparked by the Turkish refusal to cede the town to the Bulgarians as agreed in the peace negotiations. When the administration in Constantinople agreed to the cession, it was overthrown by the Young Turk Committee for Union and Progress, accompanied by demonstrations of religious students in the streets shouting 'Death rather than dishonourable peace!' Eventually Adrianople fell on 26 March 1913, leaving nearly 60,000 dead, many of them from cholera. On entering the city, the Bulgarians found the streets littered with decomposing corpses.

When further assaults on Çatalca and Gallipoli failed to achieve their aims, however, King Ferdinand of Bulgaria finally gave up for the time being his ambition of restoring and even exceeding the 'big Bulgaria' created temporarily at the Treaty of San Stefano, and on 30 May 1913 he signed the Treaty of London, brokered by the Great Powers. The agreement ratified the removal of the Ottomans from the entire region, indeed almost from Europe altogether, and sealed the creation of an independent Albania, a move backed by the Austrians in the hope that it would become a client state and cut off Serbia from the Mediterranean. Instinctively the Great Powers reached for the customary German princeling, this time Wilhelm of Wied (1876–1945), who was proclaimed head of state as Prince Vidi I, but his reign lasted less than six months; the Muslim peasants who had risen up against the Ottomans now turned against the international settlement, which they believed was imposed by Christian powers in the interests of the larger Albanian landowners. Their anger was increased by the fact that Vidi relied heavily on the military support of Catholic troops from Mirdita in the north. As the rebels entered Tirana, Vidi fled in September 1914 to join the German Army on the Western Front, though never to renounce his claim to the Albanian throne. The country fell apart, to be invaded, successively and sometimes jointly, by Serbia, Montenegro, Italy, Greece and Bulgaria in the following years.

The First Balkan War was quickly followed by a second. It was obvious to all that Bulgaria had been seriously weakened by the conflict. The Serbs concluded a secret alliance with the Greeks, and threatened to annex the Macedonian territories they occupied, on which Bulgaria had a claim. The Romanians demanded the cession of north-eastern Bulgaria (the south-eastern Dobrudja) and the Greeks began to menace the area around Salonika. Disastrously, the Bulgarian general Mihail Savov (1857–1928), instructed by the king but without sanction by the government, launched a pre-emptive attack on the Serbs on 28 June 1913. Mutinies, disease and desertions among his battle-weary troops turned the attack into a fiasco. The Serbs repulsed the Bulgarian attack, the Greeks launched a successful attack on the main Bulgarian army, and the Romanians, who had remained neutral in the First Balkan War, took the opportunity of the Bulgarian setbacks to march into southern Dobrudja. Even the Ottomans managed to reoccupy part of eastern Thrace, retaking Adrianople in the process. When the Romanian forces were within seven miles of the Bulgarian capital of Sofia, the Bulgarians reluctantly brought the month-long conflict to an end.

Some of the combatants had lost a good deal of what they had gained in the First Balkan War, but nevertheless in the Treaties of Bucharest and Constantinople, signed respectively in August and September 1913, Bulgaria enlarged its territory by 16 per cent compared to what it was before the First Balkan War, and increased its population from 4.3 to 4.7 million people. Romania enlarged its territory by 5 per cent and Montenegro by a massive 62 per cent. Greece increased its population from 2.7 to 4.4 million and its territory by no less than 68 per cent. Serbia almost doubled its territory and expanded its population from 2.9 to 4.5 million. The Ottomans had successfully defended their toehold in Europe. For Russia, however, the Balkan Wars were a catastrophe. Its carefully constructed system of Balkan alliances had collapsed in the most spectacular possible way. The most powerful state in the region, Bulgaria, was angry at the Russians' failure to support it, and now looked to Germany as an ally. Russia's only remaining friend was Serbia, and this gave the Serbs enormous leverage, which they were to use to the full in 1914. The Russian aim of gaining access to the Mediterranean had been completely frustrated. Serbia now looked to Bosnia-Herzegovina to increase its territory, having gained more or less what it wanted in other directions from the two Balkan Wars.

The Balkan Wars were remarkable for the sheer scale of troop mobilization within the combatant nations. Serbia had a population of less than three million but put into the field an army larger than any the first

Napoleon had mustered. Bulgaria mobilized half a million men, a good quarter of its entire male population. Armies dug trenches and subjected their enemy to ruthless bombardment by artillery. Troops were now dressed in camouflaged khaki or field-grey uniforms instead of the traditional identifying bright colours. Cavalry only played a subordinate part. All those involved except Romania and Montenegro put combat planes into the air and used them for bombing. Searchlights bore down on the enemy lines, allowing twenty-four-hour combat. The territorial ambitions of the combatants went well beyond annexing areas that could be argued to belong to their respective nation states by culture, language or history. The invasion of Albania by the Montenegrins, for example, or the Greater Serbia programme of the Black Hand, or King Ferdinand's desire to see himself crowned in Constantinople as ruler of a Bulgarian Empire stretching across the whole of Macedonia, were effectively examples of imperialism, now turned in towards Europe. The massacres of civilians prefigured the genocides that were to occur later in the twentieth century, as people who were seen as alien were killed in the supposed interests of the racial or religious integrity of an expanding nation state; Bulgarians burnt mosques as they advanced, and in Macedonia the occupying powers, notably Serbia, began a ruthless programme of assimilation to their own language and culture, attempting to obliterate minority cultures in the process. In November 1913 a British vice-consul in the region reported that the Muslim population in the annexed areas was 'in danger of extermination by the very frequent and barbarous massacres and pillage to which they are subjected by Servian bands'. This was far from being the last time a warning of this kind was to be issued in the twentieth century.

The Balkan Wars led directly to the deaths of 200,000 troops on all sides, and the chaos they spread caused many thousands of civilians to die from disease, especially cholera and typhus. In many ways these wars were a portent of things to come. And yet they were brief conflicts, in which all the combatant nations had clearly defined and limited aims and achieved them to a sufficient degree to allow them to agree to a ceasefire. It was not the purpose of any of the combatants to achieve regime change among their opponents. At the same time it was clear that the Great Powers were becoming increasingly drawn in to such conflicts. In the First Balkan War, when Montenegro in alliance with Serbia attacked northern Albania, where the inhabitants were mostly neither Serbs nor Montenegrins, Italy and Austria-Hungary demanded their withdrawal, Russia began to mobilize in support of the Serbs, and France declared its support for the Russians. The situation was only defused by a British intervention resulting in the international conference that guaranteed independence for Albania. The Montenegrins captured Skutari while the Russians and Austro-Hungarians squabbled about the precise borders of the new state. The refusal of the Montenegrins to withdraw threatened to escalate the situation again, until the Powers paid a huge bribe to the Montenegrin monarch King Nikola that persuaded him to remove his troops. In August 1914 defusing a renewed flare-up of these conflicts was not to be so easy.

'THE GREAT WAR WE ALL HOPE FOR'

In 1815 and for a long time afterwards, European statesmen and politicians had concluded that international co-operation was the way to prevent a recurrence of social and political revolution. The massive destruction and loss of life that the armies of the French Revolution and its successor Napoleon had visited upon Europe had to be avoided by re-establishing social hierarchy and political order. British world hegemony had prevented colonial and imperial conflicts from disturbing the European peace. European states had fought only a limited number of wars, for limited goals, and with limited means. Bismarck's concern to build a system of alliances that would allow the German Reich created in 1871 the space it needed to consolidate itself had prompted a series of arrangements designed to ward off the threat of France finding allies in its search to regain Alsace-Lorraine, annexed by Germany in the Franco-Prussian War. In 1872 he succeeded in forming the League of the Three Emperors, through which he managed to detach Russia from France and bring in Austria-Hungary, all in the interests of controlling the nationalist ambitions of the Poles, whose territory was divided between the three states. In 1882 he bolstered this system of treaties by concluding a Triple Alliance with Italy and Austria-Hungary. Five years later he signed a secret Reinsurance Treaty with Russia, in an attempt to keep it within the German fold. In the Balkans, Bismarck persuaded Austria-Hungary and Russia to accept a division of influence in which the former took the western half and the latter the eastern. Acutely aware of the risk that the turbulent politics of the Balkans could spark a European conflict, he warned repeatedly of the danger that Germany might have to fight a war on two fronts, and told the Reichstag in 1876 that Balkan conflicts were not 'worth our risking – excuse my plain speaking – the healthy bones of one of our Pomeranian musketeers'.

Bismarck was attempting to square the circle of European diplomacy. Russian and Austro-Hungarian interests, especially in the Balkans, could not in the long run be reconciled. Moreover, after his departure from office in 1890, a younger generation of German politicians and statesmen came to power imbued with a self-confidence in Germany's destiny and a disdain for the elaborate system of diplomatic alignments that Bismarck had erected to shield the young empire from its enemies. Germany, they thought, could look after itself. Without consulting the Kaiser, Bismarck's successor as Chancellor, Leo von Caprivi, let the Reinsurance Treaty lapse. Soon the German Empire was involving itself in countries outside Europe, bringing colonial issues back into European politics. The Concert of Europe began to crumble. Up to the early years of the new century Britain regarded above all Russia as its most serious potential enemy, largely because of the 'Great Game' in Asia and the continual push of the Russians towards the Mediterranean and the Middle East. France was the subject of similar suspicions, and indeed novels warning the British public about its government's lack of preparedness for a future war still saw France as the main threat well after 1900. The point was illustrated with lurid depictions of the perfidious French flying an invading army across the Channel in giant balloons, or surreptitiously digging a tunnel under the Straits of Dover to allow troops to be smuggled in under the sea without detection. This was not all fantasy. On 28 February 1900 the French Foreign Minister, Théophile Delcassé (1852–1923), reported to his Cabinet that in discussions about countering the British challenge to French colonial ambitions, 'some suggest a landing in England, others an expedition to Egypt; yet others advocate an attack on Burma by troops from Indo-China which would coincide with a Russian march on India.' The old enmity was clearly not dead.

Rebuffed by the Germans in his attempt to gain their support for these bizarre ideas, Delcassé came round to thinking that colonial questions were best solved in collaboration with the British rather than in opposition to them. In 1904, Britain and France engaged in the famous *entente cordiale*, signing a series of agreements designed to avoid the two countries being dragged into the looming Russo-Japanese war on the sides of their respective allies (the British had previously concluded an alliance with Japan as part of their efforts to prevent Russian expansion in China). This involved settling the two nations' remaining colonial difficulties, and included an understanding that Morocco belonged to the French sphere of influence. In March 1905, however, Kaiser Wilhelm II landed at Tangier, promised the sultan to help him against the French, and told the French consul he knew how to defend German interests there (phrases such as this counted as extremely bellicose in the language of diplomacy). By doing so, he was trying to undermine French interests in Morocco at a time when France's ally Russia was in trouble with Japan. He may have thought that this would persuade Britain that a strong Germany would make a better ally than a weak France, and that the *entente cordiale* should accordingly be abandoned.

But as so often with the Kaiser's interventions, the move backfired. The British responded by supporting the French, and the German government was forced to back down. The resulting Treaty of Algeçiras in April 1906 gave the French largely what they wanted. But the most significant aspect of the crisis was arguably a public statement by Lloyd George: 'If Britain is treated badly where her interests are vitally affected, as if she is of no account in the cabinet of nations, then I say emphatically that peace at that price would be a humiliation intolerable for a great country like ours to endure.' From this point onwards at the latest, the British government, Foreign Secretary Sir Edward Grey included, regarded Germany, not Russia or France, as the main threat to British interests. This view had already been adopted by British Foreign Office officials, notably Sir Eyre Crowe (1864–1925), who in January 1907 penned a celebrated memorandum arguing that either Germany was 'consciously aiming at the establishment of a German hegemony at first in Europe and eventually in the world' or that 'the great German design is in reality no more than the expression of a vague, confused and unpractical statesmanship not realising its own drift'. Either way, he concluded, the result was the same. Germany had to be opposed.

The decisive factor here was the massive build-up of German naval power in the wake of the Navy Law of 1898 and its successors. Previously there had been no effective German navy at all. But Kaiser Wilhelm and the new State Secretary of the Imperial Naval Office, Admiral Alfred von Tirpitz, were determined to build one that would boost Germany's prestige. At the same time there was an increasing feeling among Germany's ruling elite, bolstered by pressure from newly emerging nationalist associations, that the ragbag of small and insignificant colonies possessed by the German Empire was in no way appropriate for a Great Power. As the Foreign Minister, later Chancellor, Bernhard von Bülow stated, Germany needed its 'place in the sun' (a phrase later repeated by his successor Bethmann Hollweg to the French ambassador). In order to achieve it, he inaugurated a so-called 'world policy', or *Weltpolitik*. The German government and with or without its permission the Kaiser began to intervene loudly in world affairs, notably the Boer War and the Boxer Rebellion. Tirpitz's Navy Laws inaugurated a massive naval building programme that aimed to produce a fleet not of fast-moving light cruisers to defend or extend Germany's imperial interests, but of huge battleships. Their aim was to inflict such damage on the Royal Navy through a confrontation in the North Sea that the British would be forced to agree to allow an expansion of the German overseas empire by one means or another. As Tirpitz declared: 'For Germany the most dangerous naval enemy at present is England.' But Tirpitz and the Kaiser myopically failed to realize that the British would respond to this growing threat. First the British boosted their own naval construction programme, and then, in 1906, partly in response to the defeat of the Russian navy by the better-built and better-equipped Japanese navy, they launched a new type of battleship, heavily armoured, fast-moving, and armed with a much larger number of long-range guns and torpedoes than the existing models. The first one was named HMS *Dreadnought*.

By 1914 the British had twenty-nine of these battleships, many of them so much improved that they were known as 'super-dreadnoughts', whereas the Germans only had seventeen. Moreover, the whole *modus operandi* of the Royal Navy had been revolutionized in the process. In 1897 the British navy, the largest in the world, was described as 'a drowsy, inefficient, moth-eaten organism' manned by men trained to sail ships in a peaceful world. Admirals and captains took pride in the appearance of their ships, often paying for their adornment out of their own pockets. Sailors spent long hours polishing the brasswork and captains avoided gunnery practice because it dirtied the ships' paint. Captain Percy Scott (1853–1924), who invented modern naval gunnery techniques, was greatly frowned on when his ship scored 80 per cent hits in practice when 30 per cent was the fleet average. It was small wonder that Admiral 'Jackie' Fisher (1841–1920), the dynamic reformer appointed in 1902 to modernize the navy, asked two years later the plainly rhetorical question: 'How many of our Admirals have minds?' Fisher immediately stopped training in masts and yards, and in 1905 he made Scott's gunnery methods compulsory. As a result, for the first time the navy began recording more hits than misses. Yet despite opposition from what he called the 'gouty admirals' of the conservative school, Fisher was not really a modern thinker either. In 1914 the Royal Navy still thought all that counted would be a single decisive encounter in the North Sea, between rows of Dreadnoughts, of boarding parties, of a quick, total victory: a modern Battle of Trafalgar. Tirpitz thought along similar lines. Such an event never materialized. Instead naval conflict became a war of attrition in which the whip hand was held by the power that used individual submarines to sink the merchant ships of its rival and so throttle its line of supply, and battleships proved fatally vulnerable to attack from the air.

Even though they won the naval arms race, the British did not lessen their suspicions and fears of German naval ambitions. The damage, in other words, had been done and was not easily to be undone. Anxieties on both sides were reinforced by the massive publicity surrounding the launching of each new battleship. By 1914, therefore, the governments of both Britain and Germany, however divided they might have been about diplomatic tactics in the crisis, considered the other to be the major potential enemy in any broad European conflict. British anxiety was reinforced by Germany's decision in 1913 to expand its army, after a long period of focusing on the navy. This was not without consequences. In 1907, British Prime Minister Campbell-Bannerman told the French 'he did not think English public opinion would allow for British troops being employed on the Continent of Europe'. Grey and the Cabinet thought that if they sent military help to the French, it would only be in the form of a token force of two or three divisions. In any case they felt the details of military planning should be left to the professionals. They thus surrendered some of their freedom of action to the generals. Unknown to the Cabinet, Sir Henry Wilson (1864–1922), Chief of the General Staff, prepared as thoroughly as he could for a full-scale continental war. He spent his summers on cycling tours of the northern French border with Germany and in the Low Countries, where he thought the next war would take place. Without informing the Cabinet, be conducted secret negotiations with the French Army leadership, which resulted in firm plans to send over a strong British Expeditionary Force in case of a German invasion, and to put the troops wherever the French wanted them. Wilson despised democratic politicians; he knew that once the divisions were sent, more would follow; this implication of the plan was never discussed in Cabinet. Britain gained a continental commitment entirely without consideration of the consequences.

Just as admirals thought that the war at sea would be a rerun of the great naval engagements of the past, so the generals thought the war on land would be something like the conflicts of the 1860s, opening with rapid, railway-borne advances to the front, followed by a decisive encounter in which the other side would meet with a shattering defeat along the lines of Sadowa (1866) or Sedan (1870). Peace would then be concluded after a few weeks or at most a couple of months. Had they studied the Balkan Wars, the American Civil War or the Crimean War, in which the opposing sides had been relatively evenly matched, they might have thought differently. Since those days, too, barbed wire and machine guns had become standard defensive equipment, and as yet, internal combustion engines and armour-plating were not advanced enough to produce machines that could effectively overcome these obstacles and restore movement to warfare. A few recognized these inconvenient facts. In *Modern*

Weapons and Modern War (1900) the Polish banker Jan Bloch (1836–1902) argued that in the next major war 'the spade will be as important as the rifle'. He predicted that the war of the future would be a stalemate. Cavalry charges would be obsolete. Entrenched men armed with machine guns would have at least a fourfold advantage over men coming towards them across open ground. Combatant nations would have to mobilize men in their millions, and the resultant stresses and strains would lead to 'the break-up of the whole social organization'. 'The steadfastness with which the military caste clings to the memory of a state of things which has already died,' he warned, 'is . . . costly and dangerous.'

Nobody heeded his warnings, any more than they did those of the pacifist views of Wilhelm Lamszus (1881–1965), a Social Democratic teacher in Hamburg, which led him in 1912 to publish *The Human Slaughterhouse: A Picture of the Coming War*. Written as if by a participating soldier, the book described 'fields saturated with the dead', 'corpses after corpses'. 'It is as if death has thrown down his scythe [and] has now become a mechanic . . . this is what sticks in my gullet. That we will be ordered to death by technicians and mechanics. Just as buttons and needles are mass-produced, now cripples and corpses are produced by machines.' Whereas the soldiers would die in their thousands, 'the machines live on'. Conservatives described Lamszus as a 'sick person . . . who would like to suck the patriotic marrow from the bones of the German people'. But the book sold 100,000 copies in the first three months of its publication. And he was not alone. The Baltic nobleman Baron Nicholas Alexandrovich von Wrangell (1869–1927) told an acquaintance in Paris in 1914:

> We are on the verge of events the like of which the world has not seen since the time of the barbarian invasions. Soon everything that constitutes our lives will strike the world as useless. A period of barbarism is about to begin and it will last for decades.

By 1910 at the latest the idea that a war was coming was shared by many. Admiral Fisher wrote of the atmosphere he created in the Royal Navy after 1902: 'We prepared for war in professional hours, talked war, thought war, and hoped for war.' Helmuth von Moltke (1848–1916), Chief of the German General Staff from 1906 to 1914, known generally as 'Moltke the Younger' in deference to his more famous uncle, declared in 1912 that war must come 'and the sooner the better!' However, when real war actually did come two years later, he had a nervous breakdown and had to be relieved of his duties.

It was not just generals and admirals who regarded war as inevitable. As early as 1891, Émile Driant (1855–1916), the son-in-law of the political

French general Boulanger, wrote to his regiment: 'I have always desired to fight with you the great war we all hope for.' British writers enthused about the opportunity that war would present. As Horace Vachell (1861–1955) put it in his idealized novel about life at Harrow public school, *The Hill* (1905): 'To die young, clean, ardent; to die swiftly, in perfect health; to die saving others from death, or worse – disgrace – . . . to die and carry with you into the fuller, ampler life beyond, untainted hopes and aspirations, unembittered memories, all the freshness and gladness of May – is that not a cause for joy rather than sorrow?' 'How I long for the Great War!' wrote the Catholic conservative Hilaire Belloc. 'It will sweep Europe like a broom.' Speaking to Cambridge undergraduates in 1912, Viscount Esher (1852–1930), an influential figure in army reform, said that to underestimate the 'poetic and romantic aspects of the clash of arms' would be to 'display enfeebled spirit and an impoverished imagination'. War appeared to increasing numbers of men in the political elites of European nations as a release, a liberation of manly energies long pent up, a resolution to all the doubts and uncertainties, all the unresolved and insoluble problems that had plagued European politics and society in increasing measure since the late nineteenth century: a chance to do something glorious in a prosaic age. Well before August 1914 the outbreak of a general war was widely anticipated across Europe, hoped for by some, feared by others.

COUNTDOWN TO CATASTROPHE

On 28 June 1914 the heir to the Habsburg throne, the Archduke Franz Ferdinand, was carrying out a military inspection and public visit in Sarajevo, in the province of Bosnia, annexed by Austria-Hungary six years earlier. It was one of the few places under Habsburg control where he could appear at an official event with his wife, Sophie, Countess Chotek, since their marriage was a 'morganatic' one. For Serb nationalists the visit was a provocation, given Serbian claims to Bosnia and the large number of ethnic Serbs within its borders. A group of them decided to take action and prepared to assassinate the archduke. The conspirators of 28 June were as bungling and incompetent as might be expected from their age and inexperience – all of them were teenagers. Several of them were so petrified at the magnitude of their enterprise that they failed to make use of their weapons when the archduke passed them on the street in his motor car. One of them did manage to throw a bomb but it bounced off the boot and exploded under the following vehicle, injuring a number of its occupants. Instead of calling off his visit, however, Franz Ferdinand insisted on continuing with it. His Czech chauffeur did not know Sarajevo and took a wrong turning. Realizing he had made a mistake, he stopped in order to reverse, coming to a halt right in front of one of the conspirators, the nineteen-year-old Gavrilo Princip, a Bosnian Serb nationalist student. With great presence of mind, Princip let off two shots, killing the archduke and fatally wounding his wife (though in fact he had meant the second shot for the military governor of Sarajevo). To avoid capture and interrogation, Princip swallowed a cyanide capsule, but vomited it back up again. He then tried to shoot himself, but the pistol was wrested from him. Within a few years, horrified and depressed at the consequences of his act, and weakened by disease and malnutrition, he died of tuberculosis in prison in Terezín. The Emperor Franz Josef, who disapproved of Franz Ferdinand's marriage, is said on hearing the news of the assassination to have commented 'A Higher Power has restored the order I could not uphold', and ordered a third-class funeral.

In the internal debates of the Austro-Hungarian leadership during the years before his assassination, Franz Ferdinand had been a force for moderation. He realized the weakness of the empire, and consistently urged restraint in its dealings, especially with the Serbs. He sought to reform the monarchy by reducing the power of the Hungarians and making concessions to the South Slavs and the Czechs by turning the empire into a 'United States of Great Austria'. The Germans of course would have remained dominant, not least given his strong belief in their racial superiority. Franz Ferdinand's forcible removal made it easier for the war party in Vienna, led by army chief Franz Conrad von Hötzendorf (1852–1925), to follow its aggressive instincts. Conrad had already urged a war against Serbia during the Bosnian crisis of 1908–9 and again no fewer than twenty-five times between 1 January 1913 and 1 January 1914. Serbia, he declared as early as 1907, was a 'constant breeding ground for those aspirations and machinations that aim at the separation of the South Slav areas'. Now his moment had come. It was clear that the assassins had not acted entirely on their own. The Austrians rightly suspected that they had connections with Colonel Apis and the Black Hand organization, which over the previous few years had gained wide influence in the Serbian armed forces, the police and the intelligence service. Apis had recruited a number of young Bosnian Serbs, some of whom, like Princip, had taken advantage of scholarships offered by the Serbian government to study in Belgrade. Their choice of assassination as a political tactic was neither particularly new nor particularly exceptional. Assassination seemed the obvious form of protest to Princip and his comrades when the archduke's visit to

Sarajevo was announced. Colonel Apis seems to have approved of the project, and although he was not acting on behalf of the Serbian government, it was aware that an attempt might be made and even advised the archduke privately to call off his visit.

The government in Vienna decided that action had to be taken not only to punish the Serbs but also to prevent similar outrages occurring again, which was more than likely given the epidemic of assassinations that had spread across Europe over the previous few years. It also acted with an aggression that came from its knowledge that Austria-Hungary's status as a Great Power was undergoing an alarming decline. The same consciousness of weakness prompted the Austro-Hungarian government to consult the German leadership before taking any action, saying that Serbia, which it regarded as responsible for the outrage, had to be 'neutralized as a power factor in the Balkans'; otherwise, as its behaviour in the two Balkan Wars suggested, it would 'stop short of nothing' to secure a 'Greater Serbia' at the expense, among others, of the Habsburgs. Interrupting their holidays, Kaiser Wilhelm II, Chancellor Bethmann Hollweg and other members of the leadership of the German Reich agreed at a meeting held on 6 July 1914 on unconditional support for whatever action the Austrians chose to take against Serbia. This was the famous 'blank cheque', without which the government in Vienna might possibly have had second thoughts about punishing the Serbs. Nobody at the meeting seems to have thought that the Russians would actually intervene if the Austrians took action against the Serbs. The Russian Army was not ready, and the tsar would surely wait until it was, which was not likely to be before a planned reorganization and expansion of the army was completed, in 1917. The Russians had backed down in the previous Balkan crisis. They would be deterred by the Germans. Tsar Nicholas II would not condone a regicide. Such were the considerations behind the 'blank cheque': despite many allegations by later historians, there is no evidence for the claim that the Germans were using the crisis as an excuse for war with the Russians, still less with the British.

In the immediate aftermath of the assassination, international opinion was firmly on the Austrians' side. But, fatally, even though it was armed with German support, the Austrian government now let the matter rest because the French President, Raymond Poincaré (1860–1934), was on a state visit to Russia and it did not want to take any action until he was safely back home. In addition, it took time to secure agreement between the Austrian and Hungarian governments on a policy. It was only on 23 July 1914, therefore, nearly a month after the assassination, that Austria-Hungary issued the Serbian government with an ultimatum, demanding action against not only the assassins but also the men and the conditions that it alleged had encouraged them. The delay inevitably aroused suspicion. Immediate action at the end of June would probably have won widespread international approval, but a month later the shock of the murder was no longer so present, and international sympathies for the Austrians had cooled. The ultimatum, therefore, no longer somehow seemed sincere. And indeed, it was not. It was intended by the Austro-Hungarian government not as a genuine set of conditions but as an excuse for war, which had already been determined on in Vienna at the outset of the crisis.

The Serbs were shocked by the ultimatum because they had believed that Germany would have restrained the Austrians. Nikola Pašić, the Serbian Prime Minister, consulted the Russians, telling them Serbia would give in if that was what they advised. But the Russians told them to hold firm. Moreover, there was an election on in Serbia, and Pašić, like most Serb politicians, was unwilling to yield to the Austrians all along the line. In the weeks since the assassination the Serbian government had done little to investigate it and bring the culprits to justice along with those who had backed them. The government insisted that it required evidence from the Austrians before it took action. It did agree to ban the Black Hand, to suppress publications and speeches attacking Austria-Hungary and remove such criticism from the school curriculum, and to cashier officers guilty of actions against the Dual Monarchy. While the Serbian government conceded most of the points in the ultimatum, though often hedging its willingness to meet them with various conditions and equivocations, it firmly rejected Point 6, which demanded the participation of Austrian officials in the investigation of the murder, a requirement that the Serbian government declared incompatible with the country's Constitution. In effect, it suspected, this would amount to a takeover of the Serbian law-enforcement agencies by a foreign power. Declaring the ultimatum to have been rejected, and spurning any further chance of negotiation, the Austro-Hungarian government declared war on Serbia on 28 July 1914. Within twenty-four hours Austrian shells were falling on Belgrade.

Up to this point the international crisis had not been taken very seriously by the British government, preoccupied as it was with strikes and suffragette outrages and the looming threat of an armed rebellion by Ulster Protestants. Foreign Secretary Sir Edward Grey did his best to localize the conflict, pressing the Germans, French and Russians to restrain the Austrians and Serbs. All this gave the Germans the impression that Britain would remain neutral if the conflict widened. Behind the scenes, however, Grey, concerned to uphold the integrity of the 'Triple Entente', which he himself had created, was reassuring the French and Russians that they could count on British support if matters came to a head. Before the ultimatum, British public opinion was preponderantly pro-Austrian, blaming the Serbs for the assassination and saying they had to arrest the culprits. The press considered it would be ridiculous to get involved in this obscure quarrel: the *Daily News* (in a leading article headed 'Why We Must Not Fight') declared that there was no conflict of interest between Germany and the United Kingdom. A defeat for Germany would lead to Russian dictatorship over Europe. The journalist and Member of Parliament Horatio Bottomley (1860–1933), later a super-patriot, said that Serbia had to be wiped out. Only *The Times* supported British intervention. Prime Minister Asquith, preoccupied with Ulster, still thought as late as 24 July 1914 that Britain would not be involved. But Grey now attempted to get the Cabinet to intervene in the crisis with a firm declaration of support for France, in the hope that this would deter the Germans. His move was rejected by the Cabinet on 27 July. He proposed four-power mediation but did not press this idea with very much vigour or determination, and he rejected Bethmann Hollweg's offer to desist from annexations in France if Britain agreed to remain neutral. The British stance was still unclear, therefore, as the crisis moved towards its climax.

The German Kaiser Wilhelm II has often been viewed as a force for war, but in fact he was as inconsistent on this issue as he was on most others. On 6 July he wrote to Franz Joseph: 'The situation will be cleared up within a week because of Serbia's backing down', an eventuality he thus expected even before the ultimatum was issued. For his part, Moltke on 13 July expressed the view that Austria should strike against the Serbs immediately, then 'make peace quickly'. But the Austrians did not act immediately. No wonder the Kaiser and Bethmann Hollweg felt frustrated. The German leadership continued to believe France and Russia were too unprepared to intervene, however, and did not think the war would widen. On 21 July, Bethmann Hollweg informed his ambassadors: 'We urgently desire a localization of the conflict.' On 27 July, when the Kaiser learned of the Serb response to the ultimatum, he remarked: 'This does away with any need for war.' He evidently thought that the ultimatum was a genuine diplomatic document, not a pretext for war. Counsels in Berlin were divided, the civilian leadership urging caution, the military urging continued unconditional support for the Austrians. 'Who rules in Berlin?' was Conrad von Hötzendorf's question when he received two contradictory dispatches from the German leadership in the middle of the crisis. The answer was never really forthcoming, as confusion continued in the German leadership.

Military planning played a key role in the crisis. Moltke had made no attempt to amend the war plan devised by his predecessor Alfred von Schlieffen (1833–1913). The elder Moltke, victor in the wars of German unification, had thought that in the event of a general European conflict, Germany should hold the Western Front while first undertaking what he considered to be the easier task of crushing the Russians. This view had been shared by his successor Alfred von Waldersee (1832–1904). However, Schlieffen was impressed by improvements in Russian fortifications during the 1890s, by the vastness of Russia's territory, and by the growing size of the Russian Army. So he reversed the plan. A strong German army would invade Belgium. Passing round Paris, it would pin the French forces against their own fortifications on the border with Germany from the rear. Thus a war with Russia would begin with an attack on France. After the war was over when some argued that it would have been impossible to have changed mobilization plans and transfer the bulk of the German forces to the east to deal with the Russians, the German general in charge of railway operations in 1914, Wilhelm Groener (1867–1939), indignantly wrote a book, complete with maps, plans and timetables, to demonstrate that he could have performed this task in under three days had he been asked to do so. He was not. As for the Russians, military planning contained no provisions for a separate conflict with the Austrians; the mobilization plans were based on a war against Austria-Hungary and Germany combined. In addition, the partial mobilization that constituted the first stage in the process of getting an army to the front was so comprehensive that few outside Russia would be able to tell the difference from a full mobilization. Moreover, it contained manoeuvres that would impede a full mobilization, and so provided an incentive to make the transition as quickly as possible.

The opinion of the Russian press was pro-Serb, naturally enough given the influence of feelings of Pan-Slav and Orthodox solidarity. Few in St Petersburg believed that the Serbian government had really been involved in the assassination. In this view Austria had no right to take any counter-measures: the ultimatum was an act of pure aggression, like the annexation of Bosnia in 1908. The Russian government attributed this to German 'connivance'. The Russian Foreign Minister, Sergei Dmitrievich Sazonov (1860–1927), issued a press statement immediately after the publication of the Austrian ultimatum, stating that Russia would not 'remain inactive' if the 'dignity and integrity of the Serb people, brothers in blood, were under threat'. 'You are setting fire to Europe,' he told the Austrian ambassador. The French government delegation that found itself in Russia at the height of the crisis was keen above all to cement the Franco-Russian alliance in the face of Austrian provocation. As the French pressed the Russians to stand firm behind Serbia, the two Montenegrin princesses married to two Grand Dukes in Nicholas II's entourage told the Frenchmen encouragingly during a formal dinner, both speaking at the same time: 'There's going to be a war . . . There'll be nothing left of Austria . . . You're going to get back Alsace-Lorraine . . . Our armies will meet in Berlin . . . Germany will be destroyed.' On 23 July 1914, therefore, the governments of Russia and France, to whom the Austrian plan for an ultimatum had been leaked, formally agreed to defend Serbia in the face of the Austrian threat.

Following the Austrian ultimatum, issued the same day, the Russian Council of Ministers met on 24 and 25 July, concluding that the Germans were using the Austrians as their tool in the latest in a long line of provocations. As a consequence the Russian government set in motion a process of military 'pre-mobilization' on 26 July, followed by partial mobilization, announced on 29 July. This was a clear signal of solidarity with the Serbs, and there was now no chance, if there had ever been any, that the Serbs would back down. Sazonov had supported the Serbs unconditionally from the outset, and he knew since 23 July that he had the backing of the French in doing so. For their part the French were faced with the prospect of going to war to support Russian aggression in the Balkans. The two governments still hoped that a clear British declaration of approval for their actions, and those of Serbia, would deter the Germans and bring them round to restraining Austria. But the British Cabinet, which contained a number of liberals whose views bordered on pacifism, would not allow such a declaration to be issued. In addition, many felt that the United Kingdom, where imperial interests were paramount, had no real interest in a quarrel over the Balkans. Three-quarters of the Cabinet opposed entering a war unless Britain itself was attacked. Many British politicians and diplomats still thought that France and Russia, not Germany, constituted the major threats to British global interests. In 1912, Harold Nicolson (1886–1968), then a junior Foreign Office mandarin, noted: 'It would be far more disadvantageous to have an unfriendly France and Russia than an unfriendly Germany. [Germany can] give us plenty of annoyance, but it cannot really threaten any of our more important interests.' On 25 July 1914, Sir Eyre Crowe wrote: 'Should the war come, and England stand aside, one of two things must happen. (1) Either Germany and Austria win, crush France, and humiliate Russia. What will be the position of a friendless England? (b) Or France and Russia win. What would then be their attitude towards England? What about India and the Mediterranean?' British policy was still directed more by imperial considerations than by European ones.

In Germany, as the crisis became more urgent, the attitude of the Social Democratic Party, the country's largest political movement, with more seats in the Reichstag than any other, became a central consideration for Bethmann Hollweg. The German Chancellor had to secure more or less unanimous support in the legislature not only to vote the necessary credits should war break out but also to legitimize military action by the appearance of popular approval. Like other member parties of the Socialist International, the Social Democrats were formally committed to declaring a general strike in the event of war. They staged massive peace demonstrations in the major German towns and cities on 27 and 28 July 1914, involving around three-quarters of a million people. In Bielefeld the socialist editor Carl Severing (1875–1952) warned a crowd of 7,000 demonstrators that millions of workers would be led to the slaughterhouse if war broke out. International socialist solidarity seemed on the cards as the leader of the French Socialists, Jean Jaurès, issued calls for a general strike and summoned a conference of the Second International for 9 August. But on 31 July a young French nationalist, Raoul Villain (1885–1936), approached an open window in the *Le Croissant* restaurant on the corner of the rue Montmartre and the rue de Croissant, where Jaurès was dining with friends, pulled out a revolver, and shot him twice in the head. (The assassin was subsequently acquitted by a jury that was convinced of the necessity of war.) The killing threw the French and the international socialist movement into disarray. Crucially, when Russia had launched a partial mobilization on 29 July, the German leadership had panicked. The Kaiser had previously declared an official 'State of Imminent Danger of War'. Now he countermanded the order. Thus at the moment when Jaurès was shot, the German forces had still not been mobilized.

But the Russians, responding to a German threat to mobilize if they did not stand down their troops, declared a general mobilization on 31 July 1914. The delay in German mobilization convinced the leadership of the German socialist movement that the Russians were the aggressors. For the Social Democrats, Russia was a backward, uncivilized country ruled by a ruthless, antisemitic and obscurantist despotism that would crush socialism everywhere should it succeed. The war was being waged against 'Russian barbarism, for the defence of German cultural heritage, in order to protect German women and children,' wrote the young liberal officer Otto Braun (1897–1918) in his diary on 5 August. The anti-war demonstrations were abandoned. Within a few days the Social Democrats were to vote unanimously in the Reichstag in favour of war credits. Meanwhile, Bethmann Hollweg succeeded in persuading the military leadership of Germany that a formal declaration of war had to be issued against the

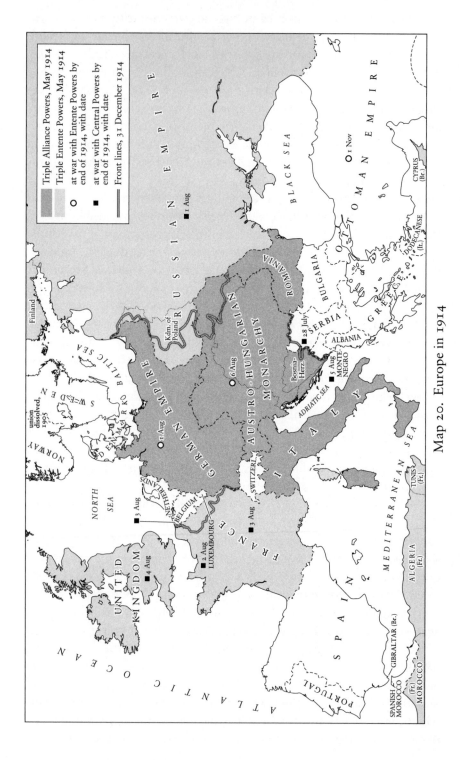

Map 20. Europe in 1914

Russians, 'otherwise I cannot pull the Socialists along'. It came on 1 August, setting the Schlieffen Plan in motion. It was now the German government's turn to issue an ultimatum, in this case to Belgium, to show no resistance to a German invasion. The ultimatum was a huge blunder. Belgium had no choice but to reject it, putting the Germans in the wrong and giving the British a reason for intervening. Asquith and Grey were now able to swing Cabinet opinion behind them. Only two ministers resigned. On 4 August 1914, Britain issued a formal declaration of hostilities against Germany. As ambassadors took leave of their hosts in foreign ministries across Europe, many of them in tears, the vacillations and tergiversations of international diplomacy came to an end. Europe was officially at war.

In the complex chain of events that led up to the outbreak of the war, it was noticeable that few, if any, of those involved thought of compromise. Ironically, the two states initially most hesitant about starting the conflict were Austria-Hungary, whose leaders asked the Germans for their support, and Serbia, whose leaders issued a similar request to the Russians. In the entire crisis the crucial moment was most probably when Germany issued the 'blank cheque' to the Austrians to do with the Serbs what they wanted. It is impossible to know whether a serious German attempt to restrain the Austrians, and a similar Russian attempt to restrain the Serbs, would have deterred the two antagonists from taking military action. The emotions running high in Vienna and Belgrade tell against this hypothesis. The rapid collapse of the Ottoman Empire in Europe had hugely raised the stakes even in comparison to the situation just over a year before, when British intervention had stopped the escalation of the Balkan Wars into a general European war. To many, including some in Vienna, the Habsburg Empire seemed next in line. From the very outset the Austrians were determined on military action, and the Serbs were determined to resist. The German, Russian and French governments never really took the idea of mediation seriously: they stood firm because they feared the consequences for their prestige and power in Europe. No serious proposal ever came anyway; the Great Power best placed to intervene, as had happened over the Balkan Wars the previous year, was Britain, but Britain did not take the crisis seriously enough until it was too late. Flexibility and cunning, the calculated instrumentalization of war in the service of policy, had been the hallmarks of an earlier generation of statesmen, the generation of Bismarck and Cavour; by 1914 they had been replaced by a generation of leaders taught by a quarter of a century of imperialist annexations, wars and conquests that only force mattered, and that the people on the other side were members of an inferior race that would be easy to defeat. Their intransigence was fortified by the belligerence of military leaders and the determination of men on all sides to display the kind of coolness and courage required of men engaging in a duel.

The statesmen who took these fateful decisions had not been carried into conflict on a wave of popular enthusiasm. Anti-war rallies, called by the leaders of the socialist movement, continued in some parts of Britain well into the second week of August 1914. The mass protests organized by the German Social Democrats in the last days of July told their own story. The huge pro-war demonstrations that followed them on the main squares of Germany's major cities, and those staged by right-wing patriotic societies on the squares of Europe's major cities a few days later, were overwhelmingly middle class in character, as attested by the seas of straw boaters discernible in contemporary photographs. In all of them there was hardly a cloth cap or a man in working clothes to be seen in the huge crowds. The first volunteers, captured on camera smiling and cheering as they set off by train to the front, were similarly drawn from the younger generation of the European bourgeoisie. Most of the vastly greater numbers of troops who followed fought because they believed their country was being attacked, their empire threatened, their way of life faced with extinction by a ruthless enemy. A good number fought only reluctantly, or because they saw no alternative.

In the pubs and bars of Hamburg, policemen disguised as workers listened to rank-and-file Social Democrats debating the issues during the last days of peace. 'What business is it of ours?' asked one worker on 29 July 1914, 'if the heir to the Austrian throne is murdered? For that we have to lay down our lives? It'll never come to it!' 'For sure, I'm married and have children too,' said another, 'but when my Fatherland is in danger, then the State will feed my family. I tell you, I don't care whether I die at work or for the Fatherland, and you'll come along like me, I tell you.' Another lamented the fact that the 'Hurrah-patriots . . . are blocking the streets as they wish, and the police don't care whether they are causing traffic jams or not. We're warned against demonstrations, and they can do what they want, just because they're for the war and sing the "Watch on the Rhine" [a patriotic German song].' For the majority of Europeans, living on a Continent that was still predominantly rural in character, war remained a distant and barely comprehensible occurrence. Peasants everywhere were worried that their harvest would be disrupted. In one village in south-eastern France the news of the war, announced by the tocsin, caused 'alarm and consternation', with everyone, men, women and children, weeping and clinging to one another. Reactions in one Cossack settlement in Russia recorded by an English traveller were equally confused: proud of their military tradition, the men were keen to fight, but the announcement of the outbreak of war had omitted to say against whom; some thought the enemy was China, others England. Nobody believed it was Germany.

The outbreak of the First World War brought to an end a century of European hegemony over the rest of the world. Of course, this was not a sudden or unheralded development. Already before 1914, America had been starting to outstrip Britain and Germany in economic terms. In the colonial empires, above all in India, the first stirrings were visible of the movements for freedom and independence that would reach fruition within a few decades. But by inaugurating a vast, global struggle lasting more than four years, the declarations of war issued in 1914 brought ruin upon Europe, destroying the sublime self-confidence that had sustained it for the better part of a century, hastening and strengthening the challenges issued to European dominance in other parts of the world. Four and more years of war shattered the European economy, which after massive inflation, a deep depression and another lengthy period of war, was not to recover for more than forty years, further undermining and finally destroying Europe's global hegemony. The United States of America entered the world stage, tilting the balance of two world wars decisively towards the Allied Powers. By 1945 the USA had become a global superpower. American culture swept across the world. The great empires of Russia, Germany and Austria-Hungary were destroyed little over four years after the beginning of the conflict; the Ottoman Empire was abolished not long after, in 1922; the Tsar of Russia was murdered with his family by revolutionaries, while the Emperors of Germany and Austria-Hungary were driven into exile, respectively in the Netherlands and in Madeira, along with the regiments of minor German princes whose fecundity had proved so useful to European diplomacy in the nineteenth century. The last Ottoman sultan, Mehmed VI (1861–1926), departed to spend the autumn of his days on the Italian Riviera.

Europe's slow and uneven march towards democracy was reversed after the First World War. New political movements, notably Communism, Nazism and Fascism, came onto the scene, prepared to use extreme violence to implement extreme policies involving the revolutionary transformation of society; 'red' and 'white' terror, with its executions and massacres, its tortures and its camps, became a feature of the post-war years. Before long, genocide was put into action on a scale that dwarfed the ethnic violence of the Balkan Wars or the Armenian massacres of the 1890s; unprecedented destruction rained down on many of Europe's greatest cities, leaving many cultural monuments in ruins. Millions more, this time civilians as well as combatants, would be killed in a Second World War whose global destructiveness was to eclipse even that of the First. The more perceptive of Europe's statesmen already suspected the magnitude of the changes the declaration of war in 1914 would bring about, if not the depths of barbarism into which Europe was about to descend. Standing at the window of his room in the Foreign Office overlooking the Mall on the evening of 3 August 1914, the British Foreign Secretary Sir Edward Grey turned to the friend who was visiting him. 'The lamps are going out all over Europe,' he said, 'we shall not see them lit again in our lifetime.'

Further Reading

GENERAL HISTORIES

Bayly, Christopher. *The Birth of the Modern World 1780–1914* (Oxford, 2004)

Berger, Stefan (ed.). *A Companion to Nineteenth-Century Europe 1789–1914* (Oxford, 2009)

Blanning, Timothy (ed.). *The Oxford Illustrated History of Modern Europe* (Oxford, 1996)

Davies, Norman. *Europe: A History* (2nd ed., London, 1997)

Gildea, Robert. *Barricades and Borders: Europe 1800–1914* (Oxford, 1987)

Hobsbawm, Eric. *The Age of Revolution 1789–1848* (London, 1963); *The Age of Capital 1848–1875* (London, 1975); *The Age of Empire 1875–1914* (London, 1987)

Merriman, John. *A History of Modern Europe from the Renaissance to the Present* (New York, 1996)

Osterhammel, Jürgen. *The Transformation of the World: A Global History of the Nineteenth Century* (Princeton, 2014)

Seigel, Jerrold. *Modernity and Bourgeois Life: Society, Politics and Culture in England, France and Germany since 1750* (Cambridge, 2012)

Sperber, Jonathan. *Revolutionary Europe 1780–1850* (Harlow, 2000); *Europe 1850–1915: Progress, Participation and Apprehension* (London, 2008)

NATIONAL HISTORIES
The Balkans

Clogg, Richard. *A Concise History of Greece* (Cambridge, 2002)

Crampton, Richard J. *Bulgaria* (Oxford, 2007)

Glenny, Misha. *The Balkans 1804–1999: Nationalism, War and the Great Powers* (London, 1999)

Hupchick, Dennis. *The Balkans: From Constantinople to Communism* (New York, 2002)

Hutchins, Keith. *Rumania 1866–1947* (Oxford, 1994)

Jelavich, Charles and Barbara. *The Establishment of the Balkan National States 1804–1920* (Seattle, 1986)

Mazower, Mark. *The Balkans* (London, 2000)

Palmer, Alan. *The Decline and Fall of the Ottoman Empire* (New York, 1992)

Quataert, Donald. *A Brief History of the Ottoman Empire 1700–1922* (Cambridge, 2005)

Britain

Devine, Thomas. *The Scottish Nation: A Modern History* (London, 2012)
Foster, Robert Fitzroy. *Modern Ireland 1600–1972* (London, 1988)
Morgan, Kenneth O. *Rebirth of a Nation: A History of Modern Wales 1880–1980* (Oxford, 1987)

The Longman History of England

Briggs, Asa. *The Age of Improvement 1783–1867* (London, 1999)
Read, Donald. *The Age of Urban Democracy: England 1868–1914* (London, 1994)

The New Oxford History of England

Hilton, Boyd. *A Mad, Bad, and Dangerous People? England 1783–1846* (Oxford, 2006)
Hoppen, K. Theodore. *The Mid-Victorian Generation 1846–1886* (Oxford, 1998)
Searle, Geoffrey. *A New England? Peace and War 1886–1918* (Oxford, 2004)

France

Gildea, Robert. *Children of the Revolution: The French 1799–1914* (London, 2008)
Tombs, Robert. *France 1814–1914* (Harlow, 1996)
Zeldin, Theodore. *France 1848–1945: Ambition, Love and Politics* (Oxford, 1973); *Intellect, Taste and Anxiety* (Oxford, 1978)

The Cambridge History of Modern France

Jardin, André, and Tudesq, André-Jean. *Restoration and Reaction 1815–1848* (Cambridge, 1984)
Agulhon, Maurice. *The Republican Experiment 1848–1853* (Cambridge, 1983)
Plessis, Alain. *The Rise and Fall of the Second Empire 1852–1871* (Cambridge, 1988)
Mayeur, Jean-Marie, and Rébérioux, Madeleine. *The Third Republic from its Origins to the Great War 1871–1914* (Cambridge, 1984)

Germany

Blackbourn, David. *Germany 1780–1914: The Long Nineteenth Century* (Fontana History of Germany, London, 1997)
Clark, Christopher. *Iron Kingdom: The Rise and Downfall of Prussia 1600–1947* (London, 2006)

Nipperdey, Thomas. *Germany from Napoleon to Bismarck 1800–1866* (Dublin, 1996)

Sheehan, James J. *German History 1770–1866* (Oxford, 1989)

The Short Oxford History of Germany

Sperber, Jonathan (ed.). *Germany 1800–1871* (Oxford, 2004)

Retallack, James (ed.). *Imperial Germany 1871–1918* (Oxford, 2008)

Habsburg Empire

Macartney, Carlile A. *The Habsburg Empire 1790–1918* (London, 1968)

Okey, Robin. *The Habsburg Monarchy c.1765–1918: From Enlightenment to Eclipse* (London, 2001)

Sked, Alan. *The Decline and Fall of the Habsburg Empire 1815–1918* (London, 1989)

Taylor, Alan J. P. *The Habsburg Monarchy 1815–1918* (London, 1941)

Iberian Peninsula

Birmingham, David. *A Concise History of Portugal* (Cambridge, 1993)

Carr, Raymond. *Spain 1808–1939* (Oxford, 1966)

Shubert, Adrian. *A Social History of Modern Spain* (London, 1990)

Italy

Clark, Martin. *Modern Italy 1871 to the Present* (London, 2008)

Duggan, Christopher. *The Force of Destiny: A History of Italy since 1796* (London, 2007)

Mack Smith, Denis (ed.). *The Making of Italy 1796–1870* (New York, 1968); *Modern Italy: A Political History* (London, 1997)

Woolf, Stuart. *A History of Italy 1700–1860: The Social Constraints of Political Change* (London, 1979)

Low Countries

Kossmann, Ernst. *The Low Countries, 1780–1940* (Oxford, 1978)

The Nordic and Baltic Regions

Derry, Thomas K. *The History of Scandinavia* (Minneapolis, 1979); *A History of Modern Norway 1814–1972* (Oxford, 1973)

Jespersen, Knud. *A History of Denmark* (London, 2011)

Kent, Neil. *A Concise History of Sweden* (Cambridge, 2011)

Kirby, David. *A Concise History of Finland* (Cambridge, 2006); *The Baltic World 1772–1993: Europe's Periphery in an Age of Change* (London, 1995)

Plakans, Andrejs. *A Concise History of the Baltic States* (Cambridge, 2011)

Tomasson, Richard F. *Iceland: The First New Society* (Reykjavik, 1980)

Poland

Davies, Norman. *God's Playground: A History of Poland* (2 vols, Oxford, 2005)

Frankel, Henryk. *Poland: The Struggle for Power, 1772–1939* (London, 1946)

Prazmowska, Anita J. *A History of Poland* (2nd ed., Basingstoke, 2011)

Wandycz, Piotr S. *The Lands of Partitioned Poland, 1759–1918* (Seattle, 1974)

Russia

Dixon, Simon. *The Modernisation of Russia 1676–1825* (Cambridge, 1999)

Hosking, Geoffrey. *Russia: People and Empire 1552–1917* (London, 1997)

Rogger, Hans. *Russia in the Age of Modernisation and Revolution 1881–1917* (London, 1983)

Saunders, David. *Russia in the Age of Reaction and Reform 1801–1881* (London, 1992)

Seton-Watson, Hugh. *The Russian Empire 1801–1917* (Oxford, 1967)

Westwood, John N. *Endurance and Endeavor: Russian History 1812–2001* (Oxford, 2003)

Switzerland

Church, Clive H., and Head, Randolph C. *A Concise History of Switzerland* (Cambridge, 2013)

Craig, Gordon A. *The Triumph of Liberalism: Zürich in the Golden Age 1830–1869* (New York, 1988)

WAR AND PEACE

Bley, Helmut. *South-West Africa under German Rule 1894–1914* (London, 1971)

Brewer, David. *The Greek War of Independence: The Struggle for Freedom from Ottoman Oppression* (London, 2011)

Clark, Christopher. *The Sleepwalkers: How Europe Went to War in 1914* (London, 2012)

Darwin, John. *After Tamerlane: The Global History of Empire since 1405* (London, 2007); *Unfinished Empire: The Global Expansion of Britain* (London, 2012)

Fieldhouse, David. *The Colonial Empires: A Comparative Survey from the Eighteenth Century* (London, 1966)

Figes, Orlando. *The Crimean War: A History* (London, 2010)

Hochschild, Adam. *King Leopold's Ghost: A Story of Greed, Terror, and Heroism in Colonial Africa* (London, 1998)

Kennedy, Paul M. *The Rise and Fall of the Great Powers: Economic Change and Military Conflict from 1500 to 2000* (London, 1988)

Lehning, James R. *European Colonialism since 1700* (Cambridge, 2013)

MacMillan, Margaret. *The War that Ended Peace: How Europe Abandoned Peace for the First World War* (London, 2013)

Otte, Thomas G. *July Crisis: The World's Descent into War, Summer 1914* (Cambridge, 2014)

Quinn, Frederick. *The French Overseas Empire* (Westport, CT, 2001)

Schroeder, Paul W. *The Transformation of European Politics 1763–1848* (Oxford History of Modern Europe, 1994)

Sluglett, Peter, and Yavuz, M. Hakan (eds), *War and Diplomacy: The Russo-Turkish War of 1877–1878 and the Treaty of Berlin* (Salt Lake City, 2012)

Taylor, Alan J. P. *The Struggle for Mastery in Europe, 1848–1914* (Oxford History of Modern Europe, 1954)

Wawro, Geoffrey. *The Austro-Prussian War: Austria's War with Prussia and Italy in 1866* (Cambridge, 1996); *The Franco-Prussian War: The German Conquest of France in 1870–71* (Cambridge, 2003)

BIOGRAPHY

Hubertine Auclert, the French Suffragette by Steven C. Hause (London, 1987)

Belzoni: The Giant Archaeologists Love to Hate by Ivor Noël Hume (Charlottesville, VA, 2011)

Bismarck: A Life by Jonathan Steinberg (Oxford, 2011)

Johannes Brahms: Life and Letters by Styra Avins (Oxford, 1997)

The Feminism and Socialism of Lily Braun by Alfred G. Meyer (Bloomington, IN, 1985)

The Education of a Self-Made Woman: Fredrika Bremer, 1801–65 by Brita K. Stendhal (Lewiston, NY, 1994)

Cavour by Denis Mack Smith (London, 1985)

Francesco Crispi: From Nation to Nationalism by Christopher Duggan (Oxford, 2002)

Marie Curie and the Science of Radioactivity by Naomi Pasachoff (Oxford, 1996)

Charles Darwin by Adrian Desmond, James Moore and Janet Browne (Oxford, 2007)

Charles Dickens by Michael Slater (London, 2009)

Disraeli by Robert Blake (London, 1966)

Bertie: A Life of Edward VII by Jane Ridley (London, 2012)

The Frock-Coated Communist: The Revolutionary Life of Friedrich Engels by Tristram Hunt (London, 2009)

Francis Joseph by Stephen Beller (London, 1996)

Frederick William IV and the Prussian Monarchy, 1840–1861 by David Barclay (Oxford, 1995)

Garibaldi: Invention of a Hero by Lucy Riall (London, 2007)

The German Worker: Working-Class Autobiographies from the Age of Industrialization, edited by Alfred Kelly (London, 1987)

Gladstone by Roy Jenkins (London, 1995)

Émile Guillaumin: The Life of a Simple Man, translated by M. Crosland (London, 1983)

Henrik Ibsen: A New Biography by Robert Ferguson (New York, 2001)

A Radical Worker in Tsarist Russia: The Autobiography of Semën Ivanovich Kanatchikov, translated and edited by Reginald E. Zelnik (Stanford, 1986)

Rosa Luxemburg by John P. Nettl (2 vols, Oxford, 1966)

Karl Marx: A Nineteenth-Century Life by Jonathan Sperber (New York, 2013)

The Unknown Matisse: A Life of Henri Matisse 1869–1908 by Hilary Spurling (London, 1998); *Matisse the Master: The Conquest of Colour, 1909–1954* by Hilary Spurling (London, 2005)

Mazzini by Denis Mack Smith (London, 1994)

John Stuart Mill: Victorian Firebrand by Richard Reeves (London, 2007)

Claude Monet: Life and Art by Paul H. Tucker (London, 1995)

Napoleon III by James McMillan (London, 1991)

Nicholas II: Emperor of All the Russias by Dominic Lieven (London, 1992)

Florence Nightingale: The Woman and Her Legend by Mark Bostridge (London, 1998)

Palmerston: A Biography by David Brown (London, 2010)

The Pankhursts by Martin Pugh (London, 2001)

A Life of Picasso by John Richardson (vols 1–2, New York, 1991 and 1996)

A Life under Russian Serfdom. The Memoirs of Savva Dmitrievich Purlevskii, 1800–1868, translated and edited by Boris B. Gorshkov (Budapest, 2005)

Radetzky: Imperial Victor and Military Genius by Alan Sked (London, 2011)

Salisbury: Victorian Titan by Andrew Roberts (London, 1999)

Clara Schumann: The Artist and the Woman by Nancy B. Reich (Ithaca, NY, 2001)

Bernard Shaw by Michael Holroyd (London, 1998)

The Feminism of Flora Tristan by Máire Cross and Tim Gray (Oxford, 1992)

The London Journal of Flora Tristan, edited and translated by Jean Hawkes (London, 1992)

Queen Victoria: First Media Monarch by John Plunkett (Oxford, 2003)

Richard Wagner: His Life, His Work, His Century by Martin Gregor-Dellin (New York, 1983)

Jakob Walter: The Diary of a Napoleonic Footsoldier, edited by Marc Raeff (New York, 1991)

Kaiser Wilhelm II by Christopher Clark (London, 2000)

Windthorst: A Political Biography by Margaret L. Anderson (Oxford, 1981)

Vera Zasulich: A Biography by Jay Bergman (Stanford, 1983)

Clara Zetkin: Selected Writings, edited by Philip S. Foner and Angela Y. Davis (New York, 1984)

Zur Mühlen, Hermynia. *The End and the Beginning*, transl. and ed. Lionel Gossman (Cambridge, 2010)

POLITICS

Anderson, Margaret L. *Practicing Democracy: Elections and Political Culture in Imperial Germany* (Princeton, 2000)

Brock, Michael. *The Great Reform Act* (London, 1973)

Eley, Geoff. *Reshaping the German Right: Radical Nationalism and Political Change after Bismarck* (London, 1980)

Elwitt, Sanford. *The Making of the Third Republic: Class and Politics in France 1868–1884* (Baton Rouge, LA, 1975); *The Third Republic Defended: Bourgeois Reform in France 1880–1914* (Baton Rouge, LA, 1986)

Figes, Orlando. *A People's Tragedy: The Russian Revolution 1891–1924* (London, 1996)

Hobsbawm, Eric. *Nations and Nationalism since 1780: Programme, Myth, Reality* (Cambridge, 1990)

Joll, James. *The Anarchists* (London, 1964)

Lichtheim, George. *A Short History of Socialism* (London, 1970)

Mosse, Werner E. *Alexander II and the Modernization of Russia* (London, 1958)

Offen, Karen M. *European Feminisms 1700–1950: A Political History* (Stanford, 2000)

Price, Roger. *The French Second Empire: An Anatomy of Political Power* (Cambridge, 2001); *People and Politics in France 1848–1870* (Cambridge, 2004)

Pulzer, Peter G. J. *The Rise of Political Anti-Semitism in Germany and Austria* (New York, 1964)

Rapport, Mike. *1848: Year of Revolution* (London, 2009)

Riall, Lucy. *The Italian Risorgimento: State, Society and National Unification* (London, 1994)

Schorske, Carl E. *German Social Democracy 1905–1917: The Development of the Great Schism* (Cambridge, MA, 1955)

Sperber, Jonathan. *The European Revolutions 1848–51* (Cambridge, 2011)

Stites, Richard. *The Four Horsemen: Riding to Liberty in Post-Napoleonic Europe* (New York, 2014); *The Women's Liberation Movement in Russia: Feminism, Nihilism, and Bolshevism, 1860–1930* (Princeton, 1978)

Venturi, Franco. *Roots of Revolution: A History of the Populist and Socialist Movements in Nineteenth-Century Russia* (London, 1960)

Vincent, John. *The Formation of the Liberal Party 1857–68* (London, 1966)

ECONOMY AND SOCIETY

Berend, Ivan. *An Economic History of Nineteenth-Century Europe: Diversity and Industrialization* (Cambridge, 2013)

Blum, Jerome. *The End of the Old Order in Rural Europe* (Princeton, 1978)

Brooks, Jeffrey. *When Russia Learned to Read: Literacy and Popular Literature 1861–1917* (Princeton, 1985)

Crowley, John et al. (eds). *Atlas of the Great Irish Famine* (Cork, 2012)

Engel, Barbara Alpern. *Between the Fields and the City: Women, Work, and Family in Russia 1861–1914* (Cambridge, 1994)

Erickson, Charlotte (ed.). *Emigration from Europe 1815–1914: Select Documents* (London, 1976)

Evans, Richard J. *Death in Hamburg: Society and Politics in the Cholera Years 1840–1910* (Oxford, 1987)

Foster, John. *Class Struggle and the Industrial Revolution: Early Industrial Capitalism in Three English Towns* (London, 1974)

Frank, Stephen. *Cultural Conflict and Justice in Rural Russia 1856–1914* (London, 1999)

Gay, Peter. *The Bourgeois Experience: Victoria to Freud* (5 vols, Oxford, 1984–98)

Glickman, Rose L. *Russian Factory Women: Workplace and Society 1880–1914* (London, 1984)

Henze, Charlotte. *Disease, Health Care and Government in Late Imperial Russia: Life and Death on the Volga 1823–1914* (London, 2011)

Hobsbawm, Eric. *Bandits* (London, 1969); *Captain Swing* (with George Rudé, London, 1969)

Hunt, Tristram. *Building the New Jerusalem: The Rise and Fall of the Victorian City* (London, 2004)

Landes, David S. *The Unbound Prometheus: Technological Change and Industrial Development in Western Europe from 1750 to the Present* (Cambridge, 1969)

Lukacs, John. *Budapest 1900: A Historical Portrait of a City and its Culture* (London, 1988)

McKean, Robert B. *St Petersburg Between the Revolutions: Workers and Revolutionaries, June 1907–February 1917* (London, 1990)

McReynolds, Louise. *Russia at Play: Leisure Activities at the End of the Tsarist Era* (Ithaca, NY, 2003)

Parthasarathi, Prasanna. *Why Europe Grew Rich and Asia Did Not: Global Economic Divergence 1600–1850* (London, 2011)

Perrot, Michelle. *Workers on Strike: France 1871–1890* (Leamington Spa, 1987)

Pollard, Sidney. *Peaceful Conquest: The Industrialization of Europe 1760–1970* (Oxford, 1981)

Porter, Roy. *The Greatest Benefit to Mankind: A Medical History of Humanity from Antiquity to the Present* (London, 1997)

Scholliers, Peter. *Wages, Manufacturers and Workers in the Nineteenth-Century Factory: The Voortman Cotton Mill in Ghent* (Oxford, 1996)

Snowden, Frank. *Naples in the Time of Cholera 1884–1911* (London, 1995)

Stern, Fritz. *Gold and Iron: Bismarck, Bleichröder and the Building of the German Empire* (London, 1977)

Weber, Eugen. *Peasants into Frenchmen: The Modernization of Rural France 1870–1914* (London, 1979)

White, Jerry. *London in the Nineteenth Century: 'A Human Awful Wonder of God'* (London, 2007)

Wohl, Anthony S. *Endangered Lives: Public Health in Victorian Britain* (London, 1983)

Wolmar, Christian. *Blood, Iron and Gold: How the Railways Transformed the World* (London, 2009)

Wood, Gillian D'Arcy. *Tambora: The Eruption that Changed the World* (Princeton, 2013)

Zelnik, Reginald E. *Labor and Society in Tsarist Russia: The Factory Workers of St. Petersburg 1855–1870* (Stanford, 1971)

NATURE, CULTURE, GENDER AND RELIGION

Abrams, Lynn. *The Making of Modern Woman: Europe 1789–1918* (London, 2002)

Anderson, Harriet. *Utopian Feminism: Women's Movements in Fin-de-Siècle Vienna* (London, 1992)

Blackbourn, David. *Marpingen: Apparitions of the Virgin Mary in Bismarckian Germany* (Oxford, 1993); *The Conquest of Nature: Water, Landscape and the Making of Modern Germany* (London, 2006)

Blanning, Tim. *The Romantic Revolution* (London, 2010)

Bracewell, Wendy. *Orientations: An Anthology of Eastern European Travel Writing Ca. 1500–2000* (Budapest, 2009)

Burrow, John W. *The Crisis of Reason: European Thought 1848–1914* (London, 2000)

Clark, Christopher, and Kaiser, Wolfram (eds). *Culture Wars: Secular-Catholic Conflict in Nineteenth-Century Europe* (Cambridge, 2003)

Corbin, Alain. *Women for Hire: Prostitution and Sexuality in France after 1850* (London, 1990)

Corton, Christine L. *London Fog: The Biography* (London, 2015)

Cunningham, Hugh. *Leisure in the Industrial Revolution c.1780–1880* (London, 1980)

Dixon, Thomas. *Weeping Britannia: Portrait of a Nation in Tears* (London, 2015)

Evans, Richard J. *Rituals of Retribution: Capital Punishment in Germany 1600–1987* (Oxford, 1996)

Facos, Michelle, and Hirsh, Sharon (eds). *Art, Culture and National Identity in Fin-de-Siècle Europe* (Cambridge, 2003)

Figes, Orlando. *Natasha's Dance: A Cultural History of Russia* (London, 2002)

Finnane, Mark. *Insanity and the Insane in Post-Famine Ireland* (London, 1981)

Frevert, Ute. *Men of Honour: A Social and Cultural History of the Duel* (Cambridge, 1995)

Harris, Ruth. *Lourdes: Body and Spirit in the Secular Age* (London, 1999)

Kern, Stephen. *The Culture of Time and Space, 1880–1918* (Cambridge, MA, 1983)

Lidtke, Vernon L. *The Alternative Culture: Socialist Labor in Imperial Germany* (New York, 1985)

Lindenmeyr, Adele. *Poverty Is Not a Vice: Charity, Society, and the State in Imperial Russia* (Princeton, 1996)

Malcolmson, Robert W. *Popular Recreations in English Society 1700–1850* (Cambridge, 1973)

McCulloch, Diarmaid. *A History of Christianity: The First Three Thousand Years* (London, 2009)

McLeod, Hugh, and Ustorf, Werner (eds). *The Decline of Christendom in Western Europe 1750–2000* (Cambridge, 2003)

McManners, John (ed.). *The Oxford Illustrated History of Christianity* (Oxford, 1990)

Ogle, Vanessa. *The Global Transformation of Time 1750–1950* (London, 2015)

Sassoon, Donald. *The Culture of the Europeans: From 1800 to the Present* (London, 2006)

Schorske, Carl E. *Fin-de-Siècle Vienna: Politics and Culture* (London, 1980)

Shubert, Adrian. *Death and Money in the Afternoon: A History of Spanish Bullfighting* (New York, 1999)

Swenson, Astrid. *The Rise of Heritage: Preserving the Past in France, Germany and England 1789–1914* (Cambridge, 2013)

Taruskin, Richard. *Music in the Early Twentieth Century* (Oxford, 2009)

Vital, David. *A People Apart: The Jews of Europe 1789–1939* (Oxford, 1999)

Vyleta, Daniel M. *Crime, Jews and News: Vienna 1895–1914* (Oxford, 2007)

Walkowitz, Judith R. *Prostitution and Victorian Society: Women, Class, and the State* (Cambridge, 1980)

Index

Prussia – *cont.*
Constitution 210, 212, 554;
Council of State 196; Criminal
Law Code 345; crop failure in
123; cultivation of land 358;
defeats by Napoleon 22–3;
Department of Trade and Industry
145; Diet 196; dominance among
German states 605; draft
constitution 196; East-Elbian 98,
100, 101, 286; 1848 revolution
195–6, 250; electorate 605; fire
brigade 441; French opinion of
687; General Law Code 458;
General Staff 262; and German
Confederation 25, 28, 33, 250,
251; and German nation state
222, 233, 600; guilds 146;
Gymnasium 491; Hegel on 175;
Herrenhaus (Upper Chamber)
280, 600; and Holstein 253; and
Holy Alliance 22–3; hunting rights
in 362; ignorance of Hungary 356;
invasion of Holstein 253; and
Italian wars of independence 242;
Kultusministerium (Ministry of
Spiritual, Educational and Medical
Affairs) 458; landowners 115,
285–6; liberalism in 182–3;
literacy in 481; Lutheranism in
458; medical profession 323;
military conscription 250; military
strength 262; militia oath 9;
Ministry of the Interior 494;
mortality crisis 125; municipal
administrative reforms 121;
national curriculum 491; Nicholas
I and 51; nobility 279; Parliament
210, 257, 281, 567–8; and Poland
178; police 250, 602; and Polish
nationalism 180, 186–7, 490, 572;
poor-law administration 441;
population 430, 433; prisons 437,
441; Progressive Party 249,
250–51; property franchise 543;

public executions in 432, 433; and
Quadruple Alliance 36; railways
153; *Realschulen* 491; reforms in
18–19, 88; religion in 458; rise of
499; and Schleswig-Holstein 199;
secondary schools in 491;
Seehandlung (state holding
company) 147; serfdom in 88, 96,
99, 287; Statute of Farm Servants
(1810) 101; tariff barriers 135,
146, 240; telegraph system 157;
troops 12, 14; typhus in 399–400;
United Diet 182–3, 195; Upper
Chamber 600; vaccination in 398;
in Wars of German Unification 27;
water supply 317; women in 508;
and women in politics 269; and
women's suffrage 566; wood theft
103, 342–3
Prussian Overseas Trading Corporation
146–7
Pryce-Jones, Pryce 328
Przhevalsky, Nicholas Mikhailovich 634
Psara 61
psychiatry 424, 424–5, 427–8, 430–31,
434
psychoanalysis 417–18
public conveniences 310
Puccini, Giacomo: *La Bohème* 525;
The Girl of the Golden West
525–6; *Madam Butterfly* 525–6;
Tosca 525–6
Puchner, Anton von 202
puerperal fever 420
Puerto Real 4
Puerto Rico 652
Pugin, Augustus 453–4; *Examples of
Gothic Architecture* 453
Pullman, George 379
Punch 296, 638
Punjab 638, 667
punishment, capital 197, 201, 433-4,
435, 436, 439-40; corporal 87,
89, 91, 101, 434-5, 440, 492,
493, 620; *see also* exile